INTERNATIONAL EDUCATION

VOLUME 2

D0338267

INTERNATIONAL EDUCATION

AN ENCYCLOPEDIA OF CONTEMPORARY ISSUES AND SYSTEMS

VOLUME 2

EDITED BY
DANIEL NESS
AND **CHIA-LING LIN**

M.E.Sharpe
Armonk, New York
London, England

The EuroSlavic fonts used to create this work are © 1986–2012 Payne Loving Trust. EuroSlavic is available from Linguist's Software, Inc., www.linguistsoftware.com, P.O. Box 580, Edmonds, WA 98020-0580 USA tel (425) 775-1130.

Library of Congress Cataloging-in-Publication Data

International education : an encyclopedia of contemporary issues and systems / edited by Daniel Ness and Chia-ling Lin.
    p. cm.
    Includes bibliographical references and index.
    ISBN 978-0-7656-2049-1 (hardcover : alk. paper) 1. Education—Encyclopedias. I. Ness, Daniel, 1966– II. Lin, Chia-ling.

LB15.I565 2012 vol. 2
370.3—dc23   2012031129

Printed and bound in the United States

The paper used in this publication meets the minimum requirements of American National Standard for Information Sciences—Permanence of Paper for Printed Library Materials, ANSI Z 39.48.1984.

EB (c) 10 9 8 7 6 5 4 3 2 1

Publisher: Myron E. Sharpe
Vice President and Director of New Product Development: Donna Sanzone
Project Manager: Henrietta Toth
Program Coordinator: Cathleen Prisco
Text Design and Cover Design: Jesse Sanchez
Typesetter: Nancy J. Connick

CONTENTS

INTERNATIONAL EDUCATION

VOLUME 2

EAST ASIA

INTRODUCTION

The East Asian region is one of the most dynamic and diverse areas in the world in terms of economic development and sociopolitical systems, both of which have significant impact on systems of education. This region encompasses countries with complicated political histories and interconnections. For example, although China and Hong Kong are not separate nations, their educational systems are distinct due to different economical and political histories and their "One Country, Two Systems" governance. This warrants separate discussions of the two educational systems.

The estimated literacy rates for these East Asian nation-states (2010–2011) range from a low of below 60 percent in Timor-Leste to a high of 99 percent in Japan, North Korea, and Taiwan. With the exception of developing nations Cambodia, Laos, and Timor-Leste, the literacy rates of the other East Asian nation-states included in this section are above the world average of 82 percent. With respect to information technology use, the reported number of Internet users per 100 people ranges from a low of below 1.0 for Cambodia, Laos, Myanmar, and Timor-Leste to a high of about 68 for Japan, South Korea, and Taiwan. (Note that the public usage of the Internet as of 2008 is prohibited in North Korea.)

The seventeen East Asian nation-states differ vastly in economic power. The region encompasses nation-states with highly successful records of economic development, including Japan and the "Asian Tigers" of Hong Kong, Singapore, South Korea, and Taiwan, as well as those developing countries where economic growth has been relatively weak. Based on the 2012 *CIA World Factbook* estimates of gross domestic product (GDP) of a list of 52 Asian nations included in the ranking, China, Japan, South Korea, Indonesia, Taiwan, and Thailand ranked among the top 10 Asian nations; Malaysia, Philippines, Hong Kong, Singapore, and Vietnam ranked among the second 10 (i.e., 11th–20th) Asian nations. The GDP ranged from a high in China of $7 trillion to $2 billion in Timor-Leste.

Precompulsory, Compulsory, and Postcompulsory Education

Enrollment in precompulsory education is generally increasing in East Asia. Although a large proportion of the nursery schools, day-care centers, preschools, and kindergartens are privately owned, some governments provide subsidies to their citizens to increase access to precompulsory education. For example, since 2000, the government in Taiwan has provided educational vouchers to aid students to attend private preschools and kindergartens, with additional financial support offered to aboriginal children and children from low-income families. In many East Asian countries, the government monitors precompulsory education whether the institution is public or private. For example, all preschools in Malaysia, whether public or private, must comply with the pedagogical and curriculum standards as well as preschool teacher training and certification requirements developed by its Ministry of Education.

The number of years of compulsory formal education ranges from a low of five years in Laos and Myanmar to six years in Malaysia, Philippines, and Singapore and nine years in the remaining nations with the exception of North Korea, which has a high of 11 years. Universal primary education was instituted in North Korea as early as 1956; during the following two decades, compulsory education was gradually extended to 11 years and was comprehensively implemented throughout the country by 1975. Compulsory schooling, however, is not necessarily accompanied by free schooling provisions; in China, Vietnam, and Laos, for example, school fees and textbooks fees must be assumed by the student's family. Primary school enrollment for each of the East Asian nation-states is near or above 90 percent, whereas secondary school enrollment is much more variable. With the exception of Cambodia, Laos, Myanmar, Timor-Leste, and Philippines, the remaining 13 nation-states have primary school completion rates near or above 90 percent. Secondary school completion rates are even more variable, with data being incomplete for some nations. Notably, in several of the largest developing countries in the region (including China, Indonesia, Malaysia, Philippines, Thailand, and South Korea), secondary school enrollment rates more than doubled from 1970 to 2001 (World Bank 2006). According to the 2005 statistics on Organisation for Economic Co-operation and Development (OECD) member countries, South Korea's high school completion rate of 97 percent was among the highest recorded in any country. On the other hand, secondary school enrollment is relatively low in Cambodia and Laos (17 percent and 35 percent, respectively, in 2000) and lower for girls than boys. In some East Asian countries, a relatively high proportion of students attend private secondary schools (e.g., 49 percent, 45 percent, and 36 percent for Indonesia, South Korea, and Philippines, respectively), whereas in others (such as China, Mongolia, Malaysia, and Vietnam), almost all students attend public secondary schools.

The vocationalization of secondary schools in East Asia is common, and the determination of the number of vocational and technical secondary programs and schools established can be related to a nation's economic goals and demands. For example, in Taiwan, the ratio of students in the academic track to those in the vocational track has varied according to the economic needs of the nation. From 1971 to 1982, the number of students in Taiwan entering the senior vocational schools increased due to the growing need for a technical workforce in the rapidly developing economy, while the number of students entering academically tracked, senior high schools gradually

declined. The educational policy, however, was later reversed due to a subsequent demand for high-quality professionals: a reduction in the number of students in the senior vocational schools was accompanied by an increase in the number of students in the senior high schools. As of 2006 the number of students in the senior vocational schools and in the senior high schools was nearly equal.

In most nation-states in East Asia, the public institutions of higher education are generally of higher quality and more desirable than private institutions. Nation-states such as Hong Kong, Malaysia, Mongolia, Philippines, Singapore, Taiwan, and Thailand have more than 25 percent of the age cohort attending higher education institutions. Taiwan has one of the highest rates of enrollment in higher education worldwide. For example, the college and university enrollment in 2005 was 56.93 per 1000 of the total population. However, in 2004, the enrollment rate estimate in higher education was only 3 percent in Timor-Leste. China has increased the proportion of the age cohort in college from a low of 4 percent in the mid-1990s to almost 20 percent in 2006. In North Korea, higher education is oriented to promote labor productivity; hence, factory colleges constitute about 40 percent of all higher education institutions. As literacy rates continue to increase and basic education becomes universal, there will be an increasing expansion of institutions of higher education in this region.

Nationalized Curriculum and Assessment

Many of the East Asian nation-states, including Cambodia, China, Malaysia, Myanmar, Singapore, South Korea, Thailand, Timor-Leste, and Vietnam, have a nationalized curriculum. Some nations have shifted toward decentralization; for example, in 1998 Taiwan shifted from a nationalized curriculum to a decentralized system in which local governments, schools, and teachers are empowered to make curricular decisions that best accommodate student needs. Other countries have assumed varying degrees of flexibility whereby schools may add curriculum of local interest provided it does not infringe upon a specified time spent on the government-specified curriculum.

The administration of nationalized examinations is a generally common practice in East Asian schools.

Such examinations are given for the purposes of determining promotion to the next grade (e.g., China, Mongolia, and Vietnam). Nationalized examinations are also given for the purpose of entering secondary school levels as well as for placement into various tracks, such as academic versus vocational tracks in secondary schools. Because these nationalized exams have significant bearing on students' subsequent education, tutoring or "cram" schools are prevalent in most East Asian nations and a common part of an Asian student's life.

Hsiu-Zu Ho

REFERENCES

Central Intelligence Agency. *The CIA World Factbook*. New York: Skyhorse, 2011. https://www.cia.gov/library/publications/the-world-factbook/index.html.

World Bank, Human Development Sector Unit East Asia and the Pacific Region. "Critical Discussions on Education: Meeting Emerging Challenges in East Asia." Working Paper Series No. 2007–2. 2006. www.usp.ac.fj/worldbank2009/frame.

CAMBODIA

Cambodia, located in southeastern Asia, is composed of four municipalities, 20 provinces, and eight islands. The majority of Cambodians are ethnic Khmers (90 percent) who speak the country's official language, Khmer, and the remainder of the population includes ethnic Vietnamese (5 percent), Chinese (1 percent), and people of other ancestry (4 percent). Theravada Buddhism is the dominant religion practiced in Cambodia (95 percent), followed by Islam and Christianity.

From the fifteenth to nineteenth centuries, the Khmer Empire in present-day Cambodia went through a period of decline. Subsequently, in 1863, the king placed the country under the protection of France, as part of the French colony of Indochina. Nearly a century later, on November 9, 1953, Cambodia gained independence from France, and the monarchy was restored under Prince Norodom Sihanouk. Since its independence, the name of the country has changed multiple times, reflecting the country's political unrest.

Cambodia transitioned into a new political system in 1993, when the country's constitution established a system of constitutional monarchy with two legislative houses: the senate and the national assembly. The prime minister is the head of government, while the king is the head of state. Whereas the prime minister exercises executive power in the government, the monarchy is symbolic and does not execute political power.

Educational System

Cambodia's current educational system is administered by the Ministry of Education, Youth and Sports (MoEYS), which oversees the implementation of the national curriculum and examinations. As of 2011, there were 84,437 teachers employed in the public schools, and there were 6,767 public primary schools and 1,980 secondary schools. The number of higher education institutions totaled 40 in 2008, of which 10 were public and 30 were private.

Preschool, Primary, and Secondary Education

Although it is not compulsory, preprimary education, designed to prepare students for primary school, was formally introduced as the Early Childhood Education (ECE) policy in 2000 by the MoEYS, targeting children three to five years old. In part, due to the rise in dual-parent working households, the demand for preschool has been slowly increasing; nevertheless, preschool attendance has been low. Objectives for schooling include structured play and social development, initial hygiene and nutrition awareness, and a more comprehensive view of child care. Although preprimary education exists in the forms of government-sponsored, community-sponsored, and private-sponsored preschools, most preschools are financially supported by nongovernmental organizations (NGOs). Preschool programs are available only in some areas and the coverage is sparse.

Compulsory education consists of nine years and includes two levels: the primary level, beginning at age six, includes grades 1 through 6; the lower secondary level, beginning at age 12, includes grades 7 through 9. The main objective of primary education is to provide students with a foundation in literacy (Khmer) and mathematics. In addition, life and learning skills, moral development, and physical appearance are emphasized.

After the completion of primary school, students enter secondary school, which includes lower secondary level and upper secondary level (grades 10 through 12). At the lower secondary level, students continue to study Khmer, mathematics, sciences, social sciences, and a foreign language.

Postsecondary Education

Cambodia's postsecondary education includes higher education and technical and professional training. The country has a low participation rate in higher education, with just 1.2 percent of the total population enrolled. As mentioned previously, there are 10 public higher education institutions, offering degree programs in agriculture, medicine, economics, technology, teacher training, science, art, and culture. As of 2008 there were 30 private universities, with the first one established in the capital city of Phnom Penh in 1997. As of 2011, however, no community or junior colleges had been established.

Curriculum, Instruction, and Assessment

The Ministry of Education, Youth and Sports is responsible for the country's national curriculum at all compulsory levels. The new curriculum is moving toward an active learning model of learning, rather than the traditional rote method seen throughout Southeast Asia. At the primary and secondary levels of compulsory education, instruction is divided into two categories, the national curriculum and local life skills programs. Grades 1 through 3 emphasize Khmer literacy, math, hygiene, and life and learning skills. Grades 4 through 6 continue to develop the skills learned in earlier grades, with the addition of science, social studies, and character and moral development. In grades 7 through 9, content knowledge development in all academic areas, such as science, mathematics, Khmer, social studies, and foreign language, is continued. The primary objective of grade 10 is to consolidate the knowledge acquired thus far. The purpose of grades 11 and 12 is to promote specialization in an academic or vocational subject area, to continue schooling in higher education, to prepare for vocational study, or to fully participate in social life. In grades 5 through 12, English and French are offered as part of the national curriculum; students

choose one of the languages to study depending on the resources of the particular school. At the higher education level, although the MoEYS will oversee the curriculum framework for higher education institutions, each institution is responsible for setting up its own system of governance and management.

Assessments, which date back to the old French model, are still practiced in Cambodia's education system. After completing grade 9 in the lower secondary level, students must pass a comprehensive exam in order to enter the upper secondary level (grades 10 to 12). Similarly, after grade 12, they must pass another comprehensive exam in order to graduate with a diploma called "bac dup."

Teacher Education

Under the MoEYS, the Teacher Training Department is overseen by the Directorate General of Higher Education. The Teacher Training Department provides in-service training at provincial teacher training colleges. In 2004 not quite 1 percent of Cambodia's primary teachers finished secondary school. To make up for a lack of wages in state-sponsored schools, teachers often work second jobs. To contend with some of these concerns, 26 teacher training centers in 24 provinces, as well as an institute focused on pedagogy located in Phnom Penh, have been established. As a means to address educational access and equity, a major goal of the MoEYS is to create a highly qualified teacher pool to serve underrepresented areas. The 2010 and 2011 goals included recruiting 5,000 teachers to the teacher training program each year, including a recruitment of 30 percent of teachers from rural and disadvantaged areas. These goals are put in place on an annual basis.

Informal Education

Informal education in Cambodia provides basic literacy skills, vocational training, and life skills for both youth and adult populations. Working collaboratively or independently, the MoEYS, NGOs, and local community groups target the country's disadvantaged populations such as females, persons with disabilities, and individuals living in remote regions. Ministry programs provide out-of-school children and illiterate, unskilled adults with vocational training and courses to develop functional literacy as well as parenting skills.

System Economics

In terms of the country's gross national product of US$4.43 billion, 2 percent or US$8.86 million was allocated to education in 2008. While 60 percent of the education budget is allocated to primary education, the gross domestic product per capita per primary student is 6 to 7 percent. In addition to governmental support, about 25 percent of education expenditure came from private sources, including nongovernmental organizations and local communities. Cambodia's National Strategic Development Plans (2006–2010 and 2010–2014) along with the Cambodian Millennium Development Goals aim for basic education to encompass a universal nine years by the year 2015.

Gender and Education

According to MoEYS, girls in Cambodian preschools represent approximately half of the enrollment. In primary school, the percentage of girls enrolled drops to a little under half of the students (47.62 percent). By the lower secondary level, girls make up 48 percent of the students and by upper secondary, less than 45 percent. One reason for the declining enrollment of girls is the high cost of education for Cambodian parents, who, if they cannot afford to educate all of their children, tend to prioritize the education of their sons. To address these inequities, the ministry developed the Education Strategic Plan (2009–2013), which focuses on the following components for girls in education: equal access, equity in management and delivery service, and a strengthening of technical capacity.

Technology and Education

As outlined in its Master Plan for ICT in Education (2009–2013), MoEYS is currently planning the future use of information and communication technology (ICT) in the ministry along with work on curriculum development, preservice and in-service teacher education, and infrastructure requirements (p. 7). However, lack of basic infrastructure, such as availability of computers, prevents the expansion of this campaign to teachers and students at all education levels. At this time, the availability of technology in education is dependent on foreign aid.

Dilemmas and Challenges

One of the main educational challenges in Cambodia is for all students to complete nine years of basic education. Female students and children in rural areas are the ones most likely to drop out of school, especially at the primary level, due to poverty. Another challenge is the wide disparities between urban and rural areas in access and quality of basic education services. For example, rural areas have fewer lower secondary and upper secondary schools. Poverty and limited resources contribute to grade repetition (18 percent) and dropout rates in the primary grades (14.2 percent). A third challenge is the recruitment and retention of trained teachers for schools in remote areas.

Future Prospects

Graduation from primary school, transition to secondary school, and free compulsory education for all are some goals under MoEYS' policy of Education for All (EFA). The Cambodian government, in collaboration with the Education Support Program, is working

---

Cambodia Education at a Glance

General Information

Capital	Phnom Penh
Population	14.80 million
Language	Khmer
Literacy rate	76%
GDP per capita	US$650
Number of phones (landline) per 100 people	0.30
Number of phones (mobile) per 100 people	40
Number of Internet users per 100 people (2010)	0.50
Number of Internet hosts (2010)	5,452

Formal Educational Information

Compulsory school age population (2010)	4.79 million
Compulsory school age population	31%
Number of years of compulsory education	9 (ages 6–15)
Student/teacher ratio (2010)	
Primary school (grades 1–6)	48.3
Lower secondary school (grades 7–9)	38.2
Upper secondary school (grades 10–12)	33.3
Average class size in primary school (2008)	38.3
Average school days per year	160
Primary school gross enrollment ratio	94.4%
Primary school entrants reaching grade 5	63%
Secondary school gross enrollment ratio	40%

Note: Unless otherwise indicated, all data are based on sources from 2011.

closely to meet the 2015 Millennium Goals. Consequently, Cambodia is focused on reducing poverty and increasing educational opportunities for those youth who are not attending school. There has also been significant effort to improve education in rural and remote areas, where girls are underrepresented, especially in the areas of early enrollment, retention, and graduation.

In addition, MoEYS is working with Project GAP (Greater Angkor Project), which focuses on curriculum reform, gender bias in textbooks, the construction of additional classrooms where there is low female enrollment, preservice teacher training, and new life skills. These new life skills include providing information on HIV/AIDS and human trafficking.

During most of the twentieth century, Cambodia's history was encumbered with foreign invasions and civil wars. Despite its turbulent educational history, Cambodia has developed extensive objectives for the future in response to the United Nations Millennium Development Goals, to be reached by 2015, including achieving educational equity. In the present economic, political, and social climate, the educational system is only now able to establish formal and systematic changes. The process of establishing a stable educational system is currently in progress, and it will take time to assess the actual implementation of these goals.

Ravy S. Lao, Rebeca Mireles-Rios,
and Vivian Lee Rhone

REFERENCES

The Cambodia Trust. www.cambodiatrust.org.uk.

Central Intelligence Agency. *The CIA World Factbook*. New York: Skyhorse, 2011. https://www.cia.gov/library/publications/the-world-factbook/index.html.

Chandler, David. *A History of Cambodia*. 4th ed. Boulder, CO: Westview Press, 2008.

Lall, Ashish. "Cambodia: Sustaining Rapid Growth in a Challenging Environment." 2009. www.worldbank.org/kh/growth.

Ministry of Education, Youth and Sports. www.moeys.gov.kh/

Nation Master. 2011. www.nationmaster.com.

Sodhy, Pamela. "Modernization in Cambodia." *Journal of Third World Studies* 31 (2004): 153–174.

Southeast Asian Ministers of Education Organization, Regional Center for Educational Innovation and Technology. www.seameo-innotech.org.

UNESCO–UIS. "Education Profile: Cambodia." www.uis.unesco.org.

US Department of State. "Background Notes: Cambodia." www.state.gov/r/pa/ei/bgn.

———. Human Rights Reports. "Cambodia." www.state.gov/j/drl/rls/hrrpt/index.htm.

World Bank Education Statistics. 2011. www.worldbank.org.

CHINA, PEOPLE'S REPUBLIC OF

The People's Republic of China (PRC) is one of the world's oldest civilizations, exhibiting nearly 5,000 years of history. As of the 2011 census, China's population reached 1.3 billion people in its 22 provinces and five autonomous regions. The main languages spoken are Mandarin (standard Chinese) and Cantonese. Other dialects include Shanghainese, Fuzhou, Hakka, and indigenous languages. The main ethnicity in China is the Han Chinese, comprising 91.9 percent of the total population; other ethnicities include Zhuang, Manchu, Hui, Miao, Uygur, Yi, Mongol, Tibetan, Buyi, and Korean, which form the remaining 8.1 percent. China is a multireligious country: Buddhism and Taoism are practiced by most of the Chinese people in the PRC, but there are also followers of Confucianism, Christianity, Islam, Hinduism, and Bon (mostly practiced in the Himalayas and Tibet as a shamanist and animalist tradition).

China's prolific history encompasses 13 dynasties, beginning with the Xia Dynasty, circa 2000 BCE, and ending with the Qing Dynasty in 1911. The Republic of China was created in 1912, and the final transition took the form of the People's Republic of China from 1949 to the present.

Since the 1970s China's economy has grown exponentially. The quest for modernization following proletarian revolutions and the death of Mao Zedong, founder and chairman of the Peoples Republic of China, in 1976 initiated significant transformations throughout the country, especially in the realms of economic, social, and cultural development and foreign relations. Immediately following the Open Door Policy of 1978 that prompted vital social, political, and economic reforms, modernization movements propelled the development of the country; efforts were rapidly made to integrate broad themes of international alliance in order to mitigate the isolation imposed by Mao Zedong's sociocultural policies. These efforts began with Secretary General Deng Xiaoping's call for modernization in the 1980s and continued with President Jiang Zemin's motto of national revitalization through science and education in the late 1990s. Since the Open Door Policy, China has grown from a reticent and sectarian nation to one that currently boasts an economy that has seen a tenfold increase in its GDP since 1978. Since Mao's death, China has swiftly repositioned itself in the race for modernization, economic prosperity, and global leadership.

Educational System

Since the era of Confucius (551–479 BCE), Chinese scholars defined education as a way to foster self-cultivation and a means to recruit the ablest administrators to oversee affairs of the state. Education has always been a key aspiration of Chinese social and political reformers. In 1921, after China was freed of imperial rule, the Chinese Communist Party (CCP) was formed. Mao Zedong, leader of the CCP, declared his support for mass education with a primary focus on improving education in the countryside. Mao's upbringing in rural China led him to believe that a rural-based education system was most important in channeling motivation and fortitude among the Chinese people; his motto was that if China were to achieve and retain collectivism and a healthy political economy, pedagogy should begin in the countryside. Because a majority of the population was concentrated in the countryside at the time, the pursuit of mass literacy in the region became a central theme for nation-building throughout the twentieth century.

In the mid-twentieth century, Mao explicitly promoted education in rural China. Peasant unions, labor schools, worker-peasant army education and training institutions, and part-time schools for workers were established in large numbers. Mao's commitment to rural China also instigated movements that prohibited Chinese urbanites from owning what he asserted were "bourgeois" items. For example, musical instruments were ordered to be destroyed, books that did not embrace his philosophies were to be burned, and artwork and other paraphernalia considered luxurious or foreign were confiscated. Nevertheless, such revolutions did not affect the philosophical value of education as it still remained integral in Communist China. Despite Mao's death and the end of the revolution in September 1976, China's leaders have continued to esteem education as a profound achievement, especially in the quest for change and rapid modernization. Education in China, long considered a civilization that placed a high value on learning, remains prevalent in all aspects of economic, political, social, and cultural life.

Precompulsory Education

Prior to the establishment of the PRC in 1949, precompulsory education (comprised of multiyear kindergarten for students age three to six) was privately funded and run by individuals. In 1949 the country had 1,300 precompulsory institutions among a population of 400 million. However, these private, precompulsory school systems lacked regulation and infrastructure. Consequently, school curricula were not standardized, teachers lacked formal training to instruct, and pedagogy was ethnocentric. In light of the Open Door Policy in 1978, new policies were formed to encourage expansion and stability in education. China turned to foreign nations for inspiration in educational restructuring, and policies for equal access to education were promptly drafted to meet the needs of the citizens. For example, in 1986, education became compulsory for children ages six to 15, and progress was also made in providing access and financial resources for children of indigenous groups and rural areas.

China's precompulsory education has become an important step in the preparation for primary school, and significant progress has been made in offering precompulsory education nationwide. In 1998 nearly 50 percent of the children in China's 22 poverty-stricken counties participated in three-year precompulsory education, and more participated in one-year precompulsory education. In 2003 the United Nations Development Programme (UNDP) reported that China had a total of 116,390 kindergartens with 613,000 teachers and over 20 million students. Access to precompulsory education was generally universal in urban areas; however, kindergartens in remote, poor, and minority areas throughout China have begun to develop rapidly as well. To further enhance precompulsory school development, the PRC formulated policies to reassess qualifications of kindergarten teachers and classroom performance in order to strengthen school leadership and educational outcomes.

Compulsory Education

Prior to 1986, compulsory education in China only comprised five years of primary school. In 1986, compulsory education was extended to nine years with the inclusion of junior secondary school. The diversification of education begins upon the completion of primary school (grades 1–6) when students are eligible to acquire vocational education. Vocational training is first introduced in junior secondary school (grades 7–9), but occupational guidance and skills training is emphasized later in the postcompulsory school years (senior secondary school, grades 10–12).

Also in 1986 the National People's Congress promulgated equal opportunity by tailoring education to the needs of children in all localities throughout China, namely minority children of indigenous groups and children in the Chinese countryside. In 1989 the PRC established the China Youth Development Foundation in order to provide basic education through the allocation of subsidies. Nevertheless, to date, millions of children from these poverty-stricken areas are either still unable to attend school or forced to drop out due to lack of resources.

In 1992 further progress was made to accomplish China's goal of providing basic education for all. Acting to complement the nine-year compulsory education law, the government sought to provide financial resources to foster equal attainment of education for children aged nine to 15, regardless of income and social standing. Three years later, in 1995, regulations were drafted to set fair standards in the collection and utilization of tuition and school fees. In 2002 statistics from the Ministry of Education (MOE) revealed that China had succeeded in universalizing the nine-year compulsory education law to about 90 percent of the population. This figure is the highest among nations under the E-9 Initiative (a grouping of the nine highest-populated countries—Bangladesh, Brazil, China, Egypt, India, Indonesia, Mexico, Nigeria, and Pakistan—who are committed under the Delhi Declaration to provide basic education for all) launched by the United Nations Educational, Scientific and Cultural Organization (UNESCO).

Further progress followed as the State Council announced the Two Waivers and One Subsidy initiative in 2005. This plan aims at relieving the financial burden of all students from the countryside and poverty-stricken areas by waiving their tuition, miscellaneous school fees, and the costs of textbooks and instructional materials. For students who have no schools available in their own locales, subsidies allow them to attend the nearest boarding school in their region. At present, China has the world's largest distance education program for students and teachers in rural areas.

Postcompulsory Education

In order to continue their secondary education, junior secondary school graduates are required to take a locally administered entrance exam. The examination results determine if the students will either enter a regular senior secondary school (i.e., an academic track) or go to a vocational secondary school. Secondary vocational education in China has grown dramatically in the last two decades in response to the demand of an increasing student population who fail entrance exams that would allow them to continue senior secondary school education. Vocational schools typically offer two- to four-year programs that train medium-level skilled workers, farmers, and technical personnel. Technical schools often provide four-year programs that train intermediate managerial and technical personnel.

With the pressure of recent educational reform to meet an increasing demand for skilled workers in a rapidly expanding economy, some regular senior secondary schools have been converted into vocational secondary schools or have allowed vocational training classes to be established in their schools. Such efforts to divert students from an academic track to a vocational or technical track in order to alleviate skill shortages as well as to ease the tough competition faced by regular senior secondary school graduates to enter higher education have resulted in a dramatic increase in the student population participating in secondary vocation education. A report by the National Research Center on Education and Development shows that there were 11.6 million students attending secondary vocational schools in the year 2011.

Throughout the years, degree-level education in China has experienced many changes. When the PRC was established in 1949, master's degree programs were a rarity and doctoral programs were nonexistent. In that year, only 200 students graduated with a master's degree and only 116,500 students were enrolled as undergraduate students throughout the nation. Students who wanted to pursue doctoral degrees needed to travel abroad for graduate training. The onset of the Cultural Revolution in 1966 further hindered the development of postcompulsory education as Mao Zedong suspended admittance to universities, terminated teaching and study, and mandated students to work in the countryside. For ten years proletarian movements replaced necessary advancements in education throughout China.

The Cultural Revolution ended upon the death of Mao Zedong in 1976, and Deng Xiaoping emerged as de facto leader until the late twentieth century. Under Deng Xiaoping's leadership, higher education and intellectual capital greatly expanded in China. To meet students' needs, bachelor's, master's and doctoral degrees were offered and forms of postcompulsory education diversified. The number of postcompulsory education institutions increased exponentially from only 598 institutions in 1976 to 2,003 institutions in 2002. In 1996 China granted over 5,000 doctoral degrees, twice the number of Great Britain, Japan, or India. Since then, the number of doctoral graduates in China has surpassed all other countries in the world except the United States. Furthermore, university enrollments throughout the nation rose from 10 percent in 1999 to nearly 30 percent in 2010, a threefold increase in just 11 years. In 2002 the total number of higher education enrollment, inclusive of students attending general senior secondary school, vocational school, adult professional schools, other special schools, and universities, amounted to over half a million. China also boasts the largest higher education system in the world, awarding more degrees than the United States and India combined. China's expansion in higher education continues. In 2006 over 34,000 doctoral degrees were granted throughout the nation. Based on this trend, China will be competitive with the United States as a leader of doctorate degrees granted.

Special Education

Despite China's extensive history and distinguished Confucian traditions in educational merit, special education was not established as a necessary and important institution until the nineteenth century. This was likely in part due to the lack of public awareness regarding disabilities as well as traditional thinking

that the responsibility for care of disabled family members lies within the family, rather than social institutions outside of the family. Social and cultural factors (including Confucian philosophies, socialist ideologies, Western cultural influences, and economic milieu) have contributed to the development of special education in China. Yet it was not until the 1980s that a comprehensive special education system began to take shape throughout the country.

Initially, special education in China focused on the teaching of blind, deaf, and mute students, but institutions have expanded to include students who have other physical and intellectual disabilities. As of 2007 special education services comprise three forms. The structure of classrooms and teaching is dependent upon the severity of the disability in that students are placed in either (1) a special education school, (2) a special education ("self-contained") classroom in a regular school, or (3) a regular classroom setting where they are fully integrated. Recent efforts have focused on the latter form of integration, called *suiban jiudu* (i.e., "learning in regular classroom"), by formulating instructional modifications to better serve the students' special needs. *Suiban jiudu* has resulted in increased enrollment of special education students in regular schools, though mostly in eastern cities. Despite progress made in recent decades, only an estimated 4.5 percent of disabled children in China receive special education services.

Minority Education

China's population is typically perceived as a monolithic Han majority. However, China also comprises 55 other ethnic nationalities. For centuries, China remained a unified multiethnic and multicultural country that collectively established the nation's rich geographical, cultural, and linguistic diversity. For over 50 years, the PRC has tried to develop and promote ethnic minority education and development. Approximately 65 percent of China's 1.3 billion inhabitants reside in the countryside, including remote mountainous and pastoral areas. Therefore, it is necessary for the Chinese government not only to provide educational funds, but also to allocate sufficient developmental funding for infrastructure.

Guidelines in education regulation have been released by the State Ethnic Minorities Commission and the former State Education Commission (now known as the Ministry of Education). For example, teaching plans and educational regulations now apply to all citizens of China, and ethnic minorities are not an exception. The PRC also plans to continually fund and develop subsidies for the development of minority education as well as provide teaching materials in such areas. Another focus is to create special classes and curriculum for the recruitment and retention of ethnic minority students. To further promote minority education, the PRC publishes textbooks in minority languages and requires all localities throughout the nation to establish in-service training schools for ethnic minority teachers. Furthermore, the government requires all general colleges and universities throughout China to meet quotas for admitting minority students.

Curriculum, Instruction, and Assessment

The Chinese government, along with local governing bodies, regulates the management of all sectors of education: precompulsory, compulsory, postcompulsory, and special education. Classroom curricula, teacher qualifications, and performance assessment are solely monitored by the MOE, which has the power to influence change and initiate necessary modifications.

In China children enter kindergarten at the age of three. The duration of precompulsory education is three years, and upon completion, students enter primary school at age six. Kindergarten can be full-time, part-time, or hourly; a selection of kindergartens replicates boarding schools as well where students have the option of living in dormitories. In rural areas, precompulsory education is mainly comprised of nursery classes that provide both child care and instruction during weather-permitting season. In minority and poor areas, activity centers, game groups, mobile aid centers, and mobile services called "caravans" are offered.

Compulsory education in China provides the most important and fundamental lessons in a child's educational career. Because essential fundamental skills are taught during the first six years of a child's schooling, the Ministry of Education seeks to regularly evaluate and modify educational policies and pedagogies. In 1986 the State Education Commission (now known as the MOE) presented the Teaching Plan for Full-

time Primary School and Junior Secondary School Compulsory Education. The plan, finalized a year later in 1987, intended to reduce a "learning burden" among students by reducing teaching content and homework assignments. For instance, the required mastery of 3,000 Chinese characters by grade six of primary school dropped to 2,500 characters. Furthermore, teaching hours committed to the Chinese language and mathematics decreased while time spent on social development, work skills, nature studies, and the fine arts curricula increased. The implementation of the plan instigated subsequent restructuring projects in compulsory education.

In 1993 the MOE implemented a revised syllabus that followed curricula developed by local and state governments as a way to ensure that instructional methods meet the needs of children residing in both urban and rural areas. In 2000 the MOE issued a nationwide pedagogical overhaul that introduced new curricula and textbooks for all subjects in all compulsory schools. Consequentially, grades 1 to 3 of primary school focus on learning the standard Chinese language (Mandarin), mathematics, nature and life studies, moral education, physical education, and arts and music. English is taught throughout compulsory school from grade 4 to grade 9, and information technology, physics, chemistry, local and global history, social sciences, politics, and labor skills are additional courses taught in the latter years of secondary school.

Assessment exams are commenced at the end of each term (a school year is divided into two terms), at the end of each school year, and immediately before graduation from primary and lower secondary school. In primary school, nationalized exams focus on students' knowledge of the Chinese language and mathematics, whereas English, natural sciences, social sciences, and history, in addition to Chinese and mathematics, are the examination subjects in secondary school. Students are allowed two attempts to pass the end-of-year examinations before being denied promotion to the succeeding grade. While graduates of primary school are not required to take entrance exams to enter junior secondary school, students planning to enter senior secondary school must pass localized entrance exams before admission.

Perseverance and effort in schoolwork are emphasized in primary and secondary school. Additionally, lessons in character development include the care of public property, as well as respect for one's own classmates, teachers, elders, family members, and the society as a whole. Students who have graduated from secondary school are expected to become moral citizens in addition to acquiring the skills that better prepare them for the workforce.

In contrast to enrollment in primary school and secondary school, which is generally controlled by local governmental bodies, enrollment in post-compulsory education in China follows a unified, nationwide procedure. The National Examination Agency of China oversees examinations for entrance into universities, adult education institutions, teacher training colleges, and postgraduate courses. Furthermore, postcompulsory education in China is primarily funded by the public and regulated by varying levels of governmental bodies. Academic courses and requirements in higher education are also regulated by the national government. In 1993, 504 academic specialties were divided into 10 major disciplines: education, law, philosophy, history, literature, economics, medicine, agronomy, natural sciences, and engineering. Four years later in 1997, higher education curriculum covered 779 specialties, including politics, military education, business, and physical education.

During the last several decades, the East Asian countries whose students outperformed those of other nations were traditionally Japan, South Korea, Singapore, and possibly Taiwan. However, during the 2010 and 2011 academic year, students in certain areas of the People's Republic of China outperformed those in nearby countries, as well as those of the United States, Canada, Australia, New Zealand, and countries of Europe. To be sure, Shanghai ranked first among 65 countries throughout the world in reading, mathematics, and science.

Teacher Education

Teachers in China form one of the largest teaching forces in the world, yet their social status has varied, especially during the Cultural Revolution. During the ten years of the revolution, a teacher's role in the classroom was rendered ambiguous, hypocritical, and discouraging, especially during the establishment of rural educational camps and the extraction of students from urban schools. Ironically, in 1956, ten years prior to the Cultural Revolution,

a campaign called "Let a Hundred Flowers Bloom" was launched to encourage intellectualism, independence, self-expression, creativity, and imagination. Today, caught between the past and the present, the old and young generations, and changing political landscapes, teachers in China face the difficult task of determining what should or should not be taught in their classrooms.

Teacher education throughout China comprises both preservice education and in-service training. Teacher training can be acquired through four-year educational institutions that include general colleges and universities or through three-year teacher programs in teacher training colleges and secondary teacher training schools. The latter primarily conduct preservice courses that enable graduates to teach in kindergartens, primary schools, junior and senior secondary schools, and special education institutions. In-service training, however, is conducted by education institutions that specifically prepare teachers for instruction in kindergarten, primary school, and secondary schools.

The curriculum for preservice institutions is based on a fixed national agenda. For teachers-in-training who plan to teach in kindergarten, the curriculum encompasses childhood development, precompulsory school education theory, child hygiene, and teaching methods for language, calculation, physical education, and arts and music. For those planning to teach in primary school, the curriculum includes Chinese language, foreign language, music and art, social science, studies of natural sciences, psychology, mathematics, and education theory and teaching methods. In addition, teachers-in-training are required to participate in classroom observations and student teaching.

In contrast to the preservice system, in-service courses are typically more oriented to the specific needs of teachers, and more open and flexible in general. Many in-service faculty members are directly involved in research and developmental work, which introduces prospective teachers to education policies and school structure, thereby shaping many to become policy makers in education.

Technology and Education

Since the turn of the century, China has made headway in technology. Students in postcompulsory schools can now enjoy the supplementation of satellite television transmission systems, Internet networks, and Internet schools. In 1999 the Ministry of Education developed a national education computer network called the China Education and Research Network (CERNET). Funded by the Chinese government and directly managed by the MOE, CERNET is the first nationwide education and research computer network in China. Constructed and headquartered in Tsinghua University in Beijing, CERNET has become an important platform in accommodating distance learning and fostering learning initiatives in the twenty-first century. CERNET has 12 regional and global channels that are connected with the United States, Canada, Great Britain, Germany, Japan, and Hong Kong. With over 8 million users and linked with more than 900 education and research institutions, CERNET has since enhanced the information infrastructure of China.

In 1999 the MOE also developed the Primary and Secondary Education Network, which provides primary and secondary school administrators, teachers, and students with information on various educational topics, such as examination resources and guides, teaching materials, teaching schemes, special topic discussion boards, and administrative data. This network, paired with CERNET, has become an educational news and information retrieval board that promotes easier access to educational services nationwide.

Gender and Education

Since China's move toward modernization in the late 1970s, girls' overall access to education has improved. Recent data show that as of 2008, 88.5 percent of females over the age of 15 were able to read and write, compared to 96 percent of males—an average of 92.2 percent. However, despite improvements in the nation, signs of gender disparity in education remain. One alarming fact is that approximately two-thirds of China's children not enrolled in compulsory school are girls. Due to economic pressures that affect poor families, especially prevalent in rural and indigenous areas, girls are also the first to drop out of school; nearly 1 million girls—particularly those belonging to ethnic minorities—drop out of school each year as a result of poverty. Studies also show that gender disparity and low enrollment rates

among girls are still linked to a deeply entrenched preference for sons.

In 1979 the PRC introduced the one-child policy—a national strategy to cap overpopulation, control economic instability, and alleviate environmental problems (the policy is strongly enforced in urban areas, but actual implementation varies in rural and indigenous areas). The policy resulted in the parental preference for the birth of sons over the birth of daughters. The social fostering of the one-child policy, however, resulted in an increased number of females in the labor force. As women were traditionally the primary caregivers, the government's cap on population growth became an incentive for women to pursue careers as they now had more time to invest in themselves. As China competes in the global labor market, gender preferences are shifting.

Informal Education

Informal education has become an increasingly important component of the Chinese education system. This form of schooling is primarily comprised of supplementary or vocational education for school-age students and continuing education for adults. In addition to the education received in the regular public school system, a vast majority of Chinese students participate in supplementary education through a variety of ways. For example, in after-school programs known as *Bu Xi Ban*, which are very popular throughout the country, public junior and senior secondary schools provide tutoring to either help students strengthen their basic academic skills or prepare them to pass entrance exams for secondary school or college. Many local community agencies and municipal education offices offer other kinds of after-school programs with instruction in children and youth centers (known as *Shao Nian Gong* or *Shao Nian Zhi Jia*). This type of supplementary schooling aims at helping gifted students excel in their talents in math, science and technology, music, art, and sports. In addition, growing numbers of private supplementary schools have emerged in China since the 1990s. These schools provide crash courses to help students prepare for specialized entrance examinations such as the Test of English as a Foreign Language (TOEFL) and the Graduate Record Examination (GRE).

In addition to secondary vocational education offered in the regular secondary school system, there are local community-based technical schools that offer a four-year, post–junior secondary school certificate program and two- to three-year post–senior secondary school training in fields like commerce, legal work, fine arts, and forestry. Some of these vocational technical schools also offer junior or senior secondary school graduates one- to three-year courses in cooking, tailoring, photography, and other specialties. Additionally, the Chinese government, in recent years, has further oriented vocational education toward helping young people obtain employment. As a result, two major vocational education projects were carried out. The first project was aimed at training skilled workers who are urgently needed in modern manufacturing and service industries, and the second program was to train rural farmers moving to urban areas for different kinds of laboring jobs (e.g., construction).

Continuing education is an indispensable part of China's education system. Many adults who were unable to finish secondary school appreciate various continuing education options available to them. They can choose to attend night schools or weekend schools (known as *Ye Da*) to obtain diplomas and certificates. Telecommunication programs (e.g., TV or radio channels of China Central Education TV) are often the preference of many people who are already in the workforce. Preservice and in-service vocational training programs offered by the government or the private sector also help many young adults become more competitive in the job market or maintain their employment position. Continuing education programs for adults, many of which are affiliated with Chinese colleges and universities, provide a wide array of distance education classes. Online education is also becoming a major trend of today's continuing education.

System Economics

At present, the central government is typically responsible for allocating funds to schools and universities that are in direct linkage. However, the central government does not have jurisdiction over funds allocated to universities in provinces, townships, and autonomous regions; the financial departments of local governments allocate their own funds for their own educational institutions.

In 1986 the PRC made a landmark decision to mandate free compulsory education. However, the goal of free compulsory education is far from being accomplished. Over a decade later, in 1998, compulsory education was still not free, even though the number of primary school students doubled to 140 million and the number of junior secondary school students increased fourteenfold to 50 million students. Each primary school student pays an average of 500 yuan (US$62) per academic year, and each junior secondary school student pays, on average, 1,000 yuan (US$125) per academic year for various school fees. For China to reach its goal of free education, an aggregate of 67.5 billion yuan (US$8.4 billion) per year will need to be invested into compulsory education.

Of China's 193 million compulsory school–level students, 70 percent reside in poor, rural, and indigenous areas. Many students in these areas are unable to attend school because they cannot afford the school fees. The central government invested 3.69 billion yuan (US$461.3 million) for schools in 12 western rural provinces to cover students' school fees. Since then, the central government has mandated local governments throughout China to allocate a minimum of 92.8 billion yuan (US$11.6 billion) from their total budget over the next five years. This would increase the total national educational expenditure to an estimated 212.8 billion yuan (US$26.6 billion).

Dilemmas and Challenges

A major challenge faced by China is the issue of access and equality of education. Despite claims that inequality in education has been eliminated, disadvantaged groups, including ethnic minorities, migrant children, and children residing in poverty-stricken and rural areas, have not shared in the economic prosperity of the rest of the nation. Budget priorities that favored primary and secondary schools and universities for the elite (termed "key schools") have led to further disparities. Local governments continue to be burdened by the central government's inadequate funds. Insufficient educational funding and investment, especially in the poor inland areas of the north, northeast, and northwest, remain a major problem in China's current effort to promote and stabilize education and educational achievement.

Another disadvantaged group is children with disabilities. Despite the passing of legislation making disability protection and compulsory education mandatory in the 1980s and 1990s, the majority of children with disabilities do not have access to general and/or special education. To date, special education services, especially in rural areas, remain underfunded, and the lack of qualified special educators and professionals, as well as insufficient assessment tools for diagnosis, instruction, and intervention, remains problematic.

China has also battled with issues of unqualified teachers. This problem not only permeates special education institutions, but also affects precompulsory and compulsory schools. Moreover, many teachers are unwilling to work in rural, indigenous, and poor regions where the majority of China's illiterate students reside.

Future Prospects

Throughout China's nearly 5,000 years of history, the Chinese have revered education. Attending postcompulsory school in the twenty-first century has become commonplace in China. With growing pressure of competition in the market economy, families want to be prepared for China's burgeoning labor market, and postcompulsory institutions now encompass opportunities for students to become competitive individuals in society. In fact, China's higher education system is recognized as the largest in the world, providing education for more than 23 million students. The connection between education and economic success is increasingly recognized throughout the nation, and future policies will strive to unite these two domains of social life. China plans to orient future reforms of its education system toward modernization, and modernization entails international alliances and collaboration.

However, education in China, amid zealous economic and cultural development, still requires improvements. The Ministry of Education, as well as the central government, recognizes that further reform of the educational system is needed. For example, China plans to optimize education and increase education acquisition by improving quality and accessibility. Yet unfinished schools and dilapidated school structures, poorly equipped classrooms, and limited curricula are major hindrances to educational development as they

People's Republic of China Education at a Glance	
General Information	
Capital	Beijing
Population (2012)	1.336 billion
Language	Mandarin
Literacy rate (2009)	93%
GDP per capita	US$6,195
Number of phones (landline) per 100 people (2009)	23.93
Number of phones (mobile) per 100 people	56.98
Number of Internet users per 100 people	38.40
Number of Internet hosts	15.251 million
Formal Educational Information	
Compulsory school age population (2005)	2.35 million
Compulsory school age population (2005)	18%
Number of years of compulsory education (2009)	9 (ages 6–15)
Student/teacher ratio	
Primary school (grades 1–6) (2008)	18
Junior secondary school (grades 7–9) (2003)	19
Senior secondary school (grades 10–12) (2003)	18
Average class size in primary school (2002)	46
Average school days per year (2006)	260
Primary school gross enrollment ratio (2009)	112%
Primary school entrants reaching grade 5 (2005)	99%
Secondary school gross enrollment ratio (2009)	77%

Note: Unless otherwise indicated, all data are based on sources from 2011.

are also a cause for high dropout rates among children in rural and indigenous areas. Additionally, because kindergartens in China are not part of the compulsory education system, children who do not attend are less prepared for primary school (kindergarten curricula provide introductory courses that facilitate a child's integration into first grade). Reforms must take place to ensure that poor, rural, minority, migrant, and disabled children receive adequate schooling as well as nutrition and health care. Furthermore, China's traditional rote learning methods compromise creativity and independent thought among the nation's students. The fast modernization of China has also caused a great divide between city dwellers and those who live in rural, indigenous areas. Due to rapid growth, household income varies greatly throughout the nation. Approximately 22 million people in China live below the "absolute poverty" line (income of US$90 or less per annum) and nearly 35 million more have a yearly income of US$125. Globalization and modernization have resulted in a misdistribution of access and opportunities. For China to address its challenges and dilemmas, government officials, educational leaders, and citizens alike must work together to support the development and education of all of China's youth.

Rose Wong, Mian Wang, and Hsiu-Zu Ho

REFERENCES

Central Intelligence Agency. *The CIA World Factbook*. New York: Skyhorse, 2011. https://www.cia.gov/library/publications/the-world-factbook/index.html.

China Daily. "China Experiences Rising School Dropout Rate." 2005. www.chinadaily.com.cn/english/doc/2005–03/04/content_421520.htm.

China Education and Research Network. 2008. www.edu.cn/HomePage/english.

Dillon, Sam. "Top Test Scores from Shanghai Stun Educators." *New York Times*, December 7, 2010.

Embassy of the People's Republic of China in the United Kingdom of Great Britain and Northern Ireland. "China Strives for Free Compulsory Education for All." 2006. www.chinese-embassy.org.uk/eng/zt/Features/t274370.htm.

Hesketh, Therese, and Wei-xing Zhu. "The Effect of China's One-Child Family Policy after 25 Years." *New England Journal of Medicine* 353 (2005): 1171–1176. http://content.nejm.org/cgi/content/full/353/11/1171.

Ministry of Education of the People's Republic of China. www.moe.edu.cn.

Nation Master. 2011. www.nationmaster.com.

Pang, Yanhui, and Dean Richey. "The Development of Special Education in China." *International Journal of Special Education* 21:1 (2006): 77–86.

Ross, Heidi A., Jingjing Lou, Lei Wang, Ran Zhang, and Yuhao Cen. "China." In *The Greenwood Encyclopedia of Children's Issues Worldwide*, ed. Irving Epstein and Jyotsna Pattnaik, vol. 1, 99–121. Westport, CT: Greenwood, 2008.

Su, Xiaohuan. "China to Overtake US on Science in Two Years." BBC World News, March 28, 2011. www.bbc.co.uk/news.

UNESCO–UIS. "Education Profile: China." www.uis.unesco.org.

UNICEF. "China." www.unicef.org/infobycountry/china_china.html.

Wang, Xiufang. *Education in China Since 1976*. Jefferson, NC: McFarland, 2003.

Washington Post. "China Sticking to One-Child Policy." January 23, 2007. www.washingtonpost.com.

World Bank, EdStats. "Education at a Glance: China." www.worldbank.org.

CHINA, REPUBLIC OF (TAIWAN)

Also known as Formosa, Taiwan is a sweet-potato-shaped island located in eastern Asia, off the southeastern coast of China. The people of Taiwan are comprised primarily of descendants of the early Han Chinese who immigrated to Taiwan from various provinces in China during the seventeenth and eighteenth century (84 percent), descendants of the later Han Chinese who immigrated from mainland China to Taiwan in the late 1940s and early 1950s to escape from communism (14 percent), and the indigenous aborigines (2 percent). While Mandarin Chinese is the official language in Taiwan, Taiwanese and Hakka languages are spoken by approximately 70 percent and 14 percent of the people in Taiwan, respectively. Japanese is also spoken by the elderly population who were educated when Taiwan was under Japan's rule (1895–1945).

Prior to the seventeenth century, Taiwan was primarily inhabited by Austronesian (Malayo-Polynesian) aborigines who migrated to Taiwan about 4000 BCE. Since the seventeenth century, Taiwan has been colonized by a number of countries, including Spain, the Netherlands, the Chinese Qing Dynasty, Japan, and the Chinese Nationalist government, Kuomintang (KMT). Martial law was in effect from 1949 to 1987, during which time Taiwan was a one-party government controlled by the KMT. Since the lifting of martial law in 1987, a number of significant constitutional changes have been made, including the direct elections of the president and vice president. Social reforms in the early 1990s have also led to the election of legislators who are representative of the people of Taiwan.

The academic excellence of students from Taiwan is evidenced in its ranking among the top nations. For example, Taiwan students ranked first in mathematics in the Three-Year Programme for International Student Assessment (PISA) conducted in 2009 by the Organisation for Economic Co-operation and Development (OECD). In the Third International Mathematics and Science Study, students from Taiwan ranked second in science and fourth in mathematics. Taiwan students have also excelled in other international competitions, including the International

Olympiads on mathematics, physics, and chemistry, and the International Animation Competitions. Taiwan is also ranked as a nation with one of the highest rates of enrollment in higher education worldwide. For example, the college and university enrollment in 2010 was nearly 57 per 1,000 of the total population.

Educational System

One of the early roots of formal education in Taiwan was the establishment of Christian churches and schools along the coastal plains of western Taiwan by the Dutch administration in the early 1600s. The Dutch missionaries hired Taiwanese aborigines as assistants for the Christian teachers. During the Qing Dynasty (1644–1911), the Han Chinese expanded educational programs in the form of public schools as well as private academies. Following the Sino-Japanese War of 1895, colonial education policy that favored Japanese language and values was established. Under Japan's rule, educational opportunities for Taiwanese students were limited; for example, opportunities for secondary and higher education were primarily reserved for Japanese students. Nevertheless, despite the inequities, significant progress in education was made under Japan's rule. Primary school education developed rapidly in terms of the number of primary schools established, the increase in student enrollment rates, and the expansion of teacher education. An additional expansion and emphasis on vocational education upgraded the professional and technical skills of the local Taiwanese and provided high-quality human resources for the rapid economic development of Taiwan during the post–World War II period.

At the end of World War II, the Chinese educational system was established in Taiwan under the rule of the Republic of China (ROC) government with emphasis on the "nation's philosophical principles and the cultivation of a national spirit in its education curriculum" (Hsieh et al. 1999). The administration adopted and embraced the spirit of Dr. Sun Yat-Sen's Three Principles of the People (nationalism, democracy, and people's well-being). As the political system shifted toward democracy and industry structure shifted from a labor-intensive to a capitalistic and technology-intensive structure, the educational system in the new millennium entered an era of transition and reform.

The education and socialization of children in Taiwan has been greatly influenced by Confucian philosophy. The child is traditionally viewed as malleable, capable of absorbing knowledge and experience with training and guidance from elders, parents, and teachers. Parents make great investments in their children's education; rooted in a strong belief in filial piety, children are expected to obey their elders, excel in school, achieve their full potential through hard work and diligence, and ultimately honor and support their parents. While parenting styles have traditionally tended to be authoritarian, child-rearing practices that encourage responsiveness to the child's viewpoint as well as the child's self-expression are becoming more common. In recent decades, educational ideals such as developing creativity and human potential, coordinating education with scientific and economic development, and promoting child-centered education have also been incorporated into Taiwan's educational model.

The Taiwanese central government consists of the Office of the President and five high branches (or *yuan*)—the Executive, Legislative, Judicial, Examination, and Control Yuan. Education in Taiwan is administered via two levels. The first is at the central government level through the Ministry of Education, which is one of the eight ministries under the Executive Yuan. The second is at the county and municipal government level through the Bureaus of Education.

The "six-three-three-four" system has been in place in Taiwan since 1922; that is, six years in elementary school, three in junior high school, three in senior high school, and four at the university level. In 1968, in an effort to include the junior high school level, the six-year compulsory education was expanded to nine years. Currently, there are more than 8,202 educational institutions in Taiwan (72 percent are public), with approximately 164 colleges and universities (66 percent are private).

Precompulsory Education

According to the Ministry of Education, the average enrollment rate of preschoolers and kindergartners from age four to six is 27.57 percent. The majority of the preschool and kindergarten programs in Taiwan are private institutions with high costs, which often cause a heavy financial burden for average-income families. In order to increase access to precompulsory education, since 2000 the government has provided educational vouchers to aid students to attend private preschools and kindergartens. Additional financial support is offered to five-year-old children from low-income families as well as aboriginal children.

Compulsory Education

In 1979 legislation was passed requiring all school-age children between six and 15 years of age to attend six years of elementary school and three years of junior high school. Moreover, in 1982, revised legislation placed fines or penalties on parents or guardians if they fail to send their school-age children to school. The net enrollment rate of elementary school students eligible for universal public education has steadily increased in recent decades and has reached 97.14 percent.

Starting from the age of six, students attend elementary school for six years with emphasis on the development of literacy. In order to improve the quality of education, the class size in elementary school has steadily decreased; for example, in 1986, the average class size was 44 students, while the current elementary class has an average size of 28.45 students and an average student/teacher ratio of 17.31. Elementary school students constitute 8.12 percent of the total population in Taiwan.

Also referred to as "lower secondary education," junior high school education in Taiwan includes grades 7 through 9. Junior high school students constitute 4.23 percent of the total population with an average class size of 34.17 students and an average student/teacher ratio of 15.24.

Postcompulsory Education

Postcompulsory education in Taiwan is a comprehensive, multilateral system with various types of educational programs for students' intellectual and career development. Choosing either an academic or vocational track, students enter one of three types of institutions: senior high school, senior vocational school (both of which are three-year programs), or a five-year junior college (which includes three years of high school). Senior high schools, which are oriented to the academic track, are usually the most difficult and competitive, whereas senior vocational schools and junior colleges are aimed at promoting diversified and specialized vocational education. The ratio of students in the academic track to those in the vocational track has varied according to economic demands. From 1971 to 1982, the number of students entering the senior vocational schools increased due to the growing need for a technical workforce in the rapidly developing economy, while the number of students entering senior high schools declined gradually. The educational policy, however, was subsequently reversed due to a demand for high-quality professionals; a reduction of the number of students in the senior vocational schools was accompanied by an increase in the number of students in the senior high schools. As of 2012, the numbers of students in senior vocational schools and senior high schools were nearly equal. In order to provide students with a wider range of selection, "bilateral high schools," which combine academic and vocational programs, were developed. To relax the pressure and keen competition of entrance examinations, an integrated junior-senior high school system was established in a number of schools.

After completion of secondary education, students from both senior high schools and senior vocational schools can enter higher education, including colleges and universities, junior colleges, and institutes of technology. As an academic track, colleges and universities, particularly the public institutions, are the most competitive and prestigious in Taiwan. Over 87 percent of senior high school graduates pursue higher education. Most colleges and universities are four-year institutions; some exceptions, including architectural, law, and medical programs, require five to seven years to complete. Junior colleges focus primarily on cultivating a workforce of well-trained technicians with skills in applied science. The fields offered by junior colleges include industry, medicine, commerce, marine, languages, home economics, tourism, and hospitality. The aim of the institutes of technology is to develop a high-level labor market in technology, engineering, and management. Upon completion of appropriate requirements, students in junior colleges and institutes of technology may still transfer to colleges and universities.

Curriculum, Instruction, Assessment

In elementary school, the academic curriculum includes Mandarin Chinese, mathematics, science, English, native languages, social studies, physical education, music, and art. Subjects covered in the junior high school include literature, mathematics, biology, physics and chemistry, English, history, geography, physical education, music, home economics and crafts, scout education, and civic and moral values. Language classes in compulsory education constitute the largest proportion of the total curricula (i.e., 20 to 30 percent). English is required beginning in third grade, and one of Taiwan's local dialects (Taiwanese, Hakka, or an aboriginal dialect) is also required in elementary school, but is optional in junior high school. In addition to the academic subjects, core character-developing components are included in the compulsory education curriculum (e.g., learning to lead a balanced life, respecting the law and democracy, developing a sense of patriotism and a global perspective, embracing lifelong learning).

In senior high school, students can choose a science or liberal arts track, depending on their interests. The liberal arts track focuses on literature and social studies, whereas the science track focuses on science and math classes to prepare students for careers in science, engineering, and medicine. In addition to the academic subjects, senior high school students are required to attend a military education class covering topics of civil defense, military drills, national defense, and basic firearms training. While a nationalized curriculum was once in place, decentralization since 1998 has empowered local governments, schools, and teachers to make curricular decisions that best accommodate student needs.

During the course of their schooling, students take two entrance examinations that have significant bearing on their subsequent education. The first exam is given upon completion of compulsory education; the results are used to determine a student's subsequent placement in a postcompulsory institution (i.e., in a particular senior high school, a senior vocational school, a combined vocational and academic school, or a five-year junior college). The examinations, held twice a year, cover five academic subjects: Mandarin Chinese, English, mathematics, natural science, and social science. Those students with the highest examination scores are eligible to attend the most prestigious schools.

The second entrance examination is taken after completion of senior high school. The results determine placement into colleges, universities, and institutes of technology and also determine the specific academic majors that students will undertake at these institutions. Although over 90 percent of high school students who take the entrance examinations go on to obtain higher education, competition remains fierce for enrollment into the limited number of prestigious public universities. To lessen the tremendous stress that the entrance examinations have placed on students, a number of alternative selection criteria, including students' academic performance, screening examinations, and teacher recommendations, have been in place since 2002. Nevertheless, many students still enroll in private "cram schools" designed specifically for increasing scores on these examinations. Although this extra study is optional, students typically stay in school (either regular or cram school) for extra classes as late as eight or nine in the evening in order to prepare for the entrance examinations.

Teacher Education

Before the 1990s Taiwan traditionally had two types of institutions for preparing teachers: "normal" colleges and universities. Normal colleges prepare teachers for kindergarten and elementary schools while normal universities prepare teachers for junior and senior high schools (including senior vocational schools). During the 1990s the liberalization of education movement opened up the channel for teacher training, resulting in the diversification of the sources for teacher education. Subsequently, upon approval, colleges and universities (other than the "normal institutions") began to develop and offer teacher-training programs to prepare teachers for elementary and secondary school levels. The number of teachers holding degrees above the bachelor degree has steadily increased in recent years. In the 2009–2010 school year, 12 percent of elementary school teachers and 17 percent of junior high school teachers held a master's or doctoral degree. Teacher training programs include basic courses (such as educational psychology, educational philosophy, classroom management, assessment and evaluation), disciplinary courses, discipline-specific courses, and a half-year of teaching practicum. Upon completion of the two-year program, participants receive a teaching certificate; however, they are still required to pass a final teacher qualification examination held by the Ministry of Education prior to their teaching appointment.

Informal Education

Informal or "social education" in Taiwan usually refers to supplementary and continuing education. Supplementary schools are typically correspondence or night schools affiliated with regular schools. Upon completion, students receive certificates or mainstream-equivalent diplomas. Other continuing educational options include adult education classes (in writing skills, practical mathematics, and civics), technical classes in basic job skills at training centers, and classes offered by some television and radio stations.

In order to provide more opportunities for citizens to access knowledge as well as to promote lifelong learning in modern society, a variety of learning channels, including libraries, museums, art education centers, science education centers, national social education centers, community colleges, tribal community colleges for indigenous populations, and social work stations, were established in 2005 in various areas in Taiwan. Additionally, students can attend extracurricular, private, supplementary institutes or classes to develop skills and talents such as playing musical instruments, chess, painting, and dancing, which might strengthen their qualifications for higher education. In order to excel in the competitive job market, an increasing number of individuals also attend supplementary computer classes and language schools.

System Economics

In 2000 the Law of Educational Budget Allocation and Management allocated for education a minimum of 21.5 percent of the average net revenue over the past three years. Approximately 19 percent of total public expenditure in Taiwan is spent on education. Total educational expenditure (including public and private sectors) for 2010 was approximately US$21 billion (5.76 percent of gross domestic product), with 38.6 percent for compulsory education, 40.25 per-

cent for higher education, 16.92 percent for secondary education, 3.46 percent for preschool education, and 0.77 percent for other types. The expenditure of private education accounted for 27 percent of total educational expenditure, whereas public education accounted for 73 percent.

Gender and Education

In Taiwan the Gender Equity Education Act of 2004 stipulated that all schools should have a gender equity education committee whose tasks include promoting curricula, teaching, and assessments that are equitable across both genders. The admission acceptance should be gender-neutral at all school levels, with the exception of a few gender-segregated schools at the junior and senior high school levels. The representation of female and male students is approximately equal from the kindergarten to the university level; however, female representation is lower at the graduate school level. With respect to gender representation of teachers, 99 percent of teachers at the kindergarten level are female; 68 percent at the elementary level; 68 percent at the junior high school level; 57 percent at the senior high school level; and 34 percent at the university and college level.

Technology and Education

In order to accommodate the rapid growth of information technology in society, the Taiwanese government since 1997 has focused on improving software and hardware at each school level, enhancing the knowledge of teachers in the field of information technology, integrating information technology into the curriculum, and establishing resource centers and computer networks at all levels of education. In 1999 the installation of teaching hardware and software for primary and secondary school was completed, enabling all schools to have computer classrooms and web access. The Taiwan Academic Network (TANet), jointly managed by the Ministry of Education, the National Science Council, and Academia Sinica, facilitates teaching and research activities as well as sharing resources among schools and research institutions of all levels nationwide. As of 2006, network services were available to an estimated 3.99 million persons; the connection rate to TANet was 100 percent for higher education institutions; and an estimated 4,000 primary and secondary schools were connected to TANet. In an effort to protect the safety of young users, the TANet specifically designed the SmartKid website to inform primary students about the web environment, the dangers hidden in the web world, and ways to protect themselves in cyberspace. Objectives such as narrowing the digital gap between rural and urban schools, establishing mechanisms to eliminate inappropriate web information, reinforcing information knowledge of teachers and students, and enriching the content of digital learning are in the forefront of the nation's focus on information education.

Dilemmas and Challenges

While equity in access to education can be evidenced by the high enrollment rate of students in compulsory education, achieving quality parity for all students still remains a challenge in Taiwan. Gaps in educational opportunities, as well as academic achievement, are found between students in different regions, reflecting not only differences in rural and urban areas, but also differences in socioeconomic status and ethnic backgrounds. Government subsidies are provided for students from low-income families as well as aboriginal students.

Additionally, a new group of children from intercultural marriages has emerged with an increasing number of foreign brides from China and Southeast Asia. In 2006, 11.70 percent of newborns were born to mothers from foreign countries, compared to 5.12 percent in 1998. Children from immigrant families constitute approximately 3.8 percent of the total number of students enrolled in elementary and junior high school. Children in intercultural families have encountered additional challenges in education due to cultural and linguistic difficulties.

Although corporal punishment in Taiwan's education system has been banned since 2006 (via an amendment to the Fundamental Law of Education), recent surveys indicate that the use of physical punishment has not been entirely eradicated. Additionally, whereas in compulsory education (grades 1–9), teachers and school administrators are responsible for student discipline, discipline in postcompulsory education is relegated to military officers, a remnant of postwar KMT practice that has been a controversial issue in Taiwan's democratic society. Educational

Taiwan Education at a Glance	
General Information	
Capital	Taipei
Population	23.025 million
Language	Mandarin
Literacy rate (2009)	97.91%
GDP per capita	US$35,100
Number of phones (landline) per 100 people	63.29
Number of phones (mobile) per 100 people	116.89
Number of Internet users per 100 people	70.01
Number of Internet hosts	6.336 million
Formal Education Information	
Compulsory school age population (2007)	2.73 million
Compulsory school age population (2007)	11.90%
Number of years of compulsory education (2007)	9 (ages 6–15)
Student/teacher ratio (2009)	
Elementary school (grades 1–6)	16.07
Junior high school (grades 7–9)	14.91
Senior high school (grades 10–12)	18.73
Average class size in primary school (2007)	
Elementary school (grades 1–6)	28.45
Junior high school (grades 7–9)	34.19
Average school days per year	200
Average hours per school day (2007)	8–9
Primary school gross enrollment ratio (grades 1–6) (2009)	97.01%
Primary school entrants completing grade 6 (2009)	99.73%
Secondary school gross enrollment ratio (2009)	95.35%

Note: Unless otherwise indicated, all data are based on sources from 2011.

reforms are in place to phase out all military personnel from civilian schools and colleges.

Despite Taiwan's political and economic progress toward becoming a democratic government with thriving economic power, its sovereignty and its demand for international recognition still remain unresolved. Given the complex interrelationships among the economic, political, and educational systems of a nation, Taiwan must remain steadfast in its progress and transformations in these domains.

Future Prospects

As Taiwan enters the highly developed information age of the twenty-first century, its ability to adequately prepare its citizens for the demands of the new millennium is key to addressing national goals of increasing the nation's competitive edge, enhancing its cultural society, preserving its ecological environment, and raising the overall quality of life for its citizens. Taiwan's shift from an agricultural society to a capitalistic and technology-intensive industrial society, along with a shift in its political system from totalitarianism to democracy during the last century, has had important influences on the nation's educational policies and reforms. Such reforms for the new millennium are geared to raising the standards of school education and moving toward a system that is more humanistic, democratic, pluralistic, creative, technology-oriented, and internationalized. In this era of rapid change and increasing global connections, as Taiwan shifts from an authoritarian to a liberal system in the political, educational, and social realms, its ability to incorporate modern ideals with age-old traditions has significant implications for the education and socialization of its children.

Hsiu-Zu Ho and Wei-Wen Chen

REFERENCES

Central Intelligence Agency. *The CIA World Factbook*. New York: Skyhorse, 2011. https://www.cia.gov/library/publications/the-world-factbook/index.html.

Ho, Hsiu-Zu, Wei-Wen Chen, and Hsin-YiKung. "Taiwan." In *The Greenwood Encyclopedia of Children's Issues Worldwide*, ed. Irving Epstein and Jyotsna Pattnaik, vol. 1, 439–464. Westport, CT: Greenwood, 2008.

Hsieh, Wen Chyuan, Chou, Y. W., and Chang, Chin-chen. *The Story of Taiwan: Education*. Taipei, Republic of China: Governor Information Office, 1999.

Internet World Stats. "Internet Usage in Asia." 2011. www.internetworldstats.com/stats3.htm.

Nation Master. 2011. www.nationmaster.com.

Republic of China (Taiwan) Ministry of Education. http://english.moe.gov.tw.

Republic of China (Taiwan) Ministry of Interior. Directorate-General of Budget, Accounting and Statistics. www.dgbas.gov.tw.

Republic of China (Taiwan) Ministry of Transportation and Communications. Directorate General of Telecommunications. www.motc.gov.tw.

World Bank Education Statistics. 2011. www.worldbank.org.

HONG KONG

The Hong Kong Special Administrative Region (HKSAR) of the People's Republic of China was formerly a collection of fishing villages and described, at one time, as an uninhabitable barren rock. Hong Kong is situated on the southeastern coast of China with a geographical size of 425 square miles (1,100 square kilometers).

The official languages are Chinese and English, with approximately 88 percent speaking Cantonese, the most widely spoken Chinese dialect in Hong Kong. However, the use of Putonghua or Mandarin, the official language of the People's Republic of China (PRC), is rapidly growing in Hong Kong and plays an essential role in business affairs with China. There are a variety of religions, including Buddhism, Taoism, Confucianism, Christianity, Islam, Hinduism, Sikhism, and Judaism. Life expectancy is about 82.7 years overall, with 79.5 years for males and 85.9 years for females.

After about 155 years of British rule, Hong Kong was returned to the sovereignty of China on July 1, 1997. The Sino-British Joint Declaration signed in 1984 allowed Hong Kong to maintain its way of life for 50 more years. The Joint Declaration provides Hong Kong continued stability within a framework of autonomy under the sovereignty of China. The Joint Declaration states that Hong Kong will function under the principle of "One Country, Two Systems," as originally proposed by Deng Xiaoping, the late leader of the Communist Party of the People's Republic of China. Deng Xiaoping stated that there can be only one China but that Hong Kong can develop its rule of law that provides an independent judiciary with free flow of information. Such principles are stipulated in the constitutional document, the Basic Law of the Hong Kong Special Administrative Region of the People's Republic of China.

Educational System

The government extended free education from nine years to 12 years—from the age of six to 17—in the 2008–2009 school year. In the 2010–11 school year, there were 572 primary (elementary) schools, 533 secondary (high school) schools, and 60 special schools for students with learning or physical disabilities.

There are three main types of local schools in Hong Kong: (1) government schools, which are operated by the government; (2) aided schools, which are fully funded by the government but are run by voluntary bodies; and (3) private schools, some of which receive financial assistance from the government. Government and aided schools deliver a curriculum recommended by the government.

The English Schools Foundation operates 15 schools that offer education to English-speaking children. In addition, there are international schools that serve primarily non-Chinese-speaking students and foreign nationals with nonlocal curricula.

Given Hong Kong's history of colonization, much of its educational system continues to be influenced by the British. In the late 1980s, preceding the handover of Hong Kong to China, a number of educational reforms was introduced to liberalize the school curriculum. The Basic Law guarantees education a great deal of autonomy and places the administration of education with the HKSAR government.

While contemporary Hong Kong education has been developed and influenced by British colonization, schools existed long before the British arrived. The migration of the Chinese into Hong Kong established schools that reflected Chinese traditions, values, and practices based on traditional Chinese models of education. After the arrival of the British, Protestant and Catholic missionaries developed social services and education, but education was still considered a luxury and limited to the upperclass. A priority to educate the Chinese elite was recommended in 1907 by an official government report, but it was not until 1971 that the colonial government introduced a six-year compulsory, free education, followed by an expansion to a nine-year compulsory, free education in 1978. The overall literacy rate is about 93 percent (95 percent for males and 88 percent for females).

Precompulsory Education

Precompulsory education is available to children age three to five in private kindergartens operated by voluntary or private bodies. These kindergartens are registered and supervised by the Education Bureau (EDB). In September 2009, 140,500 children were enrolled in 950 kindergartens. Financial assistance from the government includes rent and rates reimbursement to nonprofit-making kindergartens, waiver of fees to low-income families, and upgrade of training of professional qualifications for kindergarten principals and teachers. EDB provides a guide for curriculum development for preschool educators to develop their own school-based programs.

Compulsory Education

All children are required by law to be in full-time education between the ages of six and 15. Primary school typically begins at the age of six and lasts for six years, Primary 1–6. At about age 12, children continue to three years of compulsory junior secondary education, Secondary 1–3. Most stay on for a three-year senior secondary course, Secondary 4–6, while others start full-time vocational training. Upon completion of Secondary 6, students will take the new standard-referenced Hong Kong Diploma of Secondary Exam beginning in 2012.

Currently, there are half-day primary schools, designated as AM or PM, and whole-day schools. The half-day primary schools were intended as a temporary measure to accommodate the children of hundreds of thousands of Chinese who entered Hong Kong in 1949 when the Communists took over China. It has only been in recent years that the government has supported the adoption of whole-day schools. This has been made possible due to a decrease in the birth rate and smaller family size.

Placement into a primary school is based on a system of discretionary places (DP) and central allocation (CA). At the DP stage, parents can apply to only one government or aided primary school of their preference, with admission, based on EDB criteria, that is largely determined by exam results. At the CA stage, places are centrally allocated by EDB according to school catchment, parents' choice of schools, and through lottery. In September 2009, 289,865 children were enrolled in 473 government and aided primary schools.

Compulsory secondary education is provided at the completion of primary education. The secondary system offers three years of junior secondary (Form 1–3) and three years of senior secondary (Form 4–6).

As in the primary school allocation system, DP and CA stages also apply to secondary education. At the DP stage, secondary schools may admit students in accordance with their admission criteria. At the CA stage, students are allocated by banding (see explanation below), parental choice of schools, or random number. In September 2009, 398 government and aided secondary schools had a total enrollment of 391,573. During the 2006–2007 academic year, secondary schools changed from seven years to six years with a curriculum that implements a liberal studies approach that promotes all-round and whole-person development of students.

Postcompulsory Education

To respond to a Hong Kong that has moved from an industrial and service society such as hotel and food catering services to a rapidly growing knowledge-based economy, the government targeted 60 percent of senior secondary school graduates to have access to postsecondary education by 2010–2011. The government is planning for a 75 percent target for the 2014–2015 academic year. For students 17 to 20 years of age, the participation rate in postsecondary education increased from 33 percent in 2000–2001 to 64 percent in the 2006–2007 academic year.

Hong Kong currently has 13 degree-awarding higher education institutions, eight of which are funded through the University Grants Commission (UGC), the advisory committee responsible for advising the Hong Kong government on the development and funding needs of higher education institutions in Hong Kong. Established in 1910, the University of Hong Kong is the first and oldest tertiary education institution in Hong Kong. The Chinese University of Hong Kong followed in 1963. It was not until the 1980s that a rapid development of higher education provided additional university access. Undergraduate higher education is currently three years but will expand to four years in 2012–2013.

Of the eight UGC-funded higher education institutions, seven are universities and the eighth, a teaching training institute, the Hong Kong Institute of Education. In 2009–2010, a total of 62,215 full-time students and 4,328 part-time students pursued publicly funded subdegree or preundergraduate degrees and undergraduate and postgraduate courses. Other postcompulsory education opportunities include vocational training, retraining, and continuing education for adults.

Special Education

Children are considered to have special education needs (SEN) if they have a learning difficulty or a disability that prevents or hinders them from making use of educational facilities generally provided in schools for children of that age. The aim of special education is to provide children with an education that promotes realization of their full potential, to achieve independent living as much as they are capable, and to become well-adjusted individuals in the community. The policy encourages mainstreaming and integration of students with special needs into "ordinary" schools. Students with severe and multiple disabilities are placed in special schools for more intensive services. Class size of special schools ranges from eight to 20 students per class, with a staffing ratio of 1.5 teachers per class. As of the 2010–2011 school year, there were 61 special schools to support students with SEN such as visual and hearing impairment, intellectual disability, and social maladjustment.

Curriculum, Instruction, and Assessment

Pre-1997 colonial education in Hong Kong can be described as a curriculum originally based on a traditional English grammar school model influenced by local Chinese traditions. Curriculum was based on traditional academic subjects that directed students to the workplace or continuance in higher education. As discussed previously, the curriculum was marked by elitism, competitiveness, and examinations that were governed by a bureaucratic system.

In the years prior to the handover of Hong Kong to the People's Republic of China, initiatives to change the structure and curriculum of Hong Kong schools were introduced. Reforms and measures that promote a whole-school approach, education of the whole person, learning to learn, and lifelong learning are some examples. Such measures promote the elimination of "spoon-feeding" and rote learning and encourage critical, reflective, and creative thinking among students.

The Basic Law gives post-1997 Hong Kong the responsibility to formulate policies on the development and improvement of education. Acting on this authority, the Hong Kong government has implemented a range of organizations or advisory bodies that assist it with its policies that affect curriculum, instructions, and assessment. The EDB, the government's policy bureau, plays a policy coordination role to ensure development of full and coherent educational policies.

Currently, the basic subject matters studied in primary schools are Chinese, Putonghua, English, mathematics, music, physical education, computer studies, and general studies, which can include health, social skills, and environment. In most primary schools, Chinese is the language of instruction, with English taught as a second language.

In secondary schools, Chinese, English, and mathematics are core subjects while electives include subjects in history and the arts (e.g., world history, Chinese history, geography, and Chinese literature), science (e.g., physics, chemistry, biology, and additional mathematics) or commerce (e.g., economics, accountancy, and business studies).

In 2001 a shift to a student-centered focus was stated in the curriculum reform known as Learning to Learn—The Way Forward in Curriculum Development, issued by the Curriculum Development Council. The emphasis on learning to learn promotes whole-person development and lifelong learning as a means to enhance a productive society.

Banding

With the completion of primary school, students are placed in a secondary school based primarily on test results. Secondary schools are ranked by a banding system consisting of Bands 1 to 3. Band 1 schools are ranked the most prestigious, Band 2 schools rank in the middle, and Band 3 is ranked the lowest. The ranking of a secondary school is determined by the test scores of its students, the record of university acceptance of its student body, and the medium of instruction, with English generally given more weight than Chinese.

While primary schools do not have an official banding system, informal determination of the quality of the primary school is often based on test scores, the banding of the secondary schools where students are placed at completion of primary school, and the district or neighborhood in which the school is located.

Testing

Students are required to take tests that are used to determine their placement at various stages of their education. At the completion of Primary 5, or the fifth year of primary school, test results determine student's placement in the banding of their future secondary school. At the completion of senior secondary school for Form 6, students must take the newly developed Hong Kong Diploma of Secondary Exam (HKDSE), commencing in 2012. The results of HKDSE will determine admission to a tertiary-level institution or university.

Teacher Education

Hong Kong's Education Ordinance requires that any person who teaches in a local school must be either a registered teacher or a permitted teacher. A person who holds teacher qualification (i.e., a local teacher's certificate or postgraduate diploma or certificate in education) and is a Hong Kong citizen or a holder of a valid employment visa from the HKSAR may apply as a registered teacher. The Hong Kong Institute of Education and some of the universities provide both the academic qualifications and teacher training to become a registered teacher. In the future, it is planned that all registered teachers will be university graduates or degree holders and possess teacher education training.

A person who holds only academic qualifications but no teacher training and qualification may be considered as a permitted teacher. For kindergarten teachers, the minimum entry qualification is five passes in subject, including both Chinese and English, in the Hong Kong Certificate of Education Examination, which was replaced by the HKDSE in 2012. Since September 2003, all newly hired kindergarten teachers must possess a Qualified Kindergarten Teacher qualification or its equivalent. The EDB emphasizes the importance of continuous professional development that spans initial teacher education, induction, and in-service professional development.

Technology and Education

The government introduced the development of information technology (IT) as a tool for teaching and learning as well as a subject matter taught in schools. The goal is to prepare students for an information age and to become lifelong learners. IT facilities include broadband capabilities and e-learning platforms to conduct discussions and homework for students. Parents also participate in seminars and workshops via IT to understand their children's educational experiences.

In a survey conducted by the Education Bureau in 2006, nearly 90 percent of primary school students and nearly 80 percent of secondary school students indicated they like to use computers to learn. Ninety-five percent of primary and secondary schools students have access to computers, with 97 percent of these students stating they had access to the Internet at home. Eight-six percent of primary school teachers and 71 percent of secondary school teachers believed that IT can make teaching more effective. However, only 50 percent of the teachers used IT frequently in class.

Gender and Education

The HKSAR government is a member of the international Convention on the Elimination of All Forms of Discrimination against Women (CEDAW). As such, the government adopted the principle of equality for both sexes and equal rights and opportunities in education and males at all levels. HKSAR first established the Sex Discrimination Ordinance in 1995 to eliminate discrimination based on sex and to promote gender equality. In 1996 the Equal Opportunities Commission was established as a statutory body responsible for the implementation of the ordinance.

The majority of Hong Kong's schools are coeducational, with a roughly equal number of single-sex schools for boys and girls. The exception is at the primary school level, where entry to these schools is by parental choice and through central allocation. In regard to curriculum, the same subjects are made available to female and male students.

Females have increased their enrollment in universities. In 2001–2002, 54.4 percent of the students in the UGC-funded programs were women. In the 2010–2011 academic year, the percentage of Hong Kong women in higher education was 53.5 percent. However, concern has been expressed about the domination of male students in the fields of physical sciences, engineering, and technology, while female students tend to be in the fields of social sciences, arts and humanities, and education. With increased participation by females in all fields, these trends are shifting.

The need to reduce gender stereotyping in textbooks to avoid prejudice and promote equality between the sexes continues to be a concern. Educating teachers to be knowledgeable, sensitive, and aware of gender stereotyping in curriculum materials and in their practice is also emphasized in teacher training courses.

CEDAW expressed concern over the low percentage of women in the higher levels of the teaching profession at its last hearing with the HKSAR, held in 1999. While teaching in primary and secondary schools is dominated by women, females in higher education represented only 10 percent of academic teaching staff in 2001–2002. In 2010–2011 women made up almost 50 percent of the workforce, yet their median monthly wages were only about 85 percent of what men earned.

Informal Education

Planned school activities that are not part of the subject timetable in primary and secondary school, including extracurricular activities such as camps, student clubs and organizations, assemblies, sports activities, outside speakers, and fieldtrips, are often referred to as informal curriculum. Informal education also refers to courses that are not part of the usual formal educational structure. These include orientation courses for newly arrived children from China and education for non-Chinese-speaking children.

System Economics

The government views education as the most important long-term social investment and has been investing heavily in education in order to prepare for a knowledge-based workforce. In recent years, resources have continued to rise, and according to the 2010–2011 budget, total public expenditure on education exceeded 8.21 billion US dollars a year. This accounts for 18.9 percent of the total government recurrent expenditure, the largest expenditure of the government's budget. Additional funds will be allocated with the new initiative to introduce small class sizes in primary schools.

Funds to expand and diversify research and development will also be allocated. An additional 800 postgraduate research places were provided in phases commencing in 2009–2010 and budgeted for 38.66 million US dollars (HK$300 million) per year along with a one-time 2.32 billion US dollars (HK$18 billion) to strengthen targeted research projects.

Challenges and Dilemmas

Since 1997 there have been dramatic and sweeping educational reforms for Hong Kong schools. Tung Chee Wah, the first chief executive of HKSAR, introduced major educational reforms, particularly measures to upgrade the teaching profession and teacher education. Controversy continues over such issues as banding, the emphasis on a curriculum driven by examination, class size, medium of instruction, integration of immigrant children from China, and mainstreaming special education students into the regular classroom. Defining and shaping postcolonial Hong Kong education and development of its curriculum under a "One Country, Two Systems" framework remains a challenge. Topics of academic freedom, citizenship education, ethnic minorities, and patriotism have become part of the curriculum deliberations.

The people of Hong Kong are limited in their ability to change their government, and the legislature is limited in its power to affect government policies. Universal suffrage is strongly urged by pro-democracy groups, but it is unlikely that any significant reforms

of the electoral system will be addressed until after 2012, as set by China. The Chinese government suggested that Hong Kong may not achieve full universal suffrage in elections for the chief executive until 2017 and for the Legislative Council, or governing body, until 2020. In turn, there are efforts to democratize the classroom and the decision-making process, which demands the rethinking of the roles, responsibilities, and relationships of learners, teachers, parents, and policy makers.

The dramatic educational reforms with their changes and growth at a rapid pace must also be accompanied by quality in teaching and learning. The rapid changes represented in the educational reforms have resulted in additional workload for the schools and stress for teachers. Upgrading of teacher qualifications and the teaching profession takes time, and its realization will be a continual challenge in the future.

Future Prospects

The future of education in Hong Kong is encouraging and promising. Transformation from a culture of rote learning and memorization to one that encourages a whole-person development that embraces critical and reflective thinking highlights some of the dramatic initiatives implemented in the past decade. Hong Kong's education preparation for knowledge-based professionals, balancing local and global needs, and evolving relationship with China will continue as future challenges. The expansion of the number of student places in higher education has been impressive, and the government's ongoing commitment to strengthening education and investing in its people is very positive.

The Hong Kong government views itself as a world city and an education hub of the Asian region that attracts students and scholars internationally and from China in particular. The government strives for international competitiveness and affirms its commitment to strengthening academic exchanges and collaborative research with universities around the world.

Betty E. Ang

Hong Kong Education at a Glance

General Information

Population	7 million
Languages	English and Chinese
Literacy rate	97.1%
GDP per capita	US$31,709
Number of phones (landline) per 100 people	60
Number of phones (mobile) per 100 people	189
Number of Internet users per 100 people	70.4
Number of Internet hosts	817,701

Formal Educational Information

Compulsory school age population	554,289
Compulsory school age population	12.64%
Number of years of compulsory education	9
Student/teacher ratio (primary and secondary school)	15.2
Average class size	
Primary school	28.9
Secondary school (Form 1–Form 5)	34.4
Secondary school (Form 6–Form 7)	30.1
Average school days per year (2003)	190
Primary school gross enrollment ratio (2005)	100%
Primary school entrants reaching Form 1 of secondary school	100%
Secondary school gross enrollment ratio	100%
Child labor (ages 5–14) (2005)	0.15%

Note: Unless otherwise indicated, all data are based on sources from 2011.

REFERENCES

Adamson, Bob, and Paul Morris. "Changing Hong Kong's Schools." In *Changing the Curriculum: The Impact of Reform on Primary*

Schooling in Hong Kong, ed. Bob Adamson, Tammy Kwan, and Ka-Ki Chan, 7–20. Hong Kong: Hong Kong University Press, 2000.

Census and Statistics Department. "Statistics by Subject." www.censtatd.gov.hk/hong_kong_statistics/statistics_by_subject/.

Central Intelligence Agency. *The CIA World Factbook.* New York: Skyhorse, 2011. https://www.cia.gov/library/publications/the-world-factbook/index.html.

Government of Hong Kong. "Hong Kong: The Facts." www.gov.hk/en/about/abouthk/factsheets.

Hong Kong Special Administrative Region Government Yearbook. 2010. www.yearbook.gov.hk/2010/en.

Kennedy, Kerry John. *Changing Schools for Changing Times: New Directions for School Curriculum in Hong Kong.* Hong Kong: Chinese University Press, 2005.

Labour Department, Government of the Hong Kong Special Administrative Region.

Morris, Paul. *The Hong Kong School Curriculum: Development, Issues and Policies.* Hong Kong: Hong Kong University Press, 1995.

Nation Master. 2011. www.nationmaster.com.

Postiglione, Gerry, ed. *Education and Society in Hong Kong: Toward One Country, Two Systems.* Hong Kong: Hong Kong University Press, 1992.

Sweeting, Anthony. *A Phoenix Transformed: The Reconstruction of Education in Post-war Hong Kong.* Hong Kong: Oxford University Press, 1993.

Sweeting, Anthony, and Paul Morris. "Educational Reform in Post-war Hong Kong: Planning and Crisis Intervention." *International Journal of Educational Development* 13:3 (1993): 201–216.

University Grants Committee. www.ugc.edu.hk.

World Bank Education Statistics. 2011. www.worldbank.org.

INDONESIA

Located in southeastern Asia between the Indian and Pacific Oceans, Indonesia is the world's largest archipelagic state. The Dutch began to colonize Indonesia in the early seventeenth century; the islands were occupied by Japan from 1942 to 1945. Indonesia declared its independence after Japan's surrender, but it required four years of intermittent negotiations, recurring hostilities, and United Nations mediation before the Netherlands agreed to relinquish its colony.

Current issues in Indonesia include persistent poverty and unemployment, inadequate infrastructure, pervasive corruption, a fragile banking sector, a poor investment climate, and unequal resource distribution among regions. Significant progress has been made in rebuilding after the devastating December 2004 tsunami, and the province now shows more economic activity than before the disaster. In 2006 and early 2007, Indonesia suffered disasters including a major earthquake, an industrial accident that created a "mud volcano," a tsunami, and a major flooding, causing additional damages in the billions of dollars. Donors are assisting Indonesia with its disaster mitigation and early warning efforts. At present the Indonesian government is grappling with low-level armed conflict against the Free Papua Movement, a separatist movement.

Educational System

Prior to the Presidential Instruction Decree No. 10 of 1973, no universal educational system existed in Indonesia. Under Dutch rule, only a small proportion of Indonesians had access to education. The educational system in existence from 1892 until 1929 was, essentially, a two-class system consisting of first class for the privileged and second class for the general population. After gaining independence in 1949, the Indonesian government expended much effort on education taught in the national language and expanded the number of educational institutions. By 1960, 2.5 million students were enrolled in primary schools. However, more than half of them never completed their education.

In 1973 Indonesia's compulsory education program was initiated by the Presidential Instruction Decree No. 10. In 1976 a standardized national curriculum was first introduced throughout the school system. By 1984 basic compulsory education for children seven to 12 years old was fully implemented. In 1990 compulsory education was extended to students 15 years old by the order of Government Regulation No. 28/1990.

In 1992 a new regulation addressing educational opportunities for those struggling in the traditional, formal school system was implemented. As a result, three new types of schools were established: *Sekolah kecil*, small primary schools, in sparsely populated areas; *Pamong*, larger primary schools, serving students who dropped out of formal schools; and integrated primary schools for students with mental or physical disabilities. In 1996 Decree No. 053/U/1996 created Open *Sekolah Lanjutan Tingat Pertama* for students who could not attend traditional junior secondary schools due to learning difficulties.

Currently, the Ministry of National Education and Culture (MOEC) oversees the organizational structure of the Indonesian educational system. MOEC, which consists of seven principal units, sets the administrative structure of education, develops curriculum, finances education, establishes the infrastructure, provides equipment necessary for implementing educational activities, and trains faculty and staff who serve the educational system at the national level. At the local level, an Office of Education and Culture in each of the 27 provinces and a district office in each of the 305 districts interpret and implement MOEC's national educational and cultural policies to fit within local area needs.

Precompulsory and Compulsory Education

The purpose of precompulsory education is to stimulate the physical and mental growth of children outside the family environment and to prepare children for compulsory basic education. The subject matter at the kindergarten level includes Pancasila, the philosophical foundation of the Indonesian state, which comprises five principles held to be inseparable and interrelated: belief in the one and only God, just and civilized humanity, the unity of Indonesia, democracy led by wise guidance through consultation and representation, and social justice for the whole Indonesian people. Other subject matter includes moral education and religion, discipline, language skills, intellectual stimulation, creativity, emotional harmony, social skills, manual skills and physical ability, and health. Community support for precompulsory education is increasing. In 1969, 343,466 children were enrolled in 6,072 kindergartens. In 1995, 1.6 million children were enrolled in 40,715 kindergartens. With the increase in precompulsory education attendance, the proportion of six-year-olds enrolling in compulsory primary schools is also increasing. In 1990 about half (40.5 percent) of all enrolling students for the primary schools were six years old. As of 2012, approximately 8.5 million children are of preschool age. Moreover, approximately 25.5 million children are of primary school age. The number of adolescents of secondary school age has also surpassed

25.5 million individuals. The gross enrollment ratio for primary school children—between the ages of 6 and 12—is 115, which indicates that children over the age of 12 are enrolled or eligible for completing primary school. The net enrollment ratio for primary school, however, shows that only 94.5 percent of all primary school aged children are actually attending primary school.

Postcompulsory Education

Since the 1990s, the Indonesian government has emphasized funding and efforts related to primary education and the inclusion of junior secondary-level schools in the compulsory education system. Secondary education and higher education levels are not mandated by the government. However, development and improvement in the system's upper levels are encouraged because the government views education as the vehicle allowing Indonesia to compete and advance in science and technology and as a necessity for economic improvement.

Secondary education consists of several types. Vocational secondary education focuses on expanding students' specific occupational skills and professionalism by participating in work study or co-op programs with different companies. Religion-based secondary education facilitates students' mastery of special religious knowledge. Service-based secondary education prepares students for government work or gaining skills for the civil service sector. The special secondary education schools are for students who have physical and/or mental disabilities. The general secondary education prepares students for higher education by expanding their knowledge and skills.

In 1995 only about 39 percent of all 16- to 18-year-olds in Indonesia were enrolled in any of the different types of secondary schools. The minimum employment age of 14 years in Indonesia attracts many teenagers to work rather than to schools that require tuition payments.

Higher education in Indonesia consists of academic education or professional education at state-funded and private institutions. Academic education focuses on science, technology, and research while professional education focuses on practical skills and knowledge. Colleges, which focus on one discipline, and universities, which incorporate multiple disciplines, provide both professional and academic education.

In 1979 a semester credit unit system was adopted along with bachelor's, master's, and doctoral degrees and nondegree programs. The government entities managing higher education in Indonesia include the MOEC, Military Academy, College for Civil Servants, and Ministry of Religious Affairs (MORA).

The purpose of higher education is to increase the number of students who can apply the needed academic and/or professional skills for Indonesian society and, in turn, improve Indonesia's welfare and national culture. The number of students enrolling in higher education is increasing but is still a small percentage of the available age group (less than 10 percent of 19- to 24-year-olds in 1995 chose higher education). Most students seek jobs after secondary education rather than apply for higher education. Gaining admittance to higher education also requires students to pass a national entrance test and/or a portfolio assessment verifying achievement in secondary education subjects.

Curriculum, Instruction, and Assessment

Under Indonesian law, curriculum is defined as the arrangement of learning and assessment materials to achieve the objectives of the respective levels of education in a framework that aids in the achievement of national objectives. Ministerial Decree No. 060/U/1993 describes a "subject" as a collection of study materials, methods, and teachings that introduces concepts, basic discussion, themes, and values, combined into one discipline. It is stipulated that the minister of the MOEC organizes curriculum. Likewise, the minister of MORA is responsible for religious education, while the minister of manpower is responsible for occupational training. Decrees dating back to 1972 and including Law No. 2 of 1989 established Paket A (nonformal primary education) and Paket B (nonformal junior secondary education) programs. Paket A is designed to provide basic skills needed for junior secondary education. Paket B is to build and expand on learning within basic education, leading to employment.

Generally, the curriculum for courses of study is implemented at three capability levels: basic, intermediate, and advanced. The curriculum is to be based on valid national determination made by the MOEC and adjusted according to the condition and environmental needs of educational units. Each level of education, whether formal or nonformal, must contain Pancasila education, religious education, and citizenship education. Additionally, all basic education must contain lessons and assessments for Indonesian language, reading, and writing. Other subject areas to be addressed include technology, geography, national and general history, art, physical and health education, and English. Schools may add curriculum of local interest provided it does not reduce time spent on the government-specified curriculum. Local content may occupy as much as 20 percent of total instructional time; the remaining 80 percent must focus on government-prescribed subject matter as defined in the national curriculum.

Indonesia's current curriculum evolved over a 40-year period in four phases: (1) 1968–1975: A basic national curriculum was designed and implemented; it was criticized for not providing sufficient detail about content requirements and for providing insufficient guidance to teachers on how to implement the curriculum; (2) 1975–1984: The previous curriculum was completely revised and was highlighted by modifications of instructional time allotted to key subjects and by the introduction of a system of differentiated credits for particular subjects; (3) 1985–1989: The 1975 curriculum was revisited with increased emphasis on patriotism and the spirit of independence; (4) 1989–present: Vocation-specific curriculum was introduced to increase the relevance of junior secondary education. Skill-based education programs were introduced in the fields of health care, construction, automotive work, metalwork, electrical skills, agriculture, handicrafts, tourism, and marketing.

The national curriculum is developed in a top-down process. Every five years a document is published that contains a general elaboration of the five-year national development plan. Through this document and per the special requests of the minister of education, changes can be initiated in the curriculum. Over the past 25 years, the major calls for curricular change have come with the seating of new ministers.

Law No. 2 of 1989 states that the government is to conduct assessment related to the curriculum, staff, facilities, and infrastructure on a periodic and sustained basis. Curriculum assessment is to determine suitability. Assessment of students is to be used to determine student achievement. Teachers are to conduct student assessments and, to some degree, assess the curriculum. School principals are to assess curriculum, teachers, other staff, facilities, and infrastructure. Ministerial Decree No. 060/U/1993 states that assessment of study results are to be administered at the end of each term. There are more comprehensive assessments at the completion of the six years of primary education and again after three years of junior secondary education.

The current and future curricular trends that face Indonesia's educators include working with an overcrowded primary curriculum, a lack of integration within the curriculum, using quality textbooks, issues of national testing, and the localization of curriculum.

Teacher Education

Improvements in the areas of curriculum, instruction, and assessment along with the advent of compulsory education for all children in Indonesia have led to changes in teacher education.

While teacher education is a relatively new phenomenon in Indonesia, it has grown rapidly since World War II. Indonesian teachers had generally completed ten years of schooling to demonstrate their readiness to be a teacher and there was little or no specific training in pedagogy. However, funding from the World Bank led to rigorous, focused programs that addressed theoretical approaches to learning and teaching, a huge change from the earlier days of independence in 1949. Since 1992 basic education teachers are required to be certified by teacher training institutions with the MOE able to determine alternative routes to this form of certification. Certification is not required for teachers in nonformal programs but rather determined by ministerial regulation.

There is still little coordination between the training of teachers for primary classrooms, which takes place in teacher training facilities, and the training of those interested in teaching older students, who are educated at the universities. The greatest deficiencies in teacher education are the lack of specific, adequate training in pedagogical processes, the lack of academic resources available to teacher educators, and the academic level of certified teachers.

Informal Education

With the majority of Indonesian students staying in school for about nine years, the education of its citizenry outside of formal education may be of greater importance than in countries with more years of required education. Informal education that is not structured in any way occurs as children spend time with their parents, their peers, and in their communities. Informal education also includes "nonformal" or out-of-school education. These substitute programs were designed to eradicate illiteracy in the Indonesian language.

When compulsory education became mandatory for primary grades in the early 1990s, nonformal education became more important as efforts to help all students succeed increased. When the compulsory age was extended to include junior secondary grades, Decree No. 053/U/1996 was instituted to provide alternative, informal access to education. Typical nonstructured, informal education has continued throughout this time.

Some organizations use informal education through the media, radio, TV, and websites to deepen understanding of issues such as the environment, HIV/AIDS awareness, and other global issues. For example, Islamic Relief, a nongovernmental organization responding to the tsunami disaster, has continued to provide supplementary and information education to children displaced by the tragedy, focusing on information related to nutrition and literacy. Other Indonesians receive informal education by attending theater, workshops, lectures, or training. There are social action and philanthropic groups that provide open access to informal education and learning facilities through their organizations. For example, farmers in Bali created Subak to help enable sustainable water supplies, and people living in Jakarta formed Marsiurapan to facilitate their traditions of giving and volunteering. Companies such as Citibank and General Electric have created programs involving their employees in philanthropic activities such as helping homeless children get access to informal education and learning facilities. KOMPAK addresses issues for child workers through drop-in centers that include opportunities for children to read, write, and play sports.

Dilemmas

With its vast geographic size and ethnic diversity, Indonesia faces many challenges as it works further

Indonesia Education at a Glance

General Information

Capital	Jakarta
Population	245.6 million
Language	Bahasa Indonesia
Literacy rate	90.4%
GDP per capita	US$1,280
Number of phones (landline)	14.821 million
Number of phones (mobile)	63.803 million
Number of Internet users	16 million
Number of Internet hosts	559,359

Formal Education Information

Compulsory school age population enrolled	98%
Compulsory school age population	7
Number of years of compulsory education	9
Student/teacher ratio	
Primary school (Standard 1–6)	20.4
Secondary school (Form 1–5)	11.8
Average class size in primary school	27
Average school days per year (primary school)	240
Average number of hours per school day (primary school)	5–6
Primary school gross enrollment ratio	117.3%
Primary school entrants reaching grade 5 (2004)	89.5%
Primary school entrants reaching last grade	85.5%
Secondary school gross enrollment ratio	63.1%

Note: Unless otherwise indicated, all data are based on sources from 2011.

to develop a quality educational system that supports its desire for continued economic growth and development. Foci of reform by the national government include issues such as funding, the decentralization of decision making, and illiteracy. As an example of reform to further increase literacy, recent legislation set goals of increasing participation in primary (100 percent) and junior secondary (96 percent) education, making nine years of education compulsory.

Disparity among the many urban and rural areas has existed since the inception of formal education. The basic issues that stem from this disparity are educational access, gender equity, and socioeconomic equity. Less densely populated, rural areas show a lower percentage of six- to 12-year-old students finding access to schooling, accounting for over 1 million children not attending school. Basic education in Indonesia tends to be biased toward students from urban families, wealthy families, and schools located in Java. The percentage of females enrolled in primary schools is significantly and consistently lower than that of their male counterparts. While there are no laws discriminating against the formal education of women, there is greater illiteracy among females, fewer females complete higher levels of education, and fewer women take courses to help them gain promotions in their employment.

While Indonesia has made progress in areas of access for all students, it still struggles with inadequate funding and a deteriorating infrastructure. One example involves the fact that two government ministries oversee education. The dual control provided by these ministries can cause conflict and inefficiency, with one ministry looking at quality but having no control over budgetary issues.

Teacher quality is also a concern. Many teachers fail to meet the minimum standards set by the MOEC. Recent national efforts to encourage certification are encouraging and may address this issue over time. It is also important for Indonesia to address issues of absent teachers who increase the workload on the qualified teachers who are in their classrooms daily.

System Economics

Funding for education in Indonesia saw a large increase from 2001 through 2011 with double-digit annual growth for several years in that time span. National education expenditures grew from 11 percent to nearly 18 percent of the total budget over those 11 years. This current level of funding places Indonesia on a par with other developing countries with similar demographics and gross domestic product.

Expenditures in 2008 by the central education ministries constituted 38 percent of the total budget. Provincial expenditures were 5 percent, and spending at the district level was 57 percent of the total budget. The control structure of the budgets in Indonesia means that while the majority of expenditures happen at the district level, administrators have minimal control over how those funds are spent. As for total expenditures at different grade levels, approximately 74 percent of spending is spent on compulsory education. Total federal educational expenditures in 2011 represented 2.8 percent of the country's gross domestic product, thus ranking Indonesia 139 of 186 countries. Per capita spending in Indonesia, based on percentage of GDP education expenditure, amounts to roughly $566 per student.

Future Prospects

Corruption is a concern at many levels in Indonesian society. Work to tighten government oversight of projects and spending will be required to reduce the frequency of corruption at all levels of education. One current project from USAID is focused on improving management of existing resources, reducing corruption, and increasing parental and community participation in the educational system.

Jaesook Gilbert, Daniel Doerger,
Isaac Larison, Eric Rowley, Suzanne Soled,
and Yvonne Quintanilla

REFERENCES

Australian Agency for International Development. *Indonesia Education Program Strategy: 2007–2012.* Canberra, Australia: Australian Agency for International Development, 2012.

Central Intelligence Agency. *The CIA World Factbook.* New York: Skyhorse, 2011. https://www.cia.gov/library/publications/the-world-factbook/index.html.

Nation Master. 2011. www.nationmaster.com.

UNESCO. *Global Education Digest 2012: Comparing Education Statistics Across the World.* Montreal: UNESCO Institute for Statistics, 2012.

UNESCO–IBE. www.ibe.unesco.org/en/worldwide/unesco-regions/asia-and-the-pacific/indonesia.html.

UNESCO–UIS. www.uis.unesco.org.

UNICEF. www.unicef.org/infobycountry.

World Bank. *World Bank and Education in Indonesia.* Washington, DC: World Bank, 2011.

JAPAN

Japan (Nihon or Nippon) is a crescent-shaped archipelago located off the east coast of the Asian continent, near the Korean Peninsula and the southeast region of the Russian Federation. Japan's national language is Japanese; however, two indigenous languages—Ainu (in Hokkaido) and Ryukyu (in Okinawa)—are also used. Japan's two major religions are Shintoism (Japan's oldest and only indigenous religion) and Buddhism.

The present constitution of Japan, established in 1947 after World War II, marked the beginning of Japan as a constitutional monarchy. Under the constitution, government is a sacred trust of the people, authorized by the people, and for the benefit of the people. The emperor is to serve as the symbol of the Japanese state and the unity of the people. Japan employs a parliamentary-cabinet system with three independent branches of government: legislative, administrative, and judicial.

Japanese students have enjoyed an international reputation for high achievement in mathematics and science. For example, in the 1990s, they were among the top three high-achieving nations. This international standing, however, has somewhat declined in recent years. This decline is one of the many challenges that Japanese education faces today.

Educational System

The beginning of known education in Japan coincides with the introduction of Chinese characters in the sixth century, when both women and men of upper-class status began to receive literacy education. Slowly, literacy education spread among the samurai and peasant classes through Buddhist temples. By the end of the Edo period (1600–1867), the literacy rate increased to about 40 percent due to the establishment of schools. These included locally governed schools for children of the Samurai class and temple schools (Terakoya) for children of farmers, peasants, craftsmen, and merchants. The attendance rate in areas such as Edo (current Tokyo) exceeded 80 percent by the late Edo period. Among the attendees, approximately 80 percent were boys and 20 percent were girls.

The modern public education system was developed in the late nineteenth century at the collapse of the Edo period that marked the beginning of modern Japan. In 1885 the Ministry of Education was established. Subsequently, a school ordinance was implemented in 1872 to mandate the first four years of schooling to be compulsory (expanded to six years in 1907). Enrollment in compulsory education was approximately 50 percent in its beginning but increased rapidly to nearly 98 percent by 1910. During wartime in the first half of the twentieth century, the military influenced the course of education—for example, through the use of nationalized textbooks that taught children to fight the war for the emperor.

With Japan's defeat in World War II, the Allied nations took control of the rebuilding of Japan and a new constitution was established in 1947. In the same year, the Fundamental Law of Education and the School Education Law were created in the spirit of the new constitution and became the foundation of the current education system. Aiming to achieve equal opportunity for education, these laws established the current 6–3–3–4 school system—six years of elementary school, three years of junior high school, three years of senior high school, and four years of college or university (hereafter referred to as *university* or *universities*). Compulsory education was extended to nine years and provided free of charge. Special education was also established under these laws. The 2001 reorganization of the central government established the current Ministry of Education, Culture, Sports, and Science and Technology (MEXT). The MEXT is a result of combining the Science and Technology Agency with the former Ministry of Education, Science and Culture. One of the charges of the MEXT is to formulate and implement educational policies. Local boards of education supervise day-to-day administration under the guidance of the MEXT.

Precompulsory Education

Prior to beginning compulsory education, most children attend preschool, day care, or children's centers. Preschool typically serves children three to six years old for a few hours a day, under the jurisdiction of the MEXT. In contrast, day care was established as part of a social welfare program to assist working parents or those unable to care for their children during the day and is within the jurisdiction of the Ministry of Health, Labor, and Welfare. Day-care facilities typically serve children from birth to six years old for a longer period of time. Children's centers, established in 2006, function as a hybrid of preschool and day care under the jurisdiction of both ministries. In some cases, preschools add day-care functions and become recognized as children's centers. Likewise, day-care facilities add preschool functions to the same end. The establishment of children's centers reflects the current movement to unify preschool and day-care.

Compulsory Education

Compulsory education includes six years of elementary school and three years of junior high school. Schools at the compulsory education level are predominately public (99 percent for elementary schools and 93 percent for junior high schools). Students are typically assigned to public schools in their residential areas. The enrollment rate for compulsory education approximates 100 percent.

A typical school year for compulsory education starts in April and ends in March of the following year, with approximately 200 days of instruction. Until 2002 compulsory schools typically held classes six days a week. Currently, public schools hold classes five days a week, although some private schools maintain a six-day-a-week schedule. Elementary school teachers generally teach multiple subjects and junior high school teachers teach specialized subjects. In addition, most teachers are expected to supervise their homeroom students and oversee after-school extracurricular activities.

Postcompulsory Education

After compulsory education, graduates who wish to advance to senior high school need to satisfy entrance requirements. Nearly 98 percent of the students advance to senior high school. Approximately 74 percent of senior high schools are public. The majority of senior high schools are academic schools. Alternatives to standard academic high schools include vocational, correspondence, and night schools to meet the diverse needs of students. A recent trend is to offer diverse courses or programs within academic schools. Another recent trend is to provide junior high school and senior high school education without interruption (typically with no entrance examinations). Approximately 9 percent of senior high schools fall into this category (2010 statistics). With the implementation of a new policy in 2010, public senior high schools no longer charge tuition and the government subsidizes part of tuition for private senior high schools.

Nearly 54 percent of senior high school graduates proceed to higher education such as two-year junior colleges, four-year universities, six-year medical schools, correspondence universities, or vocational schools. Universities also offer master's and PhD programs. Approximately 78 percent of higher education schools are private. In 2010, 41 percent of students at four-year universities were female, and 89 percent of all students at two-year junior colleges were female.

Curriculum, Instruction, and Assessment

Issued by the MEXT and subject to review and revision, the Courses of Study specify basic national standards, goals of education, courses to be taught, their content, and intended instructional hours for each grade of preschool, elementary, junior high, and senior high school, including special education. The MEXT also issues teachers' manuals that teachers are expected to follow. Textbooks must adhere to the guidelines specified in the Courses of Study and be authorized by the MEXT. Textbook selection is the responsibility of local boards of education for public schools and the principal's responsibility for national and private schools. Textbooks are distributed at no charge to elementary and junior high school students.

Elementary school students study Japanese language arts, mathematics, social studies, science, music, arts and crafts, home economics, physical education, moral education, special activities, and integrated studies. Special activities include collaborative classroom activities, student councils, school events, and volunteer work in a local community. Integrated studies allow each school to augment its curriculum by focusing on areas of study deemed important. These include theme-based learning in international understanding, information, environment, or welfare and health, and activities relating to the social and cultural characteristics of the school and its local community. Since 2010, foreign language, generally English, has been required for fifth and sixth graders with focus on oral communication, in order to enhance the understanding of other languages and cultures. Junior high school students study health education and industrial arts, as well as those subjects listed for elementary school students.

Academic high schools offer general courses and courses for either a liberal arts or mathematics and science track, depending on the student's planned major at the university. Vocational schools and some academic schools offer courses such as agriculture, industry, commerce, fishery, home economics, nursing, science and mathematics, physical education, music, art, and English language for those who wish to pursue a specific academic or vocational area as their prospective career. Integrated courses cover a wide variety of subject areas and give senior high school students more options to reflect their interests as well

as academic and career plans. University students take general education courses as well as specialty courses in accord with their academic majors, declared prior to taking entrance examinations.

Teacher-led instruction has been commonly used at all levels of education. It often makes use of whole-class and sometimes small-group work known as *han* activities. Han, which typically applies to mixed-gender groups of students with diverse abilities, is most commonly seen in compulsory education. It is used for carrying out academic tasks as well as special activities such as serving school lunch, cleaning school sites, and doing daily classroom chores. Recent practices, especially in compulsory education, encourage team-teaching and use of classroom aides and volunteers. Reduced class size and ability-group instruction have become possible due to a decrease in the student population.

Beginning with elementary school all the way through senior high school, students are constantly evaluated on their academic performance, including class participation, quizzes, tests, and behavior and work habits. The MEXT specifies particular objectives to be met for each grade. Records of student academic performance, which are communicated to parents and guardians, are an important part of selection criteria for advancing to the next level of schooling. Advancement to public junior high school does not require entrance examinations. Those who wish to advance to national or private junior high schools, however, must adhere to admissions procedures specified by each school. Advancement to senior high school requires a submission of application materials, including a record of academic performance and passing an entrance examination. Applicants to public universities are required to submit records of academic performance with their applications and take a standard preliminary examination. Based on these scores, applicants choose a university and take its entrance examination. Private universities are not required to adhere to the same entrance procedures. However, a recent trend is that an increasing number of private schools are participating in the standard preliminary examination system.

Teacher Education

Students wishing to become teachers typically attend a MEXT-recognized public or private university.

Upon obtaining general teaching certificates for multiple subjects to teach at elementary school or single subjects to teach at junior high and senior high school, applicants must pass examinations administered by local boards of education. Teacher recruitment for private schools need not adhere to MEXT guidelines.

Professional development for teachers comes in various forms. These include a long-term assignment to private companies, participation in a master's program, trips abroad to observe teaching practices, and attending MEXT-mandated seminars as part of the teacher certificate renewal process. Most of these opportunities are funded by MEXT or local boards of education. As for in-service training, lesson study is a predominant method. In a typical lesson study, both novice and experienced teachers work together to design, implement, and revise a well-crafted lesson. Lesson studies may be voluntary or mandated by local boards of education and may be done by teachers within a school or across schools. The MEXT implements training of management personnel, including site principals.

Informal Education

As the nation faces the issue of aging, lifelong learning has become a recent focus. Reflecting this trend, government and private sectors offer various types of informal education to citizens of all ages. The government sector organizes events and classes at a nominal charge in order to promote social education, physical education, science and technology, cultural education, and vocational training. These events and classes are typically offered at public halls, libraries, museums, centers for children and youth, women's education centers, and culture centers. The private sector also offers various educational opportunities such as classes in music, sports, English, and computer skills. The classes tend to cover a wider range of topics and are offered more frequently at more convenient locations, but at a higher cost, than public events and classes.

After-school programs, known as *juku*, have become an indispensable component of informal education in Japan. The function of juku varies and includes helping students to develop basic academic skills. However, its most common function is to prepare students to pass entrance examinations. In order to advance to a small number of prestigious schools, many parents send their children to juku. Fueling this trend is the fact that the content of entrance examinations typically exceeds the scope of the official curriculum guidelines for public school education. The MEXT's 2002 revision of the Courses of Study was criticized for this discrepancy as this revision relaxed academic content to a significant degree. As a result, high reliance on juku is inevitable. The 2008 statistics show that about 40 percent of sixth graders, 63 percent of ninth graders, and 19 percent of eleventh graders attended juku.

Aside from juku, after-school programs are provided at public school sites, community facilities, and private institutions for children of working parents and guardians. These programs tend to serve primary-grade children and are within the jurisdiction of the Ministry of Health, Labor, and Welfare. Since the implementation of the Children's Welfare Law in 1998, the number of after-school programs has doubled, with the number of children enrolled increasing 2.4 times by 2010. However, there is a serious shortage of programs as the number of working mothers and single-parent families increases. To offset the growing demand, the MEXT began implementing a new after-school program (after-school children's classrooms) in 2009. This program, which engages children in academic learning, cultural activities, and sporting events, uses available school or other public facilities after school and on weekends.

System Economics

Japan's total expenditure on education remains among the lowest (3.4 percent of gross domestic product in 2008) when compared with other economically advanced countries listed on the Organisation for Economic Co-operation and Development (OECD) website. The education budget comes from three major sources: the national government, local governments, and private sources. Local governments provide over half of the total educational costs; the rest are almost evenly shared by the national government and the private sector. Of the national government's general budget, 9 to 10 percent (approximately US$50.9 billion in 2008) goes to the MEXT. At the local level, roughly 20 percent of the general budget of local governments (approximately US$156.5 billion in 2008) is used for education.

The MEXT in 2010 allocated 28.5 percent for compulsory education, 20.7 percent for national universities, 15.3 percent for promoting science and technology, 7.9 percent for private schools, 7 percent for tuition waivers for public high schools and tuition grants for private high schools, and 20.6 percent for supporting lifelong learning, culture, sports, exchange students, school textbooks, public school facilities, and scholarship programs. As for local governments, the 2008 data show that approximately 83.6 percent of the education budget was allocated to school education, 10.6 percent to social education, and the rest to administration and other costs.

Special Education

Special education in Japan targets students with disabilities. Since the turn of the twenty-first century, the special needs of students with multiple disabilities, as well as those with developmental disabilities such as learning disabilities (LD), attention-deficit hyperactivity disorders (ADHD), and high-functioning autism, have received considerable attention. The reform measures implemented in 2006 and 2007 aimed to provide more options to accommodate the diverse instructional needs of students and to practice more inclusive education.

Special education for students with severe disabilities used to be provided separately for the deaf, blind, and intellectually disabled from preschool through senior high school. However, the 2007 reform established a new system whereby any school that has the status of special support school can now serve students with different types of disabilities. Special support school teachers offer individualized, specialized instruction, including vocational training. At regular elementary and junior high schools, students with moderate disabilities attend special support classes, whereas students with mild disabilities, including those with LD, ADHD, and autism, attend regular classes and are provided access to resource rooms. Parents and local boards of education together make decisions regarding what is most appropriate for individual students.

The 2010 data indicate that 64.3 percent of the universities house students with disabilities, who account for 0.27 percent of the entire university population (undergraduate and graduate). Although this is a small fraction of the population of students with disabilities, postsecondary institutions admitted a greater number of students with disabilities in this decade than ever before. The Japan Student Services Organization—a legal body for the Japanese governmental organizations—serves as a channel for making local networks where local university communities research, and disseminate information about, best ways to support students with disabilities.

Gender and Education

Issues of gender in education have received much attention in response to anti–gender discrimination movements that seek gender equality in society. As a result, some gender-fair practices have been implemented. For example, many elementary school teachers have adopted a practice of organizing rosters in alphabetical order. This procedure avoids student selection for various activities to be based solely by gender. Uniforms for physical education classes have become unisex (although most senior high schools still have separate school uniforms for girls and boys). Furthermore, schools that traditionally served only girls or boys have or will become coeducational. As of 2010, about 6.7 percent of the 5,116 senior high schools are for girls only and 2.6 percent are for boys only. This trend also reflects the decreasing number of school-age children, as coeducation is seen as a way to recruit more students and to avoid school closure.

Despite increased gender-fair practices, gender differences remain prominent throughout students' learning environments. Gender-specific roles and gender-biased values are implicitly or explicitly depicted in textbooks. For example, most of the main characters in moral education textbooks are men, and when women appear they are typically introduced as mothers. In addition, Japanese reading textbooks tend to include more works by male authors than female authors. Although recent textbooks show an effort to conform to gender-fair practices, gender inequality is evident in the imbalance between the number of male and female teachers. In 2010, 93.4 percent of kindergarten teachers were women, whereas 62.8 percent of elementary school, 41.9 percent of junior high school, and 29.4 percent of senior high school teachers were women. Furthermore, men predominantly occupy administrative positions such as principals. The distribution of teachers by gender and subject matter also highlights this imbalance. In

2004 approximately 99 percent of junior high school home economics teachers were women whereas over 92 percent of shop teachers were men. Approximately 75 percent of mathematics and science teachers in senior high school were men. Additionally, more boys than girls choose to focus on mathematics and science whereas more girls than boys select literature courses.

Technology and Education

All public school facilities in Japan are equipped with computers. As of 2010, one computer is available for every eight students in elementary school, one for six students in junior high school, one for four students in senior high school, and one for three students in special education school. Furthermore, nearly 100 percent of schools have Internet connection and more than 72 percent of regular classrooms have local area network (LAN) connection. Among all public school teachers at compulsory and postcompulsory levels, nearly 60 percent are capable of teaching academic subjects using computers.

Dilemmas and Future Prospects

The current education system in Japan is hardly problem-free. One problem is a decline in academic achievement. Japanese students were among the highest achievers in mathematics and science in the 1990s. Recent results, however, no longer support such a reputation. The 2007 Trends in International Mathematics and Science Study (TIMSS) standings in mathematics dropped to fourth for fourth graders and to fifth for eighth graders. The Programme for International Student Assessment (PISA) conducted in 2009 by the OECD reported that 15-year-olds in Japan ranked ninth in mathematics, fifth in science, and eighth in reading. The 2002 revision of the Courses of Study was blamed for the decline in achievement because its academic standards were somewhat relaxed and academic instructional hours reduced. To address this problem, the MEXT revised the Courses of Study in 2011. This revision increased instructional hours for academic study, as it aims to promote academic excellence (including critical thinking skills) as well as healthy minds and bodies. Significant positive results have yet to emerge.

In the late twentieth century, the "second baby boomers"—approximately 8 million children born between 1971 and 1974—competed for entry into universities, including the most prestigious schools. Due to a sharp decline in the number of school-age children in the twenty-first century, there is room for every college applicant. Yet competition to enroll in a handful of select schools persists. For many less prestigious schools, this means that their enrollment does not reach their total student capacity. As a result, these schools have faced or are facing closure. Under such a circumstance, most private universities in recent years revised admission procedures. For example, more students are admitted through special admission processes that require essays or interviews, but not entrance examinations. These admission processes tend to select students who possess special talents in nonacademic areas. These processes are met with criticism on grounds that these students may lack necessary academic skills to pursue higher education.

Public higher educational institutions became public corporations in 2002. According to the MEXT, incorporation of public universities was to allow each institution to have flexibility and academic freedom to foster a unique intellectual environment. Critics say that this policy was implemented in order to achieve business efficiency in Japan's state institutions. This policy has been criticized for making educational institutions into for-profit entities at the expense of quality public education. It is also of concern that this is a step toward privatization of all public higher educational institutions.

The 2010 policy that waives tuition at public senior high schools and offers tuition grants at private schools has been a target of controversy. Not only does this policy strain the budget, but also it contradicts the fact that senior high school education is not compulsory. Furthermore, there is no consensus as to whether this policy should be applied to ethnic senior high schools (e.g., Korean schools, Chinese schools, and American schools).

Bullying and classroom disorder have become serious problems in recent years. As a result, an increasing number of students refuse to go to school and parents are choosing to withdraw their children from public schools. Bullying is also linked to truancy and suicide. To tackle this problem, the MEXT implemented amendments in 2000 to place school counselors on site, hire more teachers, and reduce class size at the compulsory education levels. Alternative forms of schooling have emerged in recent years for students who are victims of bullying or otherwise refuse to attend public schools. These schools aim to offer a safe place for students to learn both social skills and academic content. An increasing rate of juvenile delinquency, as well as youth prostitution, has also become a major societal concern. How to cope with these problems and improve educational systems in a timely manner is a major task for the future of the nation.

Educational dilemmas in Japan also include the education of linguistic and cultural minority children. The national government provides affirmative action, remedial education, and financial support for indigenous Ainu and Ryukyu ethnic groups. It also provided such aid for the descendants of the historically discriminated-against Burakumin—outcast people of the feudal era whose occupation involved killing (e.g., executioners and leather workers). However, affirmative action for the Burakumin expired in 2002. The systematic support for Korean immigrant children has improved over the last decade. How-

ever, de facto discrimination against these minority children remains.

Other groups of linguistic and cultural minority children who require immediate assistance include the offspring of Chinese returnees and refugees of the 1970s as well as large numbers of children of undocumented foreign workers who came to Japan from Asian countries such as Taiwan, Philippines, China, South Korea, Bangladesh, Pakistan, and Iran during the bubble economy in the 1980s and 1990s. Furthermore, with the implementation of the revised 1990 Immigration Control Law, the descendants of Japanese citizens who had emigrated to foreign countries are allowed to come back to work in Japan unconditionally. This has led to a massive population growth of Japanese descendants in Japan, especially from Latin American countries such as Brazil and Peru. The children of these recent comers have had an urgent need for various support programs, including Japanese as a Second Language classes (JSL) in school education. Although most of the support programs are currently provided by nonprofit organizations at the grassroots level, some local governments with large immigrant populations have been providing these programs, at least at the elementary school level. The national government also started to allocate special funding for JSL in 2007.

Due to the lack of financial and political support for minority students in public schools, an increasing number of heritage schools have been established. These ethnic schools were not credited as formal educational institutes in the past. In 2004, however, the Japanese government entrusted higher educational institutions to allow ethnic senior high school graduates to take entrance examinations without requiring college eligibility examinations. In contrast, children of Japanese citizens living overseas have received support from the Japanese government since the 1960s. For example, the government subsidizes all-day or weekend schools, which follow the curriculum and textbooks in Japan. It also provides teachers from Japan and accepts academic credits earned at such schools. Upon returning to Japan, however, these children receive relatively less educational support. In 2008 the MEXT issued an announcement that overseas Japanese schools would accept non-Japanese children. This announcement led to many controversies regarding the role and the function of these schools. Although Japan has emphasized in-

---

Japan Education at a Glance

General Information

Capital	Tokyo
Population	128.02 million
Language	Japanese
Literacy rate (2002)	99%
GDP per capita	US$34,000
Number of phones (landline) per 100 people	31.57
Number of phones (mobile) per 100 people	94.29
Number of Internet users per 100 people	73.91
Number of Internet hosts	54.846 million

Formal Education Information

Compulsory school age population enrolled	10.6 million
Compulsory school age population	8.24%
Number of years of compulsory education	9 (ages 6–15)
Student/teacher ratio	
Elementary school (grades 1–6)	16.7
Junior high school (grades 1–3)	14.2
Senior high school (grades 1–3)	14.1
Average class size	
Elementary school (grades 1–6)	25.2
Junior high school (grades 1–3)	29.4
Average school days per year	196–205
Elementary school gross enrollment ratio	99.96%
Elementary school entrants reaching grade 6	100%
Junior high school gross enrollment ratio	99.97%

Note: Unless otherwise indicated, all data are based on sources from 2011.

ternationalization, much work has yet to be done to internationalize domestic affairs to provide support for linguistically and culturally diverse children with respect to immigration laws, school systems, teacher education, and classroom instruction.

*Yukari Okamoto, Satoko Shao-Kobayashi,
and Kumi Hashimoto*

REFERENCES

Central Intelligence Agency. *The CIA World Factbook*. New York: Skyhorse, 2011. https://www.cia.gov/library/publications/the-world-factbook/index.html.

Ishikida, Miki Y. *Japanese Education in the 21st Century*. New York: iUniverse, 2005.

The Kodansha Bilingual Encyclopedia of Japan. New York: Kodansha America, 1998.

Ministry of Education, Culture, Sports, Science and Technology–Japan (MEXT). www.mext.go.jp/english.

Ministry of Health, Labor and Welfare—Japan. www.mhlw.go.jp/english.

Ministry of Internal Affairs and Communications, Statistics Bureau, Director-General for Policy Planning & Statistical Research and Training Institute. www.stat.go.jp/english.

Nation Master. 2011. www.nationmaster.com.

Organisation for Economic Co-operation and Development. www.oecd.org.

Passin, Herbert. *Society and Education in Japan*. New York: Bureau of Publications, Teachers College, Columbia University, 1965.

Sato, Gunei. *Internationalization and Education: Crosscultural Education in Japan*. Tokyo, Japan: Society for the Promotion of the University of the Air, 1999.

World Bank Education Statistics. 2011. www.worldbank.org.

KOREA, NORTH

The nation of the Democratic People's Republic of Korea (DPRK)—usually referred to as North Korea—is located in the northern half of the Korean peninsula, bordering China and Russia in the north and South Korea in the south. As of 2011, North Korea had 24.5 million people, the majority being ethnically and linguistically homogeneous Koreans and a very small number of ethnic Chinese and Japanese. Life expectancy is 76 years for males and 83 years for females (2011 estimation). North Korea has a communist government, structured around the communist Korean Workers' Party (KWP), to which all government officials belong. Although the capital city of Pyongyang had at one time (before the Korean War) a relatively large Christian population, autonomous religious activities are relatively restricted under the current socialist government.

Education in North Korea is centrally controlled and monitored by its government. According to the *Theses on Socialist Education*, written by the founding ruler Kim Il Sung and the most often quoted educational document in the nation, "political and ideological education is the most important part of socialist education." Hence, the education of North Korea strives to instill "the spirit of collectivism and socialist patriotism." The essential theme in educational policy is Juchae, roughly translated as concepts of "independence" and "self-reliance." The theme of Juchae permeates all educational instructions, starting from compulsory curricula to extracurricular social education and continuing adult education.

As a collectivistic society, the government revenues come from the trading of state and cooperative assets instead of taxation. The ownership of these assets is shared by the central government, local people's committees, and workers' and peasants' cooperatives. Although North Korea's economy experienced steady development in the 1970s and 1980s through heavy industry and mining, a decade of dry weather in the 1990s followed by harsh flooding left the country in severe economic hardship. During the height of the famine (from 1995 to 1998), the average life expectancy fell and the infant mortality rate climbed. Currently, economic reforms are under way and some positive changes are emerging in the gross domestic product (GDP) index and improvements in the trade deficit.

Educational System

The unified Sillar kingdom of the Korean peninsula lasted for approximately 300 years (668 CE–935 CE) until the Koryo Dynasty (935–1392) took control. The Anglicized name of "Korea" was derived from the name "Koryo" by Portuguese missionaries and merchants who first visited the land of Korea. During the Choson Dynasty (1392–1910), the royal court established one central higher educational institution in the capital and secondary schools in the provinces. State-run institutions were mostly for selected male youth of the privileged upper class. Although the

Korean language existed in an oral form since ancient Korea (approximately since 2333 BCE), Chinese characters have been used in official documents and scholarly texts. Confucian ideals were the central subject matter taught in traditional Korea. Nevertheless, Hangeul (the Korean alphabet and orthography) was developed by a group of scholars during the reign of King Sejong in 1446 to promote education of the common people.

With the influx of missionaries and merchants from European countries in the late nineteenth century, the Korean educational system went through a major change. Christian missionaries established private schools and started teaching Western curricula to children and young adults of both sexes. They initially established secondary schools, upgraded the schools to junior colleges, and eventually turned them into four-year institutions of higher education. At the turn of the century, the missionary-run schools constituted about 35 percent of the entire number of formal schools in Korea.

In 1910 Japan's annexation of Korea brought about a major upheaval in the education of Koreans. The Japanese colonial administration attempted to eradicate the Korean language and culture. Koreans were forbidden to speak their native language in schools and public settings and were required to change their names to Japanese names. In 1930 only a handful (12 percent) of Korean children aged seven to 14 attended formal schools. At the end of the colonial period in 1945, about two-thirds of school-age children in Korea did not have primary education and almost 40 percent of adults were illiterate.

After an interim period of occupation by the Allied powers of World War II, two separate nations were established in 1948: the Democratic People's Republic of Korea (North Korea) and the Republic of Korea (South Korea). The Korean War (1950–1953) devastated the two nations, destroying most cultural and educational facilities. After the war, the founding president of North Korea, Kim Il Sung, immediately launched programs to eradicate illiteracy (reported to be abolished by 1949) and to build the nation's educational system. While the primary and secondary schools retained some formats of the earlier Japanese colonial period, the tertiary-level institutions were built around Soviet models with the help of Korean educators trained

in Russia. Universal primary education was first instituted in 1956. Over the next two decades, compulsory education was gradually extended to 11 years and comprehensively implemented throughout the country by 1975.

Another noteworthy aspect of educational development was the exclusive use of Hangeul, which was instituted as the communist government's means of forming the Juchae principle. The use of Chinese orthography was banned in 1949. Moreover, military training and physical education have received special emphasis. All secondary school students over 14 years of age belong to Red Youth Guards, where they receive military training. Compulsory military service starts at age 17 and lasts for four years.

Precompulsory and Compulsory Education

Education in North Korea is designed to serve the socialist cause and follows its "cradle to grave" educational philosophy. Formal precompulsory education begins at three months of age, when almost all of North Korea's young children come under the care of government-sponsored nurseries. Universal child care, health, and education are fully funded by the central state. According to Nam Djin Ou, a professor at the Higher Teacher Training College of Pyongyang, the universal child care system is provided to allow children to "get used to a collective life from their early days" and to allow women "to take an active part in the social life and become revolutionaries" (Ou 1978).

The current compulsory education system includes one year of kindergarten (only the second year of kindergarten is compulsory), four years of primary school, and six years of secondary school (from grades 5 through 10). The academic year starts in September and ends in July but students normally spend their vacation time on work assignments in the countryside. Upon completion of primary education, around the age of 10, children may go to either a regular (academic) secondary school or special high schools that focus on vocational training, technology, or arts. One example of a special secondary school is the Mangyungdae Revolutionary Institute (named after the birthplace of Kim Il Sung), a military boarding school, which is often regarded as the first step toward a promising political career.

Postcompulsory Education

Institutions of higher education include vocational or specialized junior colleges (2–3 years), teachers' colleges (4 years), medical school (6 years), and universities (4–12 years). There are also special political colleges (3 years) where students learn the policies of the Korean Workers' Party. The enrollment of recent graduates of the secondary schools in higher education is relatively low due to the time committed to compulsory military service. More than half of the freshman class often consists of those discharged from military service.

Higher education in North Korea is technical in its orientation to promote labor productivity. Factory colleges constitute about 40 percent of all higher education institutions in North Korea. Higher education is administered under the supervision of the parallel party organization, namely the KWP. The party council of each campus enforces political education and supervises policies regarding faculty, curriculum, group activities, and sports events.

Kim Il Sung University, founded in 1946, is the prominent institution of higher education that provides comprehensive courses in liberal arts and natural sciences and offers bachelor's, master's, and doctoral degrees. The university houses 50 academic departments in 13 schools: history, philosophy, politics and economy, law, foreign languages and literature, Korean language and literature, mathematics, energy and dynamics, physics, chemistry, biology, geography and geology, and automation science.

Competition for admission to colleges is intense and is based on political considerations as well as scholastic achievement. Students submit their application documents to the education department of the local administrative body of their residence. The documents include a list of five preferred colleges, recommendations by an employer or school, a performance and academic record, an evaluation of political attitude written by a chair of the local youth league, a statement of social origin (peasant, worker, or intellectual), and special family situations if there are any. Screening is conducted by a selection committee, composed of the KWP cadres and staff members of the local administrative offices. Once the committee assigns an applicant to a college, the student then takes an entrance examination. Acceptance to the college is determined by the examination results and the student's sociopolitical status and activities.

There have been international student exchange programs between North Korea and other communist countries. Only a handful of students who are considered "politically trustworthy" by the government officials of the Korean Workers' Party are selected for the study-abroad programs.

Curriculum, Instruction, Assessment, and Teacher Education

The curriculum in North Korea is strongly influenced by its socialist ideology and the theme of Juchae. As a reaction against the traditional Confucian method of rote memorization, North Korea's education system promotes "heuristic teaching" that emphasizes methods of developing independence and creativity in each student. In addition, practical action and labor are emphasized as a way to achieve experiential learning.

Primary school curricula include both academic and political subject matters. In kindergarten, children learn the essentials of Korean language and arithmetic. They also learn from the childhood stories of the president Kim Il Sung and communist morality. During the four years of primary school, most instruction is in subjects such as Korean language, mathematics, physical education, fine arts, and music. However, instruction on communist morality and the nations' leaders is also present in all subjects. For example, textbooks in Korean language include chapter titles such as "We Pray for Our Master," "Following Mrs. Kim," and "Love of Our Father." Although primary students take biannual examinations, failure on the examinations does not result in repetition of grades. There is no foreign language instruction in primary schooling.

In secondary schools (grades 5 to 10), students used to learn Russian or English as their second language. English was removed from the school curriculum in 1950, due to the nation's detachment policy toward the United States, but later reinstated in 1964. Following the collapse of the Soviet Union in 1992, Russian was removed from the curriculum. As a part of the regular curriculum, students take politically oriented subjects such as Communist Party policy. Educational curricula are centrally developed by the State Academy for Research in Education. At the end of secondary education, students take a final examination and receive their diploma. Students who fail the examination receive only a certificate and have to retake the examination the following year in the subjects that they did not pass. However, grade retention is rare in North Korea.

The curriculum in higher education in colleges and universities is more oriented toward socialist curriculum compared to primary and secondary schools. For instance, the history of the People's Revolution is a required core course for every student. Four-year teachers' colleges prepare teachers for kindergarten, primary, and secondary instruction. In 1982 more than one-quarter of higher education institutions specialized in teacher education. Teachers are trained as "revolutionaries faithful to our Party and revolution" (Ou 1978) and receive mandatory in-service training for 10 to 16 days every six months.

Gender and Education

In terms of school curricula, emphasis is on physical education for boys and home economics for girls. However, North Korean children and youth of both genders are required to receive military training as part of their primary and secondary education. According to data from 1998, girls make up 48.7 percent of students in primary and secondary schools but only 34.4 percent at the college level. Information regarding gender differences in graduation rates and academic achievement is not readily available.

Women are proportionally represented in the workforce (40.4 percent, 1993), but very few (approximately 7 percent, as estimated in 2003) are found in the higher ranks of political organizations and in industrial sectors. Men and women of North Korea receive completely equal wages. With the universal child care provided by the government, mothers of young children, including infants and toddlers, are expected to continue their employment throughout their child-rearing period.

Informal Education and System Economics

North Korea puts special emphasis on "social education" outside of the formal structure of schools. This includes extracurricular activities during after-school hours for school-age youth and work-study education for all members of the society. Two prominent informal social organizations for school-age youth are the Pioneer Corps and the Socialist Working Youth League, where students learn collective and organizational lifestyles and also prepare for membership in the Korean Workers' Party. Cultural facilities, such as libraries, museums, monuments, and historical sites of the Korean Revolution, provide political lectures and seminars, debates, poetry recitals, and scientific forums. It was reported in the early 1990s that the daily visitors to the Students' and Children's Palace (gymnasiums and theaters) in Pyongyang included more than 10,000 children who were taking field trips as a part of their school hours and curriculum.

Since the nation's educational philosophy, as outlined in Kim Il Sung's "Theses on Socialist Education," emphasizes the education of "all members of society continuously," adult education receives a substantial portion of national funding. Adult education is organized in the forms of factory colleges, small study groups, and laborers' schools in rural areas, where the general population is provided with political and technical training. Almost all factory workers attend school part-time, free of charge. The curriculum, which emphasizes ideological training, is divided into approximately 60 percent political training and 40 percent technical training. Workers take these classes each day in two-hour study sessions after work and also through intensive summer courses.

As the country has been pushing toward rapid improvement in the rural economy, agricultural colleges and teacher training colleges have been built in rural provinces so local areas could train their own technicians and teachers. Laborers' schools have also been established in remote areas to provide basic education to peasants.

On the average, each student in North Korea receives an allocation of 16,000 *won* (North Korea *won*) for the entire academic period from kindergarten to university. This is equivalent to 10 years of earning of an average worker. North Korea's fiscal expenditure is organized around clustered categories. For example, the sociocultural category reports an aggregated spending that includes education, health, social services, housing, and cadre training. Approximately 11.4 percent of the national budget is allocated for education.

Technology and Education

North Korea was not officially present on the Internet prior to 1997, when the Korean Central News Agency, a government body, acquired its first domain server. The central government regulates the accessibility of the Internet to only a few thousand high-ranking officials who already have international phone lines. To date, Internet access is banned for citizens of North Korea. Meanwhile, the Intranet, an online network system within the country, serves as a means to disseminate information to research institutes, factories, and schools within North Korea. Cellular phone service was first introduced in 1998 and suspended in 2004, but new service was launched in 2008.

Challenges and Future Prospects

After the collapse of the Soviet Union in 1992, North Korean citizens faced severe economic hardship followed by natural disasters such as famine and flooding. In the mid-1990s, more than 6,000 school buildings were destroyed or damaged in the floods and over 300,000 textbooks were swept away. Moreover, North Korea's nuclear weapons program has been a source of complex international tension. Most international humanitarian assistance was terminated in 2005 due to the nation's nuclear program, and current assistance comes primarily from China and South Korea in the form of grants and long-term loans. These economic difficulties pose the most urgent challenge for educational improvement.

Increased use of technology and electronic media will certainly facilitate educational advancement as well as the dissemination of information. Cultural and scholarly exchanges between North Korea and the international community will foster mutual understanding and develop relations that will contribute to the advancement of education for the citizens of the Democratic People's Republic of Korea. Since the death of Kim Jong Il, it is unclear as to the path that North Korean education will take.

Piljoo Paulin Kang

North Korea Education at a Glance

General Information

Capital	Pyongyang
Population	24.46 million
Language	Korean
Literacy rate	99%
GDP per capita (2009)	US$1,800
Number of phones (landline) per 100 people (2008)	48
Number of phones (mobile) per 100 people	no data (service suspended in 2004, but new service launched in 2008)
Number of Internet users per 100 people	no data (public usage is prohibited)
Number of Internet hosts (2010)	3

Formal Education Information

Compulsory school age population	3 million
Compulsory school age population	13%
Number of years of compulsory education	11 (ages 5–16)
Student/teacher ratio (2000)	23
Average class size in primary school (2000)	23
Average number of school hours per day (1990)	8
Primary school gross enrollment ratio (1997)	96%
Primary school entrants completing grade 4	100%
Secondary school gross enrollment ratio	no data

Note: Unless otherwise indicated, all data are based on sources from 2011.

REFERENCES

Central Intelligence Agency. *The CIA World Factbook*. New York: Skyhorse, 2011. https://www.cia.gov/library/publications/the-world-factbook/index.html.

Cho, Jung-Yul. "North Korea and the Internet." Paper presented at the 2000 Annual Convention of the Association for Education in Journalism and Mass Communication Convention, Phoenix, Arizona, 2000.

Faraj, Abdulatif Hussein. "Higher Education and Economic Development in South Asian Countries." *Higher Education Review* 21 (1988): 9–26.

Kim Il Sung. *Theses on Socialist Education*. Pyongyang, North Korea: Published at the Fourteenth Plenary Meeting of the Fifth Central Committee of the Worker's Party of (North) Korea, 1977.

Kim, Ransoo, and Young Sop Ahn. "Higher Education in South and North Korea." In *East Asian Higher Education: Traditions and Transformation*, ed. Albert H. Yee, 102–121. New York: Elsevier Science, 1995.

Mercado, Stephen C. "Hermit Surfers of Pyongyang: North Korea and the Internet." https://www.cia.gov/library/center-for-the-study-of-intelligence/csi-publications/csi-studies/studies/vol48no1/article04.html.

Nation Master. 2011. www.nationmaster.com.

Ou, Nam Djin. "Some Aspects of the Educational System in the Democratic People's Republic of Korea." *Prospects: Quarterly Review of Education* 8 (1978): 116–120.

Reed, Gay Garland. "Globalisation and Education: The Case of North Korea." *Compare: A Journal of Comparative Education* 27 (1997): 167–178.

Reed, Gay Garland, and Bong Gun Chung. "North Korea." In *Asian Higher Education*, ed. Gerard A. Postiglione and Grace C.L. Mak, 231–244. Westport, CT: Greenwood Press, 1997.

Song, Jae Jung. "The *Juche* Ideology: English in North Korea." *English Today* 69/18 (2002): 47–52.

US Department of State. "Background Note: North Korea." www.state.gov/r/pa/ei/bgn.

World Bank Education Statistics. 2011. www.worldbank.org.

KOREA, SOUTH

The Republic of Korea is located between China and Japan. South Korean residents are predominantly a homogeneous ethnic group, but there is a growing population of foreign residents, including international students, temporary foreign laborers, businesspeople, English language teachers, and US military personnel, that makes up 2 percent of the total population. Although nearly half of the population declares no religious affiliation, among those with a religious affiliation, 29.2 percent are Christians, 22.8 percent Buddhists, and 0.2 percent Confucianists.

South Korea was invaded by North Korea in 1950. The Korean War lasted three years and resulted in an ongoing ideological, political, and geographical division between the north and south along a 2.5-mile (4-kilometer) stretch at the 38th parallel, known as the Demilitarized Zone. Although there have been continuous efforts to unite the two countries, an agreement has not been reached. The United States continues to have a military presence in South Korea, and all healthy Korean males are required to serve in the military to prepare for any future attacks from the north. Since the 1990s, however, symbolic steps have been taken toward a possible reunification of the two Koreas.

Following economic advancements, South Korea's educational system has expanded and developed rapidly. Among the Organisation for Economic Co-operation and Development (OECD) countries, the results of the Programme for International Student Assessment (PISA) show that Korean students rank second in reading and fourth in math (OECD 2010).

Educational System

The importance of and drive for education is deeply rooted in the mentality of all Koreans, because education is believed to establish one's social class, enabling upward social mobility as well as upholding family honor. Thus, for Korean students, there are very high personal, familial, and societal stakes attached to the attainment of a "good" education, which stems from the Confucian ideology of equating scholarship with moral and social authority.

Educational Structure

The centralization of the educational administration occurred in the 1980s. Currently, the Ministry of Education and Human Resources Development (MEHRD) formulates and implements educational policies governing K–12 institutions, including enrollment quotas, certification of schools and teachers, educational curricula and materials, and administrative and financial support for all local education offices. There are 16 metropolitan and provincial offices responsible for the educational infrastructure, management of curriculum, and implementation of national policy and regulations. Furthermore, 180 district offices of education at the local level supervise public and private schools. Each school has a council consisting of teachers, parents, community members, and the principal, who serves in an advisory role to the board.

South Korean students have six years of primary school between the ages of six and 12, three years of middle school between the ages of 12 and 15, and three years of high school between the ages of 15 and 18. Upon graduation, students can go on to a two-year junior college, three-year vocational college, or four-year comprehensive college or university. There are two types of high schools: vocational high school, offering training in agricultural, commercial, fishery, and technical skills, and comprehensive high school, providing college preparatory curricula. There are also magnet schools for the gifted and talented in the sciences, foreign languages, arts, and physical education as well as special schools for the deaf, blind, and students with other disabilities. In addition, a handful of international schools, which are not under the jurisdiction of the central government, exist for children of diplomats, military personnel, and international expatriates.

The first semester of the academic year runs from March to July and the second goes from September through February. There are approximately 205 days in the school year. Students attend schools from Monday through Friday in addition to half-day instruction on some designated Saturdays. The average school day begins about 9:00 AM and ends at 2:30 PM for primary grades and 3:30 PM for secondary grade level. The instructional class periods are between 40 and 50 minutes depending on the subject matter. Aside from regular school hours, most students attend private tutoring or learning centers (*hakwon*) covering a wide range of subject areas such as English, math, piano, and art.

Kindergarten

Kindergarten is not a part of compulsory education in South Korea. The net enrollment ratio for kindergarten is 40.6 percent (based on 2010 enrollment figures). Although most children enter kindergarten at the age of five, kindergarten programs start accepting children at age three. Since the 1980s the Ministry of Education has expanded early childhood education to accommodate the increasing number of woman entering the workforce and to enhance school readiness for all children. Today greater numbers of public kindergartens are being built to assist children from low-income families to attend kindergarten, which has generally been privately operated. Currently, there are about 4,500 national, public kindergartens and 3,887 private kindergartens, of which some are English immersion programs.

Primary School Education

Primary education (grades 1–6) in Korea is compulsory and free. All elementary schools are coeducational. There are both public and private elementary schools; private schools have more local autonomy in terms of curricula and teacher hiring practices than the public schools. The homeroom teacher typically teaches the entire curriculum; however, in some schools resource specialist teachers are available for subjects such as art, science, and English.

Middle School Education

Middle school (grades 7–9) is also compulsory and free. Starting in the middle school grades, there are both coeducational and single-sex schools as well as magnet schools for the gifted and talented. In the past, students had to take entrance examinations for middle and high schools, a practice that led to ability tracking and extreme competitiveness. The middle school entrance examination was eradicated in 1969; however, students still must pass a diagnostic evaluation (which most students are able to pass) in order to enter middle school. As a part of the "school equalization policy," students are assigned either by the proximity of the school to their primary residence by the school districts or by lottery. In middle school, students have a homeroom teacher who is responsible for the general educational guidance of the students, but they are taught by different content teachers who travel from classroom to classroom. Upon graduation, students must make a choice whether to enter a comprehensive, vocational, or another type of specialized high school.

High School Education

All high schools in South Korea consist of three years. Most high school students are between the ages of 15 and 18. High school is not compulsory and the burden of tuition is on the students. According to the 2010 figures of OECD member countries, 98 percent of South Korea's young adults complete high school, which was the highest percentage recorded in any country. Admission into high school, in the past, used to be based on a qualifying examination, but since 1974, the government has implemented an equalization policy for high schools to normalize school curriculum and minimize school differences, in particular between urban and rural areas. Students desiring enrollment in general comprehensive high schools can be selected based on a lottery system or by proximity of their primary residence, while students wanting to attend nontraditional high schools such as vocational and magnet schools focusing on foreign languages, arts, or sciences are selected by some type of entrance examination and their previous academic records. Entrance into foreign language, arts, and science high schools is extremely competitive. Students who are unable to attend high school may take the high school graduate equivalency examination to receive a high school diploma.

Higher Education

There are four categories of higher education institutions: colleges and universities with four-year undergraduate programs (a six-year program in medical colleges), junior colleges, teachers colleges, and theological colleges and seminaries. Nearly 80 percent of all Korean higher education institutions are private. Although the MEHRD oversees enrollment quotas, qualifications of faculty, and degree requirements, most universities have autonomy in their administration and course offerings. Medicine, law, pharmacy, English, engineering, and business are the most desirable majors and, hence, the most competitive to enter among Korean students.

The government sets basic requirements for college entrance to normalize public education systems and private tutoring pressures; however, the selection of students is at the discretion of each university. Universities are allowed to admit students on a year-round basis to promote diversification, specialization, and autonomy. Admission decisions are based on students' school activities records, college scholastic aptitude tests, essays, letters of recommendation, and interviews and/or performance-based assessments as well as other special criteria that may constitute extenuating circumstances, such as extremely disadvantaged backgrounds.

High school students generally apply to colleges at the end of the senior year. Students have the option of participating in either early decision plans for college (*sooshi*) or regular admissions (*jungshi*). Students take the college scholastic aptitude test (*sooneung*). The curriculum of most schools is structured around the content of this entrance examination. The test covers six areas: Korean, mathematics, English, social studies, science, and a foreign language other than English, such as Chinese characters. Because universities and colleges have strict enrollment quotas, the entrance exam makes acceptance into colleges, especially top-tier schools, very competitive. Many students who are unable to enter the college of their choice repeat the application process the next year. Students are allowed to apply to as many universities as they choose as long as the testing dates do not overlap.

Special Education

The Special Education Promotion law guarantees the right to education for children with disabilities.

The National Institute for Special Education in 1994 heightened the awareness of the importance of special education and has been responsible for training teachers and developing materials through research-based practices to improve its quality. Classes and policies to provide adequate education to children with special needs are available in public K–12 schools. There are currently 150 special schools for severely disabled children with a total enrollment of approximately 24,000 students. Mild to moderate special needs children are integrated into mainstream schools that provide special education classes.

Curriculum and Instruction

The MEHRD oversees the development of the K–12 national curriculum, which undergoes revisions every five to 10 years to reflect the changing context of society. Revised in 2009, the main objective of the current educational reform is to provide an educational plan that meets the demands of the twenty-first century. It emphasizes learner-centered education that identifies student potential, fosters individual creativity, and builds moral character.

The nationally standardized curriculum has been undergoing changes in recent years to incorporate time for creative experiential activities. The primary school curriculum, which used to consist of 10 subject areas, covers seven subject areas (Korean, social studies, math, science, physical education, arts and music, and English). In middle school, there are two main strands of the curriculum: traditional subject matters and creative and experiential activities such as after-school clubs and community service. The required content areas consist of Korean, math, social studies, science and technology, home economics, physical education, arts and music, and English. Students also take electives such as Chinese characters, environmental science, design, religion, vocational skills, or a second foreign language (German, French, Spanish, Chinese, Japanese, Russian, or Arabic) in addition to their creative and experiential activities. Similarly in high school, the curriculum covers both academic subjects and creative and experiential activities. The content areas mirror those that are offered in middle school with a greater variety of electives. The current educational reform in high schools supports schools' autonomy in developing curriculum with diversity in electives as part of an effort to offer level- and interest-differentiated courses that take into account students' career paths and aptitudes. Comprehensive high schools also have subject specialty tracks with a focus on humanities or natural sciences starting in the eleventh grade. The differences in course offerings between these two tracks prepare students for the requirements needed to select either a science-related or humanities- and social sciences-related major at the university. Specialized high schools such as vocational schools are geared toward the teaching of specialized skills needed for a particular trade. Because of the emphasis on school tests and the college entrance exam, which are generally given in a multiple-choice format, instruction is heavily geared to the "test," reinforcing the rote memorization of content facts. Reforms are currently under way to shift from this type of instruction to more creative methods of teaching and learning that promote critical thinking and effective communication skills.

Gender and Education

With the expansion of higher education institutions, female student enrollment has increased gradually during the past several decades. Historically, women were underrepresented in Korean education due to a Confucian heritage that treats education as a male-oriented activity. Korean women, whose main roles were as domestic caregivers, were traditionally educated at home by their mothers on feminine morality and virtue. During the late nineteenth and twentieth centuries, educational opportunities for women were created by Christian missionaries. Up until the 1970s it was still very common for women to have only a high school education. Today the growth in female enrollment in higher education is significant, with a greater growth at the junior college level than at the four-year university level.

Technology and Education

South Korea was the first nation in the world to provide Internet access to every primary, middle, and high school. As of 2004 every teacher has a computer and there is on average one computer for every five students. Multimedia textbooks have been developed for use in classrooms in addition to over 5,000 different kinds of educational software. There are also currently 17 cyber-universities with a rapidly growing

enrollment of 96,943 students, and this trend is continuing to rise. Moreover, the National Educational Information System, a centralized e-administration system, is now in place to assist teachers to manage student records and help parents to track their children's progress over the Internet.

Teacher Education

Teachers are trained in teachers colleges, schools of education at universities, and disciplinary programs with teacher certification programs. Kindergarten teachers can be certified through early childhood departments at universities, two-year colleges, or teachers colleges. Upon graduation, teachers automatically receive a teaching certificate; however, they must also pass the national teacher's board examination. Once employed, teachers at public schools are on a four- or five-year rotation between different schools within one district and an eight- or 10-year rotation across districts, whereas private school teachers are often employed at the same school for many years.

There are two kinds of in-service teacher training programs: one for acquiring special certificates for promotion and the other for general training on current educational theory and practices. Teachers are not mandated to attend in-service sessions; however, their participation rates and performances during the training workshops are assessed for the purposes of promotion and salary incentives. Schools have separate budgets for professional development, but compared to other OECD countries, Korean schoolteachers have limited opportunities.

Informal Education

Privately owned tutoring or instructional centers (hakwons) make up a significant portion of students' informal education. In order to have a competitive academic standing at school, most students enroll in hakwons to review and preview the content area subjects and to prepare for examinations. Hakwons cover a broad range of academic and extracurricular subjects. The cost of these hakwons can be expensive, privileging the upper socioeconomic class. Private tutors, who are generally university students attending top-tier universities, are also common. In the past, several regulations were implemented to ban such types of privatized education; however, they have not been successful.

The rising demand for English language competence has made English education one of the highest priorities for South Korean parents and students. English is now mandatory starting from third grade. At the primary and secondary levels, the focus is on conversational fluency in English with an emphasis on speaking and listening comprehension. However, because of the college entrance exam, secondary school students also focus on English grammar. To promote English language education, the government implemented a policy to have at least one native English teacher in each school. In order to advance children's English language education, the current trend is for parents to take their children abroad to English-speaking countries for an immersion experience. An estimated 80 percent of elementary schoolchildren are believed to have gone abroad for an English immersion experience.

System Economics

Government expenditure on education has been relatively generous compared to other OECD countries. The current budget for education is 7 percent of the gross national product. Approximately 20 percent of the national taxes, in addition to fiscal support from the national treasury, is given to local education agencies to fund elementary and secondary schools. The central government also provides funding for national and private universities and educational administrative and research organizations. Private schools also are able to use privately raised funds.

Dilemmas

The cutthroat competition for educational achievement among students has caused many societal problems. First, it has accentuated class differences in a society where a college degree is necessary to gain middle-class status and school networks are used as markers of social class. This kind of societal attitude prompts intense competition to win admission to the most prestigious schools, such as Seoul National University, Korea University, and Yonsei University (also referred to as SKY). The inability to attain admission into top-tier schools has led to negative effects on self-esteem and has been common reason

South Korea Education at a Glance	
General Information	
Capital	Seoul
Population	48.755 million
Language	Korean
Literacy rate (2008)	98.3%
GDP per capita	US$20,759
Number of phones (landline) per 100 people	27.3
Number of phones (mobile) per 100 people	72
Number of Internet users per 100 people	81.6
Number of Internet hosts	291,329
Formal Education Information	
Compulsory school age population	5.27 million
Compulsory school age population	9.1%
Number of years of compulsory education	9 (ages 6–15)
Student/teacher ratio	
Elementary school (grades 1–6)	19
Middle school (grades 7–9)	18
High school (grades 10–12)	15.5
Average class size in primary school	
Elementary school (grades 1–6)	26.6
Middle school (grades 7–9)	33.8
Average school days per year (2007)	205
Primary school gross enrollment ratio (grades 1–6)	99%
Primary school entrants completing grade 6	99%
Secondary school gross enrollment ratio	97.6%

Note: Unless otherwise indicated, all data are based on sources from 2011.

for adolescent suicide. Furthermore, the long hours spent in schools and hakwons take a toll on students' physical development and put immense pressures on family financial resources.

Second, the pressure to learn English has escalated the practice of taking children (*chogi yoohak*) of all ages to study abroad. It has become a societal trend for fathers to stay behind in Korea (also known as wild geese or *girogi* fathers) while mothers take their children to an English-speaking country to educate them. This has become a $600 million industry, creating a tremendous leakage of financial resources to foreign countries as well as a brain drain that threatens the economic and social future of South Korea.

Third, with the growing population of foreign laborers in Korea and the rise in interracial marriages, the numbers of foreign students and students from multicultural families has risen rapidly over the past decade. Schools are faced with challenges in providing language and educational support for children whose first language is not Korean and training for teachers in multicultural pedagogy. In addition, a growing number of students who are defectors from North Korea need services such as mentoring, counseling, and supplemental education to enable them to adjust to the new system and culture. Thus, new educational policies are being developed to address the needs of the changing student population.

Future Prospects

South Korea's long-range plan is to promote "lifelong learning and open education" (Ministry of Education). The goal is to improve education to support the development of creative and critical thinking by placing greater focus on computer education, foreign languages, and world culture and history. Educational policies and practices are being implemented to recognize the diverse and individual needs of students, and more resources are being directed toward improving the quality of teacher education and the situational constraints of the classroom, such as decreasing class size. Many areas of South Korean education need to undergo systemic reform in order to alleviate the financial and psychological pressures on students and their families that result from intense competition for entrance into a reputable university. Such reforms may curtail the current educational drain that the country is experiencing with so many individuals going abroad to attain their education.

Jin Sook Lee and Sun Ah Lim

REFERENCES

Central Intelligence Agency. *The CIA World Factbook*. New York: Skyhorse, 2011. https://www.cia.gov/library/publications/the-world-factbook/index.html.

Guo, Yugui. *Asia's Educational Edge: Current Achievements in Japan, Korea, Taiwan, China, and India*. Lanham, MD: Lexington Books, 2005.

Ministry of Education and Human Resources Development of South Korea. "Introduction: Education System." http://english.mest.go.kr/enMain.do.

Nation Master. 2011. www.nationmaster.com.

National Human Resources Development. "NHRD Statistics: HRD Indicators in Korea." www.nhrd.net/nhrd-htm/htm/eng/statistics/statistics01.html.

Organisation for Economic Co-operation and Development (OECD). "PISA 2009 Results: Executive Summary." www.oecd.org/dataoecd/34/60/46619703.pdf.

World Bank Group. *Data: Korea, Rep.* http://data.worldbank.org/country/korea-republic.

LAOS

Laos, or the Lao People's Democratic Republic (LPDR), is a landlocked country in the Indochina region of East Asia. The population of Laos consists of 49 main ethnic groups and over 100 subgroups. The Lowland Lao is the largest ethnic group, representing approximately 65 percent of the population. Languages spoken in Laos include Lao, French, English, and various ethnic tongues (e.g., Lao Theung, Lao Soung, Hmong, Yao). Lao, the official language of instruction, is spoken by about 50 percent of the population. The most common dialect is Vientiane Lao. Although the government does not recognize an official religion, the majority of the population practices Theravada Buddhism.

The country initially emerged in the fourteenth century as the Kingdom of Lan Xang (million elephants) with a monarchy government. Laos was under the rule of the Siamese before the French seized control in 1893; French rule lasted until 1945. The current border between Laos and Thailand was established by the Franco-Siamese treaty of 1907. During French colonization, Vientiane replaced Luang Prabang as the new capital; development remained a low priority. During the First Indochina War, Laos became involved in a complicated relationship between France and Vietnam. Between 1945 and 1954, Laos achieved sovereignty and formed the first coalition government. The country was declared a neutral state at the Geneva conference in 1962. At the end of the Second Indochina War in 1975, a one-party communist government emerged. The Lao People's Revolutionary Party remains the only legally recognized political party today.

Educational System

At the national level, the Ministry of Education (MOE) is responsible for the coordination, planning, policy development, and quality control of formal education. The State Planning Committee translates broad policy statements of party congresses into national plans. This highly centralized process involves many technical and administrative bodies at the national and local levels. Although provincial and district education authorities maintain compliance with national objectives, local influence can create the development of specialized projects. At the local level, management of functional responsibilities is headed by the village head, village school management committee, and the school principal.

In 1962 national educational reform became a high priority. These early reform efforts focused on teaching practical subjects, encouraging students to take an active role in the learning process, relying on local resources, and establishing educational opportunities for people of all ethnic groups across the country. Although the achievements of these early reform efforts were limited, they produced a momentum for continued reform attempts and goals to be achieved by 2020.

International organizations have been critical in financing education in the country. Since 1975 approximately US$60 million has been borrowed from the World Bank and Asian Development to upgrade primary, secondary, and tertiary schools. With a focus on economic development, the educational reform effort in Laos concentrated on school expansion and literacy. The education system has undergone a series of national plans to restructure the formal and nonformal education systems.

Formal Education

The formal education system includes up to five years of preprimary education (*anuban*), depending on when the student starts to attend; five years of primary school (*pathom*); three years of lower secondary school (*mathanyom*); and three years of upper secondary school (*udom*).

Preprimary education is structured by the MOE to prepare children for the first grade of primary school. Nursery school (*crèche*) provides education for children from two months to two years of age. Kindergarten provides education for children between three and five years of age. Unlike other levels, preprimary education is fee-based and therefore not affordable for all families. Enrollments in preprimary education vary throughout the provinces of Laos, with the highest growth of enrollment in the Vientiane Municipality.

Primary school, the compulsory component of the education system, is designed for children six to 11 years of age. National education goals include expanding access to primary education in rural and ethnic minority areas, implementing universal primary education with quality improvements, increasing the national literacy rate, improving the internal efficiency of schooling, advancing the professional training and academic status of teachers, and improving management and control of education to ensure quality. Despite an increase in enrollment trends, Laos struggles to meet these national education goals at the compulsory education level. The multiple purposes of primary education and the linguistic variability of the country's many ethnic groups challenge the government to implement a universal primary education that would meet the needs of all children.

Secondary school for students aged 11 to 17 is comprised of lower and upper divisions. Graduates from the three-year lower secondary division can join the workforce, continue to upper secondary school, or enter a three-year teacher training course that will prepare them to teach at the primary or junior secondary levels. Graduates from the three-year upper secondary division can join the workforce, attend a local university, study abroad, or enter a teacher-training program to become a teacher at a specified level.

Founded in 1995, the National University of Laos (NUOL) is located in Vientiane. NUOL has 13 disciplines: education, social sciences, sciences, letters, economics, business administration, forestry, agriculture, law and administration, medical sciences, engineering, architecture, and foundation studies. NUOL enrolls over 26,000 students and employs about 2,000 staff members. All applicants to NUOL are required to take a common entrance examination that is administered in all provinces. The quota system at NUOL requires that 50 percent of the places are reserved for students from the provinces. Any places not filled under the quota system may be filled on the basis of examination results.

Curriculum, Instruction, and Assessment

An established kindergarten curriculum uses weekly units based on a theme; daily plans include activities such as four-corner play, free play, circle play, and educational games. The objectives are to provide child care, train children for a socialist society, and stimulate young children's development based on the philosophy of learning through play.

The current primary education core curriculum

consists of Lao language, mathematics, social studies, art, physical education, music, and handicraft. Textbooks, teacher guides, and student workbooks are not available for all subject areas due to lack of funding and limited access to the printing industry. Teachers may replicate models from the teacher guides or develop their own materials. The printing of textbooks has been supported by loans from World Bank for first grade and the government of Norway for second through fifth grades. Special second-language teaching techniques and materials for students who speak Lao as a second language are not available.

Pedagogical methods are often teacher-centered. A typical classroom setting includes lectures and rote learning. Teachers are typically responsible for assessment of their students. Uniform assessment procedures are difficult to implement and monitor due to the geographical isolation of many schools and lack of other necessary resources. Without a common curriculum, subject content varies across schools and districts. In 2000 the first project to develop a systematic approach to assessment was created in an effort to provide a national educational assessment.

Teacher Education

When the socialist government came into power in 1975, it prompted an exodus of many educators. Remaining educators were forced into "reeducation" camps before reentering the country's infrastructure. Teacher training has slowly shifted from a provincial responsibility to a national priority. In the mid-1990s the MOE raised the minimum educational requirements for primary and secondary teachers and established teacher training centers. These reforms have created a dramatic increase in teacher training activity.

To become a preprimary teacher, students can enroll in a one-year program at the end of upper secondary school. To teach at the primary or the lower secondary schools, a three-year training course at the end of lower secondary school or a one-year training program at the end of upper secondary school is required. The minimum requirement to become an upper secondary teacher is the completion of a four-year teacher-training program in the Faculty of Education at NUOL.

One of the national goals is to improve teacher training through preservice and in-service teacher education. Providing in-service training has been difficult due to poor infrastructure. Raising teacher qualifications and restructuring of training resulted in a dramatic drop in teacher education enrollment. The focus of teacher training has been on the pedagogical skills necessary to teach a new integrated curriculum.

Informal Education

The informal system of education targets ethnic groups in remote areas, children and adults who have limited to no formal schooling, and government employees. The primary goals of informal education are to eradicate illiteracy for disadvantaged populations, raise the primary and secondary levels of education for government employees, and promote basic vocational training for educationally disadvantaged and low-income populations. Management of informal education exists at both the micro- and macro-levels as an effort to meet the need for social and economic development at the local and national levels. The three regional informal education resource centers, located in Luang Phrabang, Vientiane Municipality, and Champassack, assist in the development of curriculum, textbooks, and learning materials. These centers also train informal education personnel and volunteer teachers.

System Economics

Teacher training, teacher salaries, a number of textbooks, and some school construction projects are funded by the Laos government. However, the government's financial contribution and administrative oversight of individual school operations is minimal. Schools receive about US$0.73 per year per teacher from the MOE for operating expenses. Due to the lack of financial support from the central government, the education system in Laos continues to rely on the support of parents, families, and communities at the local level.

Dilemmas and Challenges

The education system in Laos is gradually making progress toward its goals and becoming more decentralized since its early reform efforts. The country faces many dilemmas and challenges while striv-

Laos Education at a Glance

General Information

Capital	Vientiane
Population	6.478 million
Language	Lao
Literacy rate (2005)	73%
GDP per capita	US$2,500
Number of phones (landline) per 100 people	2.59
Number of phones (mobile) per 100 people	25.4
Number of Internet users per 100 people	1.77
Number of Internet hosts	1,468

Formal Educational Information

Compulsory school age population enrolled (2005)	890,821
Compulsory school age population (2008)	40.85%
Number of years of compulsory education	5 (6–11)
Student/teacher ratio (2008)	
Primary school	31.48
Secondary school	24.78
Primary school completion rate (2007)	75.9%
Primary school gross enrollment ratio (2007)	115.3%
Secondary school gross enrollment ratio (2007)	46.7%
Tertiary school gross enrollment ratio (2007)	7.9%

Note: Unless otherwise indicated, all data are based on sources from 2011.

ing to achieve a national educational reform. The greatest challenge is the implementation of policies on a national level. In addition to the challenges of continued planning, coordinating, and administrating processes, the government struggles with limited funding, inadequate equipment, inadequate access to current curriculum and instructional materials, inadequate teacher education, fostering anticolonial education that would better serve the Laotian people, and shortage of teachers.

Another major challenge is to address the educational achievement gap among the various Lao ethnic groups and between males and females. The percentage of enrollment and the dropout rates among the various ethnic groups in different regions throughout Laos still vary greatly. One contributing factor is language instruction. There have been no special second-language provisions and resources for students whose first language is not Lao. Furthermore, female literacy remains a low priority. Among 10 ethnic groups, female literacy remains below 20 percent, and among six of these, average female literacy rates remain below 12 percent. Given the socioeconomic and cultural context of the country, increasing access to education among ethnic groups and females will continue to be a dilemma for decades to come.

Future Prospects

Despite the nation's high poverty level, rudimentary infrastructure, and limited external and internal telecommunications, Laos has continued to strive toward effective educational reform. From 2004 to 2007 several policy changes helped to increase economic growth. In late 2004 Laos and the United States agreed on trade relations that lowered the tariffs on exports for Laos-based producers. Laos is also in the process of reforming its trade policy in order to join the World Trade Organization. In addition, the government's tax system will be replaced by a value-added tax beginning in 2008. The economic growth combined with an efficient tax system may expedite educational reform efforts to create an effective national education system in Laos.

Rassamichanh Souryasack and Amy Lewis

REFERENCES

Central Intelligence Agency. *The CIA World Factbook.* New York: Skyhorse, 2011. https://www.cia.gov/library/publications/the-world-factbook/index.html.

Cheng, Kai-Ming. "Riding the Tide: Ministries of Education in Current Contexts of Change." *International Institute for Educational Planning*, 2003, 78–88.

Dorner, Daniel G., and Gary E. Gorman. "Contextual factors Affecting Learning in Laos and the Implications for Information Literacy Education." *Information Research* 16:2 (June 2011), paper 479. http://informationr.net/ir/16-2/paper479.html.

Nation Master. 2011. www.nationmaster.com.

Southeast Asian Ministers of Education Organization. www.seameo.org.

United Nations International Children's Emergency Fund. www.unicef.org.

US Department of State. "Background Note: Laos." www.state.gov.

World Bank. www.worldbank.org.

MALAYSIA

Malaysia is a country located in Southeast Asia. Half of its 28 million inhabitants are Malay, nearly one-quarter are Chinese, and the remaining citizens include those of Indian descent and various indigenous ethnicities. Bahasa Malaysia is the official language. Also spoken are English, Tamil, Telugu, Malayalam,

Punjabi, various Chinese dialects, and several indigenous languages.

Between 1400 and 1511 CE, Malaysia was an international seaport frequented by Arabs, Chinese, and Indian traders. Arab traders brought Islam to Malaysia, where it is now the country's official religion. However, freedom of religion is provided by the constitution; Islam (60.4 percent), Buddhism (19.2 percent), Christianity (9.1 percent), Hinduism (6.3 percent), Confucianism, Taoism, other traditional Chinese religions (2.6 percent), and tribal and folk religions (1.5 percent) are all practiced in Malaysia.

The colonial era began in 1511 with the Portuguese Malacca (Malacca is the third smallest state in Malaysia). Others who controlled the region were the Dutch (1641–1824) and the British (1826–1946). The Japanese occupied much of the area during World War II. Colonial rule ended in 1946, when British Malaya and nearby territories transitioned from the Malayan Union into the Federation of Malaya. Malaysian independence came in 1957, and in 1963, the country became the Federation of Malaysia.

Committed to global participation, Malaysia boasts the world's highest increase in total expenditure in education from 1998 to 2001. This 68 percent increase targeted greater school access, computer literacy, and gender parity. Primary school is compulsory in Malaysia, and nearly all students ages 12 to 16 attend secondary school. Those who wish to pursue tertiary education in public universities are required to complete an additional two years of preuniversity schooling. Throughout their primary and secondary years, students are promoted and tracked through the use of challenging comprehensive examinations. Public universities, which are heavily subsidized by the government, include postgraduate programs and vocational and polytechnic schools.

Educational System

Malaysia's education system during the precolonial period was informal in nature. Lessons usually took place in the teachers' homes and emphasis was given to religious studies. In some instances, education took the form of apprenticeships when students learned the rudiments of agriculture and craft-making. At a more formal level, there was also a system of small religious hut schools called *pondok* where students were taught how to read the Quran, spiritual knowledge, and morality.

The current education system in Malaysia has been heavily influenced by Great Britain. Shortly before the attainment of independence in 1957, the first attempt to introduce a national system of education was created through the Education Ordinance. Six years later, the National Language Act replaced English with Bahasa Malaysia as the language for instruction and administration. By 1982 Bahasa Malaysia was the medium of instruction at all levels in almost every public school. In all grades, English is taught as a second language.

Over the last 50 years, the Malaysian education system has evolved into a national system that reflects both global participation and national goals. According to the Ministry of Education (MOE), the mission of all public schools is to help develop students "intellectually, spiritually, emotionally and physically . . . based on a firm belief in and devotion to God." Furthermore, all Malaysian citizens should "contribute to the harmony and betterment of the society and the nation at large."

The educational structure of Malaysia is highly centralized and falls under the jurisdiction of the MOE. The government oversees the implementation of curriculum standards and the regulation of national examinations. The education system is divided into four distinct hierarchal levels: federal, state, district, and individual schools. In the primary and secondary school levels, the teacher to student ratio is 15 to 1. In 2004 the government established the Ministry of Higher Education (MOHE) to oversee postsecondary education in Malaysia. The primary and secondary school calendar runs from early January until mid-November. Three northeastern states (Kedah, Kelantan, and Terengganu) follow a slightly different calendar, beginning the school year a day earlier and ending a day earlier. This is because Fridays and Saturdays are weekends for these three states.

Preschool, Primary, and Secondary Education

Preschool education (kindergarten) is usually for children between the ages of four and six. Although preschool education is not compulsory, it is monitored by the MOE. All preschools, whether public or private, must comply with the pedagogical and curriculum standards set up by the ministry. Preschool principals and teachers are required to undergo training and certification before they can teach. In 2009 the preschool enrollment in Malaysia was 67 percent of all children from birth to five years of age.

Education is only compulsory at the primary school level and begins at age six. The duration of primary school is six years (Standard One–Six). The main goal of primary education is to provide the foundation for students to become proficient in reading, writing, and arithmetic. At the end of primary school (Standard Six), students take a standardized exam known as the Primary School Assessment Test. Although the exam serves as an assessment tool, students are automatically promoted to secondary school regardless of their performance on the test. In addition, there are private primary schools that use Mandarin Chinese and Tamil as their main language of instruction. These schools are usually run by private organizations and are also required to administer national examinations.

Upon completion of primary school, most students continue with secondary school for a period of five years (Form One–Five). Secondary education is divided into the lower secondary level (Form One–Three) and upper secondary level (Form Four–Five). At the end of Form Three, the students will sit for the Lower Secondary Assessment, a national standardized test that tracks students into the upper secondary level based on their exam results in the academic (science and arts), technical and vocational, or Islamic schools streams. In order to graduate from secondary school, students are required to pass a final national examination known as the Malaysia Certificate of Education.

Postsecondary Education

After graduation, students who wish to pursue postsecondary education in public universities are required to complete an additional two years of schooling (Form Six) and perform well on the Malaysia Higher School Certificate Examination. Public universities are highly competitive; presently, there are 20 state-run universities. Students also have the option of attending private colleges and universities in Malaysia. All tertiary institutions are required to use curricula that have been approved by the MOHE. As of 2011 there were 181 private higher education institutions registered with the MOHE.

Curriculum, Instruction, and Assessment

At the primary and secondary levels, Malaysia's education system relies on a nationalized curriculum that is regulated by the MOE's Curriculum Development Center. All textbooks are selected by the ministry's Textbook Division, with autonomy granted at the local level regarding methodology and classroom evaluation. Parents are required to buy textbooks; however, the Textbook Loan Scheme was created in 1975 to offer assistance to families in need.

In the public school system, students spend approximately one hour per day on the core subjects: Bahasa Malaysia, English, mathematics, and science. English is taught as a second language at the beginning of primary school. The curriculum also includes courses in history, civics, fine arts, physical education, and citizenship. In addition, Muslim students are required to take Islamic religious studies, while non-Muslim students take moral education. Tracking begins at the upper secondary level (Form 4). Placement in the academic (science and arts), technical and vocational, or Islamic school streams is based purely on a student's performance during a week-long standardized examination.

Special Education

At all levels of public school education, Malaysia offers services for children with special needs. Special education programs are offered to students with visual and auditory impairments, physical disabilities, and students with learning difficulties (e.g., autism, dyslexia, attention deficit hyperactivity disorder). Under the Special Education Integration Program, students attend regular classes and follow the national curriculum. However, these students also receive additional assistance through special day classes and individualized tutoring. Alternately, students may attend special education schools in a fully funded residential setting. Students in this program may use the national curriculum or an alternative educational learning plan. At the primary and secondary levels, students with special needs may extend their education by up to two years in accordance with their individual needs.

Teacher Education

The MOE's Teacher Education Division oversees the overall administration of teacher education. Candidate selection, educational training, and staff development programs are all run by the government. Primary school teacher training is done through Institutes of Teacher Education under the MOE, while secondary school teacher training is done through public universities under the MOHE. The Bachelor of Teaching Program is a five-and-a-half-year program designed for high school graduates. Those who possess the Malaysia Higher School Certificate will take four years to complete the program. Individuals with a bachelor's degree in another field can use the year-long Postgraduate Diploma in Teaching Program to become a certified public school teacher. In-service training programs offered by the MOE include various long- and short-term courses for teachers to improve their teaching and professional skills.

Technology and Education

The MOE is fully committed to the expanded use of technology in education. Beginning in 1999, a major initiative called Smart Schools was set up to fully equip all public schools with resources such as computers, high-speed Internet connection, and multimedia software. Additional teacher training programs and specific curricular goals were included to increase participation rates in science and technology at all levels. In the effort to meet the MOE's globalization objectives, starting in 2002, 30 percent of the annual education budget has been allocated for technological materials and support.

Gender and Education

In Malaysia male and female students have equal access to education. However, ongoing data from the MOE's 2000–2010 education plan revealed a steady decline in the participation of male youths at the secondary and tertiary levels. Although public university enrollment has continued to grow, these gains have been attributed to increases in female participation. However, females continue to be underrepresented in engineering and technical fields at the university level, with graduation rates at around 30 percent.

During the last decade, the decreasing numbers of male teachers in primary and secondary schools has been a major concern for the MOE. For instance, in 2008, male teachers comprised only 4 percent at the kindergarten level and 35 percent at the primary and secondary school levels. At the tertiary levels, there are equal numbers of female and male teachers.

Informal Education

All Malaysian students in the public school system are strongly encouraged to participate in cocurricular activities. Divided into three categories, these activities include clubs such as math and chess, sports such as badminton and netball, and uniform bodies such as Boy Scouts and Girl Guides. Since 10 percent of public university admission scores are based on involvement in cocurricular activities, these groups have become nearly compulsory for students applying to institutions of higher education.

Public university applicants can also boost their résumés through the National Service Program (NSP). Recognizing that 60 percent of the population is of school age, in 2004 the government instituted the NSP. Currently, students are selected through a lottery system and participate in a three-month program that involves physical training, character building, community service, and nationalism. Students learn skills ranging from hand-to-hand combat to environmental preservation. NSP is designed to bring youths from various ethnic groups together to promote patriotism and multicultural awareness.

In the 1970s adult education programs in the industrial, agricultural, and community development sectors were initiated by the government and the private sector to strengthen employment opportunities and literacy rates for the rural poor. By the mid-1990s adult education had become more accessible with the introduction of distance learning.

System Economics

In 2008 the Malaysian government allocated 4.1 percent of its gross domestic product (GDP) for education. During the same year, 17.2 percent of the government's operating expenditure was directed toward education. Primary and secondary students are not required to pay school fees. Public universities are subsidized by the government; however, attendees are also expected to pay minimal tuition fees.

Dilemmas and Challenges

As Malaysia works toward using the education system as a tool to promote national unity in a pluralistic society, attention has been drawn to the relevance of ethnic identities and home languages. In an effort to create national integration after independence, Bahasa Malaysia was declared the national language. Concerned with the needs of diverse populations, schools using other local languages (Tamil and Mandarin Chinese) were created. The MOE continues to struggle with the balance between the development of a national citizenship and the preservation of ethnic identities.

Malaysia's push toward a globally competitive national school system has also created a need for highly trained teachers. Some of the challenges the MOE is facing include attracting highly qualified men and women, developing relevant teachers training workshops, and creating current curricula to match the technological goals of a market economy.

Future Prospects

Since the recruitment of international students in higher levels of education is seen as a crucial step toward greater participation in the global market, the MOHE established four Malaysian Education Promotion Centres (MEPCs) overseas to provide support to prospective international students. Furthermore, in 2007, the Ministry of Higher Education established the International Students Affairs Unit to implement and oversee services and programs that meet the diverse needs of international students in Malaysia.

The MOE is also committed to reforming public examinations by passing initiatives that would improve assessment and increase accessibility for all students. The plan is to offer greater flexibility and more options for students. For example, in 2003, students were given the option to take public examinations in math and science subjects in Bahasa Malaysia or English.

Finally, the MOE intends to continue investing in technological upgrades throughout the public school system. The goal is to have all public schools converted to fully running Smart Schools by 2020. In addition, the government will continue to provide intensive and continuous technology training for teachers, school principals, administrators, and other educational support staff. Through the use of innovative initiatives and visionary goals, Malaysia has fostered and funded a commitment toward greater globalization and national empowerment in education. Its willingness to invest in schools continues to transform future possibilities.

Eva Wong and Cheri Scripter

REFERENCES

Almacen, Bayani Ursolino. *Teacher Training Program: The Malaysian Perspective.* Kuala Lumpur, Malaysia: University of Malaysia, forthcoming.

Central Intelligence Agency. *The CIA World Factbook.* New York: Skyhorse, 2011. https://www.cia.gov/library/publications/the-world-factbook/index.html.

Chiam, Heng Keng. "Developing Capacity in Quality Early Childhood Care and Education through Public-Private Partnership: The Malaysian Experience." Paper presented at the World Conference on Early Childhood Care and Education, Moscow, Russia, September 2010.

Department of Statistics, Malaysia. www.statistics.gov.my.

Malaysia Education at a Glance

General Information

Capital	Kuala Lumpur
Population	28.6 million
Language	Bahasa Malaysia
Literacy rate (2005)	92.9%
GDP per capita	US$7,900
Number of phones (landline) per 100 people	16.1
Number of phones (mobile) per 100 people	121.32
Number of Internet users per 100 people	55.30
Number of Internet hosts (2011)	344,452

Formal Education Information

Compulsory school age population enrolled (2011)	2.86 million
Compulsory school age population (2011)	10%
Number of years of compulsory education (2011)	6 (ages 6–12)
Student/teacher ratio (2008)	
Primary school (Standard 1–6)	15
Secondary school (Form 1–5)	15
Average class size in primary school (2008)	28
Average school days per year (primary school)	210
Average number of hours per school day (primary school)	4.8
Primary school gross enrollment ratio (2008)	97%
Primary school entrants reaching grade 5 (2008)	94%
Primary school entrant's reaching last grade (2008)	92%
Secondary school gross enrollment ratio (2008)	68%

Note: Unless otherwise indicated, all data are based on sources from 2011.

EFA. "Education For All: Global Monitoring Report." www. unesco.org.

GED. *Global Education Digest 2012: Comparing Education Statistics Across the World*. Montreal: UNESCO Institute for Statistics, 2012.

International Communications Union. www.itu.int/ITU-D/ict/ statistics.

Kiwanis Disability Information and Support Centre. 2011. www. disabilitymalaysia.com.

Langgulung, Hasan, and Che N. Hashim. "Islamic Religious Curriculum in Muslim Countries: The Experiences of Indonesia and Malaysia." *Bulletin of Education and Research* 30:1 (June 2008): 1–19.

Malakolunthu, Suseela. "Educational Reform and Policy Dynamics: A Case of the Malaysian 'Vision School' for Racial Integration." *Educational Research for Policy and Practice* 8:2 (2009): 123–134.

Malaysia Department of National Service. www.khidmatnegara. gov.

Ministry of Education, Malaysia. www.moe.gov.my/?lang=en.

Ministry of Higher Education. "Malaysia." www.mohe.gov.my/ educationmsia.

Multimedia Super Corridor. www.mscmalaysia.my.

Nation Master. 2011. www.nationmaster.com.

Penang Free School. www.pfs.edu.my.

UNESCO–UIS. "Education Profile: Malaysia." www.uis.unesco. org.

UNICEF Media Centre. "Early Investments in Education Pay Off for Malaysian Girls Today." 2005. www.unicef.org/malaysia.

United Nations Development Programme. *International Human Development Indicators*. 2011. http://hdrstats.undp.org/en/ indicators/6.html.

World Bank. "World Development Indicators." http://data.world-bank.org/data-catalog/world-development-indicators.

Mongolia

Mongolia is situated in northern Asia between Russia and the People's Republic of China. An estimated 30 percent of the population is nomadic or seminomadic. Fifty-seven percent of Mongolians live in the capital city of Ulaanbaatar and other similar urban areas, and 90 percent speak Khalkha Mongol, more commonly known as Mongolian. The remaining groups speak various Turkic languages and Russian. Due to strong historical political ties, nearly a half million Mongolians currently reside in Russia and about 3.5 million more live in China's Inner Mongolia autonomous regions.

Roughly 42 percent of the labor force raise sheep, goats, cattle, horses, and camels and produce crops such as wheat, barley, and potatoes. More recently, nonagricultural sectors have been expanding with the discovery of extensive mineral deposits of petroleum, tin, copper, coal, and gold. Nonetheless, nearly 40 percent of the population lives in poverty.

Educational System

The Ministry of Science, Technology, Education and Culture (MOSTEC) generates educational policy and sets standards for all levels of formal education in Mongolia. Promotion is determined by a series of examinations that are administered after primary school (fourth grade), lower secondary school (tenth grade), and upper secondary school (twelfth grade). Students entering higher education are also required to pass competitive entrance examinations.

Preschool, Primary, and Secondary Education

Approximately 54 percent of Mongolian children receive some form of preschool education. All kindergartens are state-subsidized and noncompulsory. Children generally attend preschool from age three to six and follow a state curriculum designed to cultivate minds, bodies, and personalities. Children usually attend kindergarten six days a week with a half day on Saturdays. Remoteness in Mongolia has become an educational issue to which MOSTEC has responded with traveling preschools and summer kindergartens. For example, in rural parts of western Mongolia, teachers are sent out to nomadic herder families seven or eight times a year to run school readiness programs for preschool children.

There are nearly 700 primary and secondary schools in Mongolia. Primary and lower secondary education are compulsory in Mongolia. Primary education lasts for five years and over one-third of the curriculum is spent on Mongolian literacy. Mathematics is also central to the curriculum. Subjects such as science, history, music, art, and physical education are mandatory as well. After primary school, students must complete four years of lower secondary school. Upper secondary school, which lasts for another two years, is not compulsory. The secondary curriculum is also focused on literacy skills and mathematics and prepares students for higher education institutions. Students must choose a foreign language, either English or Russian, and continue their previous studies in more advanced forms. In 2005 English replaced Russian as the official second language of Mongolia. After lower secondary school, students who do not attend a university may choose to enter technical and vocational schools instead and learn the skills necessary to compete in the labor market.

School dormitories are used in Mongolia to meet the needs of nomadic families and remote populations. The state has agreed to pay for dormitory expenses, but without Soviet subsidies, government funding is limited, and some of these buildings have become dilapidated and overcrowded. School dormitories are often forced to close throughout the winter because of faulty heating systems and inadequate building structures. For example, one-quarter of rural schools close during the cold winter months.

Postsecondary Education

The gross enrollment rate for higher education is 37 percent. Forty public and 131 private Mongolian universities, institutes, and colleges offer degrees ranging from technical certifications to doctorates in most areas of study. All higher education institutions are monitored by MOSTEC and must meet rigorous regulation standards to receive accreditation. In 2006 most public institutions were accredited, but only 15 percent of private postsecondary schools had received accreditation. Policy initiatives were generated to increase these numbers by 2015.

In order to pay for faculty salaries and instructional resources, student fees in higher education were initiated in 1993. Tuition approximates 250,000 Tughrik (US$234) or about four months' pay for a university professor. MOSTEC provides funds for heat, water, and electricity and oversees the academic standards of all higher education institutions. Foreign students may apply to colleges and universities in Mongolia if they have graduated from high school and passed the required entrance examinations. In postsecondary schools, Mongolian is the language of instruction, but theses and dissertations may be written in other languages.

Curriculum, Instruction, and Assessment

Prior to democracy in Mongolia, the education system was based on communist ideologies, a highly controlled nationalized curriculum, and teacher-centered pedagogies. A shift has occurred since the early 1990s, and the Ministry of Education has created greater flexibility and participation in all areas. The curriculum is still nationalized at the primary and secondary level, but it has been divided into two strands. Seventy percent of the curriculum is considered "core" and must be followed in all schools. The remaining 30 percent is "optional" and may be locally developed by individual school sites. All textbooks are published by MOSTEC. The evaluation system has also changed. Many assessments are now done at the local level and reflect student-centered learning styles. However, national examinations are still used to evaluate progress and determine promotions at each level of education.

MOSTEC has also partnered with international agencies to develop teaching methodologies and increase English language skills in Mongolian classrooms. Since 1991 the US Peace Corps has sent 660 volunteers to schools in Mongolia to teach English and organize various community development projects.

Special Education

Special education in Mongolia has followed a pattern of isolation, integration, and inclusion. Until the 1990s, children with physical and mental disabilities were required to attend segregated special education schools. In 2000 only five such schools were still in existence and disabled students were primarily mainstreamed into the regular school system. However, rural children with disabilities still have little access to education. Moreover, students with severe disabilities have historically not been served by public education. The Second Education Development Project was created to build new schools and help approximately 2,000 severely disabled children attend school for the first time.

Teacher Education

Teachers in Mongolia are required by MOSTEC to complete teacher training programs in universities and colleges. Mongolian State University of Education, the country's largest teacher training institution, operates 12 schools and five teachers colleges in various provinces. Preschool and primary school teachers attend teachers colleges; secondary school teachers receive subject specific training in one of twelve specialty schools. After four years of study, graduates receive bachelor's degrees in education and may continue with advanced degrees as desired.

Preservice and in-service teacher training and professional development opportunities have been dependent on financial resources. Recent international aid has prompted the creation and expansion of professional development workshops that address areas such as curricular reform, school and university partnerships, technology, and school management.

Technology and Education

About half of all Mongolian households own a personal computer, although this is less likely to be true in remote areas. The Mongolian government recognizes the need for growth in the information and communication technology (ICT) sector, and foreign investors have joined with the government to promote ICT Vision 2010's goal of attaining universal computer literacy in Mongolia. MOSTEC has instituted ICT classes, called Informatics for all students in grades 8 to 11. However, resources have been sparse and most classrooms have only one computer for every 25 students (Enkhjargal 2011). Furthermore, many staff members have not been adequately trained in ICT. However, as financial resources become available, MOSTEC plans to improve institutional capacity and ICT infrastructure in the education system.

Gender and Education

Male and female students have equal access to education in Mongolia. Once students enter secondary school, however, boys begin to drop out more frequently than girls, a trend that continues at each subsequent level of education. Unlike other developing nations where males tend to have greater opportunities than their female counterparts to complete their education, males in Mongolia are often needed to remain at home and work instead of traveling the necessary distance in order to attend school. According

to MOSTEC, in 2000, higher education institutions enrolled twice as many females as males. Furthermore, 60 percent of college graduates were women. Females represent 54 percent of the professional and technical work sector in Mongolia, 50 percent of the country's senior officials and managers, and 6.6 percent of the seats held in parliament (Human Development Report 2010). Nearly 90 percent of primary teachers, 70 percent of secondary teachers, and 50 percent of university professors are women.

Informal Education

The Mongolian Technical University provides distance higher education. Part-time classes and evening seminars are also offered at many institutes to meet the needs of full-time workers. Local television in Mongolia began in the mid-1970s, and 80 percent of the population is currently regular viewers. By the 1980s, the Arts Council of Mongolia began broadcasting a weekly arts and cultural heritage program. Mongolia is also developing its first education channel, which will soon cover all 21 provinces and be available in most schools.

Ten percent of Mongolian children in grades 1 to 12, many of whom were living in poverty in overcrowded urban areas, dropped out of school in 2010. In response to this crisis, MOSTEC-funded evening and correspondence classes and nonformal training opportunities are now available for children and adolescents who have left school early.

System Economics

When public schools were developed in Mongolia in the early twentieth century, the Soviet Union provided nearly one-third of Mongolia's gross domestic product (GDP). The subsequent elimination of external subsidies greatly affected Mongolia's school system; by the 1990s, underfunding was common and many buildings were left in disrepair. In 2000, 90 percent of the country's school buildings were in need of repair. More recently, international aid, mainly from nongovernmental organizations, has begun to address infrastructure limitations and resource availability throughout the public school system. Education in Mongolia is generally funded at both the state and local level. In 2009, 23.4 percent of the government's income budget was spent on education, and 5.6 per-

Mongolia Education at a Glance

General Information

Capital	Ulaanbataar
Population	3 million
Language	Khalkha Mongol
Literacy rate	98%
GDP per capita	US$1,670
Number of phones (landline) per 100 people	6.996
Number of phones (mobile) per 100 people	83.3
Number of Internet users per 100 people	12.22
Number of Internet hosts	7,942

Formal Education Information

Compulsory school age population enrolled (2005)	251,205
Compulsory school age population (2005)	9%
Student/teacher ratio	
Primary school (grades 1–4) (2008)	31
Secondary school (grades 5–10) (2005)	22.4
Average class size in primary school (2005)	31.6
Number of years of compulsory education (2005)	8 (ages 8–15)
Primary school gross enrollment ratio (2008)	89%
Primary school entrants reaching grade 5 (2007)	94%
Primary school entrants reaching last grade (2005)	92%
Secondary school gross enrollment ratio (2005)	83%

Note: Unless otherwise indicated, all data are based on sources from 2011.

cent of the nation's GDP expenditure was allocated to education. Although basic education remains free, families are required to pay for school supplies, meals, and building repair fees.

Dilemmas and Challenges

Rapid urbanization, overcrowding, and limited financial resources have created problems in Mongolia. Many schools are now operating in two shifts per day; some in Ulaanbaatar are running three shifts. Nearly 38 percent of the population does not have access to safe drinking water (Human Development Report 2010). Furthermore, poverty and inadequate housing facilities have created a generation of street children in large urban areas. To avoid freezing weather conditions, homeless children are living in manholes under the streets. Many of them are hungry and in need of health care. Local agencies estimate that Ulaanbaatar alone has 4,000 homeless children. In an effort to reunite homeless children with their parents, Mongolian officials declared 2004 the "Year of Family Development and Support." Children of

nomadic populations and those from rural areas are very limited in their access to education, proper nutrition, and health services. Local and international agencies are working together to meet the needs of all children.

While the minimum legal age for employment is 16, a significant number of children are employed as domestic workers or herders or in specific sites such as mines. With the growing awareness of the problem of child labor, the International Labor Organization (ILO) established a national office for an International Program on the Elimination of Child Labor in Mongolia. Results of the Main Report on Labor Force Survey indicate that about 65,000 children (ages five to 15) were engaged in labor. In Mongolia adult prostitution is legal, and yet data show over 200 registered cases of child prostitution each year. Greater resources are needed to meet the needs of Mongolia's homeless, nomadic, and exploited children.

Future Prospects

Mongolia is working closely with international organizations to improve its school system. MOSTEC has partnered with international groups and created long-term action plans and financial arrangements for education. The 2002–2008 Second Education Development Project was created to promote basic education rights. The 2006–2010 Third Education Master Plan targeted donor partnerships and capacity building. Schools were repaired and replaced as money becomes available. School dormitories will be renovated. More computers and Internet access sites will be provided for all primary and secondary schools. To address local needs and create a sectorwide approach to education with greater opportunities for distance learning in remote provinces, a number of projects, including MOSTEC's Third Education Development Project, are being implemented. Major changes are occurring within the education system. Mongolia's commitment to education remains steadfast.

Cheri Scripter and Hsiu-Zu Ho

References

Central Intelligence Agency. *The CIA World Factbook.* New York: Skyhorse, 2011. https://www.cia.gov/library/publications/the-world-factbook/index.html.

Human Development Report. http://hdr.undp.org/en.

Mongolian Ministry of Education, Culture, and Science. www.mecs.gov.mn/lang-English.mw.

National Statistics Office. *Main Report of Labor Force Survey*. Ulaanbaatar, Mongolia: National Statistics Office, 2010.

Nation Master. 2011. www.nationmaster.com.

Organisation for Economic Co-operation and Development (OECD). "Program Evaluation Report: Mongolia: Education Sector Development Program." 2007. www.oecd.org.

Peace Corps. www.peacecorps.gov.

UNESCO. *Achievements in Education: Mongolia*. Paris: 2007.

———. "Education for All: Mongolia: Early Childhood Care and Education Programmes." Geneva, Switzerland: 2006.

UNESCO–UIS. "Education Profile: Mongolia." www.uis.unesco.org.

World Bank. "Mongolia at a Glance." www.worldbank.org/en/country/mongolia.

MYANMAR (BURMA)

Myanmar, formerly known as Burma, is located in South-eastern Asia. Myanmar is ethnically diverse with 135 distinct ethnic groups recognized by the government. Sixty-eight percent of the population belongs to the Bamar group, followed by Shan (9 percent), Kayin (7 percent), Rakhine (4 percent), Chinese (3 percent), Mon (2 percent), Indian (2 percent) and other ethnic minorities which include the Kachin, Chin, Anglo-Indians, and Anglo-Burmese. The majority of the population is Buddhists (89 percent), followed by Christians (4 percent), Muslims (4 percent), animists (1 percent), and other religions (2 percent).

There are four major linguistic families in Myanmar: (1) Sino-Tibetan (which is the most widely spoken and includes Burmese as well as Karen, Kachin, Chin, and Chinese); (2) Kradai (of which Shan is primary); (3) Austro-Asiatic (primarily Mon, Palaung, and Wa), and Indo-European (primarily Pali, the liturgical language of Theravada Buddhism, and English). Although Burmese is the official language, more than 100 local and regional dialects are spoken throughout Myanmar.

Amid the political and economic turmoil, Myanmar faced further devastation as Cyclone Nargis ravaged the country in May 2008, leaving an estimated 1 million homeless and more than 130,000 people dead or missing. While large-scale international relief efforts were made available, Myanmar's isolationist regime delayed the entry of United Nations planes delivering food, medicine and other supplies, limited its distribution and denied entry visas to relief workers. While Myanmar's response to international relief efforts have been described by the United Nations as unprecedented, world governments remain divided on how to deal with the current military junta.

The unstable political and economic history of Myanmar since the early 1960s greatly impacted its education system. For example, because of the 1988 student protests (or referred to as the "8888" student uprising), all universities were closed for two years. A subsequent series of students' strikes in the 1990s resulted in another three years of closure. When colleges and universities were reopened in 1999, the government attempted to prevent further mass demonstrations by scattering universities in various regions. In 2011 the United States government relaxed sanctions on assistance to Myanmar and developed possibilities for trade—including the outsourcing of certain educational practice.

Educational System

The education system of Myanmar is administered by the government's Ministry of Education. The Ministry of Education is responsible for basic and higher education, while other ministries take charge of the administration and management of preschool, post-secondary, and other tertiary-levels of education. The structure and organization of the education in Myanmar include 11 years of basic education; that is, five years of primary education (kindergarten and grade one to four), four years of lower secondary or middle school (grade five to eight), and two years of upper secondary or high school (grade nine to ten). Primary education in Myanmar is compulsory. Tertiary-level and university education usually require three years to obtain a bachelor's degree, two years to obtain the masters' degree, and at least four years to obtain a doctoral degree.

Precompulsory Education

Precompulsory education targets children from ages three to five. The concept of formalized early childhood care and development is relatively new in Myanmar with an average enrollment rate of preschoolers of 7 percent in 1997. The wide variation on availability of childcare services between urban and rural areas is a major concern. The majority of preschools in Myanmar are private institutions concentrated in major cities and towns. A survey conducted by the Ministry of Education in 1998 indicated that only 1.9 percent of children entering primary school in rural Rakhine have preschool education, whereas 36.7 percent of children in urban Yangon have attended preschool classes.

Compulsory Education: Primary Education

The Myanmar Child Law enacted in 1993 indicates that children have the right to free basic education at the primary level in state schools. Primary education is the first stage of basic education, which includes two cycles: lower (one year of kindergarten and grade one to two) and upper primary education (grades three and four). Although the admission age is five, approximately 35 percent of children entering kindergarten were over age six.

The net enrollment rate of primary level was 93 percent in 2010. There is an average of 40 students in an elementary class with an average student/teacher ratio of 31 in rural areas and 26.5 in urban areas. Schools in rural and remote areas of the country are over-crowded and understaffed, especially in the lower grades.

High drop-out rates and repetition rates are increasing and pose significant problems in Myanmar primary education. Less than half of the children entering kindergarten complete the last year of primary education. The average drop-out rate and repetition rate in 1999 were 9 percent and 9.7 percent, respectively, with variations in repetition rates between rural (13 percent) and urban areas (10 percent), as well as State (9 percent in Yangon) and Divisions (17 percent in Magway). Several factors contribute to the inability of some children to attend school: insufficient resources from the government; children's lack of access to school facilities; parents' inability to afford school expenses; and children's obligations to work and take care of siblings.

Postcompulsory Education: Secondary Education

Secondary education is the second stage of basic education, which includes two cycles: lower (grade five to eight) and upper secondary education (grade nine and ten). Children in families with military connections often have easier access to enter more prestigious secondary schools. Technical and vocational education is provided in technical high schools, agricultural high schools, agricultural institutes, vocational and trade schools. The net enrollment rate of secondary education was approximately 70 percent in 2010.

Postcompulsory Education: Higher Education

Students who graduate from basic education and pass the national entrance examination in Myanmar may enter tertiary-level and university education which include technical institutes, colleges, and universities. A variety of short training courses (three to nine months of study) are also available in higher education. In the 2009–2010 school year there were nearly 160 higher education institutes in Myanmar.

Curriculum, Instruction, and Assessment

The curriculum in precompulsory education focuses on language skills as well as physical development; learning of basic numerical skills; cultivation of good behaviors and collective work habits; development of the spirit of self-reliance, self-discipline, responsibility, creative ability, and love for people and the natural environment.

Teaching materials are highly centralized and the same textbooks are used throughout the country. In elementary school, Myanmar language, English, and mathematics are the main subjects. Other subjects include: general studies (grade one and two only), basic science and social studies (grade three and four), aesthetic education, physical education, and school activities. Since the 1998–1999 school year life skills education became part of a national curriculum which aims to help students live a physically and mentally healthy life and strengthen their psychosocial competences in problem solving, creative thinking, critical thinking, self-awareness, empathy, and decision making.

Subjects covered in lower secondary school include: Myanmar language, English, mathematics, social studies, general science, life skills, moral education, vocational education, physical education, aesthetic education, and school activities. In the upper secondary school level, required courses include Myanmar language, English, and mathematics and optional courses including physics, chemistry, biology, geography, history, and economics. The school year consists of two semesters in Myanmar. Classes are scheduled for 36 weeks per year with an average of 30 (grade one and two) or 35 minutes (grade three and four) per class for primary schools and 45 minutes for secondary schools.

New assessments and evaluation procedures in basic education have shifted toward a more student-centered and learning-centered orientation. Beginning in the second grade, students' performance and progress are regularly monitored by conducting chapter-end tests for all subjects as an assessment of academic progress. In order to encourage retention in kindergarten and first grade, regular exercises (rather than chapter-end tests) are employed. In addition to chapter-end tests, a Comprehensive Personal Record (CPR) is also assessed for each student which includes a variety of components including providing assistance in their parents' livelihood, being neat and tidy, and having at least 75 percent school attendance. Students must obtain at least 40 percent in both academic performance and the CPR in order to advance to the next level in primary education.

In the lower secondary education level, the advancement of students to the upper secondary education level is determined by students' performance on the chapter-end tests, the Basic Education Standard VIII, the examination taken during the second semester of grade seven, as well as the CPR. Similarly, completion of high school is determined by results of chapter-end tests, the Basic Education Standard taken at the second semester of the tenth grade, as well as the CPR. Students who seek to enter higher education must pass the entrance examinations held by universities and vocational institutions.

Teacher Education

There are three types of teacher training institutions in Myanmar: (1) those that train primary school teachers and award students a Diploma in Educa-

tion after the completion of one-year courses; (2) those that train lower secondary school teachers and award students a Certificate in Education after the completion of two-year courses; (3) those that train upper secondary school teachers and award students the Bachelor of Education degree after completion of three to four year courses. The number of qualified teachers is relatively low. In the 1995–1996 school year a significant proportion of teachers did not have teaching qualification: 56.6 percent of primary school teachers; 57.8 percent of lower secondary school teachers; and 8.4 percent of upper secondary school teachers. In order to reduce the percentage of teachers without a teaching qualification, some training programs (typically six months in duration) for in-service teachers are offered.

Informal Education

For children whose families cannot afford the costs of basic education, monastic schools have served an important role, even before the nationalization of schools in the 1960s. It is uncertain to what degree children in monastic schools become functionally literate given the fact that monastic schools usually lack teaching capacities, techniques, and materials. There are 1,500 officially recognized monastic schools serving 93,000 children in Myanmar.

In order to improve equity and accessibility of education for every child in Myanmar, there are also some affiliated schools established in remote areas. Affiliated schools are run and built by local communities in rural areas with their own initiation and expense, and academically affiliated with nearby public schools. These schools are administratively private in nature and student fees are required.

In order to meet the demands of modernization, there are an increasing number of young people who attend private-run courses, such as foreign languages, computer studies, accounting, and business studies. However, these classes are primarily found in urban areas and attended by students from families of higher socioeconomic status.

System Economics

For the 2001 fiscal year, 18.1 percent of total government expenditure (1.3 percent of GDP) was spent on education. Total educational expenditure for the 1999–2000 school year was approximately 10,159 million kyat (US$1.5 million) with 66.9 percent for Basic Education.

Special Education

In Myanmar special education is provided to students who are mentally and physically challenged. Schools for special education are generally operated by the government as well as by nongovernmental organizations (NGOs). Institutions supported by the government include schools for students with visual impairments, schools for students with hearing impairments, and a primary school for intellectually disabled children from the kindergarten to the grade four (the school of deaf also offer preprimary classes since 1999). No fees are required in these institutions. Some NGOs have also established several special education schools including the Mary Chapman School for the Deaf, the Yangon Education Centre for the Blind, Meikhtila, and the Vocational Training Centre for the Physically Handicapped.

Gender and Education

Currently, Myanmar has little gender disparity in primary and secondary school enrollment and literacy rates. The Gender Parity Index (GPI) for gross enrollment in primary school is 1.01 for Myanmar, the highest among all countries accounted for in East Asia and the Pacific, and the GPI for gross secondary school enrollment was 1.00 (UNESCO Institute for Statistics). Half of the students in primary schools and 49 percent of students in secondary schools were females. According to the EFA Literacy Gender Parity Index, Myanmar scored 99.0 (EFA Mid-Decade Assessment). Although national enrollment figures suggest no large differences by gender, some female enrollment rates varied by state, grade level, and urban and rural areas. For example, in Kayah State, 46.72 percent of urban primary students were female and 52.92 percent of urban secondary students were female. In tertiary education, more females than males were enrolled. The GPI for gross enrollment ratio in tertiary education in the year 2000 was 1.75 (UNESCO Global Monitoring Report). A gender difference also exists with female and male enrollment in various types of vocational

institutions. Among students accepted in 2003–2004 to technical institutions, such as agricultural and commercial schools, 45.7 percent were females. However, among students accepted to weaving and home science training schools, 96.6 percent were females (EFA Mid-Decade Assessment). A gender disparity is also prevalent among teachers and school managers in basic education. In 2010 nearly 14 percent of basic education teachers were male and 86.07 percent of basic education teachers were female. Myanmar has been and is currently making efforts to address the gender inequalities in education.

Technology and Education

In order to accommodate the rapid growth of information technology in society, the Ministry of Education has in recent years emphasized the importance of Information and Communication Technology

---

Myanmar Education at a Glance

General Information

Capital	Yangon
Population	53.4 million
Language	Myanmar (Burmese)
Literacy rate	94.8%
GDP per capita	US$1,200
Number of phones (landline) per 100 people	1.69
Number of phones (mobile) per 100 people	.93
Number of Internet users per 100 people	0.23
Number of Internet hosts	172

Formal Education Information

Compulsory school age population enrolled (2006)	6.1 million
Compulsory school age population (2006)	12.6%
Number of years of compulsory education (2007)	5 (ages 6–11)
Student/teacher ratio (2007)	
Primary school (Standard 1–6)	29
Secondary school (Form 1–5)	27
Average class size in primary school (grades 1–4)	45.8
Average school days per year (primary school) (2007)	180
Average number of hours per school day (primary school)	no data
Primary school gross enrollment ratio	95%
Primary school entrants reaching grade 4 (2006)	72%
Primary school entrants reaching last grade (2005)	72%
Secondary school gross enrollment ratio (2006)	69%

Note: Unless otherwise indicated, all data are based on sources from 2011.

(ICT) on education. The use of ICT is encouraged in schools with collaborations of private sectors and local communities. Multimedia classrooms, computer laboratories as well as learning software were established in Basic Education. In the 2004–2005 school year, 100 schools had Internet connections in Myanmar. That number jumped to 172 in 2010. The government also initiated several "E-education" and "E-learning" programs. E-education programs include orientation programs on the matriculation examination and Summer English Program.

Dilemmas and Challenges

Lack of funding and resources are the major problems throughout the education system in Myanmar. The quality of teaching and teachers' salary are often low. There are high drop-out rates at the primary school level and low enrollment rates in secondary school level. Children are often taken out of schools early due to poverty—parents cannot afford fees or the children must work to assist their families. There is little assistance in terms of the provision of materials in primary schools from the government. Individual communities and private sectors are responsible for equipment as well as the construction of the schools. Due to underfunding and lack of resources, school buildings are mostly inadequately established by inferior and rough materials such as tree-trunk posts, bamboo, palm leafs, and *dani* (local materials for roofing). A 1992 survey conducted by Education Sector Study indicated that 50 percent of primary schools were constructed by such materials.

Future Prospects

Myanmar currently has plans targeted toward improving educational opportunities. The government of Myanmar launched a 30-Year Long Term Education Development Plan. The purpose of the plan is to make positive changes in educational access and quality. The plan targets educational areas in need of improvement, such as rural schooling, literacy rates, and teacher training. In regard to teacher training for example, the plan aims to increase the number of certified teachers and teacher training programs. Myanmar's goals also include improving access and quality in basic education for marginalized children, such as those who are poor, special needs, or ethnic minorities. The country is also concerned with improving assessment practices, developing new curriculum, and providing ICT for learning. With more schooling opportunities, Myanmar hopes to create a professional and skilled labor force. The education of people in Myanmar is crucial to the country's future development.

Wei-Wen Chen, Hsiu-Zu Ho,
and Connie Nguyen Tran

REFERENCES

Central Intelligence Agency. *The CIA World Factbook.* New York. Skyhorse, 2011. https://www.cia.gov/library/publications/the-world-factbook/index.html.

Economist Intelligence Unit. "Myanmar Country Profile." www.itu.int/en.

EFA. "Overcoming Inequality: Why Governance Matters." *Education for All Global Monitoring Report 2009.* Paris, France, UNESCO, 2008.

Ministry of Education. "Country Report: Myanmar Education Development Strategy Focusing on Inclusive Education." 2008. www.ibe.unesco.org/National_Reports/ICE_2008/myanmar_NR08.pdf.

———. "Myanmar EFA Mid-Decade Assessment Report: More Focus Needed on Monitoring and Capacity Building." March 27, 2008. www.unescobkk.org/education/efa.

UNICEF. "One Year After Cyclone, Myanmar on Hard Road to Recovery." May 2009. www.unicef.org/infobycountry/myanmar.html.

PHILIPPINES

The Republic of the Philippines, commonly referred to as the Philippines, is an archipelago located in Southeast Asia. Today, 95 percent of the people of the Philippines (or Filipinos) are of Malayan and Indonesian origin. Of more than 60 Filipino ethnic groups, the three largest groups are the Tagalog (28.1 percent), Cebuano (13.1 percent), and Ilocano (9 percent). While more than 180 languages and dialects are spoken, Tagalog and English are both the official languages.

Historically, the Filipino culture has been influenced by contacts with many countries. The first documented encounter was with the Chinese, who traded porcelain, silk, glass, and tin in exchange for pearls, cotton, tortoise-shell, and medicinal betelnuts in 982 CE. Before the 1500s, countries including

Borneo, China, India, Indonesia, Japan, and Malaysia helped to establish a system of political and social organization. The Philippines society was organized into community units called *barangay*, each supervised by a *datu*, or chief. Tribal leaders, who provided an informal education, were replaced with Spanish missionaries. The country's system of writing was soon lost, but the rich oral traditional literature has been preserved through folklore, songs, and poems. Spain (1521–1898), Japan (1942–1944), and the United States (1898–1942; 1944–1946) colonized the Philippines and influenced the present-day country. The Philippines was declared a sovereign and independent republic, following World War II, on July 4, 1946.

Educational System

The Philippines education system was influenced primarily by Spain and the United States. Spain introduced a Roman Catholic religion-based education system with missionaries as the first formal teachers. The clergymen provided religious instruction in *vistas* (small thatched buildings used as schools and chapels) to boys and girls in separate classrooms. Secondary and higher education institutions, modeled after the European monarchial system, served the elite few. The education of these students, who later joined the clergy, was intended to promote the religious values of the upper class. Subsequently, the landmark Educational Decree of 1863 mandated a system of free, compulsory elementary education in each village for all children age seven to 12. A normal school in Manila was also established to certify and train religious teachers. Later that year, the Royal Decree ordered separate schools for boys and girls.

The United States, in contrast, introduced a democratic public education system for the Filipino masses. By 1900 the United States had established 1,000 schools throughout the Philippines. American soldiers and Filipino teachers, who taught in English and Spanish, respectively, were temporarily recruited until more than 600 professionally trained US educators (teachers and administrators) arrived in 1901. These educators, known as *thomasites*, established an education system that replicated the US educational bureaucratic structure in order to provide basic education and teacher training to Filipinos. They propagated American ideals through education—for

example, that "all men are created equal." Filipino educators soon replaced the *thomasites* and taught Filipino children. The education system rapidly expanded to 500,000 enrolled students in 1908. Thus, more private schools were established to accommodate the large overenrollment in public schools. By 1946 private schools composed 46 percent of secondary schools and 98 percent in higher education institutions. The Philippines education system slowly evolved and now defines its own national goals and identity.

The Philippines education system has three main administrative components: the Department of Education (DepED), the Commission on Higher Education (CHED), and the Technical Education Skills and Development Authority (TESDA). The DepED has three supervisory bureaus—Bureau of Elementary Education (BEE), Bureau of Secondary Education (BSE), and Bureau of Nonformal Education (BNE)—which provides assistance with standards, staff development, policy formulation, and curricular programs. The CHED governs all public and private degree-granting higher education programs. The TESDA supervises nondegree technical and vocational training programs.

The DepED adopted UNESCO's Education for All 2015 Plan to provide quality equitable and accessible education to Filipinos nationwide. In the 2010–2011 school year (SY), there were nearly 50,600 private and public institutions at the preschool, elementary and secondary levels, with 86.9 percent being public institutions. A total of 20.4 million students were enrolled in elementary and secondary schools, with 64.3 percent at the compulsory elementary level and 34.7 percent at noncompulsory (preschool and secondary) levels. The academic year generally begins in June and ends in March. The 40-week-long school year consists of two semesters (four quarters) with about 200 six-hour instructional days. An optional summer school is offered from March to May to all students.

Precompulsory Education

The Bureau of Elementary Education manages preschool education. In the 2010–2011 SY, nearly 952,000 preschoolers were enrolled in private and public institutions, with a majority of these students (about 73 percent) enrolled in public schools. The DepEd's Preschool Service Contracting Program

(PSCP) provided education to 58 percent of all enrolled students with 2,344 PSCP classes offered in 16 regions. PSCPs serve economically disadvantaged five-year-old children from poor urban regions and municipalities, whose average annual income is less than 712 US Dollars.

Compulsory Education

Compulsory education consists of elementary school (grades 1 to 6). Students usually start elementary school at age six and graduate at age 12. In the Philippines, the first four grades of elementary education are referred to as primary school and the last two years are termed intermediate school. Some private elementary institutions offer seven grades (grades 1 to 7). Nearly 14 million children are enrolled in 42,140 elementary schools. Nearly all children (96 percent) attend public elementary schools, which make up 86.6 percent of all elementary institutions. There are about 375,000 public elementary school teachers with a ratio of one teacher for every 35 students.

Postcompulsory Education

Secondary Education. Upon the completion of elementary school, students can attend four years of secondary education, referred to as first year through fourth year. The normal age bracket for this level is 12 to 16 years. There are 8,450 public (60.1 percent) and private (39.9 percent) secondary schools. A large majority of the 6.3 million students in secondary schools are enrolled in public institutions (79.6 percent). There are nearly 180,000 secondary school teachers with a ratio of one teacher for every 39 students.

Secondary schools prepare students for future vocational or educational paths. There are four main types of high schools: general secondary, general comprehensive, vocational, and special secondary. General secondary schools educate college- and noncollege-bound students, and general comprehensive high schools prepare students specifically for college. Vocational schools train students for employment in agriculture, trade, and industry. Special secondary schools are institutions that prepare students for occupations in art, science, and technology, as well as schools for the disabled, underprivileged, and minor offenders.

Tertiary Education. Students who complete sec-

ondary schools may apply for admission into tertiary or college-level education. The Commission on Higher Education was established through the Higher Education Act of 1994. CHED oversees the promotion of quality education, academic freedom, intellectual growth, and research in the tertiary levels of education. CHED ensures accessible education to all through policy implementation, management, development, and accountability of higher education institutions (HEIs).

There are 2,036 HEIs throughout 17 regions in the Philippines. Unlike the elementary and secondary schools, most of the HEIs are private institutions (74.4 percent), which include both sectarian and nonsectarian schools. Public HEIs include state universities and colleges, local universities and colleges, other governmental schools, CHED-supervised institutions, and special HEIs. The oldest and largest private school in the Philippines is the University of Santo Tomas, a Roman Catholic institution, which was established in 1611. In the 2010–2011 SY, nearly 40,000 students were enrolled there. The most reputable public institution of higher education is the University of the Philippines (UP). UP has seven distinct campuses and more than 50,000 students registered in 246 undergraduate and graduate degree programs. The requirements for admission to private schools vary, while public schools like UP use a combination of the Philippine College Admission Test score and high school grades.

Educational System

The educational system in the Philippines ranks as one of the poorest in East Asia, due in part to a lack of physical and financial resources, relatively low gross national product, and limited educational outcomes of its students. Long periods of European colonization and Japanese subjugation may have led to this result. However, after World War II, the educational system in the Philippines has followed the dominant paradigm of precompulsory education for preschoolers and compulsory education for children and adolescents.

Precompulsory Education

Preschool programs are typically six months in duration, from October to March. The PSCP curriculum focuses on the Filipino language, communication, and mathematics. The classroom size is specified to range from 20 to 25 children. Prospective preschool teachers must meet three minimum requirements: residency in the *barangay* of the school, a bachelor's degree in preschool education or equivalent, and eligibility to take the License Exam Test. Preschool service providers, which include early learning centers, colleges, universities, and nongovernmental organizations (NGOs), must be registered and meet financial requirements of US$7 dollars per child and a teacher salary of about US$71 dollars per month.

Compulsory Education

The elementary school curriculum is designed to help students develop academic competencies. The core subjects for primary school are Filipino, English, and mathematics. Students in grades 1 to 3 take an additional course in *sibika at kultura* (civics and culture), while students in grades 3 to 6 take science and health classes. Students in intermediate school take the same primary school core subjects plus four supplemental *makabayan* courses such as *heographiya asaysayan at sibika* (geography, history, and civics). *Makabayan*, which are experiential learning subjects, focus on holistic learning, national development, and personal identity. In public schools, especially in the provinces, the vernacular language is used for instruction in the first three years of school, with English and Tagalog taught as subjects.

As students advance in elementary education, the time spent in school also increases, from five hours and 20 minutes in first grade to six hours and 20 minutes in sixth grade. Students must have a score of 75 percent to successfully pass a course. Students are also rated on 14 character traits, such as honesty, love of God, patriotism, and obedience.

Postcompulsory Education

Secondary Education. The secondary education curriculum covers five core subjects for all high school grades: Filipino, English, mathematics, science, and *makabayan*. Similar to elementary education, there are four *makabayan* classes, including *araling panlipunan* (Philippines history and government). *Makabayan* is taught for 13 instructional hours per

week, while the other four core subjects are each five hours per week.

Teachers use many types of instructional media, including prototype lesson plans, teacher-developed materials, and manuals and textbooks from the DepED's approved list. The teaching materials cover learning competencies, course scope, sequence, non-formal education accreditation, and communication technology. The language of instruction for Filipino and *makabayan* classes is Filipino, and English is used to teach math, science, and English courses.

Students must meet the minimum grade of 75 percent on the combination of tests, quizzes, homework, projects, and classroom activities to pass a course. Subject tests are divided into basic items (60 percent), advanced questions (30 percent), and superior questions (10 percent). The cumulative year grade is an average of the two semesters combined.

Tertiary Education. Tertiary schools include one- to two-year technical or vocational programs and four- to five-year professional schools. Students can attain an associate's or bachelor's degree, as well as certificates, professional training, and license examination tests. Some of the majors offered in higher education institutions are biology, musicology, Philippine studies, architecture, statistics, and fine arts. Student may also obtain master's, doctoral, or other advanced degrees, for example, in law, and medicine.

Special Education

Special education is offered in each school division throughout the country. There are 158 special education centers, which serve children with special needs (CSN). These centers support CSN learning styles with the concept of inclusive education in teacher materials, assessments, school-based in-service training, and eventual integration of individual CSN into regular schools. CSN include students who are gifted, talented, and mentally or physically challenged (e.g., visual, speech, hearing impairments). Children with behavioral difficulties, learning disabilities, and other health problems can also be considered CSN.

Teacher Education

The Philippines has more than 800 teacher education institutions to train prospective teachers. Prospective teachers are required to complete a bachelor's degree and the License Exam Test prior to employment. The bachelor's degree can be in elementary education, secondary education, and art or science combined with 18 units of professional coursework from a college of education. The Magna Carta for Public School Teachers mandates teachers not to exceed eight-hour workdays. There are more than 500,000 elementary- and secondary-level teachers in the Philippines.

Technology and Education

The use of technology is prevalent in educational institutions throughout the Philippines. The Commission on Information and Communication Technology (CICT) is the primary organization that oversees information and communication technology (ICT). CICT is responsible for planning, policy development, implementation, and development of ICT. Networks of universities, the DepEd, and NGOs work collaboratively to evaluate, plan, and implement technology usage (e.g., in teaching and online computer-assisted instruction) in educational programs.

Technical Education

The Technical Education and Skills Development Authority (TESDA) is part of the country's education system. TESDA, offered in all 17 regions throughout the nation, was created to minimize the overlap between private and public agencies' development activities. TESDA aims to mobilize the country's human resource skill development through local governments, labor units, industries, and technical vocational institutions. TESDA offers more than 100 competency-based curricula, including different levels in subjects such as medical transcription, health-care services, dressmaking, plumbing, and security services.

Gender and Education

Although education is equally accessible to both females and males, Filipino females typically achieve higher levels of education. In the 1999–2000 SY, slightly more male students (51.1 percent) were enrolled at the elementary level, but the school cohort survival rate (CSR) for females was higher than for males (73.5 vs. 64.4 percent). In 2010 there were

nearly 655,000 out-of-school primary-school-age children, 58 percent of whom were males. In addition, more males repeat a grade in primary school (3 out 100 students) than females (1 out of 100 students). The same gender trend followed in the secondary education level; the CSR for males was less than females (41 vs. 52.5 percent). The gender differences in education may in part be due to the gender-typed traditions with respect to land inheritance and schooling. Land is preferentially given to males and schooling for females.

Nonformal Education

Nonformal education (NFE) was established in the early 1970s to meet the needs of those who are unable to participate in formal education. NFE includes public and private organizations that offer organized, systematic learning outside of formal education. Most people who attend NFE systems have dropped out of formal education, due largely to poverty. The five main sectors of NFE are (1) literacy education, (2) livelihood skills, (3) certification and equivalency programs, (4) continuing education among professionals, and (5) school and university initiatives. NFE systems do not offer certifications, replace formal education, or prepare students for higher

---

Philippines Education at a Glance

General Information

Capital	Manila
Population	101.834 million
Languages	Filipino (Tagalog) and English
Literacy rate	92.6%
GDP per capita	US$3,500
Number of phones (landline) per 100 people	6.67
Number of phones (mobile) per 100 people	47.06
Number of Internet users per 100 people	8.1
Number of Internet hosts	394,990

Formal Educational Information

Compulsory school age population enrolled	13.1 million
Compulsory school age population (2005)	14.41%
Number of years of compulsory education	6 (ages 6–12)
Student/teacher ratio	
Elementary school	35
Secondary school	39
Elementary school completion rate (2006)	70%
Elementary school gross enrollment ratio (2005)	111%
Secondary school gross enrollment ratio (2005)	85%

Note: Unless otherwise indicated, all data are based on sources from 2011.

education. By the mid-1980s, the Association for Non-Traditional Education was established, followed by NFE's greatest supporter, UNESCO's Education for All (EFA) movement.

System Economics

According to the *CIA World Factbook* (2011), in the 2008 fiscal year, the Philippines government allocated 2.8 percent of its gross domestic product (GDP) to education. The DepEd received the largest portion of funds (97.1 percent) for both private and public elementary institutions. Secondary-level schools, whose enrollment is about half that of elementary schools, received only about 3 percent of the education budget. The government's GDP allocation for each student was 11.1 percent for elementary, 9.2 percent for secondary, and less than 1 percent for higher education institutions. TESDA technical vocational education received 1.92 percent. In 2008 the DepED's budget significantly increased to 3.23 billion US dollars, with most of these funds used to support compulsory elementary schools.

Dilemmas and Challenges

The Philippines faces a number of systematic educational obstacles associated with poverty. For example, indigenous people, most of who live in poverty, are often overlooked and experience discriminatory practices in formal and nonformal education. Second, although the government funds tuition and fees for secondary education, many families cannot afford the additional costs of textbooks and uniforms. Thus, many children, especially the male students, conveniently withdraw from noncompulsory secondary school and instead enter the workforce. Lastly, some teachers, especially in math and science, do not have degrees in the subjects that they teach, thus limiting the in-depth knowledge they impart to students. They cannot afford the time or finances for subject training, especially when the teaching profession can exceed the mandated 40-hour workweek.

Future Prospects

Despite the challenges that the Philippines has encountered, the educational system has developed and expanded to meet the country's demands. The DepEd is committed to the goals of the Philippines' EFA 2015 plan to achieve functional literacy for all Filipinos. EFA serves as an impetus to meet basic literacy needs of all children, youth, and adults in formal and nonformal education systems. The DepEd utilizes the education budget to meet the goals and vision of EFA 2015: (1) having measurable learning outcomes, (2) increasing achievement levels by 50 percent, (3) providing access to quality compulsory primary education, especially to girls from ethnic minorities, (4) closing the gap in gender disparities, (5) providing early education, especially to disadvantaged children, and (6) enabling access to learning and life skill programs to adults and young people. The DepEd has financially invested in the 15-year EFA project to make high-quality education accessible and equitable for all Filipinos nationwide.

Charlene Bumanglag Tomas

REFERENCES

Central Intelligence Agency. *The CIA World Factbook*. New York: Skyhorse, 2011. https://www.cia.gov/library/publications/the-world-factbook/index.html.

Commission on Higher Education. www.ched.gov.ph.

International Labor Organization. www.ilo.org.

Nation Master. 2011. www.nationmaster.com.

"Official Gazette" of the Republic of the Philippines. www.gov.ph.

Republic of the Philippines Department of Education. www.deped.gov.ph.

Technical Education and Skills Development Authority. www.tesda.gov.ph.

UNICEF. "At a Glance: Philippines. Statistics." www.unicef.org/infobycountry/philippines_statistics.html.

University of the Philippines. www.up.edu.ph/index.php.

World Bank Education Statistics. 2011. www.worldbank.org.

SINGAPORE

The Republic of Singapore is a nation-state located at the narrowest point of the Strait of Malacca in Southeast Asia. Throughout history Singapore has been a prominent trading port for Asia and the Middle East. According to ancient legend, a prince observed a good omen in the form of a lion creature and founded the settlement of Singapura, "Lion City" in Sanskrit. Singapore's history involves the reign of many colonial powers, including the Portuguese, Dutch, and British. In 1819 an influential British lieutenant governor and official of the British East India Company, Sir Thomas Stamford Raffles, established a trading post and launched free trade and immigration. In addition to nautical prominence, Singapore had many tin mines and rubber plantations that attracted laborers from nearby regions and significantly contributed to nonindigenous population growth. A multiethnic population exists today with Chinese as the primary ethnic group, followed by Malay and Indian. This unique diversity is also reflected in four official languages—English, Malay, Mandarin Chinese, and Tamil. Many Singaporeans are fluent in two languages. Singaporeans also profess a myriad of religious beliefs, including Buddhist, Muslim, Taoist, Hindu, and Christian.

Upon securing independence from Great Britain, Singapore was admitted to the United Nations and the Commonwealth of Nations. Singapore joined the Association of South East Asian Nations as a founding member in 1967. As a leading economy in the region, Singapore enjoys a high level of economic success, strong social services, and an award-winning education system. The 2011 population census indicates that the country's population surpassed 5 million persons.

Educational System

Singapore's British-influenced education system includes six years of compulsory primary school, four years of secondary school, and two years of pre-university for those seeking entrance into university degree programs. English is the primary language of instruction at all levels. The Ministry of Education is responsible for planning, coordinating, and mandating policy of the formal education system. The Singapore education system serves over 532,000 students in 355 registered schools. According to the ministry (2011), "The mission of the Education Service is to mold the future of the nation, by molding the people who will determine the future of the nation. The Service will provide our children with a balanced and well-rounded education, develop them to their full potential, and nurture them into good citizens, conscious of their responsibilities to family, society and country." Singapore's educational system often achieves recognition based on test performance scores

and international rankings. Singapore ranked fourth in the 2006 Progress in International Reading Literacy Study (PIRLS). According to a multiyear assessment analysis by the National Center on Education and the Economy, Singapore ranked first in math and second in science. Human capital is recognized as the most critical aspect to sustain Singapore's success in a global market.

Preschool, Primary, and Secondary Education

Preschool education in Singapore follows a structured three-year program for children between the ages of three and six. Preschool programs are generally offered through kindergartens and child-care centers. Kindergartens are run by a variety of social, religious, and business organizations. All kindergartens are registered with the Ministry of Education and run sessions for three to four hours during weekdays with programs in English or a second language.

Primary education in Singapore consists of six years, broken down into four years of a foundation stage and two years of an orientation stage. At the foundation stage, the core curriculum consists of English, mother tongue, and mathematics as well as classes in music, arts, physical education, and social studies. Mother tongue is the language of the student's family background. Science classes start in third grade. At the end of fourth grade, students are tracked by learning ability. At the end of sixth grade, students sit for the Primary School Leaving Examination.

Secondary education falls within three categories: government-funded, government-aided, or independent. However, all schools follow the same system that allows students to pursue a special, express, or normal course structure. The special and express courses lead up to the Singapore-Cambridge General Certificate of Education "Ordinary" Level examination, also referred to as O-level, in four years. Those following the normal course can opt for the academic or technical track. Both prepare students for the Singapore-Cambridge General Certificate of Education "Normal" (GCE "N") Level examination after satisfactory completion of four years of study, and then the O-level examination in the fifth year. Based on the course chosen, students finish secondary education in either four or five years.

After graduating from secondary school and successful passage of the O-level exams, students have the option of attending junior colleges, technical institutes, or polytechnic institutes. If students successfully pass the A-level examinations, straight university admission may be sought. In 2005 26.3 percent of the college-bound population passed the A-level exams and 86.9 percent passed the O-level.

Postsecondary

The following percentages reflect the acceptances to various institutions of higher education in recent years: 22.1 percent of students are admitted to institutes of technical education, 39.8 percent to polytechnics, 29.8 percent to preuniversity or junior colleges, and 23.1 percent to university degree programs. At the postsecondary level, Singapore maintains three universities—National University of Singapore, Nanyang Technical University, and Singapore Management University.

National University of Singapore provides a comprehensive curriculum with 14 academic faculties and a wide variety of degree programs. According to the 2011 university rankings in *The Times Higher Education Supplement*, National University is ranked thirty-fourth in the world and fourth in Asia. Its website touts its "holistic and integrated education" that "serves as a nurturing waterway where students may acquire knowledge and skills for life in an increasingly competitive global environment" (2011). The student body consists of over 24,000 undergraduate and 7,000 graduate students.

Nanyang Technical University is a research-intensive university with globally acknowledged strengths in science and engineering. Offering twelve schools within a four-college structure, Nanyang is affiliated with the National Institute of Education and Sinnathamby Rajaratnam School of International Studies. The student body comprises 20,000 undergraduate and 8,700 graduate students. The university is ranked among the top 25 technology universities in the world.

Singapore Management University is the newest addition to Singapore's higher education system. It is publicly funded and privately managed. Its administrative and educational structure is modeled after American higher education institutions. The university enrolls 5,400 students with focused stud-ies in business, accountancy, information systems, economics, social sciences, and law.

Curriculum, Instruction, and Assessment

Singapore follows a national protocol for curriculum, instruction, and assessment. The kindergarten curriculum spotlights language development, basic number concepts, and social skills. The primary school curriculum focuses on subject disciplines such as languages, humanities, mathematics, and sciences. The secondary school curriculum differs according to academic or technical trajectories. The academic curriculum provides six to eight subjects including languages, humanities, mathematics, and sciences. The technical curriculum provides five to seven subjects including languages, mathematics, and computer sciences. Although the curriculum at the preuniversity level continues to focus on arts, humanities, languages, mathematics, and sciences, the range of topics expands and targets a broader skill set.

Students advance through the levels based on standard performance indicators, assessment from principals and teachers, and national examinations. Regular testing begins at age seven, and national examinations occur at the end of primary, secondary, and preuniversity levels. The bulk of assessment is based on examinations. Other assessment methods include homework, portfolios, project work, and presentations. The Ministry of Education establishes an approved textbook list, instructional materials, and subject syllabus for primary and secondary schools.

Although registered with the Ministry of Education, international schools follow curriculum and teaching methods based on customs of the home country. For example, American schools follow the American educational system. These schools may also choose to teach in their mother tongue.

Special Education

Special education in Singapore formally began in 1974 with volunteers teaching children with leprosy. Since that time, many advances have been made for the physically and mentally challenged to assimilate into society. Singapore continues to work toward the goal of integration into a mainstream school system.

Special education for children with disabilities is provided at special education schools (SPEDs). There are 21 SPEDs run by voluntary welfare organizations receiving funding from the Ministry of Education and the National Council of Social Service. There are also private schools that cater to special education students. All schools maintain a goal of helping students with either physical or mental disabilities achieve their full potential.

Teacher Education

The National Institute of Education (NIE) is the sole teacher training institute in Singapore and a part of Nanyang Technological University. In order to be a teacher in Singapore, candidates must complete teacher certification at the NIE. There are over 26,000 teachers in Singapore from the primary to junior college level. Teacher preparation has undergone significant restructuring since 1999 to incorporate more practical experience. In 2006 NIE enrollment was 5,140 with a ratio of 69 percent female and 31 percent male students. Preschool and kindergarten teacher training is administered separately by the Preschool Qualification Accreditation Committee.

Technology and Education

Under the direction of the Ministry of Education, the Educational Technologies Division is "the champion and catalyst in harnessing educational technologies to enhance educational processes in schools." The Educational Technologies Division offers a variety of services, including consulting, professional development, and technology planning. Special pilot projects, such as FutureSchools@Singapore, are also under way to improve the use of information and communication technologies in classrooms and research for future planning.

Gender and Education

Singapore has attained gender parity for education based on literacy percentages and enrollment ratios for males and females. However, male citizens are liable for compulsory military service. All males at the age of 18 receive formal military training for a two-year period. Most men in Singapore complete national service between high school and postsecondary education, delaying their entrance into university. Women who choose to pursue higher education may receive a two-year head start and enter the workforce early compared to their male counterparts.

Informal Education

Informal education in Singapore takes a variety of forms. Starting at a young age in many different play groups offered for children, it continues through the university level with learning that extends beyond the traditional classroom walls. Residential colleges are an example of the National University of Singapore's effort to offer a broader learning environment. Students housed in these facilities regularly participate in social and recreational activities, which foster student development and community commitment.

Additional types of informal education include the Singapore Scout Association, Singapore Sports Council, and community development and volunteer programs. For instance, the Singapore Scout Association supplies leadership and citizenship development to youth. Programs are open to males and females from age eight to 26, and units are often associated with local schools.

System Economics

Singapore continues to be heralded as an "Asian Tiger" for sustained economic prosperity. A financial powerhouse, Singapore's per capita gross domestic product (GDP) ranks second-highest in Asia. The largest sectors of the GDP are service and industry, and primary services are finance and export trade. Key industries include electronics, chemicals, and rubber processing.

The government of Singapore allocates nearly 3 percent of GDP for education. The Ministry of Education for Singapore invested S$5.23 billion (US$3.24 billion) for recurrent educational expenditures and S$869 million (US$537 million) for educational development, based on figures from the 2005–2006 academic year. Recurrent expenditure on education per student includes S$3,940 (US$2,436) at the primary level, S$5,835 (US$3,607) at the secondary level, S$10,364 (US$6,407) at the preuniversity level, and S$17,681 (US$10,930) at the university level.

Singapore Education at a Glance

General Information

Capital	Singapore
Population	4.741 million
Languages	English, Malay, Mandarin, Tamil
Literacy rate	92.5%
GDP per capita	US$62,100
Number of phones (landline) per 100 people	39.06
Number of phones (mobile) per 100 people	140
Number of Internet users per 100 people	68.23
Number of Internet hosts	992,786

Formal Educational Information

Compulsory school age population enrolled (2005)	290,261
Compulsory school age population	11.8%
Number of years of compulsory education	6 (ages 6–12)
Student/teacher ratio (2005)	
Primary school	23.5
Secondary school	18.5
Average class size (2005)	
Primary school	36.1
Secondary school	36.5
Primary school completion rate	97.8%
Primary school gross enrollment ratio	no data
Secondary school gross enrollment ratio	no data

Note: Unless otherwise indicated, all data are based on sources from 2011.

Dilemmas and Challenges

Singapore strives for an education system that is internationally renowned. One of the challenges faced is maintaining cultural harmony in a nation as diverse as Singapore. The Ministry of Education's webpage on racial harmony is a step toward a goal of sharing information about all cultures in Singapore. Additionally, Singapore is looking toward new partnerships with universities around the world as well as expanding its own universities.

Future Prospects

Singapore is one of the most stable and advanced nations in Asia. Its dedication to educational excellence is evident by the high percentile spent on the education sector. In 2004 education took the largest share of expenditure in the social development sector, a total of 21 percent of the 44 percent allotted to this sector. This indicates the government's dedication to advancing the education system and upholding a position of excellence and leadership in an era of globalization. Future goals include the creation of

additional institutes and colleges with an increase in the international student population. Singapore also strives for continued services for its uniquely diverse citizenry.

Amy Lewis and Miloni Gandhi

REFERENCES

Brown Ruzzi, Betsy. *Strong Performers and Successful Reforms in Education: Lessons from PISA for the United States.* Washington, DC: National Center on Education and the Economy, 2011. www.oecd.org.

Central Intelligence Agency. *The CIA World Factbook.* New York: Skyhorse, 2011. https://www.cia.gov/library/publications/the-world-factbook/index.html.

Lepoer, Barbara Leitch, ed. *A Country Study: Singapore.* Washington, DC: Library of Congress, Federal Research Division, 1989. http://lcweb2.loc.gov/frd/cs.

Ministry of Education, Singapore. www.moe.gov.sg.

Nanyang Technical University, Singapore. www.ntu.edu.sg.

Nation Master. 2011. www.nationmaster.com.

National University of Singapore. www.nus.edu.sg.

Singapore Scout Association. www.scout.org.sg.

The Times Higher Education Supplement, 2011–2012. www.timeshighereducation.co.uk.

World Bank Education Statistics. 2011. www.worldbank.org.

THAILAND

Thailand is the only Southeast Asian country never to have been colonized. Thai people are thought to be descendants of Tai, Mon, Khmer, Chinese, and Indian peoples. The official language of Thailand is Thai, with English also a language spoken among the elite. The Thai language emerged from the Tai group of languages, and Central Thai is the language students currently learn in schools. In 1909 the present borders of Thailand were established by the Anglo-Siamese Treaty between Siam (Thailand), France, and Britain. Formerly called Siam, the country was renamed Thailand in 1939.

Numerous coups d'états have occurred throughout Thailand's history. The result of a significant coup d'état in 1972 led to a temporary civilian government, followed by a fluctuation between coalition governments and military governments. Thailand's gross domestic product (GDP) has been negatively affected by the unstable political situation and global financial crisis of the first decade of the twenty-first century, which led to decreased demand in exports and tourism. The differences in poverty levels between Bangkok and rural provinces in the northeast of Thailand are an issue of concern for the government. The differing income levels among provinces leads to schooling differences between wealthy major cities and poor provinces.

Educational System

The Ministry of Education (MOE) oversees Thailand's education system with its five offices: Office of the Permanent Secretary, Office of the Educational Council, Office of the Higher Education Commission, Office of the Basic Education Commission, and Office of the Vocational Commission. The current Thai education system is based on the 1999 National Education Act, with amendments in 2002. Formal education includes basic and higher education. Compulsory education is nine years, and the MOE states that children can attend 12 years of basic schooling for free, beginning in primary school. However, parents are expected to pay and provide for their children's uniforms, books, and transportation.

Precompulsory Education

Precompulsory education, which consists of two to three years of schooling before grade 1, is optional and for children ages three through seven. Precompulsory education varies among two-year public kindergarten programs, three-year private kindergarten programs, and one-year public preprimary programs. One-year public preprimary schools are free and part of compulsory elementary schools. Preprimary schools are meant to prepare children for grade 1 if their families cannot afford the cost of kindergarten or do not have physical access to kindergarten schools. In 2008, the precompulsory school gross enrollment rate was 89 percent. Precompulsory education is offered in both the formal and nonformal school system. The nonformal system targets disadvantaged students who do not have access to the formal school system. In 2007 about 68 percent of precompulsory education students were in the formal school system and 32 percent were in the nonformal school system.

Compulsory and Postcompulsory Education

Basic compulsory education includes six years of primary (prathom) and three years of lower secondary schooling (matthayom). Postcompulsory education includes three years of upper secondary school and two levels of degrees in higher education: Lower-than-degree level and Degree level. The Lower-than-degree, commonly known as a diploma, requires two years of study and can be obtained from vocational colleges and colleges of physical education and dramatic and fine arts. The Degree level is offered at universities and requires four to six years of study for students with a secondary school diploma. Students who receive a college diploma from a vocational college can complete the Degree level in two years, even without a secondary school diploma. In 2007 there were 1.8 million students enrolled in undergraduate degree programs, 18,215 enrolled in graduate diploma programs (additional schooling beyond a bachelor's degree), 182,357 enrolled in master's degree programs, 764 enrolled in higher graduate diploma programs (in addition to a master's degree, the higher graduate diploma is required for a professional qualification in an area such as medicine), and 16,279 enrolled in doctorate degree programs.

Curriculum, Instruction, and Assessment

Curriculum goals, plans, and methods for learning in basic education are developed by the MOE Department of Curriculum and Instruction. Teachers are expected to develop lesson plans and behavior objectives that relate to students' local context and to determine classroom activities. The MOE states that it will provide schools with expensive learning materials, such as educational technologies and reference books. Teachers further support their classrooms by purchasing additional learning materials.

Each primary school academic year includes 40 weeks of schooling. Each school day is six to seven hours and divided into periods of 40 to 50 minutes each. In the primary school curriculum, five areas of study cover subject areas such as language, mathematics, problem solving, behavior development, and career preparation. The goals of the curriculum include teaching students literacy and math skills; instilling in them a pride in being Thai; familiarizing them with social changes and their natural environment; teaching them good work behaviors; and providing them with knowledge that can be applied to issues relating to themselves, their communities, and their families.

Secondary school is six years, which is equivalent to twelve semesters. Similar to primary school, students attend school five days a week for 40 weeks in each academic year. There are seven 50-minute periods in each school day. Students must complete 90 units as part of the secondary school curriculum, which includes subjects such as Thai, science, mathematics, art, health and physical education, and social studies. Students take elective units that can also include foreign languages, vocational education, youth groups, and independent activities. In addition to completing the unit requirements, students must have 80 percent school attendance.

The MOE determines the guidelines for how students will be assessed, and school administrators and classroom teachers implement evaluation and exams. Teachers are expected to learn from the students' test scores and make improvements in their teaching in order to benefit both the teachers and students. The assessments also determine student promotions to the next grade level. After completing six years of secondary school, students are required to take national entrance examinations before applying to a university. To attend a university, test scores and grade point average from the fourth year onward in secondary school are considered in the Central University Admission System (CUAS).

Special Education

Special provisions that would allow a form of basic education for disabled children were established in 1960. Special education serves students who have hearing, visual, physical, or health impairments; who are mentally handicapped, learning disabled, or autistic; or who have emotional, behavioral, speech, or language disorders. Gifted and talented children may also be categorized as part of special education. In the MOE, the Office of the Basic Education Commission is responsible for providing education to children with disabilities. Children with disabilities are either integrated into inclusive schools or placed in special schools.

The purpose of inclusive schools, which were established in 2004, is to have integrated education. Teacher training and materials are derived from the special schools. In 2007 there were 2,700 inclusive schools with 50,000 students with disabilities enrolled. Students in the inclusive schools are each given 2,000 baht (US$55) yearly for special services needs. There are 43 special schools in Thailand, which include special schools for children with mental impairments, hearing impairments, visual impairments, and physical impairments. Admittance into those four types of special schools is not limited to children with only those disabilities. Despite these provisions, a large percentage of children with disabilities are not enrolled in the regular education system.

Teacher Education

Typically, a candidate must pass an entrance examination before entering a teacher training program. Teachers are required to have a postsecondary graduate degree. Four to five years of preservice education and training are required to earn a bachelor's of education degree. Teachers can earn a teaching degree from either a university or a teacher education college. Sixty-four public and five private institutes of higher education have preservice training for teachers of primary and secondary schooling. The teacher education curriculum for preservice training is developed by the Faculty Committee for Curriculum Planning and must be approved by the University Council and the Office of Higher Education Commission.

Students who receive a four-year bachelor's degree in education must then pass an examination to earn a teaching license. Teachers who did not earn their postsecondary degrees in Thailand must take an examination and apply for a teacher's license. Those teachers who hold a five-year bachelor's degree or a bachelor's degree in education, have completed in-service training, and can provide a letter that states their qualifications are exempt from the examination.

A teacher shortage exists in primary and secondary schools, and more teachers are needed in the areas of science, mathematics, foreign language, and special needs. The MOE has proposed more preservice and in-service training programs to increase the number of teachers in those fields. In the 1992 National Education Act, revised in 2002, the MOE states that it aims to improve the teacher licensing process, teacher salaries and benefits, and teacher training.

Technology and Education

According to the 1992 National Education Act, Thailand aims to provide educational technologies to schools and also train teachers and students in gaining skills to use new technologies. Thailand has implemented an information program called School-Net (established in 1995) that connects all schools to the Internet and allows students and teachers to access resources online. In 2002, 4,300 schools were connected to the Internet with SchoolNet. In addition to connecting schools to online resources, teachers can create programs and activities to share with other teachers and students in a digital library.

In addition to SchoolNet, a MOE project called the Interactive e-learning Project, established in 2008, intends to bridge educational inequalities with technology. The four-year project, which has engaged 3,000 schools in the country, utilizes the MOE Channel, a satellite broadcast that allows teachers in grades 4 through 10 in urban areas, such as Bangkok, to connect to remote rural areas of Thailand for learning in regards to English, math, and science. In addition to a lack of math and science teachers, students in rural schools have fewer educational resources than urban school students. The Interactive e-learning Project aims to address those areas of concern.

In 2009 the Ministry of Education and Microsoft Thailand extended their current partnership in the Partners in Learning Program to 2013. This program, which was created in 2004 to address the digital learning gap, has provided information and communication technology (ICT) training to more than 4 million students and 80,000 teachers.

Gender and Education

The Thailand constitution of 1997 states that the right to education should be equally available to all, regardless of sex; however, gender inequities in education still exist. For example, in 2000, the Gender Parity Index (GPI) for literacy rate was .95, indicating that males have higher literacy rates than females. Males also constitute a larger percentage of students at the primary school level. In 2005, 48 percent of primary school students were females and

52 percent were males, and the GPI for primary gross enrollment ratio was .95.

While primary enrollment rates are somewhat in favor of males, females make up the larger percentage of students at both the secondary and tertiary levels. In the 2005–2006 school year, school life expectancy in primary to tertiary formal schooling was 14 years for females and 13 years for males. In 2004, among students enrolled in secondary school, approximately 51 percent were females and 49 percent were males, and the GPI for secondary gross enrollment ratio was 1.05. In 2008, 77 percent of females and 71 percent of males were in secondary school. At the tertiary level in 2005, 52 percent of students were females and 48 percent were males, and the GPI for tertiary gross enrollment ratio was 1.11. Males also have a higher school dropout rate compared to females. There is also a difference in the number of female and male teachers in formal schooling at the K–12 levels. In 2006, 78 percent of preprimary teachers, 59.7 percent of primary teachers, and 55.1 percent of secondary teachers were females. However, at the tertiary level in 2001, 47 percent of teachers were female.

Nonformal Education

Nonformal education is targeted toward people who have not had the opportunity for formal education. The Department of Non-Formal Education (NFE) was established on March 24, 1979, to ensure that disadvantaged people receive basic education. The Department of NFE is also expected to provide educational technologies to formal schools. Nonformal education encompasses preschool, literacy education, vocational schooling, and programs for those who did not participate in formal schooling. Although nonformal education was initially targeted toward out-of-school people in rural areas (such as the hill tribe people), nonformal education also serves people such as the disabled, elderly, laborers, and women and children.

Basic education programs are provided for those who do not participate in or complete formal schooling. The Department of NFE provides 17 occupational certificate programs in vocational schooling. The Department of NFE also provides informal education resources for lifelong learning, such as community learning centers, village reading centers, and public libraries.

System Economics

Thailand's largest agricultural export is rice, and the country also produces maize, tapioca, rubber, and sugarcane. Thailand's manufacturing sector produces products such as garments and textiles, canned foods, jewelry and gems, and integrated circuits. In 2008, 20.5 percent of government spending, which was 3.8 percent of Thailand's GDP, was allocated to education. Total public expenditure on education has decreased over the years; for example, in 1999, 5.1 percent of Thailand's GDP was spent on education, and in 2005, 25 percent of total government spending and 4.2 percent of Thailand's GDP was spent on education. In 2008, 54 percent of Thailand's education budget was allocated for preprimary and primary education, 15 percent for secondary education, 17 percent for higher education, and 14 percent for other areas of education.

Dilemmas and Challenges

Equal access to education remains an issue in Thailand. For example, there are still disparities in preprimary school enrollment. More wealthy children compared to poor children and more children in urban areas compared to children in rural areas are enrolled in preprimary education. Opportunities for high-quality education are more difficult for the poor people of Thailand. In a 2001 World Bank survey, the average Thai household spent 16 percent of its expenditure on primary education; however, the poorest Thai households spent 47 percent of their expenditure on primary education. In addition, some groups of students, such as language minorities and those with HIV/AIDS, are struggling in basic education or do not even attend school. It is estimated that more non-Thai students are out of school than in school, likely because of language problems. Moreover, approximately half of the language-minority students in primary school do not learn in their mother tongue. Household language statistics show that in 2005–2006, 98.3 percent of households spoke Thai and 6.2 percent spoke other languages. In the 2005–2006 school year, among non-Thai-speaking households, the net attendance rate for students seven to 12 years old was 94.8 percent compared to students from Thai-speaking households, whose net attendance

rate was 98.2 percent. Furthermore, the disparity between non-Thai and Thai households increases for students aged 13 to 18; that is, net attendance rates were 81.2 percent for students from Thai-speaking households and 65.8 percent for students from non-Thai-speaking households.

The MOE also plans to find ways to include stateless children (non-Thai citizens) in the Thai educational system by including foreign education centers that serve these children in order to provide them the same rights as other Thais under the jurisdiction of the MOE. The MOE estimates that approximately half of the stateless children in Thailand are not in school. Additional funding for children in rural schools (*suksa songkhro* schools) as well as for teachers who work overtime to care for children after school is being considered. *Suksa songkhro* schools in Thailand are targeted toward children in rural areas, orphans, and children with no opportunity to attend normal schools.

Thailand Education at a Glance

General Information

Capital	Bangkok
Population	67 million
Language	Thai
Literacy rate	93%
GDP per capita	US$3,760
Number of phones (landline) per 100 people	10.48
Number of phones (mobile) per 100 people	92
Number of Internet users per 100 people	23.9
Number of Internet hosts	1.335 million

Formal Education Information

Compulsory school age population enrolled (2006)	10,631,000
Compulsory school age population (2006)	94%
Number of years of compulsory education	9 (ages 6–15)
Student/teacher ratio	
Primary school (Standard 1–6) (2008)	16
Secondary school (Lower) (2006)	22
Average class size in primary school (2006)	25
Average school days per year (primary school)	200
Primary school gross enrollment ratio (2008)	93%
Primary school entrants reaching grade 5	no data
School life expectancy in years (primary to tertiary) (2006)	14
Secondary school gross enrollment ratio (2008)	74%

Note: Unless otherwise indicated, all data are based on sources from 2011.

Future Prospects

Thailand has many education issues to address, and the nation is taking positive steps to improve the quality of education and provide equal access to education for all Thai people. The Royal Thai Government has set a goal to attain universal upper secondary education by 2015. The enrollment rate in secondary and higher education has increased over the past years, suggesting greater educational access in Thailand. Students living in poor areas of Thailand still have lower completion rates compared to students living in wealthier areas. However, the gap in enrollment ratios between rural and urban children has lessened. Although lack of financial support remains a barrier to school access and retention, Thailand has implemented programs to assist students with tuition, lunch, and transportation costs. The 15 Years Free Education with Quality Program, which was implemented in March 2009, aims to financially support poor and disadvantaged children throughout the country. This program will provide "tuition fee, textbooks, learning materials, school uniforms and activities for students' quality improvement" for free. The quality improvement activities include "academic activities," "activities to boost ethics and morals," "study trips," and "services on information technology or computer." The program supports nonformal and formal schooling from pre-elementary to high school and also vocational education. As of 2009, the Thai government has distributed 18 billion baht (US$526.8 million) among more than 40,000 local schools throughout the country. Given Thailand's goal of providing more affordable schooling, a future of increasing educational equality appears within reach.

Connie Nguyen Tran and Hsiu-Zu Ho

REFERENCES

Central Intelligence Agency. *The CIA World Factbook*. New York: Skyhorse, 2011. https://www.cia.gov/library/publications/the-world-factbook/index.html.

"Education and Schooling in Thailand." http://bangkok.angloinfo.com/countries/thailand/schooling.asp.

Ministry of Education. "The Development of Education: National Report of Thailand." 2011. www.bic.moe.go.th/en/index.php.

Ministry of Education of the Kingdom of Thailand, and Ministry of Education of the People's Republic of China. "Agreement on Mutual Recognition of Academic Degrees in Higher Education between the Ministry of Education of the Kingdom of Thailand and the Ministry of Education of the People's Republic of China." 2009. www.dpu.ac.th/dpuic/download/MutualChina.pdf.

The Nation (Bangkok, Thailand). "Thai Education for Stateless Children." May 2009. www.nationmultimedia.com.

Nation Master. 2011. www.nationmaster.com.

UNESCO. "Status of Teacher Education in Asia Pacific Region." Prepared by International Reading Association. 2008. www.unescobkk.org/education/apeid/programme-areas/teacher-education-and-training/status-of-teacher-education-in-the-asia-pacific-region.

UNICEF, Division of Policy and Practice, Statistics and Monitoring Section. www.childinfo.org.

United Nations Human Rights. Committee on the Rights of the Child Considers Report of Thailand. www.ohchr.org/EN/NewsEvents/Pages/DisplayNews.aspx?NewsID=11777&LangID=E.

World Bank. "Thailand Social Monitor on Youth: Development and the Next Generation." January 1, 2008. www.worldbank.org.

World Bank Education Statistics. 2012. www.worldbank.org.

TIMOR-LESTE

The Democratic Republic of Timor-Leste is one of the newest nations of the twenty-first century, having achieved independence in 2002. Located on the eastern edge of the Indonesian archipelago, the country consists of the eastern part of the island of Timor, the Oecussi enclave in the northwestern part of the island within Indonesian territory, and the islands of Pulau Atauro and Pulau Jaco.

The people of this nation are referred to as Timorese and include Austronesians (Malayo-Polynesians), Papuans, indigenous tribes, and a small group of ethnic Chinese. Tetum and Portuguese are the official languages, but Indonesian and English are also working languages, as stated in the constitution. In addition, as many as 33 indigenous languages are commonly spoken among the Timorese people. These languages include Galole, Mambae, and Kemak. Timor-Leste, along with the Philippines, is one of only two Asian countries that are predominantly Roman Catholic, with 98 percent of the population identifying with Catholicism. Other religions include Muslim (1 percent) and Protestant (1 percent).

Timor-Leste has had a tumultuous history in the

modern era. Formerly known as East Timor, the country was invaded in 1975 by Indonesia and was incorporated as the twenty-seventh province of the Republic of Indonesia. Timorese groups fought for independence against the Indonesian government in the decades that followed, leading to bloody massacres and human rights violations. After the Dili Massacre in 1991, widespread support for East Timor's independence in the international community led Indonesia to hold a referendum on East Timor's future. The referendum resulted in a majority in favor of independence. However, in retaliation, the Indonesian government carried out a campaign of terrorism and violence, destroying most of the country's infrastructure. Australian-led peacekeeping troops were sent to end the violence. Indonesia finally agreed to withdraw its troops after the president of the United States, Bill Clinton, threatened to cease International Monetary Fund (IMF) loans. In October 1999, administration of East Timor was given to the United Nations through the United Nations Transitional Administration in East Timor (UNTAET). After elections were held, Timor-Leste gained independence in 2002. As an independent country, Timor-Leste continued to struggle with internal political conflicts that resulted in violence, destruction, and displacement of its people. One of the greatest challenges for this emerging nation is to rebuild its infrastructure and stabilize the country.

Educational System

The Ministry of Education and Culture (MOEC) is responsible for developing, implementing, coordinating, and evaluating policies and programs related to education and culture. For example, the MOEC manages curriculum and textbook development and selects the main language of instruction and other languages taught or used in schools. In addition, the ministry is also involved in international development and planning, administration of examinations for the granting of diplomas and degrees, coordination and promotion of research, and the development of instructional technology.

As stated in the constitution of Timor-Leste, education and culture are rights afforded to all citizens. The government is responsible for establishing a public system of universal, free, compulsory basic education. The right to an education means equal opportunities for education and vocational training, as well as access to the "highest levels of education, scientific research and artistic creativity" (Section 59). Citizens also have the right to cultural appreciation, the right to foster creativity, and the duty to protect and preserve cultural heritage. The national education system consists of nine years of compulsory basic education and three years of secondary education.

Precompulsory Education

Precompulsory education begins at the age of four. Children with access to early childhood education have the option of enrolling in a two-year program. These programs are extremely rare and overall participation rate is low. There is no standard curriculum or instruction. Most of these programs receive support from community-based sources, and quality control varies across schools and districts. According to the Timor-Leste Strategic Development Plan 2011–2030 report, about 11 percent of children between the ages of three and six attend early childhood education programs.

Compulsory Education

Compulsory education, also referred to as basic education, consists of six years of primary school and three years of presecondary school. Primary school education (grades 1 through 6) begins at the age of six and presecondary education (grades 7 through 9) begins at the age of 12. According to the MOEC, there have been significant improvements in reconstructing compulsory basic education since 1999, as evidenced by increases in student enrollment and the number of teachers at both the primary and presecondary levels. In 2010, 90 percent of students within the compulsory school-age population were enrolled in basic education. However, there are challenges to achievement progress. School dropout is prevalent, with dropout rates at their highest during the first two years of primary school. Overall, 70 percent of students drop out before the completion of presecondary school. Another issue of concern is timely completion of basic education; children average 11 years to advance to the sixth grade.

Postcompulsory Education

Postcompulsory education includes three years of secondary school (i.e., general or technical education) and tertiary or higher education. Participation in secondary school in Timor-Leste ranks among the lowest in the Pacific region, with 2004 gross enrollment ratio estimates at 26 percent. The MOEC reported that the completion rate of secondary education programs was only 12 percent in 2010. Access and enrollment in higher education are limited due to lack of infrastructure and resources. There is currently only one national university in Timor-Leste, 11 higher education institutions, and 10 private institutions that offer services to students. However, limited funding and resources are challenges that have resulted in an inconsistent system of assessment and accreditation, administrative operations, and infrastructure development. Participation estimates for tertiary education are as low as 3 percent (2004). A small number of Timor-Leste students study abroad on private donor scholarships in Portugal, Indonesia, Brazil, New Zealand, and Australia.

Vocational education and training are also an option for students who want to build specific skills for the labor market. However, vocational programs are extremely rare and in the process of being developed. According to the MOEC, there are about 10 technical vocational schools, most of them funded by nongovernmental organizations (NGOs) and Catholic ministries.

Curriculum, Assessment, and Instruction

In 2003 the Ministry of Education and Culture, with UNICEF support, initiated the development of a national curriculum for the primary school level (grades 1 through 6). In addition, officials have begun the process of developing the presecondary-level curriculum (grades 7 through 9). The National Directorate of Curriculum, Materials, and Evaluations is the lead office responsible for the curriculum development process, which includes creating a program of study statement, implementation plan, syllabus, and teaching and learning materials. There is little information on the formal assessment of student progress and achievement. In general, student assessments are based on meeting learning objectives, and promotion is based on an examination process.

Primary school curriculum content includes material from local, regional, and global perspectives. Academic courses include natural sciences, social sciences, and Timor-Leste's arts and cultures. Teaching and learning methods are student-centered, encouraging students to be active participants in the classroom. The general teaching philosophy is based on meeting learning objectives outlined in the syllabus; teachers' guides are designed to provide teachers with pedagogical tools to help students accomplish these learning objectives.

At the presecondary level, the National Directorate of Curriculum, Materials, and Evaluations is working to develop a secondary-level curriculum program that will be continuous and cohesive with the content, pedagogy, and philosophy of the primary-level curriculum. Academic subjects will focus on languages (Portuguese, Tetum, and English), mathematics, physical and natural sciences, social sciences, physical education, health and hygiene, religious and moral education, arts and culture, civics education, and life and work skills. In 2005 the MOEC introduced civics education into upper secondary schools with topics on democracy, human rights, and the legal system. Subjects learned in lower secondary classes are expected to continue in the upper secondary curriculum.

Timor-Leste's National University provides training in agriculture, political science, economics, engineering, and teacher education. University students also take general education courses in civics, ethics, philosophy, and Timorese history. There are plans to expand the curriculum to include other areas of studies, such as health sciences, legal studies, media and communications, and Timor studies. To promote research as part of the curriculum, the university opened the National Research Center and the Institute of Linguistics in 2001. The National Research Center emphasizes faculty research and recruitment of research support, while the mission of the Institute of Linguistics is to promote the development and advancement of the Tetum language. Vocational education is managed by a youth council, with support from NGOs and churches. The youth centers that house vocational training programs provide services that include language and literacy as well as computing. Access is limited and program development is in progress.

Teacher Education

Programs created for the professional development and training of teachers include a three-year program offered by the Institute for Continuing Education (ICE). Located in Timor-Leste's second-largest city, Baucau, it is an Australian accredited program designed train teachers for primary school jobs. The minimum requirement for acceptance is a secondary school certificate. The National University also offers a two-year training program that is subject-specific in science, mathematics, and English for lower and upper secondary-level teachers. Another source of teacher training offered through the Ministry of Education is the Instituto Formacao Continua Professores (IFCP) professional development classes, focused on the Portuguese language, pedagogy, and education psychology. All teachers are required to attend these classes during nonschool hours. Teachers who have achieved the required proficiency in the Portuguese language have the option of enrolling in bachelor's of education courses through the IFCP. Because access and resources are limited, teachers who are not able to receive formal training must rely on workshops provided by NGOs and the United Nations Development Programme. As of 2010, over 600 teachers have completed bachelor's degree programs and nearly 40 have enrolled in postbaccalaureate programs.

Technology and Education

Information and communication technology (ICT) is still in the infancy stage of development in Timor-Leste. ICT is rarely mentioned in discussions and publications in the education field; however, the government has prioritized technical and vocational training for postcompulsory education. The country is still focusing on rebuilding structures, recruiting teachers, and providing basic materials such as pencils and books. Thus, ICT in the K–12 schools is nearly nonexistent and is not a high priority. There are a few technical colleges, but space and enrollment are extremely limited. Establishment or expansion of access and use of ICT is mostly limited to universities and colleges.

Gender and Education

During the transitional government established by the United Nations, one of the objectives was to eliminate all forms of discrimination against women, which led to a systematic approach to gender integration. A Gender Affairs Unit was created to analyze gender inequality and devise a strategic policy of gender integration. The unit explored education and literacy programs for women and girls as well as equal rights to land, employment, and investment opportunities. Even with the women's empowerment movement, gender inequality is still apparent in the education system. A survey of the labor force conducted in 2010 showed that 45 percent of women reported no educational experience compared to 34 percent of men. In the teaching profession, only 29 percent of teachers are women. Girls' academic test scores are generally lower than boys' scores. This may be due to the fact that girls' household responsibilities leave less time for studying. Attitudes toward girls' education vary between rural and urban areas. As in most countries, urban families are generally more accepting of education for girls. The barriers to girls' access to education include cultural and economic factors. Cultural attitudes and behaviors based on a patriarchal family system tend to relegate girls to domestic responsibilities.

Informal and Nonformal Education

During the UN transitional period, UNICEF, churches, and other NGOs set up informal education centers to educate displaced refugee children and families. With donations from Australia, Ireland, Japan, Netherlands, and the Unites States, UNICEF established a small operation to provide support and funds for teacher training and incentives, textbooks, uniforms, food, shelter, and other technical assistance. Other NGOs and church organizations have organized tent schools and playgroups. One of the objectives of the National Development Plan was to promote and develop nonformal education and adult literacy in a five-year plan from 2002 to 2007. Reports indicate that literacy rates in 2007 increased to 85 percent from 50 percent in 2001. The government's focus on improving literacy is one of the top priorities in rebuilding the education system. Therefore, as of 2007, the MOEC has implemented literacy programs and technical training centers in all 13 districts of Timor-Leste.

In addition, the National Equivalence Program was established to provide courses equivalent to basic education training.

System Economics

Prior to independence, there was a low level of public expenditures on education. Today, Timor-Leste ranks 1 of 186 countries in educational expenditure. Approximately 17 percent of the gross domestic product is spent on education. This large infusion of funds for education does not mean, however, that the country's education system is devoid of problems. In its 2011–2030 Strategic Development Plan report, the government pledged to improve the quality of life for its citizens through the Human Capital Development Fund, whose 2011 budget was US$25 million. Included in this budget is the plan for advancing education for all through investments in infrastructure, teacher training, and student resources.

Dilemmas and Challenges

Timor-Leste still faces many challenges ahead due to the lack of a stable infrastructure, funding, and resources. After the near complete destruction in 1999, the government has heavily invested in the reconstruction and rehabilitation of the education infrastructure. As of 2010, 70 percent of existing schools and classrooms are still in need of major repairs; additional schools are yet to be built. Timor-Leste faces the daunting task of building thousands of adequate classrooms and facilities before it can make substantial progress in educational advancement. Education reconstruction, still in the development phase, includes implementation of a national curriculum, distribution of textbooks and learning materials, and establishing languages of learning. Teachers' language fluency and teaching materials and textbooks are a mixture of Portuguese, Indonesian, and Tetum. Many schools are attempting to transition out of an Indonesian-based faculty and curriculum to a Portuguese-based curriculum, but neither teachers nor students have the fluency for a successful transition. Low student enrollment and shortages of qualified teachers pose additional problems.

Timor-Leste Education at a Glance

General Information

Capital	Dili
Population	1.18 million
Languages	Tetum, Portuguese, Indonesian, English
Literacy rate	58.6%
GDP per capita	US$551
Number of phones (landline) per 100 people	0.21
Number of phones (mobile) per 100 people	10.27
Number of Internet users per 100 people	<1
Number of Internet hosts (2010)	206

Formal Education Information

Compulsory school age population enrolled (2010)	257,501
Compulsory school age population	94%
Number of years of compulsory education	9 (ages 6–15)
Student/teacher ratio	
Primary school (Standard 1–6) (2008)	41
Secondary school (Lower) (2008)	25
Average class size in primary school	no data
Average school days per year (2004)	180
Average number of hours per school day (primary school)	no data
Primary school gross enrollment ratio	83.2%
Primary school entrants reaching grade 5 (2008)	79.77%
Secondary school gross enrollment ratio	11.74%

Note: Unless otherwise indicated, all data are based on sources from 2011.

Future Prospects

The government of Timor-Leste is dedicated to rebuilding the education sector through key projects and programs relating to access to education, quality of education, and educational administration and organization. The Ministry of Education and Culture is working to increase accessibility, particularly for children in the poorest rural areas, through programs that address school dropout prevention, school location planning, building more schools, multigrade teaching, school-based health and nutrition, and community-based preschool service. Improving the quality of education depends on reconstructing and developing curriculum, providing textbooks and materials, establishing language of instruction, training teachers and administrators, implementing national examinations, and continuing partnerships with international organizations such as UNICEF.

Julie Thuy Nguyen

REFERENCES

Central Intelligence Agency. *The CIA World Factbook*. New York: Skyhorse, 2011. https://www.cia.gov/library/publications/the-world-factbook/index.html.

East Timor and Indonesia Action Network. "Constitution of the Democratic Republic of East Timor." 2002. www.etan.org.

Nation Master. 2011. www.nationmaster.com.

"Timor Leste: Strategic Development Plan 2011–2030." 2011. www.tls.searo.who.int.

Timor-Leste Government. "2009: The Millennium Development Goals, Timor-Leste." March 2009. www.tl.undp.org.

UNESCO Bangkok. "Timor Leste." In *Status of Teacher Education in the Asia-Pacific Region*. Prepared by International Reading Association, 2008. www.unescobkk.org.

UNICEF. www.unicef.org.

United Nations Development Fund for Women. "Gender and Nation Building in Timor-Leste." Asian Development Bank, 2005. www.adb.org.

United Nations Development Programme. *Human Development Report 2011*. http://hdr.undp.org/en.

World Bank Education Statistics. 2011. www.worldbank.org.

VIETNAM

Vietnam, sometimes referred to as the "Small Dragon," has a population of some 90 million people, of which 86 percent are ethnically Vietnamese. The remaining 14 percent include ethnic groups such as Chinese, Thai, Khmer, Cham, and people of the central highlands. Vietnamese is the official language; English, French, Chinese, and Khmer are also spoken.

According to scholars, Vietnamese history dates roughly to 2,700 years ago. From 111 BCE to 938 CE, Vietnam was under the direct rule of successive dynasties from China. Vietnam gained complete independence from China in 938 CE and was subsequently ruled by various Vietnamese dynasties until French colonization in 1887. During the seventeenth century, the modern Vietnamese script, Quoc Ngu, was developed by Portuguese Jesuit missionaries. In 1954 Quoc Ngu became the official language and has been the main writing system used in public education. After World War II, the Geneva Accords partitioned the country in half. The partition led to the Vietnam War. With the fall of Saigon, the country was finally reunified in 1975 by the Vietnamese Communist Party. Although united, Vietnam suffered from internal repression and economic problems due to international isolation as a result of the Cold War and US embargo. In 1986 the Communist Party changed its economic policy and, following China's lead, began reforms in its private sector. As a result, Vietnam has become one of the fast-growing economies in Southeast Asia. Its recent membership in the World Trade Organization will continue to improve the economic environment and business sector. As Vietnam transitions into a period of national reformation, the effort to restructure education has become one of the nation's top priorities; the percentage of the national budget allocated to education increased steadily from 10 percent in 1993 to 20 percent in 2012.

Educational System

Before the mid-nineteenth century, the education system in Vietnam during the period of Chinese occupation was formed to resemble the Chinese model of education. The purpose of the education system was to prepare scholar-officials for service at the imperial court. The system was based on Confucian ideology, and only those who passed the highest level of examinations were allowed to serve in the government. After independence from China, the Vietnamese government reformed the education system to include public schools at the district and provincial levels. Education in small communities and villages was less formal, mainly private, and managed by the members of each community or village. The French colonization of Vietnam resulted in a new model for education, which consisted of six years of primary school, four years of first secondary school, and three years of second secondary school. Technical and professional schools were established to train workers for skilled labor.

From 1945 to 1986, there were massive efforts to reform education programs to reflect a national and socialist-centered system. During this period, the government established and implemented a new national curriculum, expanded schools to all liberated provinces, and created a unified education system for the entire country. Rapid socioeconomic changes in the past 25 years have prompted further educational reform.

The Ministry of Education and Training (MOET) is responsible for the overall coordination of funds and administration related to the education system. In general, the ministry handles the operations of higher education institutions, the provinces handle secondary schools, and districts manage primary and preprimary schools. The ministry's main objectives are (1) to maintain full participation of its school age population (it has essentially reached full participation of the school-age population in 2010), (2) to eliminate all fees at the secondary school level, (3) to address the problems of poverty in areas where incomes are below the national average, and (4) to increase the quality of education for all students. The Department of General Education is responsible for staffing, curriculum, textbooks, examinations, and certificates for the primary and lower secondary levels.

Precompulsory Education

There are three types of infant education, or preschool, in Vietnam. The first type of infant education is crèche (nursery school), which consists of approximately three years for children as young as three months. The second type of infant education is kindergarten, for children ages three to six years. A third type of infant education is called "young bud," which combines crèche and kindergarten into one school. About 70 percent of children from birth to five years old attend some type of precompulsory education program.

Compulsory Education

The duration of compulsory education is nine years and consists of two levels of general education. The first level is primary school education (five grades) and begins at age six. At the end of Form 5, students take a national examination in order to receive a primary education certificate that enables them to enter the second level, that is, lower secondary education.

Students begin lower secondary education (Form 6 to 9) at the age of 11. At this level, students focus on strengthening the skills learned in primary school and are introduced to technical and vocational education. The addition of technical and vocational training allows students alternatives that will assist their preparation for pursuing further academic studies in high school, vocational education, or employment. Students are required to pass a national exam in order

to receive a basic secondary education certificate.

Postcompulsory Education

Graduates of lower secondary education have the option of continuing on to specialized upper secondary level (Form 10 to 12). Students are required to pass an exit exam at the end of Form 12 to receive their general education certificates. Students who do not pursue academic tracks can choose technical and vocational education and training, which consist of three options: (1) short-term programs designed to certify students, who do not have general education certificates, in a specific skill; (2) one- to three-year programs for students with general education certificates who want to earn a vocational certificate; and (3) two- to three-year programs combining general education and vocational training to prepare students for entry into higher education.

Higher education consists of several different levels of undergraduate and graduate studies. Three-year college programs are available for students with general education or vocational certificates who want to attain college diplomas in specific career fields. There are four- to six-year undergraduate programs that award bachelor's degrees for particular fields of study. Master's (two years) and doctoral (four years) degrees provide students with a theoretical, practical, and research background in a specified area of study.

Special Education

There are two types of special education in Vietnam—programs for gifted students and programs for students with disabilities. According to the Educational Law, students at the upper secondary level exhibiting exceptional academic performance in particular subjects may enroll in gifted programs to further develop their abilities. In addition, there are special schools specifically for students who excel in arts and athletics.

Students with disabilities may attend special schools or classes designed to assist them in developing functioning skills and to provide general education, vocational training, and necessary skills for mainstreaming into the community. Children who have disabilities, who face a high risk of dropping out, or who have never attended school are often referred to as "educationally disadvantaged."

Many private and nongovernmental organizations have been working to develop special education and inclusive education programs for children with disabilities. The goal is to place students with disabilities in compulsory education classrooms with able-bodied students at the same educational level.

Curriculum, Assessment, and Instruction

Vietnam has a national curriculum that is directly supported by the government. All materials created for instruction, including textbooks and teachers' guides, go through a selection and approval process conducted by the partnership of the National Institute for Educational Science, the Educational Publishing House, the Council for Textbooks, and several divisions within the MOET. In recent years, institutions have taken on a bigger role in curriculum development, textbook selection, and distribution. A set of textbooks is used at each level of education, and textbook fees are paid by teachers and students. Instructional aids for each subject, such as reference books, guides, practice materials, and media materials, are also available.

Infant education is designed to provide children with a nurturing environment in which they can develop the bases for physical, moral, intellectual, and aesthetic skills that will prepare them for primary school. Program structure resembles family education, where teachers take on a parental role, and the program itself provides parent education, including information on family planning and child rearing.

The primary school curriculum focuses on acquiring knowledge of reading, writing, speaking, listening, mathematics, and physical education. In addition, students learn about social responsibility, nationalism, practical service care in the home, and self-care. Students may also select two optional courses in a variety of subjects: language (Vietnamese, ethnic, or foreign), music, literature, art, science, economics, and informatics (information technology).

Secondary school, divided into lower and upper, begins with Form 6. Lower secondary education instruction emphasizes the natural sciences, social sciences, arts and humanities, life skills training, and Vietnamese language and culture. Citizenship and occupational and job skills training are also curricula components at this level. In upper secondary educa-tion, there is a shift to more specialized training, focused on natural sciences, engineering, and social sciences. Upper secondary education also incorporates preparation for higher education and knowledge of socioeconomic processes.

Students following the vocational track are trained to be semiskilled or skilled workers or technicians in industry, services, and agriculture. Professional-level programs train students in economics, education, culture, medicine, and arts, while vocational programs focus on trade skills. Higher education offers advanced training in various fields in the sciences, business, and liberal arts.

Teacher Education

In order to become a teacher in Vietnam, applicants must obtain teaching certificates at either pedagogical colleges or universities. Applicants must pass an entrance exam to gain acceptance into a teacher training program. Teacher training colleges, also known as pedagogical colleges in Vietnam, provide teacher training for primary and lower secondary education. Primary school programs last two years and lower secondary school programs last three years. Each province has pedagogical colleges, which are operated by the provincial Department of Education and Training (DOET) under the supervision of the Ministry of Education and Training. Teacher training for upper secondary education can be obtained in a four-year program at nine pedagogy universities or teacher training universities (TTU).

Teacher training curricula and textbooks are normally designed and written by teams appointed from the TTU staff. The MOET provides overall policy guidance and supervision for teacher training. The ministry also delegates administrative authorities to the provincial DOET. Due to the complex nature of the teacher training administrative system, a significant degree of coordination is necessary among the central and provincial agencies in addressing issues of effective planning, management, monitoring, and evaluation.

Technology and Education

Vietnam's MOET, with the goal of advancing the field of information technology, has been continuously working with the World Bank's Millennium

Science Initiative and the Vietnamese Education Foundation to reinvent and improve education and research. As of August 2006, MOET, in partnership with the Vietnam Advanced Software Company, has been working with Connexions, an international collection of educational content run by Rice University in Houston, to develop a web-based course program that provides coursework materials to faculty and students at no cost. In addition, MOET and IBM have worked to train teachers at selected schools on teaching and learning with computers (TLC), an instructional method that integrates technology into the curriculum. By incorporating technology as an instructional tool, the MOET aims to improve and promote effective teaching strategies at all levels of education, especially in primary and secondary schools.

Gender and Education

According to MOET, Vietnam has made progress in reducing the gender gap in education. Gender equity in the classroom exists at the primary and secondary levels, where female and male students share the same learning environments, materials, and opportunities.

Enrollment rate differences in 2005–2006 for female and male students at primary and secondary schools were marginal, with female enrollment nearing 50 percent. In 2004 the gender gap in literacy rates was not significant at any level of education.

Despite advances toward equity in education, there are still disparities at various socioeconomic, regional, and cultural levels. In particular, the dropout rate for female students is higher than for male students. Girls from poor backgrounds, children from rural areas, and ethnic minority groups have the least access to education among the compulsory age population. Families with limited incomes are likely to send boys to school, while girls remain at home to assist the family by taking care of the household or by working.

Informal Education

In Vietnam, nonformal education refers to continuing education that includes the following types: complementary, distance, open, and self-study. Complementary education is designed as an accompanying system of education that supplements public institutions, and serves people of all ages in the areas of basic instruction in literacy and mathematics. It can also apply to other school subjects as well. Distance education involves online (i.e., computer-based) learning or any form of education that does not require participants to learn in the same room. Open education is available to all individuals regardless of qualifications in any particular area of study. Self-study education involves independent learning that occurs most often in the expert-apprentice setting. Students in this category generally engage in hands-on training in specific vocations. The purpose is to provide supplementary educational opportunities to promote and enhance learning experiences for students at any level of education. In addition to literacy and technology skills, education centers also focus on health information and life skills training, such as parenting and work preparation. Locations of continuing education vary, from district and community learning centers to mass media channels such as radio and television. The Department of Continuing Education, regulated by the MOET, manages education activities in the form of program development, syllabi, textbooks, and materials.

System Economics

In 2007 the government allocated 20 percent (US$4.2 million) of the total state budget to education and training, representing a 21 percent increase from funding in 2006. Of this amount, 45 percent was allocated to salaries, 35 percent for professional development and management, and 12 percent for the improvement of curriculum material and facilities. Limited funding and unequal distribution of the budget between human resources and program improvement have affected the quality of education. In 2007 the MOET reported that the increase in funding did not sufficiently meet educational demands due to rapid economic and social changes. School fees were not expected to increase, and average spending per student was low. In 2008 public expenditure on education totaled 5.3 percent of Vietnam's gross domestic product (GDP). The budget included funds for educational institutions, administration, students and families, and other private groups. Government expenditure per student at the primary level was 19.7 percent of the GDP per capita. At the secondary level, expenditure per student was 17.3 percent of the GDP.

Dilemmas and Challenges

As Vietnam transitions through reformation, changes in social and economic development necessitate changes in the education system. The transitional state of socioeconomic development of the country poses several challenges for educational reform. Schools are not able to adequately facilitate or accommodate the rising student enrollment. In addition, shortage of qualified teachers, limited funding, poor school facilities and infrastructure, and out-of-date curriculum are issues that need to be addressed. The demand for education reforms that will meet the needs of the country's rapid economic growth and modernization places considerable pressure on officials and educators to provide and improve training and resources. Unequal access to education, particularly among poor families, remains a problem. In addition, little attention is given to development of nonformal educational opportunities for those who need supplemental instruction. There are also challenges within the organization system of education, including the ability of officials at all levels to handle the increased demands of funds, enrollment, planning and development, and human resources.

Future Prospects

Education has become one of the top priorities of Vietnam. As one of the fastest-growing economies in Southeast Asia, Vietnam hopes its education system will train and prepare students to contribute to the country's efforts to attain socioeconomic success. Since 1986 there have been continuing education reform efforts. Vietnam has outlined strategy goals that are relevant to improving the overall quality of education. Policies reflect investment in teacher training, curriculum, and improving physical facilities. There is a push for a move toward institutional autonomy, which will give schools more management power. Within the classroom, educators have been working to adopt a student-centered approach that takes into account input from students and their families.

In 2012 the Ministry of Education and Train-

Vietnam Education at a Glance

General Information

Capital	Hanoi
Population	90.55 million
Language	Vietnamese
Literacy rate	94%
GDP per capita	US$1,168
Number of phones (landline) per 100 people	20.3
Number of phones (mobile) per 100 people	114.45
Number of Internet users per 100 people	27.25
Number of Internet hosts	129,318

Formal Education Information

Compulsory school age population enrolled (2009)	12.1 million
Compulsory school age population (2009)	14.1%
Number of years of compulsory education	9 (ages 6–15)
Student/teacher ratio	
Primary (Form 1–5)	20
Lower secondary (Form 6–9)	20
Upper secondary (Form 10–12)	25
Average class size in primary school	45
Average school days per year	204
Average number of hours per school day	4.5
Primary school gross enrollment ratio (2004)	106.5%
Primary school entrants completing grade 5 (2004)	
Female	87%
Male	90%
Secondary school gross enrollment ratio (2004)	67%

Note: Unless otherwise indicated, all data are based on sources from 2011.

---

ing adopted a Higher Education Reform Agenda, intended to diversify higher education in Vietnam. This includes allowing the expansion of private education. The goal is to have the private sector represent 40 percent of the higher education sector by 2020. Another aim is to diversify by decentralizing the management and administration of universities and colleges. It was widely acknowledged that higher education institutions need to operate with more autonomy and accountability in training, research, human resource management, and finance.

The educational outlook in Vietnam involves a combined vision of maintaining fundamental traditions while being open to renovations. This ideal of open education means that everyone has access to quality education programs that will foster students' creativity and talent. Educational institutions will promote scientific and technological progress, especially information technology and telecommunications. On a global level, Vietnam aims to advance knowledge development and international relations by cooperating with foreign education programs to increase the number of Vietnamese students studying abroad. Vietnam is calling on its policy makers, educators, parents, students, and the general public to work together in creating a rigorous, competitive, and accessible education system.

*Julie Thuy Nguyen, Emily Thao Tien Le,
and Mimi Tao*

REFERENCES

Central Intelligence Agency. *The CIA World Factbook*. New York: Skyhorse, 2011. https://www.cia.gov/library/publications/the-world-factbook/index.html.

Disability World. "Inclusive Education in Vietnam: A Snapshot." www.disabilityworld.org.

Do, Bich Loan. "Gender Issues in Education in Vietnam." UNESCO Bangkok. www.unescobkk.org/fileadmin/user_upload/appeal/gender/vietnam.doc.

Fry, Gerald W. "Higher Education in Vietnam." In *The Political Economy of Educational Reforms and Capacity Development in Southeast Asia*, ed. Yasushi Hirosato and Yuto Kitamura, 237–261. New York: Spring Science + Business Media BV, 2009.

Ministry of Education and Training (Vietnam). "Overview of Education and Training of Vietnam." http://en.moet.gov.vn.

Nation Master. 2011. www.nationmaster.com.

Nguyen, Loc. "Viet Nam's Education in the Transitional Period." APEC Knowledge Bank. www.apecknowledgebank.org.

Nguyen, Minh Phuong, and Thang Thi Cao. "Curriculum Planning, Development, and Reform." UNESCO–International Bureau of Education. www.ibe.unesco.org/curriculum/Asia%20Networkpdf/ndrepvn.pdf.

Statistics Documentation Centre, General Statistics Office of Vietnam. www.gso.gov.vn.

UNESCO. http://portal.unesco.org/en.

UNICEF. "Viet Nam." www.unicef.org/vietnam.

Vietnam Education Foundation. http://home.vef.gov/cat.php?id=4.

World Bank. "Vietnam." http://go.worldbank.org.

Australia, New Zealand, and Melanesia

Introduction

This section discusses the educational systems of four countries—Australia, Fiji, New Zealand, and Papua New Guinea—in the region of the world commonly known as Oceania. These countries happen to be the most populous nations in the region. With the exception of Papua New Guinea, the *CIA World Factbook* identifies 27 countries or territories that are associated with Oceania. Because only the most populous nations are discussed, the title of this section is "Australia, New Zealand, and Melanesia." It should also be noted that Melanesia includes several small countries and dependent islands that are not discussed in this section. These countries and dependent states include American Samoa, Cook Islands, French Polynesia, Guam, Kiribati, the Federated States of Micronesia, Midway Islands, Nauru, New Caledonia, Niue, Northern Mariana Islands, and Palau, to name a few. The point of excluding discussion of these systems is not to say that they are insignificant, but rather that they each exemplify the education systems of Fiji, New Zealand, Papua New Guinea, and to some extent Australia in a number of ways. Although each nation has its own system of education that is unique when compared to the systems of other countries, it is important to note that one of the purposes of this section is to present Fiji and Papua New Guinea as macrocosms of a region that consists of many smaller countries and territories that may or may not have their own formal educational systems.

In addition to a discussion of the educational systems of Fiji and Papua New Guinea, this section discusses the educational systems of Australia and New Zealand. These systems present a fairly significant contrast to those of Fiji and Papua New Guinea. First, per student spending in Australia and New Zealand is among the highest in the world, $11,826 and $9,451, respectively. Although not the lowest, at $1,027, per student spending in Fiji is significantly lower, and that of Papua New Guinea, $194, is lower still. Second, the school systems of Australia and New Zealand have been successful in accommodating students of families who reside in rural areas. These systems have been particularly successful in reaching populations through the use of information and communication technologies. The education systems of Fiji and Papua New Guinea have had much less success in reaching rural populations due to the lack of financial and physical resources. Third, unlike schooling in Australia and New Zealand, schooling in Fiji and Papua New Guinea is not compulsory. Students who are not required to attend formal educational institutions will not be as competitive in the global marketplace as students in Australia, New Zealand, and other developed nations. Fourth, the primary and secondary gross enrollment ratios of Australia and New Zealand are far higher than those of Fiji and Papua New Guinea. Moreover, the gross enrollment ratios in Australia and New Zealand are approximately the same as the net enrollment ratios in these countries—indicating that nearly all students of a particular age or grade level are attending school. In contrast, there are fairly significant gaps when comparing gross enrollment ratios and net enrollment ratios of Fiji and Papua New Guinea. This indicates that although there are many students of a particular grade level, smaller numbers of students are actually attending school. It is also likely that those who are attending school in these countries can do so because their families can afford private education. Finally, it should be noted that because there is greater emphasis on formal education in

Australia and New Zealand than in most other countries, there is also a better transition between school and work in these nations. More students tend to be marketable, and there is greater latitude for students in terms of how their schooling and expectations for a career actually become reality.

Daniel Ness and Chia-ling Lin

AUSTRALIA

Australia, the only country in the world that is also a continent, is part of a larger region known as Oceania, which consists of island nations in the South Pacific. The most common language of the country is English, spoken by nearly 80 percent of the population. Other languages include Chinese, Italian, and several indigenous languages. Ethnic groups include European (92 percent), Asian (7 percent), and aboriginal (1 percent).

The earliest people in Australia are presumed to be aboriginal settlers who arrived on the continent more than 40,000 years ago. The first signs of European settlements occurred during the seventeenth century. Originally the current six states of Australia were established as colonies in the eighteenth and nineteenth centuries. These colonies federated in 1901, when Australia was named a commonwealth of the United Kingdom. Both Australia and Great Britain were adept in using the region's natural resources to their benefit—especially during World War I and II. During this time, Australia became a major world industrial power, with its industries concentrated in the coastal regions of the country. Within the last several decades, however, the country has become increasingly important for its growth in information technologies and as an information society as a whole. According to the Organisation for Economic Co-operation and Development, Australia's economy was one of the fastest-growing economies in the 1990s. This may have been due in large part to the economic reforms of the previous decade. In future decades the Australian government will need to consider ways to control greenhouse gases as a result of pollution from former industries and to preserve the Great Barrier Reef. Although there is some ethnic tension between indigenous populations and European populations, the percent of aboriginal groups is very small, and most groups have found a sense of equitable living in the country.

It is difficult to determine the number of people or percentage of the population below the poverty line in Australia because data agencies focus attention on individuals and families whose children or relatives attend school. There is little to no information on the economic status of native Australian populations. The Smith Family website, a nonprofit children's charity that also tracks levels of poverty in Australia, has provided the following data:

- 13.0 percent of Australians live in poverty (2.86 million)
- 2.9 percent of children live in poverty
- 6.8 percent of single-parent families live in poverty

This report highlights the relationship between poverty and unemployment: the underemployed face greater risks of poverty than other populations, particularly with the increasing casualization of the workforce.

Educational System

According to the World Education Index, Australia ranks first among 179 countries in its system of education. The school year in Australia runs from January to December. Education in all states of Australia is compulsory for all children from grade 1 through grade 10—ages five through 15 years—and free for all children ages five through 18 years. Each state in Australia has its own laws regarding compulsory education. Some states, in fact, require students to attend school prior to first grade. In general, the states and territories of Australia are responsible for education laws with little, if any, interference from the central government. The following are descriptions of compulsory education requirements for each of the six Australian states and each of the two Australian territories:

Australian Capital Territory: All students whose families reside in the Australian Capital Territory, which includes the city of Canberra, are required to remain in school until achieving Year 10. They then must participate full-time in school, training, or employment until completing Year 12 (or equivalent), or reach age 17, whichever occurs first.

New South Wales: Schooling is compulsory for children and adolescents between the ages of six and 15, or from Year 1 through 10. Preschool, kindergarten, and the final two years of high school (Years 11 and 12) are optional but are still free.

Northern Territory: Education is compulsory for children between six and 15 years of age, or from grade level years 1 through 10, in the Northern Territory. As in New South Wales, preschool and Years 11 and 12 are free but optional.

Queensland: In Queensland, students are of compulsory school age from five years until they turn 16 or complete Year 10, whichever is first. Again, preschool and Years 11 and 12 of secondary school are free and optional.

South Australia: Schooling in South Australia is compulsory for children and adolescents between the ages of six and 17. Upon reaching age 17, students must participate full-time in school, training, or employment until completing Year 12 (or equivalent).

Tasmania: All children who are at least five years old must be enrolled in a school or be provided with home education until age 16 or Year 10, whichever comes first. From age 16, all students must participate in full-time education (Years 11 and 12) or training option for at least one year.

Victoria: School education is compulsory in Victoria between the ages of six and 17. Students must then participate full-time in school, training, or employment until completing Year 12 (or equivalent).

Western Australia: School in Western Australia is compulsory for children and adolescents between the ages of six and 15 (Years 1–10). Kindergarten, preschool, and the final two years of high school (Years 11 and 12) are free and optional.

Preprimary and Compulsory Education

Although mostly free, preschool in Australia is not compulsory in most states and territories. Only in Queensland and Western Australia is preschool and kindergarten education part of the primary school curriculum and system of schooling. Preschools and kindergartens are under the authority of state and territory governments and run by the Department of Education in the Australian Capital Territory, Northern Territory, Queensland, Tasmania, and Western Australia. In New South Wales, Victoria, and South Australia, however, preschools and kindergartens are under the auspices of local municipalities and private organizations. Accordingly, preschools and kindergartens are under the authority of the Department of Community Services in each of these three states. Although preschool is optional in Australia, nearly 90 percent of all families enroll their children in preschool, mostly during the year prior to the first grade of primary school.

Primary school in Australia consists of six or seven years of schooling, depending on the state. For example, six-year primary schools are prevalent in the Australian Capital Territory, New South Wales, Northern Territory, Tasmania, and Victoria. Seven-year primary schools are enforced in Queensland, South Australia, and Western Australia. The primary educational level focuses on formal studies in English, mathematics, natural sciences, and social sciences. Students also engage in sports, physical education, arts and crafts, music, and health education. Given that each state maintains its own laws regarding the number of years of primary school, the number of years of secondary school is also mandated by each state. The six-year secondary schools are the Australian Capital Territory, New South Wales, Northern Territory, Tasmania, and Victoria. The five-year secondary schools are mandated in Queensland, South Australia, and Western Australia. As stated above, although grades 11 and 12 are free, these levels are not compulsory. Nevertheless, students must provide evidence of vocational training or occupational employment upon graduating from grade 10.

There are approximately 1.8 million primary school students and 1.6 million secondary school students in Australia—thus, a total of 3.5 million students. The student/teacher ratio in the country as a whole is rather modest—17 students to 1 teacher at the primary level and 10 students to 1 teacher at the secondary level. The primary school gross enrollment rate is slightly over 100 percent—indicating that nearly all students between and including grades 1 and 6 are gaining educational access. Moreover, nearly all students reach and complete grade 5 and continue to high school and even college. The gross enrollment ratio for secondary school is 149 percent. This high ratio may be due in part to the fact that many students who are eligible to attend grades 11 and 12 decide to leave school after grade 10 and either enter a vocation or technical career or search for employment.

There are a number of college entrance examinations in Australia. Each state maintains its own test for graduating at the tenth-grade level and also the twelfth-grade level. The National Assessment Program in Literacy and Numeracy (NAPLAN) is a nationwide examination that is administered at various points throughout the secondary period. The Senior Secondary Certificate of Education is a broad term that indicates proof of high school graduation. Again, each state has its own laws and nomenclature to describe what students must accomplish by each grade level in order to be eligible for further education—whether vocational instruction at a technical institute or academic education at a college or university.

It is estimated that nearly 34 percent of all primary and secondary school students in Australia attend parochial or independent schools—in other words, schools not funded by state or federal bodies. Catholic institutions enroll the greatest number of students who do not attend public schools. In general, after students in Australia complete primary school, they continue to the secondary school or high school. Only recently did the Northern Territory adopt the middle school paradigm for its seventh- and eighth-grade students prior to entering high school.

Curriculum in Australian Schools

Although Australia has a national curriculum framework that adheres to high academic standards throughout the country, each state has autonomy in providing its own standards and curriculum. Nevertheless, nearly all schools in the country maintain provisions that follow the teaching of subjects in the eight core learning areas: English; mathematics; social studies, civics, and the environment; natural science; arts and music; languages other than English; communication and information technologies; and personal development, health and hygiene, and physical education. In addition, international students are able to enroll in English language programs as a means of supporting their studies in the other seven fields.

At the secondary school level, choice and diversity are increased as schools are able to offer a wide range of subjects, delivered by highly trained and experienced teachers and using state-of-the-art technology,

including the Internet, multimedia equipment, and laboratories. Many students use senior secondary study to gain university entry qualifications. About nine out of every 10 Australian secondary schools also offer vocational education programs in addition to the standard school curriculum.

Tertiary Education

Australia is known for some of the most prominent tertiary institutions in the world. At present there are some 1 million students enrolled in universities throughout the country. Established in 1850, the University of Sydney is the oldest institution of higher education in Australia. It has the second largest enrollment of all Australian universities. With more than 56,000 students, Monash University has the largest enrollment among all universities in the country.

There is a league of universities in Australia known as the Group of Eight. These universities have established themselves as eminent research institutions that have competed, perhaps more than any other Australian higher education institutions, for federal, state, and private funding. The Group of Eight Universities are located in the capitals of five states and one territory. Sydney is the home of two of these universities: University of Sydney and University of New South Wales. Melbourne is also the home of two of the Group of Eight universities: University of Melbourne and Monash University. The Times Higher Education and Quacquarelli Symonds World University Rankings ranked three of the Group of Eight—Australian National University, University of Sydney, and University of Melbourne—among the top 100 world universities in 2009 and 2010. The remaining five universities—University of Queensland, Monash University, University of New South Wales, University of Adelaide in South Australia, and University of Western Australia—also have high rankings among all world universities, both in research and in the academic achievement of their students.

However, the members of the Group of Eight are not the only major universities in Australia that have excelled in the areas of research and rigor among faculty and students. Established in 1986, Curtin University is the largest institution of higher education in Western Australia. With over 44,000 students annually, Curtin University was originally a polytechnic institute—the Western Australian Institute of Technology—that merged with Perth Technical College and the Western Australian School of Mines into university status in 1986. Currently it is one of the most intensive research universities in the country. Curtin has five colleges: Center for Aboriginal Studies; Business School; Faculty of Health Sciences; Faculty of Humanities, which houses schools of architecture, art, media, education, social sciences, language, and human rights studies; and Faculty of Science and Engineering, which was the original program of study prior to university status.

Another form of tertiary-level education in Australia is the polytechnic university or technical school. These schools are also known as technical and further education (TAFE) institutions. Students who enroll in TAFE institutions are those whose academic work in secondary school falls below the university level or those who wish to prepare for a vocation or technical occupation in fewer years than it takes to receive a baccalaureate at the university. Regardless, some polytechnic institutes in Australia are as rigorous, or more so, than many universities in the country. In total there are 64 polytechnic institutes and technical schools in Australia.

Teacher Education

During colonial times and most of the twentieth century, teacher education programs in Australia emulated the normal school model that originated in the United States and eventually was followed by European and East Asian countries. However, given the theory of teaching for the twenty-first century—namely, that successful teachers must also have expertise in various academic domains, not solely in pedagogical knowledge—teacher education institutions are now affiliated with universities as colleges of education. Accordingly, many universities throughout Australia maintain teachers colleges or schools of education on campus. There are at least 25 schools of education throughout Australia. Moreover, as is the case in well-known American schools of education, those in Australia are very accommodating to international students because these schools have a strong reputation for linking research in education with practice.

Although many teacher education programs in developed nations focus on master's level instruction, programs in Australian universities provide students with majors in education at the baccalaureate level as well as the master's and doctoral levels. At the baccalaureate level, students begin their freshman year with general education courses as well as human development courses. By their sophomore year, students are learning pedagogical and content-related topics associated with common subject branches—English, mathematics, science, and the like. Instruction in these domains is continued into the junior year, when students also take courses in multilingual teaching, creative arts in education, science and technology, and courses focusing on international education, poverty in education, or school psychology. By the senior year, preservice teacher education students gain insight in furthering their knowledge of the core subject areas. Moreover, they learn about assessment, curriculum and evaluation, teaching English as a second language (TESOL), and special education methods. Secondary preservice teacher education students must also major in a specific core subject area (e.g., mathematics, chemistry, history).

The purpose of graduate teacher education programs in Australia is to provide student teaching and internship experiences for students who decide to become teachers. In addition to student teaching experiences, seminars, practicums, and internships, students must also take courses in specific academic disciplines at the graduate level. Students obtaining a graduate degree in education are eligible to teach in a school depending on their area of expertise in terms of school level (i.e., early childhood, primary, or secondary).

In general, each state in Australia is responsible for teacher registration, qualification for school placement, and credentialing. On a more national scale, the program titled Teaching Australia: The Australian Institute for Teaching and School Leadership enables preservice and in-service teachers to become aware of professional standards of teachers and policy makers. The body also serves as a support system for teachers. In addition, Teaching Australia is in the process of developing a national accreditation system in teacher education.

Informal Education

Informal education in Australia is common among adults who are in the process of career change or who wish to engage in lifelong learning. There are programs in the country that focus on foundation learning, which introduces adults to basic curriculum that they need to learn or relearn for general life skills, literacy, or occupational training. The TAFE colleges, mentioned earlier, are instrumental in promulgating informal education to secondary school graduates and adults who wish to pursue career goals or engage in lifelong learning. In addition, TAFE programs are also offered for students and adults at various secondary schools throughout the country. Both within the TAFE framework and in other informal education settings, the Australian education system embraces a program known as flexible learning as part of its mission to increase student productivity at every age. Flexible learning is an educational paradigm whose aim is to accommodate learners by providing convenient times of instruction, varied instructional techniques, and appropriate curriculum for advancement in a particular academic or vocational domain. Given the diverse situations of the twenty-first-century learner, this type of learning provides nontraditional students with significant choices. For example, students can gain knowledge before or after working hours, while their children are at school, or at some other convenient time. Some informal learning settings in Australia offer classroom instruction or virtual learning, including the use of phone or laptop technology as vehicles for instruction. Many informal education settings in Australia focus on life-skill learning, particularly for adults. These include both critical thinking skills that allow learners to analyze, question, or challenge various assumptions, and metacognitive skills that are needed in order for learners to realize and monitor their own learning behaviors. Key areas of content development include improving mathematics skills, learning a foreign language, or even improving one's skills in reading or writing.

System Economics and Future Prospects

According to the United Nations Development Programme (2010), along with Tonga and Lithuania, public expenditures on education of Australia represented 4.7 percent of the gross domestic product in 2007. Given the GDP of Australia at $890 billion, educational expenditure in the country amounts to nearly $42 billion, or $11,826 per student (total amount

Australia Education at a Glance

General Information

Capital	Canberra
Population	21.7 million
Languages	English (79%), indigenous languages (11%), Chinese, Italian
Literacy rate	99%
GDP per capita	US$33,300
People below poverty line (2004)	no data*
Number of phones per 100 people	56
Number of Internet users per 100 people	72
Number of Internet hosts	7,780,000
Life expectancy at birth (years)	80

Formal Educational Information

Primary school age population	1.85 million
Secondary school age population	1.68 million
Primary school age population	9%
Number of years of primary education	7
Student/teacher ratio (primary)	17
Student/teacher ratio (secondary)	10
Primary school gross enrollment ratio	104%
Primary school entrants reaching grade 5	99%
Secondary school gross enrollment ratio	149%
Child labor (ages 5–14)	no data

Notes: *Although no figure is available, poverty is higher among native Australian (i.e., aboriginal) populations.

Unless otherwise indicated, all data are based on sources from 2011.

equivalent to US dollars divided by 3,537,000, the approximate number of primary- and secondary-age students in the country). Australia ranks 83 of 186 countries in percentage of educational expenditure.

At present Australia is one of the highest-ranking countries of the world in terms of educational access for its primary, secondary, and tertiary population. The country has some of the most prominent and rigorous tertiary institutions in the world. The Australian states have developed an education system that is innovative and competitive in terms of advances in teacher pedagogy and the development of intellectual ability in students of all backgrounds.

Australian education policy makers have revitalized e-learning throughout the country. At present, there are nearly 8 million Internet hosts in Australia—more than one host for every three people. After the United Kingdom (82.5 percent), South Korea (81.1 percent), and Germany (79.1 percent), Australia ranks fourth (78.3 percent) in percentage of total population that uses the Internet (Internet World Stats 2010). E-learning, which includes distance learning as well as the use of technology as a means of application in the workforce, is an important factor in Australian tertiary institutions. These institutions are embracing the use of advanced technologies for the purpose of increasing student knowledge of a variety of content areas. The goal is to provide students with greater opportunities for learning both in the classroom and in the workplace.

The Australian education system has also been successful in recent years in providing educational access to all indigenous groups in the country. Albeit only 1 percent of the current population, indigenous Australians had been members of approximately 250 nations on the Australian continent, each having at least one spoken language. During British colonial rule, these groups were notoriously subjugated to various forms of inequities. Further, it is surmised that disease outbreaks stemming from newly arrived British settlers during the nineteenth century wiped out large numbers of indigenous groups. However, their livelihood has improved since World War I. Within the past several decades, the study of the history of aboriginal people has become a staple of the curriculum of every state in the country.

Daniel Ness and Chia-ling Lin

REFERENCES

Center for Economic and Social Rights. *Visualizing Rights: Australia, Fact Sheet No. 3.* New York: Center for Economic and Social Rights, 2010.

Central Intelligence Agency. *The CIA World Factbook.* New York: Skyhorse, 2011. https://www.cia.gov/library/publications/the-world-factbook/index.html.

Internet World Stats. *Top 20 Countries with the Highest Number of Internet Users.* Bogota, Colombia. Miniwatts Marketing Group, 2010. www.internetworldstats.com/top20.htm.

Nation Master, 2011. www.nationmaster.com.

The Smith Family. Homepage. www.thesmithfamily.com.au/site/page.cfm.

UNESCO. *Global Education Digest 2012: Comparing Education Statistics Across the World.* Montreal: UNESCO Institute for Statistics, 2012.

———. "Strong Foundations: Early Childhood Care and Education." *Education for All Global Monitoring Report.* Paris: UNESCO, 2006.

UNESCO–IBE. www.ibe.unesco.org/en/worldwide/unesco-regions/asia-and-the-pacific/australia.html.

United Nations Development Programme. *Human Development Report 2011.* http://hdr.undp.org/en.

US Department of Labor. *2001 Findings on the Worst Forms of Child Labor.* Washington, DC: Bureau of International Labor Affairs, US Department of Labor, 2002.

World Bank Education Statistics, 2011. www.worldbank.org.

FIJI

Fiji is a country of 332 islands in Melanesia. With the exception of Papua New Guinea, Fiji is the most populous country in Melanesia. The official languages of the country are Fijian and English. A large population in the country also speaks Hindustani. The population of Fiji in the 2011 estimate (*CIA World Factbook*) was 883,125. Ethnic groups include Fijian (55 percent), Indian (37 percent), European, Chinese, and other Pacific Islander populations.

The islands of Fiji became a British colony in the late nineteenth century. During the early years of colonization, the British government brought contract laborers from India to the islands. Fiji achieved independence from the United Kingdom on October 10, 1970. After nearly two decades of relative peace, two military coups interrupted this peace in 1987—the result of perceptions by native Melanesians that Indian groups were gaining too much power. A new constitution was devised in 1990 that impelled many Fijians of Indian descent to emigrate. As tensions relaxed slightly, the election of an Indo-Fijian led to another ethnic dispute, which resulted in another coup in 2000, this time headed by Fijian civilians. Despite more equitable elections in recent years, there have still been tensions between Indian and native Fijian groups.

Educational System

Education in Fiji is free and compulsory for all children from grade 1 through grade 10—ages six through 16. Although Fiji has one of the highest attendance rates in the region, the country has had severe attrition problems, particularly during the military coups of 1987 and the civilian coup of 2000, which adversely affected Indo-Fijian school attendance. At present there are approximately 229,000 children and adolescents of primary- and secondary-level age in Fiji. The primary gross enrollment rate in the country is 103 percent. The country has been successful in keeping most students in primary schools; nearly all primary school students reach grade 5 (99 percent). The secondary school gross enrollment rate is 86 percent—still a rather high rate when compared to those of other countries in the region. The attendance rate is reflected in a rather high literacy rate of 94 percent. Unfortunately, there still remains a gap, albeit not large, between the literacy rates of males (96 percent) and females (92 percent).

Although under the umbrella of the Fijian Ministry of Education, schooling in Fiji is primarily run locally and by religious groups. It should be understood that the ethnic tension described earlier is also based on religious differences among the citizens of Fiji. The Indo-Fijian population is primarily Hindu (34 percent). The majority of the country's population, however, including most native Fijians, is Christian (53 percent). Accordingly, there are indications of friction between the two groups in most urban communities. Nevertheless, the Fijian Education Ministry is attempting to subsidize as many resources as possible so that all Fijians can gain educational access at both primary and secondary levels.

There are opportunities for preprimary education in Fiji, especially in urban communities. According to 2010 figures, there are 735 primary schools in

four districts. There are a total of 5,000 teachers and 130,378 primary school students. These numbers, particularly the student population, might be overestimated due to migration and children who reside in rural communities. The curriculum consists of a primary language (the language spoken in the community), mathematics, social studies, some natural science, physical education, and art. Some secondary schools also teach in the language of the community (Fijian, Urdu, or Hindi), but most instruction is in English. The secondary school curriculum prepares students for vocational careers or entrance into the tertiary level. The oldest and largest university in Fiji is the University of the South Pacific, with its main campus in Suva. Regional campuses include those in Labasa and Lautoka. In addition to liberal arts and sciences, the university offers programs in tourism, journalism, agriculture, technology and computing, law, business, public administration, and social work.

Teacher training programs are available in Fiji. Lautoka Teachers College offers programs that lead to a diploma in primary education and an advanced certificate in early childhood education. Teacher education students must pass the Fiji Form Seven Examination, which consists of content in English, mathematics, and at least one other language spoken in the country.

System Economics and Future Prospects

According to the United Nations Development Programme (2010), along with Jamaica and New Zealand, public expenditures on education of Fiji represented 6.2 percent of the gross domestic product in 2004. Given the GDP of Fiji at $3.792 billion, educational expenditure in the country amounts to over $235 million, or $1,027 per student (total amount equivalent to US dollars divided by 229,000, the approximate number of primary- and secondary-age students in the country). Fiji ranks 33 of 186 countries in percentage of educational expenditure.

At present, Fiji ranks rather high in educational access for its primary and secondary school-age population. However, ethnic tensions have thwarted progress in the last two to three decades. As discussed above, an Indo-Fijian minority has been perceived

---

Fiji Education at a Glance

General Information

Capital	Suva
Population	918,675
Languages	English, Fijian, Hindustani
Literacy rate	94%
GDP per capita	US$6,200
People below poverty line (2004)	25
Number of phones per 100 people	11
Number of Internet users per 100 people	11
Number of Internet hosts	9,000
Life expectancy at birth (years)	70

Formal Educational Information

Primary school age population	110,000
Secondary school age population	119,000
Primary school age population	12%
Number of years of primary education	6
Student/teacher ratio (primary)	28
Student/teacher ratio (secondary)	22
Primary school gross enrollment ratio	103%
Primary school entrants reaching grade 5	99%
Secondary school gross enrollment ratio	86%
Child labor (ages 5–14)	no data

Note: Unless otherwise indicated, all data are based on sources from 2011.

by native Fijians to have taken political control of the country. The resultant coups have disrupted free elections and the democratic process. Unfortunately, this ethnic tension has caused periods of school attrition. Second, there is a 4 to 5 percent gap separating males and females older than 15 who can read and write. In addition, male students have an edge over female students in grade promotion—particularly in tertiary level access.

One possible recommendation for improving the gap in literacy as well as the literacy rate as a whole is the promotion of informal education programs. Although schools are fairly successful in graduating students, many primary and secondary schools lack resources and facilities. One problem is the lack of busing. As a result, many families in Fiji, especially in rural communities, are unable to afford the fees that are associated with a child's education, particularly travel expenses. In addition, they must often pay for books and other supplies. At the same time, the government and the private sector have shown initiative in developing the country's information and communication technology programs as a means of supporting educational efforts.

Daniel Ness and Chia-ling Lin

REFERENCES

Center for Economic and Social Rights. *Visualizing Rights: Fiji, Fact Sheet No. 3.* New York: Center for Economic and Social Rights, 2010.

Central Intelligence Agency. *The CIA World Factbook.* New York: Skyhorse, 2011. https://www.cia.gov/library/publications/the-world-factbook/index.html.

Nation Master. 2011. www.nationmaster.com.

UNESCO. *Global Education Digest 2012: Comparing Education Statistics Across the World.* Montreal: UNESCO Institute for Statistics, 2012.

———. "Strong Foundations: Early Childhood Care and Education." *Education for All Global Monitoring Report.* Paris: UNESCO, 2006.

UNESCO–IBE. www.ibe.unesco.org/en/worldwide/unesco-regions/asia-and-the-pacific/fiji.html.

United Nations Development Programme. *Human Development Report 2011.* http://hdr.undp.org/en.

US Department of Labor. *2001 Findings on the Worst Forms of Child Labor.* Washington, DC: Bureau of International Labor Affairs, US Department of Labor, 2002.

World Bank Education Statistics. 2011. www.worldbank.org.

NEW ZEALAND

New Zealand is a country in the South Pacific Ocean that consists of two large islands (South Island and North Island) and 31 smaller islands. The official languages of the country are English, Maori, and sign language. The population of New Zealand in 2012 was 44.3 million (*CIA World Factbook*). Ethnic groups include European (70 percent), Maori (8 percent), Asian (6 percent), Pacific Islander (4 percent), and other unspecified populations.

The earliest inhabitants of the islands that compose New Zealand were the Maori, who inhabited the region as early as 800 CE. The earliest period of contact with England was 1840, when the heads of the Polynesian Maori entered a pact with the United Kingdom under the Treaty of Waitangi. This treaty enabled the tribes to maintain territorial rights while, at the same time, providing the United Kingdom with sovereignty over the region. Despite the seemingly equitable intentions of the treaty, native peoples of New Zealand were subjugated and placed under British colonial rule. A series of wars between the United Kingdom and native populations ensued. By 1872 all native groups were defeated by British forces. The colony of New Zealand became an independent nation in 1907, but still maintained its reverence and support of the United Kingdom, especially during both world wars. Since World War II, New Zealand has become a world leader in the areas of education and the global economy. The standing of Maori groups has improved since the 1980s.

The New Zealand government expects increased expenditures in education and health care in ensuing years.

Educational System

Education in New Zealand is compulsory for all children from grade 1 through grade 10—ages five through 16 years—and free for all children ages five through 19 years. The curriculum that is described in the section below is divided into eight levels—Curriculum Levels 1 through 8. The country's education system consists of 13 grade levels, which include primary, intermediate, and lower secondary levels. Senior secondary school—grade 11 through 13—prepares students for formal tertiary education.

Preprimary and Compulsory Education

The New Zealand education system is known for its unique and notable preprimary institutions. The system takes great pride in its unique schools for preschool children. Although preschool is not compulsory, most families in New Zealand send their children to preschools. There are at least five types of preprimary education schools in New Zealand. The type that most families enroll their children in is the kindergarten, which serves as a transition between home and formal schooling that commences in the first grade. A second, more informal type of setting is the Playcentre, a schooling form that is unique to New Zealand. Playcentres were founded in New Zealand in 1941 as a means of fostering family influence in child development; the teachers and administrators of the Playcentres are the parents themselves. Children from birth to age six can be enrolled in Playcentres, which afford children the opportunity to engage in cooperative learning experiences. The government provides the supplies and materials for running these institutions. The third form of preprimary education is the Kōhanga Reo school. This type of preprimary education is an offshoot of the Maori language revival, which had commenced in 1980 and continues to this day. Like the Playcentre, the Kōhanga Reo school enrolls children from birth until the entrance to formal schooling. A fourth type of preprimary school in New Zealand is the licensed early childhood center, which are typical in other parts of the world. Examples include Montessori schools, Reggio Emilia schools, and other privately owned preschools. A fifth type of preprimary school in New Zealand is the chartered early childhood school that is funded by the New Zealand government. Both licensed early childhood schools and chartered early childhood schools enroll children from birth through age five.

Primary school in New Zealand is a six-year schooling period that focuses on formal studies in four broad fields—language, mathematics, natural sciences, and social sciences. The curriculum levels consist of the following: level 1 for grades 1 and 2; level 2 for grade 3; levels 2 or 3 for grade 4; level 3 for grade 5; and levels 3 or 4 for grade 6. There are two types of primary schools. The most familiar type enrolls students from the first grade to the sixth grade. The second type enrolls students from the first grade to the eighth grade, with students remaining at the same school for grades 7 and 8. Students in grade 7 are in curriculum level 3 or 4, and those in grade 8 are in curriculum level 4 or 5. Students in the first type of primary school, namely, for grades 1 through 6, have two options for intermediate-level education. One option is the intermediate school, which consists of grades 7 and 8. A second option is the junior secondary school, which comprises grades 7 through 10, thus covering the curriculum of the lower secondary levels.

Upon graduating from intermediate school, students have the option of continuing to secondary school for the full five years—grades 8 through 13. Secondary school students also have the option of exiting secondary school after grade 11—mainly those who wish to earn a vocational or technical degree. Students in grades 11, 12, or 13 must take the National Certificate of Educational Achievement (NCEA) Examination if they wish to exit secondary school at any one of these three grade levels. Students in grade 11 are in curriculum levels 5 or 6. Twelfth-grade students are enrolled in curriculum levels 6 or 7, and those in grade 13 are enrolled in curriculum levels 7 or 8. Students who are in grade 13, at curriculum level 8, and who pass the NCEA Examination are eligible to enter the university and similar forms of tertiary education. Intermediate education students enrolled in the junior secondary school (i.e., not the intermediate school) must continue to the senior secondary school, the second type of secondary school in New Zealand. Students who enroll in the senior secondary school are more likely than their secondary school counterparts to finish grade 13 and continue to tertiary institutions upon graduation.

In 2000 an amendment to the educational system was enacted to prevent classroom overcrowding. As a result, zoning laws were enforced to limit overcrowding in schools that were deemed large in terms of class size. One problem with the amendment, its critics contend, is that it adversely affects rural New Zealand children, many of whom are Maori, who must travel even further to attend school. Present data indicate that the student/teacher ratio for primary school in the country is 15 to 1 and that of secondary school is 16 to 1. In addition, the gross and net enrollment rates for primary school are at 100 percent. With few exceptions, all primary school students in New Zealand complete primary school. The gross enrollment rate for secondary school students is 121 percent. This may perhaps be due to an insufficient number of secondary schools within particular districts or regions.

Curriculum in New Zealand Schools

Schools in New Zealand emphasize the following curriculum: English, mathematics, natural science, social science, technology, physical education and health, arts, and music. New Zealand schools emphasize these subjects as the basic core of what students learn so that they can specialize in one or more aspects of these areas in their future studies. These curriculum areas are intended to help students establish connections between different cognitive domains and to use what they learn in these areas as a means of gaining competencies in the transition from school to work.

Of the eight learning areas in the curriculum, New Zealand schools emphasize language and the learning of English as a conduit for communication in education and in the workforce. To be sure, the literacy skill of New Zealanders is an indicator of success during the adult years. Although the literacy rate in New Zealand is 99 percent, there is some gap in terms of interpretation abilities when comparing Maori with European New Zealanders. The 1996 Adult Literacy Survey allowed researchers to identify three areas of literacy that are important for interpreting information: prose, which is the ability to interpret textual information; document, the ability to interpret information in the form of charts, scheduled tables, figures, and the like; and quantitative, which is the application of arithmetic symbolism in printed sources. Individuals between the ages of 16 and 65 were tested. Level 1 indicated poor ability, level 3 indicated average ability, and level 5, high ability. Comparisons among several ethnic groups demonstrated that non-Maoris outperformed Maoris in all three areas of literacy even though both groups are considered literate.

Tertiary Education

Some of the most rigorous tertiary institutions in the world can be found in New Zealand. At present, there are some 500,000 students enrolled in universities throughout the country. The University of New Zealand was established in 1870 and eventually branched out to include six current universities in the country. The most prominent of these institutions are the University of Auckland, University of Canterbury, Massey University, University of Otago, and Lincoln University. According to the Times Higher Education and Quacquarelli Symonds World University Rankings, the University of Auckland has ranked from the low forties to the upper sixties among the world's universities. Founded in 1869, the University of Otago is the oldest institution in the country and ranks second of the eight New Zealand universities in the international rankings.

Another form of tertiary-level education in New Zealand is the polytechnic or institute of technology. Excluding the Auckland Institute of Technology, which is one of the eight universities in New Zealand, there are 20 polytechnic institutions in the country. Key areas of study include engineering, architecture, art, applied science, medical science, business and administration, computer science, nursing, and trade. Students who graduate receive bachelor's or master's degrees in technology and trade. In addition to traditional tertiary education, the New Zealand government offers students *wānanga*, which is a public institution in various parts of the country that accommodates educational advancement based on Maori, non-Western traditions. Accredited in part through the New Zealand Ministry of Education, *wānanga* schools offer baccalaureate and master's programs in a variety of fields.

Teacher Education

Teacher education in New Zealand can be obtained by enrolling in one of the country's several colleges of education. There are colleges of education in nearly all of the urban areas of New Zealand. Many of these colleges merged with the universities. For example, the Auckland College of Education merged with the University of Auckland in 2004. Some colleges of education have annexes in various parts of a particular region to serve different populations. For example, the Victoria University of Wellington Faculty of Education maintains several campuses and regional centers. Two colleges of education with individual campuses include Christchurch College of Education and the Dunedin College of Education.

Typical teacher education programs in New Zealand include those specializing in early childhood teacher education, primary teacher education, primary bilingual teacher education, secondary education, and catechetical study for students preparing to teach in religious primary and secondary schools. Students complete their program in either three or four years. The bachelor of teaching degree alone requires an average duration of three years in college. A bachelor of education studies and graduate diploma in education and teaching can be completed in four years. These periods include student teaching as well.

Informal Education

Informal education in New Zealand is appropriated in part for adults who change careers or who wish to engage in lifelong learning. Some programs focus on foundation learning, which introduces adults to basic-level curriculum that they need to learn or relearn for general life skills, literacy, or occupational training. Most important for many informal education settings in New Zealand is the acquisition of learning skills for life. These include both critical thinking skills that allow learners to analyze, question, or challenge various assumptions, and metacognitive skills that are needed in order for the learner to realize and monitor their own learning behaviors. Key areas of content development include literacy, numeracy (working with numbers, data, and measurement), spelling, writing, and oracy (speaking and pronunciation skills).

System Economics and Future Prospects

According to the United Nations Development Programme (2010), along with Jamaica and Fiji, public expenditures on education of New Zealand represented 6.2 percent of the gross domestic product (GDP) in 2007. Given the GDP of New Zealand at $119.2 billion, educational expenditure in the country amounts to over $7.39 billion, or $9,451 per student (total amount equivalent to US dollars divided by 782,000, the approximate number of primary- and secondary-age students in the country). New Zealand ranks 35 of 186 countries in percentage of educational expenditure.

At present New Zealand ranks among the highest-ranking countries of the world in terms of educational

New Zealand Education at a Glance	
General Information	
Capital	Wellington
Population	4.25 million
Languages	English, Maori, sign language
Literacy rate	99%
GDP per capita	US$26,200
People below poverty line	no data
Number of phones per 100 people	41
Number of Internet users per 100 people	72
Number of Internet hosts	2.47 million
Life expectancy at birth (years)	79
Formal Educational Information	
Primary school age population	345,000
Secondary school age population	437,000
Primary school age population	8%
Number of years of education (primary/secondary)	6/7
Student/teacher ratio (primary)	15
Student/teacher ratio (secondary)	16
Primary school gross enrollment ratio	102%
Primary school entrants completing primary school	100%
Secondary school gross enrollment ratio	121%
Child labor (ages 5–14)	no data

Note: Unless otherwise indicated, all data are based on sources from 2011.

access for its primary, secondary, and tertiary population. Although there has been some ethnic tension during the twentieth century, it has not overwhelmed the overall education system. Moreover, since the 1970s, the New Zealand government has dealt successfully with past injustices against the Maori people. In general, New Zealanders have developed an education system that is innovative and competitive in terms of teacher education method and the research and practice of the acquisition of knowledge. As stated above, New Zealand's early childhood education system is not only one of the most successful in the world, but unique in terms of its approaches to enhancing the education of young children. Early childhood education institutions in New Zealand emphasize the importance and even necessity of parental influence on children's educational growth, development, and future opportunities.

New Zealand education leaders are helping to narrow the gap in illiteracy so that more native New Zealanders, including the Maori, can succeed in school. In addition, they are attempting to improve the literacy rate as a whole through the promotion of informal education programs. In doing so, information and communication technologies have helped connect rural populations with the necessary resources for learning and competing with populations in urban centers. The New Zealand Ministry of Education has also emphasized the importance of e-learning. In short, e-learning does not necessarily refer to distance learning. Rather, e-learning is currently playing a major role in New Zealand tertiary institutions that are using advanced technologies for the purpose of increasing student knowledge of a variety of content areas. The goal is to provide students with greater opportunities for learning both in the classroom and in the workplace.

Daniel Ness and Chia-ling Lin

REFERENCES

Center for Economic and Social Rights. *Visualizing Rights: New Zealand, Fact Sheet No. 3*. New York: Center for Economic and Social Rights, 2010.

Central Intelligence Agency. *The CIA World Factbook*. New York: Skyhorse, 2011. https://www.cia.gov/library/publications/the-world-factbook/index.html.

Childinfo. Monitoring the Situation of Children and Women, 2012. www.childinfo.org/labour_countrydata.php.

Nation Master. 2011. www.nationmaster.com.

UNESCO. *Global Education Digest 2012: Comparing Education Statistics Across the World*. Montreal: UNESCO Institute for Statistics, 2012.

———. "Strong Foundations: Early Childhood Care and Education." *Education for All Global Monitoring Report*. Paris: UNESCO, 2006.

UNESCO–IBE. www.ibe.unesco.org/en/worldwide/unesco-regions/asia-and-the-pacific/new-zealand.html.

United Nations Development Programme. *Human Development Report 2011*. http://hdr.undp.org/en.

US Department of Labor. *2001 Findings on the Worst Forms of Child Labor*. Washington, DC: Bureau of International Labor Affairs, US Department of Labor, 2002.

World Bank Education Statistics. 2011. www.worldbank.org.

PAPUA NEW GUINEA

Papua New Guinea is a country that represents the eastern half of the island of New Guinea—the second-largest island in the world in area. The lingua franca of the country is Melanesian Pidgin, but English is spoken by a very small percentage of the population. The country's currency is the Papua New Guinean kina (PGK). The population of Papua New Guinea in 2011 was 6 million. Ethnic groups include Melanesian, Papuan, Negrito, Micronesian, and Polynesian populations.

In 1902 Australia occupied the British-controlled territory and eventually occupied the entire island of New Guinea in the close of World War I, when its forces seized the northern part of the Papuan section from German forces. Papua New Guinea gained independence from Australia on September 16, 1975. In 1988 the island of Bougainville attempted secession from the fledgling nation, but eventually lost to the Papua New Guinean government in 1997.

Educational System

Education in Papua New Guinea is not compulsory. Given the country's rather large indigenous populations, formal education in Papua New Guinea was administered primarily by colonial governments, most predominantly those of the United Kingdom, Australia, and, to some extent, Germany, particularly at the turn of the twentieth century. It is important to note, however, that formal education in Papua New Guinea during the early part of the twentieth century was barely noticeable and mostly consisted of religious missionary schools. These schools became more prevalent in the area during World War II and continued to grow until the 1970s—the decade of transition from colony to independent state. According to the Papua New Guinea Department of Education, the school system during the period shortly after independence consisted of 1,050 schools, over 9,000 teachers, and over 250,000 students. The department website indicates that in 2003, the number of schools more than quadrupled in number. There are approximately 3,300 primary schools, 170 secondary schools, and 140 vocational schools. Similarly, the number of teachers also nearly quadrupled. UNICEF data indicate a total of 1.7 million children and adolescents of school age. But the gross enrollment rate of primary school is only about 77 percent and the gross enrollment rate of secondary school is only about 26 percent. Of the nearly 1.8 million youth, only about half this population attends school. Church-run schools continue to maintain an important part of education in the country. According to the Department of Education, six nongovernmental church groups are governed by all 20 provinces of the country, and private autonomous schools are also growing in number. The central Papua New Guinean government has very limited responsibility for formal education. Nearly all formal education is decentralized and run by each of the 20 provinces in the country. Each province, then, is responsible for curriculum, fiduciary concerns, and the staffing of teachers and other personnel from preprimary education through the primary and secondary levels.

Definitions of educational school terms differ between the Papua New Guinea Department of Education usage and international usage. More specifically, the Papua New Guinea Education Department uses the term "elementary school" for grades 1 and 2 and "primary school" for grades 3 through 8. International terminology differs in that the term "elementary school" is used for the more generic term "primary education." Elementary school, which comprises grades 1 and 2, is instructed in the language of the community. Most often the language of instruction is Tok Pisin, Motu, or English, especially in large urban communities. Grades 1 and 2 are called "preparatory" grade levels for the primary grade levels. The language of instruction in primary grades also depends on the community of the school. Secondary school is comprised of a lower secondary level, grades 9 and 10, and an upper secondary level, grades 11 and 12. Students who succeed at the upper level often prepare for the university or another form of tertiary education. It should be emphasized, however, that few Papua New Guineans attend tertiary-level schooling.

The curriculum in the early grades consists mainly of language, particularly the language of the community, cultural mathematics, and culture and community. Cultural mathematics is an interesting notion that considers how mathematics is used in everyday life. More remarkable is an emphasis on spatial relations and measurement rather than number concepts. This may be due to the overwhelmingly rural and agrarian population and economy in the country and the need for individuals to estimate quantity in terms of space and size of a given area of land.

Curriculum content in the lower primary grades includes language learning, arts, mathematics, environmental studies, health, physical education, and community living. Content in the upper primary grades continues the curriculum of the lower grades and also includes content in science, social science,

"making a living," and personal development. Secondary school curriculum includes courses in English, "design and technology," business studies, and agriculture.

The Papua New Guinea Office of Higher Education controls the country's higher education system, which consists of six universities. The University of Papua New Guinea is the oldest and largest tertiary institution in the country. The university enrolls approximately 15,000 students annually in its several campuses and numerous study centers throughout the country. Teacher education is conducted primarily by Catholic teachers colleges in urban areas. The Papua New Guinea Department of Education sanctions these teachers colleges as the principal institutions in the country for teacher training. Other sources of teacher education include teachers colleges in Australia, New Zealand, and other countries in Asia, Europe, and North America.

System Economics and Future Prospects

It is difficult to determine educational expenditure in Papua New Guinea because education is completely decentralized. The United Nations Development Programme (2010) does suggest, however, that total public expenditure on education of the country represented 2.3 percent of the gross domestic product (GDP) in 2008. Given the GDP of Papua New Guinea at $14.93 billion, educational expenditure in the country amounts to nearly $344 million, about $194 per student (total amount equivalent to US dollars divided by 1,773,000, the approximate number of youth of primary and secondary age in the country).

The Papua New Guinean government must invest its resources in improving the extremely low literacy rate, which is presently 57 percent, with a disparity of more than 10 percent between males and females. Informal education programs can reduce the illiteracy rate among adults. Moreover, families must be committed to move beyond a solely agricultural society to an information-based system. School attendance is moderate at the primary level, but then drops precipitously thereafter, and teachers within the system are often ill-equipped to handle large class sizes. Many schools in the country lack adequate facilities and resources. Unfortunately, efforts in decentralization

Papua New Guinea Education at a Glance

General Information

Capital	Port Moresby
Population	6 million
Languages	Melanesian Pidgin, English, Motu
Literacy rate	57%
GDP per capita	US$2,700
People below poverty line	37%
Number of phones per 100 people	1
Number of Internet users per 100 people	2
Number of Internet hosts	4,285
Life expectancy at birth (years)	66

Formal Educational Information

Primary school age population	965,000
Secondary school age population	808,000
Primary school age population	16%
Number of years of education (primary/secondary)	6/6
Student/teacher ratio (primary)	36
Student/teacher ratio (secondary)	23
Primary school gross enrollment ratio	76.5%
Primary school entrants reaching grade 5	68%
Secondary school gross enrollment ratio	25.5%
Child labor (ages 5–14)	no data

Note: Unless otherwise indicated, all data are based on sources from 2011.

of schooling that seem to have given less authority to a centralized government and more to the provinces do not seem to pay off in the long run in terms of school enrollment, especially in the late primary and secondary years. Families in Papua New Guinea are unable to afford the fees that are associated with a child's education. At the same time, the Papua New Guinea government intends to reform the education system to meet present-day standards. The primary goal at the present time is to make information and communication technology more comprehensive by allowing such technologies to be shared with schools as well as institutions of higher education.

Daniel Ness and Chia-ling Lin

REFERENCES

Center for Economic and Social Rights. *Visualizing Rights: Papua Fact Sheet No. 3*. New York: Center for Economic and Social Rights, 2010.

Central Intelligence Agency. *The CIA World Factbook*. New York: Skyhorse, 2011. https://www.cia.gov/library/publications/the-world-factbook/index.html.

Nation Master. 2011. www.nationmaster.com.

Papua New Guinea Department of Education. *History: Papua New Guinea Educational System*. www.education.gov.pg.

UNESCO. *Global Education Digest 2012: Comparing Education Statistics Across the World*. Montreal: UNESCO Institute for Statistics, 2012.

———. "Strong Foundations: Early Childhood Care and Education." *Education for All Global Monitoring Report*. Paris: UNESCO, 2006.

UNESCO–IBE. www.ibe.unesco.org/en/worldwide/unesco-regions/asia-and-the-pacific/papua-new-guinea.html.

United Nations Development Programme. *Human Development Report 2011*. http://hdr.undp.org/en.

US Department of Labor. *2001 Findings on the Worst Forms of Child Labor*. Washington, DC: Bureau of International Labor Affairs, US Department of Labor, 2002.

World Bank Education Statistics. 2011. www.worldbank.org.

EUROPE

INTRODUCTION

The present section discusses the educational systems of 37 countries in Europe. The aggregate net primary school enrollment ratio for these countries is close to 98 percent, which is rather high for world standards. The aggregate net secondary school enrollment ratio is over 90 percent, which again is considerably high when compared to other areas of the world.

Like the United States, most countries in Europe, especially in western and northern Europe, enjoy high standards of living. Moreover, they have better access to improved sanitation, low rates of fertility and natural population increase, more motor vehicles, and greater access to phones, computers, and the Internet than do countries in Africa, most of Asia, and Latin America. Disease outbreaks in Europe are not as frequent as they are in impoverished regions of the world. Also the literacy rates of the overwhelming majority of countries in Europe are close to 100 percent, and the number of years of education per student exceeds 14 years—higher than the number of years in most other regions. However, there are exceptions to these data. For example, primary and secondary attendance is at times below 90 percent in Portugal and some of the former Yugoslavian countries. Although percentages are low, UNICEF data suggest that children between the ages of five and 14 are engaged in various forms of labor in these countries.

Most European countries are generally monolithic in terms of structure, content and curriculum, and overall per student spending. However, there are differences as well as socioeconomic and cultural disparities. For example, northern, western, and some southern European countries tend to have very high per student educational expenditures. Although eastern and southern European countries do not have as high educational expenditures per student as other regions of the continent, education spending in these countries is higher than that of most countries throughout the world. In addition, most European countries must attend to problems of educational equity, especially as it pertains to minority and immigrant populations. For example, Roma communities are subject to much prejudice in many central and eastern European countries, so much so that it adversely affects the educational outcomes of children and adolescents of Roma families. Also, due to the vacillating and unstable economies in a number of European countries, education on the continent is also subject to possible systemic transition. It is difficult to know, however, the types of changes that might occur.

Daniel Ness and Chia-ling Lin

ALBANIA

The Republic of Albania is located in southeastern Europe on the Adriatic and Ionian Seas. The official language is Albanian, although Greek, Vlach, Romani, and various Slavic dialects are also used. The United Nations population estimate for 2010 was 2.98 million. The population is mainly Albanian (95 percent) with some Greek and Macedonian populations. The *CIA World Factbook* places the percentage of the population practicing Islam at 70 percent; 20 percent of the people is Greek Orthodox, nearly 10 percent is Catholic, and less than 1 percent is Hindu. Albania was established in 1990, after having been under communist rule for 46 years. The country is grappling with widespread corruption, a poor infrastructure, and a high unemployment rate; nearly 25 percent of the population lives on subsistence farming below the international poverty line. Albania's gross domestic product (GDP) was about $24.5 billion (current US$) in 2011. The services economic sector represented 27 percent of GDP, industry 15 percent, and agriculture 50 percent. Although Albania's economy shows signs of improvement, it still is one of the poorest in Europe.

Educational System

An understanding of education in Albania can be attained only in the context of communist control. The communist regime considered the act of eradicating illiteracy as a high priority for all areas under its control. Education was centralized in terms of Soviet government control, textbooks, and ideology. By the 1960s a four-year primary education followed by a seven-year secondary education with general, vocational, trade, and teacher training tracks progressed into 11-year units with specific areas of specialization. Eventually the first four years of primary education were combined with the ensuing intermediate years so that compulsory education lasted eight years. High school, which lasted four years, consisted of professional (e.g., agriculture, industry, law, pedagogy, health) and vocational tracks. Tuition for tertiary education was free. Study of or interest in traditional liberal arts subjects was downplayed in nearly all Soviet bloc countries due to the association with so-called bourgeois or elitist values.

After the collapse of the Soviet Union, the schooling infrastructure in Albania became dilapidated. Vandalism was rampant and schools lacked essential supplies. With the aid of nearby countries, the Education Ministry attempted to repair the infrastructure. Rural schools suffered the worst losses; nearly 800 of the country's primary and secondary schools were dysfunctional and many of these were demolished. As a result, teachers relocated to urban areas. Accordingly, urban schools swelled in population, and, to this day, overcrowding remains a dire issue in Albanian education. Schools have altered their Soviet six-day model and shortened the school week to five days. The traditional primary school subjects—language,

mathematics, the natural and life sciences, history—have replaced the Soviet model.

Administration

Educational policy and provision are under the auspices of the Albanian government and the Parliament. Together they are responsible for passing laws regarding educational issues. Although Parliament is the highest authority, the Ministry of Education and Science handles most problems and concerns in education before they are legislated in Parliament. The Ministry of Education and Science is responsible for the implementation of laws that are passed by the Parliament. Also it presides over legal issues regarding management of school supervision. School curricula are initially approved by the ministry. Finally, the ministry is in charge of approving infrastructure improvement and educational finance.

Precompulsory and Compulsory Education

Education is compulsory for all Albanian children between six and 13 years old. Compulsory education is free. The education system comprises three levels: preschool, primary education, and secondary education. Preschool and Kindergarten, which is not compulsory, lasts for three years, serving children who enter at age three and exit at age five. In general, preschool is funded by the government. Primary education, which is compulsory, is for children entering at age six and exiting at age nine (grades 1 through 4), thereby lasting for four years. It is often referred to as the Basic First Stage. It prepares students for secondary education. At this initial level of general formal education, students acquire the necessary knowledge, skills, and competencies. Students who successfully complete their basic education advance to the so-called Basic Second Stage, which comprises grades 5 through 8, for children from 10 through 13 or 14 years old.

Secondary education is partially compulsory. The first half of secondary schooling lasts from approximately age 10 to age 13. The last four years of secondary education, ages 14 through 17, is not compulsory. Children who satisfactorily complete grade 4 enter secondary school at age 10 and remain until age 13. They may continue if their academic performance is sufficient for the second half of secondary school education. As in nearly all countries, higher education is not compulsory. Approximately 19.3 percent of students graduating from secondary schools proceed to college or the university. There are eight universities, two academies, and six private higher schools in Albania.

Postcompulsory Education

Secondary education, which is not compulsory, is for children entering at age 14 and graduating at age 17 or 18. It lasts for four years, covering grades 9 through 12. There are technical, agricultural, and vocational secondary schools, as well as the traditional liberal arts model secondary schools that prepare college- or university-bound students. In general, students receive an education that attempts to prepare them for college or entry into the labor market.

There are eight universities and three so-called higher schools that form the backbone of the tertiary system in Albania. The University of Tirana is an institution of higher education in the traditional liberal arts sense. The Polytechnic University accommodates students with a strong science and mathematics background. In addition, the Agricultural University, the High Institute of Physical Training, and the High Academy of Arts are institutions that specialize in specific professions.

Curriculum, Assessment, and Instruction

Preschool education in Albania aims to develop children's social and early intellectual abilities, developing their ability to discover and to create, and prepares them for school education.

As mentioned, compulsory education in Albania is divided into two parts: grades 1 through 4 and 5 through 8. Compulsory subjects in the first four grades include the Albanian language, literature, some history, natural science, mathematics, civics, and, to a lesser extent, art, music, technical education, and physical education. Compulsory subjects in the second set of four grades include essentially all these subjects and also one year of chemistry, three years of physical science and biology, a foreign language, history, and geography.

Secondary education is in the form of comprehen-sive school (the most common), vocational school, sport school, and art school. Students are tracked for the most part into their area of interest. In grades 9 through 12, students hone their skills in particular areas of interest, ranging from vocational skills to science, technology, or art. Students also develop their intellectual abilities, appropriate ethical dispositions, and interpersonal skills. In general, the curriculum of the comprehensive school is similar to that of the primary school. In comprehensive schools, however, students have the option of taking elective courses that may enhance their programs of study.

Higher education institutions offer two- to six-year programs leading to diplomas, as well as bachelor's and master's degrees. A number of universities offer two-year programs leading to a diploma in specializations, such as electronics, information technology, pharmacy, and dentistry. Programs of study leading to a bachelor's degree normally take four years, while engineering takes five years, and medicine six years. Two years of study beyond the bachelor's degree leads to a master's degree, whereas for engineering it is one year beyond the five-year bachelor's degree. Among the universities are Sanaa University, Aden University, and Taez University.

Teacher Education

All universities in Albania provide education for preservice teachers. However, university education programs differ in terms of the number of teaching hours allocated toward pedagogical, psychology, and methodology courses, in addition to subject matter courses of specialization. Nearly all education programs in Albanian universities include pedagogy and psychology in their curricula. Preservice teacher candidates spend on average three years in college preparation and in student teaching. Student teaching hours depend heavily on the subject of specialization.

Informal Education

Informal education is provided primarily for adults who either were not exposed to formal education or for those whose formal education occurred on the cusp of change from Soviet control to autonomous control (1980s through 1990s). It provides education in basic knowledge in reading, writing, and

Albania Education at a Glance

General Information

Capital	Tirana
Population	3.6 million
Languages	Albanian, Greek
Literacy rate	99%
GDP per capita	US$3,837
People below poverty line (2004)	25%
Number of phones per 100 people	7
Number of Internet users per 100 people	2
Number of Internet hosts	430
Life expectancy at birth (years)	78

Formal Educational Information

Primary school age population	217,000
Primary school age population	6%
Number of years of primary education (since 2008)	9
Student/teacher ratio	20
Primary school gross enrollment ratio	99%
Primary school entrants reaching grade 5	no data
Secondary school gross enrollment ratio	88%
Child labor (ages 5–14)	12%

Note: Unless otherwise indicated, all data are based on sources from 2011.

arithmetic. Informal education includes courses for particular vocations (e.g., secretarial work, cosmetics, fashion designing) and schools emphasizing foreign language instruction. Informal education programs are regulated by the Ministry of Labor if they run for six months or less; programs that run for more than six months are under the jurisdiction of the Ministry of Education and Science.

System Economics

The total public expenditure on education in 2009 represented 2.9 percent of Albania's gross domestic product. Along with Mauritania and Uruguay, Albania ranks 57 in education expenditures in percentage of GDP.

Future Prospects

Plans are under way to grapple with the numerous challenges that the country currently faces. Perhaps the most egregious challenge is the high rate of corruption in the government and those involved in the education system. Another challenge concerns the essential educational infrastructure that has been vandalized and pillaged since 1990, after the dissolv-

ing of the Soviet Union. Albanian education officials also must grapple with the large influx of students and teachers to urban schools, where resources are often scarce. One of the most disturbing problems, however, is the alienation of minority communities, particularly children of Roma families. In many eastern European countries, including Albania, the Roma are often targets of bias. This results in a perpetual cycle of stereotyping, which ultimately prevents Roma citizens from enjoying upward social mobility. Laws need to address issues of prejudice in Albanian society. Lastly, curricula and education need to place emphasis on the needs of everyday Albanians as a means of lowering poverty and increasing employment opportunities and the quality of life. Education curriculum needs to place greater emphasis on environmental improvement, clean energy, and health. For this to happen, mathematics, science, and social science curricula are essential.

Daniel Ness and Chia-ling Lin

REFERENCES

Central Intelligence Agency. *The CIA World Factbook.* New York: Skyhorse, 2011. https://www.cia.gov/library/publications/the-world-factbook/index.html.

GED. *Global Education Digest 2012: Comparing Education Statistics Across the World.* Montreal: UNESCO Institute for Statistics, 2012.

Musai, Bardhyl, et al. "National Report: Albania." In *The Prospects of Teacher Education in South East Europe,* ed. P. Zgaga. Ljubljana, Slovenia: South East European Educational Cooperation Network (SEE-ECN), Center for Educational Policy Studies, University of Ljubljana, 2006.

Nation Master. 2011. www.nationmaster.com.

UNESCO–IBE. www.ibe.unesco.org/countries/albania.htm.

UNESCO–UIS. www.uis.unesco.org.

UNICEF. www.unicef.org/infobycountry.

World Bank Education Statistics. 2011. www.worldbank.org.

ANDORRA

Andorra is a landlocked postage stamp country that is bordered to the north by France and to the south by Spain. The country has a population of 84,825 people, most of whom are Spanish (43 percent) and Andorran (33 percent). The remaining populations are mostly Portuguese and French. Most people are members of the Roman Catholic Church. Languages include French, Castilian Spanish, and Catalan.

Andorra was a monarchical principality for more than 700 years. In 1993 the system of government was modified to include a parliamentary democracy. The country's gross domestic product (GDP) is $3.3 billion. The country's natural resources include mineral water, timber, iron, lead, and hydropower.

Educational System

Schooling for Andorran children and adolescents is compulsory between the ages of six and 16—a period of 10 years. Andorra is a culturally and linguistically diverse country given its small size. Accordingly, there are French schools, Spanish schools, and Andorran schools. French schooling in Andorra is subsidized by the French government. The Spanish schools are funded primarily by the Catholic Church. The Andorran schools follow a similar curriculum as the Spanish, church-funded schools.

There is only one university in the country—the University of Andorra, which was established in 1997. Annual enrollment for the university is approximately 2,000 students. The university has competitive departments in the areas of nursing and health sciences,

as well as computer science and management. The University of Andorra has a distance education program as well that serves students on the country's periphery. It is important to note, however, that Andorra has reciprocity agreements with both Spain and France. Students attending Spanish or Andorran schools have the opportunity to apply to and enroll in universities in Spain and those attending French schools can apply to and enroll in universities in France.

System Economics and Future Prospects

The country ranks 122 out of 186 countries in terms of education expenditures as part of the national GDP. Approximately 3.2 percent of the country's GDP is allocated for educational purposes. This would amount to the equivalent of nearly $109 million, or a per capita educational expenditure of $12,100 for about 9,000 children and adolescents of compulsory age.

As a small country, Andorra has been successful in providing educational opportunities for young people. However, not all primary and secondary school-age children and adolescents attend school, despite compulsory education laws. Based on net enrollment ratio figures, primary school enrollment from 2005 to 2010, for example, was 80 percent, and figures for secondary school showed a net enrollment ratio of only 76 percent. Student/teacher ratios for primary and secondary school were approximately 14 students and 12 students for every teacher, respectively.

Roseanne Macias

REFERENCES

Central Intelligence Agency. *The CIA World Factbook*. New York: Skyhorse, 2011. https://www.cia.gov/library/publications/the-world-factbook/index.html.

Nation Master. 2011. www.nationmaster.com.

Organisation for Economic Co-operation and Development (OECD). http://stats.oecd.org.

UNESCO–IBE. www.ibe.unesco.org/en/worldwide/unesco-regions/europe-and-north-america/andorra.html.

UNESCO–UIS. www.uis.unesco.org.

UNICEF. www.unicef.org/infobycountry.

World Bank Education Statistics. 2011. www.worldbank.org.

Andorra Education at a Glance

General Information

Capital	Andorra la Vella
Population	84,825
Languages	Catalan, French, Castilian
Literacy rate	100%
GDP per capita	US$38,800
People below poverty line	no data
Number of phones per 100 people	49
Number of Internet users per 100 people	31
Number of Internet hosts	14,944
Life expectancy at birth (years)	84

Formal Educational Information

Primary school age population	5,000
Primary school age population	7%
Number of years of primary education	6
Student/teacher ratio	10
Primary school gross enrollment ratio	90%
Primary school entrants reaching grade 5	95%
Secondary school gross enrollment ratio	80%
Child labor (ages 5–14)	no data

Note: Unless otherwise indicated, all data are based on sources from 2011.

Austria

The Republic of Austria is a country in central Europe. The official language is German (nearly 89 percent), although Turkish, Serbian, Croatian, Slovene, and Hungarian are also spoken. The United Nations population estimate for 2012 was 8.2 million. The population is mainly Austrian (91 percent). Other populations include Yugoslavs, Germans, and Turks. The religion is predominantly Roman Catholic (73 percent). The remaining population consists of Protestants (5 percent), Muslims (4 percent) and others, 12 percent of whom are classified as of no religion. Austria was established in 976 CE as the Margravate of Austria. In 1156 it became the Duchy of Austria, serving as the south-central part of the Holy Roman Empire. The Austrian Empire emerged in 1804, during the Napoleonic Wars, and later became the Austro-Hungarian Empire in 1867. After World War I, Austria was proclaimed a republic in 1918 and remained so for 20 years, before the Nazi regime annexed it in 1938. This takeover was short-lived, as Austria reverted back into a republic toward the end of World War II. Austria was to remain neutral during the Cold War and its government was forbidden to reunite with Germany. Austria entered the European Union (EU) in 1995.

Educational System

Austria has a long, colorful history of education. The first school in Austria, Stiftsgymnasium Melk, located in Melk, a town in Lower Austria, began as a monastic school shortly after 1100. It is the oldest continually running school in Austria that is still in operation. It was not, however, until the end of World War II and, more specifically, after the School Organization Act of July 25, 1962, that education became a right for all Austrian citizens. Section 4 of the School Organization Act states that "every school shall be common to all, without discrimination as to birth, gender, race, social background, class, language, or religion."

The educational system of Austria is similar to that of most of the German-speaking nations of Europe in that the country has implemented a tracking system beyond the primary school level. Preprimary education exists prior to grade 1 (or before six years of age). After this point, children enter either primary schools or, in some instances, special schools, depending on their educational issues or disabilities. Primary school is for students in grades 1 through 4 (ages six or seven through 10).

There are four categories of schools within grades 5 through 8. First, students enrolled in primary special schools continue in special schools in the middle grades. Next, there is a primary school upper bracket, which consists of students in the middle grades who are continuing in a second level of primary school. The majority of students, however, enter the general secondary school. The second largest group enters the academic secondary school in grade 5. Upon completion of grade 8, academic secondary school students have the opportunity, if academically qualified, to continue to grade 12. Students who do not continue in this path can select from the following schools, if qualified, commencing in grade 9: upper-level secondary school, which is simply a continuation of the general secondary school; higher-level technical and vocational colleges (again, beginning in grade 9); training colleges for kindergarten teachers and social workers; medium-level secondary technical and vocational colleges; and finally, polytechnic school, which is followed by a dual apprenticeship program with a compulsory vocational school program. Compulsory education lasts from grade 1 to the completion of grade 9. Approximately 90 percent of all schools in Austria are public schools. Most private schools are run by the Catholic Church. It is prohibited for any public school to charge tuition.

Precompulsory Education, Compulsory Education, and Curriculum

Parents in Austria have the option of sending their children between the ages of three and six to kindergarten—an educational level that is not compulsory. By age six children must enter grade 1. Primary school, or *Grundschule*, lasts for four years until students complete grade 4. As mentioned, students who have special needs often enroll in specialized schools that focus on specific disabilities. Kindergarten children receive an education that is based primarily on the socialization of the individual and personal development. Kindergarten education also focuses on speech development and sensory and motor development. Little, if any curriculum, at this level focuses on academic subjects. The Austrian kindergarten, similar to those of neighboring German-speaking countries, infuses music and art instructional activities into its curriculum. Subjects taken in all four years of primary education include the following: religion, local history, geography, biology, German language, mathematics, music, art and drawing, technical work, use of textiles, and physical education. In addition, students practice a modern foreign language and take road safety instruction. There is also one hour per week available for remediation for those who need it.

The secondary school that usually enrolls the greatest number of students is the general secondary school, or *Hauptschule*, which lasts from grades 5 through 8. Students in the *Hauptschule* continue their general education for the first two years. This is followed in grades 7 and 8 with a preparation for careers and work. This is because most students in the *Hauptschule* often continue for vocational education. Students in the *Hauptschule* who possess strong academic skills may have the opportunity to transfer to the academic secondary school. Other options include medium-level and higher-level vocational or technical colleges. The academic secondary school consists of a four-year lower level (ages 10 to 14) and a four-year upper level (ages 14 to 18). The first two years of the first level of academic secondary school consist of a continuation of academic study. The third and fourth years consist of three branches: the *Gymnasium, Realgymnasium,* and *Wirtschaftskundliches Realgymnasium*. The traditional *Gymnasium* emphasizes languages, arts, and humanities. The *Realgymnasium* is structured on the disciplines of mathematics and science. The *Wirtschaftskundliches Realgymnasium* maintains a rigorous scientific agenda, emphasizing the fields of chemistry, biology, physics, psychology, and several other disciplines. In the final four years of the academic secondary school, some students have the opportunity to enroll in the *Oberstufenrealgymnasium*, or upper-level *Gymnasium*, which is simply a continuation of one or more of the fields of study mentioned above. The academic secondary school culminates with a mandatory matriculation examination for graduation consideration.

It is useful to compare the curricula of the general secondary school with the academic secondary school. General secondary school subjects include the following: religion, German, a modern foreign language (usually English), history and social studies, geography and economics, mathematics, biology and environmental science, chemistry, physics, music, arts, technical work, nutrition and home economics, and physical education. In contrast, the academic secondary school includes the study of Latin, philosophy, and psychology and generally emphasizes the humanities, mathematics, and the natural sciences.

Postcompulsory Education

Postcompulsory education in Austria begins at different times for different students because it depends on the educational track. Higher education in Austria is divided into four categories. One category is the postsecondary training institution, which trains individuals who wish to enter medical, agricultural, military, or technical professions. These institutions are often colleges offering two-year programs. A second category is teacher training colleges, or *Pädagogischen Hochschulen*, which generally provide programs lasting three years. Within this category are public and private universities that may include teacher training programs. A third category consists of traditional public and private colleges and universities. Finally, there are the universities of applied sciences.

There are nearly 60 universities or other higher education institutions in Austria. These institutions are divided into three categories: federal universities (*Universitäten*), private universities (*Privateuniversitäten*), and universities of applied science (*Fachhochschulen*). Over 20 universities are federal institutions, the most famous of which are the University of Vienna, Academy of Fine Arts in Vienna, University of Music and Performing Arts (Vienna), University of Graz, University of Innsbruck, University of Salzburg, and the Mozarteum University of Salzburg. The Austrian government instituted fees for federal universities in 2001. In 2008 the government decided to retract the fees for Austrian citizens.

Teacher Education

The teacher education system in Austria is partially constructed of an offshoot of the general secondary school in that one track consists of training colleges for kindergarten teachers and social workers. Programs in these training colleges last for five years, upon which students graduate after taking a diploma examination. In addition, as mentioned above, pedagogical institutions are available at federal and private universities or as separate entities. Students who wish to become teachers in the primary or secondary schools enroll in teacher training programs that last for about three years. Secondary education programs consist of courses that are aligned with each student's area of teaching interest (language, mathematics, physics, chemistry, etc.). These students must complete an exit examination prior to student teaching.

Informal Education

Informal education in Austria is often for adults who wish to continue their education. The Federal Ministry of Education sponsors both academic and vocational courses. Nonprofit organizations also play a major role in funding informal adult education in Austria. Adult education is usually defined as education for an individual who is 20 years or older. Institutions that provide adult education include colleges of further education, vocational colleges, and religious denominational organizations, as well as several other regional nonprofit adult education institutions. One major agenda of adult education in Austria is to provide adult learners with additional qualifications by attending classes. This is often for the purpose of improving workforce skills. Funding for adult education in Austria comes from a variety of sources: federal funding, provincial and municipal resources (such as chambers of commerce and labor and trade unions), occupational associations, and church organizations.

System Economics

Along with Ghana and South Africa, Austria ranks at 33 in educational expenditures as a percentage of gross domestic product (GDP). The total public expenditure on education in 2009 represented 5.4 percent of gross domestic product. About US$15.34 billion has been allocated in 2009 for education purposes.

Future Prospects

As part of the European Union since 1995, Austria plays a major role as a competitor in education and an important agent in the global economy. Along with other members of the EU, Austria maintains a strong lead in student test scores and continues to graduate students who excel in individualized areas of expertise. Austrian education excels in the areas of the humanities, mathematics, and natural and social sciences. Further, Austrian education has helped advance technological innovations as well as global communications.

Daniel Ness and Chia-ling Lin

REFERENCES

Central Intelligence Agency. *The CIA World Factbook*. New York: Skyhorse, 2011. https://www.cia.gov/library/publications/the-world-factbook/index.html.

GED. *Global Education Digest 2012: Comparing Education Statistics Across the World*. Montreal: UNESCO Institute for Statistics, 2012.

Nation Master. 2011. www.nationmaster.com.

UNESCO–IBE. www.ibe.unesco.org/countries/austria.htm.

UNESCO–UIS. www.uis.unesco.org.

UNICEF. www.unicef.org/infobycountry.

World Bank Education Statistics. 2011. www.worldbank.org.

Austria Education at a Glance

General Information

Capital	Vienna
Population	8.2 million
Language	German
Literacy rate	98%
GDP per capita	US$34,600
People below poverty line (2004)	6%
Number of phones per 100 people	45
Number of Internet users per 100 people	57
Number of Internet hosts	2 million
Life expectancy at birth (years)	79

Formal Educational Information

Primary school age population	350,000
Secondary school age population	768,000
Primary school age population	4%
Number of years of primary education	6
Student/teacher ratio (primary)	12
Student/teacher ratio (secondary)	11
Primary school gross enrollment ratio	102%
Primary school entrants reaching last primary grade	99%
Secondary school gross enrollment ratio	102%
Child labor (ages 5–14)	no data

Note: Unless otherwise indicated, all data are based on sources from 2011.

BELGIUM

The Kingdom of Belgium is located in northwestern Europe with coastline on the North Sea. The official languages are Dutch (60 percent), French (39 percent), and German (less than 1 percent). The literacy rate is 100 percent in the 2011 United Nations estimate. Schools are conducted bilingually in both French and Dutch.

The population of Belgium consists of mainly Fleming (58 percent) and Walloon (31 percent) peoples. The remaining 11 percent of the population includes populations from southern and western regions of Europe. The religion is predominantly Roman Catholic (75 percent). The remaining population consists of Protestants, Jews, and Muslims. Although occupied by Germany during the two world wars, Belgium has become a technologically advanced nation since the 1950s and a world leader in the service economy.

Educational System and Curriculum

Belgium has a 100 percent literacy rate (individuals 15 or older who can read and write). The structure of the education system is as follows. The overwhelming majority (over 90 percent) of children from two and a half to six years old attend preschool. The primary level is a six-year period of schooling from ages 6 through 12. The secondary level is also a period of six years for students 12 to 18 years. Upon graduation from secondary school, students either enter the job market or continue their education either at a university or another kind of tertiary-level institution.

Preprimary Education

Preschool is common in Belgium. It is free for all children who are two and a half or older and is run in one of three languages—Dutch, French, or German. The curriculum of most Belgian preschools consists of informal content intended to develop children's cognitive skills. Most preschools in Belgium are housed with primary schools so as to provide easy transition.

Primary Education

There are approximately 718,000 children of primary school age in Belgium. Nearly all of them attend primary school for six years. The student/teacher ratio for primary school in Belgium is approximately eleven students for every teacher. The primary school gross enrollment ratio is slightly over 100 percent, which seems to indicate that the potential number of individuals eligible to attend primary school includes students outside the typical age range. The net enrollment ratio for primary school in Belgium is about 98 percent. The basic curriculum, depending on location, includes language skills and mathematics in the morning school hours and natural science, citizenship, and music and arts during the afternoon.

Secondary Education

In general, secondary schools in Belgium are categorized in four ways: Algemeen Secundair Onderwijs (ASO: general secondary education), Technisch Secundair Onderwijs (TSO: technical secondary education), Beroepssecundair Onderwijs (BSO: vocational secondary education), and Kunstsecundair Onderwijs (KSO: art secondary education). Students who are accepted to the ASO secondary school, the most academic and broad of the four secondary types, typically prepare for the university upon graduation. Unlike the TSO or BSO, ASO students are expected to attend a university or college and are therefore frequently turned away from entering the workforce upon graduation. The ASO curriculum consists primarily of classical studies (Greek and Latin), modern languages, mathematics, natural sciences, social sciences, and the humanities. TSO students also prepare for tertiary education, but the institutions they attend are polytechnic institutes and colleges. Graduates from the TSO strand include engineers, managers, information and communication technology specialists, health professionals, and educators. Curriculum in TSO schools includes mathematics, history, physics, chemistry, earth science, environmental science, and other social sciences. Most students are eligible for the job market upon graduation, but the majority of these students continue in higher education. BSO students are the only secondary students who do not pursue higher education upon graduation. About 30 percent of all Belgian secondary students fall into this category. Graduates often pursue trade professions, such as carpentry, motor vehicle mechanics, masonry, plumbing, and the like. Although higher education is not needed in these fields, BSO students may pursue an optional seventh year of education that may make them eligible for college entrance. KSO students study general education along with their areas of expertise in one of the arts. The arts curriculum includes dancing (such as ballet), musical performance, fine arts (i.e., painting and sculpture), and acting. KSO graduates attend conservatories for music or ballet, acting schools, or schools of visual arts.

There are approximately 749,000 children and adolescents of secondary school age in Belgium. Nearly all of them attend the six years of secondary school. The student/teacher ratio for secondary school in Belgium is about 10 students for every teacher. The secondary school gross enrollment ratio is about 109 percent—again, an indication that the potential number of individuals eligible to attend secondary school includes students outside the typical age range for secondary school enrollment. The net enrollment ratio for secondary school in Belgium is about 97 percent. So the actual number of adolescents attending secondary school is lower than 100 percent.

Tertiary Education

In total there are at least 90 institutions of higher education in Belgium. Approximately 15 of these institutions are universities—six in Dutch Flemish-speaking provinces and eight in French-speaking provinces. Notable Flemish universities include the University of Antwerp and the University of Ghent. Notable French Belgian universities include the University of Liège, the University of Mons, and the Catholic universities of Leuven and Louvain. The 75 remaining institutions of higher education in Belgium include colleges of the arts, conservatories of music, university colleges, technological institutes, *hogeschools* (tertiary institutions with designated areas of specialization), and pedagogical institutes. Prior to their split the University of Leuven and University of Louvain were originally part of the Catholic University of Leuven, which, founded in 1425, is the only ancient university system in Belgium.

Teacher Education

Belgian students who wish to become teachers and have appropriate secondary school training may be eligible to enter the teacher training program offered at one of the several pedagogical institutions

of higher education in the country. Teacher education programs include early childhood education, primary education, and secondary education—depending on the subject. There is also a program in special needs education. All teacher education students must earn a baccalaureate. Teachers who plan to teach at the secondary school level must earn a master's degree.

Informal Education

Informal education in Belgium is often for adults who wish to continue their education. This type of education emphasizes both the importance of experience and the need for many adults to change careers by learning new vocations. Nonprofit organizations have contributed funding toward informal adult education in Belgium. Adult education is usually defined as education for an individual who is 18 years or older and wishes to gain skills initially as an apprentice. Institutions that provide adult education include vocational institutes, religious denominational organizations, and several other regional nonprofit adult education venues. Funding for adult education in Luxembourg comes from a variety of sources: federal funding, provincial and municipal resources (such as chambers of commerce and labor and trade unions), occupational associations, and church organizations.

System Economics

Belgium ranks 29 of 186 countries in terms of educational spending. The total public expenditure on education in 2007 represented 6.01 percent of gross domestic product. About US$23.74 billion has been allocated for education purposes. Based on these figures, total per student spending is approximately $16,182 (determined by dividing total expenditure by the approximate number of students (1,467,000) in Belgium).

Future Prospects

As one of the founding countries of the European Union, Belgium has become one of the leading technologically advanced countries in the world. This success has had a great deal to do with its generally competitive educational system. Along with other members of the EU, Belgium maintains a strong lead in student test scores and continues to graduate

Belgium Education at a Glance	
General Information	
Capital	Brussels
Population	10.39 million
Languages	Dutch (60%), French (40%)
Literacy rate	99%
GDP per capita	US$33,000
People below poverty line (2004)	4%
Number of phones per 100 people	46
Number of Internet users per 100 people	49
Number of Internet hosts	2.87 million
Life expectancy at birth (years)	79
Formal Educational Information	
Primary school age population	718,000
Secondary school age population	749,000
Primary school age population	7%
Number of years of primary education	6
Student/teacher ratio (primary)	11
Student/teacher ratio (secondary)	10
Primary school gross enrollment ratio	102%
Primary school entrants reaching grade 5	91%
Secondary school gross enrollment ratio	10%
Child labor (ages 5–14)	no data

Note: Unless otherwise indicated, all data are based on sources from 2011.

students who excel in their prospective areas of specialization. Belgian students have generally excelled in the areas of the humanities, mathematics, and natural and social sciences. In addition, the Belgian government has been fairly instrumental in providing assistance to countries that have had notoriously poor technological success. However, social factors remain a problem in Belgium. The Fleming and Walloon majorities tend to outperform ethnic minorities. It would seem that more emphasis on improving these social factors would improve the livelihood of all Belgian students.

Daniel Ness and Chia-ling Lin

REFERENCES

Central Intelligence Agency. *The CIA World Factbook.* New York: Skyhorse, 2011. https://www.cia.gov/library/publications/the-world-factbook/index.html.

Empirica. *Benchmarking Access and Use of ICT in European Schools 2012.* European Commission Staff Working Document: Progress Towards the Lisbon Objectives in Education and Training: Indicators and Benchmarks, 2012.

Nation Master. 2011. www.nationmaster.com.

UNESCO. *Global Education Digest 2012: Comparing Education Statistics Across the World.* Montreal: UNESCO Institute for Statistics, 2012.

UNESCO–IBE. www.ibe.unesco.org/countries/belgium.htm.

UNESCO–UIS. www.uis.unesco.org.

UNICEF. www.unicef.org/infobycountry.

World Bank Education Statistics. 2011. www.worldbank.org.

BOSNIA AND HERZEGOVINA

Bosnia and Herzegovina is a country located in southeastern Europe, in the west-central part of the Balkan Peninsula. After independence in March 1992, ethnic Serbs from Bosnia formed militias that served as armed resistance against the Bosnian government. The cause of this resistance was the willingness on the part of ethnic Serbs in Bosnia to partition the country and join forces with Serbia in creating a larger nation that included part of present-day Bosnia and Herzegovina. Despite years of war, the Bosnian government managed to quell the resistance militia through diplomatic means. The Dayton Peace Accords helped to bring about a peace agreement between ethnic Serbs and Bosnians. The NATO-led peacekeeping force as well as the subsequent stabilization force helped manage the Bosnian government to stabilize the country. By 2010, as a result of relative peace in the region, the peacekeeping forces had dwindled in numbers, as low as 2,500 members, and eventually became police officers. During 2010 and 2011, the Bosnian government became a nonpermanent member of the United Nations Security Council.

Approximately 40 percent of all Bosnians and Herzegovinians are Muslim. The majority of the population is Christian: about 31 percent of are Greek Orthodox and 15 percent are Roman Catholic. Members of other religions or no religion constitute 14 percent of the population.

Educational Systems

Prior to 2010 compulsory education in Bosnia and Herzegovina applied to four years of primary school and eight years of secondary school. Preprimary education was available for children ranging in age from 3 to 5 years. However, with new educational reforms in place, laws governing school attendance in Bosnia and Herzegovina mandate that children attend primary school for nine years (not four)—

namely, the lower primary school period (cycle 1, grades 1 through 3, and cycle 2, grades 4 through 6) and the upper primary school period (cycle 3, grades 7 through 9). Students in the first two cycles of primary school range from six to 11 years old, and those in the third cycle are 12 to 14 years old. There are currently about 400,000 students at the primary level. The student/teacher ratio at the primary level is about 22 students for every teacher. The primary gross attendance ratio is 102 percent, but the net attendance rate only amounts to nearly 93 percent. So not all children of primary age are attending school. The problem is more egregious in rural areas, where children often work in agriculture. Nearly all schools conduct classroom instruction in Bosnian, Serbian, or Croat.

Preschool attendance has changed as well. Parents can send their children from birth to six years of age to nursery or kindergarten. Preschool attendance, however, is dependent on whether families can afford to enroll their children into preschool programs. Compulsory education is free for all Bosnians and Herzegovinians. Nongovernmental organizations have helped to subsidize lunches and travel for primary and secondary school children of poor families or those living far from school.

Students attend secondary school from the ages of 15 to 18. There are currently nearly 200,000 students at the secondary level. The student/teacher ratio at this level is about 22 students for every teacher—similar to that of primary education classrooms. The secondary gross attendance ratio is only 70 percent; the net attendance rate amounts to 69 percent. The number of children and adolescents of secondary age who are attending school is much lower than the number attending primary school. This is an indication that students cannot afford to spend time in school because labor opportunities—no matter how minimal the pay—are more lucrative than attending school in preparation for higher education. The problem is still more acute among adolescents living in rural areas. Like secondary school systems in neighboring countries, that of Bosnia and Herzegovina is divided into two types: the Gimnazija (Gymnasia), which prepares students for higher education, and technical and vocational schools that prepare students for immediate entry into the workforce.

Tertiary Education

Bosnia and Herzegovina has a fairly large system of higher education. The system includes eight public comprehensive universities, 22 private institutions of higher education, and art academies and music conservatories. The University of Sarajevo is the oldest and largest university in the country. Originally established in 1531 as a law college, the university expanded during the last century into 24 research faculties. The other public higher education institutions in the country include the University of Tuzla, University of Banja Luka, University of Mostar, Sveuciliste Mostar, University of East Sarajevo, University of Bihac, and University of Zenica.

Higher education is funded by government authorities based in the Republic of Srpska or Federation of Bosnia and Herzegovina. The country has only recently introduced the Bologna Process as a means of adapting to uniform higher education policies throughout Europe. At present, undergraduate degrees can be completed in four years. Master's degrees typically require two more years, and doctorates take at least an additional three years to complete.

Teacher Education

All higher education students in Bosnia and Herzegovina who intend to become teacher candidates must acquire a university diploma and pass a professional examination. Bosnian and Herzegovinian teacher candidates who intend to teach at the lower primary level—grades 1 through 3—must prepare to become a classroom teacher, that is, one having a broad general knowledge, rather than specialized knowledge in one particular area. Candidates who intend to teach at the upper primary level—grades 4 through 6—must prepare to become a subject teacher. Candidates intending to become secondary teachers must also prepare for subject teacher status. This status requires candidates to enroll in a two-year degree program in a pedagogical institution or academy at one of several teacher training colleges throughout the country. Candidates from Bosnia and Herzegovina who wish to become vocational subject teachers are required to receive training in both their particular vocational skill and training in pedagogical concepts, curriculum studies, and psychology. At present, there are 16 preservice teacher education institutes in Bosnia and Herzegovina. Nearly all of them are either faculties or schools within universities. Most programs in teacher education require an initial four years of study. Some religious affiliated institutions require a minimum of two years.

System Economics and Future Prospects

Bosnia and Herzegovina is similar to other former Yugoslavian nations in that it is difficult to know precisely how much spending the government has allocated for educational purposes. Official Development Assistance (ODA) aid has been calculated in terms of different sectors of the country's economy. At nearly 43 percent of ODA, infrastructure ranked by far the highest in terms of percentage of sector share allocated in 2007. Education ranked 1.64 percent of sector share of ODA (see Magill 2010). Altogether expenditure for educational purposes includes federal spending on public and private or nongovernmental educational institutions, educational administration and policy, and subsidies for student-related and private educational expenses.

Despite a 97 percent literacy rate, Bosnia and Herzegovina has struggled with a decline in its socioeconomic and educational infrastructure, especially since the breakup of Yugoslavia. The Education Ministry of Bosnia and Herzegovina gradually improved the school infrastructure in the first decade of the twenty-first century, especially since the end of the military and civilian conflict in the late 1990s that resulted from the dissolution of the Soviet Union and Yugoslavia. Despite improvements, the nation is still struggling with its economy. One indication of this struggle is the existence of child labor, which is currently at 5 percent of all children between the ages of five and 14 years. This factor also contributes to the drop in school enrollment or attendance. Child labor increases during the third cycle of primary school, namely, for children between the ages of 12 and 14 years. To ameliorate social and economic problems among Bosnians and Herzegovinians, a number of nongovernmental organizations are working to improve the adverse living and educational conditions of families throughout the country.

Daniel Ness and Chia-ling Lin

REFERENCES

Central Intelligence Agency. *The CIA World Factbook*. New York: Skyhorse, 2011. https://www.cia.gov/library/publications/the-world-factbook/index.html.

GED. *Global Education Digest 2012: Comparing Education Statistics Across the World*. Montreal: UNESCO Institute for Statistics, 2012.

Magill, Clare. *Education and Fragility in Bosnia and Herzegovina*. Paris: International Institute for Educational Planning, 2010.

Nation Master. 2011. www.nationmaster.com.

Pasalic-Kreso, Adila, et al. "National Report: Bosnia and Herzegovina." In *The Prospects of Teacher Education in South East Europe*, ed. Uredil Pavel Zgaga, 171–208. Ljubljana, Slovenia: South East European Educational Cooperation Network (SEE-ECN), Center for Educational Policy Studies, University of Ljubljana, 2006.

UNESCO–IBE. www.ibe.unesco.org/en/worldwide/unesco-regions/europe-and-north-america/bosnia-and-herzegovina.html.

UNESCO–UIS. www.uis.unesco.org.

UNICEF. www.unicef.org/infobycountry.

World Bank Education Statistics. 2011. www.worldbank.org.

Bosnia and Herzegovina Education at a Glance

General Information

Capital	Sarajevo
Population	4,552,198
Languages	Bosnian, Croatian, Serbian
Literacy rate	97%
GDP per capita	US$5,600
People below poverty line (2004)	25%
Number of phones per 100 people	21
Number of Internet users per 100 people	18
Number of Internet hosts	31,490
Life expectancy at birth (years)	78

Formal Educational Information

Primary school age population	198,000
Primary school age population	4.5%
Number of years of primary education	4
Student/teacher ratio (primary and secondary)	approx. 22
Primary school gross enrollment ratio	no data
Primary gross attendance rate	102%
Secondary gross attendance rate	71%
Primary school entrants reaching grade 5	99%
Secondary school gross enrollment ratio	no data
Child labor (ages 5–14)	5%

Note: Unless otherwise indicated, all data are based on sources from 2011.

BULGARIA

Bulgaria is a country in southeastern Europe. The official language is Bulgarian, although Turkish and Roma are spoken by more than 10 percent of the population; 84 percent of the population is Bulgarian, 9.5 percent Turkish, and about 4.5 percent Roma. The population predominantly consists of members of the Bulgarian Orthodox Church (approximately 83 percent). About 12 percent of the population is Muslim, and the remaining 5 percent of the population is Catholic, Protestant, Hindu, and Jewish.

The Bulgarian state emerged from Bulgar tribes that emanated from present-day Turkey in the late 600s. The Bulgars held sway in the region during Byzantine rule. However, they were removed from power when the Ottomans assumed rule in the fourteenth century. Bulgaria achieved independence at two points; the first in 1878, when Bulgaria was given autonomy in the north, and in 1908, when it assumed complete autonomy from Ottoman rule. After World War II, Bulgaria came under communist rule, and it remained as one of the so-called eastern bloc countries until 1990. Bulgaria became a member of NATO in 2004 and part of the European Union in 2007. Despite its standing as a relatively poor country in Europe, Bulgaria's economy is steadily showing signs of improvement. Some of the major challenges for the Bulgarian government are administrative corruption and organized crime.

Educational System and Curriculum

Education is compulsory for all children and adolescents between the ages of seven and 16 years. The compulsory education mandate is administered by the Bulgarian Ministry of Education and Science. Education for Bulgarian students prior to tertiary education comprises 12 years of study, the first eight of which are compulsory. The first eight-year period, called basic education, is divided into two stages: forms I through IV, and forms V though VIII (similar to grades 1 through 4, followed by grades 5 through 8). The curriculum of the basic education period consists of Bulgarian, mathematics, science and the environ-

ment, and history and the community. Other areas of the curriculum at these two levels include physical education, music, art, and a foreign language, which most often commences in the second stage. Children receive graduation certificates after the completion of each of these stages.

There are three types of secondary schools in Bulgaria: comprehensive schools, profile-oriented schools, and vocational schools. Comprehensive schools provide students with a continuation of the basic education of the compulsory education period, offering more rigorous subjects for most students who plan to apply to universities and other tertiary institutions. Profile-oriented schools are secondary institutions that have a professional focus (e.g., mathematics, language, economics). Students from profile-oriented schools still have the opportunity to apply to tertiary institutions. Vocational schools emphasize skills necessary for students who wish to enter the workforce upon graduation.

Postcompulsory Education

Bulgarian higher education is divided into three types: universities, colleges, and specialized institutes. Universities in Bulgaria can only offer doctoral programs. Colleges and specialized institutes can only offer baccalaureates or diplomas in a particular specialization. Baccalaureates may be earned in a four-year period. Graduate diplomas may be earned after five years of schooling beyond the secondary level, or one to two years beyond the baccalaureate level. Doctorates take approximately three to six years beyond the master's degree level. Whereas universities in Bulgaria have several faculties of study (e.g., Sofia University has 16 separate schools and three additional departments), colleges focus on distinct areas of inquiry ranging from traditional disciplines (e.g., colleges of classics, colleges of natural science, colleges of social science, colleges of humanities) to professional studies (e.g., colleges of engineering, colleges of business and economics, institutes of medicine or law). Specialized institutes or higher schools serve as centers of vocational learning that are within the realm of tertiary education.

It is estimated that there are over 40 universities in Bulgaria. The most competitive universities in the country include Sofia University, the University of National and World Economy, Plovdiv University, and the Technical University of Sofia. Sofia University (i.e., the St. Clement of Ohrid University of Sofia) is the oldest institution in the country. The university was established in 1888, 10 years after the country's independence. With more than 20,000 students attending the university annually, Sofia University ranks as one of the largest universities in Bulgaria in enrollment.

Teacher Education

Several universities in Bulgaria provide education for preservice teachers. Specific institutes that focus on primary education include Kliment Ohridski University in Sofia, Saints Cyril and Methodius University of Valiko Târnovo, the University of Shumen, and St. Pa'ss'i Hilendarski University of Plovdiv. Nearly all education programs in Bulgarian universities include pedagogy, curriculum, and psychology in their curricula. Preservice teacher candidates spend on average four to five years in college preparation and in student teaching. Student teaching hours depend heavily on the subject of specialization. Students preparing to become secondary school teachers attend programs in one of many universities in the country. Courses must include both pedagogical and specified content-related classes (i.e., mathematics, language, natural science, and the like). These programs also last for four to five years. During the last year, students spend time in secondary school classrooms preparing to become teachers.

Informal Education

Informal education is provided primarily for adults who either were not exposed to formal education or for those whose formal education occurred on the cusp of change from Soviet control to autonomous control (1980s through 1990s). It provides basic education in reading, writing, and arithmetic. Informal education includes courses for particular vocations (e.g., secretarial work, cosmetics, fashion designing) and schools emphasizing foreign language instruction. Informal education programs are regulated by the Ministry of Labor if they run for six months or less; programs that run for more than six months are under the jurisdiction of the Ministry of Education and Science.

System Economics

Bulgaria ranks at 100 out of 186 countries in educational expenditures as a percentage of gross domestic product (GDP). Along with Malaysia, Cyprus, Rwanda, and Thailand, the total public expenditure on education in 2011 represented 4.1 percent of GDP. Nearly $15.34 billion was allocated for education purposes. Given the GDP of Bulgaria at roughly $96.78 billion, educational expenditure in the country amounts to nearly $10.15 billion, about $4,404 per student (total amount equivalent to US dollars divided by 901,000, the approximate number of primary and secondary students in the country).

Future Prospects

One of the most egregious challenges in Bulgaria is the high rate of corruption in the government and among those involved in the education system. Another challenge concerns the essential educational infrastructure that had been vandalized and pillaged since 1990, after the dissolving of the Soviet Union. Bulgarian education officials also must grapple with the large influx of students from poor farming communities, many of whom have migrated to urban areas and attend urban schools, where resources are

---

Bulgaria Education at a Glance

General Information

Capital	Sofia
Population	7.3 million
Languages	Bulgarian (84%), Turkish (10%)
Literacy rate	98%
GDP per capita	US$10,700
People below poverty line (2004)	14%
Number of phones per 100 people	34
Number of Internet users per 100 people	30
Number of Internet hosts	185,000
Life expectancy at birth (years)	73

Formal Educational Information

Primary school age population	272,000
Secondary school age population	629,000
Primary school age population	4%
Number of years of primary education	4
Student/teacher ratio (primary)	16
Student/teacher ratio (secondary)	12
Primary school gross enrollment ratio	102%
Primary school entrants reaching grade 5	91%
Secondary school gross enrollment ratio	105%
Child labor (5–14)	no data

Note: Unless otherwise indicated, all data are based on sources from 2011.

becoming scarcer. Another major challenge is dealing with the problem of alienation of minority communities, particularly children of Roma families. In Bulgaria and neighboring eastern European countries, the Roma have historically been targeted as victims of ethnic bias, particularly when local and regional economies become erratic. Alienation of Roma children and their families as well as other needy Bulgarians prevents these citizens from enjoying upward social mobility. Laws need to address issues of prejudice in Bulgarian society. Education curriculum will need to place more attention on environmental improvement, clean energy, and health care for all citizens.

Daniel Ness and Chia-ling Lin

REFERENCES

Central Intelligence Agency. *The CIA World Factbook*. New York: Skyhorse, 2011. https://www.cia.gov/library/publications/the-world-factbook/index.html.

Nation Master. 2011. www.nationmaster.com.

UNESCO. *Global Education Digest 2012: Comparing Education Statistics Across the World*. Montreal: UNESCO Institute for Statistics, 2012.

UNESCO–IBE. www.ibe.unesco.org/en/worldwide/unesco-regions/europe-and-north-america/bulgaria.html.

UNESCO–UIS. www.uis.unesco.org.

UNICEF. www.unicef.org/infobycountry.

World Bank Education Statistics. 2011. www.worldbank.org.

CROATIA

The Republic of Croatia (Republika Hrvatska) is a southeastern European country situated on the Adriatic Sea. Settled by the Croats (Hrvati) in the seventh century, Croatia has been the homeland of the Croatian people for over 1,300 years. It became the Kingdom of Croatia in the tenth century when King Tomislav was crowned the first Croatian king in Duvno in the year 925. After a period of self-rule, Croatia was subjected to the Crown of Hungary in 1102 and the Hapsburg dynasty in 1527. In 1918 the Kingdom of the Serbs, Croats, and Slovenes was formed. After World War II Croatia became one of the six republics that formed the communist country of Yugoslavia under Marshall Josip Broz Tito. The Republic of Croatia was established as a sovereign, independent democracy on June 25, 1991.

The Croats make up 90 percent of the population and are predominantly Roman Catholic. Other citizens are Protestant, Orthodox Christian, Muslim, or Jewish. The Croatian language belongs to the southern Slavic family of languages and uses the Latin alphabet as a form of writing.

Since achieving its independence, Croatia has been undergoing a major stabilization process. Croatia's economic infrastructure was damaged by a long history of communist rule and mismanagement of the economy; war-inflicted damage to bridges, factories, power lines, buildings, and houses; a tremendous Croatian and Bosnian refugee and displaced population; and struggles with the privatization of state-controlled business and industry.

Educational System

The Ministry of Science, Education, and Sports (MSES) is responsible for the overall planning, funding, evaluation, and monitoring of the educational system in Croatia. The educational infrastructure in the Republic of Croatia consists of the following institutions designed to improve and achieve education quality: Education and Teacher Training Agency, Agency for Science and Higher Education, Agency for Vocational Education and Training, National Center for External Evaluation of Education, and Agency for Adult Education.

Precompulsory Education

Preschool education in the Republic of Croatia became a subsystem of Croatia's educational system in 1997 with the passage of the Preschool Education Act. Preschool education includes educational, health-care, nutritional and social care programs for children from six months to six years of age. The primary goal of preschool education is to teach the knowledge, skills, and attitudes that would facilitate children's transition into an organized school system. Local communities establish and finance day-care centers and early childhood activities. One of Croatia's goals is to increase the number of children attending preschool from the current rate of 43 percent in an effort to bring it closer to the European standard of 90 percent. The government also aims to increase the participation of children in preschool one year before starting primary school from the current rate of 96 to 100 percent. Numerous programs and approaches are conducted in preschool institutions, including Montessori, Waldorf, Reggio Emilia, fine arts, dramatic arts, sports, music, health, religion, ecology, and early adoption of foreign languages.

Compulsory Education

Elementary education is compulsory and free for all children between the ages of seven and 15, spanning eight years. However, 12 years of public schooling is the expected norm. Compulsory elementary education is conducted in regular elementary schools and special institutions for students with developmental disabilities. Art education is taught in elementary music and dance schools. Elementary music education is also taught in certain regular elementary schools, but as a separate educational program.

Primary schooling consists of two parts: instruction as a class with a single teacher from first through fourth grade and specialized classes with teacher specialists from fifth to eighth grade. The new Croatian National Educational Standards for primary education strive to align the national curriculum with European standards and delineate competencies that students must acquire at different levels of their education. The Act on Primary Education stipulates that every student completes primary education with the knowledge of two foreign languages.

Secondary education refers to programs in grammar schools or Gimnazija, art schools, four-year vocational schools (technical, economic, health, etc.), three-year vocational schools, and programs for adult education and training. Secondary education is available to all students under equal conditions to prepare them for work or continuation of education. It is conducted by high school institutions and covers secondary education, secondary vocational education, semiskilled training, and training and skill improvement.

Grammar school programs provide extensive knowledge in the following curricular areas: general knowledge, modern languages and communication, social and humanistic knowledge, natural sciences and mathematics, technical and technological, arts, and practical work and design. Information and communications technology (ICT) and computer literacy are incorporated into all levels of education to prepare students for high-technology employment.

In order to increase the number of students who complete secondary education, the ministry has embarked on a Secondary School for All initiative to extend compulsory secondary education in Croatia. The government provides a series of incentives (i.e., free textbooks, transportation, and housing in student dormitories), program funding, and the human resources necessary to ensure access to secondary education for everyone.

The Agency for Vocational Education, established in January 2005, is designed to improve vocational education at all levels of upper secondary education. It aims to provide students with the essential skills needed in the modern labor market. The Education Management Information System will monitor secondary education enrollment and completion rates nationally.

Postcompulsory Education

Croatia has a long tradition of higher education. The first university was established in Zadar in 1396 by Dominican priests as the Universitas Jadertina or the General University. It conferred degrees of Master of Science and doctor of science. Bishop Josip Juraj Strossmayer established the foundations of higher education and advanced scholarship in Zagreb with the founding of the South Slavonic Academy in Zagreb in 1867 and the University of Zagreb in 1874.

Today Croatia has seven major universities—the universities of Dubrovnik, Pula, Rijeka, Split, Zadar, Zagreb, and the Josip Juraj Strossmayer University of Osijek. In addition, there are 12 public polytechnics, four public schools of professional higher education, two teachers' academies, eight teachers' schools of professional higher education, and 22 private institutions of higher education.

The National Council for Higher Education (NCHE) is the professional body responsible for the development and quality of the higher education system. The Act on Scientific Activity and Higher Education, adopted by the Croatian Parliament in 2003, established a framework for the reform of universities and the implementation of the Bologna Declaration principles. The Agency for Science and Higher Education, established in March 2005, is a state agency that provides logistic support to the NCHE and handles its administrative tasks related to accreditation, evaluation of bachelor's- and master's-level study programs and higher education institutions, evaluation of quality assurance systems at higher education institutions, and their integration into the European Network for Quality Assurance in Higher Education.

The reform of the Croatian higher education system is intended to become more closely aligned and adapted to the Bologna process and the European Higher Education Area. As a result, many of the higher education institutions have transformed their traditional four-year program into the predominant 3 + 2 model of the Bologna process. The intent is to enable students to enter the labor market after finishing the first cycle of study or to enroll in graduate and postgraduate study. Another reform is the separation of professional studies from university studies. In 2010 the binary system was implemented; professional studies were housed in polytechnics or schools of professional higher education while university studies were at the domain of universities.

Curriculum, Assessment, and Instruction

Traditionally the Croatian curriculum has been rigorous and highly demanding, focusing on cognitive development and extensive memorization of information. It has included the following subjects: Croatian language and literature, mathematics, physics, chemistry, biology, geography, foreign language, history, art, music, technical education, physical and health education, and religious education.

A major factor in the reform and modernization of Croatia's educational system is the development of a national curriculum. The Education Council recognized the need to bring the educational system into better alignment with European and UNESCO-approved international standards. The council recommended a compulsory national curriculum that would focus on 18 areas of literacy, with alphabetical literacy, mathematical literacy, and information technology literacy at the top of the list. These recommendations are aligned with the key competencies identified by the European Union at the Lisbon Summit as relevant for a knowledge-based society: ICT skills, technological culture, foreign languages, entrepreneurship, interpersonal and social competencies, mathematical

literacy, basic competencies in science, cultural awareness, and learning to learn. The Education Council further proposed the development of new textbooks, teaching approaches, educational programs, and course curricula sensitive to the needs of all people in Croatia, including ethnic minorities.

Teacher Education

According to the MSES Education Staff Database 2004/2005, the level of education required for primary and secondary school teachers varies greatly. Only 50.76 percent of primary school teachers possess a bachelor's degree (four-year), while 43.7 percent have an associate degree (two-year) and 5.16 percent have a high school education. In secondary school, 84.76 percent have a bachelor's degree, 6.48 percent have an associate degree, and 5.18 percent have a high school education. The level of education teachers possess does not necessarily correspond to the actual knowledge and competencies of the teachers. There are discrepancies in the quality and consistency of undergraduate studies and professional training programs. On July 5, 2007, the government of Croatia passed the Foundations of the Croatian Qualification Framework. The new framework will designate standardized education levels for qualifications and professions, which will be aligned with the International Standardized Classification of Education.

Research suggests that teachers are almost entirely a female professional group, with 92 percent of classroom teachers (first to fourth grade) and 75 percent of subject teachers (fifth to eighth grade) being women. According to Baranović et al. (2004), in contrast, the sociodemographic and professional characteristics of school principals indicate that 61 percent are male and 60.2 percent hold a university degree.

The new educational standards call for improved initial training of teachers, extended probation periods for young teachers, intensive continuous professional in-service training for teachers, and professional training for principals and other staff members. The Ordinance on Teacher Promotion in primary and secondary schools designates four levels of promotion: junior teacher, teacher, mentor-teacher, and mentor-adviser. All junior teachers must pass the state exam. Teachers are expected to participate in regular training to upgrade their skills and keep current with the latest approaches to teaching. A system of long-term support of professional training for teachers and principals will be incorporated to assist them in improving the quality of teaching and management in schools. The Institute of Education and the Agency for Vocational Education offer yearly teacher training seminars that are funded through the state budget. Traditional methods of teaching are gradually being replaced by student-centered methods that employ active teaching strategies.

Private educational institutions do exist in primary and secondary education, but receive minimal funds from the state budgets. They are financed by student entrance fees, local community contributions, and other means. They have to be aligned with the official educational system in Croatia.

Informal and Nonformal Education

The Strategy for Adult Learning, which is under the auspices of the Ministry of Science, Education, and Sports, indicates that lifelong learning is a right and obligation of all citizens of the Republic of Croatia in order to build a knowledge-based economy. However, adult education is one of the least developed areas of education. Croatia has not had a traditional focus on adult learning and lacks coherent policies and sufficient resources. One problem in particular is the integration of war veterans into the society and labor market. Their qualifications are not always commensurate with current labor market needs, and training demands outweigh the availability of educational programs. With the establishment of the Agency for Adult Education in 2006, curricular reforms are being developed to improve the quality of adult learning.

Elementary education of adults is conducted in regular schools and specialized institutions. Secondary education programs for adults can be conducted in secondary schools, colleges, and other legal institutions. Educational programs for adults cover the following: secondary vocational education, semiskilled training, retraining, training, and skill improvement.

Currently there is no recognition of informal and nonformal learning. However, one of the strategic goals of Croatia's adult education policy is setting the standards to recognize the knowledge and skills obtained in nonformal education. There is increased recognition that learning while working is an important part of professional training. In 2000 the Education Council proposed a full range of education and training programs, including continuing education and the use of the Internet to incorporate distance education as a means of teaching more skilled professionals. Adults with limited schooling will be given training in literacy, mathematics, and vocational skills—all of which increase their employability. There is also some recognition of voluntary work through the proposal of the Act on Volunteerism.

System Economics

The budget of the MSES accounted for 4.1 percent of Croatia's gross domestic product (GDP) in 2010. Taking into consideration expenditures made by other central ministries and those at the local level, public education expenditures constituted 4.6 percent of the GDP in 2009. Given a GDP of $78.09 billion, educational expenditures amount to nearly $3.6 billion, or $5,693 per student (based on 631,000 children and adolescents of primary and secondary school age). As Croatia strives to improve the infrastructure and quality of its educational system to get closer to European standards, increased financial resources from the government and other sources are critical.

Challenges and Dilemmas

Croatia is facing numerous challenges that have an impact on its economy, infrastructure, and educational system. It is confronted by the pressures of globalization and worldwide competition, the need for modernization, changes in the economy focusing on manufacturing and the service industry, the need for the rapid acquisition of new knowledge and competencies for technologically based industries, and the complexities of the process of accession to the European Community.

The Croatian educational system is confronted by a declining school-age population, need for a continuum of lifelong learning, development of a knowledge-based society, and the creation of a highly skilled labor force. The educational system itself faces the challenge of integrating students with special needs. New curricula must be developed that promote inclusion and a better system of monitoring special needs children well beyond their compulsory schooling. Moreover, teachers need to be well trained to work with special needs children.

Croatia Education at a Glance	
General Information	
Capital	Zagreb
Population	4.4 million
Language	Croatian
Literacy rate	adult 98.1%, youth 99.6%
GDP per capita	US$13,400
Number of phones (landline) per 100 people	43
Number of phones (mobile) per 100 people	133*
Number of Internet users per 100	49.7
Number of Internet hosts (2010)	1.2 million
Life expectancy at birth (years)	76.2
Formal Educational Information	
Compulsory school age population	873,000
Compulsory school age population	96.5%
Number of years of compulsory education	8 (ages 7–15)
Student/teacher ratio	18
Average class size in primary school	28
Average school days per year	181
Primary school gross enrollment ratio	96.5
Primary school entrants reaching grade 5	100%
Secondary school gross enrollment ratio	87%
Tertiary school enrollment	120,000 (31%)
Child labor (ages 5–14)	0%**

Notes: *The population of Croatia is less than the number of mobile phones in the country. **Given the partiality of governmental sources, child labor is not based on data provided by internal government publications.

Unless otherwise indicated, all data are based on sources from 2011.

Furthermore, there is a need for increased financial allocations from the state budget, social enterprises, and international funding sources. The Ministry of Science, Education, and Sports is working together with other entities, such as the Agency for Science and Higher Education, Agency for Vocational Education, Institute for Education, the Health and Social Care Ministry, Ministry of Economy, Chamber of Commerce, Chamber of Crafts, Croatian Employment Service, Croatian Association of Employers, and Croatian Association for the Education of Adults to explore funding resources, coordinate the development of national policies, and promote the achievement of their ongoing Education and Training initiative for career changers.

To ensure the successful implementation of the new educational policies, standards, and the national curriculum, it is important to define the competencies of teachers, principals, counselors, and expert associates; ensure the equalization of their prerequisite education and training; and provide ongoing professional development based on the latest educational research.

Moreover, educational institutions need financial, material, and human resources support, as well as flexibility in decision making, in order to meet the educational needs of all students and maximize learning.

Future Prospects

As Croatia strives for accession to the European Union, the quality of its educational and research systems must be competitive with the high educational standards of other advanced countries in the European Union. Competition for highly talented students, teachers, researchers, and workers is increasing on an international level. It is anticipated that the greatest growth in the labor market will be in the intellectual services area, particularly the information and communication technology sector. The globalization of the economy will require greater cooperation at the global level, produce growing competition internationally, result in changes in the employment structure, promote greater student and labor mobility, and create changes in the required knowledge and skills. Areas of educational emphasis will be acquiring language and communication skills; improving information technology and communications literacy; increasing the understanding of mathematics, natural sciences, foreign languages, and social studies; enhancing entrepreneurial skills; learning how to learn; and developing cultural literacy. The transformation to a democratic, knowledge-based society will be realized not only through the reform initiatives of the Ministry of Science, Education, and Sports, but through the collective and collaborative efforts of schools, higher education institutions, educational agencies, professional associations, parents, teachers, students, and all Croatian citizens.

Vishna A. Herrity

REFERENCES

Baranović, Branka, et al. *Evaluation of Syllabi and Development of Curriculum Model for Compulsory Education in Croatia.* Zagreb: Institute for Social Research, Centre for Educational Research and Development, 2004.

Central Intelligence Agency. *The CIA World Factbook.* New York: Skyhorse, 2011. https://www.cia.gov/library/publications/the-world-factbook/index.html.

Ministry of Science, Education, and Sports of the Republic of Croatia. http://public.mzos.hr.

Nation Master. 2011. www.nationmaster.com.

Spajić-Vrkas, Vedrana. "Visions, Provisions, and Reality: Political Changes and Education for Democratic Citizenship in Croatia." *Cambridge Journal of Education* 33:1 (2003): 33–51.

UNESCO–IBE. www.ibe.unesco.org/en/worldwide/unesco-regions/europe-and-north-america/croatia.html.

UNESCO–UIS. www.uis.unesco.org.

UNICEF. www.unicef.org/infobycountry.

World Bank Education Statistics. 2011. www.worldbank.org.

CYPRUS

Cyprus is an island country in the Mediterranean Sea, located about 50 miles from the coast of Turkey. The official languages of Cyprus are Greek, Turkish, and English. The United Nations population estimate for Cyprus in 2011 was 1.1 million. The population is mainly Greek (77 percent) and Turkish (18 percent). The religion is predominantly Greek Orthodox (78 percent). Approximately 18 percent of the population (mostly Turkish citizens) is Muslim. Cyprus was a former British colony before it became independent in 1960. Ethnic tensions between Greece and Turkey divided the country into two major regions: the southern two-thirds of the island are mostly Greek and the northern one-third is mostly Turkish.

Educational System

Education in Cyprus is controlled by the Cyprus Ministry of National Education and Culture. The system is not completely uniform in that it differs in the ethnically Turkish north and the mostly Greek south. Primary education and secondary education in the country is highly advanced when compared to systems of education in other nations of the region. Only the education systems of Greece and Israel can compete with that of Cyprus. What makes education in Cyprus most progressive is the strong emphasis on gender equality in education. The country is home to a number of all girls' and all boys' schools, primarily at the secondary level.

Precompulsory and Compulsory Education

Education has been one of Cyprus's most powerful assets in terms of its economy and success in the global marketplace. Teacher quality has been rated above average based on the credentials that teacher candidates are expected to receive at the university level.

Approximately 30,000 children are eligible to attend preschool in Cyprus; however, only about 18,000 children actually attend preschool or kindergarten. Primary and secondary schooling in Cyprus is analogous to that of Greece in the number of years that students are enrolled at each level. In general, compulsory education in the country is a nine-year period, comprised of primary education for six years and lower secondary education for three years. Although upper secondary school is not compulsory, it is attended by nearly all individuals within the upper secondary level age group.

School-age students in Cyprus have a strong record of school attendance. The net primary school enrollment ratio is 99.3 percent, which is an indicator that nearly all of the 68,000 children of primary school age actually attend school. Moreover, the survival rate to grade 5 is nearly 100 percent, and the primary completion rate is 100 percent. The student/teacher ratios for primary school and secondary school in Cyprus are about 19 students and 18 students per teacher, respectively.

Postcompulsory Education

Cyprus is home to at least three state-funded universities and 10 private universities, many of which are subsidized in part by the Cyprus government. The European University [of] Cyprus is one of the largest universities in Cyprus, enrolling between 4,000 and 6,000 students annually. Located in Nicosia, the university started as a private college in 1961 and gradually developed into a university with numerous departments. The most recent schools to open in the university were the schools of law and medicine. In 2010 the university introduced PhD degrees in education. In addition to the numerous tertiary-level institutions in Cyprus, a large percentage of Cypriot students, nearly 78 percent, study at universities abroad. Other competitive universities in the country include the University of Cyprus, a nationally funded institution in Nicosia, and the University of Nicosia. In addition to universities, Cyprus has accredited nearly 30 private colleges that specialize in individual subjects.

Cyprus Education at a Glance

General Information

Capital	Nicosia
Population	801,851
Languages	Greek, Turkish, English
Literacy rate	98%
GDP per capita	US$23,000
People below poverty line	no data
Number of phones per 100 people	53
Number of Internet users per 100 people	40
Number of Internet hosts	67,600
Life expectancy at birth (years)	78

Formal Educational Information

Primary school age population	69,000
Secondary school age population	77,000
Primary school age population	9%
Number of years of primary education	6
Student/teacher ratio (primary)	18
Student/teacher ratio (secondary)	11%
Primary school gross enrollment ratio	101%
Primary school entrants reaching grade 5	99%
Secondary school gross enrollment ratio	97%
Child labor (ages 5–14)	no data

Note: Unless otherwise indicated, all data are based on sources from 2011.

Teacher Education

All students who are preparing to become teachers in either primary or secondary school must earn a degree at the University of Cyprus or another accredited university in the areas of pedagogical studies. Secondary education teacher candidates in Cyprus must specialize in a particular area of expertise that they will teach at the secondary level. During university education, however, secondary education teacher candidates do not have time to engage in student teaching and related pedagogical practice. Accordingly, these individuals need to enroll in training courses that are available through the Cyprus Ministry of Education and Culture.

System Economics

According to the United Nations Development Programme (2011), Cyprus ranks 99 of 186 in educational expenditures as a percentage of its gross domestic product (GDP). The total public expenditure on education in 2011 represented 4.1 percent of GDP. Nearly $951.2 million was allocated for education purposes. Based on these figures, total per students spending is approximately $6,515 (determined by dividing total expenditure by 146,000, the approximate number of students in Cyprus).

Future Prospects

Education in Cyprus at all levels has been increasingly successful since the late 1980s. Teacher training is rigorous, and educational finances are used primarily for students' educational benefit. The country has also been successful in introducing technologies for both instructional use and as content for student learning. Although colleges and universities in the country demonstrate academic rigor, secondary school graduates also have the opportunity to apply to universities throughout the world, but mostly in Europe. Sectional strife between the predominantly Muslim northern third of the country and the mostly Christian southern two-thirds poses the most volatility in terms of political and educational progress in present-day Cyprus.

Daniel Ness and Chia-ling Lin

REFERENCES

Central Intelligence Agency. *The CIA World Factbook.* New York: Skyhorse, 2011. https://www.cia.gov/library/publications/the-world-factbook/index.html.

GED. *Global Education Digest 2012: Comparing Education Statistics Across the World.* Montreal: UNESCO Institute for Statistics, 2012.

Nation Master. 2011. www.nationmaster.com.

UNESCO–IBE. www.ibe.unesco.org/en/worldwide/unesco-regions/europe-and-north-america/cyprus.html.

UNESCO–UIS. www.uis.unesco.org.

UNICEF. www.unicef.org/infobycountry.

World Bank Education Statistics. 2011. www.worldbank.org.

CZECH REPUBLIC

The Czech Republic is a landlocked country in central Europe. The official language is Czech. However, a small minority speak Slovak along the country's border with Slovakia. The United Nations population estimate for the Czech Republic in 2011 was 10.2 million. The population is mainly Czech (90 percent). The religion is predominantly Roman Catholic (27 percent); however, due to association with the former Soviet Union, the country has seen a rapid growth in secularization, even to the present day.

The Czech Republic consists of 13 regions. The Czech and Slovak regions were once part of the Austro-Hungarian Empire. After World War I, the two regions formed Czechoslovakia. The Soviets gained political influence over Czechoslovakia after World War II, a political pact that lasted for nearly 45 years. The Czech region separated from the Slovak region and became independent on January 1, 1993. The country became a NATO nation in 1999 and part of the European Union in 2004.

Educational System

Education in the Czech Republic is controlled by the Ministry of Education, Youth, and Sports. The system includes preprimary education for children between the ages of two and five years, primary education for children between the ages of six and 15 years, and secondary education for adolescents between the ages of 16 and 18 years.

Preprimary education in the Czech Republic is not compulsory. In general, preschools are not free. However, parents who send their children to preschool during the year before primary school attendance need not pay tuition as this year is considered the kindergarten level.

Education in the Czech Republic is compulsory for nine years, or when students are between the ages of six and 15 years. Primary education in the country is divided into two stages. The first stage includes grades 1 through 5, and the second stage, which in neighboring countries is considered middle school or lower secondary school, includes grades 6 through 9. Both stages of schooling most often are provided within one school building. However, rural areas may be able to accommodate only grades 1 through 5, thereby requiring children to travel long distances to attend schools that accommodate grades 6 through 9.

A sample curriculum during the latter grade levels of the initial basic period (grades 1 through 5) includes Czech reading and writing; mathematics; history; biology; English, French, or German, as a foreign language; physical education; fine arts; and music. A sample curriculum during the latter grade levels of the second basic period (grades 6 through 9) include Czech language and literature; mathematics; geography; biology; chemistry; history; social studies (economics or politics); English, French, or German, as a foreign language; physical education; fine arts; and music.

Postcompulsory education in the Czech Republic includes the last three years of secondary education and tertiary education. Nearly all students completing the lower secondary school level continue to either the Gymnasium or the technical school, the two types of secondary education schools in the country, for their last three years of secondary education.

The Czech nation, both as a kingdom in medieval times and as a republic in modern times, has always had a strong tradition of public higher education at the university level. The Charles University in Prague is the oldest university in continuous operation in central Europe. Founded in 1348, Charles University was modeled on the University of Paris, serving as a central university center of theology, law, and philosophy, and remains one of the leading centers of theology, law, medicine, and education in central Europe. Today the university ranks as the second most competitive university in central and eastern Europe (according to the Quacquarelli Symonds World University Rankings). With an annual enrollment of 50,000 students, Charles University is also the largest institution of higher education in the Czech Republic. Founded as a Jesuit center of higher education in 1573, Palacký University of Olomouc is the second-oldest university in the Czech Republic. Founded in 1707 the Czech Technical University in Prague is one of the oldest technical institutions in the world and was one of the first centers of research in engineering.

At present there are about 70 universities in the Czech Republic. Of these institutions, 28 are public or state-funded institutions, and 42 are private universities and colleges. Privately run universities and colleges were generally established after 1950. Most of the private institutions are trade schools that emphasize particular specializations. For example, the *Vysoká škola ekonomie a managementu* is a college of economics and management, the *Vysoká škola podnikání* is a college of business, the *Vysoká škola regionálního rozvoje* is a college of regional development, and the *Vysoká škola zdravotnická* is a college of health and nursing.

Teacher Education

Students planning to be teachers of the basic school curriculum must enroll at one of the Czech universities that has a faculty of education or pedagogy. Candidates intending to teach at the first stage of primary school (grades 1 through 5) must enroll in a four-year program, while those intending to teach at the second stage of primary school (grades 6 through 9) must enroll in a five-year program and major in two areas of specialization: pedagogy and the desired subject taught at the lower secondary level (e.g., mathematics, Czech language and literature, biology). Secondary school teacher training at the general school requires teacher candidates to apply to university faculties of education, arts, music, philosophy, natural sciences, mathematics, physics, or physical education. Those who plan to teach at the technical school must apply to faculties of technology, economics, or agriculture. All secondary school teacher candidates must obtain a master's degree in order to be placed in a school setting.

Informal Education

The system of informal education practice in the Czech Republic provides adults with basic skills or with additional vocational skills that are necessary for competing in the workforce. Many adults who fall into one of these categories may not have been exposed to formal education. Since the change from Soviet control to autonomous control (1980s through 1990s), many educational and technological modifications have taken place. Accordingly, informal education programs provide education in basic knowledge in reading, writing, and arithmetic, foreign language instruction, as well as courses within particular vocations.

System Economics

According to the United Nations Development Programme (2011), the Czech Republic ranks 96 of 186 in educational expenditures as a percentage of gross domestic product (GDP). The total public expenditure on education in 2007 represented 4.2 percent of GDP. Nearly US$11 billion has been allocated for education purposes. Based on these figures, total per student spending is approximately $7,420 (determined by dividing total expenditure by

Czech Republic Education at a Glance	
General Information	
Capital	Prague
Population	10.2 million
Languages	Czech (95%), Slovak (2%)
Literacy rate	99%
GDP per capita	US$21,900
People below poverty line	no data
Number of phones per 100 people	32
Number of Internet users per 100 people	50
Number of Internet hosts	1.2 million
Life expectancy at birth (years)	77
Formal Educational Information	
Primary school age population	474,000
Secondary school age population	1 million
Primary school age population	4.5%
Number of years of primary education	5
Student/teacher ratio (primary)	16
Student/teacher ratio (secondary)	10
Primary school gross enrollment ratio	102%
Primary school entrants reaching grade 5	99%
Secondary school gross enrollment ratio	96%
Child labor (ages 5–14)	no data

Note: Unless otherwise indicated, all data are based on sources from 2011.

1,479,000, the approximate number of students in the Czech Republic).

Future Prospects

Education in the Czech Republic has seen rapid growth in all sectors from preprimary education to the university level. This is especially apparent with the rise of technology as a means of instruction and as part of the curriculum at all grade levels. However, it also can be said that a rift exists between grades 1 through 12 education and tertiary education. Although primary and secondary education in the Czech Republic has shown improvement, especially since the end of World War II, children and adolescents of families in urban areas, which tend to be more affluent and to live closer to competitive institutions, tend to outperform their peers in rural communities, thus creating an achievement gap. Nevertheless, the public universities in the nation have consistently ranked as some of the most competitive institutions in Europe. At the same time, private institutions in the Czech Republic do not fare as well. Most recently, private colleges and universities in the country were under investigation for education fraud, as evidenced in the Plzeň law school, which has been investigated for so-called fast-track degrees (granted after less than six months of study) and plagiarism. Accordingly, more than 300,000 university graduates have been affected.

Daniel Ness and Chia-ling Lin

REFERENCES

Central Intelligence Agency. *The CIA World Factbook.* New York: Skyhorse, 2011. https://www.cia.gov/library/publications/the-world-factbook/index.html.

Nation Master. 2011. www.nationmaster.com.

UNESCO. *Global Education Digest 2012: Comparing Education Statistics Across the World.* Montreal: UNESCO Institute for Statistics, 2012.

UNESCO–IBE. www.ibe.unesco.org/en/worldwide/unesco-regions/europe-and-north-america/czech-republic.html.

UNESCO–UIS. www.uis.unesco.org.

UNICEF. www.unicef.org/infobycountry.

World Bank Education Statistics. 2011. www.worldbank.org.

DENMARK

Denmark consists mainly of a peninsula known as Jutland that is bordered by Germany to the south and surrounded by the Baltic and North Seas to the north, east, and west. The official language is Danish, although the country has a number of German, Dutch, and English speakers as well. The population is mainly Danish (at least 95 percent). Other populations include Germans, as well as Inuit peoples in Greenland. The religion is predominantly Lutheran (95 percent) with small minorities of Catholics, Muslims, and others who are classified as no religion.

From the late Eighth Century to the middle of the Eleventh Century, the region was the home of Viking raiders, known for pillaging the possessions or property of nearby conquered Germanic tribes and Romans who had traveled to the north. Schleswig-Holstein, the southern part of the country, was conquered by Germany in 1864, but eventually returned. Denmark was controlled by German forces during World War II. After the war, Denmark emerged as one of the most economically productive countries in all of Europe.

Educational System

The education system in Denmark has more or less followed the historical trajectories of other central and northern European countries in that the primary form of schooling during the Middle Ages was the cathedral in urban settings and the monastery in both urban and rural settings. These institutions prepared young boys and adolescents for the priesthood and possibly for political administration. Some of these institutions still exist. After the Reformation in 1536, the rationale for schooling did not change—it was still a social establishment that trained male youth for theological study and law. Schooling for larger numbers of students, particularly in the eighteenth and nineteenth centuries, was, in part, a result of the post-Reformation belief that in order to be fluent in religious observance, children and adolescents needed to learn how to read. However, with the influence of the philosophers Rousseau and Kant, secularism eventually made its way into the educational system. In addition to the so-called classics disciplines, schools in Denmark included the natural sciences as part of the curriculum. The leading Danish educationist in the nineteenth century was Nikolaj Frederik Severin Grundtvig, a member of the clergy and a politician. Grundtvig was a curriculum theorist who promoted the expansion of the ancient curriculum, which focused solely on the study of Greek, Latin, and arithmetic, to include various natural sciences. Schooling for the privileged was analogous to that of other German-speaking nations. In particular, the Gymnasium served most male students. However, the first publicly funded primary school in Denmark—Folkeskole—opened in 1894. Students in the Realskole, a combined public institution that catered to both primary and secondary school students, were traditionally unable to attend the same tertiary institutions as those graduating from the putatively more prestigious Gymnasia. The Realskole was an offshoot of the Industrial Revolution: the idea was that an educational institution needed to be developed in order to train youth for the immediate workforce. University acceptance criteria, however, have changed in the last decade.

Compulsory education in Denmark is for children and adolescents between the ages of six and 16 years. The upper secondary school, which is not compulsory, is attended by more than 80 percent of those who graduate from the lower secondary, compulsory, level. This compulsory period is known as Folkeskole, or public school. Although the majority of children attend the Folkeskole, approximately 10 to

12 percent of the student population attends private schools. The Danish education system is run by the Ministry of Education for preprimary, primary, and secondary levels. The Danish Ministry of Science, Technology, and Development controls the tertiary education system in the country.

Precompulsory, Compulsory Education, and Curriculum

Parents in Denmark have the option of sending their children between the ages of three and six to kindergarten—an educational period that is not compulsory. Kindergarten children receive an education based on socialization, personal development, and real-life connections with academic subjects through a focus on speech development and sensory and motor development.

By age six children must enter grade 1. Students attend the compulsory education period at the Folkeskole for nine years. There are approximately 421,000 children and adolescents of primary school age in Denmark. There are about 10 students for every teacher in the Danish Folkeskole. The primary school gross enrollment ratio is 99 percent, an indication that nearly all school-age children are enrolled in school. This figure corroborates the primary school net enrollment ratio (96 percent). Nearly all students in Denmark complete primary school.

Upper secondary school is a three-year period for students mostly between the ages of 16 and 18. There are approximately 388,000 lower and upper secondary-level students in Denmark. The secondary school gross enrollment ratio is 123.6 percent. This large percentage is mostly due to the country's policy of admitting and enrolling large numbers of adults who need to complete their secondary education requirements, but have not done so in the past. The secondary school net enrollment ratio is 91.2 percent—indicating that nearly 10 percent of the student-age population leaves school after the compulsory period. There are approximately 10 students for every teacher at the secondary level. Secondary education is tracked into (1) upper secondary general education and (2) vocational education and training. Upper secondary general education schools are intended to prepare students for university education. This level is divided into five program types: STX, HF, HHX, HTX, and adult programs. The STX and HF programs are the most traditional in that the curricula comprehensively cover the humanities, social sciences, and natural sciences. The HHX program accommodates students whose strengths are in business and economics as well as foreign languages. The HTX program enables students with strong interest in the natural sciences and technology to prepare for tertiary education in polytechnic institutes. Most of these students major in engineering-related fields at the university level. The adult program enables students who terminated their education after the compulsory period to return and obtain upper secondary school certifications (see below). To be eligible for the upper secondary education school, particularly the STX, HHX, and HTX programs, students need to adequately complete their compulsory education and achieve a passing score on exit examinations in primary school and lower secondary school. Eligibility for the HF program requires students to be fluent in Danish and English, to have taken mathematics, chemistry, physics, and another foreign language, and to have completed their basic compulsory education requirements.

Prior to 2005 students entering the vocational track were often unable to continue their education or enter the university. However, in recent years, students with vocational interests have had the opportunity to transfer to university colleges and, in some instances, to universities. Vocational and occupational skills enable students to enter a variety of fields, such as management, paralegal positions, motor vehicle and vessel mechanics, the health profession, and maritime industries.

Postcompulsory Education

As a result of recent amendments to the Danish constitution, both upper secondary education students and vocationally oriented education and training students are eligible for higher education entry if their academic transcripts are strong and their exit examinations are above the passing cutoff score. There are three types of higher education programs: the baccalaureate, the professional baccalaureate, and certification for academic professions. The overwhelming number of students in the vocational track either prepare for the professional baccalaureate or the certificate of academic professions, while the majority of upper secondary education students continue for the general baccalaureate. Most students preparing for master's programs are in the general baccalaureate programs; however, with proper education background and credentials, those in professional baccalaureate programs may also continue for their master's degrees. Doctoral programs, such as the PhD, can be pursued only if students have obtained the master's degree.

In Denmark there are five universities, two polytechnic institutes, one business- and economics-related university, one medical university, and eight university colleges with individual specializations. The oldest and largest of these universities is the University of Copenhagen. Established in 1479, the University of Copenhagen is the only so-called ancient university in the country. In fact, it remained the only university in Denmark until 1928 with one peculiar exception: Schleswig-Holstein, a present-day state of Germany, was at one time part of Denmark, thus making the University of Kiel, which was founded in 1665 within the boundaries of Schleswig-Holstein, the second university in Denmark. However, after Germany's occupation of the region, the University of Kiel remained within German borders. Founded in 1928, Aarhus University then became the second university in Denmark. Both the University of Copenhagen and Aarhus University have high rankings among universities in Europe and have high overall international recognition. The specialization universities and the university colleges are primarily for students graduating from vocational upper secondary institutions. The polytechnic institutes enroll students from both the general upper secondary schools and the vocational secondary schools.

Teacher Education

Teacher education programs at the preprimary level are offered at university colleges and are known as social educator programs. Social educator degrees take three and one-half years to complete and require at least one year and three months of in-service training. The program requires a project leading to a baccalaureate. Students preparing to teach at the Folkeskole (primary and lower secondary levels) must complete four years at a university college education program. Students must complete at least 20 hours of in-class teaching as well as a baccalaureate project. Eligibility to teach at the upper secondary school level requires students to earn both baccalaureate and master's degrees in both pedagogical study and at least two areas of expertise.

Informal Education

Informal education is Denmark is defined as a program of learning designed for all citizens—mostly adults—for the purpose of gaining lifelong skills as a means of career advancement or for the pursuit of new knowledge at any point during the lifespan. In addition, there is an upper secondary education program for adults who did not continue their education after the compulsory period, but who now want to complete their secondary school degree. The Federal Ministry of Education sponsors both academic and vocational courses. Nonprofit organizations also play a major role in funding informal adult education in Denmark. Institutions that provide adult education include colleges of further education, vocational colleges, religious denominational organizations, as well as several other regional nonprofit adult education institutions. Education leaders in Denmark developed informal education programs as a means of providing learners with additional qualifications by attending classes either in school infrastructures or online. Most often informal education serves the purpose of improving workforce skills. Funding for adult education in Denmark comes primarily from federal and local budgets.

System Economics

According to the United Nations Development Programme (2011), Denmark ranks 11 of 186 in educational expenditures as a percentage of gross domestic product (GDP)—the highest of all countries in Europe. The total public expenditure on education in 2007 represented 7.8 percent of GDP. About US$15.730 billion has been allocated for education purposes. Based on these figures, total per student spending is $19,447 (determined by dividing total expenditure by 809,000, the approximate number of students in Denmark).

Future Prospects

As part of the European Union since 1973, Denmark is one of several European nations whose educational system is an important agent in the global economy. Similar to its neighbors, Denmark has a near 100 percent literacy rate. Along with New Zealand, Finland, and Australia, Denmark ranks extremely high on the international education index (.993). Nevertheless, the Danish Ministry of Education has recently considered lengthening the compulsory education period from nine years to 12 years. Along with other members of the EU, Denmark maintains a significant lead in student test scores and continues to graduate students who excel in the humanities, mathematics, natural and social sciences, and most professional areas of expertise. Also, Denmark has become one of the world leaders in the advancement of technological innovations as well as global communications.

Education in Greenland

Greenland is an autonomous region in the Kingdom of Denmark. Evidence of formal education in Greenland can be traced to the 1720s, when the Danish royalty planned to establish schooling in Greenland as a means of expanding the interests of Danish settlers and their offspring on the island. By 1845 an institution for training teachers was established in Ilinniarfissuaq, arguably one of the oldest formal teacher training centers in the world. The institution still exists and enrolls about 150 students annually. By 1905 school reform in Denmark had also applied to schooling procedures in Greenland. There are over 25 public schools in Greenland, mostly in the large towns. Instruction is given in Danish and to some extent Greenlandic. Greenland is also home to one university—the University of Greenland, which is located in Nuuk. The university's diverse curriculum includes programs in the humanities, social sciences, natural sciences, law, management and public administration, and medicine.

Despite inroads in improving the educational system of Greenland within the last two decades, much more needs to be done to raise the standard of educational quality and access for native Greenlanders. To reach exceptional twenty-first century levels, the administration must consider ways of installing and promoting information and communication technologies—especially for students in remote regions. Moreover, initiatives that foster articulation agreements (arrangements that allow high school students in Greenland to attend colleges or universities) between Greenland high school students and colleges and universities abroad would ease Greenlanders' participation in the global marketplace.

Daniel Ness and Chia-ling Lin

REFERENCES

Central Intelligence Agency. *The CIA World Factbook*. New York: Skyhorse, 2011. https://www.cia.gov/library/publications/the-world-factbook/index.html.

Nation Master. 2011. www.nationmaster.com.

UNESCO. *Global Education Digest 2012: Comparing Education Statistics Across the World*. Montreal: UNESCO Institute for Statistics, 2012.

UNESCO–IBE. www.ibe.unesco.org/countries/denmark.htm.

UNESCO–UIS. www.uis.unesco.org.

UNICEF. www.unicef.org/infobycountry.

World Bank Education Statistics. 2011. www.worldbank.org.

FINLAND

Finland is one of the Scandinavian countries in northern Europe. The official language is Finnish, although there are Swedish- and Russian-speaking minorities

---

Denmark Education at a Glance

General Information

Capital	Copenhagen
Population	5. 5 million
Language	Danish
Literacy rate	99%
GDP per capita	US$37,000
People below poverty line (2004)	no data
Number of phones per 100 people	61
Number of Internet users per 100 people	70
Number of Internet hosts	2.4 million
Life expectancy at birth (years)	78

Formal Educational Information

Primary school age population	421,000
Secondary school age population	388,000
Primary school age population	8%
Number of years of primary education	5
Student/teacher ratio (primary)	16
Student/teacher ratio (secondary)	10
Primary school gross enrollment ratio	99%
Primary school entrants reaching grade 5	94%
Secondary school gross enrollment ratio	124%
Child labor (ages 5–14)	no data

Note: Unless otherwise indicated, all data are based on sources from 2011.

near the borders. The population is mainly Finn (about 94 percent) with minorities of Swedish (about 5 percent), Russian, Estonian, Roma (i.e., Gypsy), and Sami backgrounds. The religion is predominantly the Lutheran Church of Finland (84 percent). The remaining population consists of members of the Russian Orthodox Church, other Christian groups, and no religion (14 percent).

For a period of nearly 700 years, from the twelfth to the nineteenth century, Finland was a province of the grand duchy under Sweden, despite cultural and language differences between the Finns and those who controlled the Finnish territory. From 1809 to 1917, Finland was an autonomous region of the Russian Empire. During World War II, the country managed to defend itself against both German and Russian forces. Soon after World War II ended, the Finnish economy suffered as result of numerous casualties and military spending in the form of reparations. However, from the early 1950s to the new century, the Finnish economy has been dramatically transformed from a forest- and lumber-based economy to a highly diversified and extremely successful information-based economy.

Educational System

Education in Finland is compulsory for nine years, for children aged seven to 15. This compulsory period is known as comprehensive school. In general, schooling in Finland lasts much longer, at the very least for a period of 14 years, because nearly all children and adolescents are enrolled in school prior to the compulsory period and after as well.

Precompulsory, Compulsory Education, and Curriculum

Compulsory education in Finland lasts for nine years for children and adolescents seven to 15 years old. This period is called comprehensive school, the first six years of which constitute primary education and the last three, lower secondary education. The overwhelming majority of students in the compulsory period attend public schools. Private schools that intend to offer comprehensive education must undergo a rigorous overview by the centralized government. In general, the curriculum of primary schools involves both play and learning; in other words, students learn but not in the confines of a teacher-centered environment that focuses on lecturing. Instruction is mostly in Finnish, but students learn in a multilingual environment where Swedish, Danish, Dutch, Russian, English, and possibly German are common second languages.

The Finnish primary and secondary school has often been touted as one of the best in the world. A number of reasons contribute to its standing as a model of education. First, in this somewhat democratic socialist system, Finnish students receive several benefits, such as full health care, free lunches, travel, and books and related materials. Finland is one of the few countries in the world that offers these and other entitlements to students. Second, by the age of seven, all students study the same curriculum regardless of their families' socioeconomic backgrounds, although the instructional method is the prerogative of the teacher. Most of the instruction is based on alternative pedagogical methods that emphasize student learning. Third, teachers are expected to earn master's degrees at a university in order to be eligible to teach in a school. Fourth, testing is unique in Finland in that norm-referencing is considered secondary to individualized performance. With the exception of the National Matriculation Examination, which helps determine strengths and weaknesses for university entrance, standardized testing essentially does not exist. Teachers develop their own examinations and provide instructional feedback as opposed to numbers or letter grades. Fifth, Finland is known as a leader in information and communication technology precisely because its education system has built in a polytechnic component—namely, as an alternative to the traditional university. Sixth, teachers have a great deal of latitude in their approach to teaching and their leverage in terms of employment. Teacher unions in Finland have had a large impact on the overall success of teacher education and retention. Teachers are well-respected by the government and society in general. Seventh, there seems to be strong collaboration between teachers, their unions, and the Finnish government in reaching educational goals. The teacher union is much more than a lobby; it is analogous to the government itself in that it examines what is best for society as a whole. In addition, the educational system as a whole is linked directly to industry through numerous networks. Professional learning communities have been formed as a way of sharing best practices that fit a particular region.

Postcompulsory Education

Postcompulsory education includes four years of study beyond the lower secondary school level and as few as two years to as many as five or 10 years of tertiary education—depending on the degree a student is pursuing. In general, the baccalaureate can be awarded in as few as two years after upper secondary school. The master's degree is awarded within two to three years after the baccalaureate, and the doctorate is awarded at any academic year thereafter.

Upper Secondary School and Vocational School

Upon graduation from comprehensive school, students enter either upper secondary school or vocational school. This conclusion depends on an individual student's academic ability and exit examination results. Students in the upper secondary school engage in four years of study, graduating when they are about 18 years old. The last two years of upper secondary school is the equivalent of the freshman and sophomore years in United States colleges and universities or the completion of two years of college. Before graduating, students take a national examination. The results of this examination determine students' academic direction. Students at this point have two possible routes upon graduation: They can either pursue a baccalaureate or enter a tertiary institution that specializes in polytechnic studies. Both programs last for a period of two years or until the individual reaches 20 or 21 years of age. Students who do not enter upper secondary school enroll in Finnish vocational schools. Like students in upper secondary schools, students in vocational schools study for a period of four years. However, the curriculum is much different and involves technical training in various vocations.

Tertiary Education

Tertiary education in Finland ranks high in comparison with neighboring countries. As in other European countries, it begins at different times for different students and depends upon one's educational track. Higher education in Finland is divided into two categories. One category is the postsecondary polytechnic institution, which educates individuals who

wish to enter medical, technological, applied science, or advanced vocational professions. These institutions offer both bachelor's (two-year) and master's (four-year) degrees. The second category is the more typical university education that leads to postgraduate degrees and licenses, including the master's degree and doctorate.

There are 10 universities in Finland. Two of them—the University of Helsinki and the Helsinki University of Technology—have consistently ranked near the top 100 institutions of higher education in the world, according to the Quacquarelli Symonds World University Rankings. The University of Helsinki is the oldest institution. Established in 1640 as the Royal Academy of Turku, the University of Helsinki enrolls more than 35,000 students, the largest enrollment of any university in the country. In addition, the University of Helsinki offers the greatest diversity and number of programs. The remaining multidisciplinary universities in the country include Åbo Akademi University in Turku, University of Turku, University of Tampere, University of Jyväskylä, University of Oulu, University of Vaasa, University of Lapland in Rovaniemi, Aalto University, and University of Eastern Finland in Joensuu and Kuopio. The Sibelius Academy in Helsinki and Kuopio is one of the largest universities specializing in music and the arts in Europe.

Teacher Education

Finnish society respects the teaching profession. Nearly all teacher education students study in universities. Traditionally, students aspiring to be secondary school teachers have always studied at the university because it was there that they could specialize in a major interest (e.g., mathematics, natural sciences, history, Finnish, English). However, by the 1970s students aspiring to become primary education teachers were also expected to complete a university education, and by 1990 this expectation was extended to teachers of kindergarten. To become teachers, students must enter a baccalaureate program that consists of 180 credits. Upon completion, students must then enter a master's degree program where they are expected to complete at least 120 credits in a specialization. In total, students are expected to complete 300 credits for two degrees within an approximate five-year period. Moreover, baccalaureates or master's degrees at polytechnic universities are permissible. In addition to areas of specialization, part of the master's degree component consists of a focus on teaching level or area—such as early childhood, primary, special education, or counseling. Another part of the teacher education component consists of courses on pedagogical study. Students who specialize in early childhood education for their baccalaureate are eligible for kindergarten (ages 1 to 6) teaching. Kindergarten teachers who have the appropriate university credentials can apply for teacher education programs that will make them eligible to teach at the preschool (age 6) level.

Students aspiring to teach at the primary level (the first compulsory period) must be accepted into a graduate-level master's program and major in education sciences. These programs cover pedagogical topics for students age seven through 12. Students aspiring to teach at the secondary level have two alternatives. One alternative is for students to complete a master's degree program in a specialized area of study. After completion, they can apply for teacher certification. A second alternative is for students to apply for teacher education certification at the same time they apply to enroll in the master's program.

Informal Education

Informal education in Finland represents a strong, vibrant part of the Finnish education system. One major role of informal education in the country is the concept of "open university," which allows nontraditional students (in terms of age) to enroll in university courses as a means of increasing skill levels. Also, those who perform well in open university courses might be eligible to enroll in a degree-granting program at the undergraduate level. Informal education in Finland also takes the form of "free education," or education for lifelong learning. Free education is funded in part by the government. Its main purpose is to provide lifelong education as well as help older students gain valuable knowledge as a means of preserving democratic goals. Free education is not new; it is a type of informal education in Finland that began in the nineteenth century as a means of educating citizens who did not receive formal education for an industrial-based society. This form of education is available through citizens' or workers' centers and institutions as well as summer university courses.

Finland Education at a Glance	
General Information	
Capital	Helsinki
Population	5.2 million
Languages	Finish (92%), Swedish (6%)
Literacy rate	100%
GDP per capita	US$33,700
People below poverty line	no data
Number of phones per 100 people	41
Number of Internet users per 100 people	84
Number of Internet hosts	4.3 million
Life expectancy at birth (years)	80
Formal Educational Information	
Primary school age population	379,000
Secondary school age population	387,000
Primary school age population	7%
Number of years of education (primary/secondary)	6
Student/teacher ratio (primary)	16
Student/teacher ratio (secondary)	12
Primary school gross enrollment ratio	100%
Primary school entrants reaching grade 5	100%
Secondary school gross enrollment ratio	112%
Child labor (ages 5–14)	no data

Note: Unless otherwise indicated, all data are based on sources from 2011.

System Economics

Finland ranks at 47 in educational expenditures as a percentage of gross domestic product (GDP). Along with Ghana, South Africa, Austria, Hungary, and Samoa, the total public expenditure on education in 2007 represented 5.4 percent of GDP. About US$15.34 billion has been allocated for education purposes. Given the GDP of Finland at roughly $188 billion, educational expenditure in the country amounts to nearly $10.15 billion, about $13,253 per student (total amount equivalent to US dollars divided by 766,000, the approximate number of primary and secondary students in the country).

Future Prospects

As part of the European Union since 1995, Finland is an important competitor in education as well as the overall global economy. Along with other members of the EU, Finland outranks other countries in secondary student test scores, and it continues to graduate students who excel in individualized areas of expertise, both in academic and technological educational environments. Finland's educational system excels in numerous areas, particularly in the humanities, mathematics and natural sciences, and the social sciences. Overall, the Finnish education system has greatly contributed to the advancement of technological innovation and global communications. The country has the potential to remain a leader in these areas in the years to come.

Daniel Ness and Chia-ling Lin

REFERENCES

Central Intelligence Agency. *The CIA World Factbook*. New York: Skyhorse, 2011. https://www.cia.gov/library/publications/the-world-factbook/index.html.

Nation Master. 2011. www.nationmaster.com.

Opetusalan Ammattijärjestö (OAJ). *Trade Union of Education in Finland. Teacher Education in Finland*. Helsinki: OAJ, 2011.

UNESCO. *Global Education Digest 2012: Comparing Education Statistics Across the World*. Montreal: UNESCO Institute for Statistics, 2012.

UNESCO–IBE. www.ibe.unesco.org/countries/finland.htm.

UNESCO–UIS. www.uis.unesco.org.

UNICEF. www.unicef.org/infobycountry.

World Bank Education Statistics. 2011. www.worldbank.org.

FRANCE

France is a large country in western Europe. The official language is French; however, some French dialects are still spoken—Provençal, Breton, Alsatian, Corsican, Catalan, Basque, and Flemish. There are numerous ethnic groups in France. These populations include members of Celtic and Latin, Teutonic, Slavic, North African, Indochinese, and Basque groups. Nearly 85 percent of all French are members of the Roman Catholic Church. The remaining population consists of Protestants (2 percent), Muslims (7 percent), Jews (1 percent), and 5 percent who are classified as no religion.

The French Republic consists of metropolitan France (in Europe), French Guiana (in South America), and the islands of Guadeloupe, Martinique, and Réunion. Today it is one of the world's leaders in technological advancement, education, and its role in the world economy. For the last 60 years, the country has maintained a stable democracy and free elections. Its collaboration with Germany led to the implementation of the euro in 1999.

Educational System

The system of education in France is highly centralized. It consists of *école maternelle* (preschool and kindergarten), *école élémentaire* (primary school), *collège* (lower secondary school), and lycée (upper secondary school). The French school system is run by the French Ministry of National Education. The national education budget for 2009 in France amounted to about US\$93.7 billion. The primary language of instruction is French. Literacy in France is nearly 100 percent for both males and females. There are approximately 15 million students in France—about 7 million in primary schools, 5 million in secondary schools, and 2.5 million in postsecondary, tertiary institutions. Nearly 80 percent of all students who enter French secondary school graduate and earn a secondary diploma. Roughly 30 percent of all students who continue for postsecondary education receive a tertiary-level diploma.

Although interest in education for the masses was of primary interest to French politicians since the eighteenth century, actual compulsory education did not commence until 1880, when Jules Ferry introduced the l'école républicaine (school of the republic), and, as a lawyer and politician, convinced the French government to require all children between the ages of six and 12 to attend school. These schools were free and secular, thereby offering education to a broader range of people with interests beyond those of the clergy. During this time, there was a surplus of schools in cities, but a lack of schools in the French countryside. This problem led to great disparity between the academic performance of city children and that of their rural peers. By the turn of the century, when a greater number of rural families moved to the cities as a result of industrial growth and increased occupation prospects, schools in Paris and other cities throughout France were unable to grapple with the large influx of rural youth who had little to no school experience. This problem led to the creation of the first intelligence test by Alfred Binet and Théodore Simon, which enabled education leaders to find the best means of educating newly arrived children from rural French communities.

In general, the French system of formal education

for the masses has served as a model for many educational systems throughout the world, including those that had begun prior to the French system in the late nineteenth century. To be sure, American educators and policy makers, with the help of Lewis Termin and other psychologists at the time, implemented Binet's intelligence test. But rather than using it as a means of identifying appropriate school settings for students of different backgrounds, Americans, Canadians, and other northern European societies used it as a means of segregating various populations. In recent years France has maintained its eminence as a world education leader.

Precompulsory, Compulsory Education, and Curriculum

Precompulsory education in France begins with *école maternelle*, which translates almost exactly to "preschool." Children at this level are between the ages of three and six years. The *petite* section is for children from three to four years old. The *moyen* section is for children from four to five, and the *grand* section is for children ages five and six. Although in part a day-care setting, the *école maternelle* conducts content-related instruction as well as serving as a means of preparation for the compulsory period.

The *école élémentaire* is a five-year period, beginning with the *cours préparatoire*, or the introductory formal grade level, for children who are six and seven years old. The subsequent four years of the *école élémentaire* include the cours *élémentaire niveau* 1, *élémentaire niveau* 2, *cours moyen* 1, and *cours moyen* 2—for children ages seven to eleven years. These levels are the equivalent of grades 1 through 5 in the United States. At present, there are approximately 3.7 million children of primary school age—about 6 percent of the population of France. The student/teacher ratio at the primary level is about 19 students for every teacher. The primary school gross enrollment ratio in France is 110 percent, and the percentage of primary school students reaching grade 5 is 98 percent. Main subjects at the primary level include French, mathematics, natural science, and social studies. All students engage in sports, health, art, and music. Many French primary schools also introduce a secondary language, usually English or German, by the *cours moyen* 1 year.

The *collège*, or upper secondary school, is a four-year period, beginning with the level titled *sixième*, and continuing with the *cinquième*, *quatrième*, and *troisième* levels (counting backward). The students enrolled in the *collège* period are 11 to 15 years old. These levels are the equivalent of grades 6 through 9 in the United States. After the collège level, students continue to the lycée, which is the upper secondary school period. The lycèe is divided into three types: *baccalauréat professionnel*, *baccalauréat general*, and *baccalauréat technologique*. In general, students entering the *baccalauréat professionnel* track are those interested in obtaining a vocation or trade and entering the workforce after three years of upper secondary school. Students entering the *baccalauréat general* track are those who intend to continue to college or university. Students entering the *baccalauréat technologique* track also wish to prepare for a college or university education, but one that emphasizes polytechnic training. Upper secondary school in France is a period that lasts for three years. The first year is the *seconde* level, followed by the *première* level, and finally the *terminale* level. At present, there are nearly 5.3 million students of secondary school age—about 8 percent of the population—in France. The student/teacher ratio at the secondary level is about 11 students for every teacher. The secondary school gross enrollment ratio in France is 114 percent, an indication that many students in the secondary level do not fall within the typical secondary-level age range.

In 2009 France was one of the top 30 countries in mathematics, natural science, and reading proficiency. French students ranked twenty-second among 65 participants in mathematics proficiency, twenty-seventh of 65 participants in natural sciences proficiency, and twenty-second of 65 participants in reading proficiency.

Students take different exit examinations depending on their interests and academic strengths. For example, students wishing to enter a university upon leaving secondary school must sit for the *baccalauréat* examination. This examination is similar to the A-Level examination that secondary school students must take in most of the United Kingdom, and the Arbitur that must be taken by students in Germany as a prerequisite for university acceptance. Other exit examinations include the *série scientifique* for students interested in the natural sciences, the *série économique et sociale* for those interested in mathematics and the social sciences, and the *série littéraire* for those interested in the humanities. The *baccalauréat technologique* and *baccalauréat professionnel* are exit examinations specifically designed for students entering specific vocations and trades.

Postcompulsory Education

Postcompulsory education in France generally begins at the same time for all students, regardless of educational track. Higher education in France is divided into five general categories. One category is the public university. There are more than 80 institutions of this kind in France. The most competitive universities in France include, but are not limited to, the College of France, École Normale Supérieure, École Polytechnique, University of Bordeaux, University of Grenoble, University of Lyon, University of Montpellier, University of Paris, University of Strasbourg, and University of Toulouse. The University of Paris was one of the premier ancient universities of Europe. At present, there are 13 successor universities to the University of Paris—all within the Paris metropolitan area. The most competitive of these are the Paris-Sorbonne University, Pierre and Marie Curie University, Denis Diderot University, and University of Paris Sud. Teacher training colleges are a second category. These include normal schools and university institutes for teacher training. Within this category are public and private institutions that may include teacher training programs. A third category consists of schools of fine arts and music conservatories. Well-known institutions of this kind include Conservatoire de Paris, Conservatoire National Supérieur d'Art Dramatique, and École des Beaux-Arts. Private universities are a fourth category of French higher education institutions. These universities are generally (but not exclusively) affiliated with a religious denomination. Nondenominational private universities include the American University in Paris, École des Hautes Études Internationales, and Baruch College, an institution in New York City with a large campus in Paris. Finally there are the universities of applied sciences and polytechnic institutes. Only universities and polytechnic institutes are capable of offering doctoral degrees.

Teacher Education

The teacher education process in France is one of the most advanced in the world. Teacher education in the early twentieth century consisted of programs that were provided by normal schools. Preservice primary education teachers were trained in *écoles normales*. Preservice secondary education teachers were traditionally trained at the university level and were required to pass an exit examination that allowed them to teach at the secondary level. After 1960 the French Ministry of Education required that all secondary students take the CAPES (certificate for teaching in secondary education) examination. By the 1980s Instituts Universitaires de Formation des Maîtres (university institutes for teacher training) were created as part of the larger university structure in several universities throughout France. These institutions both trained future primary and secondary teachers and provided settings for academic inquiry in the field of education and related disciplines. Instituts Universitaires de Formation des Maîtres offer programs for certification in numerous areas, including specific subject-related areas (e.g., mathematics, chemistry, French, history), as well as cognitive psychology, school psychology, sociology and education, movement sciences and kinesiology, international education programs, and curriculum studies. Programs in teacher training usually last from three to five years, upon which students graduate. At least one to two years must be spent in student teaching.

Informal Education

Informal education is France is provided for adults who wish to continue their education and increase their appeal among employers. The French Ministry of Education sponsors both academic and vocational courses for both traditional and nontraditional students in the effort to provide skill sets for various areas of employment. Informal adult education in France has also been sponsored by nonprofit organizations. Institutions that provide adult education include universities with continuing education facilities, vocational colleges, Catholic and Protestant organizations, and numerous regional, nonsectarian, and nonprofit adult education institutions. Funding for adult education in France comes from federal funding sources, provincial and municipal sources (such as chambers of commerce and labor and trade unions), occupational associations, and religious organizations. Formal adult education in France is controlled by an educational service called GRETA, which stands for Groupements d'etablissements (literally, "groupings of institutions"), which runs at least one adult education service center in each region of the country. Another formal adult education program is called Association nationale pour la formation professionnelle des adultes, literally, the National Association for Adult Vocational Training, which provides opportunities that direct adults to specific positions of employment.

System Economics

Along with Mongolia, Saudi Arabia, and Morocco, France ranks at 38 in educational expenditures as a percentage of gross domestic product (GDP). The total public expenditure on education in 2007 represented 5.6 percent of GDP. About US$120 billion has been allocated for education purposes. Per capita expenditure amounts to about $13,408 (the amount of education expenditure divided by 8,950,000, the approximate number of students in France).

Future Prospects

As one of the original members of the European Union, France has played a major role as a leading competitor in education, particularly in the area of higher education. Along with other members of the EU, France maintains a somewhat strong lead in student test scores and continues to graduate students who excel in individualized areas of expertise. As a result of its strong tertiary-level institutions, France is also one of the leading five countries with the largest population of international students. French education excels in the areas of the humanities, mathematics, natural science, and social sciences. French education has helped advance technological innovations as well as information and communication technologies from a global perspective.

Education in French Guiana

French Guiana is a region under France that is located in the northeastern part of South America. The official language of the region is French. It is one of the few areas of the continent that was not occupied by Spanish forces in the sixteenth century. Education in French Guiana is compulsory for children and adolescents, who must attend school for a period of eleven years—as is the case with France. There are approximately 85 schools in the region—66 primary and 19 secondary institutions.

Daniel Ness and Chia-ling Lin

REFERENCES

Central Intelligence Agency. *The CIA World Factbook.* New York: Skyhorse, 2011. https://www.cia.gov/library/publications/the-world-factbook/index.html.

Nation Master. 2011. www.nationmaster.com.

UNESCO. *Global Education Digest 2012: Comparing Education Statistics Across the World.* Montreal: UNESCO Institute for Statistics, 2012.

———. "Strong Foundations: Early Childhood Care and Education." *Education for All Global Monitoring Report.* Paris: UNESCO, 2006.

UNESCO–IBE. www.ibe.unesco.org/en/worldwide/unesco-regions/europe-and-north-america/france.html.

France Education at a Glance	
General Information	
Capital	Paris
Population	64.7 million
Language	French
Literacy rate	100%
GDP per capita	US$31,600
People below poverty line (2004)	6%
Number of phones per 100 people	56
Number of Internet users per 100 people	66
Number of Internet hosts	15.1 million
Life expectancy at birth (years)	81
Formal Educational Information	
Primary school age population	3.6 million
Secondary school age population	5.2 million
Primary school age population	6%
Number of years of education (primary/secondary)	5/7
Student/teacher ratio (primary)	19
Student/teacher ratio (secondary)	11
Primary school gross enrollment ratio	110%
Primary school entrants reaching grade 5	98%
Secondary school gross enrollment ratio	114%
Child labor (ages 5–14)	no data

Note: Unless otherwise indicated, all data are based on sources from 2011.

————. www.ibe.unesco.org/en/worldwide/unesco-regions/latin-america-and-the-caribbean/guyana.html.

UNESCO–UIS. www.uis.unesco.org.

UNICEF. www.unicef.org/infobycountry.

United Nations Development Programme. *Human Development Report 2011.* http://hdr.undp.org/en.

US Department of Labor. *2001 Findings on the Worst Forms of Child Labor.* Washington, DC: Bureau of International Labor Affairs, US Department of Labor, 2002.

World Bank Education Statistics. 2011. www.worldbank.org.

GERMANY

Germany is a large country in central Europe. The United Nations population estimate for Germany in 2011 was 81.7 million, thus making it the largest country in Europe (excluding Russia) in terms of population. The official language in the country is German. However, most people in urban areas are bilingual or multilingual—speaking English, French, Danish, Dutch, and perhaps some Flemish, Polish, and Czech, depending on the region.

The population is 90 percent German and 2.5 percent Turkish. Other populations include those from Italy, Poland, Russia, Greece, Serbia, Croatia, and Spain. Germans are generally divided into three groups in terms of religion: Protestant, Catholic, and those who are unaffiliated or have no religion. A very small percentage of the population is Muslim, particularly those who emigrated from Turkey. Germany's government system is a federal republic, consisting of 16 states.

The region that now makes up Germany was the crossroads and home to numerous tribes and ethnic groups during ancient times and through the early Middle Ages. It served as the backwoods of the Roman Empire. Later it became a central economic and political location, especially when the Franks became a dominant force in the region. Germany is also the home of some of the oldest universities in Europe, such as the University of Heidelberg, which opened its doors in 1386, and the University of Leipzig, which opened in 1409.

Germany reached independence in 1871 as a result of the so-called German Empire unification process. Despite the country's key position as a leader in economic development and education, it was the primary belligerent party in two world wars that left the country in financial and physical ruin. The unification of East and West Germany occurred in 1990 after the gradual fall of the Soviet Union. From an economic standpoint, the former West Germany was much further ahead of the former East Germany. Accordingly, the former German Democratic Republic increased its economic standing as a result of increased productivity and wages of workers.

In general, German citizens have maintained a high standard of living in comparison to other countries.

Educational System

The educational system of Germany is similar to that of most of the German-speaking nations of Europe in that the country has implemented a tracking system beyond the primary school level. After preprimary education for children before six years of age, students enter either primary schools or special schools, depending on whether they are labeled as gifted or learning disabled. Primary school is for students in grades 1 through 4 (ages six or seven through 10). The German school system consists of two general types: one type is used in the Berlin and Brandenburg region, and a second type is followed in the rest of the country. In the Berlin and Brandenburg region, the duration of primary school is six years (grades 1 to 6), and the duration of secondary school is seven years (grades 7 to 13). In most of Germany, however, primary school is only a four-year period. Secondary school begins in grade 5 and continues to grade 13.

Precompulsory, Compulsory Education, and Curriculum

Parents in Germany have the option of sending their children between the ages of three and six to kindergarten—an educational level that is not compulsory. By age six children must enter one of four types of primary school: state school, Montessori school, parochial school (either Catholic or Protestant), or Waldorf school. Again, in most German regions, primary school—or the *Grundschule*—lasts for four years, until students complete grade 4. As mentioned, students who have special needs often enroll in specialized schools that focus on specific disabilities. Kindergarten children receive an education that is based primarily on the socialization of the individual and personal development. Kindergarten education also focuses on speech development and sensory and motor development. Little, if any, curriculum at this level focuses on academic subjects, particularly in Montessori schools and most state-run institutions that accommodate early childhood programs. The German kindergarten, similar to those of neighboring German-speaking countries, infuses music and art instructional activities into its curriculum. Subjects taken in all four years of primary education include the following: local history, geography, biology, German, mathematics, music, art and drawing, technical work and use of textiles, and physical education. Many state-run and private schools also have English as part of the curriculum. Parochial schools include religion as part of the curriculum. In addition, students need to practice a modern foreign language. Remediation is also available for those who need it.

There are four types of secondary schools: the *Hauptschule, Realschule, Gymnasium,* and *Gesamtschule*. The secondary school that usually enrolls the greatest number of students is the general secondary school or the *Hauptschule*, which lasts from grade 5 through grade 9. Students in the *Hauptschule* continue their general education for the first two years. This is followed in grades 7, 8, and 9 with a preparation for careers and work. This is because most students in the *Hauptschule* continue for vocational education. Students in the *Hauptschule* who possess strong academic schools may transfer to the academic secondary school. Other options include medium-level and higher-level vocational or technical colleges.

A second type of school is the *Realschule*, which was an offshoot of the rationalist and empiricist movements of the eighteenth century. While the *Hauptshule* prepares students for vocational training, the *Realschule* emphasizes the importance of scientific inquiry as it relates to the professions. It prepares most students for both academic development as well as training in technology and both the physical and natural sciences. The common tertiary school of interest for most *Realschule* students is the polytechnic institute. The *Realschule* education falls in between the educational rigor of the *Hauptschule* and the *Gymnasium*.

The third and perhaps most prestigious secondary-level school in German-speaking countries is the *Gymnasium*. The *Gymnasium* is the most intellec-

tually and academically rigorous form of secondary education in Germany and neighboring German-speaking countries. Analogous schools include the grammar school in the United Kingdom and the preparatory school in the United States. The *Gymnasium* is essentially the only route that university-bound students can take to be considered for university education. Students who graduate from *Gymnasia* must pass the *Arbitur*, a high-stakes exit examination that, if passed, qualifies students for the university. Based in part on the German feminist movement of the nineteenth century, Gymnasia for girls were established. It has been found, however, that the greatest disparity in education attainment in Germany is between members of different socio-economic classes. Due to lower levels of academic performance, students of working-class families often enroll in *Hauptschule* and *Realschule*, and not *Gymnasia*. The curriculum of most *Gymnasia* includes the following disciplines and subjects: German, mathematics, the natural and life sciences (i.e., physics, chemistry, and biology), social sciences (i.e., psychology, sociology, geography, history, civics and political science, anthropology), information sciences (leading to engineering and computer technology), foreign languages, the fine and performing arts, and various forms of physical education. Many Gymnasia currently offer Greek and Latin as well.

The fourth and final type of secondary school in Germany is the *Gesamtschule*—also known in the United States and the United Kingdom as the comprehensive school. The *Gesamtschule*, unlike the selective Gymnasium or the vocationally based *Hauptschule* or technically based *Realschule*, has a comprehensive curriculum that includes both the study of academic disciplines found in the Gymnasium and the vocational and technological subjects found in the *Hauptschule* and *Realschule*. Students in the *Hauptschule* and *Realschule* often receive a four-year education with the intention of entering the workforce upon graduation. Graduates of the Gymnasium are nearly always college- or university-bound with the intention of obtaining a baccalaureate or higher degree. In providing a comprehensive curriculum, the primary purpose of the *Gesamtschule* is to provide a second chance to pursue a university education for those students who did not excel academically in primary school but may do so in secondary school. At the same time, the *Gesamtschule* provides technical training for students who do not perform well enough to continue to the university.

Postcompulsory Education

Postcompulsory education in Germany consists of a segment of secondary education as well as all of higher education. This section is divided into two parts: postcompulsory secondary and tertiary education, and the German university.

Postcompulsory Secondary and Tertiary Education

Compulsory education in Germany is usually a period of twelve years (from age six to 16 or 17). The number of years of education—11 or 12 years—varies depending on the region of Germany. Postcompulsory education in Germany begins at different times for different students because it depends on the educational track. In general, students who graduate from the Gymnasium have two general options: the *Fachhochschule* or the university. The *Fachhochschule* is most often translated as an institution of applied sciences, where students can earn specialization in business administration or technology. This type of higher education institution was founded in Germany. Other countries that have adopted the *Fachhochschule* include Austria, Liechtenstein, Luxembourg, Switzerland, and Greece. The *Fachhochschule* offers baccalaureate and most master's degrees. The major element that distinguishes the *Fachhochschule* from the university is that advanced master's and doctoral degrees can only be offered at the university.

The German University

Along with universities in the United States, Great Britain, Australia, New Zealand, and perhaps western Russia, those of Germany rank among the most competitive in the modern world. Many German universities also rank among the oldest in the world. There are 68 universities in Germany. Among them are several premier universities, many of which were established in the late Middle Ages. These institutions include the University of Heidelberg (1386), University of Leipzig (1409), University of Rostock (1419), University of Greifswald (1456), University of Freiburg (1457), University of Munich (1472),

University of Mainz (1477), University of Tübingen (1477), University of Hall-Wittenberg (1502), and University of Marburg (1527). These institutions were only for males from elite families who were preparing for careers in the law or clergy. The curriculum focused on the seven traditional liberal arts that were part of the trivium (grammar, rhetoric, and logic) and the quadrivium (arithmetic, geometry, music, and astronomy).

Humboldt University of Berlin, established in 1810, is the oldest continuously functioning modern German university. In general, the so-called German model of the university emphasized the importance of modern science as a major function of human development and advancement. In fact, some of the medieval universities, most notably the University of Leipzig and the University of Munich, followed the Humboldt model. In the United States the Humboldt model is evident in the curriculum of numerous universities. Johns Hopkins University, Stanford University, Cornell University, Clark University, and Northwestern University are just a few of the many examples of competitive research universities in the United States that follow the Humboldt model. Unlike other university models, the German model demonstrates an overall format of education objectives that is structured around scientific inquiry, and not philosophy, as the primary objective of higher education. German model universities, even those in non-German-speaking countries, often consist of campuses with numerous buildings that are devoted to specific areas of inquiry. Each building or group of buildings is an individual college that offers doctoral degrees.

Teacher Education

The teacher education system in Germany is perhaps the oldest in the world. In fact, after his visit to Prussia in 1843, US educational reformer Horace Mann commented in his seventh report on the effectiveness of Prussian schooling and wanted to model American schools and teacher education on the German student teaching model.

Today most student teachers in Germany study at the university level—especially those who plan to teach at the Gymnasium. German teacher education requires students to fulfill a two-year commitment to student teaching before they can apply to a school for a full-time teaching assignment. Prior to the 1970s, students who planned to enter the teaching profession enrolled in independent teacher training and pedagogical institutes. During the early 1970s, however, these institutes merged with universities, becoming affiliated colleges of education. Success in finding a full-time teaching placement depends on the subject-specific skills and expertise of students as well as cycles of retirement in specific school districts. To improve the success rate of job placement, the Standing Conference of Education Ministers from the German States issued a report in 1990 that stipulated minimal requirements of coursework for students seeking teacher education degrees at the university level. Given that the German education system is run by each of the 16 German states, this report reduced the obstacles that students faced in seeking teaching positions, especially if potential positions were located in different states from the one where the student's teacher training institution was located. For the most part, students enroll in two to four general education and psychology courses. In addition to this education core, students must enroll in about 40 courses in two major areas of study.

Teacher training at the university level generally takes four to five years to complete. This is followed by two years of student teaching. Length of teacher training also varies depending on the type of school that the candidate is considering. *Grundschule* teachers generally need three years (in addition to exit examinations) while Gymnasia teachers require five years of university education. Teachers preparing to pursue placements in *Hauptschule* and *Realschule* need about four years of university education in addition to student teaching. After the university, students entering the teaching profession must take the First State Examination, which, if passed, allows them to pursue a two-year student teaching assignment. After two years of student teaching, students take the Second State Examination before they can be professionally certified.

Informal Education

Informal education in Germany is for adults who wish to continue their education. The Ministry of Education sponsors both academic and vocational courses. Nonprofit organizations also play a major role in funding informal adult education in Germany. Adult education

Germany Education at a Glance

General Information

Capital	Berlin
Population	82.2 million
Language	German
Literacy rate	100%
GDP per capita	US$31,900
People below poverty line (2004)	11%
Number of phones per 100 people	59
Number of Internet users per 100 people	75
Number of Internet hosts	21.7 million
Life expectancy at birth (years)	79

Formal Educational Information

Primary school age population	3.2 million
Secondary school age population	8.1 million
Primary school age population	4%
Number of years of education (primary/secondary)	4/9
Student/teacher ratio (primary)	14
Student/teacher ratio (secondary)	14
Primary school gross enrollment ratio	101%
Primary school entrants reaching last primary grade	100%
Secondary school gross enrollment ratio	100%
Child labor (ages 5–14)	no data

Note: Unless otherwise indicated, all data are based on sources from 2011.

is usually defined as education for an individual who is 20 years or older. Institutions that provide adult education include colleges of further education, vocational colleges, religious denominational organizations, and various regional nonprofit adult education institutions. One major agenda of adult education in Germany is to provide adult learners with additional qualifications by offering classes to improving their workforce skills. Funding for adult education in Germany comes from a variety of sources: federal funding, provincial and municipal resources (such as chambers of commerce and labor and trade unions), occupational associations, and church organizations.

System Economics

Germany ranks 92 of 186 countries in educational expenditures as a percentage of gross domestic product (GDP). The total public expenditure on education in 2007 represented 4. percent of the country's GDP. About US$132 billion has been allocated for education purposes. Other countries whose total public expenditure on education represents 4.4 percent of GDP include Spain, Romania, Mauritania, Portugal, and Monaco.

Future Prospects

As part of the European Union, Germany is a major competitor in education throughout the world as well as an important agent in the global economy. Along with other members of the EU, Germany maintains a strong lead in student test scores and continues to graduate students who excel in individualized areas of expertise. German education excels in all areas of the physical and natural sciences, mathematics, social sciences, music, arts, humanities, law, and medicine. Further, German education has helped advance technological innovations as well as global communications. Several decades ago, education for girls in Germany was certainly available, and many women were able to study a limited number of subjects at the university level. At present, the least likely candidate to succeed in German schooling is a male immigrant from Turkey or other regions of the Middle East. The German government needs to abolish any form of discrimination so that all its citizens can benefit from a world-renowned system of education.

Daniel Ness and Chia-ling Lin

REFERENCES

Central Intelligence Agency. *The CIA World Factbook*. New York: Skyhorse, 2011. https://www.cia.gov/library/publications/the-world-factbook/index.html.

Nation Master. 2011. www.nationmaster.com.

UNESCO. *Global Education Digest 2012: Comparing Education Statistics Across the World*. Montreal: UNESCO Institute for Statistics, 2012.

UNESCO–IBE. www.ibe.unesco.org/countries/germany.htm.

UNESCO–UIS. www.uis.unesco.org.

UNICEF. www.unicef.org/infobycountry.

World Bank Education Statistics. 2011. www.worldbank.org.

GREECE

Greece is a country in the southern European mainland that includes nearly 1,400 islands, 227 of which are inhabited. The country's official language is Greek; however, a very small minority speaks English and French. The United Nations population estimate for Greece in 2011 was 10.7 million. The population is mainly Greek. The religion is predominantly Greek Orthodox (about 98 percent).

The region of Greece has often been considered by historians as one of the so-called cradles for the development of Western civilization. Known as Hellas, or Ellada, during ancient times, Greece was the location of the founding of philosophy, politics, and the notion of rule by the people (democracy), early discoveries in mathematics, and the natural sciences. Ancient Greece is also known for its development of literature (both history and legend), theater, and art. Greece is perhaps one of the first locations where evidence of an advanced writing system exists. Historians generally place ancient Greece within the period of 1600 BCE (with the Mycenaeans) to the early sixth century CE (the rise of Byzantium). Greece was also pivotal during late antiquity and the Middle Ages, during the Byzantine period, which lasted from the late fifth century to the fall of Constantinople in 1453. In 2001 Greece became the twelfth member state to enter the Eurozone.

Educational System

Education in Greece consists of preprimary, primary, secondary, and tertiary education systems. Schooling, whether public or private, is run by the Ministry of Education and Religious Affairs. At present, public schools in Greece are subsidized by both the federal government and municipal governments.

Precompulsory and Compulsory Education

In general, preschools and kindergartens in Greece are free and not compulsory. Although preprimary education in Greece was established during the middle of the nineteenth century, laws concerning the implementation of preschool education as a precursor to primary education were enacted in 1985. Preschools and kindergartens in Greece are intended to build children's psychomotor, emotional, and cognitive skills prior to formal schooling. On another level, preschools enable parents to work while children are engaged in informal schooling.

Primary school in Greece is a six-year period. Each academic year is called a class. The first two years of primary schooling are not graded. However, the last four years—classes 3 through 6—have a quite highly structured curriculum. Primary school students generally learn the following subjects during the six years: Greek language and literature, mathematics, the natural environment, music, art, physical education, theater and plays, and computer studies. In addition, most children by the fifth year begin to learn English. Students during the fifth and sixth year have the opportunity to enroll in physics, geography, politics, and another foreign language. Students from the third to sixth year of schooling usually enroll in history and religion. At present there are about 635,000 children in Greece of primary school age. The primary school gross enrollment ratio is 101 percent and the net enrollment ratio for the same period is 99 percent. This is an indication that nearly all of the 635,000 children are enrolled in school. Moreover, nearly all primary school children reach grade five and finish primary school. The primary school student/teacher ratio is about 11 students per teacher.

Secondary school in Greece consists of two levels: middle school and upper secondary school. Middle school in Greece is called the gymnasium. Upper secondary school is in two forms: the general lyceum and the vocational lyceum. Although the word "gymnasium" commonly refers to an elite school in Europe, particularly in Germany, the term comes from Greek and means "high school." However, in modern-day Greece, the middle school is the gymnasium. Students at the middle school level attend gymnasia for three years (the equivalent of grades 7 through 9). In addition, primary school students in the sixth year identify their strong subjects so that they can enroll in the appropriate gymnasium. Students need not pass examinations or requirements for gymnasium entry. The six types of gymnasia are the general gymnasium, musical gymnasium, art gymnasium, experimental gymnasium, athletic gymnasium, and religion (church-related) gymnasium. Students during the three gymnasium years must learn many subjects: modern Greek (language and literature), ancient Greek (language and literature), mathematics, biology, chemistry, physics, social science, politics, art and music, religion, computer sciences, English, a second European language, economics, geography, and at least one vocation.

Upper secondary school is also a three-year period. Students at this level are between the ages of 15 and 18 years. Students attending the general lyceum, which has a curriculum that follows the general gymnasium, prepare for university studies. Those attending the vocational lyceum receive technical and vocational training for immediate entry into the workforce upon graduation.

At present there are about 685,000 children and adolescents in Greece of lower and upper secondary school age. The secondary school gross enrollment ratio is 102 percent and the net enrollment ratio for the same period is 91 percent. The net enrollment ratio for secondary school shows that about 60,000 students either leave school by grade 9 or 10, or simply do not attend school. The secondary school student/teacher ratio is approximately 8 students per teacher. This may be a result of a drop in the number of students enrolled in secondary school.

Postcompulsory Education

There are approximately 25 universities and polytechnic institutes in Greece. Established in 1837, the National and Kapodistrian University of Athens—simply known as the University of Athens—is the oldest university in southeastern Europe. With more than 50,000 students enrolled annually, the university has the second largest enrollment of any university in Greece. The largest university in terms of enrollment is Aristotle University of Thessaloniki. On its three campuses, Aristotle University enrolls close to 90,000 students each year. Other notable institutions include the University of Macedonia (with campuses in Thessaloniki, Edessa, and Naoussa), the University of the Aegean, the Athens School of Fine Arts (established in 1837), and the Panteion University. In addition to universities, Greece has nearly 20 technical education schools. Unlike universities, these institutions have specific emphases in technological training. Other tertiary institutions in Greece include colleges, military academies, nursing schools, police and fire academies, ecclesiastical institutes, and schools of tourism. Colleges in Greece are analogous to individual schools within a university. Some colleges specialize in particular disciplines while others have broad baccalaureate programs, but do not offer graduate-level studies. In addition, the Hellenic Open University was established in 1992 to serve students through distance education.

Teacher Education

Teacher training programs at the preprimary and primary levels are available in departments of education and pedagogy at several universities throughout Greece. These programs are mostly four years in duration and often include a fifth year for practical training. Students who plan to enroll in secondary teacher training programs must also apply to one of several universities in Greece. Secondary education students must major in their specialized areas of interest that pertain directly to the subject that they plan to teach. Students who plan to teach in vocational lyceums apply to schools that are designed for technical vocational education teachers or technical pedagogy schools. Students must pass exit examinations in both general and technical secondary programs in order to be placed in a secondary school setting.

Informal Education

Informal education in Greece is provided for adults who either were not exposed to formal education or need additional skills in order to compete in the labor force. On the one hand, informal education can provide students with basic knowledge in reading, writing, and arithmetic. It can also provide students interested in honing their skills with courses for particular vocations (e.g., technical skills, updated office and clerical skills, cosmetics, fashion designing) as well as courses that emphasize foreign language instruction. Informal education programs are not necessarily regulated by the Ministry of National Education and Religious Affairs unless the programs are part of a continuing education department at a nationally funded or privately funded and accredited institute of higher education.

System Economics

According to the United Nations Development Programme (2011), Greece ranks 104 of 186 in educational expenditures as a percentage of gross domestic product (GDP). The total public expenditure on education in 2005 represented 4 percent of GDP. About US$12.72 billion has been allocated for education purposes. Based on these figures, total per student spending is approximately $9,658 (determined by dividing total expenditure by 1,317,000, the approximate number of students in Greece).

Future Prospects

Despite its status as a country with high-income citizens and a high standard of living, Greece has been faced with a sporadically impaired economy that led the government to consider severe austerity measures. Although primary and secondary education students in Greece are not directly affected by austerity measures, teachers are affected by holds on salary increases. Given the volatile economic conditions, the education system in Greece is one of the most competitive in the eastern Mediterranean region. Distance education and information and communication technologies are consistently on the rise in both curriculum and instruction throughout the country. There has also been great emphasis on environmental education in Greek schools during the last few decades.

Daniel Ness and Chia-ling Lin

Greece Education at a Glance

General Information

Capital	Athens
Population	10.7 million
Language	Greek
Literacy rate	96%
GDP per capita	US$24,000
People below poverty line	no data
Number of phones per 100 people	55
Number of Internet users per 100 people	40
Number of Internet hosts	2.5 million
Life expectancy at birth (years)	80

Formal Educational Information

Primary school age population	634,000
Secondary school age population	683,000
Primary school age population	6%
Number of years of education (primary/secondary)	6/6
Student/teacher ratio (primary)	11
Student/teacher ratio (secondary)	8
Primary school gross enrollment ratio	102%
Primary school entrants reaching grade	99%
Secondary school gross enrollment ratio	102%
Child labor (ages to)	no data*

Notes: *Although UNICEF has no data on child labor, the 2011 *CIA World Factbook* indicates that "women, men, and children are trafficked to and within Greece for the purpose of sexual exploitation and forced labor."

Unless otherwise indicated, all data are based on sources from 2011.

REFERENCES

Central Intelligence Agency. *The CIA World Factbook.* New York: Skyhorse, 2011. https://www.cia.gov/library/publications/the-world-factbook/index.html.

Nation Master. 2011. www.nationmaster.com.

UNESCO. *Global Education Digest 2012: Comparing Education Statistics Across the World.* Montreal: UNESCO Institute for Statistics, 2012.

UNESCO–IBE. www.ibe.unesco.org/en/worldwide/unesco-regions/europe-and-north-america/greece.html.

UNESCO–UIS. www.uis.unesco.org.

UNICEF. www.unicef.org/infobycountry.

World Bank Education Statistics. 2011. www.worldbank.org.

HUNGARY

The Republic of Hungary is a landlocked country located in east-central Europe. The official language is Magyar (i.e., Hungarian), which is spoken by nearly 95 percent of the population. Other languages spoken in Hungary include German, Slovak, Ukrainian, Romanian, Croatian, and Slovenian, primarily near the borders. The population is mainly Hungarian (93 percent) with some Roma (2 percent). The religion is predominantly Roman Catholic (52 percent) and, to a lesser extent, Calvinist (16 percent), Lutheran (3 percent), and Greek Catholic (3 percent). Nearly 11 percent of the population follows unspecified religions, and about 15 percent of the population is not members of any religion.

Hungary was part of the Austro-Hungarian Empire from 1867 to 1919, when the Hungarian government came under communist rule. Upon the fall of Germany at the end of World War II, Soviet troops occupied Hungary, which eventually became one of the satellite countries of the Soviet Union. In 1956 the country withdrew from the Warsaw Pact, a move that caused much resentment among Soviet authorities. By the 1960s Hungary began to diversify its economy by gradually moving away from Soviet directives. After the fall of the Soviet Union, Hungary ran multiparty elections for the first time in 1990. The country joined NATO in 1999 and the European Union in 2004.

Hungary has always excelled in education; however, this did not always translate into a sound economy for the country. For instance, although both Hungary and Austria have comparable educational systems in terms of competitiveness and level of success, the two countries differ greatly in terms of socioeconomic conditions.

Educational System

The overarching body that controls education in Hungary is the Ministry of National Resources. Within this body administration of educational concerns falls under the auspices of the Ministry of Education, the Ministry of Finance, the Ministry of Social Affairs, and the Ministry of Interior.

Precompulsory and Compulsory Education

Most of preschool education in Hungary is not compulsory. Only in the final year of preschool, namely, the kindergarten year, is attendance required. Preprimary education serves children between the ages of three years and seven years. Of these 380,000 children, close to 330,000 are enrolled at the preschool level. Preschool in Hungary is fairly advanced in terms of the promotion of academic progress and preparation for primary school. Most children attend preschool for about three and a half years (usually ages four through seven).

It is difficult to generalize ages and grade levels of primary education in Hungary because educational institutions are not necessarily aligned with grade levels; in other words, schools in Hungary have primary curriculum ranging from four to eight years of schooling. There are about 430,000 children in Hungary who are within the age range of the first four years of school, about 4 percent of the country's population. Children generally begin their formal schooling at age six. During the first four years of schooling, children learn reading and grammar in Hungarian, mathematics, environmental studies, music, art, physical education, and possibly a foreign language—most commonly, English, German, French, or possibly Russian. The student/teacher ratio for the first four years of schooling is 10 students per teacher. The primary school gross enrollment rate in Hungary is 98 percent, but the net enrollment ratio is 88 percent—indicating that not all students of primary age are attending school. Of the approximately 380,000 primary students enrolled, 98 percent of students reach grade 5 successfully.

Given the imprecise nature of the dividing line between primary and secondary school in Hungary, after the initial four years, students continue for an additional eight years of schooling. Nearly 1 million students in Hungary fall within the age group of grades 5 through 12, about 10 percent of the country's total population. Curriculum at the secondary level includes the continuation of studies at the primary grade levels and the inclusion of biology, chemistry, physics, history, geography, and history of art. The student/teacher ratio for the remaining eight years of schooling is about 11 students for every teacher. While the secondary school gross enrollment ratio is 96 percent, the actual percentage of secondary-school-age students attending secondary school is about 90 percent.

There are three types of secondary schools in Hungary: the *Gimnázium* (similar to the German Gymnasium); *Szakközépiskola*, which is a comprehensive high school that offers both curriculum for university-bound students and vocational, skills-related coursework; and *Szakmunkásképző Szakiskola*, which is solely vocational school for students who intend to enter the workforce upon graduating. Students entering the *Gimnázium* are preparing for a traditional university education. Students must take Greek or Latin in addition to two other foreign languages, as well as the usual high school level curriculum of natural sciences and social sciences, mathematics, physical education, and the arts and music. Upon graduating from the *Gimnázium*, students must pass the *Matura*—a culminating examination that is required for students who are applying to universities. Since 2005 information and communication technology courses as well as computer programming have become new staples in the secondary school curriculum in Hungary.

Postcompulsory Education

The first university in Hungary was founded in 1367 by Louis the Great in the city of Pécs. The University of Pécs eventually split into two academies—one of jurisprudence and the other of theology. The university experienced on-and-off discontinuations and openings in subsequent centuries. The modern University of Pécs that exists today was established in 1912.

Hungary is home to 20 state-funded universities, seven privately run or religiously funded universities, 10 state-funded colleges and conservatories, and 33 colleges that are affiliated with private or religious entities. Established in 1538, the University of Debrecen is the second-oldest and second-largest institution of higher education in Hungary; it enrolls 32,000 students annually. The largest and third-oldest university in the country is Eötvös Loránd University, named after the well-known physicist in 1950. Established in 1635, the university was originally named the University of Budapest. Today it has eight colleges—political sciences, education and psychology, humanities, informatics and technology, special education, social sciences, natural science, and elementary and nursery school teacher training institute—and an enrollment of nearly 35,000 students. Eötvös Loránd University is internationally recognized for its department of mathematics, whose alumni include Paul Erdős, John von Neumann, and Éva Tardos. Another competitive university in Hungary is the University of Szeged. Established in 1872 as the University of Kolozsvár, the University of Szeged enrolls about 30,500 students annually, making it the third largest university in the country in terms of enrollment. This university has a diverse curriculum, including faculties of agriculture, health sciences, food engineering, arts, economics and business, law and public administration, medicine, and pharmacy, in addition to the traditional colleges of natural sciences, technology, social sciences, education, and the humanities. Other internationally recognized institutions in the country include the Liszt Ferenc Academy of Music (which graduated renowned composers including Béla Bartók and Zoltán Kodály), the Hungarian University of Fine Arts, the Budapest Academy of Drama and Film, and the Corvinus University of Budapest. Colleges in Hungary focus on few areas of specialization, such as the Budapest Business School or the Bhaktivedanta Theological College.

Teacher Education

Most universities in Hungary provide education for preservice teachers through their faculties of education, psychology, and nursery and elementary education programs. These programs are some of the most innovative in Europe—particularly in the areas of mathematics, science, and technology.

University education programs differ in the number of teaching hours allocated toward pedagogy, psychology, and methodology courses, in addition to subject matter courses of specialization. Education programs in Hungarian universities generally include pedagogy and psychology in their curricula. Preservice teacher candidates spend about three years in college preparation and two years in student teaching. Student teaching hours depend on the subject of specialization.

Informal Education

Informal education in Hungary is provided primarily for adults who did not receive a formal education or whose formal education occurred during the change of control, especially during the time of glasnost following the transition from the Soviet Union to the Russian Federation (1980s and 1990s). In addition to improving skills for workforce entry, the general goal of informal education in Hungary is to provide retraining in skills, professional training, continuing education, acquisition of general knowledge, and foreign language instruction. Informal education includes basic knowledge in reading, writing, arithmetic, and numerous vocations and trades, such as paralegal positions, office positions, industrial management, and fashion design. The Ministry of Labor coordinates short-term informal education programs for adults attempting to increase skills for employment. Longer programs are run by the Ministry of Education. Informal education students are generally 20 years of age or older. However, younger students participate as well.

System Economics

According to the United Nations Development Programme (2011), Hungary ranks 52 of 186 in educational expenditures as a percentage of gross domestic product (GDP). The total public expenditure on education in 2007 represented 5.2 percent of GDP, similar to that of Slovenia, Switzerland, and Yemen. About US$9.8 billion has been allocated for education purposes. Based on these figures, total per student spending is approximately $6,860 (determined by dividing total expenditure by 1,422,000, the approximate number of students in Hungary).

Hungary Education at a Glance

General Information

Capital	Budapest
Population	9.9 million
Language	Hungarian
Literacy rate	100%
GDP per capita	US$17,600
People below poverty line	9%
Number of phones per 100 people	40
Number of Internet users per 100 people	59
Number of Internet hosts	2.6 million
Life expectancy at birth (years)	73

Formal Educational Information

Primary school age population	428,000
Secondary school age population	994,000
Primary school age population	4%
Secondary school age population	10%
Number of years of education (primary/secondary)	4/8
Student/teacher ratio (primary)	10
Student/teacher ratio (secondary)	11
Primary school gross enrollment ratio	98%
Primary school entrants reaching grade 5	98%
Secondary school gross enrollment ratio	96%
Child labor (ages 5–14)	no data

Note: Unless otherwise indicated, all data are based on sources from 2011.

Future Prospects

As part of the European Union since 2004, Hungary has been a leading competitor and proponent of preschool to secondary school education. Moreover, the country has been a leader in informational technologies, natural sciences, and mathematics—subjects that have contributed to the strengthening of the global economy. Along with other members of the EU, Hungary maintains a strong lead in student test scores and continues to graduate students who excel in individualized areas of expertise. Hungarian education excels in the humanities, mathematics, and natural and social sciences. Education in Hungary has advanced technological innovations as well as communications. The Hungarian government, however, is in transition in terms of its commitment to fighting racism within its borders. In particular, Roma populations are at a clear educational disadvantage when compared to their peers. The issue of combating educational and social inequities is a serious dilemma that the Hungarian government must face in ensuing years.

Daniel Ness and Chia-ling Lin

REFERENCES

Central Intelligence Agency. *The CIA World Factbook*. New York: Skyhorse, 2011. https://www.cia.gov/library/publications/the-world-factbook/index.html.

Földvári, Péter, and Bas Van Leeuwen. "Average Years of Education in Hungary: Annual Estimates, 1920–2006." *Eastern European Economics* 47:2 (2009): 5–20.

Nation Master. 2011. www.nationmaster.com.

UNESCO. *Global Education Digest 2012: Comparing Education Statistics Across the World*. Montreal: UNESCO Institute for Statistics, 2012.

UNESCO–IBE. www.ibe.unesco.org/en/worldwide/unesco-regions/europe-and-north-america/hungary.html.

UNESCO–UIS. www.uis.unesco.org.

UNICEF. www.unicef.org/infobycountry.

World Bank Education Statistics. 2011. www.worldbank.org.

ICELAND

Iceland is an island in the North Atlantic Ocean between Greenland and the United Kingdom and Ireland. Iceland has the world's oldest functioning legislative assembly—the Althing—which was established in 930. At present Iceland is known for longevity, a strong economy, and a high rate of literacy.

The official language is Icelandic, although English, German, and Norwegian are spoken throughout the country. The population is mainly descendants of Norse and Celtic peoples (94 percent). The remainder of the population comes from other lands. Claiming 85 percent of the population, the Lutheran Church of Iceland is by far the largest religious group in the country. Other groups include the Icelandic Free Church, the Catholic Church, and the Hafnarfjorour Free Church, as well as other Christian and nonreligious groups. In general, Icelanders have maintained a high standard of living.

Educational System: Precompulsory, Compulsory Education, and Curriculum

With gymnasia dating back to the eleventh century, it is safe to argue that Iceland has one of the oldest formal education systems in the Western world. There are five education levels in Iceland: playschool, primary school, lower secondary school, upper secondary school, and higher education. The second and third levels—the primary school and lower secondary school grades—are compulsory and include children between the ages of six and 16 years of age. Nearly all schools in the country are publicly or governmentally funded. There are 192 compulsory education schools, 42 upper secondary schools, and nine higher education institutions serving the students of Iceland. Although overall responsibility in education resides with the Ministry of Education, Science, and Culture, local jurisdiction in education has become more prevalent within the last 60 years, particularly when considering compulsory schools. The upper-level schools and higher education colleges and universities are run entirely by the government.

Playschool

Playschool, the first level of education in Iceland, is not compulsory, yet most parents send their children under six to playschools throughout the country. Playschools are essentially preschools where the notion of play is considered a fundamental component of child development and preparation for primary school. Despite local autonomy in general, the Ministry of Education governs the policies and curricula that are to be included in playschools. Therefore, although local districts fund the playschools, they must adhere to national guidelines regarding curriculum and policies regarding the schooling of young children. Nearly 30 percent of funding for playschools comes from tuition that is paid by children's families. The remainder is paid for by the districts and partially by the government. Three-year-old children usually attend playschool for four hours per day, while four- and five-year-old children can attend playschool for up to nine hours—especially during the winter months, when hours of light are minimal.

Primary School and Lower Secondary School

Children are required to attend school from first grade to tenth grade (ages six to 16). The curriculum during this time includes the following: Icelandic, mathematics, art and music, foreign language, history and religious studies, physical education, natural science, information and communication technology, home economics, and health and life skills. Close to

40 percent of the school day is allocated to Icelandic and mathematics. Equal amounts of time (about 10 percent) are allocated for art and music, foreign language, history and religious studies, physical education, and natural science. Approximately 10 percent of the time is allocated to technology, home economics, and health. Primary education, grades 1 through 7, and lower secondary education, grades 8 through 10, usually are offered at the same school. The school year lasts for 180 days; the success of the Icelandic model of education demonstrates that a 180-day school year can be successful. Given the country's rather low population when compared to other countries around the world, it is important to note the differences in school and class size in Iceland. As would be expected, large municipalities, such as Reykjavik and Kópavogur, have larger class sizes. Schools in these areas might have over 1,000 students. In contrast, rural villages in Iceland may have as few as 10 students. Regardless of location, however, all children are entitled to the same education.

Upper Secondary School

Although lower secondary school is compulsory, upper secondary school is not. Nearly all upper secondary schools in Iceland are gymnasia. Although all students are entitled to go to gymnasia, they must be eligible to do so. Eligibility for acceptance to a gymnasium requires high levels of academic performance in lower secondary school as well as high entrance test scores. The duration of upper secondary school is four years (ages 16 to 20). No tuition is required for students to attend gymnasia. Approximately 95 percent of all students—the overwhelming majority—who graduate from lower secondary school enter gymnasia. However, due to the rigor of the curriculum, not all students can remain in upper secondary school for the entire four-year period. As noted above, there are 42 gymnasia in Iceland—the largest having upward of 3,000 students, and the smallest having less than 100. Gymnasia are divided into four types that demonstrate a system of tracking: grammar gymnasia, industrial-vocational gymnasia, comprehensive schools, and specialized schools. Students who enter the grammar gymnasium remain for four years and are eligible to matriculate to a college or university. Students in industrial-vocational gymnasia focus on polytechnic and vocational specializations. Students who enroll in comprehensive schools are provided with a broader curriculum that includes that of the grammar gymnasium as well as that of the industrial-vocational gymnasium. Finally, the specialized school provides students with programs that focus on specific trades.

Higher Education

There are seven institutions of higher education in Iceland. The most well-known is the University of Iceland, which was established in 1911 as a result of the merging of three schools—one of which specialized in theology, a second in medicine, and a third in law. The University of Iceland is the premier research institution in the country. Since 1918 other higher education institutions have been established in Iceland; not all of these institutions necessarily specialize in research. These institutions include the Agricultural University of Iceland, Bifröst University, Hólar University College, Iceland Academy of the Arts, Reykjavik University, and the University of Akureyri. Nevertheless, all higher education institutions are both tuition-driven and funded by government sources. Depending on the academic year, approximately 20 percent of Icelandic students who graduate from gymnasia travel abroad for university education.

Teacher Education

Two universities in Iceland offer primary school teacher training: the University of Iceland and the University of Akureyri. Teacher training programs in Iceland are generally three years in length. Students who are eligible to enroll in lower secondary teacher training programs must have earned a baccalaureate at a college or university. Professional development courses for teachers who are in service are also available at the university level for those who are eligible to take them. Students who are eligible to enroll in upper secondary school teacher training programs must have completed a university education with two years devoted to a subject area specialization (e.g., mathematics, natural science, history, language) or vocation.

Informal Education

Informal education in Iceland is available for adults who wish to acquire additional skills and abilities in order to increase workforce desirability. Most informal education settings provide evening classes for working adults. These courses are similar to courses provided for younger students who enroll in upper secondary level or higher education courses during the day. Most informal education programs are funded by the government. However, they can also be funded in part by regional and municipal resources. Adult education is usually defined as education for an individual who is 20 years or older. Adults also have the opportunity to benefit from distance education, especially those who live in rural communities and remote regions in Iceland.

System Economics

Iceland ranks 15 of 186 countries in terms of educational expenditures as a percentage of gross domestic product (GDP). The total public expenditure on education in 2007 represented 7.5 percent of the country's GDP. About US$900 million has been allocated for education purposes. This amounts to a per capita education expenditure of nearly $15,000.

Iceland Education at a Glance

General Information

Capital	Reykjavik
Population	308,910
Languages	Icelandic, English, Norwegian, Swedish, German
Literacy rate	99%
GDP per capita	US$38,000
People below poverty line	no data
Number of phones per 100 people	61
Number of Internet users per 100 people	81
Number of Internet hosts	344,748
Life expectancy at birth (years)	81

Formal Educational Information

Primary school age population	31,000
Secondary school age population	31,000
Primary school age population	10%
Number of years of education (primary/secondary)	7/7
Student/teacher ratio (primary)	11
Student/teacher ratio (secondary)	11
Primary school gross enrollment ratio	98%
Primary school entrants reaching grade	100%
Secondary school gross enrollment ratio	109%
Child labor (ages 5–14)	no data

Note: Unless otherwise indicated, all data are based on sources from 2011.

Future Prospects

Iceland has consistently played a major role in education as it generally places high as a competitor in educational achievement rankings based on student test scores. More importantly, Iceland is an important agent in the global economy. The country continues to graduate students who excel in individualized areas of expertise. Education in Iceland excels in the humanities, mathematics, natural and social sciences, and information and communication technologies. The country is also a leader in alternative-based fuel production and innovative and pioneering research in medicine and the environment. Further, as in other countries of Europe, education in Iceland has helped advance technological innovations as well as global communications.

Daniel Ness and Chia-ling Lin

REFERENCES

Central Intelligence Agency. *The CIA World Factbook*. New York: Skyhorse, 2011. https://www.cia.gov/library/publications/the-world-factbook/index.html.

Nation Master. 2011. www.nationmaster.com.

UNESCO. *Global Education Digest 2012: Comparing Education Statistics Across the World*. Montreal: UNESCO Institute for Statistics, 2012.

UNESCO–IBE. www.ibe.unesco.org/en/worldwide/unesco-regions/europe-and-north-america/iceland.html.

UNESCO–UIS. www.uis.unesco.org.

UNICEF. www.unicef.org/infobycountry.

World Bank Education Statistics. 2011. www.worldbank.org.

IRELAND

Ireland, in western Europe, occupies approximately five-sixths of the island of Ireland (one-sixth of the island—Northern Ireland—is occupied by the United Kingdom). The official language is English, although Irish Gaelic is spoken by some of the population along the western coast. The population is mainly Celtic and English. The religion is predominantly Roman Catholic (89 percent). The remaining population consists of Protestants or atheists. Ireland's government system is a republic, consisting of 26 counties.

Between 600 and 150 BCE, Celtic tribes arrived on the island that is now Ireland. The people who inhabited the island were constantly invaded by Norse warriors. Fighting ended with the defeat of the Danes under the leadership of the Irish king Brian Boru in 1014. Unfortunately, peace in the region ended with the English invasion in the twelfth century. As a result, the people of Ireland were ruled by England for nearly nine centuries. As a result of the 1916 failed Easter Monday rebellion against the United Kingdom, guerrilla warfare ensued for the next six years; finally, in 1921, 26 counties succeeded from British rule and became independent. Ireland became part of the European Community—later, the European Union—in 1973. After this point the governments of the United Kingdom and Ireland collaborated to fight off terrorist groups—groups that exist to the present day.

Educational System and Curriculum

In Ireland education is compulsory for 10 years, from ages six to 16. However, most students begin their schooling at four years of age. In general, students complete 10 years of schooling, of which six to seven years constitute primary education and three to four years constitute lower secondary education. At the very least, children must finish the Junior Certificate Examination. Preschool is not compulsory and lasts for approximately three years, from age three to five. Types of preschools include day-care centers, play centers, Montessori schools, and church-run programs. As of 2009 the government of Ireland passed a law that allows parents to send their children to preschool in the year preceding primary school.

Children in Ireland are required to complete eight years of primary school: two years of kindergarten, followed by six years from first to sixth grade. Primary school students attend one of four types of schools: Gaelscoil, multidenominational school, national school, or preparatory school. The Gaelscoil is a relatively new phenomenon in Irish primary education. This type of school is run not by the government or church, but rather by private and volunteer organizations and groups. The primary language used in the Gaelscoil is Irish, which is now considered one of the official languages of Ireland. The Gaelscoil is the fastest-growing school in the

country, both in enrollment and school buildings. The multidenominational school is another relatively new phenomenon in Ireland. These schools represent children of families of all religious and ethnic backgrounds. They too are run by private and volunteer organizations. National schools are the oldest type of formal education in Ireland, created in the middle of the nineteenth century when the completion of primary education was considered an ideal. More students attend national schools than any other form of primary school education in Ireland. Since its establishment more than 150 years ago, the national school has been managed by the Catholic diocese of Dublin. Steps have been taken in recent years to secularize the national school. Finally, there are preparatory schools, which function primarily as private schools and are most often supported by the payment of tuition fees. Upon graduation, preparatory school students often continue to private secondary schools.

Like primary education in Ireland, there is more than one type of secondary school: the comprehensive school, the vocational school, and the voluntary secondary school. The comprehensive school is essentially a fusion between academic secondary and vocational schools. These secondary educational institutions are completely financed by the government and account for about 15 percent of the secondary school enrollment. The vocational school accepts students who are not academically bound and who are likely to enter the workforce upon graduation. Although this type of school is privately owned by vocational organizations and companies, it receives partial funding from the government. Approximately one-third of all students in Ireland attend vocational schools. The voluntary secondary school is the common progression for students in the national primary school. Both are run by the Catholic diocese and other private religious organizations. Again, the Irish government funds most of these schools, particularly in terms of teacher salaries and supplies. The voluntary school accounts for over one-half of all students entering secondary school. The secondary school graduation rate in Ireland is relatively high. Students are expected to complete a general examination in order to receive a secondary school diploma. There are more opportunities for school choice in metropolitan regions, such as Dublin, Cork, and Galway.

Postcompulsory Education

Postcompulsory education in Ireland has become quite competitive in recent years in its standards and rigor. At present there are 38 institutions of higher education in Ireland. The most well-known of these institutions is the University of Dublin. Established in 1592, the university is the oldest in Ireland. Also referred to as Trinity College Dublin, it was modeled after the universities of Oxford and Cambridge. Other major universities in the country include Dublin City University, the National University of Ireland, and the University of Limerick. Polytechnic institutes, such as the Cork Institute of Technology and the Waterford Institute of Technology, are quite competitive on international higher education acceptance standards. Rather than applying to a particular university, students generally select a university based on their eligibility—grades and test results are the main criteria—and apply to the country's Central Application Office, which handles the admissions process for all students. Most universities require that students are fluent in English (possibly Irish as well) and at least one additional foreign language, as well as secondary-level mathematics and the natural sciences.

Teacher Education

Teacher education in Ireland has a long history. Formal teacher education began with the establishment of national schools in the middle of the nineteenth century. It was managed under the Catholic diocese and remained fairly consistent, with little change, for nearly a century. The first signs of change occurred in 1922, when the Commissioners of National Education established two-year teacher training institutions. These institutions emphasized separation of classrooms and teachers by gender and religious denomination. Formal teacher training for secondary school teachers began in 1912, well after teacher training programs for the national primary schools. Students who received a university degree had the option to enter a one-year, part-time program in teacher training for secondary education.

Teacher education in Ireland changed significantly during the 1960s. As the economy of the republic improved, so did teacher education and the need to educate students for the then new service economy. Accordingly, the nineteenth-century infrastructure of teacher training institutions in Ireland had to be modernized. Within the decade, single-sex institutions gave way to coeducational teacher training. Institutions of teacher training began to follow the United States model of teachers colleges. By the last decades of the twentieth century, teacher education departments emerged as parts of universities. From the mid-1990s to about 2010, the European Union's Human Resources Operational Program allocated the equivalent of US$60 million to upgrade the educational system in Ireland. Specifically, the allocation was meant to update the curriculum and school management and to modify teacher education so as to prepare future teachers for twenty-first century skills.

Informal Education

In Ireland adults who wish to continue their education have the opportunity in many instances to pursue informal education. The Ministry of Education in Ireland sponsors both academic and vocational courses. Nonprofit organizations also play a major role in funding informal adult education in Ireland. Adult education is usually defined as education for an individual 18 years or older who wishes to gain experience or skills in order to pursue a second career or upward mobility. Educational institutions that provide adult education in Ireland include colleges with adult education programs, vocational colleges, and religious denominational organizations, as well as several other regional nonprofit adult education institutions. These institutions specialize in helping students improve their workforce skills for the purpose of diversifying employment opportunities. Funding for adult education in Ireland comes from a variety of sources: federal funding, provincial and municipal resources (such as chambers of commerce and labor and trade unions), religious organizations, and occupational associations.

System Economics

Ireland ranks 73 of 186 countries in terms of educational expenditures as a percentage of gross domestic product (GDP). The total public expenditure on education in 2007 represented 4.9 percent of GDP.

Ireland Education at a Glance

General Information

Capital	Dublin
Population	4.1 million
Languages	English, Gaelic, Gaeilge
Literacy rate	99%
GDP per capita	US$44,500
People below poverty line	10%
Number of phones per 100 people	54
Number of Internet users per 100 people	69
Number of Internet hosts	1,339,000
Life expectancy at birth (years)	78

Formal Educational Information

Primary school age population	446,000
Secondary school age population	281,000
Primary school age population	11%
Secondary school age population	7%
Number of years of education (primary/secondary)	8/5
Student/teacher ratio (primary)	18
Student/teacher ratio (secondary)	16
Primary school gross enrollment ratio	104%
Primary school entrants reaching grade 5	99%
Secondary school gross enrollment ratio	112%
Child labor (ages 5–14)	no data

Note: Unless otherwise indicated, all data are based on sources from 2011.

Nearly US$8.526 billion has been allocated for education purposes. Other countries whose total public expenditure on education represents 4.9 percent of GDP include Argentina, Jordan, Aruba, Canada, Thailand, Syria, and Poland.

Future Prospects

As part of the European Union since the 1970s, Ireland has increased its role as a competitor in the global economy. Along with other members of the EU, Ireland's students are increasing in global competitiveness in terms of test scores. In addition, more students are graduating from tertiary education institutions—a trend that seems to show that expertise is becoming much more individualized, with professionals demonstrating higher levels of skills. Education in Ireland excels in nearly all areas of the curriculum. Further, education in Ireland has helped advance technological innovations as well as global communications. One potential obstacle in Ireland is that almost one-half of the country's economic sector remains devoted to industry, with nearly one-third of the labor force in occupations related to industry.

Nevertheless, the country is steadily moving toward an information and services labor force.

Daniel Ness and Chia-ling Lin

REFERENCES

Burke, Andrew, ed. *Teacher Education in the Republic of Ireland: Retrospect and Prospect.* Armagh, Northern Ireland: Centre for Cross Border Studies, 2004. www.crossborder.ie/pubs/scotensreport.pdf.

Central Intelligence Agency. *The CIA World Factbook.* New York: Skyhorse, 2011. https://www.cia.gov/library/publications/the-world-factbook/index.html.

Nation Master. 2011. www.nationmaster.com.

UNESCO–IBE. www.ibe.unesco.org/countries/ireland.htm.

UNESCO–UIS. www.uis.unesco.org.

UNICEF. *Global Education Digest 2012: Comparing Education Statistics Across the World.* Montreal: UNESCO Institute for Statistics, 2012.

———. www.unicef.org/infobycountry.

World Bank Education Statistics. 2011. www.worldbank.org.

ITALY

Italy is a peninsular country in southern Europe. The official language is Italian. However, French, German, and Slovene are commonly spoken, particularly along the northern borders. The population is mainly Italian. Other groups include German, French, Albanian, Slovene, and Greek populations. The religion is predominantly Roman Catholic (90 percent). The remaining population consists of Protestants and Jews, as well as a small Muslim population.

The Italian peninsula represents one of the most important historical centers of civilization the world has known. It was home to the Roman Republic and subsequently the Roman Empire, which eventually stretched as far as England to the north, parts of Sudan to the south, and the frontiers of the Arabian Peninsula and present-day Iran to the east. Throughout the Middle Ages, the Italian peninsula was central to the mission and spread of Christianity. In the early Middle Ages, the bishop of Rome was the principal leader of the Roman Catholic Church in the world and has remained the chief figure of Roman Catholicism to this day. Italy reached statehood in 1861 under King Victor Emmanuel II, when the regional states united into a single national entity. The country was ruled by fascist dictatorship from the 1920s to the end of World War II, when the Allies defeated Italy and Nazi Germany. Italy witnessed an economic revival after the war and became an economic leader in the remaining decades of the twentieth century. In 1999 the country joined the Economic and Monetary Union. Despite substantial economic growth since World War II, a clear socioeconomic rift exists between the affluent north and the more economically disadvantaged south—a problem that is tangentially associated with education equity.

Educational System

The earliest evidence of formal and compulsory education in Italy was in 1861, shortly after the unification of the Italian states. The primary goal of formal education at this time was to reduce illiteracy levels. Accordingly, the Casati Act set provisions mandating that all children complete primary school.

Precompulsory, Compulsory Education, and Curriculum

Schooling in Italy consists of four levels: *scuola dell'infanzia* (noncompulsory preschool), *scuola primaria* (primary school), *scuola secondaria di primo grado* (first level of secondary school, also known as lower secondary school), and either *scuola secondaria di secondo grado* (second level of secondary school, also known as upper secondary school) or *formazione professionale* (professional secondary school).

Preschool education is the only noncompulsory education period in Italy. Children at this level attend school for three years, usually starting at age three and continuing to age six; however, children may start preschool after three years of age. The Reggio Emilia approach and the Montessori teaching and learning method are two of the most widespread preschool philosophies developed in Italy. These two preschool approaches have been adapted by preschools throughout the world.

Primary education is the first compulsory education period in Italy. Students who are expected to attend primary school (school years 1 through 5) are between the ages of six and 11. However, five-year-old children can enroll in primary school, depending on their date of birth as reflected in the school year. The curriculum at the primary level includes Italian, mathematics, natural science, history, geography, civics, physical education, visual arts, and music. At present, there are about 2.7 million primary school age students in Italy. The primary student/teacher ratio is 11 students for every teacher. The primary school gross enrollment ratio is 102 percent. The primary school net enrollment ratio is 99 percent, indicating that nearly all children of primary school age are attending primary school. Moreover, nearly all students attending primary school reach grade 5 and actually complete this level of schooling.

Lower secondary education is the second compulsory education period. Students in lower secondary education are between the ages of 11 and 14 years. At the end of this period students receive the Licenza di Scuola Media (middle school degree). Curriculum at this level consists of a continuation of the subjects taught at the primary level. In addition, students gain insight into polytechnic disciplines as well as more rigorous subjects in the natural sciences.

After their fourteenth birthday, or year 3 of lower secondary school, students are expected to attend either upper secondary school or professional secondary school. Either type requires students to attend for five years (ages 14 or 15 through 18 or 19). Upper secondary school prepares students who plan to attend the university. The main school types are the Liceo, the Instituto Tecnico, and the Instituto Professionale. The Liceo is divided into five types: Liceo Classico (emphasis on classical languages—particularly ancient Greek and Latin); Liceo Scientifico (emphasis on natural sciences); Liceo Scienze de Umane (emphasis on social sciences); Liceo Linguistico (emphasis on the study of language and modern languages); and Liceo Artistico (emphasis on the arts and music). The Instituto Tecnico prepares students who wish to enter disciplines related to engineering and technology. The Instituto Professionale emphasizes vocational training and trades.

There are more than 4.5 million children and adolescents in Italy who are of secondary school age. The secondary school gross enrollment rate is nearly 100 percent, and the net enrollment rate is approximately 93 percent, indicating that the overwhelming majority of students in Italy complete secondary school. The student/teacher ratio at the secondary level is 11 students per teacher. The Programme for International Student Assessment (PISA) ranks Italy thirty-sixth among 65 countries throughout the world in student academic performance. However, many of the country's universities rank among the most competitive in the world.

Postcompulsory Education

Higher education in Italy is divided into four general categories: the public and private university, polytechnic university, institute of arts or music, and the college (a non-doctoral-granting institution). There are over 90 universities in Italy. Educational researchers put the actual number of universities in the country at 93. This figure does not include the 11 distance learning universities. By far Italy has the greatest number of so-called ancient universities—namely, universities that were founded before 1500—in Europe and the world. Seventeen ancient universities are still in existence, many of which rank, according to the Quacquarelli Symonds University Rankings, among the most successful 500 universities in the world. It is important to note, however, that the missions of these universities, as of other ancient universities in the world, have changed. Originally they were affiliated with the diocese of a large area, usually a city, nearby a local cathedral. The mission was to train young men for the clergy and the law. At present a number of these universities are leaders in scientific research and medicine, in addition to law. Established in 1088, the oldest university in Italy, and arguably the oldest university in the world, is the University of Bologna. Other well-known universities in Italy include the University of Catania (1444), University of Ferrara (1391), University of Florence (1349), University of Genoa (1471), University of Macerata (1290), University of Modena and Reggio Emilia (1188), University of Naples (1224), University of Padua (1222), University of Parma (1412), University of Pavia (1361), University of Perugia (1308), Sapienza University of Rome (1303), University of Salerno (late twelfth century), University of Siena (1246), and University of Turin (1404). The Sapienza University of Rome is the largest university in Europe, enrolling more than 147,000 students annually. Other competitive institutions in Italy include the University of Messina (1548); the University of Palermo (1806), which is a leading university in medicine and law; the Ca' Foscari University of Venice, a leading university in business and economics; the Architecture Institute of Venice; the Academy of Fine Arts of Verona; and the Conservatory of Verona. In addition, there are 27 colleges and nonuniversity institutions of higher education in Italy. These are mostly institutions that grant baccalaureates and master's degrees.

At the college and university level, the bachelor's degree is usually earned in four years—traditionally between the ages 19 and 23 years. At the university level, the general master's degree requires about two years of coursework and thesis. Master's degrees in specific specializations in the natural sciences, premedicine, law, architecture, some forms of engineering, and the arts can be completed within a five-year period (ages 19 to 24). The doctoral degree usually takes an additional three to five years beyond the master's degree.

Teacher Education

Students who plan to become preprimary or primary school teachers in Italy must enroll in a four-year university curriculum, which leads to the Laurea in Scienze della Formazione Primaria (LSFP—baccalaureate in primary education). By the sophomore year of the program, students must decide between the early childhood program and the primary school teacher program. Pedagogical instruction takes place during the second two-year period of each of the programs. Training programs for prospective secondary school teachers in Italy must include a four- to five-year *corsi di laurea* (degree courses), which are available in most universities throughout the country. Secondary school teaching can take place only after the university program and after two years of student teaching service in the specific subject. Students must also pass a regional examination that is based on the specific area of study. Moreover, there are two types of subject-specific examinations: one for lower secondary school and one for upper secondary school.

Informal Education

Informal education practices in Italy emphasize the education of adults who wish to return to school to gain skills for desirability in the workforce. The Ministry of Education, Universities, and Research in Italy sponsors both academic and vocational courses. Funding for informal education also comes from nonprofit organizations. Most adults in Italy who return to school are over 20 years of age. However, this does not preclude individuals who complete upper secondary school and enter the workforce upon graduation. Institutions that provide adult education include programs through universities or colleges, religious denominational organizations, and other regional nonprofit adult education institutions, such as union groups and municipal agencies. Funding for adult education in Italy comes from a variety of sources: federal funding, provincial and municipal resources (such as chambers of commerce and labor and trade unions), occupational associations, and church organizations.

System Economics

Along with Algeria, Kosovo, Sierra Leone, and Spain, Italy ranks at 91 in educational expenditures as a percentage of gross domestic product (GDP). The total public expenditure on education in 2007 represented 4.3 percent of GDP. Nearly US$76.282 billion has been allocated for education purposes. Per capita expenditure amounts to approximately $10,571 (the amount of education expenditure divided by 7,216,000, the approximate number of students in Italy).

Italy Education at a Glance

General Information

Capital	Rome
Population	61 million
Languages	Italian (some German, French, Slovene)
Literacy rate	99%
GDP per capita	US$30,200
People below poverty line	no data
Number of phones per 100 people	35
Number of Internet users per 100 people	43
Number of Internet hosts	23.1 million
Life expectancy at birth (years)	80

Formal Educational Information

Primary school age population	2.6 million
Secondary school age population	4.5 million
Primary school age population	4.5%
Secondary school age population	7.5%
Number of years of education (primary/secondary)	5/8
Student/teacher ratio (primary)	11
Student/teacher ratio (secondary)	11
Primary school gross enrollment ratio	102%
Primary school entrants reaching grade	99%
Secondary school gross enrollment ratio	99%
Child labor (ages 5–14)	no data

Note: Unless otherwise indicated, all data are based on sources from 2011.

Future Prospects

Italy has a rather strong educational system. Its strengths lie in a well-developed early childhood system, primary school education, and highly competitive universities. However, the success of its secondary school program is mixed. Some education scholars argue that secondary schools are exceptional due to the rather high completion rate, while other education researchers maintain that socioeconomic disparities between the affluent north and the less affluent south contribute to a less than satisfactory secondary education system. In general, students leave school well-prepared for the workforce and are skilled in technologically related subjects. Another issue that is currently being addressed by education scholars and educational administrators is integrazione scolastica—inclusive education for all, regardless of ethnicity, social class, learning style, or disability. A remaining challenge in the educational system of Italy concerns what Simona D'Alesso (2011) refers to as macro-exclusions, which are forms of discrimination against non-Italian children as well as all children with specific physical challenges or learning difficulties. The implications of inclusive education implementation are multifold. Such a mandate would change the ways in which teacher education programs are administered in education institutes. It would also increase the diversity of teachers in terms of teaching styles and areas of expertise as a platform in accommodating students of different needs. In addition, inclusive education programs would potentially transform the ways in which students would be assessed, particularly in terms of criteria (what they should know at a given age) and not solely in terms of norms (how a student compares with other students). More importantly, the success of the educational system in Italy will depend upon the country's level of unemployment in the years to come.

Daniel Ness and Chia-ling Lin

REFERENCES

Central Intelligence Agency. *The CIA World Factbook*. New York: Skyhorse, 2011. https://www.cia.gov/library/publications/the-world-factbook/index.html.

D'Alessio, Simona. *Inclusive Education in Italy: A Critical Analysis of the Policy of Integrazione Scolastica*. Rotterdam: Sense Publishers, 2011.

Nation Master. 2011. www.nationmaster.com.

UNESCO. *Global Education Digest 2012: Comparing Education Statistics Across the World.* Montreal: UNESCO Institute for Statistics, 2012.

UNESCO–IBE. www.ibe.unesco.org/en/worldwide/unesco-regions/europe-and-north-america/italy.html.

UNESCO–UIS. www.uis.unesco.org.

UNICEF. www.unicef.org/infobycountry.

World Bank Education Statistics. 2011. www.worldbank.org.

LIECHTENSTEIN

Liechtenstein is the fourth-smallest country in Europe. Approximately one-third (11,852) of Liechtenstein's 34,604 inhabitants are from foreign lands, mostly from the border countries of Switzerland and Austria, as well as nearby countries, such as Germany, France, and Italy. Liechtensteiners take great interest in their educational system.

The Principality of Liechtenstein formed in 1719, when the county of Vaduz and the Barony of Schellenburg united. By 1805 mandatory education was established as a solution to problems associated with economic isolation and the lack of trade with neighboring states. As a result of the Customs Treaty with Austria-Hungary, which was concluded in 1852, Liechtenstein was essentially economically liberated. Under the leadership of Prince Johann II, Liechtenstein underwent several economic reforms, including the establishment of the first bank in 1861, a revitalization of the system of education, and the first circulating newspaper in 1862. The development of the textile industry, which had been imported to Liechtenstein from Austria a decade earlier, required the study of textiles and technical studies in the primary school curriculum. Prior to World War I, primary education was the only mandatory education that existed in Liechtenstein. The twentieth century, however, showed rapid progress in the development of the Liechtensteiner public education system. Today Liechtenstein is a highly competitive and technological society.

Educational System

The educational system of Liechtenstein is similar to that of most of the German-speaking nations of Europe in that the country has implemented a track-ing system beyond the primary school level, which usually is completed by age 11 or the end of grade 5. Compulsory schooling in Liechtenstein begins at age five or six (depending on the child's birth date) with kindergarten. Although preschools do exist in Liechtenstein, they are not compulsory. After age six the student continues on to primary school, separate from kindergarten, for grades 1 through 5 (ages seven to 11). Upon completion of primary school, the student is then tracked into one of three types of secondary school: the Oberschule, Realschule, or Gymnasium. With the Oberschule and Realschule, students are required to complete four years of schooling, from grades 6 through 9 (ages 12 to 15), and have the option to continue to grade 10. The first two tracks, discussed in more detail below, prepare the student with a professional or vocational education, whereas the third track prepares the student for an academic career and the possibility for advanced degrees in an academic discipline.

Precompulsory and Compulsory Education

Compulsory education in Liechtenstein begins as early as six years, the age when some students enter kindergarten, or as late as seven years, when students enter primary school. The second year of kindergarten is only compulsory for children whose native language is not German. German-speaking families have the option of enrolling their children in kindergarten. Recent employment figures by economic sector indicate that the country employs over 900 teachers for its kindergarten, primary, and secondary education school system. Upon completing kindergarten, children at the approximate age of seven attend primary school, which consists of five grade levels (grades 1 through 5). With the exception of children whose native language is not German, grade 1 represents the commencement of compulsory schooling. Primary school is free of cost for all students.

Nearly all primary education students enter one of the three high school tracks mentioned earlier. Students who graduate from the Oberschule or Realschule have the option of a voluntary tenth year of secondary school, where they can improve their skills in a particular profession or vocation. The Vocational High School in Liechtenstein is the only school in

Liechtenstein which allows students to pursue a high school degree (known as Matura) by grade 13. In addition to the Vocational High School, students who graduate from the Oberschule or Realschule may enroll, if accepted, in professional colleges or vocational schools in neighboring countries. Students bound for the Gymnasium must complete three years of general education and an additional five years of a more specified major (see below). Gymnasium graduates may apply to four higher educational institutions within Liechtenstein or continue their education in universities or research institutes in other countries.

Although not as popular as the public schools, kindergarten, primary, and secondary students may also enroll in the private Waldorf School, located in Schaan. The curriculum at the Waldorf School is essentially the same as that of the public schools. However, students of Waldorf education generally remain with the same teacher for a number of years, and they learn various subjects in so-called epoch form—that is, a particular subject for several days at a time.

Postcompulsory Education

There are six institutions of higher education (excluding vocational colleges, which are essentially extensions of the Oberschule and Realschule) in the country. Most educational institutions in Liechtenstein are located in Vaduz, the capital, or in Schaan, the largest city in population. Nearly 100 percent of all Liechtensteiner students who complete their compulsory education go on to higher education. Formal education for students who are older than 15 takes a number of forms. Given that the educational system in Liechtenstein implements tracking, students who graduate from the Gymnasium—the academic route—are eligible to apply to four higher education institutions in Liechtenstein: the Liechtenstein Institute, International Academy of Philosophy, Liechtenstein University of Applied Sciences, and University for Human Sciences. The Liechtenstein Institute prepares Gymnasium graduates for scientific research in the areas of law, political science, sociology, history, and economics. The International Academy of Philosophy is a private institution that prepares students in the area of philosophy. Students at the academy have the opportunity to earn a master's or doctoral degree. The Liechtenstein University of Applied Sciences offers both baccalaureate and master's degrees in the fields of architecture and business. The University for Human Sciences, founded in 2000, enrolls students who wish to study psychology, neuroscience, and cognitive science. In addition to these four universities and institutes, other higher education institutions in the country include the Liechtenstein Music School and the Liechtenstein School of Art.

Curriculum, Assessment, and Instruction

Children who attend kindergarten receive an education that is mostly based on the socialization of the individual and personal development. Kindergarten education also emphasizes speech development and sensory and motor development. Little emphasis is placed on academic subjects. The Liechtensteiner kindergarten, however, incorporates music and art instructional activities into its curriculum.

Upon entrance to primary school, children are taught the following subjects: German, mathematics, social studies, art, music, textile work and technological design, religion, and sports and exercise. In grade 3 students are required to learn English as a second language. Student assessment is based on a number of factors, including academic achievement, social interaction, and academic work habits. By grade 5, the student's teacher and parents decide which of the three tracks the student should take for secondary education. If there is no agreement between the teacher and parents, then the student has the option of taking an entrance examination before the beginning of grade 6. About 28 percent of all primary school graduates enter the Oberschule, 50 percent enter the Realschule, and 22 percent are bound for the Gymnasium.

The Oberschule offers a vocational education for students who do not perform well enough to enter the Realschule or the Gymnasium. Students, however, may transfer to the Realschule after the first or second year if their performance improves. Students who graduate from the Oberschule by grade 9 usually enter a vocational profession. The Realschule provides both an academic and a professional education. A professional education appeals to students who wish to specialize in an area of business, commerce, medicine, technology, or possibly education. Students in the Realschule have the opportunity to transfer at the end of each of the secondary grade levels to the Gymnasium.

During the first three years of the Gymnasium (i.e., lower level), students continue the academic subjects that they studied in the last year of primary school. During the upper level (grades 9 through 13), students may concentrate in one of five areas: Latin and Italian (often referred to as "Lingua"); modern languages; art, music, and education; economics and law; and mathematics and the natural sciences. Students who graduate from the Liechtensteiner Gymnasium usually enter the university, and those who do continue their higher education in Switzerland, Austria, the University of Tübingen in Germany, or within the Principality of Liechtenstein may do so without an examination.

Teacher Education

Higher education institutions in Liechtenstein do not offer degrees in teacher education. This may be partially due to the country's extremely small land area or the limited space and resources (e.g., number of schools or venues for student teaching) at the college or university level for fostering a teacher education program. Therefore, students who complete secondary school or possibly obtain a college education may further their studies in teacher education at a number of teacher education institutions in Switzerland, Austria, and Germany. Both primary and secondary schools in Liechtenstein recognize and accept teacher education diplomas from institutions in neighboring German-speaking countries. In neighboring Switzerland, teacher preparation at both the primary and secondary levels was offered in secondary schools that offered teacher education programs. Since 2004, however, most teacher education diplomas have been awarded at pedagogical institutes at 13 universities of applied sciences. In neighboring Austria, students in teacher education programs at the primary level complete three years of instruction at the postsecondary level at teacher training colleges (Pädagogische Akademien). These colleges are generally attached to (or nearby) primary schools to aid in student teaching. Students of teacher education programs at the secondary level, however, must attend a university and complete one year of teacher training upon graduation. Teacher trainees in

both Switzerland and Austria are eligible for teaching in the Liechtensteiner school system.

Informal Education

In Liechtenstein informal education is often used in reference to adults who wish to continue their education. Liechtenstein began its mission to implement adult education in the late 1970s. By 1979 the Liechtensteiner government enacted the Law on the Promotion of Adult Education, which states in Article 2, "Adult education offers the opportunity to acquire and multiply skills and abilities. It contributes to the mental realization of the individual, in particular to personality development and to increase interest of the population in contemporary issues." Since 1979 a number of informal adult education offices and programs have emerged. These include the Stein-Egerta Adult Education Institute (formerly the Office for Adult Education), the Gutenberg House, the Resch Community Center, and the Educational Association for Women. The Stein-Egerta Institute publishes the *Course Book for Free-Time and Adult Education*, which is circulated to nearly 17,000 Liechtensteiners throughout the country. From 1999 to the present, adult education services have been run by a foundation, Liechtenstein Adult Education, created by the government after the enactment of a public law.

Liechtenstein Education at a Glance

General Information

Capital	Vaduz
Population (2012)	36,713
Language	German
Literacy rate	100%
Number of phones per 100 people	93
Number of Internet users per 100 people	59
Number of Internet hosts	3,727

Formal Education Information

Compulsory school age population	5,191
Compulsory school age population	15%
Number of years of compulsory education	10 (ages 6–15)
Student/teacher ratio	16.3
Primary school gross enrollment ratio	100%
Primary school entrants reaching grade 5	100%
Secondary school gross enrollment ratio	100%
Child labor (ages 5–14)	no data

Note: Unless otherwise indicated, all data are based on sources from 2011.

System Economics

Education represents the third-largest area of fiscal responsibility for the Liechtensteiner government. Only finance and taxation (29.2 percent of the economy) and social welfare and institutions (23.3 percent of the economy) are larger. Over US$100 million was allocated in 2007 for education purposes. The GDP for Liechtenstein in 2011 was the equivalent of over US$5 billion. Funding for education in Liechtenstein differs from that of several other postindustrial countries in that both compulsory education and noncompulsory (higher education) institutions are financed by the government.

Daniel Ness and Chia-ling Lin

REFERENCES

Central Intelligence Agency. *The CIA World Factbook*. New York: Skyhorse, 2011. https://www.cia.gov/library/publications/the-world-factbook/index.html.

The Columbia Gazetteer of the World Online. New York: Columbia University Press, 2010. www.columbiagazetteer.org.

Nation Master. 2011. www.nationmaster.com.

Office for Education, Liechtenstein. *Liechtenstein*. Paris: International Associations of Universities, 2009.

Office of Economic Affairs. *Liechtenstein in Figures*. Vaduz, Liechtenstein: Office of Economic Affairs, 2011.

UNESCO–UIS. www.uis.unesco.org.

UNICEF. www.unicef.org/infobycountry.

World Bank Education Statistics. 2011. www.worldbank.org.

LUXEMBOURG

The Grand Duchy of Luxembourg is a small country in west-central Europe. The official language is Luxembourgish, although German and French are often used in educational institutions and in government. The population consists mainly of groups who migrated from Celtic regions and have cohabited with French and Germanic peoples. Other groups include populations from Portugal, Italy, and southeastern European areas. The religion is predominantly Roman Catholic (87 percent). The remaining population consists of Protestants, Jews, and Muslims. Luxembourg's government is a constitutional monarchy consisting of three administrative districts.

With the acquisition of Luxembourg Castle, Count Siegfried of Ardennes founded Luxembourg in 963. Luxembourg became fully independent in 1867. The country was taken by Germany in both world wars. In 1948 it entered the Benelux (Belgium, Netherlands, Luxembourg) Union prior to joining NATO. Ten years later Luxembourg became one of the founding nations of the European Union.

Educational System and Curriculum

Luxembourg has a 100 percent literacy rate. Preschool is common, especially in the city of Luxembourg, but it is not compulsory. Compulsory education in the country begins when children reach the age of six and continues for nine years, or until children reach the age of 15. Primary school lasts for six years. Children in Luxembourg are multilingual. The initial primary school period is taught in Luxembourgish. The second half of the primary school period is taught in German. Subjects taught in Luxembourger schools include language, grammar, arithmetic, social studies, natural science, art, music, hygiene, and physical education. Upon finishing primary school, students must enter the first few years of secondary school. At that point, most teachers will communicate with their students in French. All students are required to speak all three languages fluently by the time they graduate from secondary school. One issue of contention, however, is that many students, particularly those whose families emigrated to Luxembourg, do not reach this requirement by the end of their secondary school period. English, a fourth language, is commonly required, particularly in schools in the city of Luxembourg. Other languages include Portuguese, Italian, and Croatian—the native languages of most immigrant groups in Luxembourg. Academically inclined students have the opportunity to remain in secondary school for seven years. Successful completion of secondary school allows most graduates to continue on to the university level. The attendance rate of primary school students is essentially 100 percent. The attendance rate drops to about 82 percent for students who complete all seven years of secondary education.

Tertiary Education

Postcompulsory education in Luxembourg begins at different times for different students because it depends on the educational track. Higher education in Luxembourg is divided into two main categories with a number of subcategories. The two main categories are university education and technical or vocational education. Students who wish to enter high-level professions, such as law, medicine, and engineering, must complete secondary school and earn a baccalaureate at a college or university.

Due to the country's relatively small size, many secondary school graduates often travel abroad to attend universities in other areas of the European Union or elsewhere. The Central University of Luxembourg was founded in 1969 and was the country's premier institution of higher education until 2003, when the University of Luxembourg was established. The University of Luxembourg offers programs in law, economics and finance, natural science, technology and communication, mathematics, languages and literature, humanities, arts, and education training. Courses are usually taught in two languages. Pairs of languages are selected from French, English, and German. Students are also encouraged to study abroad—often in Europe, but also in North America and Asia. In particular, the University of Luxembourg has academic partnerships with Miami University in Ohio and Laval University in Quebec. The Sacred Heart University is another university in Luxembourg that specializes in business and finance.

Teacher Education

Luxembourger students who wish to become teachers and have appropriate secondary school training may be eligible to enter the teacher training program offered at the University of Luxembourg, Faculty of Arts, Social and Educational Sciences. Teacher education programs include early childhood education, primary education, and secondary education—depending on the subject. There is also a program in special needs education. Students who finish the program and pass all required examinations receive the Professional Bachelor in Educational Sciences degree.

Informal Education

Informal education in Luxembourg is often for adults who wish to continue their education. This type of education emphasizes both the importance of experi-

ence and the need for many adults to change careers by learning new vocations. Nonprofit organizations play a major role in funding informal adult education in Luxembourg. Adult education is usually defined as education for an individual 18 years or older who wishes to gain skills initially as an apprentice. Institutions that provide adult education include vocational institutes, religious denominational organizations, and other regional nonprofit adult education venues. Funding for adult education in Luxembourg comes from a variety of sources: federal funding, provincial and municipal resources (such as chambers of commerce and labor and trade unions), occupational associations, and church organizations.

System Economics

Along with the total public expenditures as a percentage of gross national product (GDP) in Brunei, Venezuela, Togo, Niger, and Japan, expenditure on education in Luxembourg is 3.7 percent of the overall GDP. Luxembourg ranks 125 of 186 countries in terms of educational spending. Nearly US$1.51 billion has been allocated in 2009 for education purposes.

Luxembourg Education at a Glance

General Information

Capital	Luxembourg
Population	497,538
Language	Luxembourgish
Literacy rate	100%
GDP per capita	US$71,400
Percentage of people below poverty line	no data
Number of phones per 100 people	53
Number of Internet users per 100 people	78
Number of Internet hosts	244,225
Life expectancy at birth (years)	79

Formal Educational Information

Primary school age population	35,000
Secondary school age population	38,000
Primary school age population	7%
Number of years of education (primary/secondary)	6/7
Student/teacher ratio (primary)	11
Student/teacher ratio (secondary)	10
Primary school gross enrollment ratio	101%
Primary school entrants reaching grade 5	92%
Secondary school gross enrollment ratio	96%
Child labor (ages 5–14)	no data

Note: Unless otherwise indicated, all data are based on sources from 2011.

Future Prospects

As one of the founding countries of the European Union, Luxembourg plays a major role as a competitor in education and as an important agent in the global economy. Along with other members of the EU, Luxembourg maintains a strong lead in student test scores and continues to graduate students who excel in individualized areas of expertise. Luxembourger education excels in the humanities, mathematics, and natural and social sciences. In addition, education in Luxembourg has helped advance technological innovations as well as global communications.

Daniel Ness and Chia-ling Lin

REFERENCES

Central Intelligence Agency. *The CIA World Factbook*. New York: Skyhorse, 2011. https://www.cia.gov/library/publications/the-world-factbook/index.html.

GED. *Global Education Digest 2012: Comparing Education Statistics Across the World*. Montreal: UNESCO Institute for Statistics, 2012.

Nation Master. 2011. www.nationmaster.com.

Noesen, Jos. *Vocational Education and Training in Luxembourg*. Luxembourg: Office for Official Publications of the European Communities, 2005.

UNESCO–IBE. www.ibe.unesco.org/countries/luxembourg.htm.

UNESCO–UIS. www.uis.unesco.org.

UNICEF. www.unicef.org/infobycountry.

World Bank Education Statistics. 2011. www.worldbank.org.

MACEDONIA

Macedonia is a landlocked country located in southeastern Europe, in the central part of the Balkan Peninsula. Macedonia became an independent nation when it separated from the former Yugoslavia in 1991. The new nation was unable to be called "Macedonia" since the name was seen as an affront to Greece, which objected to the name on cultural and historical grounds. As a result, the new country was designated "the Former Yugoslav Republic of Macedonia." By 2004 the country was commonly referred to as the Republic of Macedonia.

About 65 percent of all Macedonians are Macedonian Orthodox. About 33 percent of the population consists of members of Islam. The remaining 2 percent are unspecified or have no religious affiliation.

Educational System

Compulsory education in Macedonia applies to eight years of primary school and four years of secondary school. Preprimary education is available in the country, but mostly for families who can afford to send their children to preschool. Compulsory education, however, is free for all Macedonians. Most recently, nongovernmental organizations have subsidized lunches for primary and secondary school children.

One of the major difficulties in educating young Macedonians is the fact that schools use different language of instruction. UNICEF has identified 331 schools that use Macedonian as the official language of instruction, 128 schools that use Albanian, 36 schools that use Turkish, and 12 schools that use Serbian. Given the limited budget for education and the dire need to standardize teaching methodologies and plans for instruction, the lack of consistency in the consideration of an official language for instruction has added to inequitable circumstances, especially those of students in schools that are not taught in Macedonian. Despite Article 48 of the constitution of the Republic of Macedonia, which states that the "representatives of the ethnic minorities have the right to education in their languages in the primary and secondary education in a way determined by law," inequitable circumstances still exist because schools accommodating ethnic minorities receive less funding than do so-called mainstream schools. In schools that use the language of an ethnic minority, the Macedonian language is also taught.

The Macedonian system of education requires that children attend primary school for eight years—the longest duration for primary school attendance (out of 181 nations). The country's net enrollment ratio at the primary school level is 97 percent (approximately 116,700 students in any single academic year). Three percent (2,861 students) do not attend primary school. This relatively high percentage of students may be due to the country's 6 percent child labor rate. The primary school completion rate is approximately 96 percent, and the student/teacher ratio is 19 students for every teacher.

There are over 90 public high schools in Macedonia. In addition, four high schools accommodate students with disabilities, and an additional three high schools are privately run. In general, secondary school is divided into three types: the gymnasium, the vocational school, and the art and music academy. Students who are accepted to the gymnasium most often prepare for the university or polytechnic institute. The gymnasium accounts for roughly half of all secondary education students in the country, probably because attending one of the universities is considered highly desirable. Students entering the vocational high school either enter the workforce upon graduating or enroll in a tertiary-level institution that emphasizes vocational or technical training. Students who graduate after three years often continue to a vocational college. Those graduating after four years will often enter the workforce. The arts or music academy aims at developing students' skills in these areas. Again, the major issue in secondary school education in Macedonia is the segregation of schooling based on language: 90 secondary schools offer instruction in Macedonian, 22 in Albanian, and four in Turkish.

There are five publicly funded universities in Macedonia: Sts. Cyril and Methodius University of Skopje, St. Clement of Ohrid University in Bitola, Goce Delčev University of Štip, State University of Tetovo, and the University for Information Science and Technology "St. Paul the Apostle" in Ohrid. There are also a number of private universities in the country. Established shortly after the end of World War II, the University of Skopje is the largest institution of higher education in Macedonia, accounting for more programs, faculties, and research institutes than any other university in the country. Since 1948 most universities in Macedonia have offered doctoral degrees. Most students, however, graduate with the baccalaureate degree or one of several master's degrees.

Teacher training programs are provided at the university level. For example, the University of Skopje provides teacher training at the St. Clement of Ohrid Faculty of Pedagogy, which provides six undergraduate study programs. Students deciding to teach at the primary school level must complete one of these six programs. Those who decide to teach at the secondary school level must also enroll in one of the other faculties in order to specialize in a particular subject, such as mathematics, one of the natural sciences, language, or history.

In addition to primary, secondary, and traditional tertiary education, the education system in Macedonia, given the country's poor economic circumstances, has developed a process whereby adults can complete their education degrees and gain skills and qualifications. These courses and programs range in areas. Most common subjects are information science and technologies, computer systems, foreign languages, and business-related fields.

System Economics and Future Prospects

According to the World Bank (2011), public spending on education as a percentage of total government expenditure in Macedonia was reported to be slightly over 13 percent in 2008. This amount is not, however, based on gross national product (GDP) education expenditures. Rather, public expenditure on education is based on current and capital public expenditure. This expenditure includes federal spending on public and private educational institutions, educational administration and policy, and subsidies for student-related and private educational expenses. Data on educational expenditure as a percentage of GDP are unknown.

Macedonia Education at a Glance

General Information

Capital	Skopje
Population	2 million
Languages	Macedonian (66%), Albanian (25%), Turkish, Roma, Serbian
Literacy rate	96%
GDP per capita	US$8,300
People below poverty line	30%
Number of phones per 100 people	22
Number of Internet users per 100 people	41
Number of Internet hosts	60,533
Life expectancy at birth (years)	74

Formal Educational Information

Primary school age population	293,997
Secondary school age population	91,083
Primary school age population	14%
Number of years of education (primary/secondary)	8/4
Student/teacher ratio	19
Primary school gross enrollment ratio	92%
Primary school entrants reaching grade 5	99%
Secondary school gross enrollment ratio	82%
Child labor (ages 5–14)	6%

Note: Unless otherwise indicated, all data are based on sources from 2011.

Despite a 96 percent literacy rate, Macedonia, like Serbia, its northern neighbor, has grappled with a decline in its socioeconomic and educational infrastructure, especially since the dismantling of Yugoslavia. The Education Ministry of Macedonia has lacked sufficient school resources, as well as the ability to make schooling equitable for all citizens. The rather large minority of Muslims in the country is struggling economically and in terms of educational access when compared to the Christian majority. This lack of resources, along with years of military and civilian conflict resulting from the dissolution of the Soviet Union and Yugoslavia, led to drops in school enrollment and attendance. Another reason for a steady drop in enrollment is child labor. According to UNICEF, 6 percent of all children between 5 and 14 years of age are engaged in labor in Macedonia, particularly in agriculture and industry. This high rate of child labor seems to account for the high rates of attrition of students, particularly those in secondary schools.

Due to the dire economic circumstances of Macedonia, a number of nongovernmental organizations are working with the Macedonian government to improve the adverse living and educational conditions of young Macedonians. Like its northern and eastern neighbors, Macedonia must deal with an unstable economy, poor health care, a large number of minors working (often without pay), and poor educational quality. Nongovernmental organizations helping the nation in the sphere of education have supported initiatives to supply funding that will alleviate travel burdens for schoolchildren, particularly those in rural areas, as well as funding allocated for educational supplies and materials.

Daniel Ness and Chia-ling Lin

REFERENCES

Central Intelligence Agency. *The CIA World Factbook.* New York: Skyhorse, 2011. https://www.cia.gov/library/publications/the-world-factbook/index.html.

Dizdarevič, Jasmina D., Snežana Adamčeska, and Lena Damovska. "National Report: Macedonia." In *The Prospects of Teacher Education in South East Europe,* ed. Pavel Zgaga, 325–360. Ljubljana, Slovenia: Faculty of Education, University of Ljubljana, 2006.

Nation Master. 2011. www.nationmaster.com.

UNESCO. *Global Education Digest 2012: Comparing Education Statistics Across the World.* Montreal: UNESCO Institute for Statistics, 2012.

UNESCO–IBE. www.ibe.unesco.org/en/worldwide/unesco-regions/europe-and-north-america/the-former-yugoslav-republic-of-macedonia.html.

UNESCO–UIS. www.uis.unesco.org.

UNICEF. www.unicef.org/infobycountry.

World Bank Education Statistics. 2011. www.worldbank.org.

MONACO

Because of its small geographical area (1.95 square kilometers, or 0.75 of one square mile), the Principality of Monaco is called a postage stamp country. In 2011 the estimated population of the country was 30,539, making it the most densely populated nation in the world. Given the principality's mild climate, attractive coastline, and railroad transportation hub, Monaco has been known for its casino and tourism economy since the end of the nineteenth century.

Educational System

Compulsory education in Monaco is similar to that of France; however, unlike in France, where students are required to attend school from age six to 18, children in Monaco must attend school from age six to 16.

There are seven schools in Monaco that function as both preschools and primary schools. Collège Charles III, the single general secondary school, and Lycée Albert I, the only secondary school that provides technological education in the principality, prepare students who wish to pursue college- and university-level degrees. The Lycée Technique et Hôtelier de Monte Carlo is a secondary school that prepares vocationally bound students. The country is also home to two religious denominational private secondary schools as well as an international secondary school that focuses primarily on business and tourism.

Preschool in Monaco typically lasts three years for children between three and five years old. The duration of primary school, the first compulsory period, is five years (ages six to 10), and the duration of secondary school, the second compulsory period, is seven years (ages 11 through 17). Gross and net enrollment ratio data as well as entrance, transition, repetition, and completion data are either too old to be useful or nonexistent, due in part to the large number of foreign primary and secondary students in the country. The student/teacher ratio for primary school in Monaco is about 14 students per teacher. The student/teacher ratio for secondary school is about nine students for every teacher.

The International University of Monaco, located in Monte Carlo, is the only university in the country. Although the university offers all major subjects, its main focus is international business. Most students who enroll in the International University of Monaco major in business administration, financial engineering, finance and wealth management, tourism, international trade, global studies, luxury retail management, international sports business management, or communication and entertainment.

System Economics and Future Prospects

According to the United Nations Development Programme (2011), Monaco ranks 163 of 186 in educational expenditures as a percentage of gross domestic product (GDP). The total public expenditure on education in 2004 represented 1.2 percent of GDP, similar to educational expenditures of the United

Arab Emirates. Nearly US$11,715,600 was allocated in 2004 for education purposes. Based on these figures, total per student spending is approximately $2,130 (determined by dividing total expenditure by 5,500, the approximate number of students in Monaco). It is important to note, however, that this per capita amount does not reflect the total per student spending from government and private sources.

Through its 10 public and three private educational institutions, Monaco has been somewhat successful in providing education for its youth. Given Monaco's position as a leader in business and tourism, students who graduate from secondary school or the university in Monaco generally have strong backgrounds in tourism, business, economics, and construction. It is difficult, however, to determine how much of this success is due to schooling in Monaco or schooling abroad. This is because Monegasques (citizens of Monaco) are outnumbered by foreign groups, particularly the French, by nearly three to one (47 percent French versus 16 percent Monegasque).

Daniel Ness and Chia-ling Lin

REFERENCES

Central Intelligence Agency. *The CIA World Factbook*. New York: Skyhorse, 2011. https://www.cia.gov/library/publications/the-world-factbook/index.html.

Nation Master. 2011. www.nationmaster.com.

UNESCO. *Global Education Digest 2012: Comparing Education Statistics Across the World*. Montreal: UNESCO Institute for Statistics, 2012.

UNESCO–IBE. www.ibe.unesco.org/en/worldwide/unesco-regions/europe-and-north-america/monaco.html.

UNESCO–UIS. www.uis.unesco.org.

UNICEF. www.unicef.org/infobycountry.

World Bank Education Statistics. 2011. www.worldbank.org.

Monaco Education at a Glance

General Information

Capital	Monaco
Population	30,586
Languages	French, English, Italian, Monegasque
Literacy rate	99%
GDP per capita	US$30,000
Percentage of people below poverty line	no data
Number of phones per 100 people	114.8
Number of Internet users per 100 people	72
Number of Internet hosts	23,621
Life expectancy at birth (years)	80

Formal Educational Information

Primary school age population	no data
Primary school age population	no data
Number of years of education (primary/secondary)	5/7
Student/teacher ratio (primary)	14
Student/teacher ratio (secondary)	9
Primary school gross enrollment ratio	no data
Primary school entrants reaching grade 5	83%
Secondary school gross enrollment ratio	no data
Child labor (ages 5–14)	no data

Note: Unless otherwise indicated, all data are based on sources from 2011.

MONTENEGRO

Montenegro is a country located in southeastern Europe, along the coast of the Adriatic Sea. After World War I, the region became part of greater Yugoslavia, which also included the regions of Bosnia and Herzegovina, Serbia, Kosovo, Croatia, Macedonia, and Slovenia. When Yugoslavia dissolved in 1992, Montenegro and Serbia united to form the new

Federal Republic of Yugoslavia. However, within the ensuing decade, the federation between the two regions became loose. By 2006 Montenegro became an independent nation, thus making the country one of the newest states in Europe.

The country's population was 661,807 in the United Nations' 2011 estimate. Religions in Montenegro include Greek Orthodox Christianity, Islam, and Roman Catholicism.

Educational System

Free education in Montenegro is not new. By 1875 there were over 70 schools in the principality. In 1869 the country also opened one of the first teacher education schools in the region. At present the educational system in Montenegro is governed by the Ministry of Education and Science. Preprimary education is available for children from birth to six years of age. Preprimary education for children from birth through three years of age is conducted in nursery schools. Education for children ages four and five is provided in kindergartens. Compulsory education in the nation is a nine-year period that lasts from age six to 14.

It is estimated that there are 80,000 students of primary and secondary age in Montenegro. Of these, about 27,000 children are between the ages of six and nine—the age range for primary school—and about 53,000 students are between the ages of 10 and 18—the age range for upper primary school (ages 10 through 14) and secondary school (ages 15 through 18). The Osnovnaškola—primary school—enrolls children who have turned six years old.

Compared to some of the other post-Yugoslavian nations, Montenegro seems to be more successful in integrating children of all ethnic backgrounds into the schools. One reason may be the inclusion of the history and culture of all the country's ethnic groups in the curriculum. The language of instruction is Montenegrin, which is considered a hybrid of Serbian, Bosnian, and Croatian. In addition, many schools have integrated Albanian, especially schools in Podgorica, the capital, and along the Albanian border, as a means of accommodating Albanian children; textbooks are published in Montenegrin and Albanian. These policies were adopted by the Ministry of Education and Science in 2009.

There are three types of secondary schools in Montenegro—similar to those in neighboring countries: the gymnasium, professional school, and vocational school. The gymnasium, like other gymnasia in other countries, is the most competitive type of secondary school in Montenegro. The main purpose of the Montenegrin gymnasium, which lasts for four years (ages 15 through 18), is to prepare students for university education. Students must also pass an exit examination in order to enter a tertiary-level institution. The professional school, which lasts for three or four years (ages 15 through 17 or 18), provides students with a broad curriculum that includes subjects taught at the gymnasium as well as subjects involving specializations in particular occupations. Students at the professional school may have the opportunity to continue to a higher education institution. The vocational school, which lasts for three years (ages 15 through 17) prepares students for specific vocations and trades. Students entering the vocational school do not generally continue toward a higher education degree. Rather, they enter the workforce using the skills they have learned through the vocational school curriculum.

The University of Montenegro is the largest university in the country, enrolling about 11,000 students annually. At present the university consists of 20 faculties (i.e., departments) and three institutes (Institute of Foreign Languages, Institute of History, and Institute of Marine Biology). The university, like most higher education institutions in the country, also has a teaching college that prepares preservice teachers at the primary and secondary levels. A number of university-bound students attend institutions in Serbia. For example, students majoring in special education and related services must apply to the University of Belgrade in Serbia in order to be certified for a particular area of special education.

System Economics and Future Prospects

Given the country's recent independence as a republic, it is difficult to know precisely how much educational spending the government of Montenegro has allocated for educational purposes. Although public spending on education as a percentage of gross domestic product (GDP) is unknown at this time, public spending on education as a percentage of all public spending is 30 percent. This figure is based on the Institute for Educational Policy figure for 2000,

Montenegro Education at a Glance

General Information

Capital	Podgorica
Population	666,730
Languages	Serbian, Montenegrin, Bosnian, Albanian
Literacy rate	100%
GDP per capita	US$3,800
People below poverty line	12%
Number of phones per 100 people	54
Number of Internet users per 100 people	44
Number of Internet hosts	6,247
Life expectancy at birth (years)	75

Formal Educational Information*

Primary school age population	381,000
Secondary school age population	847,000
Number of years of education (primary/secondary)	4/8
Student/teacher ratio (primary)	20
Student/teacher ratio (secondary)	14
Primary school gross enrollment ratio	98%
Primary school entrants completing primary school	96%
Secondary school gross enrollment ratio	89%
Child labor (ages 5–14)	4%

Notes: *Formal education data are combined with data for Serbia (see Serbia).

Unless otherwise indicated, all data are based on sources from 2011.

when Montenegro was still part of the Republic of Yugoslavia. This amount was based on capital public expenditure for 2000. This expenditure included federal spending on public and private educational institutions, educational administration and policy, and subsidies for student-related and private educational expenses.

Unlike Serbia, its neighbor and former federation partner, Montenegro has not suffered from decline in its formal system of education. Education in Montenegro is demonstrating some success in student learning and school infrastructure. This cautiously positive outlook on education in the fledgling nation is due, at least in part, to the willingness of the government to unite the various cultures and social groups within its boundaries. The Montenegrin Education Ministry has maintained the educational infrastructure and included the aid of nongovernmental organizations in order to improve the quality of education and provide funding for students of poor families, minority groups, and rural dwellers.

Daniel Ness and Chia-ling Lin

References

Central Intelligence Agency. *The CIA World Factbook.* New York: Skyhorse, 2011. https://www.cia.gov/library/publications/the-world-factbook/index.html.

Institute for Educational Policy. *Education in Montenegro: Needs Assessment.* Budapest: Institute for Educational Policy, 2000.

Nation Master. 2011. www.nationmaster.com.

UNESCO–IBE. www.ibe.unesco.org/en/worldwide/unesco-regions/europe-and-north-america/republic-of-montenegro.html.

UNESCO–UIS. www.uis.unesco.org.

UNICEF. www.unicef.org/infobycountry.

Vujacic, Lidija, Jasmina Djordevic, and Natasa Micovic. "National Report: Montenegro." In *The Prospects of Teacher Education in South East Europe,* ed. Pavel Zgaga, pp. 431–436. Ljubljana, Slovenia: Faculty of Education, University of Ljubljana, 2006.

World Bank Education Statistics. 2011. www.worldbank.org.

Netherlands

The Kingdom of the Netherlands is a country of coastal lowlands along the North Sea. The official languages are Dutch and Frisian. However, most Dutch are bilingual or multilingual and speak French, German, or English. The population is mainly Dutch (83 percent). Approximately 8 percent of the population consists of Dutch citizens from other western European regions, and 9 percent of the population consists of individuals from Turkey, Morocco, Antilles, Suriname, and Indonesia. About 30 percent of the population is Roman Catholic, 20 percent is Protestant, 5 percent is Muslim, and 2 percent are members of other religions. The remaining 43 percent do not belong to any religious group.

Since World War II, the country has become an economic power in Western Europe. The Netherlands is one of the founding countries to introduce the euro as the currency of the European Union.

Educational System

The Netherlands has a fairly long history of comprehensive formal education for all children and adolescents. While most countries in Europe during the Industrial Revolution sanctioned child labor, the Netherlands was one of the first to forbid labor by children less than 12 years of age. One result of this law was the institutionalization of compulsory education in 1901 for all children six to 12 years of age. From 1901 to 1968, education in the Netherlands consisted of kindergarten (*Kleuterschool*) for children ages four to six and the so-called *lagere* school—primary education for children between six and 12 years of age. After 12 years of age, students could leave school entirely or apply to one of seven different types of school. One school type was individual technical education, where students would get individualized training in a particular technical field. A second type was vocational training (*Ambachtschool*), which was a more comprehensive vocational institution. A third type was extended primary education, which had a basic curriculum that was essentially a continuation of the primary curriculum. These three types enrolled adolescents between the ages of 12 and 16. A fourth school type was the *hogere burgerschool* (HBS), or higher commoner's school, which offered a more diverse curriculum for adolescents between 12 and 17 years. A fifth school type was the middle-level girls' school, which was analogous to the *hogere burgerschool*, which enrolled mostly boys. Finally, there were the elite schools—namely, the gymnasium and athenaeum. Students who wished to continue with a classical university education would need to graduate from one of these two institutions. The athenaeum differed from the gymnasium in that it included both a classical and the commoner school (HBS) curriculum. Students graduating from the commoner's school were more than likely to attend technical colleges or polytechnic institutes. Gymnasium or athenaeum graduates were more than likely bound for university education.

A 1963 education law streamlined secondary education into four tracks and expanded compulsory education from six to nine years. This law was enacted in 1968. Seven years later compulsory education was extended to ten years. This educational overhaul allowed for a more complete transition from an industrial to a service economy and strengthened the country's influence in the area of information and communication technology.

Schools in the Netherlands are mostly public; however, there are private and parochial schools as well. The Dutch Ministry of Education, Culture, and Science is the chief administrative body of education in the Netherlands. Compulsory education commences at age five and continues to age 16. After age 16 students must enroll in school for at least two days per week—partial compulsory education. However, the largest segment of the student population attends school on a full-time basis in order to be eligible for university status. Partial compulsory education continues to age 23.

Precompulsory, Compulsory Education, and Curriculum

Early childhood programs in the Netherlands are among the most advanced in the world. Preschools in the country strongly emphasize informal cognitive development through the use of constructive play—particularly in the form of block play or brick (e.g., Lego®) play. Prior to 1986, nursery school accommodated children from four to six years of age. This was primarily a period when children would be cared for during the day. After 1986, however, a government mandate encouraged the merging of nursery school with primary school. This merge has provided more opportunities for cognitive activity and instruction for four- to six-year-old children, one of the primary objectives of preschool (the first two grade levels in the primary education period).

Primary Education

Children begin what is known as *basisschool*—translated as basic school—at age four and continue through age 12. Many public schools in the Netherlands are encouraged to follow specific educational philosophies. Common curricular themes are the Montessori method, the Rudolf Steiner (Waldorf) method, the Dalton plan, and the Pestalozzi plan. The first two years are essentially akin to preschool and kindergarten. These two years are followed by six years of basic primary education. In the third year children begin to learn mathematics, language skills, basic natural science, and history, along with music, physical education, and art. By the last two years of *basisschool*, children are encouraged to learn how to read, write, and speak in English. Before completing the *basisschool*, students are expected to take an exit examination that is administered by the country's Central Institute for Test Development. This examination provides information regarding a student's academic performance as well as the best-fit secondary school.

Secondary Education

After the *basisschool* and the national exit examination, children have one of three options: *voorbereidend middelbaar beroepsonderwijs* (VMBO); *hoger algemeen voortgezet onderwijs* (HAVO); and *voorbereidend wetenschappelijk onderwijs* (VWO). VMBO is preparatory middle-level applied education, which provides a combination of applied education with a continuation of traditional subjects from primary school. With VMBO, students have the option to enter the job market after four years (age 16), enter an applied two-year higher education program and enter the job market (age 18), or transfer to a HAVO school after the third or fourth year. Students who enter the HAVO track are prepared for a polytechnic education. The HAVO school is a five-year program that prepares students for entrance to a tertiary polytechnic institute. These institutions award baccalaureates after four years of education and master's degrees after a further two years of education. Students who enter the VWO track enter either the gymnasium or lyceum. These secondary institutions differ in one respect: the gymnasium emphasizes the study of classical languages—namely, Greek and Latin—whereas the lyceum offers the classics but does not emphasize them. Both institutions prepare students for the traditional university education, which offers the baccalaureate, master's, and doctoral sequence.

Postcompulsory Education

There are at least 67 institutions of higher education in the Netherlands. Of these, roughly 20 are universities. The remaining 47 institution are *hogescholen*, also known as vocational universities or vocational institutions. These tertiary institutions are in the form of pedagogical institutes (teacher training colleges), colleges of agriculture, technological colleges, nursing institutes, art institutes, and music conservatories. This form of higher education is entitled *hoger beroepsonderwijs* (HBO), meaning higher professional education. Students need a HAVO diploma in order to be considered for acceptance at an HBO institution. Requirements for graduation from an HBO include four years of schooling and the completion of at least 240 credits.

Universities are the research institutions of higher education in the Netherlands, providing *weten-schappelijk onderwijs* (WO), which means scientific education. Of the 20 universities, three are polytechnic institutes, one is an open university, six are comprehensive universities, and four are universities with distinct specializations. Founded in 1575, the University of Leiden is the oldest higher education institution in the country. Other so-called ancient universities include the University of Groningen (1614), the University of Amsterdam (1632), and the University of Utrecht (1636). The University of Amsterdam has the largest enrollment of any university in the Netherlands, and the University of Utrecht has the largest endowment. These and other universities include professional programs, such as schools of law, medicine, and business and economics. In addition, the specializations of universities with academic or professional concentrations include engineering, natural science, and agriculture. Requirements for graduating with a baccalaureate from a WO include three years of schooling and the completion of at least 180 credits. WO students are also eligible to continue for a master's degree (two years) and a doctorate (at least four additional years after earning the master's degree).

Teacher Education

The teacher education system in the Netherlands takes place in *hogescholen* that are specifically designed to prepare teachers, educational leaders, and curriculum specialists.

Informal Education

Informal education in the Netherlands is often for adults who wish to continue their education. The Dutch Ministry of Education, Culture and Science sponsors both academic and vocational courses for adults wishing to return for both degree and nondegree programs. Nonprofit organizations also play a major role in funding informal adult education in the Netherlands. Adult education is usually defined as education for an individual who is 20 years or older. This is because compulsory education statutes require children and adolescents to attend formal schooling through 18 years of age. Institutions that provide adult education include programs within universities, vocational colleges, religious denominational organizations, and other regional, nonprofit adult education

Netherlands Education at a Glance

General Information

Capital	Amsterdam
Population	16.7 million
Languages	Dutch, Frisian
Literacy rate	99%
GDP per capita	US$32,100
People below poverty line	10.5%
Number of phones per 100 people	44
Number of Internet users per 100 people	85
Number of Internet hosts	12.6 million
Life expectancy at birth (years)	79

Formal Educational Information

Primary school age population	1.1 million
Secondary school age population	1.2 million
Primary school age population	7%
Number of years of education (primary/secondary)	6/6
Student/teacher ratio (primary)	17
Student/teacher ratio (secondary)	13
Primary school gross enrollment ratio	106.5%
Primary school entrants reaching grade 5	99%
Secondary school gross enrollment ratio	118%
Child labor (ages 5–14)	no data

Note: Unless otherwise indicated, all data are based on sources from 2011.

institutions. Adult education in the Netherlands aims to provide adult learners with additional qualifications and skills for work. Funding for adult education comes from a variety of sources: federal funding, provincial and municipal resources (such as chambers of commerce and labor and trade unions), occupational associations, and church organizations.

System Economics

The Netherlands ranks at 50 in educational expenditures as a percentage of gross domestic product (GDP). The total public expenditure on education in 2007 represented 5.3 percent of GDP. Nearly US$35.881 billion was allocated in 2007 for education purposes. With about 2,403,000 primary and secondary school students, per student spending amounts to about $14,932.

Future Prospects

As part of the European Union, the Netherlands has become one of the leading nations in student scores, educational access, and educational quality at all levels. Along with students in other countries of the EU, students in the Netherlands excel in all academic and vocational areas. This is evidenced, in part, by results from the Programme for International Student Assessment (PISA), which, in 2009, ranked the Netherlands at nine in overall academic performance among countries throughout the world—higher than the Organisation for Economic Co-operation and Development (OECD) country average. Education in the Netherlands has helped advance technological innovations and global communications. Moreover, the Dutch Ministry of Education, Culture and Science, in collaboration with the Dutch government, has promoted and advocated for educational access for its minority populations reasonably well.

Daniel Ness and Chia-ling Lin

REFERENCES

Broekhof, Kees. *Preschool Education in The Netherlands.* Utrecht, Netherlands: Sardes Educational Services, 2006.

Central Intelligence Agency. *The CIA World Factbook.* New York: Skyhorse, 2011. https://www.cia.gov/library/publications/the-world-factbook/index.html.

Nation Master. 2011. www.nationmaster.com.

OECD Programme for International Student Assessment (PISA). *PISA 2009 Country Profiles.* Paris: OECD, 2011. http://stats.oecd.org/PISA2009Profiles/#.

UNESCO. *Global Education Digest 2012: Comparing Education Statistics Across the World.* Montreal: UNESCO Institute for Statistics, 2012.

UNESCO–IBE. www.ibe.unesco.org/countries/netherlands.htm.

UNESCO–UIS. www.uis.unesco.org.

UNICEF. www.unicef.org/infobycountry.

World Bank Education Statistics. 2011. www.worldbank.org.

NORWAY

Norway is a country of northern Europe. After centuries of raids throughout coastal Europe, Norway eventually adopted Christianity under King Olav Tryggvason in 994. Norway dissolved its union with Sweden in 1905 after years of nationalistic sentiment. During World War II, the country was occupied by Nazi Germany, despite the fact that Norway claimed neutrality. Norway became a member of NATO in 1949. Its economy improved after discovery of offshore oil and natural gas.

The official language is Norwegian, a language of two systems—Bokmal and Nynorsk. A small minority speak Sami and Finnish. English is spoken in Oslo and other urban areas. The currency is the Norwegian *krone* (NOK), and one US dollar is equivalent to almost 6 NOK. The population is mainly Norwegian and Sami. At 85 percent of the population, the Church of Norway is by far the largest religious group in the country. Other Norwegians follow various Protestant Christian sects, Catholicism, Islam, and no religion.

Educational System: Precompulsory, Compulsory Education, and Curriculum

Dating back to the eleventh century, the emergence of cathedral schools made the education system of Norway one of the oldest in the Western world. Compulsory education in Norway is an 11-year period from ages six to 16. There are three general periods in the school system of Norway: primary school (*Barneskole*), lower secondary school (*Ungdomsskole*), and upper secondary school (*Videregåendeskole*). The first two levels fall within the compulsory schooling period. Unlike in other school systems, children must switch schools when leaving primary school to go to lower secondary school, and again when moving from lower secondary school to upper secondary school.

Primary School

Primary school is a seven-year period (grades 1 through 7, or ages six to 13). In grades 1 and 2, children mostly learn the alphabet and basic arithmetic skills. Since 1997 primary schools have included English as part of the curriculum. In grades 2 through 7, students study Norwegian, physical and life sciences, religion, physical education, and mathematics, spending less time on social sciences, such as geography and history. English is also mastered by the end of primary school. Although students are not given formal grades, they are tested at each grade level, not so much to determine grade promotion as to determine which subjects need more emphasis in future grades.

Lower Secondary School

Lower secondary school, a three-year period (grades 8, 9 and 10), is essentially a continuation of what students have learned in the primary grades, yet at a more rigorous level. In addition to the curriculum mentioned above, students in lower secondary school have the option of taking a foreign language, such as French or German, as well as advanced literature courses in Norwegian and English. Academic performance at the lower secondary level often determines whether students continue to upper secondary school or acquire vocations that will enable them to enter the workforce. The key indicator of promotion to upper secondary school is the specific subject test of the grade 10 examination. Students must perform well on the exit examination for grade 10 in order to enter grade 11. They also have the option to take portions of the examination before the 10th grade if they are granted an exemption from a particular subject. Performance on the international assessment known as the Programme for International Student Assessment (PISA) in 2009 demonstrated that Norwegian students outperformed their Scandinavian peers, but performed less well than students from Shanghai in mathematics.

Upper Secondary School

Entry to upper secondary school, also a three-year period (grades 11, 12 and 13), depends on student performance on examinations and schoolwork in the lower secondary school grades. Upper secondary school is generally the equivalent of senior high school in the United States; however, it differs from American senior high school in that it is not compulsory. However, given the need for highly skilled labor, a greater number of students than before are accepted into upper secondary schools. Prior to 2005 the Norwegian government instituted a mandate that did not permit the establishment of private schools that did not have either a religious or pedagogical context. After 2005, however, secular private schools were established. Other changes to the Norwegian education system include a single upper secondary school system in 1994. Prior to this time, the upper secondary school system consisted of three components: general school; mercantile, or business, school; and vocational school. This format was based on the German upper secondary school model. However, since the early 1990s, the separation of high schools through tracking proved unsuccessful in increasing academic performance. The general idea behind the merging of these three components is a practical one: in order to ensure access to higher education, it is necessary to provide students with a comprehensive education that will provide that opportunity. In addition, students who enter vocations or technological occupations need increasingly more content knowledge that they would appropriately receive from a general upper secondary education.

Higher Education

Higher education is in the form of universities, university colleges, and private schools of higher learning. Completion of upper secondary school is a requirement for entry into a higher education institution. Another way that students can be admitted to a higher education institution is by showing evidence of five years of experience in a particular occupational or professional area. These students, 23 years of age or older, can obtain a general admissions certificate if they have passed exit examinations in Norwegian, English, mathematics, and most of the natural and social sciences at the upper secondary school level. Students who graduate from upper secondary school and who have been enrolled in general education also have the opportunity to be admitted to the university if academic performance is adequate.

All programs and degrees are generally provided at the university level. Baccalaureates are earned after three years (given that the last year of upper secondary school in Norway is often analogous to the freshman year at college in the United States). Master's degrees are awarded after five years of study and doctorates are usually awarded after eight years of study and the completion of a dissertation. Professional studies, particularly those in law and health professions, are also provided at universities. University colleges are institutions where students specialize in a highly skilled profession that does not necessarily require the earning of advanced degrees beyond the baccalaureate. Such professions include engineering, nursing, and careers in technology and information science. Private schools of higher education usually specialize in business-related professions. Other private schools include institutions of music and art. Prior to 1800, students who planned to enter the military had the opportunity to attend the Norwegian Military Academy, which taught mathematics, geography, engineering, and other technological areas

of study. Otherwise, the nearest university at the time was the University of Copenhagen in Denmark. The University of Oslo, the premier university in Norway, opened its doors in 1811 and was modeled after the then University of Berlin—the present-day Humboldt University of Berlin—which was the first institution to emphasize modern scientific inquiry. Since then, eight universities were established in various regions of Norway. In addition to the University of Bergen, which was established in 1946, the University of Tromsø, which serves students in the fairly remote northern part of the country, opened its doors in 1972.

Teacher Education

Teacher education in Norway is available for students; the method of teacher education depends on the level that a student wished to teach. Students who plan to teach at the primary school or lower secondary school level attend regional colleges or university colleges that have teacher training programs. These programs provide students with the necessary prerequisite coursework and student teaching experiences that they will need in order to teach in the public or private schools. Students who plan to teach at the upper secondary school level must take prerequisite education courses or a year-long pedagogical course in addition to a major in a specified discipline at the university level. The Norwegian government requires students to complete at least 20 courses in a field of study.

Informal Education

Informal education in Norway is an option for adults who wish to acquire additional skills and abilities in order to increase workforce desirability. Most informal education settings provide evening classes for working adults. These courses are similar to courses provided for younger students who enroll in upper secondary level or higher education courses during the day. As described above, adults over 23 may enter programs at the university level if they can show evidence of five years of combined school and professional work experience. Most informal education programs are funded by the government. However, they can also be funded in part by regional and municipal resources as well as private and reli-

Norway Education at a Glance

General Information

Capital	Oslo
Population	4.6 million
Language	Norwegian
Literacy rate	100%
GDP per capita	US$46,300
People below poverty line	no data
Number of phones per 100 people	41
Number of Internet users per 100 people	84
Number of Internet hosts	3.3 million
Life expectancy at birth (years)	80

Formal Educational Information

Primary school age population	438,000
Secondary school age population	365,000
Primary school age population	9.4%
Number of years of education (primary/secondary)	7/6
Student/teacher ratio (primary)	11
Student/teacher ratio (secondary)	9
Primary school gross enrollment ratio	98%
Primary school entrants reaching grade 5	100%
Secondary school gross enrollment ratio	113%
Child labor (ages 5–14)	no data

Note: Unless otherwise indicated, all data are based on sources from 2011.

gious organizations. Adults also have the opportunity to benefit from distance education, especially those who live in rural communities and remote regions, particularly in the north of Norway near the Finnish and Russian borders.

System Economics

Norway ranks 27 of 186 countries in terms of educational expenditures as a percentage of gross domestic product (GDP). Along with public expenditure on education of Barbados and Sweden, the total public expenditure on education for Norway in 2007 represented 6.8 percent of the country's GDP. Nearly US$18.6 billion was allocated for education purposes. This amounts to per capita education expenditure over $23,000.

Future Prospects

Norway has consistently played a major role in education as it generally places high as a competitor in educational achievement rankings based on student test scores, such as TIMSS and PISA. Norway's education system has had a positive impact on the global economy. The country continues to graduate students who excel in individualized areas of expertise. Education in Norway excels in the areas of the humanities, mathematics, the natural and social sciences, and information and communication technologies. Norway is also a leader in the production and use of alternative-based fuels as well as innovative and pioneering research in medicine, physics, chemistry, and environmental studies. Further, similar to other countries of Europe, education in Norway has helped advance technological innovations and global communications.

Daniel Ness and Chia-ling Lin

REFERENCES

Central Intelligence Agency. *The CIA World Factbook.* New York: Skyhorse, 2011. https://www.cia.gov/library/publications/the-world-factbook/index.html.

Nation Master. 2011. www.nationmaster.com.

UNESCO. *Global Education Digest 2012: Comparing Education Statistics Across the World.* Montreal: UNESCO Institute for Statistics, 2012.

UNESCO–IBE. www.ibe.unesco.org/en/worldwide/unesco-regions/europe-and-north-america/norway.html.

UNESCO–UIS. www.uis.unesco.org.

UNICEF. www.unicef.org/infobycountry.

World Bank Education Statistics. 2011. www.worldbank.org.

POLAND

Poland is located in central Europe. The official language is Polish—spoken by nearly 99 percent of the population. The population is mainly Polish (97 percent); however, there are some people of German, Belarusian, and Ukrainian descent. The religion is predominantly Roman Catholic (90 percent); however, there are also citizens who are members of the Eastern Orthodox Church as well as a very small Protestant population. The religions of about 8 percent of the population are unspecified.

After World War II, Poland became a Soviet satellite nation. By 1980 corrupt labor practices led to the formation of the Solidarity movement, headed by Lech Walesa. A decade later Poland witnessed its first presidential elections. Poland became a member of NATO in 1999 and the European Union in 2004. At present, although widespread corruption has been curtailed, the country still suffers from rather harsh differences in socioeconomic status among citizens in both urban and rural areas.

Educational System

Preschool exists for children between the ages of three and six years. The compulsory educational system in Poland is divided into three levels: primary school, lower secondary school, and upper secondary school. Primary school and lower secondary school have set durations, namely, six years for primary education and three years for lower secondary education. Lower secondary school is called the gymnasium. The duration of upper secondary school varies depending on the academic or educational direction of the student. In general, the total duration of education for students in Poland ranges from 12 to 13 years, depending on the type of upper secondary school attended. Types of upper secondary schools in Poland include the specializing lyceum (3 years), general lyceum (3 years), technical secondary school (4 years), vocational school (2 to 3 years), complementary lyceum (2 years), and complementary technical secondary school (3 years). At the end of upper secondary school, students are expected to take the national secondary school achievement examination in order to receive a graduation certificate for university acceptance or workforce entry.

Administration

Educational policy and provision for both early education and compulsory education are under the auspices of the Polish Ministry of National Education. The offices include the minister of education as well as the ministers of education and behavior, ministers of national education and sport, and ministers of education and science. Tertiary education, however, is under the auspices of the Ministry of Science and Higher Education.

Precompulsory and Compulsory Education

The Ministry of Education introduced a new time line for primary and secondary education in the 1999/2000 academic school year, which mandates that children of primary school age must attend school for a six-year period. Under this mandate the ministry identified two stages. The first stage covers grades 1 through 3—a period that is designed to accommodate the social and academic needs of children who are transitioning from preschool and nonformal education to a more formalized school curriculum. The second stage covers grades 4 through 6, which includes a more formalized curriculum that prepares students for lower secondary school general education.

The curriculum in the six years of primary school includes Polish, mathematics, natural science, social studies (mostly the history of Poland), music, art, and physical education. By the second stage (grades 4 through 6), the curriculum includes religion, ethics, other modern foreign languages (usually English, French, German, Ukrainian, Lithuanian, or Russian), and computer technology. Students also have the option in the second stage to focus on a particular area of study. These areas include ecology, health education, reading and media, education, and culture. According to UNESCO, there are approximately 2.6 million children of primary school age, representing 7 percent of the total population of Poland. The student/teacher ratio at the primary level is about 12 students per teacher. The primary school gross enrollment rate is 98 percent, and the percentage of students reaching grade 5 is nearly 100 percent.

Lower secondary education in Poland is provided through gymnasia—three-year schools that generally adopt the basic formal curriculum provided in the last three grades of primary education. Generally, students in gymnasia are between the ages of 13 and 16 years. The Polish gymnasium school period allows each student to determine academic direction. Accordingly, based on academic performance and subjects of interest, students are counseled to enroll in one of five types of upper secondary schools: (1) the basic vocational school (*zasadnicze szkoly zawodowe*—with a duration of 2 to 3 years); (2) the general secondary school (*licea ogólnoksztalcace*—3 years); (3) the vocational secondary school (*technika*—4 years); (4) supplemental general high school (*uzupelniajace liceum ogólnokształcące*—2 years with possible transfer to general secondary school); and (5) the supplemental secondary vocational school (*technika uzupelniajace*—3 years).

Approximately 3.3 million children and adolescents in Poland are in the secondary school age range, roughly 8 percent of the total population of the country. The student/teacher ratio is 13 students for every teacher. The secondary school gross enrollment ratio is close to 100 percent. However, the net secondary school enrollment ratio is nearly 93 percent.

Postcompulsory Education

There are 10 types of university in Poland: the traditional comprehensive university, polytechnical institutes, medical universities and institutes, agricultural colleges and universities, pedagogical institutes, music conservatories, theological seminaries, universities of economics and business, maritime institutes, and military academies. To date there are 18 traditional universities in Poland. In total there are 395 institutions of higher education in Poland. Most of these institutions are private denominational colleges with individual specializations.

Founded in 1364, the Jagiellonian University in Kraków is the oldest university in Poland, and, after the University of Prague, the second-oldest university in central Europe. The university's faculties include law, medicine, philosophy, philology, mathematics and computer science, chemistry, biology and earth sciences, Polish language and literature, biochemistry and biophysics, physics and astronomy, management and social communication, and international studies and political science. With a student body of over 49,000 students, Jagiellonian University ranks as one of the two most competitive universities in Poland. The other leading university in the country is the University of Warsaw, which was established in 1816. With an enrollment of nearly 57,000 students and an administrative and academic staff of nearly 6,000 individuals, the University of Warsaw is known for its departments in the fields of physics, Polish studies, philosophy, applied mathematics, geography and regional studies, journalism, and business and economics.

Poland is also the home to notable music conservatories. With its origin as the Music School for Singers and Theater Actors in 1810, the Fryderyk Chopin University of Music eventually became affiliated with the University of Warsaw before it separated into its own entity. Famous alumni include internationally recognized composers and pianists such as Fryderyk Chopin, Wanda Landowska, Witold Lutoslawski, Ignacy Jan Paderewski, and Alexandre Tansman. Another notable music conservatory in Poland is the Academy of Music in Krakow, whose graduates include the famed composer Krzysztof Penderecki and the conductor Stanislaw Skrowaczewski.

Teacher Education

Teacher education and training in Poland has been a field of tertiary education since 1990. The teacher education field takes place primarily in university departments of education. Most of the 18 universities include department faculties of education. However, there are several pedagogical institutes that offer degrees specifically for students who plan to enter the field of teacher education. Three of these institutions are the Akademia Pedagogiczna (Pedagogical Academy) in Krakow, the Akademia Świetokrzyska (Holy Cross Academy) in Kielce, and Akademia Pedagogiki Specjalnej (Academy of Special Education) in Warsaw.

In general, students planning to prepare for primary school or gymnasium teaching are required to attend a teacher training college (*kolegium nauczycielskie*) or a specialized college for foreign language instruction (*nauczycielskie kolegium języków obcych*). The duration of programs is generally between four and six years. Secondary school teachers must receive a

---

Poland Education at a Glance

General Information

Capital	Warsaw
Population	38.4 million
Languages	Polish
Literacy rate	100%
GDP per capita	US$14,300
People below poverty line	17%
Number of phones per 100 people	27
Number of Internet users per 100 people	49
Number of Internet hosts	10.5 million
Life expectancy at birth (years)	75

Formal Educational Information

Primary school age population	2.6 million
Secondary school age population	3.3 million
Primary school age population	7%
Number of years of education (primary/secondary)	6/6
Student/teacher ratio (primary)	11.5
Student/teacher ratio (secondary)	13
Primary school gross enrollment ratio	98%
Primary school entrants reaching grade 5	99%
Secondary school gross enrollment ratio	100%
Child labor (ages 5–14)	no data

Note: Unless otherwise indicated, all data are based on sources from 2011.

master's degree in their specialization and must also take courses in pedagogical studies.

Informal Education

Informal education in Poland includes postsecondary education for people who left secondary school. Students in this category are usually between 19 and 21 years of age. Subjects in postsecondary, nontertiary schools include medical studies, technology, agriculture studies, forestry, transportation and communication, hotel services, business and administration, and teaching. The duration of programs is between three and five years. In addition to postsecondary education, informal education is provided primarily for older adults who either were not exposed to formal education or for those whose formal education occurred during the change of political administration—from Soviet intervention to autonomous control (1980s through 1990s). Adult informal education focuses on furthering basic skills in language and mathematics. Informal education includes courses for particular vocations and foreign language instruction.

System Economics

According to the United Nations Development Programme (2011), Poland ranks 62 of 186 in educational expenditures as a percentage of gross domestic product (GDP). The total public expenditure on education in 2007 represented 4.9 percent of GDP, the same percentage of educational expenditure as in Syria, Argentina, Grenada, Estonia, Ireland, and Canada. Nearly US$35.344 billion was allocated for education purposes. Based on these figures, total per pupil spending is $5,893 (determined by dividing total expenditure by 5,998,000, the approximate number of students in Poland).

Future Prospects

As part of the European Union since 2004, Poland has been consistent in its commitment to education for children and adults. The country has been successful in the areas of informational technology, the natural sciences, mathematics, the arts, and music. Along with other members of the EU, Poland continues to graduate students who excel in individualized areas of expertise, particularly in the humanities, mathematics, and natural and social sciences. The Polish government, however, is in transition in terms of its commitment to improving the status of its citizens. Poland has a high rate of disparity between affluent individuals living in urban areas and a majority of low-income laborers in rural areas. The issue of combating educational and social inequities between social classes in Poland needs to be addressed by the Polish government.

Daniel Ness and Chia-ling Lin

REFERENCES

Central Intelligence Agency. *The CIA World Factbook*. New York: Skyhorse, 2011. https://www.cia.gov/library/publications/the-world-factbook/index.html.

Nation Master. 2011. www.nationmaster.com.

UNESCO. *Global Education Digest 2012: Comparing Education Statistics Across the World*. Montreal: UNESCO Institute for Statistics, 2012.

UNESCO–IBE. www.ibe.unesco.org/en/worldwide/unesco-regions/europe-and-north-america/poland.html.

UNESCO–UIS. www.uis.unesco.org.

UNICEF. www.unicef.org/infobycountry.

World Bank Education Statistics. 2011. www.worldbank.org.

PORTUGAL

Portugal is located in Europe's Iberian Peninsula along the Atlantic Ocean to the west and the Mediterranean Sea to the south. The official language is Portuguese. The population consists mainly of people who have lived along the Mediterranean coastal regions in the southwestern part of Europe. Eastern European populations have immigrated to Portugal since the early 1990s. The religion is predominantly Roman Catholic; however, like Spain, its neighbor, Portugal has seen a growth in secularization, away from religion in general.

Portugal was initially established as a kingdom in 1143 and became a republic in 1910, more than 750 years later. Portugal was one of the leading world powers in the fifteenth and sixteenth centuries. Its strength on the world scene, however, diminished after a devastating earthquake near Lisbon in 1755 and Napoleon's occupation of the region in the early

1800s. A republican government was introduced after the overthrow of the monarchy on October 5, 1910. In 1975, after more than 60 years of exploitive leadership, the government of Portugal granted independence to all its colonies in Africa. The country became a member of the European Union in 1986.

Educational System

The primary and secondary education system in Portugal is run by the country's Ministry of Education. Higher education administration is run by the Portuguese Ministry of Science, Technology and Higher Education. Compulsory education in Portugal lasts for nine years. Primary school comprises the first six years of the compulsory education period, and the first three years of secondary school are the last three years of the compulsory period.

Precompulsory and Compulsory Education

Preprimary education is available for parents who can afford to send their children between the ages of three and six years to preschool. Therefore it is not free or compulsory. The combined period of primary school and the first three years of secondary school constitute the basic education curriculum. This combined period is divided into three cycles (cycles 1, 2, and 3). After the third cycle (lower secondary school), students are awarded the Diploma Certificate. Public or private secondary education is a three-year optional period that is accessible for students who earn the basic education Diploma Certificate at the end of the ninth year of schooling. Two types of secondary schools are available for students: general secondary schools and technical or vocational schools. Students who earn the Certificate of Secondary Education/High School Diploma are eligible to apply to one of the many universities in Portugal or abroad.

There are approximately 650,000 students of primary school age in the country. Nearly all of them, about 99 percent, attend primary school. The primary school completion rate is approximately 104 percent, indicating that individuals older than the typical age for primary school are enrolled in primary school and complete this course of study. The primary school student/teacher ratio is about eleven students for every teacher. Data suggest that nearly 680,000 children and adolescents of secondary school age live in Portugal. However, only 82 percent (based on the country's net enrollment ratio for secondary school) of these individuals are enrolled in secondary school at any given time. This accounts for close to 558,000 students. The student/teacher ratio for secondary school in Portugal is about seven students for every teacher.

Postcompulsory Education

Tertiary education in Portugal is divided into public and private institutions of higher education. Within this dichotomy, institutions are further categorized as universities, polytechnic institutes, and specialized institutes emphasizing vocations and trades. In addition to public and private institutions, Portugal recognizes institutions run by the Catholic Church, as introduced by decree of the Holy See. Private institutions in Portugal must be recognized by the Ministry of Science and Higher Education if they are to be eligible for accreditation and operation in the country. The Portuguese system of higher education also regulates state higher education institutions by the same procedures as those for private institutions. Accordingly, students are able to transfer between university and polytechnic institute as well as between public institution and private institution, and vice versa.

There are about 80 institutions of higher education in Portugal. It is important to note that the private institute in Portugal is similar to a college with a distinct specialization or a college with a broad curriculum that awards only baccalaureate degrees. In terms of public institutions, there are 13 state-run universities, one university institute, and one distance education teaching university. In addition, the state runs 16 polytechnic institutes as well as three nursing schools. Data show that there are at least 10 private universities, 16 private institutes, at least five private polytechnic institutes, and at least four private nonintegrated nursing schools. The country also has an air force academy, a military academy, a naval school, and a police academy.

Before the 1960s, higher education in Portugal was primarily for the elite. In general, formal study in theology, law, medicine, or the classics was appropriated for young people, mostly young men, whose families were able to afford quality education. However, this changed with the opening of numerous public and private universities between the 1970s and the 1990s.

Portugal is home to the University of Coimbra, one of the 20 oldest institutions of higher education in Europe. Founded in 1290, the University of Coimbra prepared boys and young men for the clergy and law in its early years. Today the university includes eight faculties: the Faculties of Law, Medicine, Humanities, Science and Technology, Pharmacy, Economics, Psychology and Education Sciences, and Sports Sciences and Physical Education. In addition, the University of Coimbra houses nearly 30 research institutes, mostly in the natural sciences, social sciences, and technological sciences. With nearly 30,000 students, the University of Porto is the largest university in the country in terms of enrollment.

Teacher Education

Portuguese students at the tertiary level who plan to become teachers at the basic or secondary levels must enroll in higher education courses that lead to the *licensiado* degree. These courses must be based on curriculum that meets the needs associated with the grade or level of schooling for which the candidate is training. Teacher education for the first, second, and third cycles within the basic education period is offered in faculties of education at universities or at colleges of education (*escolas superiores de educação*) throughout the country.

Students who plan to be secondary school teachers must enroll in one of the several universities in the country that offer degrees in secondary education. Candidates who wish to be qualified to teach in vocational schools or arts and music academies must complete degree courses in the specialization of interest as well as courses related to pedagogy. This holds true for candidates who major in one of the five branches of secondary study (i.e., mathematics, language and literature, one of the several social studies, natural sciences, or foreign language). Length of study generally depends on the educational level and the content or area of specialization; teacher candidates must study for at least four years in order to receive an initial degree in teacher education.

Portugal Education at a Glance

General Information

Capital	Lisbon
Population	10.7 million
Language	Portuguese
Literacy rate	93.3%
GDP per capita	US$19,800
People below poverty line	no data
Number of phones per 100 people	38
Number of Internet users per 100 people	42
Number of Internet hosts	3.2 million
Life expectancy at birth (years)	78

Formal Educational Information

Primary school age population	652,000
Secondary school age population	679,000
Primary school age population	6%
Number of years of education (primary/secondary)	6/6
Student/teacher ratio (primary)	10.5
Student/teacher ratio (secondary)	7
Primary school gross enrollment ratio	116%
Primary school entrants completing primary school	104%
Secondary school gross enrollment ratio	97%
Child labor (ages 5–14)	3%

Note: Unless otherwise indicated, all data are based on sources from 2011.

Informal Education

Informal education in Portugal is a rather novel initiative, given that education for lower- and middle-class citizens emerged during the 1960s and 1970s. More recently, initiatives to eradicate illiteracy in the country have led to the creation and development of informal education programs in higher education institutions as well as in places of worship, union halls, and municipal offices. Informal education practices in Portugal provide adults who were not exposed to formal education with basic knowledge in reading, writing, arithmetic, and vocations that increases skill levels for potential growth and increased pay in the workforce. Informal education includes courses in technical skills as well as in foreign language instruction. Informal education programs held in state-run higher education institutions are regulated by the Ministry of Science, Technology and Higher Education.

System Economics

According to the United Nations Development Programme (2011), Portugal ranks 88 of 186 in educational expenditures as a percentage of gross domestic product (GDP). The total public expenditure on education in 2008 represented 4.4 percent of GDP. Nearly US$10.8 billion has been allocated for education purposes. Based on these figures, total per student spending is approximately $8,165 (determined by dividing total expenditure by 1,331,000, the approximate number of students in Portugal).

Future Prospects

The most important challenge for the education system in Portugal is the eradication of illiteracy, particularly among its adult population. In addition, data from UNICEF's "Monitoring the Situation of Children and Women" (2010) show that 3 percent of all children between the ages of five and 14 are engaged in some form of labor. It can further be speculated that children who engage in labor either fail to attend or drop out of school. Moreover, as adults, these individuals, nearly all of whom are members of the working class, may not learn how to read or write. Therefore a major initiative for the Portuguese Ministry of Education is to ensure educational equity for all children and adolescents as a means of achieving 100 percent literacy and to encourage the Portuguese government to pass laws that end child labor practices. Despite these drawbacks in the Portuguese system of education, the country increased its ranking from 37 in 2006 to 27 in 2009 in student Programme for International Student Assessment scores in the areas of reading, mathematics, and science.

Daniel Ness and Chia-ling Lin

REFERENCES

Central Intelligence Agency. *The CIA World Factbook.* New York: Skyhorse, 2011. https://www.cia.gov/library/publications/the-world-factbook/index.html.

Nation Master. 2011. www.nationmaster.com.

UNESCO. *Global Education Digest 2012: Comparing Education Statistics Across the World.* Montreal: UNESCO Institute for Statistics, 2012.

UNESCO–IBE. www.ibe.unesco.org/en/worldwide/unesco-regions/europe-and-north-america/portugal.html.

UNESCO–UIS. www.uis.unesco.org.

UNICEF. www.unicef.org/infobycountry.

World Bank Education Statistics. 2011. www.worldbank.org.

ROMANIA

Romania is a country in southeastern Europe, in the northeastern part of the Balkan Peninsula. In medieval times the region of Romania comprised the principalities of Wallachia and Moldavia, which were under the suzerainty of the Ottoman Empire. The two principalities united into Romania in 1862. The country gained independence in 1878. During World War I, the country sided with the Allied powers. However, during World War II, Romania became one of the Axis regimes that aided Germany in the battles against the Soviet Union. The eventual defeat of Nazi Germany led to Soviet occupation of Romania. The country was ruled by Nicolai Ceausescu from 1965 to the late 1980s. In 1989 the Ceausescu regime was overthrown by protesters, dissident members of the Romanian Communist Party, and the Romanian army. Ceausescu and his wife were executed shortly thereafter. Eventually communist rule was overtaken by a republic form of government in 1996. The country joined NATO in 2004 and the European Union three years later.

Approximately 87 percent of all Romanians are Eastern Orthodox. The remaining 13 percent of the population consists of Roman Catholics and Protestants. The official language is Romanian (spoken by 91 percent of the population), followed by Hungarian (7 percent) and Romany (1 percent).

Educational System

The Ministry of Education and Research runs the educational system in Romania. The educational system in the country has undergone several changes since the 1989 Revolution. Although schooling in urban areas has improved, schooling in rural areas has remained static or worsened. Compulsory education mandates in the country require students to be enrolled in school for the entire primary school period (four years), lower secondary school period (four years), and the first two years of the four-year upper secondary school period—a total of 10 years.

Preprimary and Primary Education

Preprimary education in Romania is available for children between three and six years of age. Preschools, however, are most prevalent in urban settings. Few, if any, preschools are found in Romania's rural areas or farming regions. Children who are able to attend kindergarten are often introduced to basic foreign language instruction. Large cities also have day-care facilities for working parents.

Primary education is a four-year period designated for children from six to 10 years old. This period consists of four grade levels. The first two levels emphasize basic language and reading skills, mathematical proficiency, and basic science literacy. Children in the first two levels are also required to engage in physical education, music, and art. By the third and fourth grade levels, students in primary school have a diverse and extended curriculum. Courses offered include mathematics, Romanian, history, geography, natural science, art, music, French or English, and computer knowledge. The subject of religion is an elective. There are approximately 900,000 children of primary school age in Romania. The primary student/teacher ratio is about 17 students per teacher. The primary school net enrollment ratio for Romania is 91.3 percent, relatively low when compared to other European nations. The low enrollment rate might be related to the lower numbers of rural children attending school. However, the percentage of children reaching grade 4 is 95 percent, and the percentage of children completing primary school is nearly 99 percent.

Secondary Education

Secondary education in Romania is divided into lower secondary education (grades 5 through 8) and upper secondary education (grades 9 through 12). Lower secondary schools include *gymnaziu*, which is analogous to the German *gymnasium*, the *ciclul inferior al liceului* (which translates as comprehensive junior high school), and arts and trade school. The most competitive upper secondary schools in Romania are the national colleges. These institutions have at least a century-long tradition of classical education curricula along with strong natural science and mathematics departments. Saint Sava National College, the oldest high school in Romania, was founded in 1688 and enrolls approximately 1,000 students per year. Other comprehensive gymnasia include military schools, high schools of economics, and high schools for academically gifted students.

It is important to note, however, that secondary education in Romania has suffered from relatively high levels of attrition and truancy. There are nearly 2.3 million children and adolescents who are of secondary school age in Romania. Of these, about 1.9 million are enrolled in a secondary school program. In other words, slightly less than half a million children and adolescents do not attend secondary school. This problem may have to do with an overwhelmingly large percentage of families in rural, farming regions whose incomes fall below or at the international poverty line. Children and adolescents are often obliged to work, mostly in agricultural labor, and therefore do not realize the significance of formal schooling as a benefit.

Tertiary Education

Romania is home to over 110 public and private universities, many of which were founded after the Revolution of 1989. At present, 56 universities are funded or subsidized by the federal government, and 57 universities are privately funded. About 10 of the private universities are currently undergoing the accreditation process. Romania is also home to several higher education institutions that focus on specific professional domains, such as education and pedagogy, law, and business and economics.

The most competitive university in the country is the University of Bucharest. Established in 1864, the University of Bucharest often ranks among the 500 to 600 of the most competitive universities throughout the world. The university has 18 faculties, including departments within the humanities, natural sciences and mathematics, social sciences, law, and religion. More than 34,000 students enroll every year. The oldest continuously running university in the country is Alexandru Ioan Cuza University, founded in 1860, in Iasi, Romania. In contrast, Babeş-Bolyai University, in Cluj-Napoca, was founded in 1581 but closed its doors in the seventeenth century, reopening in 1872. Babeş-Bolyai University, along with the University of Bucharest and Alexandru Ioan Cuza University, is one of the highly competitive institutions in the country.

Despite the long heritage of higher education in Romania, the country's universities do not often show up on lists of the most competitive European tertiary-level institutions. Several higher education ranking organizations have not included Romanian universities within the top 500 worldwide rankings.

Teacher education in Romania is available, in part, through universities for content instruction and also at pedagogical institutions for actual teacher training. Students intending to teach at the preprimary or primary school levels are trained in pedagogical higher schools (i.e., teacher training institutions) at the tertiary level. These students must pass a special examination in order to be placed in a school setting. Students intending to teach in both lower and upper secondary school must be awarded specialized degrees from higher pedagogical institutes. However, upper secondary certification requires a longer period of study. All students in this category must have completed pedagogical courses as well as university-level content courses.

System Economics and Future Prospects

According to the United Nations Development Programme (2010), along with Algeria, Italy, Kosovo, Sierra Leone, and Spain, total public expenditures on education in Romania represented 4.3 percent of the gross domestic product (GDP) in 2007. Given the GDP of Romania at $264 billion, educational expenditure in the country amounts to over $11.35 billion, or $3,504 per student (total amount equivalent to US dollars divided by 3,239,000, the approximate number of primary and secondary students in the country). Per student spending was greater during the Soviet and Yugoslavian era. Although Romania ranks 92 of 186 countries in terms of percentage of educational expenditure, the amount of funding needed to support a strong educational system in the country requires financial subsidies from municipal, regional, and nongovernmental sources. Accordingly, due to the lack of assistance from the central government, funding per student is severely handicapped in comparison with Romania's neighbors, particularly countries to the north and west.

Romania has a literacy rate of 97 percent, which is defined as the percentage of citizens 15 years of age or older who can read and write. The Education Ministry of Romania lacks sufficient resources for rural schools, particularly those in poor farming communities. As a result, school enrollment is high in urban areas and relatively low in rural hinterlands. There is also an element of child labor in Romania, most prevalent in farming and animal husbandry in rural areas. Poor families in these regions depend on the labor of individuals of school age in order to eke out a living. According to UNICEF, 1 percent of all children between five and 14 years of age are engaged in labor in Romania. Most apparently, underage labor is the result of high rates of attrition of students, particularly those in secondary schools.

Nevertheless, a number of nongovernmental organizations (NGOs) are working with the Romanian government and Ministry of Education to improve the adverse conditions in education, which range from the country's unstable economy to a lack of health-care facilities and the number of underage workers. NGOs helping the nation within the sphere of education have supported initiatives to supply funding that will alleviate travel burdens for schoolchildren, particularly those in rural areas, as well as funding allocated for educational supplies and materials. Moreover, although advanced school technologies are prevalent in large urban areas, NGOs are helping to prepare rural Romanians to benefit

Romania Education at a Glance

General Information

Capital	Bucharest
Population	21.9 million
Languages	Romanian (91%), Hungarian, Romany
Literacy rate	97%
GDP per capita	US$9,100
People below poverty line	25%
Number of phones per 100 people	23
Number of Internet users per 100 people	28
Number of Internet hosts	2.4 million
Life expectancy at birth (years)	72

Formal Educational Information

Primary school age population	895,000
Secondary school age population	2.3 million
Primary school age population	4%
Secondary school age population	10.5%
Number of years of education (primary/secondary)	4/8
Student/teacher ratio (primary)	17
Student/teacher ratio (secondary)	13
Primary school gross enrollment ratio	105%
Primary school entrants completing primary school	95%
Secondary school gross enrollment ratio	86%
Child labor (ages 5–14)	1%

Note: Unless otherwise indicated, all data are based on sources from 2011.

from the use of information and communication technologies as well.

Daniel Ness and Chia-ling Lin

REFERENCES

Bîrzea, Cezar, Ioan Neacşu, Dan Potolea, Mihaela Ionescu, Olimpius Istrate, and Luciana-Simona Velea. "National Report: Romania." In *The Prospects of Teacher Education in South East Europe*, ed. Pavel Zgaga, 437–486. Ljubljana, Slovenia: Faculty of Education, University of Ljubljana, 2006.

Central Intelligence Agency. *The CIA World Factbook*. New York: Skyhorse, 2011. https://www.cia.gov/library/publications/the-world-factbook/index.html.

Nation Master. 2011. www.nationmaster.com.

UNESCO. *Global Education Digest 2012: Comparing Education Statistics Across the World*. Montreal: UNESCO Institute for Statistics, 2012.

UNESCO–IBE. www.ibe.unesco.org/en/worldwide/unesco-regions/europe-and-north-america/republic-of-serbia.html.

UNESCO–UIS. www.uis.unesco.org.

UNICEF. www.unicef.org/infobycountry.

World Bank Education Statistics. 2011. www.worldbank.org.

SAN MARINO

Because of its small geographical area (61.2 square kilometers, or 23.63 square miles), the Republic of San Marino is called a postage stamp country. San Marino is a landlocked country and an enclave that is entirely within the borders of Italy. After the Holy See and Monaco, San Marino is the third-smallest country in Europe. In 2011 the estimated population of the country was 31,817, thus making it the twenty-first most densely populated state in the world. Founded in 301 CE, San Marino is claimed by many historians to be the oldest continuous republic in the world, despite invasions from axis forces during World War II. Despite its independent nation status, San Marino has aligned itself politically and socially with Italy. San Marino has become known for its tourism economy.

Educational System

Preschool in San Marino is typically for three years for children between three and five years. Compulsory education in San Marino is similar to that of Italy. Both countries require children to begin primary school at age six. Primary school in San Marino is a five-year period, and secondary school in the country lasts for eight years. Students are expected to enroll in public primary and secondary schools. Primary schools (scuola elementare) enroll students from six to 11 years of age. Upon receiving the primary school certificate, students continue to lower secondary school (scuola medie inferiore), which lasts for three years and enrolls students between the ages of 11 and 14 years. Upon finishing lower secondary school, students have the option to attend one of the several types of upper level secondary schools, similar to those in Italy. Upper secondary schools (scuola secondaria superiore) are three years in duration and enroll students between the ages of 15 and 18 years. Upon graduation, students are awarded the Diploma di Maturità, which is one of several requirements for university enrollment.

The student/teacher ratio for primary school in San Marino is about eight students per teacher. The student/teacher ratio for secondary school is about six students for every teacher. There are no institutions of higher education in San Marino. However, students who graduate from the upper secondary school have the same opportunities to attend colleges and universities in Italy as do Italian citizens.

Students who successfully complete upper secondary school have two general options: (1) they can apply for enrollment for tertiary education in San Marino, or (2) tertiary education in Italy or abroad. In San Marino tertiary education is available at the Università degli Studi della Repùbblica di San Marino, which provides both undergraduate and graduate offerings. The university offers baccalaureate, master's and doctoral programs. The most common majors are economics and tourism, business administration, nursing, communication, sports management, and engineering. The training of preprimary, primary, and secondary school teachers is conducted in teacher training institutions in Italy. Preservice teachers who wish to teach in San Marino must participate in a nearly month-long student teaching course in San Marino during the month of September.

System Economics and Future Prospects

Due to a lack of government resources on education, it is difficult to ascertain how much of San Marino's

San Marino Education at a Glance

General Information

Capital	San Marino
Population	31,477
Language	Italian
Literacy rate	96%
GDP per capita	US$34,100
People below poverty line	no data
Number of phones per 100 people	68
Number of Internet users per 100 people	54
Number of Internet hosts	8,895
Life expectancy at birth (years)	82

Formal Educational Information

Primary school age population	no data
Secondary school age population	no data
Primary school age population	no data
Number of years of education (primary/secondary)	5/8
Student/teacher ratio (primary)	8.2
Student/teacher ratio (secondary)	6.3
Primary school gross enrollment ratio	no data
Primary school entrants reaching grade 5	88%
Secondary school gross enrollment ratio	no data
Child labor (ages 5–14)	no data

Note: Unless otherwise indicated, all data are based on sources from 2011.

gross domestic product of $1.137 billion is spent on education. However, given the similarity between the country's education system and that of Italy, researchers have estimated total education spending at about US$48.9 million. With a student population of about 5,700 children and adolescents, per student spending would amount to $8,579. It is important to note that this per capita amount does not reflect the total per student spending by government and private sources. Given San Marino's position as a leader in business and tourism, students who graduate from secondary school in San Marino generally have strong backgrounds in numerous disciplines in both traditional education and vocational education.

Daniel Ness and Chia-ling Lin

REFERENCES

Central Intelligence Agency. *The CIA World Factbook*. New York: Skyhorse, 2011. https://www.cia.gov/library/publications/the-world-factbook/index.html.

Nation Master. 2011. www.nationmaster.com.

UNESCO. *Global Education Digest 2012: Comparing Education Statistics Across the World*. Montreal: UNESCO Institute for Statistics, 2012.

UNESCO–IBE. www.ibe.unesco.org/en/worldwide/unesco-regions/europe-and-north-america/san-marino.html.

UNESCO–UIS. www.uis.unesco.org.

UNICEF. www.unicef.org/infobycountry.

World Bank Education Statistics. 2011. www.worldbank.org.

SERBIA

Serbia is a landlocked country in southeastern Europe, in the northern part of the Balkan Peninsula. After Tito's death in 1980 Yugoslavia managed to continue its political connections for an additional 10 years. The newly formed Serbian government's ultranationalist policies, which favored Serbs over neighboring groups, eventually led to the dissolution of Yugoslavia. In 1991 Croatia, Macedonia, and Slovenia became independent nations. One year later Bosnia declared independence. The only region that was left from the Socialist Federal Republic of Yugoslavia (1945–1992) was the Federal Republic of Yugoslavia, which included both Serbia and Montenegro. The policy of ethnic cleansing led to several years of bitter internal war and genocide. NATO eventually bombed Serbia in 1999. The bombing eventually lead to the disbandment of the Federal Republic of Yugoslavia in 2003. Internal conflict within the federation of Serbia, Montenegro, and Kosovo led to the secession of Montenegro in 2006, followed by the secession of Kosovo in 2008.

Approximately 85 percent of all Serbians are Serbian Orthodox. The remaining 15 percent of the population are Roman Catholics, Protestants, Muslims, atheists, and people of no religious affiliation.

Educational System

Education in Serbia comprises the preprimary, primary, secondary, and tertiary levels. The ages of children attending preschools range from three to six years. Parents generally send their children to preschool for one to four years. Compulsory schooling takes place for the entire primary school period and the first three years of secondary school. The population of children of primary school age is nearly 850,000 individuals. Primary schooling is divided into the lower grades (grades 1 through 4) and the upper grades (grades 5 through 8). Topics in the curriculum for the lower grades include Serbian, mathematics, physical science, and community and global issues, as well as art, music, and physical education. By the first year of the upper grade levels (i.e., grade 5), schools begin to diversify the curriculum according to student interests and abilities. For example, fifth graders usually take a second foreign language, and possibly biology, chemistry, history, and geography. Based on the fifth-grade curriculum, Serbian students in subsequent grade levels are able to focus on specific subjects in which they can excel. By grade 8, students' grades and scores will determine how they proceed in secondary school. All primary school children in Serbia have the option to take two elective courses—one in civics and social studies, and the other in religion.

The primary school gross enrollment ratio in Serbia is about 98 percent. The primary school net enrollment ratio of 96 percent seems to suggest that most children of primary age attend or are enrolled in primary school. Moreover, the survival rate to the last primary grade is the same percentage of students. The student/teacher ratio at the primary level is about 20 students for every teacher.

Secondary Education

Secondary school lasts from three to four years, for students from 15 to 18 years old. There are four categories of secondary schools in Serbia: special schools for the gifted (*matematička gimnazija*), grammar schools (*gimnazija*), professional schools, and vocational schools. To date, the Serbian Ministry of Education created two special schools for gifted students. These schools enroll students as young as 12 years of age for the study of mathematics and the sciences. Students who are accepted to these institutions have excelled in these subjects during the primary school period. Grammar schools are equally competitive in that students accepted to grammar schools excel in the areas of language and the social sciences, as well as mathematics and the natural sciences. Both special schools for the gifted and grammar schools prepare students for university education—both in Serbia and at universities in other countries. Professional schools enroll students who are interested in specific areas of expertise—such as certain types of engineering, medical professions, and the like. These schools are much broader and comprehensive in content-related scope than other secondary school types. Moreover,

professional schools have the greatest student population. Vocational schools accommodate students who wish to enter the workforce upon graduation without having to attend tertiary education. These programs last for three years and train students in a variety of skills and vocations. Common vocation courses include machine science, pharmacology, medical science, veterinary school, and technical or computer-related disciplines.

The secondary school gross enrollment ratio in Serbia is about 89 percent. However, no data exist on the secondary school net enrollment ratio. The student/teacher ratio at the primary level is about 14 students for every teacher.

Tertiary Education

Serbia has attempted to conform to the directives of the Bologna Process, which has provided European governments with a more or less uniform structure of their higher education institutions. Accordingly, universities in Serbia follow a specified time period for offering baccalaureates, master's degrees, and doctorates.

There are a total of seven public universities and seven private universities in Serbia. In addition, there are individual institutes that specialize in professional subjects in a host of cities throughout the country. The most competitive university in the country is the University of Belgrade, which is the oldest and largest university in the country. The University of Belgrade was founded in 1808 as a means of educating members of elite classes. At present nearly 90,000 students enroll in the university annually. There are 31 faculties in the University of Belgrade—the largest number of faculties of any university in Serbia. Other public universities include the University of Novi Sad, the University of Niš, the University of Kragujevac, the University of Priština, the Belgrade University of Arts, and the University of Novi Pasar. Acceptance to most universities and faculties in Serbia is based in part on exit examinations from secondary schools. Nearly all Serbian universities offer master's degrees and doctorates.

Teacher Education

Students who enter the teaching profession in Serbia must satisfy two levels of training. First, students must have a university degree in order to become a teacher at any level. Faculties of education are available in nearly every public university in the country. Second, after university students become employed at schools, they must pass a sequence of teacher certification and licensing examinations in order to become tenured. Examination reforms have taken place after 2003 because teacher certification examinations were unclear in identifying what was expected of the new teacher. Students have the opportunity to earn master's-level degrees in education, although students wishing to become teachers need not continue beyond the baccalaureate level.

System Economics and Future Prospects

According to the United Nations Development Programme (2010), along with Iran, Dominica, and Lithuania, total public expenditures on education in Serbia represented 4.7 percent of the gross domestic product (GDP) in 2008. Given the GDP of Serbia at $80.1 billion, educational expenditure in the country amounts to nearly $3.77 billion, or $3,065 per student (total amount equivalent to US dollars divided by 1,228,000, the approximate number of primary and secondary students in the country). Per student spending was greater during the Soviet and Yugoslavian era. Serbia ranks 73 of 186 countries in terms of percentage of educational expenditure.

Despite a 96 percent literacy rate, Serbia's socioeconomic and educational infrastructure has suffered from decline since Kosovo's separation from Serbia in 2008. The Education Ministry of Serbia lacks sufficient resources for its schools. This lack of resources, along with years of military and civilian conflict, led to a steady drop in school enrollment. Another reason for a steady drop in enrollment is child labor. According to UNICEF, 5 percent of all children between five and 14 years of age are engaged in labor. This rather high rate of child labor in the region most likely accounts for the high rates of attrition of students, particularly those in secondary schools.

Serbia has very limited association between education and the private sector. In fact, the primary school level is almost entirely publicly funded. However, due to the poor economic circumstances of Serbia, there are a number of nongovernmental organizations working with the Serbian government to improve the adverse conditions young Serbians are facing. These conditions range from the country's unstable economy to problems with health care, child labor, and education. Nongovernmental organizations helping the nation within the sphere of education have supported initiatives to supply funding that will alleviate travel burdens for schoolchildren, particularly those in rural areas, as well as funding allocated for educational supplies and materials.

Daniel Ness and Chia-ling Lin

Serbia Education at a Glance

General Information

Capital	Belgrade
Population	9.1 million*
Languages	Serbian (88%), Hungarian, Romany, Bosniak, Romanian, Croatian, Albanian (in Kosovo)
Literacy rate	96%
GDP per capita	US$4,400
People below poverty line (2004)	30%
Number of phones per 100 people	35
Number of Internet users per 100 people	32
Number of Internet hosts	528,253
Life expectancy at birth (years)	75

Formal Educational Information**

Primary school age population	381,000
Secondary school age population	847,000
Number of years of education (primary/secondary)	4/8
Student/teacher ratio (primary)	20
Student/teacher ratio (secondary)	14
Primary school gross enrollment ratio	98%
Primary school entrants completing primary school	96%
Secondary school gross enrollment ratio	89%
Child labor (ages 5–14)	10%

Notes: *Population figures include Kosovo. **Formal education data (excluding "Child labor") are based on student populations in both Serbia and Montenegro.

Unless otherwise indicated, all data are based on sources from 2011.

REFERENCES

Central Intelligence Agency. *The CIA World Factbook*. New York: Skyhorse, 2011. https://www.cia.gov/library/publications/the-world-factbook/index.html.

Kovács-Cerović, Tünde. "National Report: Serbia." In *The Prospects of Teacher Education in South East Europe*, ed. Pavel Zgaga, 487–526. Ljubljana, Slovenia: Faculty of Education, University of Ljubljana, 2006.

Nation Master. 2011. www.nationmaster.com.

UNESCO. *Global Education Digest 2012: Comparing Education Statistics Across the World.* Montreal: UNESCO Institute for Statistics, 2012.

UNESCO–IBE. www.ibe.unesco.org/en/worldwide/unesco-regions/europe-and-north-america/republic-of-serbia.html.

UNESCO–UIS. www.uis.unesco.org.

UNICEF. www.unicef.org/infobycountry.

World Bank Education Statistics. 2011. www.worldbank.org.

Slovakia

Slovakia is a landlocked country in central Europe. The population is mainly Slovak (85 percent). About 10 percent of the population is Hungarian. The official language is Slovak. However, about 11 percent of residents are Hungarian speakers. The religion is predominantly Roman Catholic (69 percent). Slovakia consists of eight regions. The Slovak region separated from the Czech region of Czechoslovakia and became independent on January 1, 1993. Slovakia became a NATO nation in 1999 and part of the European Union in 2004.

Educational System

The system of education in Slovakia is run by the Ministry of Education and the Higher Education Council. School types include state-run schools, church-owned schools, and private schools. Educational levels include preschool and kindergarten (ages three through six years), primary education (ages six through 15), secondary schools (ages 16 through 19), and colleges and universities.

Preprimary education in Slovakia includes preschools, which enroll children as young as three years of age. However, children do not have to attend formal schooling until kindergarten, which is the year preceding first grade. All kindergartens are free. Activities at the preschool level include drawing and coloring, learning numbers, experiencing nature and surroundings, singing, and free play. Kindergarten children engage in the introduction to geometric thinking, notions of time, learning the formal alphabet, and introduction to reading.

Compulsory education in the Slovak Republic lasts for nine years and comprises nine grade levels of primary education. Like the system in the Czech Republic, the primary education system in Slovakia is divided into stages of four years (grades 1 through 4) and five years (grades 5 through 9), respectively. In the first stage, students are introduced to a basic curriculum that includes the Slovak language, mathematics, the natural environment, physical education, art, and music. In the second stage, students are introduced to new subjects, such as one or two foreign languages (chosen from English, German, Spanish, or Russian), biology, physics, history, religion, and technical education.

Unlike secondary education in the Czech Republic, secondary education in Slovakia consists of four school types: the gymnasium, the secondary professional school, the secondary vocational school, and the general secondary school. The gymnasium, also called the grammar school, prepares students for university education. Students have two points of entry: after the first primary school stage (age 10 or 11) or after the second primary school stage (age 15 or 16). The secondary professional school also prepares students for higher education, but mostly in the areas of professional studies.

Universities in Slovakia have existed since the fifteenth century. However, the earliest institutions closed their doors within the same century they had opened. A number of these universities, such as Universitas Istropolitana (Danube University) and the University of Trnava, were founded as centers for theology, philosophy, and law. The oldest continuously functioning institution of higher education in present-day Slovakia is Comenius University in Bratislava, which was established in 1919. Comenius University, named after the famed educator, is the largest university in the country, enrolling more than 30,000 students annually. The university is prized for its traditional faculties of humanities, mathematics, natural sciences, and social sciences, as well as its new faculties of education, pharmacy, physical education and sports, and medicine. Higher education in Slovakia is also known for its rigor and emphasis in the area of transportation science and engineering. The University of Žilina, which was established in 1953, is an international leader in the areas of aeronautics, civil engineering, electrical engineering, mechanical engineering, management science and informatics, and flight training.

At present there are about 35 institutions of higher education in Slovakia, of which 20 are public and over 10 are private. Nearly all of the public institutions

Slovakia Education at a Glance

General Information

Capital	Bratislava
Population	5.4 million
Languages	Slovak (84%),
	Hungarian (11%), Roma, Ukrainian
Literacy rate	100%
GDP per capita	US$18,200
People below poverty line	21%
Number of phones per 100 people	20
Number of Internet users per 100 people	65
Number of Internet hosts	1.1 million
Life expectancy at birth (years)	75

Formal Educational Information

Primary school age population	235,000
Secondary school age population	679,000
Primary school age population	4%
Number of years of education	
(primary/secondary)	4/9
Student/teacher ratio (primary)	17.5
Student/teacher ratio (secondary)	13.3
Primary school gross enrollment ratio	99%
Primary school entrants completing	
primary school	97%
Secondary school gross enrollment ratio	96.5%
Child labor (ages 5–14)	no data

Note: Unless otherwise indicated, all data are based on sources from 2011.

are universities or academies of art or music. Most of the private institutions are colleges with distinctly emphasized disciplines, or colleges that provide a broad curriculum with a baccalaureate as the highest terminal degree.

Teacher Education

Teacher training in Slovakia initially involves a university degree. Most universities in the country have faculties of education. These faculties are involved in the training of teachers for both the first and second stages of primary school. Like the system in the Czech Republic, the system in Slovakia requires four-year programs for teacher candidates in the first stage and five-year programs for those in the second. Candidates for the second stage of primary education must major in two areas: education or pedagogy and one of the school disciplines (mathematics, Slovak language and literature, one of the natural sciences). Secondary school teacher candidates are required to enroll in a university and major in a specialized field that is taught at the secondary level. Fields must be in the faculties of humanities, natural sciences, physical education, mathematics, arts, and educa-

tion. Programs for candidates majoring in secondary education are five years in duration. At the end of this period, candidates must pass a national teacher examination in order to be placed in a secondary school setting. Students must also take pedagogical courses.

System Economics

According to the United Nations Development Programme (2011), Slovakia ranks 114 of 186 in educational expenditures as a percentage of gross domestic product (GDP). The total public expenditure on education in 2007 represented 3.6 percent of GDP. Nearly US$4.3 billion was allocated for education purposes. Based on these figures, total per student spending is approximately $4,735 (determined by dividing total expenditure by 914,000, the approximate number of students in Slovakia). Despite this seemingly low figure, per student spending is subsidized by both additional government sources and private funding as well.

Future Prospects

The trends of education in Slovakia are similar to those in the Czech Republic. Specifically, the Slovak education system witnessed growth from preschool to the tertiary education sectors. Technology for instruction and as part of the curriculum has become an essential part of the education process. At the same time, as in the Czech Republic, the level of advancement and competitiveness at the primary and secondary levels lags behind that of the tertiary level. This is evidence in the 2009 Programme for International Student Assessment (PISA) results of the two countries: the Czech Republic ranked 34th out of 65 countries participating, and Slovakia ranked 35th.

Daniel Ness and Chia-ling Lin

REFERENCES

Central Intelligence Agency. *The CIA World Factbook.* New York: Skyhorse, 2011. https://www.cia.gov/library/publications/the-world-factbook/index.html.

Nation Master. 2011. www.nationmaster.com.

UNESCO. *Global Education Digest 2012: Comparing Education Statistics Across the World.* Montreal: UNESCO Institute for Statistics, 2012.

UNESCO–IBE. www.ibe.unesco.org/en/worldwide/unesco-regions/europe-and-north-america/slovakia.html.

UNESCO–UIS. www.uis.unesco.org.

UNICEF. www.unicef.org/infobycountry.

World Bank Education Statistics. 2011. www.worldbank.org.

SLOVENIA

Slovenia is located in southeastern Europe. Slovenia was originally part of the Austro-Hungarian Empire until 1918, when Slovenes, Serbs, and Croats joined forces. The regions of present-day Slovenia, Serbia, and Croatia became Yugoslavia in 1929. After World War II, the Slovene portion of Yugoslavia kept economic ties with Western European countries, despite its political allegiance to Moscow. Slovenia became independent in 1991 after the dissolution of the Soviet Union and Yugoslavia. The country's relatively strong education system and stable political system have contributed to the nation's relatively successful economy.

The country's population was 2 million in the 2011 United Nations estimate. Approximately 60 percent of all Slovenes are Roman Catholic. The remaining 40 percent of the population consists of members of Protestant sects, Greek Orthodox, and those who have no religious affiliation. Slovenia's gross domestic product (GDP) for 2010 amounted to $56.58 billion.

Educational System

Preprimary education in Slovenia is quite advanced when compared to other former Yugoslavian states. Preschool education in the country is an integrated form of schooling that combines some instruction with play and child care. The preschool system in Slovenia is based on legislation from 1996 that emphasizes individualized attention to children rather than a more or less pluralistic "one size fits all" program.

Compulsory Education and Upper Secondary Education

Compulsory education in Slovenia consists of an eight-year period; the primary school lasts for six years and lower secondary school for two years. Modifications are currently under way that call for a restructuring of compulsory education to include three three-year cycles for a total of nine years. At present there are nearly 200,000 children who are of primary or lower secondary school age (4.5 percent of the total population of the country). The student/teacher ratio for the primary level is about 15 students for every teacher. Nearly all students entering primary school complete the primary school level.

Upper secondary school is divided into three types: vocational school, technical school, and traditional general education school (similar to the German gymnasium). Vocational schools enable students who will not continue to tertiary education to enter the workforce with specialized skills. The duration of the Slovenian vocational school is generally three years. Slovenian technical schools enable students to qualify for various professional disciplines that require tertiary education, particularly polytechnic disciplines such as engineering fields, architecture, and computer programming. Technical school education usually lasts for four years (grades 9 through 12). General education schools are traditional secondary schools that prepare university-bound students. There are different types of general education schools, including classical gymnasia, polytechnic gymnasia, social science gymnasia, and arts academies. Although the gross and net enrollment ratios for secondary school are lower than those of primary school, most students who enter secondary school complete a degree in one of the three types of schools in the country.

Slovenia is one of the few post-Yugoslavian countries that have attempted to accommodate students of different cultures and backgrounds. This can be seen in the multilingual classrooms that are evident in most primary and secondary schools. The four most common languages spoken are Slovenian, Hungarian, Serbo-Croatian, and Italian.

Tertiary Education

Higher education in Slovenia is divided into two types: public universities and private colleges, schools, or institutes. The oldest and largest university in Slovenia is the University of Ljubljana, located in the nation's capital. Founded in 1919, the University of Ljubljana enrolls approximately 61,000 students annually. The University of Ljubljana maintains 23 faculties and three academies—the Academy of Music, Academy of Fine Arts and Design, and Academy of Theater, Radio, Film, and Television. One of the most competitive faculties in the university is the Faculty of Economics, which offers an undergraduate degree in marketing, 10 master's programs, and one doctoral program in economics and business.

Other public universities in the country include the University of Maribor, the University of Primorska, and the University of Nova Gorica. The University of Maribor emphasizes engineering and polytechnic disciplines. All three universities have strong faculties in the natural sciences. Private institutions include individual and autonomous schools or institutes that specialize in distinct professional areas. Examples include the European Faculty of Law in Nova Gorica, the Faculty of Information Studies in Novo Mesto, the Celje Higher School of Commerce, the Polymer Technology College in Slovenj Gradec, and the Academy of Visual Arts in Ljubljana.

Teacher Education

Similar to teacher training programs in neighboring countries, teacher education in Slovenia takes place at the university level. Nearly all universities in Slovenia have faculties of education for the purpose of training teachers. Programs for preprimary and primary teachers last for four years, followed by a year for preparing a thesis. Students also must prepare for a state-produced examination for teachers that must be passed in order to be placed in a school setting. Students preparing for secondary school teaching must be enrolled in a four- to five-year program that emphasizes one of the key areas taught in secondary school. Subjects include mathematics, linguistics or languages, one of the natural sciences, history, or sports. Students must also take courses in pedagogy and psychology. These students must also take an additional year to write a thesis and prepare for the comprehensive teachers' examination for secondary school candidates. Teacher candidates in vocational schools enroll in a similar program, but also must have at least three years of experience working in the vocation of specialization.

System Economics and Future Prospects

According to the United Nations Development Programme (2010), along with Hungary, Switzerland,

Slovenia Education at a Glance	
General Information	
Capital	Ljubljana
Population	2.3 million
Languages	Slovenian (91.1%),
	Serbo-Croatian (4.5%)
Literacy rate	100%
GDP per capita	US$23,400
People below poverty line	13%
Number of phones per 100 people	50.5
Number of Internet users per 100 people	56.2
Number of Internet hosts	137,494
Life expectancy at birth (years)	77
Formal Educational Information	
Primary school age population	93,000
Secondary school age population	183,000
Primary school age population	4.5%
Number of years of education (primary/secondary)	5/8
Student/teacher ratio (primary)	15
Student/teacher ratio (secondary)	11
Primary school gross enrollment ratio	98%
Primary school entrants completing primary school	99%
Secondary school gross enrollment ratio	96%
Child labor (ages 5–14)	no data

Note: Unless otherwise indicated, all data are based on sources from 2011.

and Yemen, total public expenditures on education in Slovenia represented 5.2 percent of GDP in 2007. Given the GDP of Slovenia at $56.58 billion, educational expenditure in the country amounts to nearly $2.95 billion, or $10,660 per student (total amount equivalent to US dollars divided by 276,000, the approximate number of primary and secondary students in the country). Per student spending was greater during the Soviet era. Slovenia ranks 51 of 186 countries in terms of percentage of educational expenditure.

With a near 100 percent literacy rate, Slovenia has one of the highest rates of literacy in the region. Unlike many of its eastern and southern neighbors, Slovenia has not suffered from decline in its formal system of education. Many post-Soviet-bloc countries were provided few resources for running schools, which made enrollment drop. In contrast, education in Slovenia saw drastic improvement over the decades since the dissolution of the Soviet Union and breakup of Yugoslavia.

The Slovenian Ministry of Education has rebuilt the educational infrastructure in the country. To this end, the Slovenian government and nongovernmental organizations have succeeded in improving the quality of education in the country and have also provided funding for students of poor families and rural dwellers. For example, rural families and farming families need not pay for travel fees to and from school or classroom supplies. Teacher education in Slovenia has been significantly more successful than in some of the neighboring nations.

Daniel Ness and Chia-ling Lin

REFERENCES

Central Intelligence Agency. *The CIA World Factbook*. New York: Skyhorse, 2011. https://www.cia.gov/library/publications/the-world-factbook/index.html.

Nation Master. 2011. www.nationmaster.com.

UNESCO. *Global Education Digest 2012: Comparing Education Statistics Across the World*. Montreal: UNESCO Institute for Statistics, 2012.

UNESCO–IBE. www.ibe.unesco.org/en/worldwide/unesco-regions/europe-and-north-america/slovenia.html.

UNESCO–UIS. www.uis.unesco.org.

UNICEF. www.unicef.org/infobycountry.

World Bank Education Statistics. 2011. www.worldbank.org.

Zgaga, Pavel, Tatjana Devjak, Janez Vogrinc, and Igor Repac. "National Report: Slovenia." In *The Prospects of Teacher Education in South East Europe*, ed. Pavel Zgaga, 527–570. Ljubljana, Slovenia: Faculty of Education, University of Ljubljana, 2006.

SPAIN

Spain is located in southwestern Europe and covers most of the Iberian Peninsula. Spain has a population of 43 million people. The official language is Castellano or Spanish. All Spanish citizens are obligated to learn Castellano. Spain also has four co-official languages that are spoken in specific regions of the country. Catalan, Gallego, and Valenciano are Latin-based languages, while Euskera is a distinct language unrelated to the Latin-based Spanish. Catalán is spoken in Catalonia and the Balearic Islands, Valenciano in Valencia, Gallego in Galicia, and Euskera in the Basque country and Navarre. Approximately three-quarters of the population speak Castellano Spanish as their first language. There is no official religion in Spain, but most citizens identify themselves as Roman Catholic. Most of the population of Spain is located in the coastal regions and the city of Madrid; about 76 percent of the population lives in urbanized regions. The population has in-

creased after birth rates dropped in the 1990s. This current expansion in population is primarily due to increased immigration from northern Africa and South America. Immigration in Spain was up 7.28 percent in 2005. Spaniards have high life expectancy rates at 80 years for the entire population: 76.7 years for men and 83.2 years for women. In 2006 the unemployment rate for the working population was 8.15 percent.

Curriculum, Instruction, and Assessment

The core curriculum of compulsory education is developed by the state with adaptations made at the school level. The core curriculum at the primary level includes mathematics, art, physical education, environmental education, Spanish language and literature, a foreign language, and the language and literature of the autonomous community. Religion is offered but optional. The core curriculum at the secondary level includes mathematics, physical education, natural sciences, social studies, geography and history, technology, music, the Spanish language and literature, and the language and literature of the autonomous community. Religion is offered but optional. Textbooks are chosen by subject departments at each school.

The academic performance of each student is assessed through state guidelines. Students in Spain do not take standardized tests in primary or secondary school. At the primary level, the classroom teacher assesses the students' performance and promotes them to the next grade. At the secondary level, the teachers, in collaboration, promote the students based on objectives developed from the curriculum. Students can repeat a grade if they are not passed by their teachers.

Students who complete primary and secondary schooling receive a certificate of completion (*Graduado en Educación Secundaria*). After completion of compulsory education, students can choose to attend postcompulsory education.

Upper secondary school students in the Bachillerato as well as the vocational training programs are assessed throughout the school year. If they do not perform adequately in more than two subjects in the first year or more than three in the second year, they are required to repeat the year. Students who successfully complete upper secondary school can apply for institutes of higher education.

Educational System

The education system of Spain is run by the Ministry of Education and Science. The Spanish constitution of 1978 ensured that all Spanish citizens have the right to an education and established a structure and set of guidelines for the management of compulsory education. Spain is divided into 17 municipalities called *comunidades autónoma* (autonomous communities). Autonomous communities have the right to interpret and uphold educational policy according to their own regional interests. The autonomous communities are also concerned with maintaining the culture and language of their region. All students at the primary and secondary level are required to take courses in the Spanish language as well as the local language of the autonomous community.

Education in Spain is divided into three categories: precompulsory education, compulsory education, and postcompulsory education. Precompulsory education is preprimary school (*escuelas de educación infantil*) for children age one to six. Compulsory education is divided into two phases: primary school (age six to 12) and lower secondary school (age 12 to 16). All Spanish citizens are required to attend school from the age of six to 16. Postcompulsory education consists of upper secondary school (age 16 to 18), university education, and vocational training. Compulsory education in Spain is free of charge for all citizens, though parents may be required to pay for the cost of books and transportation. Parents have the option of sending their children to private schools, which are primarily Roman Catholic. Private schools have an operating agreement with the state. Private institutions have the freedom to select admission requirements and teacher qualifications. They also designate their own tuition rates.

Precompulsory and Compulsory Education

Compulsory education in Spain is divided into two areas: primary education (six to 12 years of age) and lower secondary education (12 to 16 years of age). Preprimary school (up to the age of six years) is noncompulsory in Spain. Children have the op-

tion of attending preprimary school through the age of six years. Preprimary school is divided into two stages according to age; stage 1 (age one to three) and stage 2 (age three to six). At the preprimary level, students are introduced to reading and writing, a foreign language, numbers, and the arts. In addition to academic content, children in preprimary school learn to socialize and communicate with others.

The goal of primary school is to teach students basic skills like reading and writing and increase their personal development. The main objective of lower secondary school is to help students learn the core curriculum and prepare for future studies and life outside of school. The school year is 180 days for primary school and 175 days for secondary school. The school year for both phases begins in mid-September and ends in late June. The maximum class size, determined by the state, is 25 students in primary school and 30 in lower secondary school. In primary school one teacher teaches all the core subjects except for music, physical education, and foreign languages, which are taught by additional specialized teachers.

Postcompulsory Education

After students complete compulsory primary and lower secondary school, they have the option of attending upper secondary school (*bachillerato*). Upper secondary school is for students age 16 to 18. Students and families have the option of attending a specified vocational training school instead of upper secondary school. Tuition for both types of education is free and provided by the state. Upper secondary school is divided into four types of schools that emphasize humanities and social sciences, art, natural science and health, or technology. Specified vocational training schools help students prepare for the job market and increase their own personal development.

When students successfully complete the *Bachillerato* or the vocational training program, they have the option of applying to a university or advanced, specific vocational or art training. Students interested in attending a university or an art school must pass an entrance examination in addition to successful completion of the *Bachillerato*. Students planning to attend an advanced, specific vocational training school must either have a *Bachillerato* certificate or pass an entrance exam.

University

The function of the modern university in Spain is to create knowledge, engage in original research, and train future professionals and scholars. Reforms made in the 1980s have led to more self-governance of the university system. Institutes of higher education in Spain are divided into universities and nonuniversity institutions. Universities are academically based institutions in which students receive academic degrees. Nonuniversity programs provide students with advanced levels of specialized vocational training to prepare them for the workforce. Universities in Spain include public and private institutions. Sixty-seven of the universities in Spain are public. Students attending public university or nonuniversity tertiary education are required to pay a portion of their tuition. In 2004, 38 percent of the adult Spanish population between 25 and 34 and 26 percent of adults between 25 and 63 had degrees in higher education.

At present the university is divided into three phases. The first stage is intended for students who plan on pursuing a professional career and do not plan on continuing in higher education. These students take courses in fine arts, information technology, library science, nursing, health, social work, engineering, or architecture. The first phase generally lasts for three years. After completion of academic requirements, they receive the *diplomado* (university diploma) or *diplomado* in architecture or engineering degree. Students who choose to continue on to the second stage of university must take an additional year of academic coursework. The second stage takes two to three years of additional general education courses as well as coursework specialized to their field of study. After completing the requirements of the second stage, students are awarded the *licenciado* or professional degree. The final and third stage of university is the doctorate. Students who choose to pursue the doctorate take an additional two to three years of coursework and are expected to write a dissertation. The university system has been reorganized. The reorganization was fully implemented in 2010/2011. All the stages were merged into one stage and will take three to four years to complete. Postgraduate work will include a master's degree (an additional one to two years) and a doctorate degree (no time frame specified).

Established in 1134, the University of Salamanca is the oldest institution of higher education in Spain and the third-oldest university in the world. Other medieval, continuously operating universities in Spain include the University of Murcia (1272), the University of Madrid (1293), the University of Lleida (1300), the University of Barcelona (1450), the University of Santiago de Compostela (1495), the University of Valencia (1499), the University of Seville (1505), and the University of Granada (1531).

Nonuniversity Tertiary Education

Nonuniversity tertiary education consists mainly of advanced specific vocational training programs. These vocational programs are divided into 22 different areas of study. Students who graduate from advanced specific vocational training are prepared to enter the workforce as professionals in fields like graphic arts, marketing, furniture making, automobile maintenance, dental hygiene, or the development of computer applications. Advanced specific vocational training programs are one to two years in length. Students take coursework specific to their area of study and learn the necessary job skills for their industry or place of business. Students who successfully fulfill the requirements receive the *Técnico Superior* certificate. Additional types of nonuniversity tertiary programs include art and sports education. Students in arts and sports-based programs receive comparable degrees to the *Diplomado* and *Licenciado*.

Teacher Education

Those interested in teaching at the primary school level attend teacher training universities. After three years of coursework, teachers will receive a *Título de Maestro* (Title of Teacher). The *Título de Maestro* is a single subject credential that permits teaching at the preprimary and primary level. Primary and preprimary teachers choose a specialization field: preprimary education, primary education, foreign language (English and French), physical education, music education, special education, or hearing and speech therapy. Candidates choosing to specialize in preprimary education and primary education are trained to teach all the school subjects, while specialized teachers instruct physical education, music, special education, and hearing and speech therapy. Teacher training courses primarily include content relating to what candidates will be teaching at the preprimary and primary school level. They also learn about the psychological and social foundations of education and general and current theories of education. The final requirement of the *Titulo de Maestro* is over 300 hours of practicum or teaching at a school site. Candidates are accepted into teacher education programs as long as there is space and as long as they hold a *Bachillerato*.

Candidates interested in teaching at the secondary school level must hold a university degree. Secondary teachers specialize in a specific subject. After one year of coursework and 300 hours of teaching at a school site, teachers will receive a *Licenciado*. The curriculum is centered on courses relating theory to practice with a focus on effective pedagogy and the social and psychological foundations of education. An additional component of the teacher education curriculum is the opportunity for teachers to practice their teaching methods with students in secondary school settings.

Informal Education

The field of informal education in Spain is primarily concerned with nonformal adult education. These sites of informal learning help adults develop basic literary and life skills as well as offer personal and social development opportunities. Adult education programs outside of traditional education promote the maintenance of language and culture (i.e., Basque language and culture) and offer Spanish language and co-official language courses for immigrants. Additional adult education courses include job training and programs for groups with special needs, such as gender equality, support for immigrant rights, and increased access to health care. Nonformal education extends to community organizations that emphasize culture, arts, and sports for youth and adults.

Education in the Canary Islands

The Canary Islands consists of seven islands located southwest of Spain and approximately 100 kilometers off the coast of Morocco and Western Sahara. The Islands are known as a hub that has served travelers to North and South America as well as countries in western Africa. Approximately 37 percent of Spain's GDP in the region is devoted to tourism and construction.

Primary and secondary education schools on the Canary Islands have the same regulations as those on the Spanish mainland. In general, all children are expected to attend school from six to 16 years of age. If they wish to pursue college or university education, they must take an additional three years of upper secondary school (ages 16 through 18). Schooling on the Canaries has been notoriously worse than that in Spain in several respects. Student test scores rank lower than those in other Spanish schools. Also, course offerings are limited due to the limited number of specialists in certain content areas. Further, it has been difficult for Canary Islanders to find employment. Given possible austerity measures being taken in Spain, the outlook for employment on the Canaries is starker. This brings to attention the need for the two major higher education institutions in the Canaries to reconsider their focus so that Canary Islanders will be able to find employment.

Two main universities as well as a distance education university (Nacional de Educacion a Distancia), serve the Canary Islands. One university is the University of La Laguna, on in Tenerife Island, which has a traditional liberal arts and science focus. The second university, Universidad de las Palmas de Gran Canaria, which is in Gran Canarias, has a more polytechnic and vocational focus. These universities have had a difficult time in competing with the standards and rigors of those on the mainland. For example, pass rates for students taking the admission examinations for these institutions are much lower than those of students who take entrance examinations in Spain. However, initiatives are being sought in order to identify ways in which the two institutions can benefit the economy of the Islands.

Dilemmas

Since Spain's transformation into a democratic nation in 1978, it has experienced tremendous growth in its economy as well as an increase in social and political rights. Like most industrialized nations, Spain has faced social and political dilemmas that challenge the education of its citizens. While Spain is currently making efforts to improve the education of all its students, it is still struggling with how to increase the educational opportunities of underrepresented students, particularly immigrants, low-income residents, and students with special needs. Spain is also seeking a way to deal with the growing trend of school dropouts.

An often overlooked group in education is students with special needs. Spanish schools have not figured out how to integrate special needs students into mainstream education and provide support to classroom teachers in meeting the needs of these students. Spain is also grappling with how to address the social inequality of its students and schools. A greater number of middle-class students are leaving the public school system for the private school sector, resulting in a devaluing of the public school system.

In the last 10 years Spain has experienced an increase in the number of immigrants from South America and northern Africa. This increase in immigration brings the challenge of integrating immigrant youth into the educational system and preparing them for future economic opportunities. There is also the debate of whether immigrants should be assimilated into Spanish culture or allowed to maintain their cultural identity and language. In order to integrate immigrant youth into Spain's educational system, some argue that teachers need to be trained in multiculturalism and

tolerance to help them ease the transition of immigrant youth into schools and society. Curriculum in the native language of the immigrant youth also needs to be integrated into the schools.

A serious challenge facing Spanish youth and Spanish society is a high youth dropout rate. Spain has one of the highest youth dropout rates from upper secondary school in OECD nations. In 2009, 27.9 percent of Spanish youth age 16 to 24 did not graduate from upper secondary school. In comparison, youth from other OECD nations have a dropout rate of only 13.6 percent; youth from European Union (EU) nations have a dropout rate of 11.1 percent. Attending upper secondary school is not mandatory in Spain. Youth who drop out of upper secondary school have limited options for long-term employment and financial security. While jobs for young people in Spain have increased by 50 percent over the last 10 years, many young people entering the workforce are taking long-term jobs that are not permanent, eventually leading to unemployment.

System Economics

In 2010 the gross domestic product (GDP) of Spain was $1.369 trillion. In 2007 Spain allocated 4.3 percent of its GDP to education (while OECD nations spent an average of 4.96 percent of their GDP on education). This amounts to approximately $58.867 billion. Accordingly, Spain spends approximately $11,795 per student (based on an estimated student-age population of 4,991,000 children and adolescents). Compulsory education is subsidized by the government. However, families sometimes pay for additional costs (textbooks, transportation, and some extracurricular activities, depending on location).

Future Prospects

Improving the quality of education at all levels continues to be a social and economic priority for Spain. Over the years Spain has made considerable efforts to make its educational system competitive with other European nations through educational reforms. Spain has focused on strengthening its overall educational structure and providing more autonomy to the regional governments.

Spain's future goals for improving preprimary education are to increase the enrollment of children in the

---

Spain Education at a Glance

General Information

Capital	Madrid
Population (2012)	47 million
Languages	Spanish (Castellano), Catalan, Gallego, Valenciano, Euskera
Literacy rate (15–24 years)	97.9%
GDP per capita	US$30,600
People below poverty line	20%
Number of landline phones per 100 people	43
Number of Internet users per 100 people	67
Number of Internet hosts	4.2 million
Life expectancy at birth (years)	81

Formal Educational Information

Primary school age population	2.3 million
Secondary school age population	2.6 million
Primary school age population	5.1%
Number of years of compulsory education (primary/secondary)	6/6
Student/teacher ratio (primary)	14
Student/teacher ratio (secondary)	11
Primary school gross enrollment ratio	105%
Primary school entrants completing up to age 12	100%
Secondary school gross enrollment ratio	118%
Child labor (ages 5–14)	no data

Note: Unless otherwise indicated, all data are based on sources from 2011.

first phase of preprimary education (under the age of three), increase the number of preprimary schools, and increase the number of students attending preprimary school (age three to six) to 100 percent by 2016. Spain is also currently making significant reforms to strengthen its higher education system. The most significant educational reform in higher education has been the implementation of the Bologna Reform Process. This reform measure attempts to reorganize the university system and change the current structure of higher education. The current three-phase system of university will be reorganized to match the structure of other European universities. This reform will allow for easier exchange of students from Spain to other European universities and will also increase the employment opportunities of Spanish citizens abroad. The Bologna Reform Process has been implemented in 2010 or 2011.

Additional reform efforts in the university system include increasing the autonomy of individual universities. This reform allows universities more power in setting the requirements for hiring teachers. Additional reforms are being implemented to improve the training of teachers at all levels of teaching. As Spain continues to improve its educational system and compete economically with other European nations, it must continue to address the high rate of long-term unemployment of its young people and other social issues like immigration and school dropouts.

Roseanne Macias

REFERENCES

Central Intelligence Agency. *The CIA World Factbook*. New York: Skyhorse, 2011. https://www.cia.gov/library/publications/the-world-factbook/index.html.

The Economist. "Country Briefings: Spain." www.economist.com.

Eurydice, Information on the Education Systems and Policies in Europe. http://eacea.ec.europa.eu/education/eurydice.

Nation Master. 2011. www.nationmaster.com.

Nicaise, Ides, et al. "Success for All? Educational Strategies for Disadvantaged Youth in Six European Countries." Synthesis report presented at the European Conference on Educational Research, Lahti, Finland, 1999. www.leeds.ac.uk/educol/documents/00001297.htm.

Organisation for Economic Co-operation and Development (OECD). http://stats.oecd.org.

Pereyra, Miguel, and Pablo Castillo. "The Official Discourse of Social Integration in Education in Spain: A Text Analysis Report." In *Public Discourses on Education Governance and Social Integration and Exclusion: Analyses of Policy Texts in European Contexts*, ed. Sverker Lindblad and Thomas Popkewitz. Uppsala, Sweden: Department of Education, Uppsala University, 2000.

Sedgwick, R., ed. "Education in Spain." *World Education News and Reviews.* 2002. www.wes.org/ewenr/02July/Practical.htm.

UNESCO–IBE. www.ibe.unesco.org/en/worldwide/unesco-regions/europe-and-north-america/spain.html.

UNESCO–UIS. www.uis.unesco.org.

UNICEF. www.unicef.org/infobycountry.

World Bank Education Statistics. 2011. www.worldbank.org.

World Resources Institute. "Population, Health, and Human Well-Being, Spain." Earth Trends Country Profiles. http://earthtrends.wri.org.

SWEDEN

Sweden is a country of northern Europe. Indigenous groups in Sweden engaged primarily in subsistence farming and fishing. After religious clashes in the early seventeenth century, many Swedish groups engaged in overseas trade. Some Swedes eventually settled on what are now the southern banks of the Delaware River in present-day New Jersey and Pennsylvania. Although Sweden was an important military power in the sixteenth and seventeenth centuries, it has avoided nearly every major war—including both world wars—to the present day. Like many citizens in Europe, the people of Sweden benefit from universal medical coverage as well as other types of social systems throughout the country.

The official language is Swedish. A small minority speak Sami and Finnish. English is spoken in Stockholm and other urban areas. The population is mainly Swedes and Sami-speaking minorities. Other minority groups include immigrants from Finland, Croatia, Denmark, Norway, Greece, and Turkey. At 87 percent of the population, the Lutheran Church is by far the largest religious group in the country. Other groups include various Protestant Christian sects, as well as Roman Catholics, Jews, Muslims, and Buddhists.

Educational System: Precompulsory, Compulsory Education, and Curriculum

Education is compulsory for all children of Sweden between the ages of six and 16 years, or grades 1 through 9. The country's education system is divided into four categories: preprimary, primary, secondary, and tertiary levels.

Preprimary Education

Many children in Sweden between the ages of one and four years attend preschool—known as *förskola*. The *förskola* presents a curriculum that is consistent with many preschool curricula throughout the world, namely, one that emphasizes social, emotional, motor, and intellectual development. Kindergarten is attended by nearly all Swedish children between the ages of four and six. Swedish kindergarten combines the developmental approaches found in typical preschools with the formal aspects of schooling that children will encounter when they reach grade 1.

Primary and Lower Secondary Education

The overwhelming majority of schools in Sweden are run by municipal governments. Most of the remaining schools are publicly funded. However, a small number of schools are private institutions, some of which run boarding schools, especially in urban locations. Primary education in Sweden is compulsory for six years and enrolls children between the ages of seven and 12 years. The school year in Sweden begins in the last two weeks of August and continues to the middle of June, an academic year that is somewhat longer than that of other European and North American countries. Compulsory education in Sweden consists of both the primary school and lower secondary school levels, also known as *Grundskola*. In total, this period consists of nine years of compulsory schooling. The curriculum of this period is known as basic. The curriculum is controversial to the extent that all students must learn the same content at each grade level. This poses some conflict in allowing students who are advanced in particular subjects to study at higher levels. For example, the study of mathematics is the same for all children until grade 7, when students have the opportunity to select out of the basic mathematics curriculum. This phenomenon indicates a lack of concern for academically able students at younger ages. Moreover, nontraditional forms of education, such as homeschooling, are nonexistent in Sweden.

Nevertheless, it is important to note that Sweden has one of the highest numbers of so-called free schools in the world. A Swedish free school is similar to the American charter school in that it is partially subsidized by federal and municipal taxes. In addition, these schools are available through school choice vouchers for families who do not want their children attending local public schools. Although these schools are considered independent, for-profit institutions, they cannot discriminate against students, nor can they charge additional fees or set standards for acceptance. The curricula in free schools are often implemented according to various curriculum philosophies (e.g., Montessori, mathematics and science emphasis, Rudolph Steiner).

Lower secondary school in Sweden lasts from grades 7 through 9—ages 13 to 15 or 16 years. During this period, the curriculum becomes more varied and diverse; students must learn English as well as Swedish and are able to enroll in more advanced mathematics courses, as well as those in the natural sciences, social sciences, art, music, and physical education. The majority of lower secondary school graduates enroll into upper secondary school. In general, there are four levels of grading: (1) pass with special distinction (equivalent to grade of A); (2) pass with distinction (equivalent to grade of B); (3) pass (equivalent to grade of C); and (4) not passing.

Upper Secondary School

Known as the *Gymnasieskola*, the upper secondary school in Sweden enrolls students between the ages of 16 and 18 years—grades 10 through 12. Acceptance to the *Gymnasieskola* depends on student grades in the *Grundskola*. The overarching purpose of the upper secondary school is to prepare students for either academic study or vocational training. This preparation depends on the assessment outcomes of each student. The *Gymnasieskola* is generally divided into two curricula: preparatory and vocational. The preparatory curriculum includes at least three categories of specialization: humanities, social sciences, and natural sciences. The vocational track enables students to gain skills for early workforce entry. Nearly half of all secondary school students are in the vocational track, which includes 15 weeks of workplace training and experience.

Higher Education

Upon completion of the *Gymnasieskola*, most students are eligible for university entrance. Higher education in Sweden consists of universities, colleges, and private schools of higher learning. Completion of upper secondary school is a requirement for entry into a higher education institution. Another way that students can be admitted to a higher education institution is by providing evidence of a certain number of years of work experience, depending on the particular occupational or professional specializations. A baccalaureate can be earned in most higher education institutions in Sweden after three years. More than one-third of all Swedes (about 37 percent) have completed three years or more of higher education. A master's degree in Sweden can be earned typically in two additional years, and a PhD degree in an additional four years. Sweden has the fourth-highest percentage in the world of students holding tertiary degrees. Only Canada, Japan, and the United States have higher percentages.

There are 14 universities in Sweden. Established in 1477, Uppsala University is the oldest university in the country and the oldest ecclesiastical center in the Scandinavian region. Uppsala University has an enrollment of over 20,000 students. Lund University is another highly competitive research university in Sweden. Founded in 1666, Lund University enrolls nearly 27,000 students annually. Other competitive institutions are the University of Gothenburg and Stockholm University, which enrolls nearly 30,000 students per year—making it the largest university in the country. In addition to these institutions, there are three private university-level institutions that are certified to award postgraduate degrees. In addition, the *högskola* is a third type of higher education institution in Sweden. The *högskola* is similar to the university, but offers doctoral degrees in only one or two specializations; it does not offer doctoral degrees in most or all levels of study. There are more than 10 *högskola* throughout Sweden; nearly all are public institutions.

Teacher Education

Teacher education in Sweden depends on the level that a student teacher would like to teach. Students who plan to teach at the primary or lower second-ary level attend local colleges or university colleges that have teacher training programs. These programs provide students with the necessary prerequisite coursework and student teaching experiences that they will need in order to teach in the public or private schools. Students who plan to teach at the upper secondary school level must take prerequisite education courses or a year-long pedagogical course in addition to a major in a specified discipline at the university level.

Informal Education

Informal education in Sweden is an option for adults who wish to acquire additional skills and abilities in order to increase workforce desirability. Most informal education settings provide evening classes for working adults. These courses are similar to courses provided for younger students who enroll in upper secondary level or higher education courses during the day. As described above, adults who are past the traditional university-level period (i.e., 17 to 22 years old) may enter programs at the university level if they can show evidence of five years of combined school and professional work experience. Most informal education programs are funded by the government. However, they can also be funded in part by regional and municipal resources as well as private and religious organizations. Adults also have the opportunity to benefit from distance education, especially those who live in rural communities and remote northern regions.

System Economics

Sweden ranks 28 of 186 countries in terms of educational expenditures as a percentage of gross domestic product (GDP). Along with public expenditure on education of Barbados and Norway, the total public expenditure on education for Sweden in 2007 represented 6.7 percent of the country's GDP. Nearly US$29.8 billion was allocated for education purposes. This amounts to per capita education expenditure over $21,500.

Future Prospects

Like its Scandinavian neighbors, Sweden has consistently played a major role in education, generally

---

Sweden Education at a Glance

General Information

Capital	Stockholm
Population	9 million
Languages	Swedish
Literacy rate	99%
GDP per capita	US$32,200
People below poverty line	no data
Number of phones per 100 people	59
Number of Internet users per 100 people	89
Number of Internet hosts	4.3 million
Life expectancy at birth (years)	81

Formal Educational Information

Primary school age population	656,000
Secondary school age population	727,000
Primary school age population	7%
Number of years of education (primary/secondary)	6/6
Student/teacher ratio (primary)	10
Student/teacher ratio (secondary)	10
Primary school gross enrollment ratio	98%
Primary school entrants reaching grade 5	100%
Secondary school gross enrollment ratio	103%
Child labor (ages 5–14)	no data

Note: Unless otherwise indicated, all data are based on sources from 2011.

---

placing high as a competitor in educational achievement rankings based on student test scores, such as TIMSS and PISA. Sweden's education system has had a positive impact on the global economy. The country continues to graduate students who excel in individualized areas of expertise. One of the most promising aspects of education in Sweden is that the differences between the academic performance of native and ethnic minority students are low to insignificant when compared to other European Union nations (such as Belgium or Germany). Education in Sweden excels in the areas of the humanities, mathematics, the natural and social sciences, and information and communication technologies. The country is also a leader in producing and using both traditional and alternative-based fuels and has been innovative in pioneering research in medicine, physics, chemistry, and environmental studies. Further, as in other countries of Europe, education in Sweden has helped advance technological innovations and global communications.

Daniel Ness and Chia-ling Lin

REFERENCES

Central Intelligence Agency. *The CIA World Factbook*. New York: Skyhorse, 2011. https://www.cia.gov/library/publications/the-world-factbook/index.html.

Empirica. *Benchmarking Access and Use of ICT in European Schools 2012*. European Commission Staff Working Document: Progress Towards the Lisbon Objectives in Education and Training: Indicators and Benchmarks, 2012.

Nation Master. 2011. www.nationmaster.com.

UNICEF. *Global Education Digest 2012: Comparing Education Statistics Across the World*. Montreal: UNESCO Institute for Statistics, 2012.

UNESCO–IBE. www.ibe.unesco.org/en/worldwide/unesco-regions/europe-and-north-america/sweden.html.

UNESCO–UIS. www.uis.unesco.org.

UNICEF. www.unicef.org/infobycountry.

World Bank Education Statistics. 2011. www.worldbank.org.

SWITZERLAND

Switzerland is a confederation, but its current government is modeled after a federal republic. The official languages are German, French, and Italian. Other languages in Switzerland include Serbian, Croatian, Albanian, Portuguese, Spanish, English, and Romansch. The population is mainly German (65 percent). Other populations include French (18 percent), Italian (10 percent), and Romansch (1 percent). Roman Catholic (42 percent) and Protestant (35 percent) populations are the largest religious groups. The remaining population consists of Muslims (4 percent) and people profession either no religion or others (17 percent). Switzerland consists of 26 administrative divisions called cantons. Founded in 1291, the Swiss Confederation consisted of three cantons, which are similar to states. Over the years, the confederation increased in size. By the sixteenth century, the Swiss Confederation declared its independence from the Holy Roman Empire. Switzerland has prospered as a sovereign and neutral nation, thereby managing to avoid the two world wars. Since the end of World War II, the country has been involved in many international organizations as a neutral power. Switzerland did not become a member of the United Nations until 2002.

Educational System

Switzerland's educational system has a nearly 800-year history. The first institution of formal education in Switzerland was the University of Basel, which was established in 1460. Its specializations over the years included medicine and the sciences, and to this day, Switzerland maintains its role as a leading exponent of scientists and medical researchers. Students in Switzerland scored 15 out of 57 in the science portion of the Programme for International Student Assessment (PISA). Switzerland was also the home of many famous educators and theorists throughout history—most notably the pedagogue and reformer Johann Heinrich Pestalozzi (1746–1827) and the genetic epistemologist Jean Piaget (1896–1980).

The educational system of Switzerland is similar to that of most of the German-speaking nations of Europe in that the country has implemented a tracking system beyond the primary school level. With a required period of nine years, compulsory education in Switzerland is also similar to that of its neighbors. Children attend preprimary schools before grade 1 (or before six years of age). After this point children enter either primary schools or, in some instances, special schools, depending on their educational issues or disabilities. Primary school is for students in grades 1 through 6 (ages six through 12).

There are three general categories of secondary schools (grades 7 through 11): *écoles de maturité gymasiale* (high school), *écoles de culture générale* (middle school), and *écoles professionnelles* (professional schools). Students enrolled in primary special schools do not necessarily have an analogous system of schooling in the secondary grades. Students who successfully complete their first six years of compulsory education in the primary grade levels may continue to high school for three to four years. Upon completion, they have the opportunity to enter the traditional university, initially for a baccalaureate and subsequently for a master's degree or a doctorate. A second option is for students to enroll in middle schools. Doing so prepares students for four options: traditional college or university education, the normal school (teachers college), the specialized school (where a master's degree can be earned), or a polytechnic institute. The third option is for students who attend the professional secondary school for two to four years. These students are unable to enroll in the university or normal school, but are able to continue for professional certificates in various vocations. Nearly all schools are public and federally funded.

Precompulsory, Compulsory Education, and Curriculum

Parents have the option to send their children who are three years or older to kindergarten (*Vorschule*) for one to three years. Compulsory education begins when children enter primary school (*Primarschule*), a period that lasts from four to six years depending on the canton in which the children reside. The primary language of instruction during the compulsory period depends on the location of the school. German is the dominant language of instruction in schools in the northern and eastern regions of the country, while French is the dominant language in the western part of the country. Some schools in the south of Switzerland are conducted in Italian. There are approximately 531,000 primary school children in Switzerland. The primary school student/teacher ratio is 13 students for every teacher, and the primary school gross enrollment rate is 98 percent. Nearly 92 percent of all primary school entrants complete primary school.

Children must continue to lower secondary school (*Sekundarschule*) for three to five years, depending on the number of years of primary school. For example, a child enrolled in primary school for six years will enroll in lower secondary school for three years, while a child in another canton who is enrolled in primary school for four years must enroll in lower secondary school for five years. Upon completion of lower secondary school, which is a continuation of the basic curriculum taught in primary school, students have one of three options: the *Gymnasium* (high school), *Fachmittelschule* (secondary school), or *Berufsfachschule* (professional school). The *Gymnasium* is the most competitive track. It provides the most traditional education, which includes classical studies, natural sciences, social sciences, mathematics, philosophy, religion, foreign language, physical education, and the fine and performing arts. Most students of the *Gymnasium* prepare for entry to a traditional university education. The curriculum at the *Fachmittelschule* is a combination of traditional courses with vocational courses. Students who are interested in entering one of the polytechnic institutions often are selected into the *Fachmittelschule*. The curriculum at the *Berufsfachschule* is primarily vocational; it prepares students who wish to enter the workforce upon graduation or continue for one to three years at a tertiary vocational institution. There are approximately 630,000 secondary school students in Switzerland. The secondary school gross enrollment rate in the country is at 93 percent. PISA results show that secondary school students rank 15 out of 57 in mathematics and natural sciences scores.

Postcompulsory Education

There are approximately 80 institutions of higher education in Switzerland. Of these, 12 are universities that offer nearly all degrees up to the doctorate (two of these schools are federal polytechnic institutes), 11 are universities of applied sciences, 16 are art institutes or music conservatories, 18 are pedagogical universities, and 16 are private colleges. The University of Basel is the only so-called ancient institution of higher education in Switzerland. Established in 1460, the University of Basel enrolls about 11,000 students annually. Its famous alumni include Daniel Bernoulli (mathematician and naturalist), Leonhard Euler (mathematician and philosopher), Friedrich Nietzsche (philosopher, philologist, and composer), Carl Jung (psychologist), and Hans Urs von Balthasar (theologian). The university is perhaps most known for its faculties of theology, law, medicine, and humanities. The highest-ranking university in Switzerland, though, is the University of Zurich. Established in 1833, the University of Zurich enrolls more than 33,000 students, the largest enrollment of any institution of higher education in Switzerland. Six alumni from the University of Zurich were Nobel Prize laureates, including Albert Einstein. Other notable universities include the University of Geneva, the University of Fribourg, the University of Bern, the University of Neuchâtel, the University of Lausanne, and the University of Lucerne.

Teacher Education

The teacher education system in Switzerland is an option for students who graduate from the *écoles de maturité gymasiale* (high school) or *écoles de culture générale* (middle school), but not any of the

professional schools. Students who graduate from the *écoles de maturité gymasiale* may be eligible to enroll in one of the 18 pedagogical universities that serve preservice teachers. The 1990s saw the implementation of important educational reforms at the national level. These reforms emphasized the process of professional training and career prospects, as well as the creation of compatible degrees for teachers across Europe as a means of facilitating mobility. In 2004 all pedagogical institutes were in place. The training of teachers is currently the responsibility of 13 HEPs and institutes attached to three universities. Training in vocational schools is provided by the Federal Institute for Advanced Studies in Vocational Training.

In the fall of 2003, nearly 2,400 students began training to become teachers in preschool and primary school. Almost everywhere in Switzerland, this sector of student teacher candidates is housed in HEPs. Only the cantons of Bern and Geneva offer this training in university institutes. Nearly 1,800 students began their training for teaching secondary

---

Switzerland Education at a Glance

General Information

Capital	Bern
Population	7.6 million
Languages	German (official, 64%), French (official, 20%), Italian (official 6.5%), Serbo-Croatian, Albanian, Portuguese, Spanish, English, Romansch
Literacy rate	99%
GDP per capita	US$34,000
People below poverty line	no data
Number of phones per 100 people	63
Number of Internet users per 100 people	75
Number of Internet hosts	4.8 million
Life expectancy at birth (years)	81

Formal Educational Information

Primary school age population	531,000
Secondary school age population	630,000
Primary school age population	7%
Number of years of education (primary/secondary)	6/7
Student/teacher ratio (primary)	13
Primary school gross enrollment ratio	98%
Primary school entrants completing primary school	91.5%
Secondary school gross enrollment ratio	93%
Child labor (ages 5–14)	no data

Note: Unless otherwise indicated, all data are based on sources from 2011.

school in the same year. The implementation of the Bologna Declaration, the document that declares the ability of students to attend universities anywhere in Europe and Russia, applies to the entire sector of high schools, including the HEP. Introduction to phased training for the bachelor's and master's degrees in teaching began in 2005. The working conditions of teachers are determined by the administrations of the cantons. These students must complete an exit examination prior to student teaching.

Informal Education

Informal education is Switzerland is often for adults who wish to continue their education. This form of education is funded by the central government, individual cantons, and nonprofit organizations. Students in this category usually have been out of school for at least three years. Institutions that provide adult education include colleges of further education, vocational colleges, and religious denominational organizations, as well as several other regional nonprofit adult education institutions. Adult education in Switzerland attempts to provide adult learners with additional qualifications for making them desirable in the workforce.

System Economics

According to the United Nations Development Programme (2011), Switzerland ranks 53 of 186 in educational expenditures as a percentage of gross domestic product (GDP). The total public expenditure on education in 2007 represented 5.2 percent of GDP. Nearly US$16.874 billion was allocated for education purposes. Based on these figures, total per student spending is approximately $14,534 (determined by dividing total expenditure by 1,161,000, the approximate number of students in Switzerland).

Future Prospects

Given that schoolchildren in Switzerland enter compulsory schooling at a rather late age (six to seven years), new reforms, in part due to recent PISA results, are addressing the need to lower the entry age for compulsory schooling. The following educational reform measures have been planned by the Swiss government: first, the cantons are committed to a system that ensures the teaching of content that meets current needs while, at the same time, adapting to the evolution and future needs of the global society; second, the cantons are committed to promoting diversity; third, the cantons and the Swiss Confederation are attempting to enable all young people to reach postcompulsory training and earn diplomas; finally, the government is attempting to institute less demanding curriculum for young people facing difficulty in school or those from socially disadvantaged backgrounds as a way to increase their chances of integration and social promotion.

Daniel Ness and Chia-ling Lin

References

Central Intelligence Agency. *The CIA World Factbook*. New York: Skyhorse, 2011. https://www.cia.gov/library/publications/the-world-factbook/index.html.

Nation Master. 2011. www.nationmaster.com.

UNESCO. *Global Education Digest 2012: Comparing Education Statistics Across the World*. Montreal: UNESCO Institute for Statistics, 2012.

Organisation for Economic Co-operation and Development (OECD). Programme for International Student Assessment Results. 2009. http://stats.oecd.org/PISA2009Profiles/#.

UNESCO–IBE. www.ibe.unesco.org/countries/switzerland.htm.

UNESCO–UIS. www.uis.unesco.org.

UNICEF. www.unicef.org/infobycountry.

World Bank Education Statistics. 2011. www.worldbank.org.

Turkey

Often referred to as part of Asia Minor, Turkey is a country that is part of two continents: Thrace, the northwestern part of the country, bordering Greece and Bulgaria, forms part of southeastern Europe, and Anatolia, the remainder of the country, is the western part of Asia. The official language is Turkish. However, some populations speak Kurdish, Dimli, Azeri, and Kabardian. The population is mainly Turkish (80 percent); there is a minority Kurdish population (20 percent). The religion of almost the entire population is Islam; however, there are traces of Christian and Jewish populations.

The ancient cities in the region commonly traded with Greece and other nations on the Mediterranean

Sea. During the first three centuries of the Common Era, Christianity burgeoned in a number of Turkish cities, particularly Ephesus (present-day Selçuk) and Antioch (present-day Antakya). Constantinople, present-day Istanbul, was home to the emperor of the Roman Empire, mostly after the third century, when Rome, the capital of the western half of the empire, was waning in importance. The region was the center of Byzantium, an empire that lasted for nearly 1,000 years. Ottoman Turks ruled the country for several centuries until 1923, the year that Turkey was established as a successor state to the Ottoman Empire. The country became a member of the United Nations in 1945 and of NATO in 1952. Turkey has been grappling with problems associated with anti-immigrant sentiment, particularly among Turks in the southeastern part of the country—an area with a large percentage of Kurds. The country has also intervened in what the Turkish government believed to be a Greek occupation of Cyprus. Since 2000, however, Turkey has attempted to make positive strides toward economic security through collaboration with the European Union.

Educational System

The preprimary, primary, secondary and tertiary education systems in Turkey are run by the Ministry of National Education. Formal education (i.e., primary and secondary education periods) comprise a total of twelve years, of which the first eight are compulsory. The most egregious problems in the education system in Turkey are related to disparate income levels of families.

Precompulsory and Compulsory Education

Preprimary education is available to children of families who can afford the tuition. Children who are enrolled are usually between the ages of three and five years—a period of generally three years. Preschools in Turkey serve the dual purpose of providing both intellectual and social development for children on the one hand, and providing care for children while parents are at work on the other. Preschool education is neither free nor compulsory.

Compulsory education in Turkey requires children between the ages of seven and 15 years to attend and complete primary education—a period of eight

years. The net enrollment ratio for primary school during the 1990s was nearly 100 percent. However, 2008 data show that the gross enrollment ratio for primary school dropped to 94 percent, and the net enrollment ratio for the same period of schooling dropped to 90 percent, an indication that 10 percent of children of primary school age do not attend school. Reasons for this drop in enrollment include a growing agricultural economy that has contributed to the country's increased economy, a large gap between affluent and poor families, the finding that 3 percent of all children between five and 14 years are engaged in work, large class sizes (an average of 31 students for every teacher at the primary level), a relatively low percentage of gross domestic product (GDP) contributed for educational purposes (see below), and a lack of motivation on the part of students to go to school. In most schools, the curriculum at the basic primary level includes Turkish language, mathematics, natural science, social studies, religion, physical education, art, and music.

Most students in Turkey who are 15 to 18 years of age continue for four years of secondary school, which enables them to apply to universities and other institutions of higher education. However, perceived shortcomings and weaknesses of public schools have contributed to a decline in public secondary school enrollment as children and adolescents of affluent families are sent to private secondary schools. Poor families do not have the financial wherewithal to choose this option.

In Turkey there are high schools that specialize in numerous fields. Unlike the European tracking model, which usually includes three or four tracks—for example, one traditional, a second professional, and a third vocational—high schools in Turkey are highly specialized. Public high schools and Anatolian high schools (which emphasize foreign language study) are the most prevalent; they cover a comprehensive curriculum. Other types of high school include the following: science high schools, social science high schools, pedagogical or teacher training high schools, military academies, Imam-Hatip secondary schools that emphasize religion, vocational secondary schools (which teach distinct vocations such as tourism, business, mechanical repair, industrial arts, plumbing, and electricity technical training), and private high schools. The overarching curriculum at most secondary schools in Turkey includes Turkish language and literature, mathematics, biology, chemistry, physics, history, geography, and at least two foreign languages (chosen from English, German, French, Italian, Spanish, Japanese, Chinese, Arabic, or Russian).

Specialized high schools, particularly those for the mathematically and scientifically gifted and talented, are available in large urban areas. Three examples of this type of high school are the Ankara Science High School in Ankara, the country's capital; the Malatya Science High School in Malatya; and Robert College of Istanbul, whose curriculum and structure are based on the American science high school model, specifically, Stuyvesant High School and the Bronx High School of Science (both in New York City).

Students intending to continue to a higher education institution must be administered a high school exit examination that indicates student strengths and weaknesses in a variety of academic domains. The examination is in four parts: writing and mathematics, science, social science, and languages.

Postcompulsory Education

Turkey is home to nearly 170 universities and academies. About 75 percent of these institutions are public or state-run, while the remaining 25 percent are privately run. Most of the state-subsidized institutions are technical schools, polytechnic institutions, and one fine arts academy. Of the nearly 45 private institutions, four are military academies and one is a police academy. İhsan Doğramacı Bilkent University, the first private, nonprofit university in Turkey, is the most competitive university in the country. It is also worthy of note that Bilkent University is a rather young institution, established in 1984. With an annual enrollment of roughly 13,000 students, the university is especially known for its faculty of administrative and social sciences and faculty of law. The Middle East Technical University, established in 1956, is ranked the most competitive polytechnic institution in the country. Not far behind in competitive status is Istanbul Technical University, which was founded in 1773, making it the third-oldest engineering university in the world and the oldest continuously running tertiary institution in Turkey. Established in 1958, Anadolu University is the fourth-largest university in the world when combining both residential students and distance education students—1.5 million students in all.

Teacher Education

Students who are training to become primary school teachers must pass the high school exit examination and apply to universities where the *lisans diplomasi*—teaching license—can be earned. Students must be enrolled in pedagogy programs for at least four years. Prospective secondary school teachers must also prepare for the high school exit examination. However, in their case, a five-year program at the university level must be completed, the *lisans diplomasi* must be earned, and two majors must be declared, one in pedagogy and the other in the area of teaching specialization at the high school level.

Informal Education

Informal education in Turkey is available for individuals—mostly adults—who were not exposed to formal education in their primary or secondary years or who need additional skills for employment. Informal education can provide students with basic knowledge in language and mathematics, experience in particular vocations or trades, and foreign language instruction. Informal education programs are regulated by the Ministry of National Education and are available in training centers throughout the country. Some of these programs are also funded by nongovernmental organizations or private organizations that are accredited in particular academic or vocational domains. In addition, distance education instruction toward a two-year or four-year degree is offered through the Open Education Faculty of Anadolu University in Eskişehir, Turkey. This is an example of a nonformal education program that accepts applicants based on scores on the Central National University Entrance Examination.

System Economics

According to the United Nations Development Programme (2012), along with Algeria, Italy, Kosovo, Sierra Leone, and Spain, total public expenditures on education in Turkey represented 2.9 percent of the gross domestic product in 2006. Given the GDP of Turkey at over $1 trillion, educational expenditure in the country amounts to nearly $27.855 billion, or $1,760 per student (total amount equivalent to US dollars divided by 15,289,000, the approximate num-

Turkey Education at a Glance

General Information

Capital	Ankara
Population	77.8 million
Languages	Turkish, Kurdish, Dimli, Azeri, Kabardian
Literacy rate	87.5%
GDP per capita	US$9,000
People below poverty line	20%
Number of phones per 100 people	22.5
Number of Internet users per 100 people	31.5
Number of Internet hosts	3.4 million
Life expectancy at birth (years)	73

Formal Educational Information

Primary school age population	8.3 million
Secondary school age population	6.8 million
Primary school age population	11%
Number of years of education (primary/secondary)	6/5
Student/teacher ratio (primary)	30
Student/teacher ratio (secondary)	24
Primary school gross enrollment ratio	94%
Primary school entrants reaching grade 5	97%
Secondary school gross enrollment ratio	74%
Child labor (ages 5–14)	5%

Note: Unless otherwise indicated, all data are based on sources from 2011.

ber of primary and secondary students in the country). Per pupil spending was greater during the Soviet and Yugoslavian era. Since Turkey ranks 136 of 186 countries in percentage of educational expenditure, the amount of funding needed to support a strong educational system requires financial subsidies from municipal, regional, and nongovernmental sources.

Future Prospects

As described above, several factors contribute to substandard educational conditions in Turkey at the present day. The most problematic issue is the presence of child labor, which involves 3 percent of the Turkish population between five and 14 years old. Child labor stifles educational productivity, particularly for potential students who come from poor families or who resort to agricultural labor as a means of providing for parents and siblings. In addition, the widening gap between poor and affluent families has made it prohibitive in some cases for poor children to compete with other children on an academic basis.

In addition, the high rate of corruption in the government and the education system in recent years, particularly after the breakup of the Socialist Federal Republic of Yugoslavia, a former neighbor, has repressed educational progress among the country's youth. Moreover, frequent skirmishes and small wars with neighboring nations and ethnic groups— including, at present, the Kurdish population in Turkey as well as neighboring Iraq—have hindered Turkey's progress in furthering its educational agenda as a means toward economic prosperity. Another disturbing problem is the government's overall alienation of minority communities, particularly children of Roma communities. In many countries of eastern Europe and the Near East (such as Turkey), members of Roma are often targets of inequality, which results in a perpetual cycle of stereotyping. Turkey's education curriculum also needs to place greater emphasis on environmental improvement, clean energy, and health. Accordingly, mathematics, science, and social science curricula will be essential in carrying out a more modern educational agenda in Turkey.

Daniel Ness and Chia-ling Lin

REFERENCES

Central Intelligence Agency. *The CIA World Factbook*. New York: Skyhorse, 2011. https://www.cia.gov/library/publications/the-world-factbook/index.html.

Nation Master. 2011. www.nationmaster.com.

Nohl, Arnd-Michael, Arzu Akkoyunlu-Wigley, and Simon Wigley, eds. *Education in Turkey*. Münster, Germany: Waxmann Verlag, 2008.

UNESCO. *Global Education Digest 2012: Comparing Education Statistics Across the World*. Montreal: UNESCO Institute for Statistics, 2012.

UNESCO–IBE. www.ibe.unesco.org/countries/albania.htm.

UNESCO–UIS. www.uis.unesco.org.

UNICEF. www.unicef.org/infobycountry.

World Bank Education Statistics. 2011. www.worldbank.org.

UNITED KINGDOM

The United Kingdom (UK) of Great Britain (which includes England, Scotland, and Wales) and Northern Ireland comprises an area of 94,526 square miles (244,820 square kilometers). The official language is English, although 26 percent of the population of Wales speaks Welsh and a small number of Scottish residents speak the Scottish form of Gaelic. The United Nations population estimate for 2010 was 62.3 million. The population is mainly white (92 percent), followed by black (2 percent), Indian (2 percent), and Pakistani (2 percent). The religion is predominantly Christian (72 percent). The remaining population consists of Muslims (2.5 percent) and Hindus (1 percent). Other populations (23 percent) have not specified their religion or indicate no religion.

The UK has been a world power for centuries. The country has assumed prominence as a model of parliamentary democracy. In terms of education, it has been a leader in both literature and the sciences. The country achieved its greatest land acquisition during the nineteenth century, when the British Empire controlled nearly one-fourth of the earth's land. World War I and II contributed to the downsizing of the UK, with much of its empire dismantled. Nevertheless, during the second half of the twentieth century, the UK developed into a prosperous nation. Although the UK is a member of the European Union, the country is not part of the Economic and Monetary Union, so the British pound is in use. The UK's gross domestic product (GDP, current US$) is about $2.123 trillion. The services economic sector represents 73.4 percent of the GDP, industry 25.6 percent, and agriculture 1 percent. Despite the UK's generally high standard of living, approximately 17 percent of the population falls below the international poverty line.

Educational System

Compulsory education in the United Kingdom lasts from a child's fifth birthday to the school year when the child turns 16 years of age. This mandate will change in 2013, when children will be expected to attend school until 17 years of age, and again in 2015, when school attendance will be mandatory for all children until they reach their eighteenth birthday. These changes are mostly due to increased rates of college and university attendance, as well as changes in the number and types of occupations. Approximately 93 percent of all schools in the UK are public schools. Most private schools are run by the Church of England and some by the Roman Catholic Church.

Precompulsory Education, Compulsory Education, and Curriculum

It should be noted that since the United Kingdom is divided into four so-called countries—England, Scotland, Wales, and Northern Ireland—one educational system might not be parallel with another. This is evident by the autonomous role that each country has in educational control. The national curriculum is divided into five key stages: key stage 1 (ages five to seven), key stage 2 (ages seven to 11); key stage 3 (ages 11 to 14); key stage 4 (ages 14 to 16), and key stage 5, which serves as the curriculum for college-bound students. Accordingly, what is stated below emphasizes the generalities, and not the specifics, of the UK educational system.

Preprimary and Primary Education

Parents in the UK have the option of sending their children between the ages of three and six to kindergarten—an educational level that is not compulsory. By age six children must enter grade 1. Primary school lasts for six years, until students complete grade 5. Students with special needs often enroll in specialized schools that focus on specific disabilities. Kindergarten is the first year of formal education, serving as a transition from informal to formal learning. Children receive an education that is based primarily on early formal academic learning skills, the socialization of the individual, and personal development. Kindergarten education also focuses on speech development and sensory and motor development. Subjects taken in all six years of primary education include the following: regional history, geography, English language and literature, mathematics, music, art and drawing, technical work, use of textiles, and physical education. In addition, by the end of the primary school period, students need to learn a modern foreign language.

There are approximately 4.3 million children of primary school age in the UK. Almost all of these children attend school between the ages of five and 10 years. This is evident in the close to 100 percent primary school net enrollment ratio (98.7 percent). The primary school gross enrollment ratio is 107 percent, indicating that some children outside the age range are enrolled at the primary school level. The student/teacher ratio in preschools in the UK is about 21 children for every teacher. For primary school in the UK, the student/teacher ratio is between 17 and 18 students for every teacher. Nearly all students who are enrolled in primary school are able to complete the fifth grade or the final year of the primary school period.

Secondary Education

There are about 5.5 million secondary school–age children and adolescents in the UK. Given the secondary school net enrollment ratio of 95.3 percent, nearly all children and adolescents between the ages of 11 and 17 attend secondary school. The secondary school gross enrollment ratio is 105 percent, indicating that some students outside the age range are enrolled in secondary school. The student/teacher ratio in secondary schools in the UK is 14 to 15 students for every teacher. About three-fifths of all teachers at the secondary school level are female (compared to four-fifths at the primary school level).

The curriculum at both the primary and secondary education levels is mandated by the central government. However, some regulations do not apply to the educational system in Scotland. All students between the ages of four and 17, regardless of grade level, must enroll in mathematics, English, and science. Depending on the grade level, students at some point in their schooling must enroll in the following areas: fine arts (key stages 1, 2, and 3), citizenship (key stages 3 and 4), design and technology (key stages 1, 2, and 3), geography (key stages 1, 2, and 3), history (key stages 1, 2, and 3), information and communication technology (key stages 1, 2, and 3), one or more modern foreign languages (key stage 3), music (key stages 1, 2, and 3), and physical education (all four key stages before preparing for college or university entrance).

Compulsory Education in Each of the Countries of the United Kingdom

What follows is a description of the educational systems in each of the four countries of the United Kingdom: England, Scotland, Wales, and Northern Ireland. In general, there are more similarities than differences. Differentiation has occurred because

the central government has allowed each of the four countries to control the educational system.

England

Precollege education involves 15 years of schooling. The first year of schooling, nursery school, is not compulsory. Primary schooling begins by age four and continues to age 10, or Year 6 (the equivalent of "sixth grade") of schooling. There are three types of primary schools in England: infant school, primary school, and first school. Infant school enrolls children between the ages of four and six, or the reception year (analogous to kindergarten), Year 1, and Year 2. After infant school, children attend junior school from Years 3 through 6. The more popular alternative is primary school, where children attend school from the reception year through Year 6. A less popular alternative is the first school, which enrolls children from the reception year to Year 4. After first school, children enroll in middle school, and subsequently in upper school or high school, which prepares college-bound students. Students who complete Year 6 in the more typical primary school enroll in either a secondary school with the so-called sixth form or one without the sixth form. The sixth form consists of the final two years of secondary education that prepares college- or university-bound students. Students who do not enroll in the sixth form often do not continue their studies beyond the secondary school grades.

Scotland

Albeit under the same central government as England, Wales, and Northern Ireland, the Scottish system of education is the most divergent among the four systems. Unlike the other three systems, the Scottish education system has the most autonomy. This is in part a result of the Scotland Act of 1998, which allowed the Parliament of Scotland control over all educational administration. Traditionally, the Scottish system of education emphasized breadth in the curriculum, while the systems of the other three countries of the United Kingdom emphasize depth in specific subjects—particularly at the secondary school levels. Accordingly, some of the higher education programs in Scotland consist of five-year baccalaureates.

Unlike the systems of England, Wales, and Northern Ireland, the educational system of Scotland consists of seven (not six) years of primary school (P1 through P7, ages four or five to 10 or 11). Secondary school attendance in Scotland is compulsory for six years (S1 through S6, ages 11 through 17). Nearly all students are administered the Scottish Qualifications Certificate, which determines where they attend their postsecondary studies. The overwhelming majority of schools in Scotland are nondenominational. The majority of denominational schools are Roman Catholic.

Wales

The primary and secondary education system in Wales is fairly consistent with that of England. For example, the first stage in primary education is called Early Years, a precompulsory period for children between three and five years of age. Compulsory education begins with the second stage, key stage 1, which is the first part of the compulsory education period (for children ages five to seven years), and continues all the way to key stage 4, which enrolls students in Years 10 and 11 (adolescents between 14 and 16 years of age). Key stage 5 is for college-bound students. The curriculum is similar to that in the rest of the UK; however, unlike the other three UK countries, the Welsh system of education mandates that students learn both English and Welsh.

Northern Ireland

Education and schooling from preschool to secondary school in Northern Ireland are controlled by the Northern Ireland Executive Department of Education. Higher education is run by the Department of Employment and Learning. The Department of Education provides resources to local school and library boards that oversee five distinct regions of Northern Ireland. Northern Ireland is the only region of the UK that maintained grammar schools instead of primary schools. Grammar schools traditionally enrolled students for their entire compulsory education. Students in Years 8 through 12 attend either secondary schools or grammar schools. Upon the successful passing of the General Certificate of Secondary Education examination, students can apply to college or the university. The education system in Northern Ireland is the most segregated in all of the UK. Students attend either Protestant- or Catholic-run institutions. Although integrated schools exist, they are a small minority.

Postcompulsory Education

There are roughly 125 universities or other higher education institutions in the UK. This figure does not include colleges, schools, or institutes that are housed within these universities. In addition to the two so-called ancient universities (i.e., universities founded between 1000 and 1500) in England, the University of Oxford and the University of Cambridge, other competitive institutions in England include the following: University of London, which houses the well-known School of Economics, University College London, and School of Advanced Study; University of the Arts London; University of Birmingham; Bournemouth University; University of Buckingham; University of Chichester; University of Exeter; Imperial College London; University of Leeds; University of Leicester; University of Manchester; the Open University (famous for distance learning); University of Sheffield; University of Sussex; University of Warwick; and the University of York.

Of these estimated 125 universities, 34 are in Scotland. Three universities—namely, the University of St. Andrews, University of Glasgow, and the University of Aberdeen—were founded before 1500. Other competitive universities in Scotland include the University of Edinburgh, the University of Dundee, and the University of Strathclyde. The so-called ancient universities of Scotland contributed to the reputation of Scotland as a center for philosophy and the natural sciences. In addition, Scottish universities have been known for their success in medicine.

Wales is home to 11 universities and 20 further education colleges. Further education colleges are common in the UK and parts of Ireland. These colleges are analogous to institutions of continuing education and are not the same as universities. The purpose is to prepare or possibly retool students for specific occupations and vocations. As such, they are similar to the American community college model. Competitive universities in Wales include Cardiff University, University of Gamorgan, Swansea University, Bangor University, and Aberystwyth University.

Teacher Education

Teacher education in the UK may be provided in universities, university colleges, or specialist institutions. In general, in England, Wales, and Northern Ireland, teacher education programs last five years. In Scotland teacher education programs are available for both four and five years. Overall, the general phenomenon in teacher education is that the length of teacher preparation programs has increased, perhaps due to the call for teachers to earn a master's degree. Primary teacher education must be completed in at least four years, and in some institutions, five years. Secondary school preparation programs take at least five years to complete. In-class student teaching, often called professional training, is an important part of UK teacher education programs. In most programs, students engage in professional training more than 50 percent of the time in primary education settings, and more than 30 percent of the time in secondary education settings.

In the UK early childhood teacher education is similar to study for teacher education at the primary level. Programs in early childhood in the UK take about five years to complete. This time period also includes student teaching qualifications. The teacher education model in the UK follows both a concurrent model, where the general, theoretical, and practical professional training take place concurrently, and a consecutive model, where general courses are introduced and are followed by theoretical courses and subsequently practical courses. Some preservice teachers follow the concurrent model while others follow the consecutive model. The UK has one of the highest levels of information and communication technologies (ICT) preparation in Europe for the country's prospective teachers. A recent study found that nearly 90 percent of all in-service teachers in the UK use ICT for lesson preparation, and 74 percent of these teachers use ICT for instruction.

Informal Education

Informal education in the UK is becoming a major factor not only in providing opportunities for adults pursuing second or third careers, but as a means of stimulating the economy. The Ministry of Education sponsors both academic and vocational courses. Nonprofit organizations also play a major role in funding informal adult education in the UK. Adult education is usually defined as education for an individual who is 20 years or older. Institutions that provide adult education include colleges of further education, vocational colleges, religious denominational organizations, and several other regional nonprofit adult education institutions. One major agenda of adult education in the UK is to provide adult learners with additional qualifications and the enhancement of skills for employment. Funding for adult education in UK comes from a variety of sources, including the federal government, country and municipal resources, occupational associations, and religious organizations.

System Economics

The UK ranks at 31 in educational expenditures as a percentage of gross domestic product. The total public expenditure on education in 2009 represented 5.6 percent of GDP. Nearly US$118.88 billion was allocated in 2009 for education purposes. Based on these figures, total per student spending amounts to $12,000 (determined by dividing total expenditure by 9,763,000, the approximate number of students in the UK). Total public expenditure on education as a percentage of total government expenditure is approximately 12 percent.

Future Prospects

In the summer of 2004 the Department for Education and Skills in England published its *Five-Year Strategy for Children and Learners*. The *Five-Year Strategy* identifies an education strategy for the decade beyond 2010 that attempts to address chronic educational weaknesses by emphasizing children, students, parents, and potential employers. The *Five-Year Strategy* discusses eight reforms that are intended to rectify current educational problems:

- assured three-year budgets for every school from 2006, based on student numbers
- universal specialist schools and better specialist schools
- latitude for all secondary schools to own land and buildings, manage assets, employ staff, and build partnerships with outside sponsors and educational foundations

- more places in popular schools
- halving the existing inspection burden on schools and replacing the existing system of local authority "link advisers" with a single annual review carried out by a "school improvement partner," usually a serving head teacher from a successful school
- provision of 200 independently managed academies to be open or in the pipeline by 2010
- every secondary school to be refurbished or rebuilt to a modern standard over the next 10 to 15 years
- the creation of foundation partnerships as a means of enabling schools to group together to raise standards and take on wider responsibilities in areas such as provision for students with special educational needs

In March 2006 the Department for Education and Skills (which no longer exists) published the Further Education Reform White Paper titled *Raising Skills, Improving Life Chances*. This document outlines the importance of improving the opportunities of young people and adults.

Education in Wales has also made strides for improvement in recent years. In 2001 the National Assembly in Wales published *The Learning Country*, an overall strategy to ensure education for all and lifelong learning, thus providing the basis for a unique outline for education and training in the British region over the ensuing decade. Plans for revitalizing the agenda set forth in *The Learning Country* are under way. The general goal in *The Learning Country* is to deliver better educational outcomes in schools, colleges, universities, and work-based training centers. The general plan is to build stronger foundations for teaching and learning by placing more emphasis on education in the early years, providing support for special needs students, improving the transition between primary and secondary school, developing more flexible practice in schools so as to provide students with more desirable outcomes when they graduate, ensuring better services for students while in school, providing more productive assistance to teachers and other practitioners, overhauling career placement practices so they adhere to twenty-first century practices, promoting greater access to post–grade 16 (i.e., postbaccalaureate) learning, improving overall skills of students in all grade levels, and modernizing higher education communication.

According to UNESCO, the educational system in Northern Ireland had undergone the most considerable changes. Based on the Education Reform Order of Northern Ireland in 1989, these changes were set in place in 1996 and were based on both curriculum- and assessment-related reforms. The government allowed the legislature to make necessary modifications so that the reforms would be successful. A new set of educational reform proposals that involved radical restructuring was introduced in 2006. The Education Curriculum Minimum Content Order of 2007 then required the implementation of these radical curricular reforms from 2007 to 2009. The revised curriculum mandates that the general curriculum remain the same as before. However, the main difference is the emphasis on skills to meet present and future societal demands. Students in Northern Ireland in grades 1 through 10 are witnessing somewhat of a renaissance by being introduced to the importance of community involvement as a means of supporting a sustainable environment. In addition, the new curriculum emphasizes health and hygiene, cultural awareness, and sustainability in the workforce. The Classroom

---

United Kingdom Education at a Glance

General Information

Capital	London
Population	62.3 million
Languages	English, Welsh, Scottish, Gaelic
Literacy rate	99%
GDP per capita	US$31,800
People below poverty line	17%
Number of phones per 100 people	53
Number of Internet users per 100 people	78
Number of Internet hosts	7 million
Life expectancy at birth (years)	79

Formal Educational Information

Primary school age population	4.2 million
Secondary school age population	5.4 million
Primary school age population	7%
Number of years of education (primary/secondary)	6/7
Student/teacher ratio (primary)	17.5
Student/teacher ratio (secondary)	15
Primary school gross enrollment ratio	107%
Primary school entrants reaching grade 5	no data
Secondary school gross enrollment ratio	105%
Child labor (ages 5–14)	no data

Note: Unless otherwise indicated, all data are based on sources from 2011.

2000 initiative (C2K) has enabled the five education boards of Northern Ireland to sustain ICT services to all schools of the country.

Current educational trends in Scotland show that the curriculum in the region is currently under reform. Known as "Curriculum for Excellence," the curricular reform in Scotland is intended to focus on developmental curriculum aimed at students of all levels between the ages of three and 18. The goals of implementing "Curriculum for Excellence" are to promote success in learning, confident students, a developing workforce, and a strong and informed citizenry. In 2007 the reform was introduced to the Scottish legislature. Implementation of the curriculum began in 2008.

Daniel Ness and Chia-ling Lin

REFERENCES

Central Intelligence Agency. *The CIA World Factbook*. New York: Skyhorse, 2011. https://www.cia.gov/library/publications/the-world-factbook/index.html.

Empirica. *Benchmarking Access and Use of ICT in European Schools 2012*. European Commission Staff Working Document: Progress Towards the Lisbon Objectives in Education and Training: Indicators and Benchmarks, 2012.

Nation Master. 2011. www.nationmaster.com.

UNESCO. *Global Education Digest 2012: Comparing Education Statistics Across the World*. Montreal: UNESCO Institute for Statistics, 2012.

UNESCO–IBE. www.ibe.unesco.org/en/worldwide/unesco-regions/europe-and-north-america/united-kingdom-of-great-britain-and-northern-ireland.html.

UNESCO–UIS. www.uis.unesco.org.

UNICEF. www.unicef.org/infobycountry.

World Bank Education Statistics. 2011. www.worldbank.org.

Middle East and South Central Asia

Introduction

In this section, the educational systems of 21 countries are discussed, of which 13 are in the Middle East and eight in south-central Asia. In some countries in these two regions, social and political inequities based on gender, ethnicity, religion, and language, as well as poverty and war, among other factors, have a profound and detrimental effect on their education systems.

The World Education Forum on Education for All (EFA) Conference, held in Dakar, Senegal, in 2000, focused on achieving six key education goals by 2015: early childhood care and education, universal primary education, learning opportunities for youth and adults, adult literacy, gender parity and equality, and quality of education. Data on key education indicators from the Institute for Statistics of the United Nations Educational, Scientific and Cultural Organization (UNESCO) in 2012 show that a few countries in the Middle East region are close to achieving some of the EFA goals, while others are far from doing so, particularly in poor, conflict-torn countries. As of 2010, the population in the Middle East region ranged from 1.3 million in Bahrain to 27.4 million in Saudi Arabia. The number of years of compulsory education ranged from six (ages six to 11) in Iraq and Saudi Arabia to 12 (ages six to 17) in Qatar and 13 (ages five to 17) in Israel. The regional gross enrollment ratio (GER) in preprimary education was 22 percent, ranging from 1 percent in Yemen and 6 percent in Iraq to 81 percent in Lebanon and 104 percent in Israel. The regional GER in primary education was 98 percent, ranging from 84 percent in Oman and 87 percent in Yemen to 118 percent in Syria. The regional GER in lower and upper second-

ary education was 69 percent, ranging from 44 percent in Yemen and 51 percent in Iraq to 96 percent in Bahrain and 101 percent in Saudi Arabia. The survival rates to grade 5 in primary education ranged from 66 percent in Yemen and 77 percent in Iraq to 98 percent in Bahrain and Oman and 99 percent in Israel. The regional number of students per teacher in primary education was 21, which is below 40 and the most widely used international ceiling, ranging from 8 in Kuwait and 11 in Saudi Arabia to 28 in Palestine and 31 in Yemen. The regional number of students per teacher in lower and upper secondary education was 15, ranging from 8 in Kuwait and 9 in Lebanon to 23 in Palestine and 25 in Yemen. The regional adult literacy rate, ages 15 years and over, was 75 percent (83 percent for males and 66 percent for females), ranging from 64 percent in Yemen and 78 percent in Iraq to 95 percent in Qatar and 97 percent in Israel. The regional youth literacy rate, ages 15 to 24, was 89 percent (92 percent for males and 86 percent for females), ranging from 83 percent in Iraq and 85 percent in Yemen to 100 percent in Bahrain. The regional public expenditure on education varied between 1.0 percent and 5.8 percent of gross domestic product (GDP). The total public expenditure on education in Lebanon was 1.8 percent of GDP, which represents 7.2 percent of the total government expenditure. The total public expenditure on education in Oman was 4.3 percent of GDP, which represents 31.1 percent of the total government expenditure.

As of 2010 the population in the south-central Asia region ranged from 726,000 in Bhutan to 1.2 billion in India. The number of years of compulsory education ranged from five (ages five to nine) in Pakistan and five (ages six to 10) in Bangladesh to nine (ages five to 13) in Sri Lanka, nine (ages six to 14) in India, and nine (ages seven to 15) in Afghanistan. Key education indicators show that a few countries in the south-central Asia region have made strides toward achieving the EFA goals. The regional GER in primary education was 106 percent, ranging from 95 percent in Bangladesh and Pakistan to 115 percent in Nepal and 117 percent in India. The regional GER in lower and upper secondary education was 59 percent, ranging from 34 percent in Pakistan and 44 percent in Nepal to 87 percent in Sri Lanka and 91 percent in Iran.

The survival rates to grade 5 in primary education ranged from 62 percent in Nepal and Pakistan to 96 percent in Bhutan and 99 percent in Sri Lanka. The regional number of students per teacher in primary education was 39, ranging from 20 in Iran and 24 in Sri Lanka to 43 in Bangladesh and 44 in Afghanistan. The regional number of students per teacher in lower and upper secondary education was 27, ranging from 20 in Sri Lanka and 21 in Bhutan to 41 in Nepal and 42 in Pakistan. The regional adult literacy rate, ages 15 years and over, was 63 percent (74 percent for males and 52 percent for females), ranging from 53 percent in Bhutan and 55 percent in Pakistan to 85 percent in Iran and 91 percent in Sri Lanka. The regional youth literacy rate, ages 15 to 24, was 81 percent (87 percent for males and 75 percent for females), ranging from 71 percent in Pakistan and 74 percent in Bhutan to 98 percent in Sri Lanka and 99 percent in Iran. The regional public expenditure on education varied between 2.1 percent and 4.7 percent of GDP The total public expenditure on education in Bangladesh was 2.2 percent of GDP, which represents 14.1 percent of the total government expenditure. The total public expenditure on education in Bhutan was 4.0 percent of GDP, which represents 9.4 percent of the total government expenditure.

Emad Alfar

AFGHANISTAN

Afghanistan is a small, landlocked country in southwest Asia. It is a mountainous land that has long been one of the turbulent regions of Asia. Afghanistan was formally established in 1747 and given its name by Ahmad Shah Durrani (1723–1773). The nineteenth century marked three Anglo-Afghan Wars while the

twentieth century had almost three decades of war in the region. After the Soviet Afghan War (1979–1989), Afghanistan spun into a civil war (1992–1996) and later fell into the hands of the repressive Taliban regime (1996–2001). Now, in the twenty-first century, Afghanistan is on the road to reconstructing its civil infrastructure despite Taliban uprisings in rural areas. Ambitious despite potential turmoil, Afghanistan's Ministry of Education has succeeded in procuring foreign aid to rejuvenate the educational system.

History of Education in Afghanistan

Afghanistan's educational system has been practically destroyed by multiple post-Soviet wars. Foreign assistance to create a modern system has been vital since the very beginning of Afghanistan's educational history. The Islamic madrassa system, which taught Islamic scripture, Persian and Pashtu language, mathematics, and literature (such as the classic Persian poems of Rumi, Firdawsi, and Sa'adi), has twelve centuries of history in the nation. The first attempt to develop schools outside of the madrassa system was in the nineteenth century when Amir Sher Ali (1825–1879) built two schools that concentrated on military strategy. The development of these schools was stopped by the first Anglo-Afghan war. In 1853 Amir Abdur Rahman (circa 1840–1901) wrote in his autobiography that his father had built a school for him in Balkh. However, what is lacking from the memoir is the mention of classmates. The future amir was trained in military strategy, surgery, blacksmithing, religion, and Persian and Pashto language skills. Early schools in this era served members of the royal family, soldiers, and the servants of royal family.

In 1904 Amir Habibullah (1872–1919) established the first Indian British school in Kabul. Lycée Habibia opened its doors to receive recent graduates of madrassas and began a new phase of modern education in Afghan history. In 1905 Mahmud Tarzi (1865–1933) returned to Afghanistan from exile. He was the leading proponent of modernization for Afghanistan within an Islamic framework. As editor of the famous *Siraj al-Akhbar* (Lamp of the News), he spread modernity and a new literary tradition after translating James Joyce and other modernist writers. His form of modernity for Afghanistan was the cornerstone of Afghanistan's educational system.

By 1912 the French schooling system had entered Afghanistan, and young Afghans learned French instead of English as the European language option. After years of struggle against British colonialism, it is not a surprise that Afghans preferred French instead of English as the European language of choice. In 1921 Queen Soraya (1899–1968), the wife of the modernizing King Amanullah (son of Amir Habibullah), established the first girls' primary school, which she named Masturat. By 1928, 800 girls were enrolled in this school. Under the reign of Shah Amanullah (1892–1960), young women were granted scholarships to study education and nursing in Turkey. In 1924 Shah Amanullah received German-backing to build Lycée Amani. This was the first high school built after Afghan independence from the British in 1919. After the fall of Shah Amanullah, all schools were closed down from 1929 to 1931 as a result of the civil war that was waging in Afghanistan between modernists and conservatives.

In the 1931 constitution drafted under the new king, Nadir Shah (1883–1933), school was made mandatory for all students. However, girls' schools did not reopen until 1939. Nadir Shah was assassinated in 1933 by a young student while he was distributing pens to the students at a high school graduation ceremony in Kabul as encouragement for enrollment at Lycée Amani (which he had renamed Lycée Nejat). His young son, Zahir Shah (1914–2007), succeeded him immediately after his death. Under his son's reign, Afghanistan's education system flourished and even spread to rural areas. Teachers from Germany, Turkey, France, and India were invited to teach in newly built schools, most of them located in the capital Kabul and in Jalalabad City in Nangarhar Province in eastern Afghanistan. Mandatory education was reinstituted by the new constitution in 1964. This new law applied to both boys and girls and drastically changed the rural areas of Afghanistan. The central government was now strong enough to spread schooling to even the mountainous regions. The age for compulsory enrollment was seven years old. High school choices were either humanities- or science-oriented. Students chose their field before beginning the lycée. Vocational schools that offered training as primary school teachers, lower-level health professionals, and government clerks had the largest enrollment of rural students. Many of these students returned to their villages and served their community

there. Members of the elite were sent abroad to study in the United States, Europe, Canada, Australia, and the Middle East.

Mohammed Daoud Khan (1909–1978), the prime minister of Afghanistan, invited international aid to assist Afghanistan in the 1950s. In 1954 USAID and Columbia Teacher's College restructured the primary school educational system. By 1962 primary schools as distant from Kabul as Nangarhar Province were giving multiple-choice exams, and lessons required less memorization of texts and more analysis. The transition from a madrassa to modern education was not a smooth trajectory. Wars and the collapse of civil infrastructure made a return to madrassas a necessity in order to maintain some form of literacy. From 1978 to 1989, the building of schools was a major part of the Sovietization of Afghanistan. Although enrollment ranked the highest in the 1980s, the heavy political environment affected the quality of education that Afghan children received. The repressive Soviet regime imprisoned and murdered thousands of educators who were speaking against communism. This left very few education professionals in Afghanistan. The lucky ones were able to flee the country, creating a significant "brain drain." In the 1980s, during the Soviet-Afghan war, madrassas were the only form of education available to Afghan refugees in the camps of Peshawar, Pakistan. These madrassas were very different from the traditional ones that taught Islamic scripture as well as other subjects such as Pashto and Persian language, classic Persian poetry, mathematics, geography, and history. These were highly politicized centers that promoted militancy, emphasized memorization (without analysis), and even taught young boys about weapons. A few of their hand-stapled textbooks were also distributed to the places of the Afghan Diaspora, and mosques taught basic Persian and Arabic from textbooks that spelled the words for "gun" and "grenade."

Under the reign of the Taliban (1996–2001), women were banned from education. Both teachers and students had to find alternatives to proper schools in order to read and write. Countless underground schools were set up in makeshift spaces in a rebellious spirit to teach women and girls to read. International feminist organizations became involved in assisting women's and girls' education in Afghanistan. The war on terror (October 7, 2001, to the present) and American involvement in Afghanistan have aided in reconstructing the educational system in Afghanistan. Foreign aid has been focused on building schools, training teachers, and constructing a curriculum that includes human rights, peace building, and gender awareness courses. There is also greater focus on developing vocational schools since many students are either the primary wage earners for their families or help bring income to their families.

Educational System

Kindergarten and early childhood programs are in their nascent stages in Afghanistan. According to a 2007 UNESCO Report, Afghan educators are only now going through training to be qualified for such institutions. As mentioned above, compulsory education begins at age six or seven. Grades 1 to 8 make up primary school and grades 9 to 12 are secondary school (lycée). The first middle school, Azizi Middle School, was promoted from primary school to middle school and was built with funding from the International Security Assistance Force (ISAF). According to UNICEF, as of 2011 more than half of the Afghan population was under the age of 18. The primary school enrollment ratio for boys is 108 and for girls it is 64. About 92 percent of primary school students reach the fifth grade. The male to female ratio of enrollment in secondary school is 24 males to 8 females. There is no report yet on how many students graduate from secondary school. Students who graduate from the lycée can apply to numerous universities in Afghanistan after passing a qualifying exam.

The Ministry of Higher Education released a report in 2005 stating the need to reform curriculum, train faculty and obtain qualified faculty members, reconstruct buildings and libraries, and create more equality for female students (which included building a dorm for women students at Kabul University). The ministry is also developing a rigorous entry exam to raise the standards of higher education. Kabul University is the first center of higher education in Afghanistan. In 1946 it unified the Faculty of Medicine, Faculty of Agriculture, and Faculty of Engineering under one university. In 1960 the university was made coeducational and women began enrolling, although in modest numbers. Universities in the health sciences include the University of Herat, College of Medicine; Avicenna State Medical Institute

of Kabul; and State Medical Institute of Nangarhar (founded in the 1960s). Other institutions of higher education in the country include the American University in Kabul, Heart University, Balkh University, Polytechnic University, Al Berouni University, Khost University, Kandahar University, Takhar University, Nangarhar University, Bamyan University, and Paktia University.

Curriculum, Assessment, and Instruction

There were three kinds of education available in Afghanistan as of 2008: public schools, Islamic schools (madrassas), and vocational schools. Since 2002 the Department of Compilation and Translation was designated as the administration responsible for developing curriculum and textbooks. It was successful in standardizing primary school. Classes are taught in either Pashto or Dari, depending on the population. Students in grades 1 to 3 study art, handwriting, life skills, math, and Pashto. Grades 4 to 6 have the addition of Dari, Islamic studies, science, social studies, and English. Grades 7 to 9 add economics, geography, geometry, geology, history, biology, chemistry, and trigonometry. Grades 10 to 12 add physics to their curriculum. Afghan students study a total of four languages in school. Islamic studies begin in the fourth grade and end in the sixth grade. The final year of secondary school includes a qualifying exam for Afghan universities.

The Islamic madrassas of Afghanistan still operate, particularly in remote regions where one schoolhouse opens its doors to students from seven to 15 years old. Due to their tradition and their significance in religious training, the schools operate with curriculum consultation from the Ministry of Education.

Technical and vocational education and training (TVET) is an essential type of schooling in order to help the country recover from economic disaster; the rapid reconstruction of the country requires trained skilled and technical workers. Recently international funders have contributed millions for vocational training of young Afghans. These are short-term courses that train students in appropriate trades and management skills regardless of gender, ethnicity, or religion. The result of these programs has not been fully assessed due to lack of funding.

Teacher Education

The first teachers college was established in 1912 under the reign of Amir Habibullah. Between 1919 and 1928 Afghans were granted scholarships to study abroad in France, Germany, and Turkey; in the latter year 28 young Afghan women were sent to Turkey to be trained as nurses and teachers. In 1948 the first girls' university for teaching was established. In 1973, under the reign of President Mohammad Daoud, Ibn Sina Lycée became a vocational school to train teachers for primary schools in rural villages. The student population of this school came primarily from the villages they would return to serve. During the Soviet-Afghan wars, teachers were either brought in from the Soviet Union to teach Afghan children or Afghans were sent to Moscow to be trained as teachers. During the civil war and later Taliban regime, teachers who had this communist past were forbidden to work in Afghanistan. Many fled the country while others chose different professions. The pay for teachers in Afghanistan was so low under the Taliban that teachers would leave classes early to sell merchandise in the streets. The harsh regime fired women teachers, destroying the educational quality of schools during this period.

In 2004 Columbia University's Teachers College embarked on rewriting the educational curriculum for primary schools in Afghanistan. In 2007 a delegation of Afghan educators headed by Columbia Teachers College alumna Susan Wardak made a trip to Mysore, India, to train secondary school educators. UNESCO has supported the Ministry of Education to provide the following curriculum for primary school children: reading, writing, arithmetic, sports, and language classes. Secondary school education includes literature, social studies, natural science, or vocational studies. Additions that are being developed for secondary schools are human rights, culture of peace, and gender awareness courses. UNESCO has encouraged programs for preschool and early childhood education. However, these programs require new training for educators. Another area of education that has been important to develop in postwar Afghanistan has been emphasis on vocational schools. Given the need for trained technical workers, this has been considered a more important form of education than the traditional humanities education. Currently Afghanistan has been working on setting teacher standards so that Afghani children and adolescents are all, rural and urban, on the same educational level depending on their age. The World Bank, UNESCO, and UNICEF have worked with the Ministry of Education to establish higher standards for teacher education in Afghanistan. As of 2010 a large percentage of teachers were hardly qualified themselves to teach primary, secondary, or university students. The faculty members of Kabul University had completed only a bachelor's degree. A small population had earned master's degrees and an even smaller percentage (with only two women professors) had PhDs. Given ongoing war, the Ministry of Education has instituted the Our Way Forward initiative to make teacher education and the setting of educational standards a priority and in place by 2015. In 2008 Afghanistan's Ministry of Education was given a grant of $30 million from the World Bank to train teachers and to rehabilitate schools. The Education Quality Improvement Program encourages direct involvement from parents, students, and teachers in rebuilding the school system one schoolhouse at a time. Other countries, such as Canada, have pledged to contribute millions of dollars to support this program.

Informal Education

The illiteracy rate among the adult population in Afghanistan is staggering. As of 2011 there were over 13.6 million Afghans above the age of 15 who could not read or write—approximately 28 percent of the adult population. To make matters worse, there is much gender disparity in terms of literacy; 43 percent of the male population can read and write while only 12.6 percent of the female population can. The Ministry of Education is working on a new program aimed at young people who wish to learn. The high illiteracy rate is a challenge that is beyond school-age. Small nongovernmental organizations and feminist organizations have developed programs to teach women literacy skills. However, there are few programs to teach men to read and write. This is a serious issue that is currently being addressed. The project requires a considerable amount of funding in order to be successful.

System Economics

Funding to support Afghanistan's education system has come from abroad, mainly the United States,

Afghanistan Education at a Glance

General Information

Capital	Kabul
Population	31.4 million
Languages	Persian, Pashto
Adult literacy rate (ages 15 and over)	no data
Youth literacy rate (ages 15–24)	no data
GDP per capita	US$1,207
Number of phones (mobile) per 100 people	41
Number of Internet users per 100 people	4
Life expectancy at birth (years)	48

Formal Educational Information

Enrollment in preprimary school (ages 3–6)	24,000
Enrollment in primary school (ages 7–12)	4.9 million
Enrollment in lower and upper secondary school (ages 13–18)	1.7 million
Number of years of compulsory education (ages 7–15)	9
Preprimary school student/teacher ratio	7
Primary school student/teacher ratio	44
Lower and upper secondary school gross student/teacher ratio	32
Preprimary school gross enrollment ratio	1%
Primary school gross enrollment ratio	97%
Lower and upper secondary school gross enrollment ratio	46%
Primary school entrants reaching grade 5	89%

Note: Unless otherwise indicated, all data are based on sources from 2011.

France, Germany, Japan, and Australia. Data have not been released that report a comprehensive examination of how this funding has impacted Afghanistan's education system. As of 2011 no data exist regarding the percentage of gross national product spending on education. Many projects were implemented in 2002, but it is difficult to determine how these projects have affected educational outcomes.

Future Prospects

Afghanistan has had a turbulent educational history. The implementation of a modern educational system within the respectful frame of Islam has been quite a challenge. Remarkably, despite the near collapse of modern education, Afghanistan has remained committed to reconstructing its educational infrastructure. The international community has donated billions of dollars to build Afghanistan's education system. Its success will prove not only the determination of Afghanistan to rise enlightened after decades of war, but also the commitment of the international community to build peace through establishing schools and train-

ing teachers. However, the main problem threatening these ambitious goals for a postwar Afghanistan has been the rising of the Taliban and the continued battles against international forces in Afghanistan. The future of Afghanistan's educational system is still uncertain, although hopeful.

Zohra Saed

REFERENCES

Brodsky, Anne E., et al. "Beyond (the ABCs): Education, Community, and Feminism in Afghanistan." *Journal of Community Psychology* 40:1 (2012): 159–181.

Central Intelligence Agency. *The CIA World Factbook.* New York: Skyhorse, 2011. https://www.cia.gov/library/publications/the-world-factbook/index.html.

Khan, Mir Munshi Sultan Mahomad, ed. *The Life of Abdur Rahman, Amir of Afghanistan*, vol. 1. Chestnut Hill, MA: Elibron Classics, 2005.

Malikyar, Helena. "An Eyewitness Report on Women and Education in Northern Afghanistan: Opportunities and Problems." www.rawa.org/sajida.htm.

———. "What Is to Be Done?" In *Modernist Islam: 1840–1940*, ed. Charles Kurzman, 126–132. New York: Oxford University Press, 2002.

Minister of Education, Islamic Republic of Afghanistan. *Afghanistan National Development Strategy, 2008–2013.* 2007.

Ministry of Higher Education. *Strategic Action Plan for the Development of Higher Education in Afghanistan.* May 2004.

Sadat, Hekmat. "Modern Education in Afghanistan." *Lemar-Aftaab Magazine.* www.afghanmagazine.com.

UNESCO–IBE. www.ibe.unesco.org/en/worldwide/unesco-regions/asia-and-the-pacific/afghanistan.html.

UNICEF. "Afghanistan Statistics." www.unicef.org/infobycountry/afghanistan_statistics.html.

BAHRAIN

The Kingdom of Bahrain, an island Arab country in the Persian Gulf, is located in southwestern Asia, east of Saudi Arabia and north of Qatar. The official language is Arabic. Other spoken languages include English, Urdu, and Persian. About two-thirds of the population are Bahraini citizens; the rest are nonnational Arabs, South Asians, Iranians, and British. The official religion is Islam. The majority of the population is Muslim, with small numbers of Christian and Hindu communities. Bahrain gained independence from Britain in 1971.

Educational System

The Ministry of Education administers public education, including higher education, and supervises private education. Higher education institutions, such as the University of Bahrain and the Arabian Gulf University, are autonomous and have a board of trustees chaired by the minister of education. Under the authority of the Ministry of Education, each school has an autonomous administrative and educational unit composed of the school principal and the school council, which consists of the principal as chair, assistant principal, a social worker, an elected senior teacher, a learning resources center specialist, a registrar, and five elected teachers. Article 7 of the Bahraini constitution states, "The education is compulsory and free in the early stages as specified and provided by law." Education is compulsory during the first nine years of the educational ladder and is free to all Bahrainis at all levels of education. Public schools are not coeducational.

The general public education system comprises four cycles: kindergarten, elementary, intermediate, and secondary. There is religious education, for boys only, that follows the same curriculum and educational ladder (elementary, intermediate, and secondary) as general public education, but emphasizes the study of Islam and the Quran. Higher education is provided by universities, colleges, and institutes. The two main institutions are the University of Bahrain and the Arabian Gulf University.

Precompulsory and Compulsory Education

Kindergarten, which is not compulsory, lasts for three years, for children entering at age three and exiting at age six. The Ministry of Education supervises the private sector that runs kindergartens.

Elementary education, which is compulsory, lasts for six years, from grades 1 through 6, for children entering at age six and exiting at age 12. Students receive basic general education and skills, with emphasis on English language starting in grade 3, Arabic language, and mathematics. Students who successfully complete their elementary education move on to the intermediate level.

Intermediate education, which is also compulsory, lasts for three years, covering grades 7 through 9, for children entering at age 12 and exiting at age 15. Students receive general and practical education, as well as the necessary studies to prepare them for the various tracks of secondary education.

Postcompulsory Education

Secondary education, which is not compulsory, lasts for three years, covering grades 10 through 12, for children entering at age 15 and exiting at age 18. It has four main tracks: general (scientific or literary), commercial, technical, and applied studies. Based on the chosen secondary education track, students receive an education that prepares them for higher education or for entry into the labor market. Students who successfully complete their secondary education are awarded the General Secondary Education Certificate (Tawjahiya) in the chosen track of study. Tawjahiya is also awarded to students at the end of their secondary religious education.

Higher education is provided by universities, colleges, and institutes. In addition to University of Bahrain and Arabian Gulf University, other institutions that provide higher education are College of Health Sciences; Hotel and Catering Training Center, and Bahrain Training Institute.

Curriculum, Assessment, and Instruction

Kindergarten education develops attitudes and behaviors of children based on Islam and tradition. It also develops children physically, socially, mentally, and psychologically, as well as their skills and abilities. It prepares them for elementary education. An evaluation form prepared by the teacher includes description and comments about the development of students' skills and performance in various settings.

Subjects taught at the elementary level are Islamic education, Arabic language, mathematics, science and technology, social studies, art education, songs and music, and physical education. English language is taught in grades 3 through 6, and family life education in grades 4 through 6. Emphasis is on Arabic language and mathematics. In religious schools, grades 1 through 3, the subjects taught, in addition to the general subjects (Arabic language, mathematics, social studies, art and practical education, and physical education), are holy Quran, Islamic theology, and prophetic biography. In religious schools, grades 4 through 6, the subjects taught, in addition to the general subjects (Arabic language, English language, mathematics, science, art and practical education, physical education, and social studies), are holy Quran, Islamic traditions, Islamic theology, Islamic jurisprudence, and prophetic biography. Teachers evaluate their students through continuous systematic observation, diagnostic and cumulative tests, planned activities, and daily training and practicing, in addition to individual and group projects. Students who successfully complete their elementary education continue on to the intermediate level.

Subjects taught at the intermediate level are the same as those at the elementary level, with some minor differences. Art education is replaced by practical studies. The songs and music subject is not taught at the intermediate level. Emphasis is on Arabic language, English language, science and technology, and mathematics. In religious schools, grades 7 through 9, the same general subjects are taught as in elementary education, grades 4 through 6, plus holy Quran, Quranic exegesis, Quranic intonation, Islamic traditions, Islamic theology, Islamic jurisprudence, and prophetic biography. Teachers apply similar evaluation methods as those in elementary education, plus midterm tests and final examinations at the end of each semester. Students who successfully complete the intermediate level receive the Intermediate Education Certificate and continue on to the secondary level.

Subjects taught at the secondary level are divided into four groups of courses: core, compulsory specialized, elective specialized, and free electives. These courses depend on the chosen track: general (scientific or literary), commercial, technical, or applied. Students are required to complete 180 credit hours for the technical track and 156 credit hours for all other tracks. Core subjects taught in all tracks, except for the technical track, are Arabic language, English language, Islamic education, science, mathematics, social studies, physical education, and family life education. Core subjects taught in the technical track are Arabic language, English language, Islamic education, social studies, physical education, computer education, and industrial

relations. Compulsory specialized subjects taught in the general scientific track are mathematics, physics, chemistry, biology, and geology. Compulsory specialized subjects taught in the general literary track are Arabic language, English language, Islamic education, history, geography, economics, sociology, philosophy, and psychology. Compulsory specialized subjects taught in the commercial track are accounting (Arabic and English), banking, basis of commerce, economics, insurance, office practice (Arabic and English), information technology, computer applications, trade and labor, travel and tourism, and financial mathematics. Compulsory specialized subjects taught in the technical track are industrial principles, technical drawing, practical studies, science, mathematics, and mechanics. Compulsory specialized subjects taught in the applied studies track are textile technology, measurement and cost, technical drawing, and practical training. In religious schools, grades 10 through 12, subjects taught, in addition to the general subjects (Arabic language, English language, mathematics, science, social studies, sociology, economics, psychology, philosophy, logic, physical education, and practical studies), are holy Quran, Quranic exegesis, Islamic traditions, Islamic theology, and Islamic jurisprudence.

Assessment of students' academic performance is accomplished through a variety of methods, including midterm and final examinations each semester, which, depending on the subject, can be oral, written, or practical examinations, plus research and written reports. A new assessment system is being introduced in which three different kinds of evaluation compose the final course grade: 30 percent for internal continuous evaluation by the teacher, 20 percent for internal mid-semester examination, and 50 percent for external unified examination. Students must attain an overall score of at least 50 percent in each subject. Students who successfully complete the secondary level receive the General Secondary Education Certificate (Tawjahiya), and can continue on to higher education.

Higher education is provided by universities, colleges, and institutes offering programs ranging from two-year associate degrees to four-year bachelor's degrees; further study of two to four years leads to a master's degree. The University of Bahrain includes the following main colleges: Arts, Science,

Education, Business Administration, Engineering, and Information Technology. The Arabian Gulf University in Bahrain was established in 1979 by the Gulf Cooperation Council countries (Qatar, Oman, Saudi Arabia, Kuwait, United Arab Emirates, and Bahrain). It includes two main colleges: Medicine and Medical Sciences, and Postgraduate.

Teacher Education

Elementary school teachers must hold a bachelor's degree in education. Those who teach grades 4 through 6 have two ways for qualifying: a bachelor's degree in Arabic, social studies, or religious education and a strong academic background in other basic subjects; or a bachelor's degree in chemistry, physics, biology, or mathematics and a strong academic background in other basic subjects. Intermediate and secondary school teachers must hold a bachelor's degree in a specialized subject with a minor in education. Preference in employment is given to university graduates who receive the highest marks on proficiency tests in their academic subjects. The University of Bahrain offers preservice and in-service programs. Preservice programs include mastery of the subject matter, pedagogical and methodological skills, and teaching methods. Long-term in-service programs include a bachelor of education degree, diploma in elementary education, postgraduate diploma in education, and master's degree. Short-term in-service programs offering short training courses include comprehensive training for holders of a nonspecialized bachelor's degree in elementary school mathematics, intensive training in the Arabic language, and English language development for English teachers.

Informal Education

Article 7 of the Bahraini constitution states, "The necessary plan for eradication of illiteracy is laid down by law." Educational programs for illiterates and for those who wish to continue their education are provided by the Directorate of Adult Education, under the Ministry of Education. These programs cover six years and are divided into three stages: literacy, follow-up, and consolidation. The literacy stage, covering two years, is for those who cannot read or write. Subjects taught include Arabic language, mathematics, and Islamic religion. The follow-up stage, covering two years and equivalent to grade 6 of formal elementary education, is for those who have completed the literacy stage. The curriculum is the same as that of grades 5 and 6 in formal elementary education. In addition to subjects taught at the literacy stage, other subjects taught include English language, sciences, and social studies. The consolidation stage, covering two years, is for those who have completed the follow-up stage or did not complete their formal education. The curriculum is the same as that of formal intermediate education. The subjects taught, in addition to subjects taught at the literacy and follow-up stages, are history and geography.

Numerous courses, under continuing adult education programs, are provided by the Directorate of Adult Education. Depending on each program, these courses vary in length and serve those who wish to master more information and knowledge in various fields. These courses aim to meet labor market demands and people's training and educational needs. Courses offered include English language, Arabic

---

Bahrain Education at a Glance

General Information

Capital	Manama
Population	1.3 million
Language	Arabic
Adult literacy rate (ages 15 and over)	91.9%
Youth literacy rate (ages 15–24)	100%
GDP per capita	US$25,799
Number of phones (mobile) per 100 people	124
Number of Internet users per 100 people	55
Life expectancy at birth (years)	75

Formal Educational Information

Enrollment in preprimary school (ages 3–5)	24,000
Enrollment in primary school (ages 6–11)	88,000
Enrollment in lower and upper secondary school (ages 12–17)	79,000
Number of years of compulsory education	9 (ages 6–14)
Preprimary school student/teacher ratio	16
Primary school student/teacher ratio	16
Lower and upper secondary school gross student/teacher ratio	12
Preprimary school gross enrollment ratio	59%
Primary school gross enrollment ratio	107%
Lower and upper secondary school gross enrollment ratio	96%
Primary school entrants reaching grade 5	98%

Sources: Education for All, 2011; Global Education Digest, 2011; UNESCO–UIS, 2012; UNICEF, 2012; United Nations Development Programme, 2011.

language for non-Arab expatriates, French language, Japanese language, Islamic studies for foreigners, family life education, office practice programs, computer programs, and library science.

System Economics

The total public expenditure on education in 2008 represented 2.9 percent of Bahrain's gross domestic product (GDP). It represented 11.7 percent of the total government expenditure. For the year 1997, 30 percent of public education spending was at the primary level and 35 percent at the secondary level.

Future Prospects

Currently, teaching of English language starts at grade 3 of elementary education, but there are plans to start it at grade 1 of that stage. Bahrain's future educational policies include the unification of academic secondary education tracks, the interaction of the curriculum with overall development and labor market demands, and curriculum response to the communication and information age. In response to the World Conference on Education for All (EFA) challenge, held in Jomtien, Thailand, in 1990, focusing on achieving six key education goals by 2015, Bahrain has a high chance of achieving the adult literacy goal.

Emad Alfar

REFERENCES

"Bahrain." In *The Europa World Yearbook*, vol. 1. London: Routledge, 2007.

Central Intelligence Agency. *The CIA World Factbook*. New York: Skyhorse, 2011. https://www.cia.gov/library/publications/the-world-factbook/index.html.

Education for All. "The Hidden Crisis: Armed Conflict and Education." *Education for All Global Monitoring Report*. Paris: UNESCO, 2011.

Global Education Digest. *Global Education Digest 2011: Comparing Education Statistics Across the World*. Montreal: UNESCO Institute for Statistics, 2011.

Programme on Governance in the Arab Region. www.pogar.org/countries/country.aspx?cid=2.

UNESCO–IBE. www.ibe.unesco.org/countries/Bahrain.htm.

UNESCO–UIS. www.uis.unesco.org.

UNICEF. www.unicef.org/infobycountry/bahrain.html.

United Nations Development Programme. "Sustainability and Equity: A Better Future for All." *Human Development Report 2011*. New York: Palgrave Macmillan, 2011.

BANGLADESH

Bangladesh is located in southern Asia, bordered by Burma to the southeast, India to the east, north and west, and the Bay of Bengal to the south. The official language is Bangla, and English is widely spoken. Bangladesh is one of the most densely populated countries in the world. Nearly all Bangladeshis are of Bengali ethnicity. The official religion is Islam. The population is predominantly Muslim, and the remaining population is Hindu, Buddhist, and Christian. After the end of British rule in 1947, the subcontinent was partitioned into two independent countries, India and Pakistan, with Bangladesh as the eastern province of Pakistan. In 1971 Bangladesh gained its independence from Pakistan.

Educational System

The Ministry of Primary and Mass Education is responsible for primary education, and the Ministry of Education is responsible for postprimary and postsecondary education. Article 17 of the constitution stipulates that education is free and compulsory for all children. The Compulsory Primary Education Act of 1990 made five years of primary education compulsory for children aged six to 10.

The general school system is divided into five cycles: preprimary, primary, junior secondary, senior secondary, and higher secondary. Besides the general education system, there are two other parallel streams: the technical-vocational education stream and the religious education stream (madrassa). Higher education includes public and private institutions, with studies lasting two to four years, leading to certificates, diplomas, and degrees.

Precompulsory and Compulsory Education

Nongovernmental organizations (NGOs) administer preprimary schools. Preprimary school, which is not compulsory, lasts for three years, for children entering at age three and exiting at age six. It familiarizes children with schooling.

Primary school, compulsory and free for all Bangladeshis, lasts for five years, from grade 1 through 5, for children entering at age six and exiting at age 11. It is a foundation for secondary school. Students receive basic and general broad-based education.

Postcompulsory Education

Secondary school, which is not compulsory, consists of three cycles: junior, senior, and higher. Junior secondary school is for children entering at age 11 and exiting at age 14, lasts for three years, and covers grades 6 through 8. Senior secondary school is for children entering at age 14 and exiting at age 16, lasts for two years, and covers grades 9 and 10. Higher secondary school is for children entering at age 16 and exiting at age 18, lasts for two years, and covers grades 11 and 12. Secondary education develops students' abilities, preparing them for the labor market or higher education, and enables them to become good and responsible citizens.

Higher education institutions include public and private universities, colleges, and institutes of technology. The president of Bangladesh is the chancellor of the universities. Programs of study at institutes of technology lead to a diploma or certificate; university programs lead to (pass/honors) bachelor's, master's, and doctorate degrees. Higher education institutions include Bangladesh National University, Bangladesh Open University, and University of Rajshahi. Universities are funded mainly by the government, and the rest of the cost is covered by tuition fees.

Curriculum, Assessment, and Instruction

In preprimary school, students are familiarized with the school environment and are helped with developing social skills and good hygiene.

Subjects taught in primary school, grades 1 through 5, include Bangla, mathematics, English, science, social studies, religious education (Islam, Hinduism, Buddhism, and Christianity), environmental studies, art and crafts, and physical education. Recently a system of continuous assessment of students has been implemented. Teachers evaluate students frequently through observation, as well as oral and written as-

sessment. Children in grades 1 and 2 are promoted automatically, whereas students in grades 3 through 5 are promoted based on their achievement in annual examinations.

Subjects taught in general secondary school, grades 6 through 12, include mathematics, science, language, history, geography, religion, economics, civics, art and crafts, home economics, and environment. At the end of the senior secondary cycle, grade 10, students who pass the SSC examination can move on to the higher secondary cycle, grades 11 and 12, or to nonuniversity-level higher education institutions. Upon completing grade 12, students who pass the HSC examination can move on to university-level institutions.

Programs in various fields offered by higher education institutions include the two-year ordinary first degree; a three-year specialized degree; a four- to five-year professional first degree; a one- or two-year master's degree; a two-year master of philosophy degree after a master's degree; and a doctorate degree (requiring at least three years) after a master's degree.

Teacher Education

Female primary school teachers, trained at primary training institutes (PTIs), must hold the SSC; male teachers must hold the HSC. PTIs provide one-year training courses leading to a Certificate in Education. Secondary school teachers are provided with training at teacher training colleges, offering one-year bachelor of education degrees and a master of education degree after one further year's study. Distance education courses offered by Bangladesh Open University lead to a bachelor of education degree. In-service training is provided to both secondary and college teachers by higher secondary teachers training institutes.

Informal Education

Both NGOs and the government have implemented two major goals: to make primary education universal and to provide informal education programs for out-of-school and dropout children (ages eight to 10), adolescents (ages 11 to 14), and adult illiterates (ages 15 to 35). The adult illiteracy rate is high. Libraries provide lifelong continuing education to

Bangladesh Education at a Glance

General Information

Capital	Dhaka
Population	148.6 million
Language	Bangla
Adult literacy rate (ages 15 and over)	56.8%
Youth literacy rate (ages 15–24)	77%
GDP per capita	US$1,659
Number of phones (mobile) per 100 people	46
Number of Internet users per 100 people	4
Life expectancy at birth (years)	68

Formal Educational Information

Enrollment in preprimary school (ages 3–5)	1 million
Enrollment in primary school (ages 6–10)	16.5 million
Enrollment in lower and upper secondary school (ages 11–17)	10 million
Number of years of compulsory education	5 (ages 6–10)
Preprimary school student/teacher ratio	23
Primary school student/teacher ratio	43
Lower and upper secondary school gross student/teacher ratio	27
Preprimary school gross enrollment ratio	13
Primary school gross enrollment ratio	95%
Lower and upper secondary school gross enrollment ratio	51%
Primary school entrants reaching grade 5	66%

Sources: Education for All, 2011; Global Education Digest, 2011; UNESCO–UIS, 2012; UNICEF, 2012; United Nations Development Programme, 2011.

knowledge-based and technologically oriented learning society by improving and maintaining access.

Emad Alfar

REFERENCES

"Bangladesh." *The Europa World Yearbook*, vol. 1. London: Routledge, 2009.

Central Intelligence Agency. *The CIA World Factbook*. New York: Skyhorse, 2011. https://www.cia.gov/library/publications/the-world-factbook/index.html.

Education for All. "The Hidden Crisis: Armed Conflict and Education." *Education for All Global Monitoring Report*. Paris: UNESCO, 2011.

Global Education Digest. *Global Education Digest 2011: Comparing Education Statistics Across the World*. Montreal: UNESCO Institute for Statistics, 2011.

UNESCO–IBE. www.ibe.unesco.org/en/worldwide/unesco-regions/asia-and-the-pacific/bangladesh.html.

UNESCO–UIS. www.uis.unesco.org.

UNICEF. www.unicef.org/infobycountry/bangladesh.html.

United Nations Development Programme. "Sustainability and Equity: A Better Future for All." *Human Development Report 2011*. New York: Palgrave Macmillan, 2011.

new literates to prevent them from relapsing into illiteracy.

System Economics

The total public expenditure on education in Bangladesh in 2008 represented 2.7 percent of the gross domestic product (GDP). It represented 14.2 percent of the total government expenditure. Moreover, 2 percent of public education spending was at the preprimary level, 35 percent at the primary level, 48 percent at the secondary level, and 14 percent at the tertiary level.

Future Prospects

Poverty, widespread illiteracy, low per capita income, and rapid population growth are among the major challenges facing Bangladesh.

The goals of the Education for All National Action Plan for 2003–2015 are to retain and provide quality basic (formal and informal) education to meet the needs of all citizens of all ages and to establish a

BHUTAN

Bhutan, once called Druk Yul, "the land of the thunder dragon," became a kingdom under the Wangchuk dynasty in 1907 and is currently governed by Fourth King Jigme Singye Wangchuk. The Himalayan kingdom has followed the Buddhist Drukpa tradition of neighboring Tibet since the visit of Guru Rimpoche Padma Sambhava in 746 CE. Bhutan remains relatively isolated with a tourism program that, according to the Bhutan Tourism Corporation website, limited the number of visitors entering the country in 2007 to 21,000. Given its powerful neighbors, Bhutan has remained remarkably independent and free of colonial rule. In 2008 Bhutan broke with its theocratic past in becoming a fully fledged democracy with an elected National Assembly and Supreme Constitution.

Educational System

Historically, education in Bhutan was the province of the monasteries and largely limited to boys whose families had dedicated them to the service of Buddhism. Monastic education began at Trongsa in 1540, with informal teachings based on the prevailing Tibetan Kagyud School, and was formalized with the ordination of Bhutan's first monks in 1622. Centered at Tharpaling Monastery in Bumthang and headed by the Je Khenpo (the leading religious hierarch), monastic education was based on the rote learning of liturgy and ritual practice. More recent expansion includes the study of literature, philosophy, meditation, and arts and languages at tertiary-level *shedras*, where learning is experiential and discursive. Students elect to follow a master and are trained in the habits, practices, rituals, and arguments constituting a body of traditional knowledge, the mastery of which over five or six years prepares students to become monks, nuns, and other religious officiaries. Monastic graduates are an integral part of the civil service whose training includes moral education and self-discipline, and whose growing maturity and competence are recognized in increasingly prominent official and religious postings. Once supplied by the communities they served, monasteries are now supported by the government. Early Bhutanese agrarian society did not require mass education, which only arrived in the mid-twentieth century.

Considerable Western input over the past four decades has resulted in the emergence of a secular education system. India, Canada, Denmark, Japan, New Zealand, Sweden, and Switzerland offer sustained support. The Canadian International Development Agency runs a partnership program with the University of New Brunswick, while the influence of key individuals such as the Montreal-based Jesuit Father William Mackey is legendary. Although Bhutan bears operating costs, Denmark contributes between 10 to 12 percent of the education budget. Access to education is currently impeded by limited infrastructure, underdeveloped transportation, and rapid urbanization of the country's major cities. Nevertheless, basic education (for students of roughly five to 15 years of age) is free, including board where necessary, but not yet compulsory. Changes in 2008 have affected access to education on many levels and spurred the implementation of a countrywide comprehensive English-language mass education system largely following Western precepts. In many ways Bhutan exemplifies best practice in using international sources of aid and expertise to develop a sophisticated education system that nevertheless remains focused on Bhutanese needs and knowledge.

Precompulsory and Compulsory Education

Because of the challenges associated with access to schooling, no levels of education are compulsory in Bhutan. Third King Jigme Dorje Wangchuck introduced secular mass education in 1961 as part of the Five-Year Plan programs for economic development and modernization. The first Western-model school, established in Ha in 1914, taught Dzongkha (Bhutan's official language), English, Hindi, and arithmetic. By 1960 there were 400 students in eleven schools teaching languages, literacy, science, and technology by rote. Early teachers were trained in India, and English became the standard medium in 1962. The secular education system has grown in strength and sophistication over the past 45 years, from limited accessibility and an average grade level expectancy of second or third grade, to one that now includes secondary education to tenth grade.

Age eight or nine is the normal starting point of education for most Bhutanese students. Primary and preprimary education is open to everyone, while secondary schooling to grade 12 and beyond is based upon grade point average (GPA) achievement and merit. Places are limited, and successful students are invited to continue their education. Students can choose which schools they attend, but are often constrained by lack of mobility. Although relative choice is based on access and schools vary in quality and provenance, higher GPAs afford greater choice. The final decision to accept a student, however, is at the discretion of the school principal.

The school system is divided into five levels: community school, consisting of preprimary to grade 3 (ages six to nine); community primary school, grade 4 to 6 (ages 10 to 12); lower secondary school (LSS), grade 7 to 8 (ages 13 to 14); middle secondary school (MSS), grade 9 to 10 (ages 15 to 16); and higher secondary school (HSS)—grade 11 to 12 (ages 17 to 18). Students move up between schools after successfully completing public exams.

The average student/teacher ratio in 2001 was 32, but some urban classes can reach 50 to 60. Forty percent of children are educated at urban institutions. As academic and administrative head of the education system, the director of education reports to the secretary general of development in Thimphu, while management is currently decentralized into 20 district education offices and a growing number of block development committees.

Postcompulsory Education

Bhutan has 10 vocational, technical, and community colleges and the Royal University of Bhutan, which comprises a number of campuses countrywide. The colleges are federated, with each location developing a specific disciplinary focus. Concentrations include arts and sciences, engineering and technology, three centers for health and traditional medicine, a college of art, and the Center for Agriculture, Land and Resource Management at Lobessa. Various medical, paralegal, and technical degrees are offered, as well as a master's degree in professional leadership. Areas not covered in Bhutan but considered necessary for the country are provided overseas until Bhutan develops its own programs.

Curriculum, Assessment, and Instruction

Three branches of the government oversee aspects of the educational system. The Bhutan Board of Exams (BBE) monitors assessment; curriculum development and quality control are overseen by the Education Monitoring and Support Division (EMSD); and program support is offered by the Curriculum and Professional Services Division (CAPSD). Each department has a minister and a deputy minister or secretary.

The Bhutanese curriculum is based on Lovat and Grundy's "three ways of knowing"—technical, hermeneutic, and critical. Adopted from British and Indian systems, the original content bore little relation to Bhutanese life. During the 1970s, the curriculum began focusing on Bhutan's need to manage modernization, change, and the concomitant loss of traditional culture. The first curriculum policy paper appeared in 1976, presenting four key developmental areas: (1) relevant, practical knowledge; (2) civic love, respect, and loyalty; (3) values, traditions, and moral standards; and (4) economic participation. This paper was comprehensively revised in 1984. Linked to the idea of "gross national happiness" as a develop-

mental philosophy, labeled "wholesome education" and grounded in what the Bhutanese describe as the principles of good living, the new curriculum was to be responsive, relevant, effective, and efficient. It aimed to encourage creativity, include practical as well as academic subjects, and be environmentally and technologically astute. While placing Bhutan in its global context, the focus remained on the preservation of the country's rich traditions and respect for its monarchy. *The Purpose of School Education* (1996) gave clear curriculum guidelines and, from 1997 onward, became the annually updated "Education Policy Guidelines and Instructions."

The current curriculum has eight key learning areas: Dzongkha; English; math; science and technology; human society and environment; creative and practical arts; health and physical and personal development; and socially useful and productive work. The development and provision of curricular materials are centralized at the Center for Educational Research at Paro, opened in 2001, where the board of curriculum meets twice yearly.

Students are assessed through continuous, formative assessment of their schoolwork and through biennial public examinations. Examination issuing and marking is centralized at the BBE in Thimphu, although the exams themselves are administered in schools.

Teacher Education

There are two colleges of education in Bhutan, at Paro and Samtse. Dzongkha teachers attend a separate program. Every teacher must complete a four-year bachelor of education program, entry requirements for which have risen from grade 7 to grade 12 over the past decade. India still trains and provides a large proportion of Bhutanese civil servants, including education administrators and high school teachers, many with education backgrounds.

The first Bhutanese primary-level teacher training institute (TTI) was established at Samtse in 1968 with an intake of 40 boys. The Teacher Training Center and Demonstration School was built at Paro in 1975. The 1970s also saw the first university graduates returning from India, Britain, and the Philippines to form the core of secondary school teachers. In 1983, with the introduction of its first bachelor of education program, the Samtse TTI transformed into the National

Institute of Education (NIE). The first twelve teachers graduated in 1986, when teaching qualifications were also formalized. A postgraduate certificate of education was introduced in 1990, helping in-service teachers meet the new specifications. In 1992 Paro began a diploma in teaching Dzongkha, and introduced its own degree program to become the second National Institute of Education in 2000. Higher degrees were still earned at overseas universities in London, Fredericton, New Brunswick (Canada), and Sydney, New South Wales (Australia).

By 2003 the primary and Dzongkha teacher certificates were phased out in favor of degrees from Paro and Samtse. Five-year distance education programs were introduced to facilitate in-service upgrading. In 2004 Paro began a three-year, part-time, in-service diploma in school management.

Informal Education

Most informal education in Bhutan focuses on adult and functional literacy in writing, reading, business, personal hygiene, and domestic science, and is aimed primarily at women who were largely excluded under the country's earlier monastic system. Although English is the medium of instruction throughout the formal system, most informal teaching is conducted in the country's dominant language of Dzongkha. Monastic education is also still offered alongside the secular system.

Dilemmas

A system barely half a century old is bound to face problems. Many dilemmas stem from the country's isolation and lack of infrastructure, but the most pressing concern is the shortage of Bhutanese teachers. Civil service jobs confer prestige and security, but the remuneration is modest for the expectations of a demanding job. The Bhutanese school system runs for five and a half days, including Saturday mornings, with 24-hour days not uncommon. Without a substitute teacher system, any absences have to be absorbed by the schools and borne by colleagues. Resources are modest but improving, the major emphasis being on classroom activities rather than "invisible" office work. As civil servants, teachers may be deployed anywhere in the country, disrupting home and community life. Many schools are located at several days' walk from bus routes and roads; although regional centers are being developed, such isolated postings tend to lack support and collegial contact. Conversely, with growing urban enrollment, class size is also becoming an issue.

Decentralized district educations offices (DEOs) monitor education at a local level, establishing education resource centers for their regions. Yet Bhutan's intensive process of urbanization means that many of those with higher levels of education are moving from rural homes to the major urban centers at Thimphu, Paro, and Phuentsholing. While the role of the DEOs emphasizes support rather than monitoring, the tremendous rate of change borne by the current teaching cohort has proved onerous. Many teachers still come from India and elsewhere, inevitably introducing outside influences at a fundamental level and compounding difficulties in maintaining quality teaching.

Recruitment is further undermined by the significant failure rate in the early grades. Children are expected to pass all the basic subjects at each level in order to advance, and failure at any stage, for whatever reason, precludes further education. The Bhutanese are developing a dropout safety net in order to meet the need for educated personnel throughout society, including teachers competent across the full range of subject areas and levels. Counseling is being introduced, as are methods of inclusion to cater for students with special needs. In this context too, the Danish have taken a leading role in helping the Bhutanese develop programs for exceptional learners.

The Bhutanese government is now encouraging private schools to meet the growing demand that its own primary schools cannot satisfy. High school graduate recruits and extended classrooms (small local classes held by peripatetic regional-school teachers) go some way toward relieving demand. But admission to preprimary school has now risen from five to six years of age to enable more children to attend the basic primary grades.

The medium of instruction is a related issue. Although Dzongkha is the country's official language and Sharchop is the language of the indigenous majority, most formal teaching is in English. Quite apart from the fact that most Bhutanese students enter the formal system with English as a second or third language, there is growing concern about the potential loss of the country's indigenous languages.

While traditional customs such as national dress have been legislated to be worn in public, there is no similar protection for the country's indigenous languages. This problem has become even more crucial since satellite television and Internet access were introduced in 2001.

Finally relinquishing some less palatable elements of its past, Bhutan recently passed a law banning the physical disciplining of students—an inherited norm still prevalent in monastic education—and held a conference on alternative forms of discipline in November 2006. Despite inheriting the male-dominated monastic system, secular education is committed to fair and balanced gender access.

System Economics

The Bhutanese economy is based on yak and cattle herding, agriculture, and forestry, which employs roughly 60 percent of the population (which was 798,427 according to the *CIA World Factbook* figures from 2011). Bhutan's 18,147 square miles (47,000 square kilometers) of largely uninhabitable mountainous terrain makes infrastructure development difficult and expensive. Production is more cottage- than industrially based, with strong trade, monetary, and labor links to India. Tourism and hydro development represent potential growth areas, yet foreign investment is hampered by insufficiently developed trade, labor, and financial policies. Traditionally, private enterprise has not been encouraged, and income taxation has only recently been introduced, with money allocated to local municipalities rather than to education institutions themselves. The value of educational institutions to stimulate local industry is now being recognized, however, through the process of decentralization in anticipation of the change to democratic governance.

Evelyn M. Plaice and John Stewart

REFERENCES

Bhutan Tourism Corporation. www.kingdomofbhutan.com.

Central Intelligence Agency. *The CIA World Factbook*. New York: Skyhorse, 2011. https://www.cia.gov/library/publications/the-world-factbook/index.html.

Childs, Ann, Wangpo Tenzin, David Johnson, and Kiran Ramachandran. "Science Education in Bhutan: Issues and Challenges." *International Journal of Science Education* 34:1 (2011): 1–26.

Dolker, Tshering. "Perceptions of Early School Leavers in Bhutan." *RABSEL: The CERD Education Journal* 1 (Autumn 2002).

Dorji, Jagar. *Quality of Education in Bhutan*. 2nd ed. Thimphu: KMT, 2005.

Government of Bhutan. www.bhutan.gov.bt/government/index.php.

Lokamitra, Dharmachari. "The Centrality of Buddhism and Education in Developing Gross National Happiness." In *Gross National Happiness and Development: Proceedings of the First International Seminar on Operationalization of Gross National Happiness*, ed. Karma Ura and Karma Galay. Thimphu: Center for Bhutan Studies, 2004.

Ura, Karma, and Karma Galay, eds. *Gross National Happiness and Development: Proceedings of the First International Seminar on Operationalization of Gross National Happiness*. Thimphu: Center for Bhutan Studies, 2004.

VanBalkom, W. Duffie, and Ann Sherman. "Teacher Education in Bhutan: Highlights and Challenges for Reform." *Asia Pacific Journal of Education* 30:1 (2010): 43–55.

World Bank Group. "Bhutan Data Profile." http://data.worldbank.org/country/bhutan.

Bhutan Education at a Glance

General Information

Capital	Thimphu
Population	726,000
Language	Dzonkha
Adult literacy rate (ages 15 and over)	52.8%
Youth literacy rate (ages 15–24)	74.4%
GDP per capita	US$5,329
Number of phones (mobile) per 100 people	54
Number of Internet users per 100 people	14
Life expectancy at birth (years)	67

Formal Educational Information

Enrollment in preprimary school (ages 4–5)	300
Enrollment in primary school (ages 6–12)	109,000
Enrollment in lower and upper secondary school (ages 13–18)	57,000
Number of years of compulsory education	no data
Preprimary school student/teacher ratio	12
Primary school student/teacher ratio	26
Lower and upper secondary school gross student/teacher ratio	21
Preprimary school gross enrollment ratio	2%
Primary school gross enrollment ratio	111%
Lower and upper secondary school gross enrollment ratio	66%
Primary school entrants reaching grade 5	96%

Sources: Education for All, 2011; Global Education Digest, 2011; UNESCO–UIS, 2012; UNICEF, 2012; United Nations Development Programme, 2011.

INDIA

Located in South Asia, India, the seventh-largest country in the world, is home to many languages, religions, and ethnicities. The country is also the second most populated in the world. Moreover, it is the world's largest democracy in population. India's history dates to the Indus Valley civilization that flourished in the northwestern part of the Indian subcontinent from 3300 to 1300 BCE and grew into what is known as the Harappan civilization (2600 to 1900 BCE). After the collapse of the Harappan era, a number of monarchs ruled various parts of India. The Indian subcontinent was also an important trade route, a cultural hallmark, and the origin of four of the major world religions, Hinduism, Buddhism, Sikhism, and Jainism. In the first millennium the subcontinent came in contact with Zoroastrianism, Islam, Christianity, and Judaism, which have continued to shape its culture and governance.

In the 1600s European companies established trading partnerships with the subcontinent. India soon became annexed to the British East India Company and later became a colony of England. Beginning with the first war of independence against the company in 1857, a strong anticolonial struggle involved participation and leadership from various religious and ethnic groups. India and Pakistan became independent nations in 1947, following the postcolonial political reorganization in South Asia. Education was one of the major challenges of the newly independent Indian government, and "free and compulsory education" became the priority of the state. There have been several barriers in universalizing education in India, and the goal remains unaccomplished after 60 years of independence. In contemporary India, educational realities reveal stark regional contrasts. For instance, in 2001 the literacy rate for the southern state of Kerala was 90.92 percent whereas for Bihar it was recorded as 47.53 percent (Census of India 2011). In 2007 the expenditure on education in India was 3.8 percent of the gross domestic product (GDP) and 10 percent of total government expenditure. The net enrollment in primary school was recorded as 89 percent in the year 2005 (Human Development Report 2007).

Educational System

The Ministry of Human Resource Development (HRD) oversees educational affairs in India. HRD has two main divisions: the department of school education and literacy, and the department of higher education. Central and state governments are important actors in designing educational policy, curriculum, assessment, accreditation, and funding. Education is organized in the following divisions: preprimary and primary education, secondary education, higher education, distance education, and nonformal education. The K–12 programs are broadly divided into preprimary, primary (for students from six to 11 years old), secondary (11 to 15 years old), and higher secondary (15 to 17 years old). However, these programs exhibit a great deal of variation in their structures depending on the institutions and regions. Educational planning is carried out over successive five-year plans. In the initial years after independence, the provision for free and compulsory education was included in Directive Principles of State Policy that serve as guidelines to central and state governments in policy formation and practice. Article 45 of part IV of the directive principles states that children under the age of 14 should be entitled to free and compulsory education. A directive principle is not enforceable by law but is a moral and social obligation of the government. In recent years the state's role in providing education has attracted a great deal of attention in light of the debates around equal opportunity and access, universal literacy, and social justice. In 2005 the Right to Education bill attempted to shift the provision of elementary education from a directive principle to a legally enforceable, fundamental right.

Universalization of primary education has attained the utmost importance since independence. However, widespread social inequality and uneven development pose serious impediments to educational access and retention. Integrated Child Development Services and *Anganwadis* (courtyard areas and shelters that were transformed in 1975 for the purpose of combating and preventing malnourishment of children so that they can attend school) have been two of the early child care and preprimary education projects undertaken by the state. Numerous private institutions have become increasingly involved in primary and preprimary education. The preprimary programs have two stages, lower kindergarten and upper kindergarten. As for primary schools, the government has put in place measures to make them accessible, especially for rural populations that had been left outside of institutional arrangements. Thus, by the year 2000 rural India had primary schools within 0.6 miles (1 kilometer) of the places of habitation. Primary school enrollments rose steadily over the years, from 3.1 million in 1950 to 124 million in 2008. Policy responses such as the District Primary Education Programme (DPEP) and Mid-Day-Meals have been introduced to address the dropout rate in primary education.

Secondary education serves as a necessary link between primary and higher education and is expected to prepare young students to enter higher education as well as the workforce. At the end of secondary schooling, students appear for board examination and their performance determines admission to higher education. Secondary school instruction is offered in a number of languages throughout the country. English is mandatory as a second language or language of instruction, depending on the institution. Additionally, students are required to learn Hindi and a regional language at the minimum. Science, math, history, social sciences, geography, and introductory computer science are some of the subjects taught at the secondary stage. The secondary sector has expanded a great deal over the past few years. A ban on child labor, remedial classes, and nutritional support for enrolled students in government-run schools are some of the measures carried out to increase enrollment.

India has one of the largest higher education systems in the world. While HRD is the chief institutional body overseeing higher education, the central and state governments administer various institutions of higher education. In addition to several hundred state universities, there exists a large network of research and technological institutions focusing on divergent disciplines. Additionally, the University Grants Commission (UGC) is a statutory organization established by the government to coordinate research and teaching efforts and to maintain quality of the institutions. UGC provides research and teaching grants to institutions and also advises the governments on policy issues. Most universities are managed by state governments except for the 18 central universities that are governed by the union government. Central universities receive more funding than state-managed

universities and are often research-oriented. State universities are affiliated to various colleges and serve as degree-granting institutions for students enrolled in the colleges. Institutions focusing on science, engineering, agriculture, and information technology have expanded greatly in the postindependence era. The development of Indian Institutes of Technology (IIT) is a strong case in point in thinking about the direction of Indian higher education. IITs are heavily subsidized, include facilities for advanced research and learning, and have managed to maintain high standards. In their overall quality, the IITs now rank second in the world. Given the support for technical education in recent years, the HRD Ministry hopes to graduate 500,000 engineers and 1.2 million scientists each year. The private sector has increasingly invested in higher education, especially in disciplines such as medicine and engineering. In contrast, humanities and social sciences have received far less financial and institutional support over the years. Colleges, state and central universities, and a handful of private and public research institutions continue to pursue research, teaching, and training with young scholars.

Curriculum, Assessment, and Instruction

The National Council for Educational Research and Training (NCERT) is an overarching organizational body involved in curriculum design, along with other supporting organizations. National curriculum frameworks are introduced periodically to update and reform the curriculum. A wide range of languages is used in instruction, although higher education is increasingly taught in English. Preprimary and primary education lay out the foundation for learning. Schools vary in terms of the medium of instruction; however, the common subjects introduced at the primary level include math, one or two languages, science, geography, and arts. Learning emphasis for primary education begins with local contexts and concrete examples that are followed by abstraction in later stages. Secondary education offers students opportunities to learn geometry, biology, chemistry, physics, history, civics, physical training, computers, and other electives. Students are evaluated by their teachers all through the academic year and their performance determines their promotion to the next level. Student assessments are conducted by schools until secondary school certification examinations, which are carried out by educational boards. Performances on secondary examinations and some of the entrance tests determine college admission. Curriculum in higher education is designed by the state and central universities in charge, which also conduct evaluations.

History of Teacher Education in India

Teacher education in postindependence India has undergone massive expansion and transformation over the past six decades. The changes in policy production as well as practices of teacher education have evolved in sync with the broader developments in educational policy in India. An overview of teacher education is therefore connected to the conceptions of educational philosophy as well as changing social contexts that have influenced teacher education. The following three shifts can be observed in teacher education in India: a mix of indigenous and Western traditions of knowledge in the nineteenth century, a redefinition of mass education to suit nationalist orientation in the early twentieth century, and a sustained emphasis on decentralization and community involvement in education since the 1980s. In addition to the questions of epistemology, pedagogy, curriculum practices, and institutional norms, teachers' work is significantly shaped by changing assumptions about the roles teachers play in a particular cultural economy. In the Indian context, teacher preparation programs have emerged out of a variety of reasons: to help shape the citizenry, to create equal opportunity, to prepare a competent workforce, and to streamline learning.

Historians of Indian education draw attention to a wide range of philosophical traditions that informed learning and knowledge production. From self-realization and awakening to complete liberation, education in ancient India was integral to the religious and social order. In its conception and practice, education was understood to be nonobjective, noninstitutionalized, and centered on the individual person. In *Ancient Indian Education* (1947 [1989]), Radhakumud Mookerji gives the following account of a common educational practice: "The pupil must find the teacher. He must live with him as a member of his family and is treated by him in every way as his

son. The school is a natural formation, not artificially constituted. It is the home of the teacher. . . . The pupil is to imbibe the inward method of the teacher, the secrets of his efficiency, the spirit of his life and work, and these things are too subtle to be taught." Poromesh Acharya (1978) argues that Indian education began to fade away as British educational policies set in: "It is interesting that the indigenous system did not die a natural death. In fact, it was extinguished by the British rulers through their policy of a complete system of education. They introduced a primary school system leading to higher education on the British model, which was completely different from the *Pathsala* system." The breadth of the traditional Indian educational system, however, makes for an incomplete picture without the mention of its exclusionary structure. Historically, educational opportunities in South Asia were not open to all. While traditional Hindu education was organized on the basis of caste, Islamic education was open only to aristocrats and higher classes.

In order to think about the shifts in Indian education and the emergence of modern, institutionalized forms of education, it would be instructive to consider the changes in the political economy of India. In the sixteenth century, the Indian subcontinent became an important center for the spice, tea, cotton, and opium trades. Following the Dutch, Portuguese, and French companies in the region, the British East India Company began trading with the Indian subcontinent and Southeast Asia. In 1600 the company was granted an English royal charter with the intention of favoring trade privileges to India. Expansion of European trade posts brought new changes to South Asia. In the beginning the East India Company confined itself to trade deals in ivory, silk, spices, and cotton, but its expanding economic power was a precursor to the future British colonial power in the subcontinent. The British hold over India grew amid a number of political transformations. With the Industrial Revolution under way, England asserted its dominance over the company's growing military and economic power. After concentrating on India to satisfy their imperial ambitions, the British took advantage of the collapse of the Mogul empire. In 1764 the resistance put forth by the rulers of Bengal and Oudh was crushed by the British, and the year 1765 marked the real beginning of the British Empire in India as a territorial dominion. By 1835 the direction of British intervention in India changed gears and education came to be deployed as an important tool to create model subjects of the empire. The British were dependent on administrative and service labor in India. Thomas Macaulay's articulation (1835) draws attention to the centrality of education in sustaining the colonial rule: "We must do our best to form a class who may be interpreters between us and the millions whom we govern, a class of persons Indian in blood and colour, but English in taste, in opinions, words and intellect." Simply put, the purpose of British schools and colleges in India was to meet the needs of service professionals and to create a class of Indians who would support British colonization. Macaulay was not alone in maintaining the cognitive superiority of the English language and using it to defend the empire. J.N. Farquhar wrote, "The new educational policy of the Government created during these years the modern educated class of India. These are men who think and speak in English habitually, who are proud of their citizenship in the British Empire, who are devoted to English literature, and whose intellectual life has been almost entirely formed by the thought of the West; large numbers of them enter government services, while the rest practice law, medicine or teaching, or take to journalism or business" (*South Asian History* n.d.).

The history of teacher education programs is a testament to the overall changes in education steered by the British. The transition from a noninstitutional to an institutional setting of education also signaled a reworking of the goals and meanings of being a teacher. It is useful to understand the context that produced the discourse of "new Indian education." This discourse was based on a range of seemingly contradictory reasons that brought education to the forefront. The role of education and the educated classes in England's industrial and scientific progress was an important part of the context of changing aspirations in India. Similarly, the colonial logic and convenience behind spreading education in the colonies was a significant factor. Finally, India's political leaders and their visions of linking education to the cause of national liberation played an important part in popularizing education. The beginning of an official teacher education program can be traced to the Bethune school in Calcutta that stated the need to train female teachers for girls. From 1868 to 1872 a number of teacher training centers were established in the eastern part of India. Philanthropists such as

Mary Carpenter became involved in teacher training programs for women. Teacher preparation institutions in the nineteenth century focused on orienting teachers toward Western science and philosophical traditions. English education had a tenuous relationship with the Indian elite and the emerging political leaders. While the prominent leadership in the Indian National Congress (INC) viewed English education as synonymous with colonial rule, some reformers supported it. Raja Ram Mohan Roy, for instance, saw English education as an important step in creating a society based on science and rationalism. Jyotirao Phule's support for English education was based on its hoped-for ability to dismantle the age-old Brahmanical system of oppression.

In the early twentieth century, the intensification of the anticolonial struggle in India translated into new ways of thinking about education. In particular, education became closely associated with the development of a strong national character. According to Glyn Richards's account in *Gandhi's Philosophy of Education* (2001), Mohandas Gandhi opposed British education for its elitism as well as its lack of relevance to everyday life in India. Stating his vision, Gandhi wrote, "My plan to impart primary education through the medium of village handicrafts like spinning and carding, etc., is thus conceived as the spearhead of a silent revolution fraught with the most far reaching consequences." The Indian National Congress became an influential national political organization by integrating the agenda of nationalism, inclusion, and social reform. Education played an important part in the ways INC envisioned future democratic society in India. On October 22, 1937, the first Congress of National Education was held in Wardha, where Gandhi spelled out the important tenets of education he envisioned: free education for all, mother tongue as medium of instruction, focus on self-reliance, productive labor and enhancement of skills. This structure sought to bring about the change with distinct, Indian characteristics. In this view, the role of teachers became explicitly connected to creating productive citizens with national character. It was during this time that the political consensus emerged declaring education to be the responsibility of the state. Thus national ideology and aspirations were key agents in the construction of the vision for the public education system in India.

The postcolonial Indian state continued to share this vision of education and made it a central project of nation-building as well. The first education commission of independent India declared that the real task ahead was "to create, not a *lesser* England but a *greater* India" (Naik 1997). Creating opportunities for education was given importance in the hope that education would be instrumental in equalizing a population segregated along the lines of caste, class, and gender. Establishing a growing network of state-run schools (known as "municipal/government schools"), the state promised free, compulsory education for all children. Partially state-funded schools and a few private schools were also introduced, although the affordability of government schools was crucial in opening up participatory spaces for disadvantaged communities. Teacher education programs for primary schools were established at first, overseen and funded by the state. The rapid expansion of these primary-level teacher preparation programs soon led to the formation of programs focusing on secondary school education, managed by both state and private institutions. The teacher's role was understood in terms of specific goals and expectations. In the words of NCERT (1988), "The new teacher we have in mind has to translate national goals [into] educational actions. He has to communicate to his pupils the importance of and the feeling for national integrity and unity; the need for a scientific attitude, a commitment to excellence in standards of work and action and right attitudes and values besides being proficient in the skills related to teaching." Teacher education programs expanded rapidly in order to meet the needs of the growing educational sector. Given that a large number of historically excluded people were receiving institutional access to education for the first time, the mission of teacher education programs centered on creating a teaching force that would impart values such as equality, empathy, and unity.

Policy Perspectives on Teacher Education

The development of teacher education programs is shaped by larger policy changes in education. The government of India founded the National Council of Educational Research and Training (NCERT) in 1961 to carry out curriculum design, educational research, and teacher preparation. NCERT assumes national leadership and works with numerous state and district organizations. The entire teacher education system involves "more than 2,200 teacher education institutions and 225 university departments of education. Additionally, there are networks of resources and training centers such as the District Institutes of Education and Training (DIET) (500), Institute of Advanced Studies in Education (IASE) (38) and State Councils of Educational Research and Training (SCERT) (32)" (Panda 2005). The estimated teaching force is close to 5 million, of which about 90 percent are formally trained in teacher education programs.

Preservice programs for secondary school teachers, also known as bachelor of education programs, require one year of coursework for student teachers. Elementary and pre-elementary education programs (Diploma in Education) involve two years of coursework. The courses for elementary and secondary teacher education have the following common elements: (1) foundation courses on education, (2) teaching methodology, and (3) practicum. Student teachers are exposed to the issues of teaching multiple subjects, including language, math, science, environmental studies, art, and physical education. The National Council of Teacher Education (NCTE), a central body responsible for preparing curriculum frameworks, oversees teacher education programs and monitors quality. NCTE develops a national curriculum framework (NCF) in the form of guidelines for various states, institutions, and teaching practitioners. Following the guidelines prepared by NCTE, the State Council of Educational Research and Training (SCERT) and State Directorate of Education prepare the teacher education curriculum for the primary level. The curriculum for secondary teacher education is prepared by the universities offering the teacher education programs. The first framework of teacher education (1978) sought to highlight the relevance of education to focus on the needs and concerns of children who enroll in schools. According to this framework, teacher training must focus on practical connections of school to everyday life so that students can benefit as adults. Further, the framework states that teacher education must include curriculum that reflects the social transformations in Indian society. The following broad visions of the teacher's role were identified in the first framework:

- To develop Gandhian values of education such as nonviolence, truthfulness, self-discipline, self-reliance, dignity of labor
- To act as an agent of social change in the community
- To act as liaison between the school and the community, and to employ suitable ways and means for integrating community life and resources with schoolwork
- To not only use but also conserve environmental resources and preserve historical monuments and other cultural heritage
- To express warm and positive attitudes toward growing children and their academic, socio-emotional, and personal problems, and to use professional skills to guide and counsel them
- To develop an understanding of the objectives of school education in the Indian context and awareness of the role of the school in achieving the goals of building up a democratic, secular and socialist society

The second framework (1988) goes on to include environmental and aesthetic components of learning in the objectives.

- To develop in students qualities of democratic citizenship, tolerance, concern for others, cooperation, responsibility, and commitment to social justice
- To promote environmental consciousness, a secular outlook, and a scientific temper
- To organize and participate in programs of community service and development
- To engage in developmental activities in the community, extension activities, and community service
- To understand social, cultural, and moral values oriented toward the unity and integration of the Indian people—democracy, secularism, scientific temper, egalitarianism, cultural heritage, conservation of the environment, and civic responsibility
- To develop aesthetic interests and appreciation—literary, cultural, and artistic pursuits

Similarly, the National Policy of Education (NPE) (1986) had an important role in shaping primary education in India. NPE advocated the following recommendations for primary education: (1) child-centered approach in teaching, (2) at least two rooms in every school with all-weather usable learning materials, (3) expansion of child-care programs, (4) measures to address dropouts, (5) enhancement of the nonformal stream of education, and (6) strengthening of teacher education programs. Specifically, NPE advised the following goals, addressing issues of equity, access, and equality:

- A common educational structure to be envisaged by the government
- Regular updates of the national curriculum framework
- Education to be used as an agent of basic change and to be accessible to women and minority populations
- Proper measures to address students with disabilities

Since 1986 local districts became important units that housed teacher education programs and resource centers. Each district was prepared with a district-level resource center and district institutes of education and training (DIET). As for secondary teacher education, the teacher preparation programs were strengthened with infrastructural support as well as enhanced professional expertise. Additionally, nearly 50 branches of Institute of Advanced Studies in Education (IASE) were established as model resource centers and education programs for preservice and in-service teachers. In this direction, the Project Mass Orientation of School Teachers was initiated in order to upgrade and streamline teacher education programs.

The District Primary Education Programme (DPEP) was another important policy initiative that was introduced in the 1990s, addressing two issues: universal literacy and reduction in the dropout rate. As part of the Structural Adjustment Program, DPEP was planned to offset any adverse impacts of India's policies of economic liberalization. The policies advocated decentralized management of education. Further, DPEP sought to get more community involvement in primary education. The participation of community here is articulated within the provisions of para-teachers who are members of the local community and hired on a contract basis in schools. The growing number of para-teachers points at the trend of casualization of teaching labor.

While the proposed objectives of various policy

India Education at a Glance

General Information

Capital	New Delhi
Population	1.2 billion
Languages	Hindi, English
Adult literacy rate (ages 15 and over)	62.8%
Youth literacy rate (ages 15–24)	81.1%
GDP per capita	US$3,582
Number of phones (mobile) per 100 people	61
Number of Internet users per 100 people	8
Life expectancy at birth (years)	65

Formal Educational Information

Enrollment in preprimary school (ages 3–5)	40.4 million
Enrollment in primary school (ages 6–10)	145.4 million
Enrollment in lower and upper secondary school (ages 11–17)	101.7 million
Number of years of compulsory education	9 (ages 6–14)
Preprimary school student/teacher ratio	40
Primary school student/teacher ratio	40
Lower and upper secondary school gross student/teacher ratio	25
Preprimary school gross enrollment ratio	55%
Primary school gross enrollment ratio	117%
Lower and upper secondary school gross enrollment ratio	63%
Primary school entrants reaching grade 5	69%

Sources: Education for All, 2011; Global Education Digest, 2011; UNESCO–UIS, 2012; UNICEF, 2012; United Nations Development Programme, 2011.

documents are laudable, since an equitable, just education is one of the most important needs of contemporary India, the policies have not translated into practice. A large population remains excluded from social progress. It is also important to understand the larger context, working conditions, and constraints with which teachers in India work. Less than desirable working conditions, especially in the government-run schools in impoverished rural and urban regions, would perhaps top the list of concerns. Government-run schools continue to be understaffed; numerous schools in rural areas are run as one-teacher-schools. Large-scale disparities affect the work of teachers working in small towns, rural areas, and remote areas. Manabi Majumdar (2004) contends that in 1998, the average rural schools had only two instructional rooms and only 41 percent of schools had drinking water. Similarly, the PROBE report (1999) found that only one-fourth of the surveyed schools had a minimum of two teachers, two classrooms, and some teaching aids. Additionally, the report documents the status of the facilities in Indian schools that are nonfunctioning.

More specifically, 26 percent of blackboards are either nonfunctioning or not available. Only 48 percent of all schools have playgrounds. Forty-one percent of all schools have running drinking water, and only 11 percent of all schools have working toilets. Also, 22 percent of all schools have libraries.

Teachers receive less than adequate institutional support for enhancing their professional skills or experimenting with their teaching. Even within the decentralized system, the curriculum is prepared by higher authorities, away from the crowded, underfunded classrooms. As India reorients its educational policy, emphasizing the knowledge economy and the quality of education in order to suit global pressures, a serious rethinking of its teacher education programs is necessary.

Rearticulation and capacity-building of India's teacher education programs are essential to develop quality education centered on equality, empathy, and inclusion.

Shivali Tukdeo

REFERENCES

Acharya, Poromesh. "Indigenous Vernacular Education in Pre-British Era: Traditions and Problems." *Economic and Political Weekly* (Bombay) 13, December 2, 1978, 1981, 1983–1988.

Burton, Antoinette. *At the Heart of the Empire: Indians and the Colonial Encounter in Late-Victorian Britain.* Berkeley: University of California Press, 1998.

The Census of India. *Number of Literates & Literacy Rate.* 2011. http://censusindia.gov.in/2011census/censusinfodashboard/index.html.

Central Intelligence Agency. *The CIA World Factbook.* New York: Skyhorse, 2011. https://www.cia.gov/library/publications/the-world-factbook/index.html.

Government of India. *Know India: State and Union Territories.* www.india.gov.in/knowindia/state_uts.php.

Hall, Catherine. *Civilising Subjects: Metropole and Colony in the English Imagination, 1830–1867.* Cambridge, UK: Polity Press, 2002.

Human Development Report. *Human Development Index Value.* 2007. http://hdrstats.undp.org/countries/data_sheets/cty_ds_IND.html.

Kosambi, Meera. *Pandita Ramabai's American Encounter: The Peoples of the United States.* Bloomington: Indiana University Press, 2003.

Macaulay, Thomas. "Minute of 2 February 1835 on Indian Education." In *Macaulay: Prose and Poetry*, ed. George Malcolm Young, 721–729. Cambridge, MA: Harvard University Press, 1970.

Majumdar, H.B. "Origin and Development of Teacher Education in India" In *Education of Teachers in India*, ed. Shridhar Nath. Mukerji. New Delhi: S. Chand, 1963.

Majumdar, Manabi. "'Classes for the Masses?' Social Capital, Social Distance and the Quality of the Government School System." In *Interrogating Social Capital: The Indian Experience*, ed. Bhattacharyya, et al. New Delhi: SAGE, 2004.

Mookerji, Radhakumud. *Ancient Indian Education: Brahmanical and Buddhist*. Delhi: Motilal Banarasidas, 1947 [2011].

Naik, Jayant Pandurang. *The Education Commission and After*. New Delhi: APH, 1997.

National Council on Educational Research and Training (NCERT). *Human Rights: A Source Book*. New Delhi: NCERT, 1996.

———. *National Curriculum for Elementary and Secondary Education: A Framework*. New Delhi: NCERT, 1988.

———. *The National Curriculum Framework for School Education*. New Delhi: NCERT, 2000.

Panda, Pranati. "Responsiveness of Teacher Education Curriculum Towards Human Rights Education in India." *Human Rights Education in Asian Schools* 1:8 (2009). www.hurights.or.jp/archives/human_rights_education_in_asian_schools/.

PROBE team. *Public Report on Basic Education in India*. New Delhi: Oxford University Press, 1999.

Richards, Glyn. *Gandhi's Philosophy of Education*. New Delhi: Oxford University Press, 2001.

Scharfe, Hartmut. *Education in Ancient India*. Leiden, the Netherlands: Brill, 2002.

Sinha, Mrinalini. *Colonial Masculinity: The 'Manly Englishman' and the 'Effeminate Bengali' in the Late Nineteenth Century*. Manchester, UK: Manchester University Press, 1995.

UNESCO. *Global Education Digest 2012: Comparing Education Statistics Across the World*. Montreal: UNESCO Institute for Statistics, 2012.

UNESCO–IBE. www.ibe.unesco.org/en/worldwide/unesco-regions/asia-and-the-pacific/india.html.

IRAN

The Islamic Republic of Iran is located in western Asia. The principal language is Farsi (Persian), spoken by about 50 percent of the population; it is also the national language. Turkic-speaking Azerbaijanis make up about 27 percent of the population, and Kurds, Arabs, Balochis, and Turkomans less than 25 percent. The majority of Persians and Azerbaijanis are Shiite Muslims, while the other ethnic groups are mainly Sunni Muslims. There are also small minorities of Christians, Jews, and Zoroastrians. The official religion is the Shia branch of Islam.

During World War II Iran supported Nazi Germany. The Allied forces occupied Iran and forced Reza Shah to abdicate in favor of his son, Mohammad Reza Pahlavi. Pahlavi was deposed in 1953 in a military coup engineered by the US and British intelligence services. The shah fled the country but returned to power the next year. The shah's policy, which included the redistribution of land to small farmers and the enfranchisement of women, provoked opposition from landlords and the conservative Muslim clergy. Following intense civil unrest in Tehran, the shah left Iran with his family in 1979. The Ayatollah Ruhollah Khomeini returned from exile and took power, and Iran was declared an Islamic republic. Iran's macroeconomic performance has been strong. In the first five years of the twenty-first century, Iran's gross domestic product (GDP) grew by an average annual rate of 5.1 percent. The growth is largely owing to rising oil prices, but the private sector has also seen strong growth.

Educational System

The Ministry of Education is in charge of the school system and has the responsibility for some teacher training and technical institutes. The ministry employs the highest number of civil servants—42 percent of the total—and receives 22 percent of the national budget. The school system is divided into six cycles: preschool, primary, middle (or guidance), secondary, preuniversity, and postsecondary. Primary education is mandatory under the Iranian constitution. Admission to postsecondary institutions is through a nationwide entrance examination. In general, education is free of charge, though private schools and universities authorized by law are allowed to charge tuition fees. Most primary, middle, and secondary schools are state schools. Preschool, which is not mandatory, starts at age five for a duration of one year. Primary school starts at age six for a duration of five years. Middle school, also known as the guidance cycle, covers grades 6 to 8 for children aged 11 to 13. This guidance cycle aims at evaluating the student's proficiency to pursue higher education or vocational or technical education during secondary school. Secondary school covers grade 9 to grade 11 for children from 14 to 17 years old for a duration of three years, and is divided into two main branches, academic/general and technical/vocational. The one-year preuniversity program prepares students to enter university and higher education institutions.

Precompulsory and Compulsory Education

Preschool is a noncompulsory one-year program for children who are five years old. There is no exam at the end of the cycle and students automatically proceed to the following cycle. Primary school (*dabestan*) is a five-year program for children aged six to 11 in which students receive a broad-ranging general education. Promotion to each grade is based on annual examinations. Students complete this cycle of their education by passing the primary school leaving examination held at the end of grade 5. Those who fail must wait a whole year before taking the exam again. If they fail a second time, they cannot go on to the next phase of education and must instead pursue basic vocational training. Middle school is a three-year program for children between 11 and 14 years old in which students receive further general education. The subjects emphasize both theoretical and applied knowledge with the aim of determining whether students will pursue academic or technical/vocational studies. Students who successfully pass a regional examination conducted at the end of the cycle are awarded a Certificate of General Education. Those who receive acceptable grades then continue their education in either the academic or technical/vocational tracks.

Postcompulsory Education

Eighty-five percent of Iranian students who complete the middle school go on to the secondary school cycle, a three-year program for students aged 14 to 17. It is divided into academic/general and technical/vocational branches. The choice of either branch is up to students and is dependent on their qualifications.

The academic branch is divided into literature and culture, socioeconomic studies, physics and mathematics, and experimental sciences. At the end of this cycle, students take national examinations conducted by the Ministry of Education. Successful candidates are awarded the *diplom-motevaseteh* (national high school diploma), which provides access to the preuniversity year or employment.

Students who complete the academic branch and pass a national examination are eligible to enter the preuniversity cycle. This phase of education lasts for one year, leading to the Certificate of Completion/Diploma. Students who complete the pre-university cycle are eligible to take the konkur (university entrance examination) for admission to the first year of undergraduate study.

The technical branch covers technical, business, and agriculture studies. Students who enter the technical/vocational track continue with a two-year vocational or agricultural program or a four-year technical program at a technical school. The two-year vocational program (ages 14 to 16) is designed to train skilled workers and farmers and leads to the Trade Certificate. The four-year technical program, which trains lower-grade technicians, is divided into three main branches: technical, services, and agriculture. It leads to a Second Class Technician's Certificate. Higher skilled workers are trained at postsecondary institutes of technology.

Iran has about 46 universities, 60 postsecondary technical institutions, 200 colleges/higher institutes/professional schools, and a number of teacher training colleges. When the Islamic Republic was proclaimed in 1979, the High Council of the Cultural Revolution was established as the supreme policy-making body for higher education. Although Iran has a number of private colleges, most of the country's universities are state-run. The 13 most prominent ones are the University of Tehran, Tarbiat Modaress University, Shahid Beheshti University, Sharif Technical University, Amirkabir Technology University, Iran Science and Technology University, Tabriz University, Isfahan Technology University, Shiraz University, Isfahan University, Mashhad University, Ahwaz University, and Tarbiat Moallem University.

Curriculum, Assessment, and Instruction

During preschool, students receive the basic notions needed to enter primary schools. Preschool develops children's physical and mental power. In bilingual areas of Iran, a one-month preparatory course is offered prior to the first grade of primary school to ensure students' ability to communicate in Persian.

The subjects taught in primary school are the Quran, religious teaching, Persian composition, dictation, Persian reading and comprehension, social studies, arts (painting, calligraphy, and workmanship), mathematics, and physical education.

The subjects taught in middle school are Persian language and literature, mathematics, natural sciences, foreign language, Arabic language, Quran, religion and ethics, social studies, sports, arts, and vocational and technical studies. English as a second language is introduced from grade 7. In this cycle the abilities and interests of students are recognized. At the end of the cycle students take a regional examination under the supervision of provincial boards of education. Those who pass become eligible to proceed to the next cycle.

The academic branch of secondary school is divided into literature and culture, socioeconomic, physics and mathematics, and experimental sciences sections. The courses offered in the first year are common, followed by specialized subjects based on the student's aptitude, interest, and grades. The technical branch offers general courses followed by specialized industrial, agricultural, or business and vocation courses. This branch is particularly designed to train technicians for the labor market. The preuniversity program prepares students to enter university and higher education institutions. It entitles students to sit for the Konkur (national entrance examination). Qualified students entering the technical-vocational branch can continue studies leading to the postdiploma degree (technician) or sit for the preuniversity examination.

Higher education is provided by comprehensive universities, specialized universities, universities of technology, medical universities, teacher training centers, and private institutions. The main subjects currently offered in the Iranian universities comprise natural and basic sciences, humanities, medical and health sciences, arts and literature, engineering, and agriculture. The highest number of students, 26 percent, is found in engineering branches. This figure is followed by 24 percent in medical and health fields of study, 13 percent in pedagogic and teacher training, and 8 percent in literature, humanities, and academic theology.

Teacher Education

Primary and middle school teachers are trained in a number of institutions under the auspices of the Ministry of Education. They are trained in two years in teacher training centers where they obtain an associate degree. After students finish grade 10 in secondary school, they can be admitted to this special teacher training program. The graduates are entitled to teach in either rural or urban primary schools. Rural teacher training centers are designed to train teachers who will be teaching in rural areas. After finishing middle school (grade 8), students are trained in rural teacher training centers for four years. The graduates will teach schools in rural areas. Middle school teachers are trained in middle school training centers designed for students who have already graduated from secondary school and hold their diploma through a nationwide examination. They are required to study for another two years in teacher training institutions that offer courses in 14 specialized subjects. They are awarded an associate diploma upon graduation. Each student is supposed to specialize in only one subject. The major subjects are primary education, Persian language, English language, French language, experimental sciences, social sciences, mathematics, vocational and technical training, Islamic ethics and Arabic language, art, fostering affairs (child development), physical education, and children with special needs. Secondary school teachers are trained in universities under the jurisdiction of the Ministry of Culture and Higher Education. Students must hold a university-level bachelor's degree. There are two ways to qualify: a bachelor's degree holder in a field other than education can complete a one-year teacher training program, or a secondary school graduate can complete a four-year program leading to a bachelor of education degree. The universities devoted to the task of training secondary school teachers include Tarbiat Moallem (Teacher Training) University in Tehran, faculties of education at major universities, and colleges of education run by the Ministry of Education; the Faculty of Education at the University of Tehran trains educational specialists and not classroom teachers. Several major universities, such as Tabriz, Mashhad, and Isfahan University, offer postgraduate degrees in education.

Informal Education

There are about 2,300 adult education schools for adults who would like to continue their education. Community learning centers, run by the Literacy

Movement Organization, are designed to provide training opportunities for those in rural and underdeveloped areas and throughout the country who never learned to read and write. With more than 2,000 centers throughout Iran, community learning centers comprise the greatest number of adult education schools in the country. They have employed some 55,000 instructors, distributed 300 easy-to-read books and manuals, and provided literacy classes to about 1 million people, both men and women. The initiative paid particular attention to the needs of women who headed households. In addition to teaching basic academic skills and vocational training, the program offers classes in "skills for life," such as child care, communication, and self-esteem. Mosques provide informal education in Islamic studies. For Afghan refugees living in Iran, various international organizations, in a joint venture with the Iranian government, are providing education. The program supports home schooling and informal education, as well as classes given in regular schools.

System Economics

Education represents 5 percent of Iran's GDP, which is US$6.9 billion. It represents 22 percent of the total government expenditure. Thirty-two percent of education spending is appropriated for primary and middle schools, 46 percent is appropriated for secondary schools, and 22 percent is appropriated for postsecondary schools.

Future Prospects

International education researchers have consistently argued that Iran must reconsider its treatment of its citizens, particularly women, if it is to improve its educational system and transform its society into a knowledge-based economy. To be sure, men, with an 86 percent literacy rate, have an 11 percent edge over women, whose literacy rate is 75 percent. Moreover, the hierarchical nature of social class in the country has placed much of its population in dire financial straits and poverty. According to most agencies, approximately 18 percent of the population in Iran is below the poverty line. Modifications to the traditionalist judicial and political order of Iran are needed in order to eradicate practices of alienation and provide oppressed Iranians with upward mobility through formal education.

Charles Lin

REFERENCES

Central Intelligence Agency. *The CIA World Factbook*. New York: Skyhorse, 2011. https://www.cia.gov/library/publications/the-world-factbook/index.html.

Earth Trends, Country Profiles. "Iran." http://earthtrends.wri.org/country_profiles/index.php?theme=5.

The Economist. "Iran." In *Pocket World in Figures*. 2011.

Embassy of the Islamic Republic of Iran in Oslo, Norway, Student Advisory. "Education System in Iran." www.iran-embassy-oslo.no/embassy/educat.htm.

"Iran." In *The Europa World Yearbook*, vol. 1. London: Routledge, 2009.

Sedgwick, Robert, ed. "Education in Post-Revolutionary Iran." *World Education News and Reviews* 13:3 (2000). www.wes.org/ewenr/00may/practical.htm.

Shahidian, Hammed. "The Education of Women in the Islamic Republic of Iran." *Journal of Women's History* 2:3 (2010): 6–38.

Iran Education at a Glance

General Information

Capital	Tehran
Population	73.9 million
Language	Farsi (Persian)
Adult literacy rate (ages 15 and over)	85%
Youth literacy rate (ages 15–24)	98.7%
GDP per capita	US$11,570
Number of phones (mobile) per 100 people	91
Number of Internet users per 100 people	13
Life expectancy at birth (years)	72

Formal Educational Information

Enrollment in preprimary school (age 5)	456,000
Enrollment in primary school (ages 6–10)	5.6 million
Enrollment in lower and upper secondary school (ages 11–17)	7.9 million
Number of years of compulsory education	8 (ages 6–13)
Preprimary school student/teacher ratio	27%
Primary school student/teacher ratio	20%
Lower and upper secondary school gross student/teacher ratio	no data
Preprimary school gross enrollment ratio	42%
Primary school gross enrollment ratio	114%
Lower and upper secondary school gross enrollment ratio	91%
Primary school entrants reaching grade 5	94%

Sources: Education for All, 2011; Global Education Digest, 2011; UNESCO–UIS, 2012; UNICEF, 2012; United Nations Development Programme, 2011.

UNESCO–IBE. www.ibe.unesco.org/en/worldwide/unesco-
    regions/asia-and-the-pacific/iran-islamic-republic-of.html.
UNICEF. www.unicef.org/infobycountry/iran.html.

IRAQ

The Republic of Iraq, an Arab country, is located in western Asia. The official languages are Arabic and Kurdish. Other spoken languages are Assyrian, Armenian, Turkmen, and English. The majority of the Iraqi population is Arab, followed by Kurds; the rest are Assyrian and Turkmen. The official religion is Islam. Almost all Iraqis are Muslim; the rest are Christian. Iraq's government system is a multiparty republic with one legislative house, the Council of Representatives.

Educational System

The Ministry of Education administers public education and supervises private education. The Directorates General of Education in the governorates implement the plans and policies of the ministry and supervise the educational process. The Ministry of Higher Education is in charge of postsecondary and higher education. Education is free at all stages for all Iraqis. Education is compulsory at the primary level, lasting for six years, for children ages six through 11.

The education system comprises three stages: kindergarten, primary, and secondary (intermediate and preparatory cycles). Higher education is provided by public and private institutions: universities, technical institutes, and private colleges. These institutions offer programs leading to diplomas, as well as to bachelor's, master's, and doctorate degrees.

Precompulsory and Compulsory Education

Kindergarten, which is not compulsory, lasts for two years, for children entering at age four and exiting at age six. Kindergarten education aims at removing the boundaries between school subjects and encouraging integrated educational situations to stimulate children's interests and enhance their energy. It prepares children for primary school.

Primary education, which is compulsory, lasts for six years, covering grades 1 through 6, for children entering at age six and exiting at age 12. Primary school students receive foundation education and basic general knowledge, preparing them for intermediate education.

Postcompulsory Education

Secondary education, which is not compulsory, comprises two cycles: intermediate and preparatory. Intermediate education lasts for three years, covering grades 7 through 9, for children entering at age 12 and exiting at age 15. Intermediate education aims at enriching students' knowledge received in the primary stage, especially in the area of language and general education. Students who successfully complete their intermediate education are awarded the Intermediate Education Certificate and can continue on to preparatory education.

General preparatory education lasts for three years, covering grades 10 through 12, for children entering at age 15 and exiting at age 18. Preparatory education aims at preparing students for higher education or the labor market. During the three years of general preparatory education, students choose a track of study from two available tracks (scientific and literary). There also are vocational preparatory schools, which last for three years, offering four tracks: industrial, agricultural, commercial, and veterinary. Students who successfully complete their preparatory education are awarded the Preparatory Education Certificate or the Vocational Baccalaureate in the chosen track and can continue on to higher education or join the labor market.

Higher education is provided by public and private institutions: universities, technical institutes, and private colleges. These institutions offer two- and three-year programs leading to diplomas, four- to six-year programs leading to bachelor's degrees, and further study beyond the bachelor's degree leading to higher diplomas, master's, and doctorate degrees. Among the universities are Baghdad University, Al-Basrah University, Al-Kufa University, Al-Mosul University, Babil University, Kirkuk University, Koya University, Al-Anbar University, Al-Qadisiya University, Deyali University, Wassit University, and University of Tikrit.

Curriculum, Assessment, and Instruction

Kindergarten education develops the child's personality: physically, psychologically, socially, and mentally. It also takes into consideration individual differences.

Subjects taught in primary education, grades 1 through 6, are Islamic education, Arabic language, mathematics, science, art education, and physical education. Additional subjects taught are songs and music in grades 1 and 2; social studies in grade 4; English language in grades 3 through 6; history, geography, and national and social education in grades 5 and 6. Emphasis is on Arabic language and mathematics.

Subjects taught in intermediate education, grades 7 through 9, are Islamic education, Arabic language, English language, history, geography, mathematics, chemistry, physics, biology, art education, physical education and sports, and national and social education. Emphasis is on Arabic language, English language, and mathematics.

In the first, second and third years of general preparatory education, grades 10 through 12, two tracks are offered: scientific and literary. Subjects taught in the scientific track are Islamic education; Arabic language; English language; mathematics; chemistry; physics; biology; physical education, and art education. Plus, Kurdish language in grade 10 Emphasis is on mathematics, chemistry, physics, biology, English language, and Arabic language. Subjects taught in the literary track are Islamic education; Arabic language; English language; history; geography; mathematics; physical education, and art education. Plus, Kurdish language and sociology in grade 10, philosophy and psychology in grade 11, and economics in grades 11 and 12. Emphasis is on Arabic language and English language.

School and general examinations aim at measuring and evaluating students' achievement. Evaluation and examination instruments are periodically revised and developed by a specialized committee. School examinations measure students' performance throughout the year. The Ministry of Education also holds three general examinations: at the primary level to qualify graduates for admission to the intermediate level; at the intermediate level to qualify graduates for admission to the various tracks of the preparatory level; and at the preparatory level to qualify graduates for admission to higher education or for entry into the labor market.

Higher education is provided by public and private institutions in various specializations, such as arts, science, medicine, and engineering. Technical institutes and colleges provide higher technical education programs in many fields, such as engineering, administration, applied arts, agricultural, and medical studies. These programs last for two years, with most of the study hours devoted to practical education, leading to diplomas. Most bachelor's degree programs last for four years. Programs in architecture, veterinary medicine, dentistry, and pharmacy last for five years, and in medicine for six years. Master's degree programs last for two years beyond the bachelor's degree. Some specialized institutions provide programs in some medical fields, leading to higher diplomas. Doctorate degree programs last for three years beyond the master's degree, including one year for coursework and two years for research and dissertation. Some specialized institutes offer a two-year postgraduate higher diploma.

Teacher Education

Primary school teachers can qualify in two ways: teachers receive training in a five-year program after intermediate education at teacher training institutes, leading to a diploma in primary education, or students are admitted to two-year teachers institutes after completing their preparatory education. Most of these institutes were converted into four-year teachers colleges at university level. Intermediate and preparatory school teachers must be graduates of the colleges of education based in universities. Preservice and in-service teacher training programs are available in the governorates. In-service training programs provide teachers with new experiences and acquaint them with innovations in various fields of education and science.

Informal Education

Informal education is considered to be within the framework of lifelong education. It includes juvenile classes, private institutes, training centers, and lifelong educational activities. Juvenile classes, lasting for four years, are for out-of-school children aged 11 through 14 years. Students study primary school curriculum, including practical and theoretical elements. Those who graduate qualify to pursue their studies or join the labor market. Private institutes provide vocational courses and training opportunities for those who wish to learn a particular trade, such as typewriting, sewing, or hairdressing. Training centers offered by women's, farmers', and workers' mass organizations provide cultural and health education programs. Lifelong educational activities provided by training centers, workshops, and vocational sections in vocational schools aim at expanding Iraqis' involvement in vocational, industrial, and agricultural activities, acquainting them with the latest developments in these areas, and providing them with basic skills that serve the development plan in the country.

Adult education is linked to the Overall National Literacy Campaign, which began in 1978. The campaign's objectives are to eliminate illiteracy and raise the cultural level of Iraqis, teaching them to read, write, and calculate; provide students with basic and supplementary education, each of which is seven months in duration, qualifying them for admission to grade 4 of primary education; help Iraqis in achieving self-sufficiency to pursue their education and to develop their skills and abilities; and enable those who wish to complete primary education to pursue their studies in popular schools.

Popular schools are considered a parallel path to primary schools. They adopt special curriculum and specifications related to psychological and educational characteristics. Grades 1 and 2 subjects are taught in the first year, grades 3 and 4 subjects in the second year, grade 5 subjects in the third year, and grade 6 subjects in the fourth year.

System Economics

Current data are not available. The total public expenditure on education in Iraq in 1989 represented 5.1 percent of gross domestic product. For the year 1992, 3 percent of public education spending was at the preprimary level, 53 percent at the primary level, 24 percent at the secondary level, and 21 percent at the tertiary level.

Future Prospects

The 1991 and 2003 wars in Iraq have created many challenges. The country needs to provide and main-

Iraq Education at a Glance

General Information

Capital	Baghdad
Population	31.6 million
Languages	Arabic, Kurdish
Adult literacy rate (ages 15 and over)	78.2%
Youth literacy rate (ages 15–24)	82.6%
GDP per capita	US$3,562
Number of phones (mobile) per 100 people	76
Number of Internet users per 100 people	6
Life expectancy at birth (years)	68

Formal Educational Information

Enrollment in preprimary school (ages 4–5)	109,000
Enrollment in primary school (ages 6–11)	4.8 million
Enrollment in lower and upper secondary school (ages 12–17)	2 million
Number of years of compulsory education	6 (ages 6–11)
Preprimary school student/teacher ratio	15
Primary school student/teacher ratio	17
Lower and upper secondary school gross student/teacher ratio	14
Preprimary school gross enrollment ratio	6%
Primary school gross enrollment ratio	103%
Lower and upper secondary school gross enrollment ratio	51%
Primary school entrants reaching grade 5	77%

Sources: Education for All, 2011; Global Education Digest, 2011; UNESCO–UIS, 2012; UNICEF, 2012; United Nations Development Programme, 2011.

tain adequate school buildings; provide adequate numbers of teachers at various levels; provide instructional materials, such as stationery and school furniture; provide prerequisites for curriculum, teaching aids, and educational technologies; and develop education and examination techniques through the introduction of modern technologies. Prior to the two wars, Iraq was a leader in education in its region. However, the country's ranking in education has dropped as a result of violent conflict.

Plans that are under way include the following: accelerate the rebuilding of the infrastructure of education, and rehabilitate damaged educational institutions; provide more educational opportunities for girls, rural residents, and displaced people; reform and diversify secondary and vocational education to offer students various fields of study; introduce elective subjects, such as scientific, aesthetic, and cultural activities, particularly at the preparatory level; develop the process and methods of assessment in various fields; introduce computer studies in some secondary schools and use computers as an aid in the teaching and learning process; and unify primary and intermediate education into a nine-year program.

Emad Alfar

REFERENCES

Central Intelligence Agency. *The CIA World Factbook*. New York: Skyhorse, 2011. https://www.cia.gov/library/publications/the-world-factbook/index.html.

Education for All. "The Hidden Crisis: Armed Conflict and Education." *Education for All Global Monitoring Report*. Paris: UNESCO, 2011.

Global Education Digest. *Global Education Digest 2011: Comparing Education Statistics Across the World*. Montreal: UNESCO Institute for Statistics, 2011.

"Iraq." In *The Europa World Yearbook*, vol. 1. London: Routledge, 2007.

Programme on Governance in the Arab Region. www.pogar.org/countries/country.aspx?cid=6.

UNESCO–IBE. www.ibe.unesco.org/en/worldwide/unesco-regions/arab-states/iraq.html.

UNESCO–UIS. www.uis.unesco.org.

UNICEF. www.unicef.org/infobycountry/iraq.html.

United Nations Development Programme. "Sustainability and Equity: A Better Future for All." *Human Development Report 2011*. New York: Palgrave Macmillan, 2011.

ISRAEL

Israel is situated on the eastern shore of the Mediterranean Sea. The country's official languages are Hebrew and Arabic. In 2011 the country's population was 7.5 million people, nearly 5.7 million of them Jews. In addition to Jews, other Israelis include 1.2 million Muslims, about 170,000 Bedouins, nearly 152,000 Christians, and 129,000 Druzes.

The State of Israel achieved its political independence in 1948. Jewish and Arab affairs were handled differently. The administrative separation of Jewish and Arab affairs happened as a matter of course from the moment the British Army had taken control. The education function was a prime example of this separation. The British administration took over the Arab educational system, especially in villages. Once the villages built their school buildings, the administration provided the rest of the schools' needs, including the classroom teachers. The Jewish Agency

administered the Jewish educational system. For example, it established three educational "trends" (general schools, religious schools, and labor schools in communes and cooperative villages). Each trend created its own supervisory oversight. In 1932 the Jewish Agency transferred control of the Jewish educational system to the National Committee but continued to provide some financial support. To provide higher education, both the Hebrew University in Jerusalem and the Technion (now known as the Israel Technological Institute) in Haifa were established in 1925. Since 1948 immigrants have arrived from over 70 countries. Immigrants' social adjustments to the country and their upward economic mobility have been enhanced mostly by education (followed by health, employment and welfare services).

Educational System

Israel has no written constitution as yet because of the still-unresolved issue of religion in the administrative structure of the state. It was the first prime minister, David Ben-Gurion, who convinced his political contemporaries to avoid dealing with the volatile issue of the relationship between religion and state, the resolution of which was simply not creating a written constitution. Selected laws enacted during the Ottoman period and the British rules are still used in Israeli courts, along with laws enacted since independence. Two additional reasons for not writing a constitution emerged later. One was the Arab minority that is both Israeli and Muslim, and the other involved difficulties in deciding what is an appropriate constitutional framework (as compared to the United States, Great Britain, and France).

Educational legislation was enacted soon after statehood was achieved. The objectives of this legislation over the 60 years since independence have included defining and designing a social vision through education and creating the formal framework of the educational system. Other legislative objectives covered laws regarding who has the right to public education, what are the state's obligations in this regard, and what are the connections between the Ministry of Education and the local municipal authorities.

Precompulsory and Compulsory Education

The 1949 Compulsory and Free Education Law was enacted one year after the achievement of independent statehood. The law states that all children from five to 18 years old may study free of charge and that education for all children aged five to 15 will be compulsory. This law was considered a central piece of legislation in the country and in its educational system. It reflected the recognition that human capital is the major resource of the social and technological strength of the country. It was also considered the major right of the individual and the major force that enhances equal opportunities. In 1982 mandatory education was extended to age 16. In 2006 mandatory and free education for all was extended to age 18.

The National and Sectoral Education Law specifies the country's obligation to provide education to each and every student while permitting the maintenance of kindergartens and schools within separate sectors. These sectors reflect the demographic structure of the Israeli society: the national sector (Jews and Arabs); the national religious sector (Jews); the nonofficial sector (unsupervised by the state; Jews and Arabs); and the ultra-Orthodox sector (Jews). This law also defines the system of relationships between the Ministry of Education and the local authorities. In most schools the teachers are employees of the Education Ministry. Some teachers, however, are employees of nongovernmental agencies such as the world ORT (Organization for Rehabilitation through Training) organization and the Labor Federation's Amal organization. Some teachers work for private institutions.

In 1968 the Israeli Knesset decided to change the structure of the educational system from the eight-year elementary school (grades 1–8) and the four-year secondary school (grades 9–12) model to a new system consisting of six years of elementary education, three years of middle school education, and three years of secondary education. This parliamentary decision followed at least eight years of political debates at the national level. The decision itself was also political rather than legal in nature, possibly implying that it may not be as binding as a law. The purposes of this reform were several. Operationally, it was designed to create changes in school curricula and in teacher training in academic colleges. The overall goal was to raise the school achievement of all students and to speed up the social integration of schoolchildren coming from different socioeconomic and cultural backgrounds. The 2000 Student Rights Law places responsibilities on the Ministry of Education, local authorities, schools, and parents with regard to students' learning (including matters such as requests and complaints by students or their parents) and behavior (including matters such as violence and justification of expulsion). According to this law, each student receives a booklet describing student's rights in Hebrew and Arabic.

Postcompulsory Education

In 2007 Israel had seven universities that awarded undergraduate and graduate degrees: the Israel Technical Institute in Haifa, the Hebrew University in Jerusalem, Tel Aviv University, Bar Ilan University in Ramat Gan, the Weizmann Institute of Science in Rehovot (which confers only graduate degrees), the University of Haifa, and Ben-Gurion University in Beersheba.

In 1948 about 3,000 students received a bachelor's degree from colleges, including teacher training colleges. In 2003 that number was 68,000. The corresponding numbers of students in universities were 44,000 and 77,000. Today 46 percent of the people in Israel between the ages of 24 and 65 (including Jews and non-Jews) hold a bachelor's degree. This is the highest percentage in the world.

Curriculum, Assessment, and Instruction

In 2011 close to 1.9 million students in Israel attended prekindergarten to twelfth grade classes and close to 300,000 students attended institutions of higher education. About 440,000 students attended prekindergartens and kindergartens. This distribution included about 20 percent in prekindergartens and kindergartens, 38 percent in elementary schools, 29 percent in secondary schools, and slightly less than 14 percent in higher education. Among those who were two to five years of age, 45 percent of the two-year-olds, 78 percent of the three-year-olds, 89 percent of the four-year-olds, and 95 percent of the five-year-olds were enrolled in educational institutions. Of the six to 13 year olds, 95 percent attended schools, and of the 14 to 17 year olds, 96 percent attended school.

The following subjects are taught in the Israeli schools. In the Jewish elementary schools, children study Hebrew, arithmetic, history, geography, literature, science, civics, English, computers, art, physical education, Arabic, French and other languages, theater, film, music, dance, photography, and (in religious schools) additional Jewish topics. In Islamic and Christian schools, the respective religious topics are also taught. In elementary schools, the mean number of weekly hours of instruction is 46. The numbers in junior high schools and senior high schools were somewhat higher.

Until 2004 children attended school six days a week. In 2004 the Knesset approved a transition to a five-day school week. The Education Committee of the Knesset worked out the transition procedures, and schools that gained the approval of their local authority and that of the Ministry of Education started implementing this transition that year.

In addition to teacher-administered tests, a number of national tests are given in Israeli schools. For example, annual tests designed by the Ministry of Education are administrated locally to fifth and eighth graders. These are tests in English, native tongue (Hebrew or Arabic), mathematics, and science. Both teachers and students are also required to complete questionnaires that include questions about the school climate and levels of school safety and violence. Various European and American tests are also administered.

The Israeli matriculation exams are the most important tests administered to students. The number of students in Israel who were 17 years old in 2007 was about 114,800. Of them, about 86,600 took these examinations and about 52,700 succeeded in receiving the matriculation certificate. Sixty-two percent of the Hebrew education examinees and 49 percent of the Arabic education examinees received the coveted matriculation certificate.

Significant innovations have been made in recent years. Among them is the option of writing a thesis instead of taking some exams for the twelfth grade matriculation. Another option is for capable students to complete the high school diploma at age 16 and then to attend an institution of higher education. Other innovations in the high schools and in the postsecondary institutions include curricula linked to modern industries. Elementary school students now study about the environment, alternative sources of energy, and biomedical innovations.

Teacher Education

In recent years the Council for Higher Education approved the establishment of 12 regional colleges that award bachelor's degrees and 23 publicly supported training colleges that award bachelor's degrees to elementary school teachers. There are also some partly or totally government-supported postsecondary private institutions. Secondary school teachers have been required (since 1948) to study in a university in order to receive a bachelor's degree with the teaching credential.

The gender-related composition of enrollees in teachers colleges has determined the corresponding gender-related composition of schoolteachers in Israel. The percentages of women teaching in schools in 2000 were as follows: close to 90 percent in Hebrew elementary education, close to 70 percent in Arab elementary education, close to 75 percent in Hebrew secondary education, and close to 40 percent in Arab secondary education.

Special Education

A major special education law was enacted in 1988. Its two major goals were (1) to enhance the achievement of children with physical, mental, psychological, and behavioral disabilities so that they will be able to perform skills, engage in school-related activities, and communicate their ideas; and (2) to enable the children to function in society as well as to be integrated into the world of work. This law mandated the provision of systematic learning and medical and psychological treatment to all individuals aged three to 21 who needed such help. Special education is offered in the educational system in two main ways: (1) in separate institutions and schools, and (2) in a modified inclusionary form in regular classrooms. Most of the separate schools are boarding schools serving disabled students, such as students with severe autism, the deaf, the blind, and those with severe illness. In 2010 there were about 45,000 such students in Israel (both Arab and Jewish).

System Economics

The total budget of the Israeli educational system in 2010 (excluding monies earmarked for the seven universities) was about $12 billion. In addition, the

Ministry of Education provided about $65 billion. All local authorities together spent over $1.5 billion. Parents paid about half a billion dollars and the rest of the funding came from external sources. According to data published by the Paris-based Organisation for Economic Co-operation and Development (OECD), Israel's national expenditure per student (NES) in public schools is somewhat below countries such as Japan, Norway, Sweden, Denmark, Finland, Spain, Portugal, Belgium, Switzerland, and France. It is substantially below that of the United States, Great Britain, Australia, Italy, Holland, and Germany. The Israeli NES is somewhat higher than that in the Czech Republic, Slovakia, and South Korea.

Israel Education at a Glance

General Information

Capital	Jerusalem
Population	7.4 million
Languages	Hebrew, Arabic
Adult literacy rate (ages 15 and over)	97%
Youth literacy rate (ages 15–24)	no data
GDP per capita	US$28,546
Number of phones (mobile) per 100 people	133
Number of Internet users per 100 people	67
Life expectancy at birth (years)	82

Formal Educational Information

Enrollment in preprimary school (ages 3–5)	440,000
Enrollment in primary school (ages 6–11)	861,000
Enrollment in lower and upper secondary school (ages 12–17)	619,000
Number of years of compulsory education (preprimary–12)	13 (ages 5–17)
Compulsory school age population	1.7 million
Compulsory school age population (preprimary–12)	97.1%
Preprimary school student/teacher ratio	no data
Primary school student/teacher ratio	13
Lower and upper secondary school gross student/teacher ratio	9
Average class size in primary school	27.5
Average school hours per school calendar year (weekly)	51.1
Preprimary school gross enrollment ratio	104%
Primary school gross enrollment ratio	111%
Lower and upper secondary school gross enrollment ratio	89%
Primary school entrants reaching grade 5	99%

Sources: Central Bureau of Statistics (Israel), 2010; Education for All, 2011; Global Education Digest, 2011; Ministry of Education (Israel), 2011; UNESCO–UIS, 2012; UNICEF, 2012; United Nations Development Programme, 2011.

Future Prospects

There are significant challenges in the educational system in Israel. Immigrants continue to come from countries in which education is not a high priority. Some students require a basic orientation about school, and their families may also need such explanations. There is a shortage of highly qualified teachers in some areas of the country. Average class size still approaches 40 students in several schools. Progress is slow in the attempt to decentralize the educational system and provide increased autonomy to local school leaders. Having few natural resources, Israel's pivotal resource is its population and, thus, the national education budget is second only to the security budget. Another problem in several cities and towns throughout Israel is the growing virulent hostility on the part of the ultra-Orthodox community (approximately 10 percent of the country's population) toward both other Jews and non-Jews alike. This hostility is particularly apparent in neighborhoods in and near Jerusalem as well as other politically sensitive areas of Israel. Much of the animus is directed against Jewish women and girls who do not adhere to the extreme religious and political positions of the ultra-Orthodox community. This problem is adversely affecting the education of the majority, mostly girls, who are often intimidated in school settings. Despite Israel's political and military conflicts with some of the neighboring countries, the nation continues to work vigorously toward ensuring equality and human rights to all of its citizens, as well as protecting them from harm and violence.

Israel's educational system has produced several outstanding results over the years. For example, Israel has developed sophisticated advanced technology for use in agriculture, water purification, and irrigation as a result of extensive research at the Israel Technical Institute, the Weizmann Institute, and Tel Aviv University. Since the 1960s Israel has provided help in these and related areas to several African nations. Also, Israel's high-tech research, innovation, and development, particularly in the areas of medicine and medical engineering, have expanded exponentially in recent years.

Naftaly S. Glasman and Gideon Ben-Dror
with Lynette D. Glasman

REFERENCES

Ben-Dror, Gideon. "Initial Administrative Steps in Implementing the Reform in the Israeli Educational System: 1968–1972." PhD dissertation, University of California, Santa Barbara, 1979.

Central Intelligence Agency. *The CIA World Factbook.* New York: Skyhorse, 2011. https://www.cia.gov/library/publications/the-world-factbook/index.html.

Ephron, Dan. "Israel's Ultra-Orthodox Problem." *Daily Beast*, January 2, 2012. www.thedailybeast.com.

Glasman, Naftaly S. "Developments Toward a Secondary Education Act: The Case of Israel." PhD dissertation, University of California, Berkeley, 1968.

Government of Israel. "The New Horizon Plan: Advancing the Status and Pay of Teachers." Jerusalem, 2006 (in Hebrew).

Knesset Committee of Education and Culture. "Implementation of the Inclusion Legislation: A Special Hearing." Jerusalem, 2006.

Ministry of Education, State of Israel. http://cms.education.gov.il/educationcms/units/owl/english/about/ministry+structure.htm.

State of Israel, Central Bureau of Statistics. www1.cbs.gov.il/reader/?MIval=cw_usr_view_Folder&ID=141.

JORDAN

The Hashemite Kingdom of Jordan, an Arab country, is located in western Asia. The official language is Arabic, but English is used and understood widely in government and among educated citizens. The majority of the population is of Arab ethnicity, and the remaining smaller portion is Circassian and Armenian. Many Jordanians are of Bedouin and Palestinian descent, and most of the remaining population is Iraqi or Egyptian. The number of displaced people and Palestinian refugees living in Jordan, most as citizens, is about 3 million. It is estimated that between 700,000 and 1.7 million Iraqis are living in Jordan, most of them in the capital, Amman. Due to wars and conflicts in neighboring countries and in the region, substantial influx of migration into Jordan has and will continue to put a strain on its services, infrastructure, and limited resources. The official religion is Islam. The majority of Jordanians are Muslim, and a small portion is Christian.

Educational System

The Ministry of Education administers all public schools and supervises all private and vocational schools. The private sector is in charge of private schools, and the United Nations Relief and Works Agency (UNRWA) is in charge of schools for Palestinian refugees. The Vocational Training Corporation administers formal apprenticeship, both in-service and preservice programs for adult employees. The Higher Education Council administers higher education institutions. All other educational institutions are supervised by the Ministry of Education. The Ministry of Social Development administers schools for students with special needs.

Starting in the mid-1980s, a comprehensive review of Jordan's education system produced the Provisional Education Act Number 2 of 1988, which became the Education Act Number 3 of 1994, regulating kindergarten, basic, and secondary education. Some of the outcomes of this act were to extend the duration of free compulsory education from nine to ten years, to provide the necessary infrastructure for the development of the education system, to focus on the quality of education and social development, and to prepare the education system to meet the needs of the twenty-first century.

The school system is divided into three cycles: kindergarten, basic, and secondary. Higher education is comprised of two levels: community college and university. Community colleges are accessible to holders of all types of general secondary education certificates. Depending on the specialization of study, universities admit students who meet a required minimum score on specific streams on the general secondary education certificate.

Precompulsory and Compulsory Education

Nongovernmental organizations and the private sector administer kindergarten schools. Kindergarten, which is not compulsory, lasts for two years, for children entering at age four and exiting at age six. Attendance of classes is not mandatory. One of the goals of kindergarten education is to provide students with a sound educational environment for their well-balanced growth.

Basic school, which is compulsory and free for all Jordanians, is for children entering at age 6 and exiting at age 16, lasts for 10 years, and covers grades 1 through 10. Students receive basic general broad-based education, including civics and science, and those who complete basic school move on to secondary school. Students are given a certificate at the end of each academic year from grades 1 through 10, showing results from the first and second terms along with the final average. Scores in grades 8 through 10, and commonly in addition to student preference, are used to determine the appropriate enrollment in one of the two major streams of secondary school, but the final decision is made by the Ministry of Education. Basic school students are offered education, as a foundation for secondary school, in the following areas of basic academic subjects: physical, technical, artistic, spiritual, social, foreign language, health, and information technology.

Postcompulsory Education

Students who have completed basic school enter secondary school at age 16 and exit at age 18. The two years of secondary school, grades 11 and 12, lead to higher education or the labor market. Secondary education is free but not compulsory. Secondary school comprises two major streams: (1) the comprehensive secondary education stream (academic substream or vocational sub-stream); and (2) the applied secondary education stream (apprenticeships and training centers). The comprehensive academic substream consists of a common core curriculum and optional specialized academic courses (scientific, literary, or Islamic law). At the end of two years and upon successful passing of the general secondary examination, students are awarded the General Secondary Certificate (*Tawjihi*) and are prepared for entrance to universities. In the comprehensive vocational substream, students are prepared for the labor market with a specialization in commercial, agricultural, industrial, hotel, nursing, or home economics studies. Depending on their specialization, those students who pass two additional subjects (listed in respective order to area of specialization: Arabic and English, chemistry and biology, mathematics and physics, mathematics and biology, chemistry and biology, chemistry and biology) qualify for entrance to community colleges, universities, or the labor market. Generally, students in the comprehensive vocational secondary school substream go on to community colleges, while those in the comprehensive academic secondary school substream go on to universities, even though entrance to either option is determined by the student's scores of

the *Tawjihi* exam and financial means. In the second major stream, the applied secondary school stream, students are offered apprenticeship and intensive vocational training leading to a certificate (not the *Tawjihi*). The Vocational Training Corporation, a number of voluntary organizations, and UNRWA provide this second major stream education and prepare students for direct entry into the labor market. Training centers are run mostly for basic school dropouts and nearly entirely in the field of industrial and women's craft. Most students in Jordan, both males and females, enroll in the comprehensive academic secondary education substream.

Higher education institutions are supervised by the Higher Education Council, which is chaired by the prime minister. There are two levels of higher education: a community college level and a university level. Public community colleges as well as private, other governmental, and UNRWA institutions offer two- to three-year practical education in specialization programs. Al-Balqa' Applied University supervises all public community colleges. Students who pass a comprehensive examination (*Al-Shamel*), given at the end of the two- or three-year program, are awarded an associate degree. Public and private universities offer programs that last for at least four years, leading to a bachelor's degree. After the completion of the bachelor's degree, with a minimum rating of good, and a further two years of study at the postgraduate level, a master's degree is awarded. Candidates who hold a master's degree with a minimum rating of very good are awarded a doctorate degree after three to five years of further study. Among the public universities are the University of Jordan, Yarmouk University, Mu'tah University, Jordan University for Science and Technology, Al-Albayt University, and Hashemite University. Among the private universities are Amman Private University, Philadelphia University, Jerash Private University, Irbid Private University, and Jordanian University of Applied Science. Each university is autonomous, with a board of trustees that is responsible for setting policy and managing the internal affairs of the university. Public universities are funded by the government, student tuition, and grants. Private universities charge student tuition, which is about four times that of public universities.

Curriculum, Assessment, and Instruction

Kindergarten students are prepared for a smooth transition from home to school, helped with developing social skills and a positive disposition toward school, and educated about the practice of good hygiene. Kindergarten students are evaluated by their performance in a variety of activities and by their growth in social and cognitive skills aimed at developing the personality of the student. A practical applications manual for kindergarten teachers was developed by a national team, comprised of public as well as private and voluntary organizations, in order to improve kindergarten education. Progress assessment updates are provided regularly to parents of kindergarten students.

In basic school there are three types of curriculum: core, civics, and science. Subjects taught in the core curriculum are Islamic education and culture, Arabic language, mathematics, music and anthems, art education, physical education, and vocational education in grades 1 through 10; English language in grades 5 through 10; and computer science in grade 10. There are plans to introduce English language in grade 1. Subjects taught in the civics curriculum are social and national education in grades 1 through 5, and history, geography, and national education in grades 6 through 10. Subjects taught in the science curriculum are general science in grades 1 through 8, and physics, biology, and chemistry in grades 9 and 10. Students are given a certificate at the end of each academic year in grades 1 through 10. Each certificate includes the results of the two terms and the final average. Based on results in grades 8 through 10, individual interest, and space availability in schools, students enroll in one of the two major streams of secondary education. Through the Diagnostic Education Project, a diagnostic evaluation method used by teachers for basic school students, an appropriate educational plan is created to challenge those with high-achieving performance and to offer a remedy to those with learning difficulties.

In the first major stream of secondary education, the subjects taught in the comprehensive academic substream, with the option of scientific or literary specializations, are Islamic education and culture, Arabic language, English language, scientific education, and civics as part of the common general educa-

tion. Additional subjects in the scientific option are mathematics, physics, chemistry; one subject from biology, geology and environment; one subject from literary or vocational streams; and one subject from vocational education and home economics. Additional subjects in the literary option are Arabic language, English language, history; one subject from Islamic education and culture, geography, and mathematics; and one subject from computer science, music, physical education, and foreign languages other than English. As for the comprehensive vocational secondary school substream, the subjects taught in the common general education are the same as those taught in the comprehensive academic secondary school substream. Additional specialization-related subjects taught in this substream include vocational sciences and practical training, depending on the specialization (commercial, agricultural, industrial, hotel, nursing, or home economics). Successful secondary students receive the General Secondary Education Certificate (*Tawjihi*) at the end of the secondary cycle. The *Tawjihi* certificate includes the results of the two terms and the student's final average on the General Secondary Education examination. Students who enroll in the comprehensive academic substream can transfer easily to the comprehensive vocational substream, in theory. The converse is only possible provided that the minimum required results of grade 10 are met, but this rarely occurs in practice. In the second major stream of secondary education, the applied secondary school stream (apprenticeships and training centers), students receive training mainly in the field of industrial and women's craft. Apprenticeships, in cooperation with employers, provide two years of vocational training and one year of supervised employment in the following occupational groups: electric power, vehicle repair and maintenance, electronics, metal and mechanical maintenance, air conditioning and plumbing, printing and binding, hotel and restaurant management, chemical industries, construction, and carpentry. Apprenticeship students receive three days of school education, which include one day for general subjects, one day for vocational subjects, and one day for practical training in a workshop. These students also receive another three days of practical work in a company, where they are joined by instructors to focus on required skills.

In higher education, community colleges provide vocational and nonuniversity-level programs to holders of all types of general secondary education certificates. These are two- to three-year programs offered in computer science, education, agriculture, hotel management, engineering, applied fine arts, administration and finance, medicine, nursing, interior design, pharmacology, social work, commerce, and meteorology. At the undergraduate university level, a bachelor's degree usually takes four years, for a total of 126 to 164 credit hours, according to the field of study. Dentistry, pharmacy, and engineering take five years. Medicine takes six years, ending with a one-year internship. At the postgraduate university level, a master's degree takes two years beyond the bachelor's degree and can be earned in one of two ways: either through 33 credit hours of coursework and a comprehensive examination, or through 24 credit hours of coursework and nine credit hours of research. A doctorate degree takes three to five years beyond the master's degree. It requires 24 credit hours of coursework and 24 credit hours of research, depending on the subject, culminating with the submission of an original dissertation.

Teacher Education

The Ministry of Education is continuously upgrading credentials of teachers and improving the teaching and learning process. This is consistent with the Education Act Number 3 of 1994, which requires teachers from kindergarten through secondary school to hold a university degree, and their supervisors a postgraduate degree. Kindergarten and basic school teachers must hold a bachelor's degree. Secondary school teachers must hold a bachelor's degree and a one-year postgraduate Higher Diploma in Education. To achieve these requirements, two types of certification training are available, preservice and in-service. Preservice training focuses on critical thinking, cooperative teaching, skills for applying knowledge to practical life, teaching methods, and skills related to work. In-service training courses focus on modern teaching methods, new curricula, and textbooks. By collaborating with educational experts and international and regional organizations, the General Directorate of Training in the Ministry of Education plans these preservice and in-service programs for the purpose of training, certifying, and supervising teachers, and for upgrading qualifications of administrators at the central and field levels. Employment of teachers

is based on existing demand, experience, academic qualifications, specialization, and year of graduation. An employment quota is given to orphans of fathers who served in the Jordanian army, poor families, and the handicapped who hold academic qualification, provided that the percentage of these employment exceptions does not go over 5 percent. Promotion is generally given after five years in a grade, class, or category. Earlier promotion is possible if a teacher has a distinctive performance or has earned a higher academic degree. Generally, higher education teachers must hold a doctorate degree, although in some cases a master's degree is sufficient.

Informal Education

A variety of informal education programs are offered to adults, such as evening classes, literacy programs, and home studies. These programs provide education for adults to continue self-learning and sit for school and general examinations. By focusing on literacy and adult programs as well as informal education programs, the Jordanian government aimed to reduce the rate of illiteracy; develop the capabilities of trainers and supervisors in illiteracy and adult education programs; improve the quality of informal education programs; reinforce literacy programs by introducing health, cultural and agricultural education skills to meet labor market needs; and diversify teaching methods and content. In addition, informal vocational training and cultural programs are offered to adults. These programs are provided by cultural centers through more than 115 vocational and academic training short courses. Students receive a certificate at the end of these courses, recognized by the Ministry of Education. Cultural centers are spread out across various directorates of education in the governorates and districts.

System Economics

Current data are not available. Jordan's total public expenditure on education in 1999 represented 4.9 percent of gross domestic product (GDP). It represented 20.6 percent of the total government expenditure. For the year 1997, 40 percent of public education spending was at the primary level, 36 percent at the secondary level, and 23 percent at the tertiary level.

Jordan Education at a Glance

General Information

Capital	Amman
Population	6.1 million
Language	Arabic
Adult literacy rate (ages 15 and over)	92.2%
Youth literacy rate (ages 15–24)	98.9%
GDP per capita	US$5,749
Number of phones (mobile) per 100 people	107
Number of Internet users per 100 people	38
Life expectancy at birth (years)	73

Formal Educational Information

Enrollment in preprimary school (ages 4–5)	105,000
Enrollment in primary school (ages 6–11)	817,000
Enrollment in lower and upper secondary school (ages 12–17)	700,000
Number of years of compulsory education	10 (ages 6–15)
Preprimary school student/teacher ratio	21
Primary school student/teacher ratio	20
Lower and upper secondary school gross student/teacher ratio	18
Preprimary school gross enrollment ratio	32%
Primary school gross enrollment ratio	92%
Lower and upper secondary school gross enrollment ratio	87%
Primary school entrants reaching grade 5	94%

Sources: Education for All, 2011; Global Education Digest, 2011; UNESCO–UIS, 2012; UNICEF, 2012; United Nations Development Programme, 2011.

Future Prospects

There is a high commitment in Jordan to education reform, both in government and among the main education stakeholders. Education reform, which began in the mid-1980s and is ongoing, is supported by a considerable budget. Since that time, significant achievements have been made. The country has completed the implementation of the first (1989–1995), second (1996–2000), and third phase (2000–2005) of its Educational Development Plan. Recent policies support early childhood care and education programs, such as opening kindergartens in remote and disadvantaged areas. In response to the World Conference on Education for All (EFA), held in Jomtien, Thailand, in 1990, focusing on achieving six key education goals by 2015, Jordan has already achieved the goal of gender parity in primary and secondary education and has a high chance of achieving the goals of universal primary education and adult literacy.

Emad Alfar

References

Central Intelligence Agency. *The CIA World Factbook*. New York: Skyhorse, 2011. https://www.cia.gov/library/publications/the-world-factbook/index.html.

Education for All. "The Hidden Crisis: Armed Conflict and Education." *Education for All Global Monitoring Report*. Paris: UNESCO, 2011.

Global Education Digest. *Global Education Digest 2011: Comparing Education Statistics Across the World*. Montreal: UNESCO Institute for Statistics, 2011.

"Jordan." In *The Europa World Yearbook*, vol. 1. London: Routledge, 2007.

Programme on Governance in the Arab Region. www.pogar.org/countries/country.aspx?cid=7.

UNESCO–IBE. www.ibe.unesco.org/countries/Jordan.htm.

UNESCO–UIS. www.uis.unesco.org.

UNICEF. www.unicef.org/infobycountry/jordan.html.

United Nations Development Programme. "Sustainability and Equity: A Better Future for All." *Human Development Report 2011*. New York: Palgrave Macmillan, 2011.

Kuwait

Kuwait, an Arab country, is located in western Asia along the northwestern shores of the Persian Gulf. The official language is Arabic, and English is widely spoken. Roughly one-third of the population are Kuwaiti citizens; the rest are non-Kuwaiti citizens. The majority of the population is of Arab ethnicity, and the rest are Kurd, South Asian, and Persian. The official religion is Islam. Most Kuwaitis are Sunni Muslim and Shiite Muslim, with a substantial number of Christian, Hindu, Sikh, and Buddhist communities. Suffrage is universal for all adult Kuwaiti males, and since May 16, 2005, to all adult Kuwaiti females, with all voters having been citizens for 20 years and not in the security forces. Kuwait gained its independence from the British in 1961. In 1990 Iraq invaded Kuwait, which was then liberated in 1991.

Educational System

The Ministry of Education administers all public education through the last grade of secondary education and supervises all nongovernmental and private education. The Ministry of Higher Education administers higher education beyond secondary education. Public education, including kindergarten and higher education, is free for all Kuwaiti citizens. Enrollment in public schools is limited to Kuwaiti citizens. Arab and non-Arab students who are not Kuwaiti citizens enroll in private (Arabic or foreign) schools. Private Arabic schools follow the public education system. Private foreign schools, such as British, American, French, and Indian schools, follow the education system of their home country.

The general education system is divided into four stages: kindergarten, elementary (primary), intermediate (lower secondary), and secondary. Higher education, which covers postsecondary and university education and training, is provided by two main institutions: Kuwait University and the Public Authority for Applied Education and Training.

In addition to the general education system, there are three other types of education: religious education, vocational education, and special education (for disabled students). Religious education is an eight-year-long study, at the intermediate and secondary levels, after four years of general elementary education. In religious education, most weekly lessons are on two subjects, Islamic studies and Arabic language; the rest are on other subjects taught in the general education system. Vocational education is a four-year study, at the intermediate level, after four years of general elementary education. In vocational education, most weekly lessons are on general technical subjects: fundamentals of industry, engineering drawing, and industrial safety. Special education offers various levels (elementary, intermediate, and secondary) of education according to the type of disability: mental, visual, physical, and hearing.

Precompulsory and Compulsory Education

Kindergarten is not compulsory, but is free to all Kuwaiti citizens. Kindergarten school, for children entering at age four and exiting at age six, lasts for two years.

Elementary school, which is compulsory, is for children entering at age six and exiting at age 11. It lasts for five years, covering grades 1 through 5. It is a preparatory stage for the intermediate level. Students are provided with basic education in arithmetic, reading, and writing, with emphasis on Arabic language.

Intermediate school, which is compulsory, lasts for four years, covering grades 6 through 9, for children entering at age 11 and exiting at age 15. It is a preparatory stage for the secondary level. This stage aims for students to develop their creativity, acquire technical knowledge, and gain an understanding of their national identity. Students are provided with general, broad-based education, with emphasis on Arabic and English languages and Islamic education.

Postcompulsory Education

Secondary school, which is not compulsory, lasts for three years, covering grades 10 through 12, for children entering at age 15 and exiting at age 18. It is a preparatory stage for practical life and the postsecondary level. Secondary education has two systems: the syllabi (units/credits) system and the two-semester system. The syllabi system, which began in the academic year 1978–1979, is similar to that of the United States. It consists of 40 units, each unit being equal to five lessons each week for 15 weeks, which is a semester. Typically a student enrolls in five units each semester, two semesters each year, for a total of six semesters in the entire secondary stage. This system has the following branches: information technologies, arts, sciences, commercial and industrial studies, and foreign languages. The other system, the two-semester system, which began in the academic year 1984–1985, is similar to that of the French Baccalaureate or the German *Arbitur*. This system has two streams: science and humanities. Each academic year consists of two semesters. During the first year of secondary education, students from both streams study the same subjects. In the second and third year of secondary education, students are divided into science and humanities streams. Students study different subjects in each stream. Students who successfully complete the requirements of the syllabi system or the two-semester system receive the General Secondary School Certificate (*Thanaweya 'Ama*), preparing them for enrollment in higher education institutions.

The Ministry of Higher Education administers higher education, which is offered by two main institutions: Kuwait University and the Public Authority for Applied Education and Training. There are two other specialized institutions: the Higher Institute of Dramatic Arts and the Higher Institute of Musical Arts.

Curriculum, Assessment, and Instruction

Kindergarten education aims to develop the child mentally, physically, socially, emotionally, and spiritually. It is a preparatory stage for the elementary level. The government provides educational services to children in kindergarten schools in which children develop kinetic skills, rationality, and their senses, besides playing and learning.

Subjects taught in grades 1 through 5 at the elementary level are Islamic education, Arabic language, English language, science, mathematics, physical education, art education, and music. Social studies is introduced in grade 4. English language was first introduced to grade 1 in the academic year 1993–1994.

All subjects taught at the elementary level are also taught at the intermediate level, in grades 6 through 9, plus computer studies, practical studies, and home economics (for girls). Recent curriculum changes made at the intermediate level include adding information technology to the curriculum and introducing new topics in social studies, such as the Iraqi invasion and the role of coalition countries in liberating Kuwait. In the last year of intermediate education, grade 9, all students study the same subjects. Subjects taught are Islamic education, Arabic language, English language, mathematics, integrated sciences, social studies, practical studies/art education/computer studies, physical education, and home economics (for girls). At the end of each year, an overall percentage is calculated for all compulsory subjects. Based on this percentage, a general evaluation is obtained for a student: excellent, very good, good, and passing. Students who successfully complete this stage are awarded the Intermediate School Certificate, allowing them to move on and enroll in secondary education.

In the two-semester system of secondary education, during the first year, the same subjects taught in grade 9 are also taught in grade 10 except for replacing integrated studies with biology, physics, and chemistry. Upon completing the first year, grade 10, students enroll in either the science stream or the humanities stream. In the science stream, subjects taught are Islamic education, Arabic language, English language, mathematics, biology, geology (second year only, grade 11), physics, chemistry, physical education, and home economics (for girls). In the humanities stream,

subjects taught are Islamic education, Arabic language, English language, French language, mathematics, scientific knowledge, history, geography, economics, sociology, physical education, and home economics (for girls); in the third year, grade 12, mathematics, scientific knowledge, economics, and sociology are dropped, and psychology and philosophy are added. At the end of the third year of secondary education, students who receive at least 50 percent of the maximum grade for each subject on the government final exam are awarded the General Secondary School Certificate. As for the syllabi system, consisting of 40 units, students enroll in one of its branches: information technologies, arts, sciences, commercial and industrial studies, and foreign languages. Generally, more than half of the units students enroll in are in their branch; the rest are units that are relevant and complementary to their branch, plus elective units. Students who successfully complete the 40 units requirement of their branch, with a minimum grade of D, are awarded the General Secondary School Certificate. Holders of this certificate are eligible to enroll at higher education institutions.

Kuwait University, the only public university in the country, offers undergraduate and graduate programs, lasting for at least four years, in the following fields: Islamic law (Shari'ah) and Islamic studies; science; arts; education; medicine; Women's College; allied health and nursing; graduate studies; commerce, economics and political science; law; and engineering and petroleum. A bachelor's degree normally takes four years, except for the College of Engineering and Petroleum, which requires five years, and the College of Medicine, which requires seven. A master's degree takes one or two years beyond the bachelor's degree. The Committee for Scientific Affairs, affiliated with Kuwait University, conducts periodical review and evaluation of science programs, besides updating curriculum. The Public Authority for Applied Education and Training (PAAET) offers technical and vocational training programs, most of them lasting for two years, in the following fields: business studies, basic education, health sciences, and technological studies. The College of Basic Education programs last four years.

Teacher Education

Preuniversity teachers must hold a bachelor's degree. Both Kuwait University and PAAET offer four-year teacher training programs leading to a bachelor's degree. In order to enroll at these two institutions, candidates must hold the General Secondary School Certificate, with the required percentage of marks, and pass aptitude tests.

Kindergarten and elementary school teachers receive 100 credit hours of training from the Faculty of Basic Education, at PAAET, in three areas: academic, pedagogical, and cultural. Each area requires roughly one-third of the 100 credit hours.

Also, kindergarten, elementary, intermediate, and secondary school teachers receive training from the Faculty of Education, at Kuwait University, which offers two diploma programs: pedagogical training and pedagogical guidance. The university offers teachers higher studies programs, leading to a master's degree in teaching or a Higher Teaching Diploma.

Teacher training programs at both institutions combine pedagogical training with specialized and general curriculum. Preservice training includes principles of Islam, mastery of basic knowledge, and principles of self-learning. In-service training includes information technologies training, completion of pedagogical training, and upgrading of skills and knowledge. All employees, including teachers, of the Ministry of Education receive annual training on the latest developments in education. The ministry supports training abroad so teachers can learn about the latest educational developments and trends.

A master's degree is required for assistant teachers at Kuwait University and for instructors at technical colleges. A PhD is required for university professors.

Informal Education

Informal education is provided through literacy courses and adult education, the Kuwait Institute for Scientific Research, the Child and Motherhood Center, and the Sultan Educational Society. The Child and Motherhood Center, a nongovernmental center, offers computer, secretarial, and foreign language courses. Governmental community centers provide continuous education and courses in specialized areas.

According to Law Number 4/1981, issued on January 11, 1981, illiterate male Kuwaiti citizens, ages 14 through 40, and illiterate female Kuwaiti citizens, ages 14 through 35, are required by law to enroll in literacy programs. Upon completing the literacy stage, adults can enroll in the Adult Education Center, starting at the intermediate level. This also holds for students who drop out from an earlier level and want to resume their education. The center offers its students a course of study that leads to the General Secondary School Certificate, which allows certificate holders to enroll at Kuwait University or PAAET. There are 70 learning centers, including evening religious institutes.

System Economics

The total public expenditure on education in 2006 represented 3.8 percent of gross domestic product. It represented 12.9 percent of the total government expenditure. Ten percent of public education spending was at the preprimary level, 21 percent at the primary level, 38 percent at the secondary level, and 30 percent at the tertiary level.

Kuwait Education at a Glance

General Information

Capital	Kuwait
Language	Arabic
Population	2.8 million
Adult literacy rate (ages 15 and over)	93.9%
Youth literacy rate (ages 15–24)	98.6%
GDP per capita	US$52,657
Number of phones (mobile) per 100 people	161
Number of Internet users per 100 people	38
Life expectancy at birth (years)	74

Formal Educational Information

Enrollment in preprimary school (ages 4–5)	71,000
Enrollment in primary school (ages 6–10)	211,000
Enrollment in lower and upper secondary school (ages 11–17)	255,000
Number of years of compulsory education	9 (ages 6–14)
Preprimary school student/teacher ratio	11
Primary school student/teacher ratio	8
Lower and upper secondary school gross student/teacher ratio	8
Preprimary school gross enrollment ratio	76%
Primary school gross enrollment ratio	95%
Lower and upper secondary school gross enrollment ratio	90%
Primary school entrants reaching grade 5	96%

Sources: Education for All, 2011; Global Education Digest, 2011; UNESCO–UIS, 2012; UNICEF, 2012; United Nations Development Programme, 2011.

Future Prospects

Prior to the academic year 2004-2005, the education system followed a 4–4–4 model (four years for the elementary level, four years for the intermediate level, four years for the secondary level). Secondary education has two systems: the syllabi system and the two-semester system. After a period of implementing these two systems, a national conference for the development of education in Kuwait was held in April 2002. As a result of this conference, the Ministry of Education decided, in decree Number 76/2003, to adopt a new system that follows a 5–4–3 model: five years for the elementary stage, four years for the intermediate stage, and three years for the secondary stage, beginning in the academic year 2004–2005. The new educational ladder extends the duration of compulsory education from eight to nine (covering both elementary and intermediate education). Preparations are under way for a unified system (a combination of the syllabi system and the two-semester system) of the secondary stage and for the 5–4–3 model.

Emad Alfar

REFERENCES

Central Intelligence Agency. *The CIA World Factbook*. New York: Skyhorse, 2011. https://www.cia.gov/library/publications/the-world-factbook/index.html.

Education for All. "The Hidden Crisis: Armed Conflict and Education." *Education for All Global Monitoring Report*. Paris: UNESCO, 2011.

Global Education Digest. *Global Education Digest 2011: Comparing Education Statistics Across the World*. Montreal: UNESCO Institute for Statistics, 2011.

"Kuwait." In *The Europa World Yearbook*, vol. 1. London: Routledge, 2009.

Programme on Governance in the Arab Region. www.pogar.org/countries/country.aspx?cid=8.

UNESCO–IBE. www.ibe.unesco.org/countries/Kuwait.htm.

UNESCO–UIS. www.uis.unesco.org.

UNICEF. www.unicef.org/infobycountry/kuwait.html.

United Nations Development Programme. "Sustainability and Equity: A Better Future for All." *Human Development Report 2011*. New York: Palgrave Macmillan, 2011.

LEBANON

The Lebanese Republic, an Arab country, is located in western Asia, bordered by the Mediterranean Sea to the west, Israel to the south, and Syria to the east and north. The official language is Arabic. Other spoken languages are French, English, and Armenian. The population is diverse, consisting mainly of Lebanese citizens plus other ethnic and religious groups, including Palestinians, Kurds, and Armenians. The population comprises various Muslim and Christian groups, as well as Druze. Lebanon gained its independence from the French in 1943.

Educational System

The Ministry of Education and Higher Education is responsible for public education in all levels, as well as for higher education, and supervises private education. Basic education is compulsory for all Lebanese children from six to 14 years old. Education is free at all stages for all Lebanese.

The education system comprises three stages: kindergarten, basic education (elementary and intermediate), and secondary. Higher education is provided by private institutions and one public institution: the Lebanese University. These institutions offer programs leading to licenses and diplomas, as well as to bachelor's, master's, and doctorate degrees.

Precompulsory and Compulsory Education

Kindergarten, which is not compulsory, lasts for three years, for children entering at age three and exiting at age six. Kindergarten prepares students for a smooth transition from home to school. Attendance of classes is not mandatory.

Basic education is compulsory, comprising two cycles: six years of elementary and three years of intermediate. Elementary education, which is compulsory and lasts for six years, from grades 1 through 6, is for children entering at age six and exiting at age 12. Students are provided with the necessary knowledge, skills, and values essential to their integration into society, according to their growth level and age, allowing them to participate effectively in the learning process. This stage prepares students for social integration and for the intermediate cycle. Intermediate education, which is compulsory, is for children entering at age 12 and exiting at age 15. It lasts for three years, covering grades 7 through 9. It is an extension of elementary education and an integral part of secondary education. Students acquire the necessary knowledge, skills, and values to become educated citizens, allowing them to discover their own abilities and preferences. This cycle prepares students for secondary education, pursuing their technical study, or entering directly into the labor market. Students who successfully complete their basic education are awarded the Intermediate Education Certificate and can continue on to secondary education.

Postcompulsory Education

General secondary education, which is not compulsory, is for children entering at age 15 and exiting at age 18; it lasts for three years, covering grades 10 through 12. It aims to strengthen the links between school and everyday life by providing students with knowledge and skills, allowing them to enter the labor market or to pursue higher education, as well as by providing them with theoretical and practical education in the fields of culture, science, and modern technology. In the first year of secondary education, grade 10, students study a common curriculum, enabling them to choose a track of study in the next two years. In the second year, grade 11, two tracks are offered: humanities and sciences. In the third year, grade 12, four tracks are offered: arts and humanities, socioeconomics, general sciences, and life sciences. There are also technical and vocational secondary schools, which last for three years, in three fields of study: agriculture, industry, and services (including finance, trade, management, tourism, information technology, hospitality, and health). Students who successfully complete their secondary education are awarded the Secondary Education Certificate, called the Lebanese Baccalaureate, and can continue on to higher education.

Higher education is provided by public and private institutions. There is only one public institution: the Lebanese University. Admission to higher education institutions is based on the Lebanese Baccalaureate. The administrative structure of the largest universities, including the Lebanese University, is divided into four models: the governmental model, Arab model, French model, and American model. These institutions offer programs leading to licenses and diplomas, as well as to bachelor's, master's, and doctorate degrees. Among the institutions are Beirut Arab University, Saint Joseph University, American University of Beirut, Lebanese American University, Imam Ouzai University College, Notre-Dame University–Louizeh, Holy Spirit University of Kaslik, and University of Balamand.

Curriculum, Assessment, and Instruction

Kindergarten education develops the child physiologically, intellectually, and morally. It provides children with a positive environment that encourages them to communicate with others and to express themselves. It develops their spirit of cooperation to be able to live in society. It prepares them for school education.

Basic education comprises two cycles: six years of elementary and three years of intermediate education. Subjects taught in elementary education, grades 1 through 6, are Arabic language; French (or English) language; civic education, history, and geography; sciences; mathematics; art education (including drawing, singing, music, dance, and theater) agriculture; and physical education. Emphasis is on Arabic language and French (or English) language.

Subjects taught in intermediate education, grades 7 through 9, are Arabic language, first foreign language, second foreign language, civic education, history, geography, mathematics, sciences, technology, informatique (computer sciences), art education, agriculture, and physical education. Emphasis is on Arabic language, first foreign language, mathematics, and sciences. Students who successfully complete their basic education (elementary and intermediate cycles) are awarded the Intermediate Education Certificate and can continue on to secondary education.

In the first year of general secondary education, grade 10, all students are taught the same subjects: Arabic language, foreign language, second foreign language, sociology and economics, civic education, history, geography, mathematics, physics, chemistry, life sciences, technology, informatique (computer sciences), art education and other educational activities, and physical education. Emphasis is on Arabic language, foreign language, and mathematics.

In the second year of general secondary education, grade 11, two tracks are offered: humanities and sciences. Subjects taught in the humanities track are Arabic language, foreign language, second foreign language, philosophy and civilizations, sociology and economics, civic education, history, geography, mathematics, scientific culture, technology, informatique (computer sciences), art education and other educational activities, and physical education. Emphasis is on Arabic language and foreign language. Subjects taught in the sciences track of grade 11 are the same as those in the humanities track, except that scientific culture is replaced by physics, chemistry, and life sciences. Emphasis is on mathematics and physics.

In the third year of general secondary education, grade 12, four tracks are offered: arts and humanities, socioeconomics, general sciences, and life sciences. Subjects taught in the arts and humanities track are the same as those taught in the humanities track of grade 11, except for sociology and economics. Emphasis is on philosophy and civilizations, Arabic language, and foreign language. Subjects taught in the socioeconomics track in grade 12 are the same as those taught in the humanities track of grade 11. Emphasis is on sociology and economics. Subjects taught in the general sciences track in grade 12 are the same as those taught in the humanities track of grade 11, except for sociology and economics, plus scientific culture is replaced by physics and chemistry. Emphasis is on mathematics, physics, and chemistry. Subjects taught in the life sciences track in grade 12 are the same as those taught in the general sciences track of grade 12, plus life sciences. Emphasis is on mathematics, physics, chemistry, and life sciences.

There are also technical and vocational secondary schools, which last for three years. At the end of the three-year cycle of general academic, technical, and vocational secondary education, students take the Lebanese Baccalaureate exam in their chosen track. Successful students are awarded the Lebanese Baccalaureate Certificate of Secondary Education. Holders of this certificate can continue on to higher education or enter the labor market.

Higher education is provided by public and private institutions. Three- to five-year programs are offered at some institutions leading to a license, diploma, or a bachelor's degree. One- to two-year study beyond the bachelor's degree leads to a master's degree. Three years of further study beyond the master's degree leads to a doctorate degree. The number of colleges and institutes has increased in recent years, as well as the number of specializations offered, including nursing, physical therapy, dentistry, technology and science, computer science, management, tourism, hotels, and translation.

Teacher Education

Kindergarten and basic (elementary and intermediate cycles) school teachers receive training at colleges of education in public and private universities. Students must hold the Lebanese Baccalaureate for admission into a college of education. Students enroll in a three-year program of study leading to the bachelor's degree in basic education. Secondary school teachers must hold a teaching diploma, offered by colleges and universities in various fields, such as literature, mathematics, history, and physics. Or they can enroll in a five-year program, offered by the College of Education at the Lebanese University, leading to the certificate of pedagogical aptitude in secondary education. Teachers receive professional development training in contents of new curricula, teaching methods, assessment of educational achievement, theoretical academic subjects, technology subjects, learning techniques, practical applications, global education, environmental education, and international issues, such as democracy, solidarity, peace, human rights, and freedoms. Job training is mandatory in the public education sector, five hours monthly. It includes the following steps: a survey of the main problems encountered, analysis and categorization of problems, a discussion and presentation of solutions to problems by trainers, screening of films on types of lessons, and evaluation.

Informal Education

Adult education is provided for all Lebanese citizens, regardless of their age, educational background, socioeconomic status, or occupation, giving them an opportunity for training, retraining, or promotion. Educational opportunities are available to employed technicians and professionals, through continuous technical training, in order to update their skills and knowledge, as well as to introduce them to the latest

Lebanon Education at a Glance

General Information

Capital	Beirut
Population	4.2 million
Language	Arabic
Adult literacy rate (ages 15 and over)	89.6%
Youth literacy rate (ages 15–24)	98.7%
GDP per capita	US$14,067
Number of phones (mobile) per 100 people	68
Number of Internet users per 100 people	31
Life expectancy at birth (years)	72

Formal Educational Information

Enrollment in preprimary school (ages 3–5)	153,000
Enrollment in primary school (ages 6–11)	464,000
Enrollment in lower and upper secondary school (ages 12–17)	391,000
Number of years of compulsory education	9 (ages 6–14)
Preprimary school student/teacher ratio	16
Primary school student/teacher ratio	14
Lower and upper secondary school gross student/teacher ratio	9
Preprimary school gross enrollment ratio	81%
Primary school gross enrollment ratio	105%
Lower and upper secondary school gross enrollment ratio	81%
Primary school entrants reaching grade 5	90%

Sources: Education for All, 2011; Global Education Digest, 2011; UNESCO–UIS, 2012; UNICEF, 2012; United Nations Development Programme, 2011.

technological innovations. This training falls into the framework of lifelong learning. Upon the completion of their study, trainees receive a certificate of specialization.

At the centers of modular professional training, students receive training at three levels. The first training module is carried out within an autonomous training module, allowing students the flexibility to move vertically (i.e., a training module that is linked to and leads to a higher level module) or horizontally (i.e., moving to another trade at the same level within the same group of trades). After passing each module, students receive an official work certificate, allowing them to practice their trade or to continue further training at a higher modular level. In each training module students receive 600 to 900 hours of training, of which 25 percent is theory and 75 percent is practical work. At the end of the third module, students receive a professional certificate, allowing them to work or to pursue a higher technical level of formal education.

Students who did not complete their formal basic education can attend courses as part of the training modules. These courses are also open to adults who wish to benefit from these programs in order to be retrained in another profession or who desire a promotion while remaining in the same professional field. Admission to these various training modules depends on the requirements of each specialization and on regulations set by the Ministry of Technical and Vocational Education in collaboration with the Ministry of Labor and the National Agency for Employment.

The education system provides trade training in any profession recognized by the labor market to holders of the basic education certificate who wish to leave formal schooling early. The National Commission on Literacy was created in 1995 to develop programs for eliminating illiteracy, in collaboration with the Ministry of Social Affairs and community groups. The Ministry of Social Affairs, created in 1997 for the elimination of illiteracy and adult training, provides programs whose goals include enabling illiterates to learn trades that require basic knowledge in reading, writing, and arithmetic and to become autonomous in their daily life; strengthening the workers' sense of dignity and self-confidence; and improving the quality of life and adapting individual and social behavior.

System Economics

The total public expenditure on education in 2009 represented 1.8 percent of Lebanon's gross domestic product. It represented 7.2 percent of the total government expenditure. For the year 2005, 33 percent of public education spending was at the primary level, 30 percent at the secondary level, and 31 percent at the tertiary level.

Future Prospects

Plans are under way that aim to maximize the quality of education and training in preuniversity levels; establish a balance between general academic education and technical and vocational education; diversify higher education; match education with the Lebanese and Arab labor market; and reflect technical progress and the development of technologies in education.

Emad Alfar

REFERENCES

Central Intelligence Agency. *The CIA World Factbook*. New York: Skyhorse, 2011. https://www.cia.gov/library/publications/the-world-factbook/index.html.

Education for All. "The Hidden Crisis: Armed Conflict and Education." *Education for All Global Monitoring Report*. Paris: UNESCO, 2011.

Global Education Digest. *Global Education Digest 2011: Comparing Education Statistics Across the World*. Montreal: UNESCO Institute for Statistics, 2011.

"Lebanon." In *The Europa World Yearbook*, vol. 2. London: Routledge, 2009.

Programme on Governance in the Arab Region. www.pogar.org/countries/country.aspx?cid=9.

UNESCO–IBE. www.ibe.unesco.org/countries/Lebanon.htm.

UNESCO–UIS. www.uis.unesco.org.

UNICEF. www.unicef.org/infobycountry/lebanon.html.

United Nations Development Programme. "Sustainability and Equity: A Better Future for All." *Human Development Report 2011*. New York: Palgrave Macmillan, 2011.

NEPAL

Nepal lies between China to the north and India to the east, south, and west, making it a landlocked country in South Asia.

In 1951 Nepal witnessed a dawn of democracy by setting itself free from the family rule of the Ranas. Since then various models and forms of democratic governments have been introduced, providing a ground for the rise of an absolute monarch, King Gyanendra, in the country. Ten years of Maoist insurgency led by Puspa Kamal Dahal Prachanda and the Popular Movement led by Girija Prasad Koirala, forming a seven-party alliance, succeeded in reinstating the parliament in 2006, leading to the suspension of the monarchy. The seven-party coalition government formed under Koirala's leadership was also joined by the Maoists, making it an eight-party alliance, which became a seven-party alliance again after the integration of the Nepali Congress (Democratic) into the Nepali Congress in 2007. The alliance agreed to hold elections to form the Constituent Assembly to write a constitution and decide about the fate of the king. As indicated in the interim constitution of 2007, Nepal was supposed to enter into a new phase of restructuring and reconstruction, adopting a decentralized federal framework and a republican

political order. These changes were to set the tone of the reform agenda and provide policy directions for education to materialize the vision of a new Nepal. Unfortunately, due to disagreement among political parties, although the interim constitution was to become finalized in the spring of 2011, extensions have been added.

Nepal's population consists of two major groups: Indo-Europeans, who constitute roughly 74 percent, and Sino-Tibetans, who constitute about 26 percent. More than 80 percent of the population practices Sanatan Dharma (a faith system in Hindu that means "eternal law"). Other religions include Buddhism (10 percent), Islam (4 percent), Kirant (4 percent), and other religions (2 percent). As of 2011, the population of Nepal was 29.4 million. According to the Nepalese Central Bureau of Statistics, the current estimated population growth rate is 2.2 percent per annum. Nepal's estimated infant mortality rate as of 2011 is 44.54 per 1,000 live births, and the estimated life expectancy at birth as of 2011 is 66.2 years. There are 101 distinct caste and ethnic communities and more than 92 languages in Nepal. The Nepali language, as the mother tongue of 48 percent of the population, serves as a language of wider communication. Although the Pahadi language spoken in the far west has been considered part of Nepali, the reality is that the Pahadi language (which is spoken and not written) and the Nepali, the official language, are not mutually intelligible. Other languages documented in the census have been recognized as the languages of the nation by Nepal's extension of the interim constitution.

Educational System

The responsibility for the execution of education functions lies with the Ministry of Education and Sports (MOES). MOES provides policy directions and develops the statutory framework for the attainment of educational goals in the country. The ministry's mandate with regard to these broad functions includes the following: (1) formulating policy, (2) setting standards, (3) coordinating sectoral programs, (4) generating and mobilizing resources, and (5) monitoring and evaluation. With a view to carrying out these functions, the MOES service delivery system is supported by central and local-level institutions.

The central-level agencies within the MOES system

are responsible for implementing and monitoring education programs across the country. The principal responsibility for the delivery of school-level education services lies with the Department of Education (DOE). At the technical level, there are several constituent agencies that work as technical arms of the MOES system. These institutions include the Curriculum Development Center, National Center for Educational Development, Nonformal Education Center, Controller of Examinations, Higher Secondary Education Board, and Council for Technical Education and Vocational Training.

Each of the regional educational directorates acts as the liaison between the centers and district-level programs. District education offices (DEOs) are the key implementing units for delivering education services in the districts. DEOs are responsible for developing strategies and providing support for the functioning of the education system at local levels. Resource centers as part of district-level delivery provide technical backstopping to schools and help teachers carry out curricular intents. At the school level, the school management committee is entrusted with the responsibility for managing teachers and resources, attaining targets, and ensuring students' learning.

Traditionally, Nepal has been a home for the preaching in Hindu Vedic ashrams and Buddhist teachings in monasteries following traditions of *gurukul* education, which is deeply rooted in the Hindu tradition of devotion to the guru (teacher). In *Gurukul* education, students are regarded as the disciples of their guru, who is considered the source of knowledge and wisdom. Owing to the influence of these local imperatives, a majority of teachers still possess the legacy of *Gurukul* tradition, which manifests in their pedagogical practices in schools.

Education in the Western sense did not take place until the middle of the nineteenth century. Only after 1851 when Prime Minister Jung Bahadur Rana brought British and Bengali tutors to Kathmandu to teach the children of the Ranas and the royals did the country witness the formal start of education in the Western sense. This historic step, though self-centered, gave birth to the Durbar School (the school for the palace), which catered to the children of the ruling-class families for the first time inside Nepal.

The spread of English is clearly visible in the education system and has become pervasive in people's

Figure 1: **Napal Ministry of Education and Sports Service Delivery System**

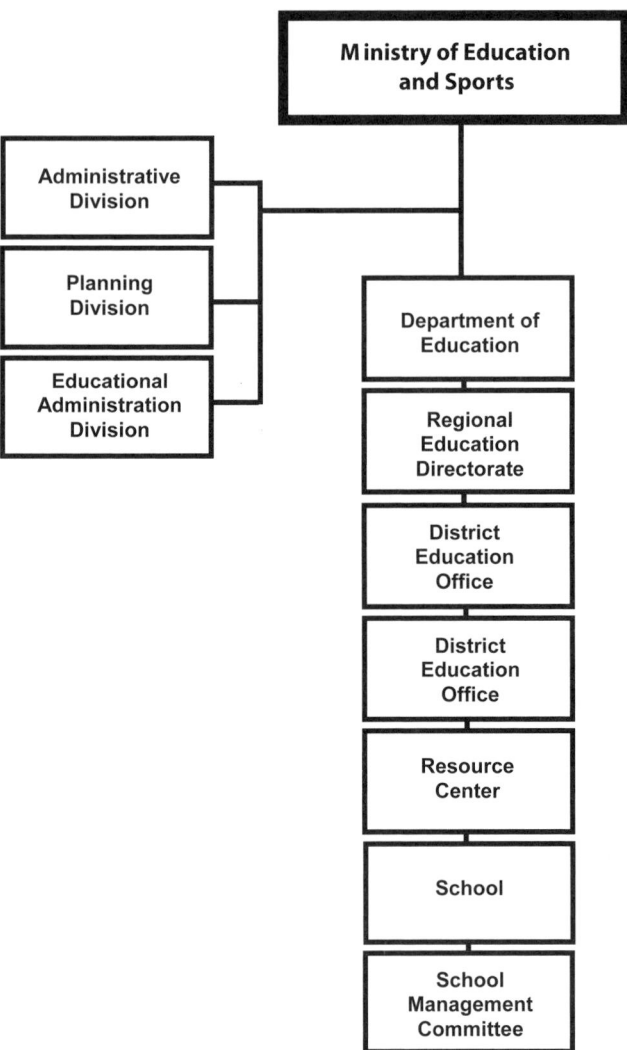

Source: DOE 2010.

everyday life in Nepal. The medium of instruction in public schools is Nepali, whereas private schools tend to opt for English instead. The mother tongues in Nepal appear to be sandwiched between English and Nepali. Nepal's education system has witnessed a rapid expansion of schools over a decade or so, leading to the spread of both public and private schools. At present the number of schools has reached 28,000, with 8,000 schools run by the private sector to satisfy the interest of anglophile parents across the country.

Primary and Secondary Education

Nepal is committed to compulsory school education as stipulated in the interim constitution of Nepal. However, due to resource limitations, Nepal has not yet been able to introduce compulsory basic education.

Nepal's education structure entails both formal and nonformal education, ranging from school education to university education. School education comprises five years of primary education (grades 1–5) for children starting at five years of age, three years of lower secondary education (grades 6–8), two years of secondary education (grades 9–10), and two years of higher secondary education (grades 11–12). Over a period of years, early childhood development and preprimary programs have come to be seen as an integral part of school education.

Tertiary Education

The university system operates under the University Grants Commission (UGC). UGC is responsible for allocating resources and determines educational standards in higher education. UGC gives recommendations to the government about establishing universities and provides universities with a framework for enhancing the quality of education. At present, the following universities are in operation in Nepal:

1. Tribhuvan University was Nepal's first university, established in 1959 and funded by the government. It is the largest university with 60 constituent campuses and 348 affiliated campuses spread across the country.
2. Nepal Sanskrit University was established in 1986 with a view to promoting Sanskrit studies and research in the country. It is a government-funded university, with 12 constituents and 17 affiliated campuses.
3. Kathmandu University was established 1991 through public initiatives. It has six schools and 11 affiliated campuses.
4. Purbanchal (eastern) University was established in 1995 as a state-funded institution whose mission is to expand the opportunities for higher education at the regional level.
5. Pokhara University was established in 1996 as a state-funded regional university.
6. Lumbini Buddhist University was established in 2004 to promote research and higher studies in Buddhism.

Considering the emerging needs of the educational reform in the country, the Ministry of Education has initiated a process for restructuring school and university education. Under the school sector reform (SSR), a new school structure is proposed in the light of Nepal's interim constitution. The SSR intends to expand the present grade 1 to 5 primary school structure to grade 1 to 8 basic education; however, given that the interim constitution is still in place, it is unclear if the SSR will execute this policy. Likewise, the SSR aims at harmonizing the secondary and higher secondary education structure by integrating the curricular, examination, standard-setting, and management functions of grades 9 to 12. The reform plans also provide also for general and vocational streams of education in grades 9 to 12 to cater to the needs of students who opt for acquiring general vocation qualifications.

Curriculum, Assessment, and Instruction

The Curriculum Development Center (CDC) is entrusted with the responsibility for developing the national curriculum framework (NCF) and for designing school curricula. On the basis of these guiding principles, CDC develops pro forma templates for writing textbooks and prepares teachers' guides and supplementary materials as aids for students. In 2006 CDC developed the NCF for school education, focusing on quality enhancement, inclusion, decentralization, local-level capacity building, continuous assessment, multilingual education, and core and flexible curricula.

According to the NCF (2006), school education is planned to be organized into two levels: basic education (grades 1–8) and secondary education (grades 9–12). The basic education curriculum entails languages, including mother tongues, Nepali, and English; mathematics; social studies; creative art; and science, comprising general science, environment science, health, and physical education. At this basic level, Nepali, English, mathematics, social studies, and science are arranged under core learning areas, whereas two subjects, including a local language or

Figure 2: **Education Structure of Nepal**

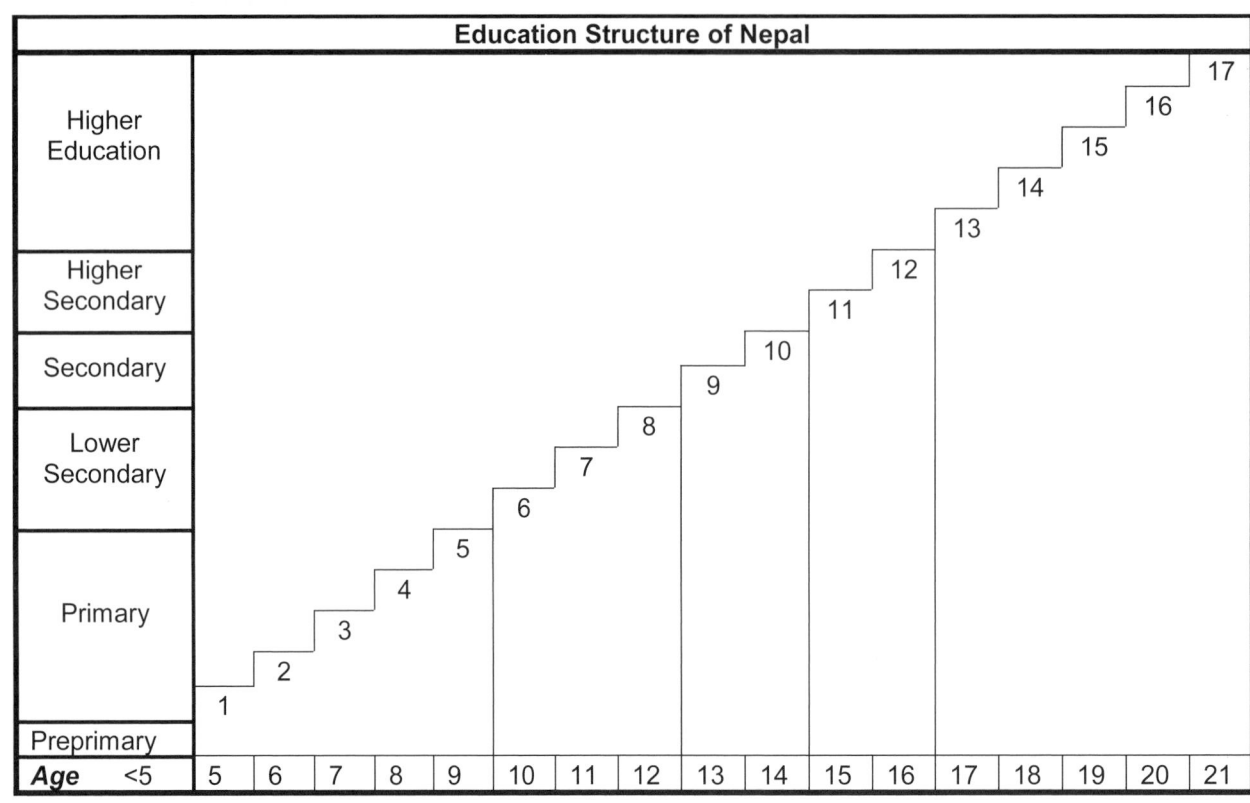

Source: Ministry of Education and Sports 2010.

Sanskrit and a locally determined subject relating to occupation, history, culture, and so on, are offered as optional subjects.

At the secondary level, the core learning areas include languages, science, mathematics, social studies, and technical and vocational subjects. From grade 9 onward, provisions have been made for a separate technical and vocational stream.

CDC has developed implementation guidelines for the continuous assessment system (CAS) for the early grades of primary education. In the school sector reform, the CAS is employed as a major strategy in basic education for student evaluation and progress monitoring.

The grade-level examinations are school-based. However, the fifth- and eighth-grade examinations are conducted under the aegis of the district education offices. The Office of the Controller of Examinations (OCE) has been established by the government to carry out examination functions. The first School Leaving Certificate (SLC)—which is awarded to students who complete the secondary school level examinations—were held in 1934. Since then, changes have been made in the examination system.

Teacher Education

Teacher development has been recognized as a major strategy to improve the quality of education in Nepal. The government has placed emphasis on two sets of activities for teacher development: (1) recurrent teacher training and professional support, and (2) certification of teacher training. The Department of Education provides support for conducting recurrent teacher training through district and subdistrict networking, and coordinates on-the-job teacher development programs across the country. The National Center for Educational Development (NCED) provides 10-month in-service courses to untrained primary school teachers through educational training centers, which are located across the country. MOES has developed a strategic plan for the training of primary school teachers. The Faculty of Education under Tribhuvan University is involved in preservice teacher education and development programs. Its role is crucial for the supply of competent teaching personnel in the school system. In order to improve the quality of instruction in primary schools, MOES has planned to upgrade the present entry qualification for primary school teachers from the SLC to the higher secondary level of education that is provided at tertiary institutions.

In order to increase the coverage as well as improve the quality of education in Nepal, the Ministry of Education has been implementing the Teacher Education Project through NCED. Still, about 30 percent of teachers in primary schools are yet to be trained. The major challenge in teacher development in Nepal appears to be how the population of female teachers can be increased from the current level of less than 30 percent to at least 50 percent in primary schools. Another challenge in this regard seems to be how the participation of the disadvantaged and minority groups can be ensured in the teaching profession. Besides, the teacher development programs for the secondary and higher secondary schools are yet to be streamlined and strengthened to enhance the quality of instruction at upper levels of school education.

Informal Education

Adult literacy programs are a priority of the government. Likewise, at the school level, nonformal education programs are emphasized to ensure children's access to education. The government has mobilized internal and external resources to expand nonformal education and literacy programs in the country. An administrative setup for nonformal education has been established under the Ministry of Education. Based on past experiences, the government established the Nonformal Education Center in 1999 in order to lead and coordinate nonformal education activities in the country.

Nonformal education aims to provide educational opportunities to children between eight and 14 years of age who missed primary schooling at the appropriate age. Graduates of such programs are mainstreamed to formal schools so that they can complete their primary education cycle. Adult literacy programs focus on reading, writing, and arithmetic, especially for adults between the ages 15 and 45. In addition, functional knowledge and skills are imparted in order to build self-confidence and enhance quality of life. Women are given special priority in these programs. School outreach and flexible schooling programs aim at providing primary education to children who are unable to attend formal schools due to family financial hardships.

The Adult Literacy Program (ALP) and Women Literacy Program (WLP) are two major interventions that target the illiterate population between the ages 15 and 45. ALP is for all illiterate people and WLP specifically targets women. Both programs have two levels. The first phase of the programs aims at literacy and vocational skills, whereas the second phase aims at stabilizing literacy and strengthening skills and knowledge gained during the first phase. In addition to literacy and vocational skills, WLP also provides knowledge and skills appropriate for household and family matters. The Community Learning Center is a new and innovative approach to increasing literacy with a view to providing opportunities for basic and continuing education and establishing linkages between education and development.

The Community-Based Alternative Schooling Project aims at building a nonformal education model and improving the existing alternative schooling programs for out-of-school children.

System Economics

The government of Nepal has allocated 17 percent of its total budget to the education sector, with a 55 percent share in basic and primary education. Past trends show a gradual increment in investment in education. The government aims at allocating 3.7 percent of its gross domestic product to the education sector (at present the amount is about 3 percent). However, owing to resource constraints, Nepal has not yet been able to introduce compulsory basic education as envisioned in the United Nations Education for All and Millennium Development Goals.

To cater to diverse needs of the target populations, different funding modalities, including block grants, earmarked grants, performance-based grants, and per capita funding grants, have been introduced. The Annual Strategic Implementation Plan (ASIP) has been a major instrument to allocate resources for targeted interventions through decentralized and strategic planning in education. A school sector approach has been initiated to harmonize programs and resources in education. A joint financing arrangement has been developed to blend resources received from pooling partners. Earmarked funding from nonpooling partners has also been utilized to meet funding requirements in the sector. About 30 percent of external resources from both pooling and nonpooling partners has been mobilized in the education sector. Major external partners in the sector include Asian Development Bank, Denmark, European Union, Finland, Japan, Norway, UNESCO, United Nations Population Fund (UNFPA), UNICEF, UNDP, United Kingdom, World Bank, World Food Program, and other nongovernmental organizations (NGOs).

At present, primary education (grades 1–5) is free of cost. That is, tuition and textbooks are free. However, due to inadequate mechanisms to reinforce this provision, schools have continued raising fees from students. The government pays 100 percent of salary of primary, lower secondary, and secondary teachers (for approved posts) and also

provides administrative and stationery expenses of community schools.

In order to ensure inclusion in education and provide access for girls and children from disadvantaged, marginalized communities and children with disabilities, the government has introduced different incentive schemes, such as free textbooks, 50 percent scholarships for girls, 100 percent scholarships for Dalit (so-called untouchables at the lowest strata of the caste hierarchy), scholarship for marginalized students, and midday meals and cooking oil, targeting children in remote and food deficit districts.

Sustainable financing for the education system requires commitment from central and local governments. Besides the commitment from the center, the country needs to mobilize resources from local governments, communities, NGOs, civil society organizations, and the private sector in order to ensure children's basic education. This is also crucial to fulfill Nepal's commitment to compulsory school education as stipulated in the interim constitution.

Lava Deo Awasthi

REFERENCES

Awasthi, Lava Deo. "Exploring Monolingual School Practices in Multilingual Nepal." PhD dissertation, Danish School of Education, Copenhagen, 2004.

Central Bureau of Statistics. *Statistical Pocket Book: Nepal.* Kathmandu: Central Bureau of Statistics, 2010.

Central Intelligence Agency. *The CIA World Factbook.* New York: Skyhorse, 2011. https://www.cia.gov/library/publications/the-world-factbook/index.html.

Curriculum Development Center. *National Curriculum Framework for School Education in Nepal.* Sanothimi, Nepal: Curriculum Development Center, 2006.

Department of Education, Nepal. *The Flash Report.* Sanothimi, Nepal: Department of Education, 2010.

Ministry of Education and Sports, Nepal. *Nepal in Educational Figures.* Kathmandu, Nepal: Ministry of Education and Sports, 2007.

Nepal Demographic Health Survey. Kathmandu, Nepal: Ministry of Health and Population, New Era and Macro International, 2010.

University Grants Commission. *Annual Report 2005/06.* Bhaktapur, Nepal: University Grants Commission, 2006.

Whelpton, John. *A History of Nepal.* Cambridge, UK: Cambridge University Press, 2005.

Nepal Education at a Glance

General Information

Capital	Kathmandu
Population	27.2 million
Language	Nepali
Adult literacy rate (ages 15 and over)	60.3%
Youth literacy rate (ages 15–24)	83.1%
GDP per capita	US$1,199
Number of phones (mobile) per 100 people	31
Number of Internet users per 100 people	7
Life expectancy at birth (years)	68

Formal Educational Information

Enrollment in preprimary school (ages 3–4)	947,000
Enrollment in primary school (ages 5–9)	4.9 million
Enrollment in lower and upper secondary school (ages 10–16)	2.3 million
Number of years of compulsory education	no data
Preprimary school student/teacher ratio	41
Primary school student/teacher ratio	32
Lower and upper secondary school gross student/teacher ratio	41
Preprimary school gross enrollment ratio	12%
Primary school gross enrollment ratio	115%
Lower and upper secondary school gross enrollment ratio	44%
Primary school entrants reaching grade 5	62%

Sources: Education for All, 2011; Global Education Digest, 2011; UNESCO–UIS, 2012; UNICEF, 2012; United Nations Development Programme, 2011.

OMAN

The Sultanate of Oman is an Arab country located in southwestern Asia on the Arabian Peninsula. The official language is Arabic. Other spoken languages include English, Urdu, Baluchi, and Hindi. Its currency is the Omani rial, which is equivalent to about US$2.60. Roughly half of the population is Omani, one-third is South Asian, and the remaining groups include Iranians, East Africans, and Arabs from other countries. The official religion is Islam. The majority of the population is Muslim, with small numbers of Christian and Hindu communities. Oman gained independence in 1650 after the expulsion of the Portuguese. In July 1970—the year in which the sultan acceded to the throne and achieved full international recognition—the country's name was changed from the Sultanate of Muscat and Oman to the Sultanate of Oman.

Educational System

The Ministry of Education is responsible for public education and supervises private education. As a result of recent education reforms, two education systems operate simultaneously: the old general education system, comprising six years of elementary, three years of preparatory, and three years of secondary schooling, and the new basic education system, which comprises ten years of basic education and two years of secondary. The new basic education system is being phased in gradually, while the old general education system is being phased out. Education is not compulsory at any level, but it is free for all Omanis.

The new general education system, called the new basic education, comprises four stages: (1) kindergarten, (2) cycle one of basic education, (3) cycle two of basic education, and (4) secondary education. Kindergarten lasts for two years, for children entering at age four and exiting at age six. All private schools, established mainly by the private business sector, provide kindergarten education. Cycle one of basic education lasts for four years, covering grades 1 through 4, for children entering at age six and exiting at age 10. Cycle one prepares students for the next stage. It enables students to understand and appreciate social, environmental, and economic relations in their community through the development of their skills, competencies, and knowledge. Cycle two of basic education lasts for six years, covering grades 5 through 10, for children entering at age 10 and exiting at age 16. Cycle two provides students with the necessary knowledge, skills, and competencies to advance to the secondary stage.

Secondary education, also called postbasic education, lasts for two years, covering grades 11 and 12, for children entering at age 16 and exiting at age 18. Secondary education comprises two streams, arts and science. It strengthens students' intellectual, social, and spiritual development and improves their scientific thinking and self-learning ability. Students are prepared for continuing on to higher education or entering into the labor market. Students who successfully complete their secondary education are eligible for enrollment into higher education institutions.

The Ministry of Higher Education is in charge of higher education institutions. These institutions offer one- to ten-year programs leading to certificates, diplomas, and bachelor's, master's, and doctoral degrees.

Curriculum, Assessment, and Instruction

Kindergarten education fosters a balanced intellectual, spiritual, emotional, and social development of the child's personality. It prepares children for school education.

Subjects taught in cycle one of basic education, grades 1 through 4, are Islamic education, Arabic language, English language, mathematics, sciences, physical education, art education, music education, environmental life skills, and information technology. Social studies is also taught in grades 3 and 4. Emphasis is on Islamic education, Arabic language, English language, and mathematics. Subjects taught and emphasized in cycle two of basic education, grades 5 through 10, are the same as in cycle one, except that the teaching of music education ends after the students complete grade 9 and information technology is replaced by computer science.

The new general secondary education, grades 11 and 12, comprises two streams, arts and science. Subjects taught in the arts stream are Islamic education, Arabic language, English language, mathematics, sciences, social studies, physical education, economics and administrative sciences, art education, and environmental life skills. Emphasis is on Arabic language, English language, and social studies. Subjects taught in the science stream are the same as those in the arts streams, except for social studies and economics and administrative sciences. Emphasis is on Arabic language, English language, mathematics, and sciences. Each academic year consists of two semesters. An all-inclusive end-of-year final exam has been replaced by mid-semester and end-of-semester exams. Increased emphasis is placed on assessing higher-order thinking skills instead of factual recall. The new basic education system promotes a student-centered instead of teacher-centered approach to teaching and learning. Students are also evaluated through a wide range of assessment instruments, including continuous classroom assessment, such as short written or oral tests, quizzes, performance assessment tasks, projects, and student self-assessments. Depending on the education system in which they are enrolled, students who successfully complete their secondary education are awarded the General Certificate in General Education or the General Education Diploma in Postbasic Education, allowing them to continue on to higher education.

Higher education is provided by Sultan Qaboos University and several specialized colleges and institutes: colleges of education (four-year programs), technical industrial colleges (two-year programs), higher Islamic institutes, health institutes, and a banking institute. Sultan Qaboos University includes the Colleges of Medicine, Science, Engineering, Agriculture, Education, Arts, and Economics.

Teacher Education

Teachers at all levels must be trained in education. Elementary school teachers must hold a bachelor's degree and be trained for four years at one of the colleges of education. Preparatory and secondary school teachers must be trained at one of the colleges of education and hold a university degree in education or a postgraduate diploma in education of at least one year after graduation. The Ministry of Education provides in-service training programs for teachers, including short-term programs (week-long innovation courses, workshops, and seminars), mid-length programs (designed to prepare elementary teachers to teach at the preparatory level), and specialized courses (designed to provide training according to teachers' needs).

Informal Education

Informal education is offered at literacy centers, special education centers, and through society development programs. The Ministry of Education provides literacy and adult education programs. Literacy programs, designed for Omanis who are more than 10 years old and have not received formal education, last for two years and provide an education that is similar to that of grades 1 through 4, at the end of which students are awarded a literacy certificate. Those who complete the literacy program can continue on to the adult education program. Adult education programs provide education that parallels grade 5 of elementary education through grade 12 of secondary education. They offer a choice of attending regular adult education classes or home study. Students take exams similar to those given in formal general education.

System Economics

The total public expenditure on education in Oman in 2009 represented 4.3 percent of gross domestic

---

Oman Education at a Glance

General Information

Capital	Muscat
Population	2.7 million
Language	Arabic
Adult literacy rate (ages 15 and over)	86.6%
Youth literacy rate (ages 15–24)	97.6%
GDP per capita	US$26,791
Number of phones (mobile) per 100 people	166
Number of Internet users per 100 people	63
Life expectancy at birth (years)	73

Formal Educational Information

Enrollment in preprimary school (ages 4–5)	44,000
Enrollment in primary school (ages 6–9)	302,000
Enrollment in lower and upper secondary school (ages 10–17)	322,000
Number of years of compulsory education	no data
Preprimary school student/teacher ratio	19
Primary school student/teacher ratio	12
Lower and upper secondary school gross student/teacher ratio	15
Preprimary school gross enrollment ratio	45%
Primary school gross enrollment ratio	84%
Lower and upper secondary school gross enrollment ratio	91%
Primary school entrants reaching grade 5	98%

Sources: Education for All, 2011; Global Education Digest, 2011; UNESCO–UIS, 2012; UNICEF, 2012; United Nations Development Programme, 2011.

product. In the year 2006, 31.1 percent of the total government expenditure was on education. Thirty-three percent of public education spending was at the primary level, 40 percent at the secondary level, and 27 percent at the tertiary level.

Future Prospects

The Ministry of Education is gradually implementing educational reforms, including structural changes at the ministry, regional, and school levels. As a result of a conference, titled "Oman 2020: The Vision Conference for Oman's Economy," held in July 1995, among the goals the country aims to achieve by 2020 are promoting the acquisition of global knowledge, information, and human skills; spreading education and making it accessible to all; and the Omanisation (replacing foreign workers with Omani citizens) of the country's economy in order to reduce dependency on foreign labor. The seventh Development Plan (2006–2010), prepared by the Ministry of Education, aims to eradicate illiteracy among male and female Omanis between the ages of 15 and 44. Curriculum is being developed for grades 11 and 12 of the new secondary education as the first cohort of students completes grade 10 of the new basic education.

Emad Alfar

REFERENCES

Central Intelligence Agency. *The CIA World Factbook*. New York: Skyhorse, 2011. https://www.cia.gov/library/publications/the-world-factbook/index.html.

Education for All. "The Hidden Crisis: Armed Conflict and Education." *Education for All Global Monitoring Report*. Paris: UNESCO, 2011.

Global Education Digest. *Global Education Digest 2011: Comparing Education Statistics Across the World*. Montreal: UNESCO Institute for Statistics, 2011.

"Oman." In *The Europa World Yearbook*, vol. 2. London: Routledge, 2009.

Programme on Governance in the Arab Region. www.pogar.org/countries/country.aspx?cid=13.

UNESCO–IBE. www.ibe.unesco.org/countries/Oman.htm.

UNESCO–UIS. www.uis.unesco.org.

UNICEF. www.unicef.org/infobycountry/oman.html.

United Nations Development Programme. "Sustainability and Equity: A Better Future for All." *Human Development Report 2011*. New York: Palgrave Macmillan, 2011.

PAKISTAN

The Islamic Republic of Pakistan is located in South Asia. While Islam is the religion of the majority of population, a small minority follow Christianity, Hinduism, Buddhism, Ahmadiyya, Zoroastrianism, and Sikhism. Pashto, Punjabi, Sindhi, Balochi, and Saraiki are some of the languages spoken in Pakistan. Urdu is the national language while English serves as an official language.

Delivering his presidential address on December 29, 1930, the president of the Punjab Muslim League, Allama Iqbal, voiced the idea of an independent state for Muslims in India. As the prospects for British withdrawal from South Asia became clear, the Pakistani statesman Mohammad Ali Jinnah declared his support for the Lahore Declaration which was adopted by the league in 1940. One year later, Jama'at-e-Islami, the most powerful Islamist organization, was founded. The subsequent negotiations between the British, the Muslim League, and the Indian National Congress gave birth to the reality of the idea of Pakistan as an independent state. Pakistan became independent from the United Kingdom on August 14, 1947. Pakistan's formation was based on the idea of creating a homeland for Indian Muslims, a state that was built upon hopes to offer social welfare, prosperity, and a sense of justice to its citizens. However, the discrepancy between these early aspirations and reality profoundly points to the severe challenges Pakistan had to face. In the early years, Pakistan developed its economy based on agriculture that was diversified in later years. While the Punjab region had an excellent advantage in its irrigation system, the other three provinces did not have the same benefits.

Educational System

Founded at the annual All India Muhammadan Educational Conference in Shahbagh, Dhaka, in 1906, the Muslim League was largely dominated by wealthy landowners and was secular in its initial political orientation. One of its principle concerns, however, was the place of Indian Muslims within the Hindu-dominated political structure of India.

Universal primary education and quality improvement of existing institutions were identified as immediate goals by the new government. When Pakistan became independent, the country had only one institute of higher education, Punjab University. In order to address the immediate needs of the country, the government focused on developing higher education in the next 20 years. The changes in Pakistan's education policy have, to no small extent, reflected the larger political changes the country has experienced over time. In the last few decades Pakistan has struggled with varied tensions. Differences over the tenets and extent of religious influence in the public sphere continue to stir passionate responses. Additionally, the tensions between emerging civil society and growing military influence, the self-centered elite and the socially excluded masses, are contentious issues that cannot be ignored in the contemporary political culture of Pakistan.

Education in Pakistan is divided into the following stages: primary education (grades 1 through 5), middle school education (grades 6 through 8), high school education (grades 9 and 10, leading to the Secondary School Certificate), intermediate education (grades 11 and 12, leading to a Higher Secondary School Certificate), and higher education. Additionally, other streams include technical and vocational studies, adult education, distance education, nonformal education, and religious education. Technical and vocational studies can be started after completing the coursework up to grade 8. Provincial governments are responsible for managing academic institutions while the federal government is involved in curriculum development, accreditation, and funding matters. Urdu, Sindhi, and to a lesser degree Pashto are used in instruction in various schools. Historically, numerous schools in Pakistan used English as the medium of instruction. Along with its modern educational system, Pakistan also has the system of religious education to impart knowledge about Islamic traditions. These madrassa institutions include *muktabas* (primary schools), *durul ulooms* (secondary schools), and *jaamias* (universities) that are managed independently of provincial or federal governments.

Following independence, the Pakistani state took upon itself the task of providing accessible education. The first Pakistan Education Conference was convened at Karachi on November 27, 1947, focusing on linking educational policy to the needs of Pakistan as an evolving nation. Muhammad Ali Jinna, the leader of the All-India Muslim League, gave a speech at the conference in which he voiced the priority of public education: "There is no doubt that the future of our State will and must greatly depend upon the type of education we give to our children and the way in which we bring them up as future citizens of Pakistan. Education does not merely mean academic education. There is an immediate and urgent need to give scientific and technical education to our people in order to build up our economic life. We should not forget that we have to compete with the world which is moving very fast in this direction" (Government of Sindh 2009). In the same vein, the conference identified teacher education as an important cause and recommended that provinces take necessary steps to ensure proper training of teachers and an adequate salary scale for them.

Pakistan's educational planning and policy decisions involved investment in higher education, teacher education, and an expansion of basic education. In the 1970s, during the government of Zulfikar Ali Bhutto, education in Pakistan was nationalized, making the system state-run for the next decade. However, the capacity of government-run institutions could not accommodate the growing demand for higher education. In 1978, Pakistan experienced major political instability when the civilian government of Prime Minister Bhutto succumbed to a coup and General Zia ul Haq took power. General Zia introduced deregulation and privatization measures in general that had far-reaching implications for education. Following a review of Bhutto's nationalized educational policy, Zia cleared the way for private institutions that resumed operating by the early 1980s. Further, he called for Islamization of education, including establishing *muktabas* (primary schools) and madrassas (religious educational institutions) and reorienting school contents in conformity with principles of Islam (Boissiere et al. 2007).

Curriculum, Assessment, and Instruction

The *katchi*, early childhood, preprimary education classes, are places where children receive basic learning that prepares them to enter into primary classes. In most cases, primary schools house preprimary classes. The preschools focus on developing children's mental as well as physical skills through play activities. In the next stage of primary education, children are introduced to formal learning of language, problem solving, and developing motor skills. In addition to language and mathematics, primary schools focus on reading comprehension and introduction of art. Although children are evaluated, their performance does not hold them from progressing to the next grade.

The required criteria for completing primary and middle school are determined by specific institutions in which children are enrolled. The curriculum taught in middle school includes language, mathematics, social studies, natural sciences, and introduction to English (where applicable). The high school curriculum is divided into three streams: natural sciences, humanities, and religion. Students write the "matric" examination after completing secondary school. Successful completion of this examination earns them the Secondary School Certificate (SSC). The next stage after SSC is the Higher Secondary Certificate (HSC) examination, conducted by affiliated colleges. Humanities, natural sciences, premedical education, pre-engineering, and domestic sciences are some of the streams students can choose from. The Higher Secondary Certificate (HSC) is required for entering higher education. Examination papers are graded based on a maximum of 100 points. Universities and colleges set their own requirements regarding admission. Higher education courses are offered by universities, specialized institutions, and colleges. From one university in 1947, Pakistan has come a long way in creating necessary infrastructure and building opportunities for the population. As of 2012, Pakistan has over 230 universities that enrolled students specializing in a range of disciplines. Throughout secondary schooling and higher education, students are evaluated on a scale of 1 to 100 and awarded corresponding divisions A through F. Division A is awarded to marks above 60 percent and above; division B for marks between 46 percent and 59 percent; division C for marks between 33 percent and 45 percent; and marks below 33 percent are given F.

Teacher Education

Teacher education is organized through preservice and in-service programs. Most teacher education institutions are managed by the state, with a handful of privately run institutions. The number of teachers in the public sector is about 500,000, while nearly 100,000 teachers work in the private sector. About 135 institutions are involved in teacher education, focusing on both preservice and in-service programs. The organization and management of teacher education programs are decentralized up to district levels in order to familiarize teachers with local needs. Preservice programs are organized in the form of certificate, degree, or diploma, focusing on educational theories, pedagogy, and content areas. In-service programs, organized by specific provincial governments, emphasize curriculum design and the development of administrative and management skills. The Provincial Institute of Teacher Education is involved in overseeing teacher education on the state level. Federally, the National Institute of Science and Technology is involved in teacher education. Numerous universities, educational institutions, and colleges offer programs in teacher education and supervisor education. Colleges offer two programs in elementary teacher education: the Primary Teaching Certificate and Certificate in Teaching. The curriculum wing of the Ministry of Education, in conjunction with several educational boards, develops curriculum for these two programs, which enroll undergraduate students. Similarly, two programs are offered to train secondary school teachers: a year-long bachelor of education program and a three-year, integrated BA/BSc and BEd program. Supervisor education and administrator education programs are offered by universities and other institutions. While the curriculum for the BEd degree is designed by the Higher Education Commission of Pakistan, the in-service teacher education curriculum is designed by specific institutions that offer the program. The Higher Education Commission of Pakistan is responsible for reviewing and revising the curricula.

The Primary Teaching Certificate requires completion of the following courses: Principles of Education and Methods of Teaching; Child Development and Counseling; School Organization and Management; Health and Physical Education; Six Methods of Teaching in Subject Areas; and one short-term and one long-term practicum. The following courses are offered in the secondary teacher education program: Perspectives on Education in Pakistan; Human Development; School Organization and Management; Evaluation and Guidance; Society, Schools, Teachers;

Method Course; and Practicum. A total of 14 courses are offered in the BEd program; ten of these are core and the rest are electives.

In 1993 the Commonwealth Secretariat produced a report focusing on teacher development in South Asia. Laying out a historical account of education in Pakistan, the report drew attention to the void between policy prescription and practice: "Development of Education system in Pakistan suffered from stagnation and slow growth. Teacher education has been brought to the forefront especially in the wake of attempts to reorient the focus of educational system. It is assumed that training will satisfy both practical and theoretical needs—practical aspects of classroom management and theoretical issues in child development." Since independence, Pakistan has implemented more than 15 educational policy regimes. The National Education Policy of 1992 articulated the following tasks to be implemented by 2002: promoting universal primary education, improving overall quality, reassessing teacher education programs, modernizing curricula, and introducing computer literacy at early stages. Although some implementations have occurred, the goals of the National Education Policy have not come to fruition.

System Economics

By 1990 Pakistan spent 2.1 percent of its gross domestic product (GDP) on education. The expenditure dipped in the next 10 years, accounting for about 0.8 percent in the year 2001. By 2009 the percentage of GDP expenditure on education increased to 2.7 percent. Pakistan thus ranks 142 out of 186 countries in terms of educational expenditure.

Future Prospects

A UNESCO report on Pakistan's educational policy in 2006 states, "A common feature of all policies, plans, programs, and schemes is that all of them, with the sole exception of the Second Five-Year Plan, failed to achieve their objectives." The report goes on to document a series of policy decisions that did not yield anticipated results. For instance, under Social Action Program, Pakistan spent over 3.56 billion US\$ (327 billion PKR) but despite this initiative the enrollment rates decreased. In response to this report, the

Pakistan Education at a Glance	
General Information	
Capital	Islamabad
Population	173.5 million
Languages	Urdu (official, 8%), Punjabi (48%)
Adult literacy rate (ages 15 and over)	54.9%
Youth literacy rate (ages 15–24)	70.7%
GDP per capita	US\$2,688
Number of phones (mobile) per 100 people	59
Number of Internet users per 100 people	17
Life expectancy at birth (years)	65
Formal Educational Information	
Enrollment in preprimary school (ages 3–4)	4 million
Enrollment in primary school (ages 5–9)	18.4 million
Enrollment in lower and upper secondary school (ages 10–16)	9.4 million
Number of years of compulsory education	5 (ages 5–9)
Preprimary school student/teacher ratio	41
Primary school student/teacher ratio	40
Lower and upper secondary school gross student/teacher ratio	42
Preprimary school gross enrollment ratio	49%
Primary school gross enrollment ratio	95%
Lower and upper secondary school gross enrollment ratio	34%
Primary school entrants reaching grade 5	62%

Sources: Education for All, 2011; Global Education Digest, 2011; UNESCO–UIS, 2012; UNICEF, 2012; United Nations Development Programme, 2011.

Ministry of Education declared a four-part agenda to improve teacher education:

1. Increasing the effectiveness of in-service and preservice education programs
2. Introducing regular quality assessment measures and upgrading teacher education programs
3. Introducing attractive incentives for teachers
4. Emphasizing management and administrative training

While the directions mentioned above are important and timely, teachers overwhelmingly work under less than desirable conditions. First, most teacher education programs operate under stringent budgetary constraints that ultimately impact student teachers' access to essential resources such as libraries, equipment, and teaching aids. Second, teachers move from training programs to a range of difficult classes. Crowded classes and inadequate schooling facilities are common problems. Teaching is increasingly geared toward performance on tests and the examination system in general, thus privileging performance over creativity. Third, teacher absenteeism has been a common cause of concern. Finally, setting up quality assessment and accountability measures is essential for the progress of Pakistan's educational system.

The connection between social progress and equitable education is by now a part of common wisdom. As Pakistan stands at a significant political juncture, its education system calls for serious attention. Moreover, as the current global economy increasingly shifts toward information-centric development, the significance of education is enhanced.

Shivali Tukdeo

REFERENCES

Boissiere, Maurice, Safiullah Baig, Manisha Modi, and Fareeha Zafar. *Evaluation of World Bank Assistance for Primary Education in Pakistan: A Country Case Study.* Washington, DC: World Bank, 2007. www.worldbank.org/ieg.

Central Intelligence Agency. *The CIA World Factbook.* New York: Skyhorse, 2011. https://www.cia.gov/library/publications/the-world-factbook/index.html.

Cohen, Stephen P. *The Idea of Pakistan.* Washington, DC: Brookings Institution Press, 2004.

Commonwealth Secretariat. *Initial Teacher Training: South Asian Approaches.* London: Commonwealth Secretariat, 1993.

EFA. "Strong Foundations: Early Childhood Care and Education." *Education for All Global Monitoring Report.* Paris: UNESCO, 2006.

GED. *Global Education Digest 2012: Comparing Education Statistics Across the World.* Montreal: UNESCO Institute for Statistics, 2012.

Government of Pakistan, Ministry of Education. National Curriculum. www.moe.gov.pk.

Government of Sindh. Education & Literacy Department. 2009. www.sindh.gov.pk/dpt/EducationFinal/index.htm.

"Pakistan." In *The Europa World Yearbook*, vol. 1. London: Routledge, 2009.

UNESCO. *Strengthening Teacher Education in Pakistan.* Islamabad: UNESCO, 1998.

UNESCO–IBE. www.ibe.unesco.org/en/worldwide/unesco-regions/asia-and-the-pacific/pakistan.html.

———. *Public Expenditure Review*, vol. 1. Washington, DC: 2004.

Zafar, Fareeha. "Fiscal Devolution in Education: Case Study Reflecting Initial Responses." UNESCO/MOE-Pakistan, 2003.

Ziring, Lawrence. *Pakistan in the Twentieth Century: A Political History.* New York: Oxford University Press, 2000.

PALESTINE

Palestine, known today as the Palestinian Autonomous Territories or Areas, is an Arab state, comprising the noncontiguous West Bank and Gaza Strip. The official language is Arabic. Other spoken languages are English and Hebrew. According to the United Nations, the population for 2011 in Palestine was 4.2 million, of which 2.5 were in the West Bank and 1.6 in Gaza. Palestinians are of Arab ethnicity. The vast majority is Muslim; Christians are a minority.

The West Bank was part of the British Mandate of Palestine until the end of the 1948 Arab-Israeli War, after which it became part of Jordan in accordance with the 1948 armistice agreement. It remained under the sovereignty of Jordan in spite of the Israeli occupation in 1967 until King Hussein of Jordan formally relinquished legal and administrative control on July 31, 1988. The first uprising (intifada) against Israeli occupation began in 1987.

Gaza was an administrative province under the British Mandate of Palestine until it was transferred to Egypt after the 1949 armistice. It remained under Egyptian administration until June 1967, when it was occupied, and later administered, by Israel. In 1993 the Palestine Liberation Organization and Israel signed the Declaration of Principles on Interim Self-Government Arrangements (DOP) in Washington, DC, providing for Palestinian self-government in the West Bank and Gaza until a permanent settlement is achieved. In 1994, as a result of transfer of authority, the Palestinian Authority (PA) assumed some of the civil responsibilities that were performed by a military government. The second uprising, known as the Al-Aqsa intifada, against Israeli occupation began in late 2000. Since October 2000 most of the West Bank has remained under Israeli military occupation or control. In 2003 the United States, European Union, United Nations, and Russia presented a "roadmap" to a final settlement of the conflict by 2005 based on reciprocal steps by the two parties leading to a two-state solution, Israel and Palestine. The proposed date for a permanent status agreement has been postponed indefinitely due to the resumption of conflict. In 2005 Israel unilaterally disengaged from Gaza, dismantling Israeli military installations and settlements there, and withdrew from four settlements in the West Bank.

However, from December 2008 to January 2009, Israel began launching rocket attacks on Gaza as a means of curbing the strength of Hamas, an Islamic Palestinian party. Fighting between the Palestinian Authority and Hamas has been ongoing since 2006.

Educational System

The Ministry of Education and Higher Education (MOEHE), established in 1994, administers public education and higher education and supervises private education. Since 1950 the United Nations Relief and Works Agency for Palestine Refugees in the Near East (UNRWA) has provided free education in grades 1 through 9 to all refugee children and youth in the West Bank and Gaza in accordance with the local education systems. After completing grades 1 through 9 at UNRWA schools, students transfer to government schools for grades 10 through 12. Even though UNRWA schools operate under a separate management and delivery system, they use the same curriculum as the one used in government schools. The MOEHE is responsible for supervising UNRWA, especially regarding the use of curriculum.

At the start of the academic year 2005–2006, government schools accounted for about 70 percent of total enrollments, UNRWA schools 24 percent, and private schools 6 percent. About 60 percent of total enrollments were at schools in the West Bank, and 40 percent were in Gaza. There is a large concentration of UNRWA schools in Gaza, accounting for about 44 percent of total enrollments in Gaza. In the academic year 2006–2007, UNRWA operated 92 schools in the West Bank and 193 in Gaza. In the academic year 2001–2002, about two-thirds of children from refugee households enrolled in UNRWA schools; the rest enrolled in government and private schools. About 10 percent of total enrollments at UNRWA schools are nonrefugee children. The Palestinian Central Bureau of Statistics estimates that 42 percent of the Palestinian population under 18 year are refugees.

Before the academic year 2000–2001, there were two education systems, or a dual curriculum, in operation in the Palestinian Territories. Students in the West Bank studied the Jordanian curriculum, and students in Gaza studied the Egyptian curriculum. In 1994 the PA assumed responsibility for education in the both areas. The MOEHE completed the First Palestinian Curriculum Plan in 1998 and began

gradual implementation of a new, unified Palestinian curriculum in the academic year 2000–2001. The first cohort of students to have completed the entire new Palestinian curriculum, grades 1 through 12, will graduate at the end of the academic year 2011–2012.

Basic education, lasting for 10 years, is compulsory and free for all Palestinian children from six to 15 years old. Of all the schools in the West Bank and Gaza, roughly a third are boys' schools, a third are girls' schools, and a third are coeducational schools. Most coeducational schools provide basic education, grades 1 through 4.

The education system comprises three stages: kindergarten, basic (comprises preparatory and empowerment cycles), and secondary. Higher education is provided by institutions according to three categories: governmental; public nonprofit, funded by the PA; and private. These institutions offer two- to five-year university and nonuniversity programs, as well as graduate university studies.

Precompulsory and Compulsory Education

Kindergarten, which is not compulsory, lasts for two years, for children entering at age four and exiting at age six. Kindergarten education aims at developing children's abilities physically, socially, mentally, and emotionally. It is provided mainly by the private sector under the supervision of the MOEHE. It prepares children for basic education.

Basic education, which is compulsory, lasts for ten years, comprising two cycles: four years of preparatory cycle and six years of empowerment cycle. Preparatory education consists of grades 1 through 4, for children entering at age six and exiting at age 10. Empowerment education consists of grades 5 through 10, for children entering at age 10 and exiting at age 16. Basic education provides students with foundation education, basic general knowledge, and a balanced education among different subjects, preparing them for secondary education.

Postcompulsory Education

Secondary education, which is not compulsory, lasts for two years, covering grades 11 and 12, for students entering at age 16 and exiting at age 18. It is divided into two branches: academic and vocational. The vocational branch offers four tracks: agriculture, commerce, hotel management, and industry. Secondary education provides students with maximum help and opportunity to acquire knowledge and develop their skills according to their interests and capabilities. It builds students' abilities in the areas of critical and analytical thinking, creativity, and communication. Students who successfully complete their secondary education are awarded the Secondary Education Certificate (*Tawjihi*) and can continue on to higher education or join the labor market.

Out of the institutions of higher education, ten are traditional universities, one is an open university, 11 are university colleges, and 19 are community colleges. Four of them are UNRWA colleges and training centers. They offer programs leading to two-year diplomas, bachelor's and master's degrees, and doctorates. The traditional universities are Al-Azhar University, the Islamic University, Al-Aqsa University, Hebron University, Polytechnic University, Bethlehem University, Al-Quds University, Birzeit University, An-Najah University, and Arab American University. The only open university is Al-Quds Open University.

Curriculum, Assessment, and Instruction

Kindergarten education is provided through a variety of activities and worksheets focusing on the understanding of language, science, society, music, drama, physical education, and the environment.

Subjects taught in preparatory education, grades 1 through 4, are Islamic education, Arabic language, English language, general science, mathematics, social sciences and national education, arts and crafts, physical education, free activity (including computers, sports, library visits, and scientific investigations), and civics.

Subjects taught in empowerment education, grades 5 through 10, are the same as those taught in preparatory education. These grades also include technology and applied sciences and elective subjects such as a third language (French, Hebrew, or German), home economics, or health and environmental sciences. Emphasis is on Arabic language, general sciences, and mathematics. Grade 10 includes vocational education and technical subjects.

Subjects taught in the academic secondary educa-

tion, grade 11, are Islamic education, Arabic language, English language, mathematics, chemistry, physics, biology, history, geography, arts and crafts, technology and applied sciences, economics and administration, and physical education. Subjects taught in the academic secondary education, grade 12, are Islamic education, Arabic language, English language, mathematics, arts and crafts, physical education, and two subjects chosen from chemistry, physics, biology, economics and administration, history, or geography.

As for higher education, community colleges mainly provide programs in higher technical and vocational education. These are two-year programs leading to diplomas, requiring 70 credit hours. Studies leading to bachelor's degrees normally take four years at universities and some university colleges, while engineering and agriculture take five years. Studies leading to master's degrees normally take two years beyond the bachelor's degree. Studies leading to postgraduate diplomas in some subjects take one or two years beyond the bachelor's degree without research training. Studies leading to doctorates in some subjects take three years beyond the master's degree.

Teacher Education

Basic education teachers must hold a bachelor's degree and/or a teaching diploma from a university. However, basic education teachers of sports, arts, and home economics generally hold community college degrees. Generally, secondary education teachers must hold a bachelor's degree and a teaching diploma from a university. The MOEHE requires all teachers to receive training at the tertiary level. There are preservice and in-service teacher training programs. Preservice training programs focus on disciplinary knowledge. In-service training programs provide teachers with orientation to the new curriculum, teaching methodologies, and subject knowledge. Teachers represent the largest employment sector in Palestine. Roughly 66 percent of teachers are employed by the government, 18 percent by UNRWA, and 16 percent by the private sector.

Informal Education

Informal education provides flexible curriculum, programs, and study hours according to the needs of learners and society. It includes two main types: literacy and adult education, and continuing education.

Literacy and adult education is a two-year program provided by the MOEHE since 1997. It is designed for school-age children and adults who are not enrolled in formal schools and aim at acquiring basic skills in reading, writing, and arithmetic to develop their abilities and build their personalities. It enables learners to continue their formal education. Those who pass an examination at the end of the two-year program are awarded a literacy certificate, qualifying them to take the grade 9 examination of formal education; they later can move on to take the *Tawjihi* examination. Continuing education is designed for those who wish to acquire new vocational and technological skills or to receive job retraining. It aims at developing individuals' capabilities to learn, as well as improving their skills and productivity level to contribute to Palestine's social, economic, and intellectual development.

System Economics

Data are not available.

Palestine Education at a Glance

General Information

Language	Arabic
Population	4.2 million
Adult literacy rate (ages 15 and over)	94.6%
Youth literacy rate (ages 15–24)	99.2%
GDP per capita	no data
Number of phones (mobile) per 100 people	no data
Number of Internet users per 100 people	no data
Life expectancy at birth (years)	no data

Formal Educational Information

Enrollment in preprimary school (ages 4–5)	91,000
Enrollment in primary school (ages 6–9)	395,000
Enrollment in lower and upper secondary school (ages 10–17)	714,000
Number of years of compulsory education	10 (ages 6–15)
Preprimary school student/teacher ratio	19
Primary school student/teacher ratio	28
Lower and upper secondary school gross student/teacher ratio	23
Preprimary school gross enrollment ratio	395
Primary school gross enrollment ratio	91%
Lower and upper secondary school gross enrollment ratio	86%
Primary school entrants reaching grade 5	no data

Sources: Education for All, 2011; Global Education Digest, 2011; UNESCO–UIS, 2012; UNICEF, 2012; United Nations Development Programme, 2011.

Future Prospects

Remarkable achievements have been made in the last five years in the education sector in Palestine despite the extremely severe conditions in which schools operate. However, many challenges lie ahead to build on these achievements and take the necessary steps forward. One of the main future challenges is to consolidate the education system and introduce strategic choices to improve the quality of education. Improvement in learning outcomes requires shifting spending policies from construction, textbooks, and increased number of teachers to developing pedagogical methods and practices, monitoring and evaluation, and human resources.

Other challenges include economic stability, efficient use of human and financial resources, universal basic education, improvement of educational quality, an update of the Palestinian national curriculum, evaluation and monitoring capabilities at all levels of the education system, efficient system management, school improvement policies, and relevance of education through reform of vocational education at secondary and tertiary levels. Also, besides its potential gains in quality of education, the best possible response to occupation, closures, curfews, and other constraints on physical mobility is the use of alternative delivery modes and intensive use of information and communication technology (ICT) in education.

Emad Alfar

REFERENCES

Central Intelligence Agency. *The CIA World Factbook*. New York: Skyhorse, 2011. https://www.cia.gov/library/publications/the-world-factbook/index.html.

Education for All. "The Hidden Crisis: Armed Conflict and Education." *Education for All Global Monitoring Report*. Paris: UNESCO, 2011.

Global Education Digest. *Global Education Digest 2011: Comparing Education Statistics Across the World*. Montreal: UNESCO Institute for Statistics, 2011.

Ministry of Education and Higher Education. www.mohe.gov.ps.

Palestine Human Development Report 2004. Birzeit University, Development Studies Programme. home.birzeit.edu/dsp.

"Palestine." In *The Europa World Year Book*, vol. 2. London: Routledge, 2007.

Palestinian Curriculum Development Center. www.pcdc.edu.ps.

Palestinian Education Initiative. www.pei.ps.

Programme on Governance in the Arab Region. www.pogar.org/countries/country.aspx?cid=14.

UNESCO–IBE. www.ibe.unesco.org/en/worldwide/unesco-regions/arab-states/palestine.html.

UNESCO–UIS. www.uis.unesco.org.

UNICEF. www.unicef.org/infobycountry/oPt.html.

United Nations Development Programme. "Sustainability and Equity: A Better Future for All." *Human Development Report 2011.* New York: Palgrave Macmillan, 2011.

World Bank. go.worldbank.org/OM4QIEVVE0.

QATAR

Qatar is located on the Arabian Peninsula. The official language is Arabic. Other spoken languages include English, Urdu, and Persian. About half of the population is Arabs from other countries and Qatari citizens; the rest are South Asians and Iranians. The majority of the population is not Qataris. The official religion is Islam. The majority of the population is Muslim, with small numbers of Christians and Hindus. Qatar's government system is a constitutional emirate.

Educational System

The Ministry of Education (MOE) and the Supreme Education Council administer public education, including higher education, and supervise private education. The Girls' Education Department, in affiliation with the Ministry of Education, administers female public education and is autonomous. Higher education is provided by Qatar University, the main higher education institution, founded in 1973. Recently, Western higher education institutions have been opening satellite campuses in Qatar. Education is free at all levels for all Qataris. In 2001 Law Number 25 was approved and amended in 2009 regarding free and compulsory education. Education is compulsory from the start of primary education to the end of secondary education, a duration of 12 years, unless the student reaches the age of 18, whichever comes first.

The general public education system comprises four cycles: kindergarten, elementary, preparatory, and secondary. Preparatory and secondary religious education is for boys only. Higher education institu-tions offer programs leading to bachelor's and master's degrees, as well as postgraduate diplomas.

Precompulsory and Compulsory Education

Kindergarten, which is not compulsory, lasts for three years, for children entering at age three and exiting at age six. The private sector manages kindergartens.

Elementary education, which is compulsory, lasts for six years, covering grades 1 through 6, for children entering at age six and exiting at age 12. It is a foundation stage in the educational ladder. Students receive education in basic reading, writing, and arithmetic. Students who successfully complete their elementary education advance to the preparatory level.

Preparatory education (general or religious), which is compulsory, lasts for three years, covering forms 1 through 3, for children entering at age 12 and exiting at age 15. This intermediate stage between elementary and secondary education prepares students for the practical life. They receive basic human and scientific education. For some students, after receiving an appropriate vocational training and because of their individual situation, it is a final stage; they do not continue on to secondary education. Other students who successfully complete the preparatory education advance to secondary education.

Secondary education includes four types: general, commercial, technical, or religious. It is compulsory. Secondary school lasts for three years, covering forms 1 through 3, for students entering at age 15 and exiting at age 18. This stage is a bridge to higher education and to employment in the labor market. Boys can enroll in any of the four types of secondary education, whereas girls can enroll only in general secondary education. Students who successfully complete secondary education are awarded the Secondary Education Certificate (*Thanawiya*) in their chosen type of study. Holders of the *Thanawiya* are eligible for enrollment into higher education institutions.

Postcompulsory Education

Higher education institutions offer four- and five-year programs leading to a bachelor's degree depending on the specialization, and further studies lead to a master's degree and postgraduate diploma.

Curriculum, Assessment, and Instruction

Kindergarten education develops the skills of children in reading, numeration, and applied capabilities through the introduction of games and entertainment. It prepares children for elementary education.

Subjects taught at the elementary level are religious studies, Arabic language, English language, mathematics, hygiene and science, art education, and physical education. Social studies is taught in grades 3 through 6. Emphasis is on Arabic language, religious studies, and mathematics. In grades 1 through 4, students take four examinations each year, which constitute the following percentages of the final course mark: November exam, 20 percent; January exam, 20 percent; March exam, 20 percent; and end-of-school-year exam, 40 percent.

Subjects taught at the general preparatory level, forms 1 through 3, are religious studies, Arabic language, English language, mathematics, hygiene and science, social studies, fine arts, physical education, and home economics (for girls only). Emphasis is on Arabic language, English language, religious studies, and mathematics. Subjects taught at the religious preparatory level, forms 1 through 3, are almost the same as those of the general preparatory level, plus jurisprudence in Islam, Islamic theology, Quranic studies, Islamic tradition, and biography of the prophet. The hygiene and science subject is replaced by science.

In form I of general secondary education, students study a common curriculum: religious studies, Arabic language, English language, mathematics, integrated science, history, geography, civics, computer science, study skills, physical education, and home economics (for girls only). At the end of Form I of general secondary education, students enroll in either the literary or the science sections of general secondary education, forms 2 and 3. Subjects taught in the literary section, distributed among forms 2 and 3 of general secondary education, include religious studies; Arabic language; English language; French language; history; geography; civics; sociology; computer science; philosophy, ethics, and psychology; study skills; fine arts; physical education; and home economics (for girls only). Mathematics and science are taught in some subsections of the literary section. Subjects taught in the science section, distributed among forms 2 and 3 of general secondary education, include religious studies, Arabic language, English language, mathematics, physics, chemistry, biology, computer science, study skills, physical education, and home economics (for girls only). Subjects taught in religious secondary education, distributed among forms 1 through 3, include jurisprudence in Islam, Islamic theology, Quranic studies, Islamic tradition, Islamic studies, Arabic language, English language, science, mathematics, geography, history, civics, sociology, philosophy, study skills, computer science, and physical education. In the other two types of secondary education, commercial and technical, some subjects taught are similar to those of general secondary education, plus other specialized subjects related to the chosen type of study.

From grade 5 of elementary education through form 2 of secondary education, students take regularly organized examinations throughout the school year and are also evaluated on other factors, such as growth, activity, behavior, effectiveness, interaction, and participation. Students must attain a mark of at least 50 percent in each subject. In form 3 of secondary education and at the end of that school year, students take a final general examination administered by the Ministry of Education. Those who pass receive the Secondary Education Certificate (*Thanawiya*) in their chosen type of study and can continue on to higher education.

Qatar University is the main institution providing higher education. It is autonomous and comprises the Colleges of Islamic Law (Shari'ah) and Islamic Studies; Education; Human Sciences; Science; Engineering; Administration and Economics; and Technology.

Teacher Education

All teachers must hold a bachelor's degree from the College of Education at Qatar University by studying a program, four years in length, for a total of 144 credit hours. Holders of this degree, with the mark "good," are offered further study through postgraduate courses, provided by the Ministry of Education in cooperation with Qatar University, for a total of 22 credit hours leading to a special diploma in education. This special diploma qualifies for a master's degree in education. The College of Education also offers evening courses to a large number of teachers who hold university degrees, but lack knowledge of the teaching profession. These are one-year evening courses, for a total of 36 credit hours. The Ministry of Education provides a large database of teaching strategies through teachers' guidebooks. It also provides in-service training courses on new curriculum and textbooks. Teachers, educational leaders, and other education professionals receive preservice and in-service training courses provided by the Teacher's Qualifying Institute, the Education Leaders' Training Center, and the Ministry of Education's Training Center.

Informal Education

The Ministry of Education provides literacy and adult education programs. There are two integrated courses for adults at evening schools: a literacy course paralleling elementary education to grade 6 and an adult education course, which comes after the literacy course, covering both preparatory and secondary education.

Qatar Education at a Glance

General Information

Capital	Doha
Population	1.7 million
Language	Arabic
Adult literacy rate (ages 15 and over)	94.7%
Youth literacy rate (ages 15–24)	97.8%
GDP per capita	US$80,944
Number of phones (mobile) per 100 people	132
Number of Internet users per 100 people	69
Life expectancy at birth (years)	78

Formal Educational Information

Enrollment in preprimary school (ages 3–5)	25,000
Enrollment in primary school (ages 6–11)	85,000
Enrollment in lower and upper secondary school (ages 12–17)	67,000
Number of years of compulsory education	12 (ages 6–17)
Preprimary school student/teacher ratio	15
Primary school student/teacher ratio	12
Lower and upper secondary school gross student/teacher ratio	10
Preprimary school gross enrollment ratio	53%
Primary school gross enrollment ratio	103%
Lower and upper secondary school gross enrollment ratio	94%
Primary school entrants reaching grade 5	96%

Sources: Education for All, 2011; Global Education Digest, 2011; UNESCO–UIS, 2012; UNICEF, 2012; United Nations Development Programme, 2011.

System Economics

The total public expenditure on education in 2008 represented 2.4 percent of Qatar's gross domestic product. It represented 8.2 percent of the total government expenditure. For the year 1978, 39 percent of public education spending was at the primary level, 29 percent at the secondary level, and 11 percent at the tertiary level.

Future Prospects

The Secondary Education Diversification Plan has led to many recent changes in secondary education. There are two new types of secondary education that are being introduced, agricultural education and applied education. Agricultural secondary education includes soil and irrigation technology, gardening, livestock, and fisheries. Applied secondary education includes postal service technology, typing technologies, electronic photography technology, hotel services, and nursing. Furthermore, general secondary education consists of two scientific sections (physics and mathematics; chemistry and biology) and two literary sections (languages; social studies). Technical secondary education consists of four sections that include 11 specializations: building and construction technology section (building technologies; carpentry and decoration); mechanics section (light vehicles; heavy vehicles); electricity and electronics section (industrial electronics; radio and television; air conditioning and refrigeration; electricity); and minerals section (fitting and turning; blacksmithing and welding; metal shaping). Commercial secondary education consists of three sections: office administration; banking and insurance; and intermediate accounting.

Emad Alfar

REFERENCES

Central Intelligence Agency. *The CIA World Factbook*. New York: Skyhorse, 2011. https://www.cia.gov/library/publications/the-world-factbook/index.html.

Education for All. "The Hidden Crisis: Armed Conflict and Education." *Education for All Global Monitoring Report*. Paris: UNESCO, 2011.

Global Education Digest. *Global Education Digest 2011: Comparing Education Statistics Across the World*. Montreal: UNESCO Institute for Statistics, 2011.

Programme on Governance in the Arab Region. www.pogar.org/countries/country.aspx?cid=15.

"Qatar." In *The Europa World Yearbook*, vol. 2. London: Routledge, 2009.

UNESCO–IBE. www.ibe.unesco.org/en/worldwide/unesco-regions/arab-states/qatar.html.

UNESCO–UIS. www.uis.unesco.org.

UNICEF. www.unicef.org/infobycountry/qatar.html.

United Nations Development Programme. "Sustainability and Equity: A Better Future for All." *Human Development Report 2011.* New York: Palgrave Macmillan, 2011.

Saudi Arabia

The Kingdom of Saudi Arabia is located in southwestern Asia. The official language is Arabic. English is widely spoken in urban areas. The United Nations population estimate for 2011 was 27 million. More than three-quarters of the population are Saudi citizens; the rest are other Arabs, Africans, and South Asians. The official religion is Islam. The country is home to two of the holiest places in Islam: Mecca and Medina. The population is almost entirely Muslim. Saudi Arabia is a monarchy based on Islam and the Quran; the Consultative Council, consisting of 150 appointed members, is an important factor that greatly impacts the educational infrastructure and student outcomes.

Educational System

Issued by the Council of Ministers, Resolution Number 779 in 1969, the Educational Policy Document is a comprehensive guideline for the goals of education in Saudi Arabia. The educational policy is based on Islam and the Quran. Even though there was no specific law regarding compulsory education until recently, Article 233 of the Educational Policy states that the government provides free education at all stages to all male and female Saudis. In 2004, compulsory basic education in the first six years was enforced, followed by three years of intermediate education and three years of secondary education.

Schools are not coeducational, except for kindergarten, but follow the same educational ladder and curriculum, with some minor differences. The Supreme Committee for Educational Policy, chaired by the king, is the highest authority supervising education in the country, under which are four main ministries and agencies. The Ministry of Education administers public education for males and supervises private education. The Presidency General for Girls' Education administers public education for girls. The Ministry of Higher Education is in charge of higher education. The General Organization for Technical Education and Vocational Training is in charge of technical education and vocational training. The private sector provides and contributes to education under state supervision.

The general public education system comprises four cycles: kindergarten, elementary, intermediate, and secondary. In addition to general secondary education, technical education as well as teacher training education are offered at the secondary level. There are Quranic schools that follow the same educational ladder (elementary, intermediate, and secondary) of general education schools, but emphasize the study of Islam and the Quran. Higher education is provided by public and private institutions, teachers colleges, girls' colleges, and higher technical institutes.

Precompulsory and Compulsory Education

Kindergarten, which is not compulsory, lasts for three years, for children entering at age three and exiting at age six. It is a preparatory stage for elementary education. Attendance is not mandatory. Private and nongovernmental institutions provide nurseries and kindergartens for children between the ages of three and five. Elementary education, which is compulsory, lasts for six years, covering grades 1 through 6 for children entering at age six and exiting at age 12. It is a foundation of the educational ladder. Emphasis at this stage is on Islam, the Quran, and Arabic language. Students who successfully complete their elementary education receive the General Elementary Education Certificate and can move on to the intermediate level.

Postcompulsory Education

Intermediate education, which is not compulsory, lasts for three years, covering grades 1 through 3, is for children entering at age 12 and exiting at age 15. It is a preparatory stage for secondary education. Students who successfully complete their intermediate education receive the Intermediate Education Certificate and can choose to pursue general or specialized secondary education.

Secondary education (general or specialized), which is not compulsory, lasts for three years, covering grades 1 through 3, for children entering at age 15 and exiting at age 18. In addition to general secondary education, technical education (postal, health, technical supervision, agricultural, commercial, and industrial) and teacher training education are offered at the secondary level. In the first year of general secondary education, students study a common curriculum. In their second and third years, besides studying common subjects, students study subjects from their chosen track: scientific or literary. There are Quranic schools that follow the same educational ladder (elementary, intermediate, and secondary) of general education schools, but emphasize the study of Islam and the Quran. Students who successfully complete their secondary education are awarded a certificate or a diploma according to their choice of study: General Secondary Education Certificate (*Tawjihiyah*), Secondary Vocational School Diploma, Secondary Commercial School Diploma, or Secondary Agricultural School Diploma. Students who hold a secondary education certificate or equivalent are eligible for enrollment into higher education institutions. Higher education is provided by public and private institutions, teachers colleges, girls' colleges, and higher technical institutes, each having its own university or institute council. They offer nonuniversity programs leading to certificates and diplomas, as well as university programs leading to bachelor's, master's, and doctoral degrees. Some of the main universities are King Saud University, the Islamic University, King Abdul Aziz University, Imam Mohammad Bin Saud Islamic University, King Fahd University for Petroleum and Minerals, King Faisal University, Um Al-Qura University, and King Khaled University.

Curriculum, Assessment, and Instruction

Kindergarten education familiarizes students with the school environment and nurtures their moral, mental, and physical growth in accordance with the teachings of Islam. It encourages their imaginative thinking and prepares them for elementary education.

Subjects taught at elementary level are religious subjects (the Holy Quran, Quranic intonation, Islamic theology, Islamic jurisprudence, Islamic traditions and culture, and conduct and behavior), Arabic language, mathematics, science and health education, art and work education, and physical education. Additional subjects taught in the last three years of elementary education are geography, history, and national education. For girls, the curriculum is the same as that for boys, but physical education is replaced by women's and art education. Emphasis is on religious subjects and Arabic language. By passing the examinations at the end of each of the two semesters, students are promoted from one grade to the next. Those who pass the examination at the end of grade 6 receive the General Elementary Education Certificate and can move on to intermediate education.

Subjects taught at the intermediate level are religious subjects (the Holy Quran, Islamic theology, Quranic exegesis, Islamic jurisprudence, Islamic traditions and culture); Arabic language, history, geography, science and health education, mathematics, English language, art education, national education, and physical education. For girls, the curriculum is the same as that for boys, but physical education is replaced by women's and art education. Emphasis is on religious subjects and Arabic language. The examinations system is similar to that of the elementary level. Upon successful completion of their intermediate education, students are awarded the Intermediate Education Certificate and can continue on to secondary education. Students can choose to enroll in general secondary or technical secondary schools.

In the first year of general secondary education, all students study the same subjects: religious subjects (the Holy Quran, Islamic theology, Quranic exegesis, Islamic jurisprudence, Islamic traditions and culture); Arabic language, history, geography, physics, chemistry, biology, mathematics, English language, computer science, library and research, national education, and physical education. At the end of the first year of general secondary education, students are divided and enroll for the final two years in different sections based on their interests and marks in the first-year subjects. Girls can enroll in either the arts or the sciences sections. Boys can enroll in the following sections: religious and Arabic sciences, administration and social sciences, natural sciences, and technical sciences. During the final two years of general secondary education, common subjects taught for boys in all these sections are religious subjects (the Holy Quran, Islamic theology, Quranic exegesis, Islamic jurisprudence, Islamic traditions and culture), Arabic language, English language, computer science, national education, and physical education. Additional subjects are taught, mostly related to the chosen section. In the religious and Arabic sciences section, the additional subjects are history, geography, psychology, sociology, and library and research. In the administration and social sciences section, they are history, geography, psychology, sociology, administrative sciences, economics, accounting, mathematics, library and research, and activities. In the natural sciences section, they are physics, chemistry, biology, earth science, and mathematics. In the technical sciences, they are sciences and technical sciences, and mathematics. For girls, the curriculum is the same as that for boys with some minor modifications, and physical education is replaced by sewing and tailoring, and home economics. Upon successful completion of their general secondary education, students are awarded the General Secondary Education Certificate (*Tawjihiyah*) and are eligible for enrollment into higher education institutions.

Holders of the Intermediate Education Certificate can choose to enroll in technical secondary schools. These schools offer the following specializations: postal, health, technical supervision, agricultural, commercial, and industrial. These studies lead to the Secondary School Diploma in the chosen specialization. Holders of some of these diplomas are eligible for enrollment into community colleges, health colleges, and junior technical colleges.

Students can enroll in Quranic schools, which are religion-oriented schools, covering the entire 12 years of general education. These schools follow the same educational ladder as that of general education: elementary (grades 1 through 6), intermediate (grades 1 through 3), and secondary (grades 1 through 3). These secondary schools include the Quranic Secondary Schools and Dar-Al-Tawheed School; others are under the Imam Mohammad Bin Saud Islamic University. Quranic schools emphasize the study of Islam and the Quran. These studies lead to the General Secondary Education Certificate (*Tawjihiyah*), and certificate holders are eligible for enrollment into higher education institutions.

There are teacher training secondary schools for girls who hold the Intermediate Education Certificate. Upon the completion of their studies, students can enroll in girls' junior colleges.

Higher education is provided by public and private institutions, teachers colleges, girls' colleges, and higher technical institutes, each having its own university or institute council. They offer nonuniversity programs leading to certificates and diplomas, as well as university programs leading to bachelor's, master's, and doctoral degrees. Higher technical institutes and colleges of technology offer one- and two-year programs at a nonuniversity level in higher technical and vocational training, leading to certificates and diplomas. At the postsecondary level, the General Organization for Technical Education and Vocational Training provides two-year technical programs. Most universities admit both men and women, except for Imam Mohammad Bin Saud Islamic University and King Fahd University for Petroleum and Minerals, which admit men only. A bachelor's degree takes four years in humanities and social sciences, and five to six years in engineering, pharmacy, and medicine. A master's degree takes two years after a bachelor's degree and requires coursework and dissertation. A doctorate takes three years after a master's degree and requires coursework and dissertation. The primary language of instruction in technological and scientific subjects is English; Arabic is used in all other subjects.

Teacher Education

For elementary school, teachers are required to hold the General Secondary Education Certificate (*Tawjihiyah*). Then, after two years of training at junior colleges, they are awarded the Diploma for Junior College Training for Teachers. Those with a B average or higher qualify to enroll in a university and earn undergraduate credits. Male teachers qualify to teach intermediate and secondary schools in two ways: holding a bachelor of education degree; or by completing a bachelor's degree course followed by one year of intermediate and secondary school teacher training leading to a Higher Diploma in Education or by studying abroad. Female teachers qualify to teach intermediate school by completing a Diploma from Junior College Training for Teachers. Female teachers qualify to teach secondary school by completing a four-year program leading to a bachelor in education degree at a college of education.

Informal Education

Regardless of age, the education system provides options for all Saudis to learn and study at any time. At centers for eliminating illiteracy, students enroll at any age for a three-year program in adult education. The first year is equivalent to grade 2 of elementary education, the second year is equivalent to grade 4, and the third year is equivalent to grade 6. In the summer, the government runs eliminating illiteracy campaigns in Bedouin regions and remote areas. There are evening schools for male and female students. They provide education that qualifies students to take the Intermediate Education Certificate and the General Secondary Education Certificate examinations as in formal schools. Nonformal education programs are also provided by the Secretariat General for Adult Education under the Ministry of Education. These programs are carried out through summer education campaigns, participation in cultural activities of the Social Service Center, and training courses for adult education workers. There are special training programs for girls in tailoring, sewing, nutrition, and first aid. Vocational training centers provide dropout students, ages 14 to 17, with training in electricity, mechanics, welding, and carpentry. Training in-service programs are offered by the private sector to employees in computer, typewriting, and languages.

System Economics

The total public expenditure on education in Saudi Arabia in 2008 represented 5.6 percent of gross domestic product. It represented 19.3 percent of the total government expenditure. For the year 1975, 44 percent of public education spending was at the primary level, 16 percent at the secondary level, and 40 percent at the tertiary level.

Future Prospects

Besides requiring compulsory basic education in the first six years, some of the other objectives of the Seventh Development Plan (2000–2004) were to expand the participation of the private sector in

---

Saudi Arabia Education at a Glance

General Information

Capital	Riyadh
Population	27.4 million
Language	Arabic
Adult literacy rate (ages 15 and over)	86.6%
Youth literacy rate (ages 15–24)	97.8%
GDP per capita	US$22,713
Number of phones (mobile) per 100 people	188
Number of Internet users per 100 people	41
Life expectancy at birth (years)	74

Formal Educational Information

Enrollment in preprimary school (ages 3–5)	186,000
Enrollment in primary school (ages 6–11)	3.2 million
Enrollment in lower and upper secondary school (ages 12–17)	2.9 million
Number of years of compulsory education	6 (ages 6–11)
Preprimary school student/teacher ratio	11
Primary school student/teacher ratio	11
Lower and upper secondary school gross student/teacher ratio	11
Preprimary school gross enrollment ratio	11%
Primary school gross enrollment ratio	106%
Lower and upper secondary school gross enrollment ratio	101%
Primary school entrants reaching grade 5	94%

Sources: Education for All, 2011; Global Education Digest, 2011; UNESCO–UIS, 2012; UNICEF, 2012; United Nations Development Programme, 2011.

---

education and to move toward a knowledge-based economy. Recently, the Ministry of Education was given the authority to administer public education for males and females. It prepared a 10-year plan, 2004–2014, designed to improve the quality of the educational system, develop an infrastructure of information technology and communications for teaching and learning, and develop adult education and eliminate illiteracy.

Emad Alfar

REFERENCES

Central Intelligence Agency. *The CIA World Factbook.* New York: Skyhorse, 2011. https://www.cia.gov/library/publications/the-world-factbook/index.html.

Education for All. "The Hidden Crisis: Armed Conflict and Education." *Education for All Global Monitoring Report.* Paris: UNESCO, 2011.

Global Education Digest. *Global Education Digest 2011: Comparing Education Statistics Across the World.* Montreal: UNESCO Institute for Statistics, 2011.

Programme on Governance in the Arab Region. www.pogar.org/countries/country.aspx?cid=16.

"Saudi Arabia." In *The Europa World Yearbook*, vol. 2. London: Routledge, 2007.

UNESCO–IBE. www.ibe.unesco.org/countries/SaudiArabia.htm.

UNESCO–UIS. www.uis.unesco.org.

UNICEF. www.unicef.org/infobycountry/saudiarabia.html.

United Nations Development Programme. "Sustainability and Equity: A Better Future for All." *Human Development Report 2011*. New York: Palgrave Macmillan, 2011.

Sri Lanka

Formerly known as Ceylon until 1972, the Democratic Socialist Republic of Sri Lanka is an island nation located off the coast of southern India in the Indian Ocean. The official languages are Sinhala and Tamil. The English language is also spoken and used as a link language between Sinhala and Tamil. Sri Lanka's population is predominantly Sinhalese, with small numbers of Moor and Tamil. The population is 76.6 percent Buddhist, 8.5 percent Muslim, 7.9 percent Hindu, 6.1 percent Roman Catholic, and 0.8 percent other Christians. Sri Lanka gained its independence from the United Kingdom in 1948. The Liberation Tigers of Tamil Eelam (LTTE), a separatist group, has been fighting the government since 1983 to create a Tamil state in the northern and eastern provinces. In May 2009, the government declared victory over the LTTE and an end to the 26-year civil war. The legislative capital of Sri Lanka is Sri Jayawardenepura Kotte.

Educational System

The Ministry of Education is responsible for making policy in the general public education and *pirivena* schools (for training young students to become Buddhist clergy, from grade 1 to higher education) and for supervising private education. Education policies are implemented in nine provinces by Provincial Councils of Education. The nine provinces are central, eastern, north central, northern, north western, sabaragamuwa, southern, uva, and western. According to gazette notification 1003/5 of November 25, 1997, education is compulsory for all Sri Lankan children from five to 13 years old. Education is free in all stages for all Sri Lankans. The Ministry of Higher Education is in charge of postsecondary education.

The education system comprises five stages: preprimary, primary, junior secondary, senior secondary, and collegiate. Universities, technical colleges, open university, and national colleges of education provide postsecondary and higher education.

Precompulsory and Compulsory Education

Preprimary education is not compulsory and lasts for two years. It is for children entering at age three and exiting at age five. Institutions that provide preprimary education include daycare centers, Montessori schools, crèches, early childhood development centers, and preschools. These institutions are managed by private, nongovernmental, and local (urban and municipal councils) governmental organizations.

Primary education, which is compulsory, is for children entering at age five and exiting at age 10. It lasts for five years, covering grades 1 through 5. It prepares students for junior secondary education.

Junior secondary education, which is compulsory, is for children entering at age 10 and exiting at age 14, covering grades 6 through 9, and lasts for four years. It develops the students' creative imagination and provides them with a suitable environment for attaining emotional maturity. It is an extension of primary education and prepares students for senior secondary education.

Postcompulsory Education

Senior secondary education, which is not compulsory, lasts for 2 years, covering grades 10 and 11, for children entering at age 14 and exiting at age 16. It helps students achieve their social, moral, physical, and psychological growth. It develops students' abilities in critical thinking and abstract reasoning. Students who successfully complete their senior secondary education can move on to the collegiate stage (grades 12 and 13) or enter technical colleges.

The collegiate level, which is not compulsory, lasts for 2 years, covering grades 12 and 13, for children entering at age 16 and exiting at age 18. Upon completing the collegiate level, students can enroll in universities or national colleges of education.

Institutions of postsecondary and higher education offer programs leading to diplomas, as well as bachelor's, master's, and doctorate degrees.

Curriculum, Assessment, and Instruction

Preprimary education fosters a balanced social and emotional development of the child's personality, develops the child physiologically and morally, and promotes good health habits. It prepares children for a smooth transition from home to school.

Subjects taught in primary education, grades 1 through 5, are first language (Sinhala/Tamil), mathematics, environmental-related activities (an integrated subject that includes social studies, health and physical education, science, art, music, and dancing), religion, and co-curricular activities (which include participation in religious festivals, cultural events, or meditation). Two more subjects added, starting from grade 3 through grade 5, are English language and second language (Sinhala/Tamil). If the students' first language is Tamil, they study Sinhala as a second language. Similarly, if their first language is Sinhala, they study Tamil as a second language. In general, Sinhala and Tamil are used as a medium of instruction in schools. In grade 5, students take an additional subject, called optional curriculum, chosen from dancing, arts, or agriculture. Emphasis is on first language (Sinhala/Tamil), environmental-related activities, and mathematics. Students who pass the grade 5 scholarship and placement examination at the end of primary education move on to the junior secondary level.

In junior secondary education, grades 6 through 9, subjects taught are first language (Sinhala/Tamil), English language, second language (Sinhala/Tamil), mathematics, religion, health and physical education, and aesthetic subjects (including oriental and western music, Sri Lankan and Karnatic dancing, and art). The subject environmental-related activities is taught in grade 6 only. In grades 7 through 9, three subjects are added: science and technology, social studies and history, and life competencies/practical skills. After completing their junior secondary education, students move on to senior secondary education.

Subjects taught in senior secondary education, grades 10 and 11, are the same as those taught in grades 7 through 9, however the subjects second language (Sinhala/Tamil), health and physical education, life competencies/practical skills are dropped. Another subject, called technical subject, is added, plus two more subjects chosen from history, a modern or classical language, health and physical education, development studies, second language (Sinhala/Tamil), literature (Sinhala, Tamil, English, or Arabic), or geography. Emphasis is on first language (Sinhala/Tamil), social studies and history, science and technology, English language, and mathematics. Students who pass the general certificate of education ordinary-level (GCE O-level) examination at the end of their senior education move on to the collegiate level or enroll in technical colleges.

At the collegiate level, grades 12 and 13, based on their performance on the GCE O-level examination, students can choose from three streams: science, art, or commerce. Students who pass the general certificate of education advanced-level (GCE A-level) examination at the end of their collegiate level education can enroll in universities or other higher education institutions.

There are four types of government schools in Sri Lanka: Type 1AB schools (grades 1 through 13, up to the GCE A-level, in the science, commerce, and arts streams), Type 1C schools (grades 1 through 13, up to the GCE A-level in the commerce and arts streams), Type 2 schools (grades 1 through 11, up to the GCE O-level), and Type 3 schools (grades 1 through 5, with a few Type 3 schools offering classes up to grade 8). For the year 2010, the number of schools by type was 716 schools of Type 1AB, 2005 schools of Type 1C, 4094 schools of Type 2, and 2870 schools of Type 3.

In postsecondary and higher education, students who pass the GCE O-level examination can enroll in technical colleges that provide two-year programs leading to a vocational diploma. Students who pass GCE A-level examination can either enroll in national colleges of education that provide three-year programs leading to a teacher certification diploma, or enroll in universities that offer four- to six-year programs leading to a bachelor's degree: four years in most fields, five years in medicine and architecture, and six years in traditional medicine. Two years of study beyond the bachelor's degree leads to a master's degree. Three to five years of study beyond the master's degree leads to a doctorate degree.

Teacher Education

Preservice and in-service teacher training programs are provided by the national institute of education, teacher centers, national colleges of education, departments of education in universities, and regional English support centers. National colleges of education offer two-year programs, plus one-year internship in schools leading to a teacher certificate diploma for grades 1 through 11. Universities and the national institute of education offer bachelor's degree holders postgraduate programs leading to a postgraduate diploma in education or master's degree for grades 12 and 13. National colleges of education provide preservice teacher training, focusing on the professional development of new teachers. Teacher centers, national colleges of education, and the national institute of education provide in-service teacher training, focusing on the ongoing professional development of current teachers. Regional English support centers provide in-service teacher training for English language teachers.

Informal Education

One of the goals of the initiative Education Sector Development Framework and Program (ESDFP) is to develop informal education in Sri Lanka. The ESDFP initiative targets out-of-school adolescents who are in need of work-related skills in order to enter the labor force. Informal education in Sri Lanka aims to eliminate illiteracy, provide work and training opportunities through vocational courses, promote the objectives of compulsory education, support community learning centers for young adolescents, develop programs for children affected by the 26-year civil war, and provide equal access to education through distance learning and open admission schools.

System Economics

The total public expenditure on education in 2009 represented 2.1 percent of Sri Lanka's gross domestic product. It represented 8.1 percent of the total government expenditure. For the same year, 31 percent of public education spending was at the primary level, 56 percent at the secondary level, and 13 percent at the tertiary level.

Future Prospects

The initiative Transforming the School Education System as the Foundation of a Knowledge Hub Project (TSEP) was conceived as part of a $US100 million agreement between Sri Lanka and the World Bank in 2012. The TSEP initiative aims to enhance access and quality in primary and secondary education and provide a foundation for the knowledge-based economy in the country. Its main goals include increasing completion rates in primary and secondary education, improving management of schools, and updating school curriculum to meet the new demands and needed skills of the global economy.

Emad Alfar

REFERENCES

Central Intelligence Agency. *The CIA World Factbook.* New York: Skyhorse, 2011. https://www.cia.gov/library/publications/the-world-factbook/index.html.

Education for All. "The Hidden Crisis: Armed Conflict and Education." *Education for All Global Monitoring Report.* Paris: UNESCO, 2011.

Global Education Digest. *Global Education Digest 2011: Comparing Education Statistics Across the World.* Montreal: UNESCO Institute for Statistics, 2011.

Sri Lanka Education at a Glance

General Information

Capital	Colombo
Population	20.8 million
Languages	Sinhala (official), Tamil (national), English
Adult literacy rate (ages 15 and over)	90.6%
Youth literacy rate (ages 15–24)	98%
GDP per capita	$US5,078
Number of phones (mobile) per 100 people	83
Number of Internet users per 100 people	12
Life expectancy at birth (years)	75

Formal Educational Information

Enrollment in preprimary school (ages 3–4)	no data
Enrollment in primary school (ages 5–9)	1.6 million
Enrollment in lower and upper secondary school (ages 10–17)	2.3 million
Number of years of compulsory education	9 (ages 5–13)
Preprimary school student/teacher ratio	no data
Primary school student/teacher ratio	24
Lower and upper secondary school gross student/teacher ratio	20
Preprimary school gross enrollment ratio	no data
Primary school gross enrollment ratio	99%
Lower and upper secondary school gross enrollment ratio	87%
Primary school entrants reaching grade 5	99%

Sources: Education for All, 2011; Global Education Digest, 2011; UNESCO–UIS, 2012; UNICEF, 2012; United Nations Development Programme, 2011.

Ministry of Education, Sri Lanka. www.moe.gov.lk.

"Sri Lanka." In *The Europa World Yearbook*, vol. 2. London: Routledge, 2008.

UNESCO–IBE. www.ibe.unesco.org/countries/SriLanka.htm.

UNESCO–UIS. www.uis.unesco.org.

UNICEF. www.unicef.org/infobycountry/sri_lanka.html.

United Nations Development Programme. "Sustainability and Equity: A Better Future for All." *Human Development Report 2011.* New York: Palgrave Macmillan, 2011.

SYRIA

The Syrian Arab Republic is located in western Asia, bordered by Turkey to the north, the Mediterranean Sea and Lebanon to the west, Israel to the southwest, Jordan to the south, and Iraq to the east. The official language is Arabic. Other spoken languages are French, English, Kurdish, Armenian, and Circassian. Syria's population consists of mainly Syrian citizens; the rest are Kurds, Palestinians, Armenians, and Circassians. The population is mainly Muslim, with small numbers of Christians and Druze. Syria gained its independence from the French in 1946. Syrian protests, which seem to have blossomed as a result of recent social upheaval in other countries of the Middle East, have escalated into one of the bloodiest examples of a government's ruthless hegemony over its peacefully dissenting citizens.

Educational System

The Ministry of Education administers public education and supervises private education. Some responsibilities are delegated to the Directorate of Education and to the Governorate Council for each of the 14 governorates in order to decentralize the process. The Ministry of Higher Education is in charge of postsecondary education. According to Law Number 32 of April 4, 2002, basic education is compulsory for all Syrian children from six to 14 years old. Education is free in all stages for all Syrians.

The education system comprises three stages: kindergarten, basic education (elementary and intermediate cycles), and secondary. Higher education is provided by public and private institutions: universities, higher institutes, and intermediate institutes. These institutions offer programs leading to licenses and diplomas, as well as to bachelor's, master's, and doctorate degrees.

Precompulsory and Compulsory Education

Kindergarten, which is not compulsory, lasts for three years, for children entering at age three and exiting at age six. Kindergarten education aims at developing children's personality physically, mentally, socially, morally, emotionally, and verbally. It prepares children for a smooth transition from home to school.

Basic education is compulsory, comprising two cycles: six years of elementary and three years of intermediate schooling. Elementary education lasts for six years, covering grades 1 through 6, for children entering at age six and exiting at age 12. Elementary education provides students with basic knowledge and develops their skills in reading, writing, and arithmetic. It prepares students for intermediate education. Intermediate education lasts for three years, covering grades 7 through 9, for children entering at age 12 and exiting at age 15. Intermediate education provides students with a suitable environment for attaining emotional maturity, and it develops their creative imagination and aesthetical appreciation. It is an extension of elementary education and prepares students for secondary education. Students who successfully complete their basic education are awarded the Basic Education Certificate, which allows them to continue on to secondary education.

Postcompulsory Education

Secondary education, which is not compulsory, lasts for three years, covering grades 10 through 12, for children entering at age 15 and exiting at age 18. Secondary education helps students achieve their physical, psychological, social, moral, and human growth. It develops students' abilities in abstract reasoning, logical thinking, and constructive criticism. In the first year of general secondary education, grade 10, students study a common curriculum, enabling them to choose a track of study in the next two years. In the second and third years, grades 11 and 12, two tracks are offered: scientific and literary. There are also vocational secondary schools, which last for three years, offering three tracks: industrial, commercial, and arts (for girls only). Students who successfully complete their secondary education are awarded the Secondary Education Certificate (*Thanawiya*) in the chosen track and can continue on to higher education.

Higher education is provided by public and private universities, as well as by higher and intermediate institutes of professional and technical training. These institutions offer two-year programs leading to associate degrees, four- to six-year programs leading to licenses or bachelor's degrees, and further study beyond the bachelor's degree leading to postgraduate diplomas, master's degrees, and doctorate degrees. The universities include Damascus University, Aleppo University, Tishreen University, Al-Ba'ath University, Al-Furat University, and Syrian Virtual University.

Curriculum, Assessment, and Instruction

Kindergarten education develops the child physiologically, intellectually, and morally. It provides children with a suitable environment and care for a well-balanced growth in developing positive social skills, gaining good health habits, and achieving a positive attitude toward school. It prepares children for a smooth transition from home to school.

Basic education comprises six years of the elementary cycle and three years the intermediate cycle. Subjects taught in elementary education, grades 1 through 6, are religious education, Arabic language, English language, mathematics, social studies, science and health education, music education, physical education, and art education. Emphasis is on Arabic language and mathematics.

Subjects taught in intermediate education, grades 7 through 9, are religious education, Arabic language, English language, French language, mathematics, social studies, science and health education, music education, physical education, art education, and vocational education. Plus, informatics (computer sciences) is taught in grades 7 and 8. Emphasis is on Arabic language and mathematics. Students who successfully complete their basic education (elementary and intermediate cycles) are awarded the Basic Education Certificate and can continue on to secondary education.

In the first year of general secondary education, grade 10, all students are taught the same subjects, which are religious education, Arabic language, English language, French language, philosophy and humanities, history, geography, mathematics, informatics, physics, chemistry, biology, art education, physical education, and national socialist education. Emphasis is on Arabic language and mathematics.

In the second and third years of general secondary education, grades 11 and 12, two tracks are offered: scientific and literary. Subjects taught in the scientific track of general secondary education are religious education, Arabic language, English language, French language, mathematics, informatics, physics, chemistry, biology, and national socialist education. Additional subjects taught in grade 11 are philosophy and humanities, history, informatics, and physical education. Emphasis is on mathematics, physics, and Arabic language.

Subjects taught in the literary track of general secondary education are religious education, Arabic language, English language, French language, philosophy and humanities, history, geography, physical education, and national socialist education. Additional subjects taught in grade 11 are mathematics, scientific culture, informatics, and art education. Emphasis is on Arabic language and foreign languages (English and French).

There are also vocational secondary schools, which last for three years, offering three tracks: industrial, commercial, and arts (for girls only). The academic year in basic and secondary education is divided into two semesters, in which students are evaluated according to four tools: oral examinations, homework and exercises, written examinations, and semester final examination. The overall mark for each semester is obtained by averaging the first three tools and the fourth tool. The mark for the year is obtained by averaging the two overall semester marks. Students who successfully complete their secondary education are awarded the Secondary Education Certificate (*Thanawiya*) in the chosen track, which allows them to continue on to higher education.

Higher education is provided by public and private institutions. All intermediate and higher institutes are public. Intermediate institutes offer two-year programs in industry, agriculture, medical sciences, economics, administration, transport, and tourism, leading to an associate degree. Universities offer four- to six-year programs leading to a license or a bachelor's degree: four years in basic sciences, arts, humanities, law, Shari'ah (Islamic law), economics,

Syria Education at a Glance

General Information

Capital	Damascus
Population	20.4 million
Language	Arabic
Adult literacy rate (ages 15 and over)	83.4%
Youth literacy rate (ages 15–24)	94.9%
GDP per capita	US$5,285
Number of phones (mobile) per 100 people	57
Number of Internet users per 100 people	21
Life expectancy at birth (years)	76

Formal Educational Information

Enrollment in preprimary school (ages 3–5)	145,000
Enrollment in primary school (ages 6–11)	2.3 million
Enrollment in lower and upper secondary school (ages 12–17)	2.6 million
Number of years of compulsory education	9 (ages 6–14)
Preprimary school student/teacher ratio	17
Primary school student/teacher ratio	18
Lower and upper secondary school gross student/teacher ratio	18
Preprimary school gross enrollment ratio	10%
Primary school gross enrollment ratio	118%
Lower and upper secondary school gross enrollment ratio	72%
Primary school entrants reaching grade 5	92%

Sources: Education for All, 2011; Global Education Digest, 2011; UNESCO–UIS, 2012; UNICEF, 2012; United Nations Development Programme, 2011.

social sciences, nursing, and fine arts; five years in engineering, architecture, agriculture, pharmacy, dentistry, and veterinary science; six years in medicine. Two years of study beyond the license or bachelor's degree leads to a master's degree. At least three years of study beyond the master's degree leads to a doctorate degree, including research and dissertation.

Teacher Education

According to the decision of the Ba'ath Socialist Party in March 1997, teacher training is to be provided by colleges of education instead of teacher training institutes. Furthermore, according to Decree Number 61 of 1999, four colleges of education at four universities (Damascus, Aleppo, Tishreen, and Al-Ba'ath) are designated to provide teacher training for all stages of education, including kindergarten and elementary. Teachers in all stages of education must hold university degrees. Elementary school teachers must hold the Elementary Teaching Certificate. Intermediate school teachers must hold a bachelor's degree plus a diploma in education. Secondary school teachers must hold a bachelor's degree in their respective fields of specialization (from colleges of sciences, letters, mechanical and electrical engineering), plus a diploma in education.

Informal Education

The aim of Decree Law Number 7 of 1972 is to eliminate illiteracy among all Syrians who are over eight years old, do not read or write, and are not enrolled in school. This law specifies that the state is responsible for providing free education to illiterate citizens. The Directorate of Education and the Governorate Council in each of the 14 governorates, as well as technical ministries, official and popular organizations, and employers participate in the process of eliminating illiteracy. In coordination with other authorities, the Ministry of Culture is in charge of adult literacy centers and programs. These programs provide literacy classes to illiterates and semiliterates who are between the ages of 13 and 45 years old and offer work and training opportunities through vocational and apprenticeship courses.

System Economics

The total public expenditure on education in 2007 represented 4.9 percent of Syria's gross domestic product. It represented 16.7 percent of the total government expenditure. For the year 1997, 54 percent of public education spending was at the primary level and 43 percent at the secondary level.

Future Prospects

Plans are under way that aim to develop educational management, enhance the potential of educational staff through preservice and in-service training, modernize methodologies and technologies, emphasize research and experimentation, develop the educational assessment process, and introduce computers and informatics into the core of educational activity. However, many of these innovations have been put on hold as a result of political unrest and national demonstrations and protests against the authoritarian regime. Military intervention by the Syrian government has left scores of the country's citizens dead. Educational improvements may be possible when the government ceases violent intervention against its citizens.

Emad Alfar

REFERENCES

Central Intelligence Agency. *The CIA World Factbook.* New York: Skyhorse, 2011. https://www.cia.gov/library/publications/the-world-factbook/index.html.

Education for All. "The Hidden Crisis: Armed Conflict and Education." *Education for All Global Monitoring Report.* Paris: UNESCO, 2011.

Global Education Digest. *Global Education Digest 2011: Comparing Education Statistics Across the World.* Montreal: UNESCO Institute for Statistics, 2011.

Programme on Governance in the Arab Region. www.pogar.org/countries/country.aspx?cid=19.

"Syria." In *The Europa World Yearbook*, vol. 2. London: Routledge, 2007.

UNESCO–IBE. www.ibe.unesco.org/countries/Syria.htm.

UNESCO–UIS. www.uis.unesco.org.

UNICEF. www.unicef.org/infobycountry/syria.html.

United Nations Development Programme. "Sustainability and Equity: A Better Future for All." *Human Development Report 2011.* New York: Palgrave Macmillan, 2011.

UNITED ARAB EMIRATES

The United Arab Emirates (UAE) is located in western Asia, on the Arabian Peninsula. The seven emirates that form the UAE are Abu Dhabi, Dubai, Sharjah, Umm Al-Qaywayn, Ajman, Fujayrah, and Ras Al-Khaymah. The official language is Arabic. Other spoken languages include English, Hindi, Urdu, and Persian. The United Nations population estimate for 2011 was eight million. Less than one-quarter of the population is UAE citizens, also known as Emiratis; the rest are other Arabs and South Asians. The official religion is Islam. The majority of Emiratis are Sunni Muslims and Shiite Muslims. There are substantial numbers of Christians, Hindus, and Sikhs. The UAE is a federation of the seven emirates, each having its own ruler and government.

Educational System

Established in 1971, the Ministry of Education (MOE), which is responsible for public educational affairs and the supervision of private education,

followed Kuwait's syllabi system for all educational levels until 1977. From 1977 to 1991, the ministry embarked on its first major curriculum reform for the elementary and intermediate levels in order to reflect the country's identity, needs, and goals. Among the achievements of this reform are a unified mathematics and general science curriculum for grades 1 through 9 among the Arab Gulf Cooperation Council (GCC) countries (Bahrain, Kuwait, Oman, Qatar, Saudi Arabia, and UAE); the addition of topics about GCC to social science and Arabic language textbooks; and teaching the English language in all grades beyond kindergarten. The second major curriculum reform began in 1992 and had four phases. The first phase, 1991–1992, assessed current curriculum and instruction materials; the second phase, 1992–1994, developed textbooks and teaching materials for Islamic education, philosophy, psychology, and other subjects; in the third phase, 1994–1998, these textbooks and materials were introduced into the classroom and teachers received in-service training for them; in the fourth phase, 1994–2000, the new curriculum was analyzed for its effectiveness. Higher education is under the responsibility of the Ministry of Higher Education and Scientific Research. Article 17 (1971) of the UAE constitution states that "education is compulsory in the primary stage and free in all its stages." The Ministry of Education reported in 2001 that basic education (covering nine years, grades 1-9) is compulsory starting at age six.

The public education system comprises four cycles: kindergarten, primary, lower secondary, and upper secondary. Higher education is offered at public and private institutions.

Precompulsory and Compulsory Education

Kindergarten, which is not compulsory, lasts for two years, for children entering at age four and exiting at age six. Attendance is not mandatory. Primary education, which is compulsory, lasts for five years, covering grades 1 through 5, for children entering at age six and exiting at age 11. Lower secondary education, which is compulsory, lasts for four years, covering grades 6 through 9, for children entering at age 11 and exiting at age 15. Students receive a foundation education for upper secondary education, with similar emphasis on subjects as that in the primary education.

Postcompulsory Education

Upper secondary education, which is not compulsory, offers two streams: general and technical. It lasts for three years, covering grades 10 through 12, for children entering at age 15 and exiting at age 18. The general stream has two substreams: arts and science. The technical stream offers three areas of study: agricultural, commercial, and technical. In the first year of secondary education, all students study the same core subjects. In their second and third years, besides studying common subjects, students study subjects from their chosen substream. As for higher education, some colleges offer two- and three-year degree programs, leading to a diploma, while others offer bachelor's and master's degree programs.

Curriculum, Assessment, and Instruction

Kindergarten students are provided with social and emotional education that promotes their physical and mental capabilities and develops their overall personality. This cycle prepares students for primary education, serving as a bridge between their home environment and primary school.

Subjects taught at both the primary level are Islamic studies, Arabic language, English language, mathematics, science, art, social studies, health and physical education, civics, information technology, home economics, life skills, and music. The same subjects are taught at the lower secondary education level, except for social studies, civics, home economics, life skills, and music. Additional subjects taught at the lower secondary level are history and geography.

In the first year of the general secondary education stream, common subjects taught are Islamic studies, Arabic language, English language, history, geography, mathematics, physics, chemistry, biology, geology, health and physical education, and information technology. In the second and third years of the general secondary education stream, subjects are taught according to the chosen substream (arts or science). In the arts substream curriculum, subjects taught are Islamic studies, Arabic language, English language, history, geography, economics, psychology, mathematics, physics, biology, health and physical education, and information technology. One more added subject in the second year is chemistry. In the science substream, subjects taught are Islamic studies, Arabic language, English language, mathematics, physics, chemistry, biology, geology, health and physical education, and information technology. As for the technical substream, the curriculum is the same as in the general secondary education, with more emphasis and more time spent on technical subjects in one of three areas of study: agricultural, commercial, or technical.

Each academic year consists of two terms, and each term is an independent and separate unit. At the primary level, students receive continuous assessment (written, oral, and activities). Marks for each term are based on two tests. Marks from the two terms are added to make the final result. Successful students move on to the lower secondary level. At both the lower and upper secondary levels, students take tests at the end of each term. Students are also evaluated throughout the year based on their coursework. The coursework mark is added to the tests mark to make the final result. Students who successfully complete the requirements of secondary education and pass the general examination are awarded the General Secondary Education Certificate (*Thanaweya 'Ama*). Holders of this certificate are eligible to enroll in higher education institutions.

The national institutions of higher education are the United Arab Emirates University (UAEU), Zayed University, and the Higher Colleges of Technology (HCT). Both UAEU and HCT have separate campuses for men and women. Bachelor's degree programs normally take four years and require a minimum of 132 credit hours, except for Shari'ah law, which requires 150 credit hours, and engineering, which takes five years and requires 172 credit hours. A medical degree takes six years, plus one year of residence beyond graduation. Master's degree programs in engineering, environmental sciences, and business administration take one year of study beyond the bachelor's degree. Two-year and three-year programs at the HCT, which lead to a diploma, train Emiratis for technological and professional occupations in the fields of engineering, health, communication technology, and business. The primary language of instruction is English, except for the Shari'ah law program, which is in Arabic.

Teacher Education

All teachers must hold a university degree and have classroom experience. The Ministry of Education provides preservice training for primary school teachers and in-service training for secondary school teachers. Training courses are intended to improve teaching skills, update curriculum knowledge, teach about the latest teaching methods and aids, and provide remediation for inadequate performance. English language skills and computer competency are of particular importance. In-service training is mandatory for new teachers. The College of Education of the UAEU trains secondary school teachers. UAEU, Zayed University, and some of the HCT offer a bachelor of education diploma. UAEU also offers a postgraduate diploma in education.

Informal Education

Article 17 (1972) of the UAE constitution states that "The law shall develop plans necessary for spreading and universalizing education at all levels and eradicating illiteracy." The Ministry of Education provides adult education and literacy centers in all areas of the country. To facilitate and expedite its goals for eradicating illiteracy, MOE located these centers in government schools. The centers, following the curriculum of government schools, offer two branches of study: a literacy curriculum for two years and the next stage curriculum, which covers grades 5 through 12. The Women's Associations, in cooperation with MOE, provide adult literacy and literacy programs, which include social centers and heritage revival centers. MOE provides these centers with all teaching materials and instructors.

System Economics

The total public expenditure on education in UAE in 2009 represented 1 percent of gross domestic product (GDP). It represented 23.4 percent of the total government expenditure. In the year 1997, 7 percent of public education spending was at the preprimary level, 48 percent at the primary level, and 45 percent at the secondary level.

Future Prospects

Strategic plans for a new educational reform, known as Education Vision 2020, are under way, covering the years 2000 through 2020. These plans include the newly created 5–4–3 educational ladder, in which the first nine years form a compulsory basic education, followed by three years of secondary education. Among the goals of the reform are to enable students to become knowledgeable, critical thinkers, active, creative, proficient in needed skills, healthy, lifelong learners, and productive individuals.

Emad Alfar

REFERENCES

Central Intelligence Agency. *The CIA World Factbook*. New York: Skyhorse, 2011. https://www.cia.gov/library/publications/the-world-factbook/index.html.

Education for All. "The Hidden Crisis: Armed Conflict and Education." *Education for All Global Monitoring Report*. Paris: UNESCO, 2011.

Global Education Digest. *Global Education Digest 2011: Comparing Education Statistics Across the World*. Montreal: UNESCO Institute for Statistics, 2011.

United Arab Emirates Education at a Glance

General Information

Capital	Abu Dhabi
Population	7.8 million
Language	Arabic
Adult literacy rate (ages 15 and over)	90%
Youth literacy rate (ages 15–24)	95%
GDP per capita	US$47,215
Number of phones (mobile) per 100 people	145
Number of Internet users per 100 people	78
Life expectancy at birth (years)	76

Formal Educational Information

Enrollment in preprimary school (ages 4–5)	117,000
Enrollment in primary school (ages 6–10)	304,000
Enrollment in lower and upper secondary school (ages 11–17)	322,000
Number of years of compulsory education	9 (ages 6–14)
Preprimary school student/teacher ratio	18
Primary school student/teacher ratio	17
Lower and upper secondary school gross student/teacher ratio	12
Preprimary school gross enrollment ratio	94%
Primary school gross enrollment ratio	105%
Lower and upper secondary school gross enrollment ratio	95%
Primary school entrants reaching grade 5	97%

Sources: Education for All, 2011; Global Education Digest, 2011; UNESCO–UIS, 2012; UNICEF, 2012; United Nations Development Programme, 2011.

Programme on Governance in the Arab Region. www.pogar.org/countries/country.aspx?cid=21.

UNESCO–IBE. www.ibe.unesco.org/countries/UAE.htm.

UNESCO–UIS. www.uis.unesco.org.

UNICEF. www.unicef.org/infobycountry/uae.html.

"United Arab Emirates." In *The Europa World Yearbook*, vol. 2. London: Routledge, 2009.

United Nations Development Programme. "Sustainability and Equity: A Better Future for All." *Human Development Report 2011*. New York: Palgrave Macmillan, 2011.

Yemen

Yemen, an Arab country, is located in southwestern Asia on the Arabian Peninsula. The official language is Arabic. The population is mainly Yemeni citizens; the rest are South Asians and Europeans. The official religion is Islam. The majority of the population is Muslim, with small numbers of Christians and Hindus. The Republic of Yemen was established in 1990, after the unification of Yemen Arab Republic (North Yemen) and People's Democratic Republic of Yemen (South Yemen).

Educational System

The administration of education is divided into three levels: Ministry of Education (MOE), Governorate Education Office (GEO), and District Education Office (DEO). The MOE administers public education at the central level and is responsible for higher education. The GEO carries out the policies of the MOE and supervises education in each of the 20 governorates in the country. The DEO is in charge of education at the local level. The Ministerial Decree Number 1319/1994 stipulates the merging of the two educational systems that existed before the unification into one: basic education for nine years, followed by secondary education for three years. Basic education is compulsory for all Yemeni children from six to 14 years old. Education is free in all stages for all Yemenis.

The education system comprises three cycles: kindergarten, basic education, and secondary education. Higher education is provided by public and private institutions. These institutions offer programs leading to diplomas, as well as to bachelor's and master's degrees.

Precompulsory and Compulsory Education

Kindergarten, which is not compulsory and lasts for three years, is for children entering at age three and exiting at age six. The majority of kindergarten schools are public, funded by the government; the rest are private.

Basic education, which is compulsory, lasts for nine years, covering grades 1 through 9, for children entering at age six and exiting at age 15. Students who acquire the necessary knowledge, skills, and competencies to successfully complete their basic education advance to the secondary level.

Postcompulsory Education

Secondary education, which is not compulsory, lasts for three years, covering grades 10 through 12, for children entering at age 15 and exiting at age 18. In the first year, all students study the same curriculum. In the final two years of general secondary education, students enroll in either the scientific or literary track. Yemen also has technical, agricultural, and vocational secondary schools, as well as religious institutes that emphasize the study of the Quran and Islam. Students receive an education that prepares them for higher education or entry into the labor market. Student who successfully complete their secondary education are awarded the Secondary Education Certificate (*Thanawiya*) in their chosen track.

Higher education institutions offer two- to six-year programs leading to diplomas, as well as bachelor's and master's degrees.

Curriculum, Assessment, and Instruction

Kindergarten education develops the children's spiritual, religious, and human values, as well as their physical and linguistic capabilities. It develops their ability to discover and to create, preparing them for school education.

Subjects taught in basic education, grades 1 through 9, are learning the Quran, Islamic education, Arabic language, mathematics, health sciences, and extracurricular activities, including physical education and sport. Other subjects taught are introduced at various grades: moral and civic education at grade 3, both history and geography at grade 5, and English language at grade 7. Emphasis is on Arabic language and mathematics. Student who successfully complete their basic education advance to the secondary level.

In general secondary education, grade 10, all students are taught the same subjects: learning the Quran, Islamic education, Arabic language, history, geography, Yemeni society and culture, mathematics, biology, chemistry, physics, English language, and extracurricular activities, including physical education and sport. After the first year of general secondary education, students enroll in either the scientific or literary track. Subjects taught in the scientific track in grades 11 and 12 are learning the Quran, Islamic education, Arabic language, mathematics, biology, chemistry, physics, English language, and extracurricular activities, including physical education and sport. Emphasis is on mathematics, Arabic language, and English language. Subjects taught in the literary track in grades 11 and 12 include learning the Quran, Islamic education, Arabic language, history, geography, social science, economy, psychology, philosophy and logic, arithmetic, English language, and extracurricular activities, including physical education and sport. Emphasis is on Arabic language and English language.

In both basic and general secondary education, students' final results, represented as a percentage of the overall mark, are obtained as follows: continuous monthly assessment, 20 percent; semiannual assessment, 20 percent; and annual assessment, 60 percent. Students who successfully complete their basic and secondary education are awarded the Intermediate Education Certificate and the Secondary Education Certificate (*Thanawiya*) in the chosen track, respectively.

Higher education institutions offer two- to six-year programs leading to diplomas, as well as bachelor's and master's degrees. A number of universities offer two-year programs leading to a diploma in specializations, such as electronics, information technology, pharmacy, and dentistry. Programs of study leading to a bachelor's degree normally take four years, while engineering takes five years, and medicine six years. Two years of study beyond the bachelor's degree leads to a master's degree, whereas for engineering it is one year beyond the five-year bachelor's degree. Among the universities are Sanaa University, Aden University, and Taez University.

Yemen Education at a Glance

General Information

Capital	Sanaa
Population	24 million
Language	Arabic
Adult literacy rate (ages 15 and over)	63.9%
Youth literacy rate (ages 15–24)	85.2%
GDP per capita	US$2,507
Number of phones (mobile) per 100 people	46
Number of Internet users per 100 people	11
Life expectancy at birth (years)	65

Formal Educational Information

Enrollment in preprimary school (ages 3–5)	no data
Enrollment in primary school (ages 6–11)	3.2 million
Enrollment in lower and upper secondary school (ages 12–17)	no data
Number of years of compulsory education	9 (ages 6–14)
Preprimary school student/teacher ratio	15
Primary school student/teacher ratio	31
Lower and upper secondary school gross student/teacher ratio	25
Preprimary school gross enrollment ratio	1%
Primary school gross enrollment ratio	87%
Lower and upper secondary school gross enrollment ratio	44%
Primary school entrants reaching grade 5	66%

Sources: Education for All, 2011; Global Education Digest, 2011; UNESCO–UIS, 2012; UNICEF, 2012; United Nations Development Programme, 2011.

Teacher Education

Basic school teachers are offered training and programs of study at the postsecondary level for two years at teacher training institutes, some of which are women's teacher training institutes. Secondary school teachers are offered training and programs of study at the colleges of education at the universities, leading to the Bachelor of Arts in education degree. Topics covered in teacher training include methods of teaching subjects at various grade levels, child development and psychology, use of textbooks, communication and learning, difficulties of learning, and use of instructional material.

Informal Education

Informal education is offered to youths who did not receive an education and to adults, ages 10 to 45 years. Students gain basic knowledge in reading, writing, arithmetic, and the basic principles of Islamic religion and Islamic law. Informal education aims to help students, mainly adults, solve problems they confront in their daily lives and adapt to changes in the surrounding world. In addition to helping students learn to read, memorize, and recite Quranic verses by heart, Quranic schools provide education in Arabic language, reading, writing, and arithmetic.

System Economics

The total public expenditure on education in Yemen in 2008 represented 5.2 percent of gross domestic product. For the year 2008, the public expenditure on education represented 16 percent of the total government expenditure.

Future Prospects

Plans are under way to tackle many of Yemen's educational challenges. Among these challenges are high rates of illiteracy; low enrollment numbers of school-age population; lack of gender parity and equality; shortage of required infrastructure; poor quality of school facilities and educational materials; too few classrooms; and low numbers of trained teachers.

Moreover, increasing internal political tension poses an obstacle to the country's educational efforts.

Emad Alfar

REFERENCES

Central Intelligence Agency. *The CIA World Factbook*. New York: Skyhorse, 2011. https://www.cia.gov/library/publications/the-world-factbook/index.html.

Education for All. "The Hidden Crisis: Armed Conflict and Education." *Education for All Global Monitoring Report*. Paris: UNESCO, 2011.

Global Education Digest. *Global Education Digest 2011: Comparing Education Statistics Across the World*. Montreal: UNESCO Institute for Statistics, 2011.

Programme on Governance in the Arab Region. www.pogar.org/countries/country.aspx?cid=22.

UNESCO–IBE. www.ibe.unesco.org/en/worldwide/unesco-regions/arab-states/yemen.html.

UNESCO–UIS. www.uis.unesco.org.

UNICEF. www.unicef.org/infobycountry/yemen.html.

United Nations Development Programme. "Sustainability and Equity: A Better Future for All." *Human Development Report 2011*. New York: Palgrave Macmillan, 2011.

"Yemen." In *The Europa World Yearbook*, vol. 2. London: Routledge, 2009.

NORTH AMERICA AND CARIBBEAN

INTRODUCTION

This section discusses the educational systems of 17 countries and one territory in North America and the Caribbean. There is great disparity both among countries and within countries of this region. Indeed, the United States, the most affluent nation in the world, is only about 625 miles (about 1,000 kilometers) from Haiti, the poorest country in the Western Hemisphere. Both countries are discussed in this section. To illustrate, the average student/teacher ratio in the United States is 15.4 to 1 while that of Haiti is nearly 34 to 1. Primary students in the United States have a completion rate of essentially 100 percent, while the rate in Haiti cannot be determined because the educational infrastructure is in a state of ruin. The United States has greatly benefited from public education—it was celebrated in the latter half of the twentieth century as perhaps the world's finest institution that other countries have tried to emulate. Haiti has no public education option: poor families who want to send their children to school must spend at least one-third of their entire earnings to provide that education.

It is also true that socioeconomic disparities (as well as ethnic and educational disparities) exist in nearly all the countries mentioned in these sections (and of course other sections as well). It should be self-evident that not all people in the United States, for example, are equal in terms of their socioeconomic status, educational experience, family background (which can be defined as ethnicity, cultural milieu, and general mind-set), and commitment to education—which many people forget serves as the backbone of educational success. At the same time, both the United States and Haiti do have something very important in common—as do essentially all the nations in this section: there are families in each region that are committed to improving their children's livelihood by sending them to school because the parents know that people with an education have more opportunities than those who do not have an education. It is important to emphasize, however, that not all alienated groups, such as most people of Haiti, have a commitment to improving their children's education and overall economic well-being. Amerindian populations who have been historically alienated in their own countries—for example, Mexico, Guatemala, Honduras, El Salvador, and Panama—have few alternatives; most live in agrarian regions where labor is an essential part of a family's livelihood. Accordingly, these regions tend to have high levels of child labor. These regions also have sprawling rural areas with few resources and little to no electricity or running water. Children who are schooled in these areas must often travel several miles, most often at the family's expense, to attend school that is taught on video or by a teacher located in another part of the country—which is possible, of course, only if the school has electrical power.

In sum, this section, perhaps more than any other, demonstrates the greatest disparities in terms of wealth, conviction, and attitude toward educational and economic goals.

Daniel Ness and Chia-ling Lin

BAHAMAS

The Commonwealth of the Bahamas is a Caribbean island chain located southeast of Florida and northeast of Cuba in the North Atlantic Ocean. About 85 percent of all Bahamians are black, 12 percent are white, and 3 percent are Asian or Latino. In the fifteenth century, when Europeans set sail to the Americas in large numbers, the islands that constitute the Bahamas were inhabited by the Lucayan—a native people who were eventually enslaved by the Spanish aristocracy. The islands were occupied by English settlers by 1650 and eventually became a British colony by 1783. The commonwealth established independence in 1973 and since then has flourished thanks to its popular tourism industry and offshore banking business. The commonwealth's primary concern is its centralized location for illegal drug trafficking and a large number of HIV/AIDS cases. The rate of HIV/AIDS among Bahamian adults is 3 percent (nearly 5,600 cases).

Educational System

The Bahamas Ministry of Education runs the commonwealth's school system, which provides compulsory education for all students between five and 16 years of age. In general, education in the Bahamas consists of public elementary and secondary education as well as higher education.

The Bahamian government, under the auspices of the United Kingdom, has encouraged and promoted an educational system that emphasizes cognitive skills, social skills, and life skills as essential elements of a democratic society. According to its mission statement, the charge of the Bahamian Ministry of Education is "to provide all persons in The Bahamas an opportunity to receive an education that will equip them with the necessary knowledge, skills, beliefs and attitudes required for work and life in a democratic, Christian society."

Higher education is provided by universities, colleges, and institutes. There are over 50 institutions of higher education in the Bahamas. The College of the Bahamas and the University of the West Indies have the largest enrollment.

Precompulsory and Compulsory Education

Compulsory education in the Bahamas is for children between the ages five and 16, covering 11 or 12 years. Prior to the 1990s, compulsory education in the com-

monwealth had been two years less (meaning 9 or 10 years of education). By the late 1980s, the Bahamian Ministry of Education oversaw 226 schools. Of these schools, 188 were government-run and the remaining 38 were independently run. New Providence, the most populous island of the Bahamas, ran 38 government schools and 13 independent schools, while the Family Islands and Grand Bahama ran 150 government schools and 25 independent schools. At the time, the government classified the school system into three categories: primary education, secondary education, and all-age education. Primary education includes preschools, whose students range from three to five years old, and primary schools, whose students range in age from five to 10. Parents of three- and four-year-old children have the option of enrolling their children in preschool. Secondary school students range in age from about 11 to 16 or 17 years. Students 11 to 14 attend junior high schools, and those between 14 and 16 or 17 attend senior high schools. The all-age schools educate students between 5 and 16 years of age, most of whom reside on the Family Islands—areas with lower population than New Providence.

Between 1991 and 1997, the government's budget and expenses for education rose nearly 6 percent. In 1991, 15.5 percent of the national budget was allocated for education. By 1997 this allocation rose to well over 21.5 percent.

Postcompulsory Education

Primary and secondary education is compulsory in the Bahamas. Tertiary education is not. Higher education is provided by universities, colleges, and institutes offering programs ranging from certificates in learning and achieving proficiency in a trade or vocation to two-year associate degrees, four-year bachelor's degrees, and, after further study of two to four years, master's degrees. The two primary institutions of higher learning in the commonwealth are the College of the Bahamas and the University of the West Indies. Other institutions include Atlantic College, Galilee College, Access Bible Academy, Bahamas Baptist Community College, Institute of Business and Commerce, McHari Institute, Nova Southeastern University (with a campus in the United States), Omega College, Shaw University, Sojourner Douglass College, and the University of Miami extension in the

Bahamas. Most institutions of higher education in the Bahamas are affiliated with a number of sects from the Protestant Church or with the Catholic Church.

Curriculum, Assessment, and Instruction

In general, from the early grades to the high school level, curriculum in Bahamian schools include language arts, health and family life education, art and design, foreign language (Spanish and French), religious studies, and social studies.

For the Bahamas Ministry of Education, the subject of language arts serves as the core of the school curriculum. According to the ministry, the aim of the language arts curriculum is to prepare students in effective communication in speech, reading, and writing. The language of focus is English. One of the main objectives of the language arts curriculum is for students to connect what they are learning with everyday life situations and events. Components of instruction include grammar, writing, literature, reading, speaking, syntax, and handwriting. Students at both the primary and secondary school levels are assessed in language arts through national examinations, which are created to evaluate students' listening and reading comprehension and written communication.

Health and family life education also plays a crucial part of the curriculum. Health and family life education seems to either substitute for or complement students' study in the area of life science. This curriculum is intended to serve students based on age level with respect to family structure, family roles and responsibilities, maturation and development, human sexuality, disease control and prevention, substance abuse prevention, and environmental issues. The following forms of assessment have been used by teachers from kindergarten to the high school level: research projects, summative assessment tools (e.g., tests and quizzes), portfolios, games and puzzles, role playing, artistic and written expression, and field trips.

Art and design are a requirement for all students. Through the medium of art and design, students are able to demonstrate their knowledge in other subject areas, such as history and cultural studies. This aspect of the curriculum includes fine arts, graphic design, observational study, and crafts. Art and design is often taught in tandem with literature, mathematics, and science.

Foreign language study in schools in the Bahamas commences in the fourth grade (sometimes the third grade) with Spanish. The primary foreign languages taught in high school are Spanish and French. Spanish at the primary grades emphasizes speaking and listening through repetition, songs, rhymes, and dramatic play. Yet at the same time, reading and writing skills are also part of the curriculum. Secondary school students who are proficient in English have the option of continuing with Spanish and including French as a second or third language.

The Ministry of Education states that Christianity is "embedded in Bahamian culture." As a result, religious studies play a central part in education from the early grades to the high school grades. Religious history and Christian doctrine are included in religious studies. Despite the title "religious studies," with the exception of the primary grades, there is little, if any, examination and study of non-Christian religions. One possible benefit of religious studies is that students may gain knowledge of the origins and influences of the legal system and moral codes that have been undergirded by Judeo-Christian rituals and values.

The social studies curriculum in the Bahamas is essentially an amalgamation of the social sciences. It provides young students in the primary grades with knowledge about different cultures, history, religion, and location and tourism. In general, however, social studies in the early grades focus on the local environment and community. Not until the fourth and fifth grades do students begin to learn about neighboring societies and countries throughout the world. The social sciences at the secondary level are divided into geography, civics, government, economics, and history. Students in the secondary grades learn about civic responsibility, democracy, global equity, environmentalism, and diplomatic relations.

Mathematics is required as a subject in primary and secondary education. Nevertheless, it has been noted that the state of mathematics education in the Bahamas is severely lacking. Due to shortages of qualified teachers of mathematics and technical sciences, class sizes have grown in recent years to accommodate these shortages. As a result, there have been many instances of poor student behavior, lack of structure, and student attrition in these subject areas. The Ministry of Education has demonstrated a need for improvement in mathematics, earth science, and physical science disciplines.

Teacher Education

Teachers in the Bahamas must have teacher certification. Prior to 1980, there were few, if any qualifications for teachers in the commonwealth. By 1981, however, the College of the Bahamas began programs preparing teacher candidates with a modicum of courses leading to an associate of arts degree and certification. After 1993 the commonwealth upgraded teacher requirements and mandated that all students preparing for teacher candidacy must earn a bachelor of arts or an equivalent in order to be eligible for certification. By 1997 the commonwealth hired enough certified teachers to be able to accommodate its entire primary student enrollment.

The primary higher education institution of teacher education in the Bahamas is the College of the Bahamas. Since 1993 the college has been attempting to improve its teacher education programs to award bachelor's degrees, which were introduced in 1997. In that year, the College of the Bahamas introduced the bachelor of education degree for primary school teachers. Those presently awarded an associate degree are still hired; however, the encouragement for individuals to seek baccalaureates is growing. Teacher certification, or its equivalent, is a mandatory requirement for all teachers in the Bahamas.

Informal Education

In 2004 the Bahamas Ministry of Education, Youth, Sports, and Culture established the Department of Higher Education and Lifelong Learning, which primarily serves adults of all educational levels. The department consists of the following units: Tertiary/Quality Assurance Division, Scholarships and Educational Loans, Bahamas Library Service, National Literacy Services, and the Bahamas Technical Cadet Corps. The overall mission of the department is to accommodate the commonwealth's workforce with personal enrichment and lifelong learning as a means of the population's involvement in the global economy.

The Tertiary/Quality Assurance Division controls all the fiscal and academic aspects of tertiary education in the Bahamas. The division's charges include programs in teacher training; quality assurance of institutions whose constituents are applying for primary, secondary, or all-age status; and accreditation

of teacher education. The division is also responsible for the Future Teachers of the Bahamas Programme, which recruits adults from a variety of occupations to pursue teaching in most of the academic areas for primary and secondary school.

The Education Loan Authority was established in 2002, prior to the Department of Higher Education and Lifelong Learning, but was subsumed under the department in 2004. The authority was established as a result of Parliament's decision to raise funds for the Education Loan Guarantee Scheme, an initiative founded under the 2001 Education Guarantee Fund Act. The authority's responsibility is to enable all citizens with the resources to return to school for professional studies or lifelong learning. The Bahamas Library Services unit enables the citizens of the commonwealth to readily access library related resources. This branch of the department evolved from two primary constituents: local communities and the government. The National Literacy Services unit was created as a means of developing a functionally literate society. Under the auspices of National Literacy Services is Let's Read Bahamas, which was created in 1994 in an effort to improve literacy. This program was developed to raise standards in literacy. Two major primary departments are operated by National Literacy Services: Adult Literacy and Family Literacy. The Program in Adult Literacy serves students who are either nonschooled or left school and do not have basic reading skills, as well as adults in the workplace who need basic literacy skills. The Family Literacy Program helps young "at-risk parents" who do not have a high school degree.

Finally there is the Bahamas Technical and Vocational Institute. Also known as the Bahamas Technical Cadet Corps, the Bahamas Technical and Vocational Institute aims to educate and train Bahamians in the various vocational and technological occupations that are needed for economic success in the twenty-first century. The institute is also a haven of lifelong learning for any citizen of the Bahamas. One of the criticisms of the organization is that it has not updated its facilities, leaving its courses unchanged and equivalent to the standards of the last century.

System Economics

Public expenditure on education for the world in 2010 was approximately 4.9 percent of the gross domestic product (GDP), 4.7 percent for developing

Bahamas Education at a Glance

General Information

Capital	Nassau
Population	305,655
Languages	English, Creole
Adult literacy rate (ages 15 and over)	95.6%
GDP per capita	US$21,600
People below poverty line	9.3%
Number of phones (landline) per 100 people	45.8
Number of phones (mobile) per 100 people	60.9
Number of Internet users per 100 people	30.4
Life expectancy at birth (years)	66

Formal Educational Information

Enrollment in primary school (ages 5–10)	36,000
Enrollment in lower and upper secondary school (ages 11–16)	36,000
Enrollment in tertiary school	over 21,000
Number of years of compulsory education	12 (ages 5–16)
Primary school student/teacher ratio	17
Lower and upper secondary school student/teacher ratio	14.2
Primary school gross enrollment ratio	100%
Secondary school gross enrollment ratio	100%
Tertiary school gross enrollment ratio	no data
Primary school entrants completion rate	100%

Note: Unless otherwise indicated, all data are based on sources from 2011.

countries, and 5.0 percent for countries in the Caribbean region. No data exist, however, that capture the percentage of GDP spent on education by the Bahamian government. At present, no data exist on the public expenditure on education as a percentage of government expenditure. Moreover, there is no data on spending per student as a percentage of GDP per capita at the primary and secondary education levels.

Future Prospects

Recent trends show that there is an emphasis to promote and continue literacy education in the Bahamas. Within the last five years, the United States ambassador to the Bahamas has urged support of the literacy program in the schools on New Providence that had begun years earlier by the preceding ambassador. More importantly, however, given the paucity of literacy promotion outside of New Providence, the ambassador pledged to further support the literacy program and take the program to numerous locations on the Family Islands, where literacy rates are poor.

There are initiatives in the Bahamian government to update educational facilities for institutions of both compulsory and noncompulsory education. For instance, media attention on the lack of up-to-date equipment at the Bahamas Technical and Vocational Institute seems to have stimulated a push for the institution to run semiautonomously for the attraction of private donors.

Daniel Ness and Chia-ling Lin

REFERENCES

Central Intelligence Agency. *The CIA World Factbook*. New York: Skyhorse, 2011. https.www.cia.gov/library/publications/the-world-factbook/index.html.

"Bahamas." In *The Europa World Yearbook*, vol. 1. London: Routledge, 2007.

Nation Master. 2011. www.nationmaster.com.

UNESCO–IBE. www.ibe.unesco.org/countries/Bahamas.htm.

UNESCO–UIS. www.uis.unesco.org.

UNICEF. www.unicef.org/infobycountry/bahrain.html.

United Nations Development Programme. "Beyond Scarcity: Power, Poverty and the Global Water Crisis." *Human Development Report 2012*. New York: Palgrave Macmillan, 2012.

World Bank Education Statistics. 2011. www.worldbank.org.

BELIZE

The parliamentary democracy of Belize is located in the southern part of North America, bordered on the north by Mexico and on the west by Guatemala. About half of the Belizeans are mestizo (48.7), followed by Creole (24.9 percent), Maya (10.6 percent), Garifuna (6 percent), and other groups (9.4 percent). Nearly half of the population is Roman Catholic, 27 percent are Protestant, and 24 percent are either members of non-Judeo-Christian religions or those who do not belong to a religious faith. During the late 1600s and for a good part of the 1700s, the area that is now Belize was in dispute between Spanish and British colonists. By 1852 the area formally was named the colony of British Honduras. Belize did not become an independent nation until 1981. Despite a rather promising tourism industry, the country's major concerns include high unemployment, a high crime rate, a high dependency on the South American drug trade, and a large number of HIV/AIDS cases. The rate of HIV/AIDS among Belizean adults is 2.4 percent (nearly 3,200 cases).

Educational System

The Belize Ministry of Education runs the country's school system, which provides compulsory education for all students between five and 14 years of age—approximately 10 years of compulsory schooling. In general, education in Belize consists of public elementary and secondary education as well as higher education. Aside from institutions of higher education, there are a total of 480 schools in Belize—142 of which are preschool, 288 primary, and only 50 secondary.

The goals of education include students' understanding of Belizean history and nationhood, an appreciation of cultural diversity, commitment to social justice, development of social skills, development of intellectual and cognitive skills, and personal hygiene.

Higher education is provided by universities, colleges, and institutes, including Central America Health Sciences University and Belize Medical College, Galen University, Medical University of the Americas (Belize Campus), St. John's Junior College, St. Matthews University, and the University of Belize.

Precompulsory and Compulsory Education

Although compulsory education in Belize begins at age five, parents have the opportunity to send their children under five to preprimary school. Nearly 34 percent of all children under the age for compulsory education are enrolled in what Belize refers to as preprimary education (i.e., preschool education). Compulsory education in Belize is for children between the ages five and 14, a period of about 10 years. Since 1994 the percentage of primary-school-age children enrolled in primary education increased from 94 percent to 97 percent. All students who enter primary school seem to finish (104 percent). However, the percentage of Belizean students enrolled in secondary school has been much lower. Given that all students generally complete primary school, 69 percent of girls and 64 percent of boys continue in secondary education. Despite these unfavorable numbers, the percentage of students enrolling in secondary school has increased nearly 35 percent (from 31 percent in 1991 to about 37 percent in 2006).

Postcompulsory Education

Primary education is compulsory in Belize. Secondary education is becoming increasingly required, but is not yet enforced as compulsory for students beyond the sixth-grade level. Tertiary education is not compulsory. In fact, of the total resources allocated for state-sponsored higher education in Belize, only 1 percent funds tertiary education. Higher education is provided by universities, colleges, and institutes offering programs ranging from certificates in learning and achieving proficiency in a trade or vocation to two-year associate degrees, four-year bachelor's degrees, and, after further study of two to four years, master's degrees.

Curriculum, Assessment, and Instruction

The vision for curriculum in Belizean schools is to promote what the Ministry of Education refers to as "character education." This term encompasses citizenship, morality, a commitment to freedom and diversity, social responsibility, self-esteem, and care for the physical environment. In general, from the early grades to the high school level, curriculum in Belizean schools includes Spanish, English, mathematics, history and economics, health and hygiene education, fine and performing arts, and the physical and life sciences.

The primary school grades are divided into three categories: the lower division, middle division, and upper division. The lower division focuses on English, mathematics, science, and social studies, as well as Spanish, physical education, and music. The curriculum of the second division at the primary level is basically similar to the first; however, rather than music, the middle division calls for "expressive arts." In the third division, children learn about health and hygiene as well as various forms of technology.

The primary areas of study in the Belizean primary school curriculum are divided into four areas: (1) Language (English and Spanish); (2) mathematics, science, work and technology; (3) social studies and personal development (as it relates to social and cultural connections); and (4) the expressive arts, physical education, and health.

The Belizean Ministry of Education refers to the origins and development of a nationalized curriculum as one that follows a logical contingency approach.

According to the ministry, this approach is founded upon a "top-down" and "bottom-up" way of pursuing educational goals, in which a research-based (top-down) program is mediated by an experiential (bottom-up) focus that is dependent on the individual student. In other words, the fundamental, core aspects of a particular subject (e.g., mathematics, social studies) are supported by research within that field of study, yet at the same time the educational system in Belize emphasizes the importance of the child's own experiences and everyday connections with a specific subject.

The following are the "Goals of Education" as illustrated in the nationalized curriculum established by the Belize Ministry of Education in 2011:

1. A knowledge of Belize and a commitment to and involvement in its nationhood and development
2. An appreciation of and respect for different people and cultures and a commitment to justice and equity for all
3. Spiritually, social skills and personal qualities
4. Intellectual skills and qualities
5. A knowledge and practice of healthy lifestyles
6. An understanding of the economics of Belize and of the world, the appreciation of work, the capacity to participate in economic activities, skills in design, and the ability to use a range of technologies
7. A knowledge of the universe and an understanding of the solar system with special attention to the earth
8. An understanding of systems and subsystems in the physical world, including the natural environment and the need to preserve it
9. An understanding of number, quantity, and space and the application of relevant concepts
10. An appreciation of, and participation in, artistic ventures, particularly within the Belizean culture
11. The ability to communicate proficiently in English
12. The ability to communicate effectively in Spanish

One of the main problems in Belizean education is the attrition rate of students in secondary school. Attrition has been the result of poor financial resources among families, teenage pregnancy, and disciplinary issues among teenagers. In addition, the earning of a diploma has always been seen as a positive indicator of upward mobility in terms of financial success in Belize. However, according to Merrill (1992) and Norris and Callco (2010), academic credentials began to lose power and importance when students began to realize that a secondary school diploma failed to provide them with higher-paying jobs and economic mobility.

Teacher Education

Teachers in Belize must have teacher certification. The Teacher Education and Development Unit (TEDU) is the highest overseer of prospective teacher candidates in Belize. It is run by the Ministry of Education. According to the ministry, TEDU is responsible for quality assurance with regard to teacher preparation and professional development during teacher candidacy and as a teacher. TEDU's mission, then, is to enforce accountability, promote improvement in teacher education and preparation, and provide "leadership for reform in teacher education." TEDU, as well as the Ministry of Education that subsumes it, seems to follow the typical doctrine that student achievement and success are dependent on so-called high-qualified teachers. This is a pattern in most government-sponsored educational systems throughout the world.

The charge of TEDU is to manage all functions that have to do with the education and professional development of teachers and educators before and during their careers. The agency serves as the monitor of teacher education programs in Belizean higher education institutions. Its aim is to support and monitor, against established standards, the delivery of teacher education programs in institutions offering such programs. TEDU coordinates a new teacher induction program, which requires preservice teachers to undergo a one-year training period prior to certification. TEDU also provides training for in-service teachers who need to meet certification requirements. Further, TEDU's mission also includes a resource center, which serves as an enrichment venue for prospective and in-service teachers who wish to locate information and research on issues related to education.

Informal Education

Informal education in Belize is a branch of educational development that is run by Educational Support Services (ESS), a branch of the Ministry of Education. The mission of ESS is to promote lifelong learning, as well as general education and holistic learning for all children and adults. Another aspect of the agency's mission is to increase enrollment, particularly in secondary school, where enrollment is significantly lower than in primary education in Belize. ESS is also charged to ensure that children attend school regularly, are healthy, and are secure from external influences that may affect their abilities or well-being in school.

ESS aims to ensure that students do not come to school hungry or spend their time in school with poor nutritional habits. This is mostly problematic for students whose families fall below the poverty line. Another goal of ESS is to ensure that students with learning difficulties or physical difficulties receive the appropriate care and assistance for furthering their

education. The objective is to prepare all students for opportunities within a global market economy.

System Economics

Public expenditure on education for the world in 2008 was approximately 4.9 percent of the gross domestic product (GDP), 4.7 percent for developing countries, and 5.0 percent for countries in the Caribbean and Central American region. Public expenditure on education for Belize in 2008 was approximately 5.8 percent of the GDP. In 2004 the public expenditure on education as a percentage of public expenditure was 87.6 percent, nearly 5 percent lower than the world average and Caribbean average, and 2 percent below the "developing country" average. Spending per student by the end of the 2004 academic year as a percentage of GNP per capita at the primary level was 13.7 percent. Spending as a percentage of GNP per capita at the secondary education level was 19.9 percent.

Future Prospects

One of the key issues that the Belizean government will need to consider in coming years is the condition of secondary education and advancement of students to the college and university levels. At present, although most students complete primary education, the attrition rate for students at the secondary level is high. In recent years, there have been some indications that this may change, especially given the difficulties of the global economy and recent global food shortages. To address the issue of attrition and other problems in Belizean secondary education, the Ministry of Education set out to identify strengths within the educational system. One of these strengths has been the emphasis on food and nutrition. In December 2007, several secondary students were nominated to enter the finals of the Caribbean Food and Nutrition Institute (CFNI) Regional Nutrition Quiz Competition. The Ministry of Education has also focused on increasing technological knowledge and enriching secondary school teachers with alternative approaches to teaching through initiatives that encourage partnerships with other countries, such as South Korea and Canada.

Daniel Ness and Chia-ling Lin

Belize Education at a Glance

General Information

Capital	Belmopan
Population	294,385
Languages	Spanish, Creole
Adult literacy rate (ages 15 and over)	76.9%
GDP per capita	US$8,400
People below poverty line	33.5%
Number of phones (landline) per 100 people	11.3
Number of phones (mobile) per 100 people	31.6
Number of Internet users per 100 people	11.9
Life expectancy at birth (years)	69

Formal Educational Information

Enrollment in primary school (ages 5–10)	40,000
Enrollment in lower and upper secondary school (ages 11–16)	39,000
Enrollment in tertiary school	9,000
Number of years of compulsory education	10 (ages 5–14)
Primary school student/teacher ratio	22.8
Lower and upper secondary school student/teacher ratio	14.3
Primary school gross enrollment ratio	127%
Secondary school gross enrollment ratio	84%
Tertiary school gross enrollment ratio	3%
Primary school entrants completion rate	95%
Child labor (ages 5–14)	40%

Note: Unless otherwise indicated, all data are based on sources from 2011.

REFERENCES

"Belize." In *The Europa World Yearbook*, vol. 1. London: Routledge, 2009.

Central Intelligence Agency. *The CIA World Factbook*. New York: Skyhorse, 2011. https:www.cia.gov/library/publications/the-world-factbook/index.html.

Merrill Timothy, ed. *Belize: A Country Study*. Education. Washington, DC: GPO for the Library of Congress, 1992. http://countrystudies.us/belize/32.htm.

Ministry of Education and Youth, Belize. 2011. www.moe.gov.bz/.

Nation Master. 2011. www.nationmaster.com.

Norris, Jordan, and Molly Calico. "Belize as a Classroom." *Impact Belize*. Paper 3. 2010. http://digitalcommons.wku.edu/impact/3.

UNESCO–IBE. www.ibe.unesco.org/countries/Belize.htm.

UNESCO–UIS. 2011. http://stats.uis.unesco.org/unesco/TableViewer/document.aspx?ReportId=121&IF_Language=eng&BR_Country=580.

UNICEF. www.unicef.org/infobycountry/belize.html.

World Bank Education Statistics. 2011. www.worldbank.org.

BERMUDA

Bermuda consists of a group of islands in the Atlantic Ocean located due east of South Carolina (United States). The official language is English, although Portuguese is also spoken. Given its small size, it has a relatively high population density. About half of all Bermudans are black and 34 percent are white. Despite its relatively small population, Bermuda is religiously diverse. The breakdown is Anglican, 23 percent; Roman Catholic, 15 percent; African Methodist Episcopal, 11 percent; and other Protestant denominations, 18 percent. Members of non-Christian religions are approximately 12 percent of the population, while the remaining 21 percent either are not affiliated or profess an unspecified or no religious belief.

Bermuda was at first settled by British colonists who were members of the Virginia Company. Headed for Virginia in 1609, the colonists were instead shipwrecked on the Bermudan islands. The islands have been a British possession since then. Bermuda has been a popular tourist destination since the mid-nineteenth century and has been established primarily as a tourist economy. In recent years, Bermuda has become a popular center for international business and a well-known offshore financial center.

Educational System

The Ministry of Education of Bermuda administers public education, including higher education, and supervises private education. The Bermudan Ministry of Education runs the country's school system, which provides compulsory education for all students between five and 17 years of age—approximately 13 years of compulsory schooling. In general, education in Bermuda consists of preprimary, primary, and secondary education as well as higher education. Aside from institutions of higher education, there are a total of 37 government-run schools in Bermuda—12 preschools, 17 primary schools, 5 lower secondary schools, 2 upper secondary schools, and 1 special needs school. The emphasis on education and academic achievement in Bermuda is rather high, despite its relatively low population, small area, and hence, low number of schools. There are also at least 10 private schools in the country, most of which are run parallel with the British educational system.

The goals of education include a strong emphasis on the four main subject strands: language (English), social studies, science, and mathematics. In addition, educators in Bermuda, particularly in government-run schools, intend to establish an environment that is conducive to each student's growth in terms of academic achievement, practical applications, physical development and education, critical thinking processes, and aesthetic, social, and moral development. A related goal is the importance of using formal education as a means of promoting community and civic life.

Most students in Bermuda who graduate from secondary school are encouraged to enter higher education. Since there is only one institution of higher education in Bermuda—Bermuda College—most students who seek college- or university-level education study abroad, primarily in the United States, Canada, Great Britain, and Australia.

Precompulsory and Compulsory Education

Preschool, which is not compulsory, is for children entering at age four years and exiting at five years.

The Ministry of Education supervises the private sector educators who run kindergartens.

Primary or elementary education, which is compulsory, is for children entering at age five and exiting at age 11 or 12; it lasts for six to seven years, covering grades 1 through 6. Students receive basic general education and skills, with a strong emphasis on mathematics, English, social studies, and the sciences. Students who successfully complete their primary education will continue to lower secondary school.

Lower secondary school, for children entering at age 12 and exiting at age 15, lasts for three years, covering grades 7 through 9. Students receive general and practical education, as well as the necessary studies to prepare them for high school. Secondary education, for students entering at age 15 and exiting at age 18, lasts for 3 years, covering grades 10 through 12. Secondary students who are unable to complete their program at age 18 may have an additional year to complete their studies.

Postcompulsory Education

In Bermuda, higher education is provided by Bermuda College. However, most students are encouraged to eventually attend college overseas. Bermuda College is a public institution that awards associate degrees in the fields of business administration, computer information systems, actuarial sciences, education, construction, culinary studies, electronics, motor vehicle technology, plumbing, woodworking, the humanities, fine and performing arts, social and human services, the natural sciences, and Internet development. Many students who wish to pursue the baccalaureate degree enroll in Mount St. Vincent University, which is both an online degree program and an in-person matriculation program in Halifax, Nova Scotia. Aside from this educational route, most students seek baccalaureate programs in colleges and universities throughout the world.

Curriculum, Assessment, and Instruction

The curriculum of preschool education is quite formalized in comparison to preschool programs of other countries. At Bermudan preschools, the curriculum focuses on social, cognitive, and motor skills

development. In addition, the formal foundations of language, mathematics, social studies, and science are introduced. In primary school, the core studies of English, mathematics, social studies, and the sciences are continued and increasingly formalized.

Teacher Education

Teachers, especially those employed by government-run schools, must be certified by the government of Bermuda and also must be members of the Bermuda Union of Teachers. The union strongly encourages private teachers to apply for membership. In July 2002 the government enacted the Bermuda Educators Council Act. This legislation was ratified as a means of raising the academic level and preparedness of new teachers.

Students wishing to pursue studies in teacher education must receive a baccalaureate degree in elementary education or a baccalaureate degree in secondary education with a specialization in a particular discipline (e.g., mathematics, Spanish, earth science). Students can complete two-year degrees that have a liberal arts emphasis. These courses, which serve as the core, must be in the disciplines of computer information systems, the humanities (English, foreign language, philosophy, fine and performing arts), mathematics, the social sciences, and the natural sciences. In addition to the core courses, students must enroll in courses in educational foundations, educational psychology, and human development.

Informal Education

Informal education in Bermuda is also a major function for the Bermudan Ministry of Education, which emphasizes the importance of lifelong learning. In most Central American and Caribbean nations, the subject of literacy represents a mainstay in lifelong learning or informal education programs. This is also the case in Bermuda, despite the fact that the country has a near 100 percent literacy rate. Bermuda is a small country and, therefore, does not have a need to fund multiple organizations in the area of lifelong, informal learning. One major program, however, is located at Bermuda College in the Centre for Professional and Career Education (PACE). PACE complements the college—as stated above, a two-year vocational and liberal arts institution—by providing a center for lifelong learning opportunities, particularly for students who wish to change careers or gain additional vocational skills. The program hires specific personnel who have experience in optimizing the level at which students can engage in a particular vocation and, at the same time, compete in a global economy. The skills and vocations that PACE provides include, but are by no means limited to, the following: business education, paralegal education, culinary studies, food safety, human services (which include childcare and preschool education as well as geriatric care), auto maintenance and mechanics education, navigation and pilot training, horticulture and landscaping, jewelry making, and technical education involving computer maintenance and operations.

System Economics

Public expenditure on education for the world in 2005 was approximately 4.9 percent of the gross domestic product, 4.7 percent for developing countries, and 5.0 percent for countries in the Caribbean region. Public expenditure on education for Bermuda is not known as of this time. Public expenditure on education in Bermuda as a percentage of government expenditure is also not known. In 2010 the public expenditure on education as a percentage of public expenditure was 96.9 percent, nearly 5 percentage points higher than the world average and Caribbean average, and 3 percentage points higher than the "developing country" average.

Future Prospects

In 2011 a group of Bermudan educators referred to as the Educational Review Team made the following 10 recommendations for improving the school system of Bermuda. The team recommended that the first six have priority in terms of implementation.

1. Improving teacher quality: This recommendation is based on classroom observations in which the teacher observers concluded that one in four lessons were below average in quality of content and pedagogy.
2. Improving leadership from principals: Principals need to spearhead initiatives that promote curriculum advancement, student preparation, and teacher quality.
3. Modernizing outmoded beliefs and conditions in the Ministry of Education: The team seems to believe that the ministry impedes the advancement of education into the twenty-first century. The team seems to be recommending a business or corporate approach to running the school system.
4. Creating an executive board to implement the review for the creation of a three-year strategic plan for updating the educational system.
5. Creating greater accountability and transparency in the schools: That is, schools should have more autonomy, yet at the same time be accountable for educational outcomes. Schools should also be responsible for developing annual school reviews.
6. Raising the age for compulsory schooling: Students should be required to remain in school until the age of 18 (up from 17) so that they become more experienced in vocational skills. The team also advocates the creation of a senior school federation. Curriculum should be standardized in all high schools in order to prepare students for entrance into Bermuda College, the primary vocational institution in Bermuda.
7. Creating federations for each primary and lower secondary school partnership with the authority to oversee the functions of primary and secondary schools, hire personnel (i.e., teachers and administrators), and control the allocation of resources.
8. Modifying curriculum throughout the country so students will have an easier experience being promoted from one grade to the next and all students will learn the same content regardless of the school they attend.
9. Addressing student behavioral problems and learning difficulties: That is, a central authority should be created to deal with students who fail to conform to classroom regulations. In addition, this central authority would be involved in controlling issues pertaining to students with learning disabilities and conditions (e.g., attention deficit disorder, Asperger's syndrome, dyslexia).
10. Establishing a system by which members of the federation boards are elected in a more

Bermuda Education at a Glance

General Information

Capital	Hamilton
Population	66,163
Languages	English, Portuguese
Adult literacy rate (ages 15 and over)	98%
GDP per capita	US$69,900
People below poverty line (2000)	19%
Number of phones (landline) per 100 people (2002)	84.6
Number of phones (mobile) per 100 people (2004)	74.1
Number of Internet users per 100 people (2005)	59
Life expectancy at birth (years)	78

Formal Educational Information

Enrollment in primary school (ages 5–10)	5,000
Enrollment in lower and upper secondary school (ages 11–16)	5,000
Number of years of compulsory education	13 (ages 5–17)
Primary school student/teacher ratio	9.3
Lower and upper secondary school student/teacher ratio	6.9
Primary school gross enrollment ratio	102%
Secondary school gross enrollment ratio	89%
Tertiary school gross enrollment ratio	61.2%
Primary school entrants completion rate	97%

Note: Unless otherwise indicated, all data are based on sources from 2011.

or less democratic voting process. The team believes this will allow more interaction from the various communities.

One egregious problem with some of these recommendations has to do with the contradiction between encouraging autonomy on the one hand and mandating strict standards as well as the adherence to a national curriculum on the other.

Daniel Ness and Chia-ling Lin

REFERENCES

"Bermuda." In *The Europa World Yearbook*, vol. 1. London: Routledge, 2007.

EFA. "Strong Foundations: Early Childhood Care and Education." *Education for All Global Monitoring Report 2012*. Paris: UNESCO, 2012.

Forbes, Keith A. "Bermuda's Education in Public or Private Schools: Island Options Before Going to University Abroad If Academically Qualified." 2008. www.bermuda-online.org/educate.htm.

GED. *Global Education Digest 2012: Comparing Education Statistics Across the World*. Montreal: UNESCO Institute for Statistics, 2012.

Nation Master. 2011. www.nationmaster.com.

UNESCO–IBE. www.ibe.unesco.org/countries/Bermuda.htm.

UNESCO–UIS. www.uis.unesco.org.

UNICEF. www.unicef.org/infobycountry/bermuda.html.

World Bank Education Statistics. 2011. www.worldbank.org.

CANADA

Canada is the second-largest country in the world in terms of area (when including inland water). Canada has two official languages: English (spoken by nearly 60 percent of the population) and French (spoken by 23 percent of the population). Most of the remaining 17 percent of the population speak Chinese, Punjabi, Spanish, Italian, Arabic, German, Tagalog, Vietnamese, Portuguese, Urdu, Polish, Korean, Persian, and Russian. Ethnic groups in Canada are divided as follows: British origin, 28 percent; French origin, 23 percent; other European groups, 15 percent; Amerindian, 2 percent; Asian, African, and Middle East origin, 6 percent. The remaining 26 percent of the population are of mixed backgrounds. Roman Catholics make up nearly 43 percent of the population. Another 28 percent belong to one of the Protestant sects, nearly 2 percent are Muslim, and nearly 28 percent have an unspecified religion, or none.

Between the mid-sixteenth century and 1867, parts of Canada were controlled predominantly by either the British or the French. Fur trading was one of the first industries. By the late eighteenth and early nineteenth centuries, timber production became increasingly common.

Canada declared its independence from Great Britain in the summer of 1867. Since the nineteenth century, Canada's economic and technological output paralleled that of the United States. French Quebecois separatist movements have been common throughout Canadian history; however, all separation or separatist efforts have been thwarted. Since 2000 the number of AIDS-related cases and deaths appear to have decreased.

Educational System

Education in Canada is supervised by federal, provincial, and regional forms of government.

Preprimary and Compulsory Education in Canada

Compulsory education in Canada consists of both primary school and secondary school. Again, Canadian schooling and education are under the auspices of each of the provinces. It is interesting to note the different nomenclature associated with virtually the same notion of schooling for a particular educational level or period. For example, "elementary school" in Alberta and British Columbia, "primary school" in Newfoundland and Labrador and Quebec, and "school" in Manitoba are synonymous.

For the most part, with the exception of Quebec and parts of Newfoundland and Labrador, formal education is instructed in English in all the provinces and territories of Canada. Formal education in Quebec and in certain regions of Newfoundland and Labrador (and to a lesser extent, New Brunswick) is instructed predominantly in French.

Alberta

Formal education in Alberta consists of kindergarten and 12 compulsory grade levels. College or university education follows the twelfth grade. The preprimary kindergarten level is part of the primary (elementary) school. In general, public school in Alberta at the primary level consists of kindergarten through grade 6. Secondary school in Alberta is divided into two parts—junior high school and senior high school. Junior high school consists of grades 7 through 9, and senior high school consists of grades 10 through 12. Children and adolescents must attend school from kindergarten to grade 12.

British Columbia

Formal education in British Columbia consists of kindergarten and 12 compulsory grade levels. College or university education follows the twelfth grade. The preprimary kindergarten level is part of the primary (elementary) school. In general, public school in British Columbia at the primary level consists of kindergarten through grade 7. Secondary school in British Columbia is divided into two parts—junior secondary school and senior secondary school. Junior secondary school consists of grades 8 through 10, and senior high school consists of grades 11 and 12.

Children and adolescents must attend school from kindergarten to grade 12.

Manitoba

Formal education in Manitoba consists of kindergarten and 12 compulsory grade levels. College or university education follows the twelfth grade. The preprimary kindergarten level is part of the primary (early) school. In general, public school in Manitoba at the primary level consists of kindergarten through grade 6. Secondary school in Manitoba is divided into two parts—junior high school and senior high school. Junior high school consists of grades 7 through 9, and senior high school consists of grades 10 through 12. Children and adolescents must attend school from kindergarten to grade 12.

New Brunswick

Formal education in New Brunswick consists of kindergarten and 12 compulsory grade levels. College or university education follows the twelfth grade. The preprimary kindergarten level is part of the primary (elementary) school. In general, public school in New Brunswick differs from the models in the previously listed provinces in that the primary level consists of kindergarten through grade 5 (not 6). Secondary school in New Brunswick is divided into two parts—middle school and high school. Middle school consists of grades 6 through 8, and high school consists of grades 9 through 12. Children and adolescents must attend school from kindergarten to grade 12.

Newfoundland and Labrador

Formal education in Newfoundland and Labrador is somewhat different from that in most of the other provinces. This province's educational system consists of kindergarten through grade 9, followed by Levels I through III. These 13 years, as in the other provinces, are all compulsory grade levels. College or university education follows Level III. The preprimary kindergarten level, unlike the previous models, is not part of the primary school. In general, public school in Newfoundland and Labrador at the primary level consists of two levels: primary school and elementary school. Primary school consists of grades 1 through 3 and elementary school consists of grades 4 through 6.

Secondary school in Newfoundland and Labrador is divided into two parts—intermediate school and senior high school. Intermediate school consists of grades 7 through 9, and senior high school consists of Levels I, II, and III. Children and adolescents must attend school from kindergarten to Level III of senior high school.

Nova Scotia

Formal education in Nova Scotia consists of the "primary" level—which is kindergarten—and 12 compulsory grade levels that follow. College or university education follows the twelfth grade. The preprimary "primary" level is part of the elementary school period. In general, public school in Nova Scotia at the elementary level (the term "elementary" is used in place of "primary" school because the term "primary" is the distinct term used by the Nova Scotia educational system that refers to kindergarten) consists of the primary level through grade 6. Secondary school in Nova Scotia is divided into two parts—junior high school and senior high school. Junior high school consists of grades 7 through 9, and senior high school consists of grades 10 through 12. Children and adolescents must attend school from the "primary" (kindergarten) level to grade 12.

Ontario

Unlike the formal education systems of other Canadian provinces, that of Ontario includes a fourteenth additional year of education. Altogether, children and adolescents of Ontario must attend school from junior kindergarten (followed by kindergarten) through 12 subsequent compulsory grade levels. College or university education follows the twelfth grade in secondary school. Both junior kindergarten and the subsequent kindergarten are part of the primary (elementary) school period. In general, public school in Ontario at the primary level consists of seven years of schooling from junior kindergarten through grade 5. Secondary school in Ontario is divided into two parts—middle school and secondary (high) school. Middle school consists of grades 6 through 8, and secondary school consists of grades 9 through 12. Children and adolescents must attend school from junior kindergarten to grade 12. Compared to the educational systems of other provinces,

the formal education system of Ontario spans the longest period.

Prince Edward Island

Formal education in Prince Edward Island consists of 12 compulsory grade levels—i.e., grades 1 through 12. College or university education is available for students who graduate from senior high school after finishing the twelfth grade. The preprimary kindergarten level in Prince Edward Island is not part of the primary (elementary) school. In general, public school in Prince Edward Island at the primary level consists of grades 1 through 6. Secondary school is divided into two parts—intermediate school and senior high school. Intermediate school consists of grades 7 through 9, and senior high school consists of grades 10 through 12. Children and adolescents must attend school from grade 1 to grade 12.

Quebec

Of all the educational systems in Canada, the formal education system of Quebec is the most distinctive. Formal education in Quebec consists of six primary grade levels (grades 1 through 6) followed by five secondary school levels (Section I through Section V). College or university education follows the successful completion of Section V. Prior to formal education, parents have the option of sending their children to the *garderie*—which translates to "day care." Following the *garderie*, the year prior to grade 1 is called *maternelle*, which means infant school, or, more appropriately, early childhood preschool. In sum, the preprimary levels in Quebec are not compulsory (like those of Newfoundland and Labrador and Prince Edward Island as described above, and Saskatchewan as described below), nor are they part of the primary school. In general, public school in Quebec at the primary level consists of grade 1 through grade 6. Secondary school in Quebec consists of five academic school levels—Sections I through V. Section I is similar to grade 7, Section II is similar to grade 8, Section III is similar to grade 9, Section IV is similar to grade 10, and finally, Section V is similar to grade 11—the last compulsory grade level in the province. Children and adolescents must attend school from grade 1 in the primary level to Section V in the secondary level. Students who graduate from secondary school in Quebec have the option of enrolling in a college, university, or other related tertiary-level institution.

Saskatchewan

Formal education in Saskatchewan consists of 12 compulsory grade levels—i.e., grades 1 through 12. College or university education is available for students who graduate from senior high school after finishing the twelfth grade. The preprimary kindergarten level in Saskatchewan is not part of the primary (elementary) level. In general, public school in Saskatchewan at the primary level consists of grades 1 through 5. Secondary school in Saskatchewan is divided into two parts—middle school and secondary school. Middle school consists of four grade levels—namely, grades 6 through 9, and secondary school consists of grades 10 through 12. Children and adolescents must attend school from grade 1 to grade 12.

Northwest Territories

The Northwest Territories is one of three federal territories in Canada. Schooling in the Northwest Territories is similar to that of Newfoundland and Labrador. It is also interesting to note that in 1949, Newfoundland and Labrador was the last province to enter into confederation with Canada. Accordingly, much of the north country of Canada seems to have had a similar structure and system of education. Formal education in the Northwest Territories consists of kindergarten and 12 compulsory grade levels. College, university, or similar tertiary education follows the twelfth-grade level. The preprimary kindergarten level is part of the primary school period. In general, public school in the Northwest Territories at the primary level consists of kindergarten through grade 3. Primary school continues from grades 4 through 6 and is called intermediate school. Following intermediate school, students continue to junior secondary school from grades 7 to 9. This is followed by senior secondary school from grades 10 to 12. Children and adolescents must attend school from kindergarten to grade 12.

Nunavut

Nunavut is one of three territories of Canada. It was part of the Northwest Territories until 1999, when it formally separated and became the newest federal territory. Formal education in Nunavut consists of kindergarten and 12 compulsory grade levels. College or university education follows the twelfth grade. It is not so clear, however, how to determine levels of education in Nunavut because different schools have different grade ranges. The majority of primary schools run from kindergarten through grade 5, kindergarten through grade 6, kindergarten to grade 7, and sometimes kindergarten through grade 8—depending on the school. Depending on the community or village, a school can range in grade levels from kindergarten to grade 4 or kindergarten to grade 12. Schools that cover all grade levels are usually located in remote villages or hamlets. Secondary school in Nunavut ranges from grades 6 through 12 to grades 9 through 12. In sum, due to the remoteness of most villages of Nunavut, there is no standard "elementary school," "middle school," and "high school" in the region, but rather small schools that function as both primary and to some extent secondary schools as well. Children and adolescents must attend school from kindergarten to grade 12.

Yukon

Formal education in Yukon, one of the three federal territories of Canada, consists of kindergarten and 12 compulsory grade levels. College or university education follows the twelfth grade. The preprimary kindergarten level is part of the primary (elementary) school. In general, public school in Yukon at the primary level consists of kindergarten through grade 7. Secondary school in Yukon is divided into two parts—junior secondary school and senior secondary school. Junior secondary school consists of grades 8 through 10, and senior secondary school consists of two grades—grades 11 and 12. Children and adolescents must attend school from kindergarten to grade 12.

Tertiary Education in Canada

Tertiary education in Canada differs from that of the United States and other so-called Westernized societies to a degree. The most noticeable difference is that Canadian colleges grant most certificates and degrees up to and including the baccalaureate. The associate's degree, which is commonly the degree earned at the American community college level, is available at most colleges in Canada. In addition, Canadian colleges offer specialized degrees and certificates in many vocations and technical subjects, as well as in applied arts and sciences. Most universities in Canada do not grant certificates and specialized degrees, but they do offer the baccalaureate degree as well as postgraduate degrees, including the master's degree and the doctorate. All universities in Canada offer advanced academic degrees in graduate schools with distinct specializations (e.g., graduate schools of arts, science, law, and journalism).

Tertiary education in Quebec, however, is slightly different from that of other Canadian provinces. As described above, there is no "twelfth grade" year in the province. Rather, the "eleventh grade" year in Quebec is referred to as Secondary V. Upon successful completion of Secondary V, students can opt in to a preuniversity program that lasts for two years. These students are usually more academically inclined than their classmates. Successful completion of a two-year period at the preuniversity level, most often in the areas of arts and science, social sciences, or engineering, leads students to the university, which consists of a three- or four-year period when students prepare for the baccalaureate. A second option is a three-year professional program in a specialized tertiary institution for students who wish to obtain a vocation or trade. These students enter the workforce after three years of training. Graduates then have the option of continuing for a master's degree for a two-year period or a doctoral degree for a three-year period or longer.

In total, there are 83 universities in Canada that award both baccalaureate and graduate degrees. Most of these universities are located in urban areas. Leading research institutions include the following:

Alberta: University of Alberta in Edmonton, University of Calgary, University of Lethbridge, Athabasca University

British Columbia: University of British Columbia, Simon Fraser University, University of Victoria, University of Northern British Columbia

Manitoba: Collège universitaire de Saint-Boniface in Winnipeg, University of Manitoba, University of Winnipeg, Brandon University

New Brunswick: University of New Brunswick, Crandall University in Moncton, University of Moncton, Mount Allison University

Newfoundland and Labrador: Memorial University of Newfoundland, College of the North Atlantic

Nova Scotia: University of King's College in Halifax, Dalhousie University

Ontario: University of Toronto, Carleton University in Ottawa, Lakehead University in Thunder Bay, Laurentian University, McMaster University in Hamilton, Queen's University in Kingston, Ryerson University in Toronto, Trent University in Peterborough and Oshawa, University of Guelph, University of Ontario Institute of Technology in Oshawa, University of Ottawa, University of Waterloo, University of Western Ontario in London, University of Windsor, Wilfrid Laurier University in Waterloo, York University in Toronto

Prince Edward Island: University of Prince Edward Island in Charlottetown

Quebec: Université Laval in Quebec City (established in 1663, the oldest institution of higher education in Canada), University of Montreal, Concordia University in Montreal, École des Hautes Études commerciales de Montréal (a university of business and commerce), École Polytechnique de Montréal, McGill University in Montreal, University of Sherbrooke, University of Quebec in Montreal, University of Quebec in Three Rivers

Saskatchewan: The University of Saskatchewan, University of Regina

The institutions of higher education in the three territories of Canada each maintain their own systems of tertiary education. In Nunavut higher education has focused on ways to increase productivity and economic growth. These areas include mining, fishing, tourism, engineering, and government administration. Nunavut Arctic College, with campuses in Cambridge Bay, Rankin Inlet, and Iqaluit, is the principle institution of higher education in Nunavut. This institution has built partnerships with major universities in Quebec and other provinces. The principle institution of higher education in the Northwest Territories is Aurora College in Inuvik. Aurora College also has campuses and training sites in Yellowknife and Hay River. Higher education in Yukon began in 1963 with the Whitehorse Vocational Training Center, which eventually evolved in terms of growth in enrollment and curriculum. In 1988 the center became Yukon College. The main campus of Yukon College is in Whitehorse, the territory's capital.

Teacher Education

Teacher education in Canada is provided almost exclusively through the universities, where preservice teachers are able to receive teacher training at the undergraduate and graduate levels. Ontario has the largest number of teacher training universities in the country. Some of the most well-known teacher training universities include: British Columbia: University of British Columbia; Newfoundland and Labrador: Memorial University; Ontario: York University, University of Western Ontario, University of Waterloo, Carleton University, University of Guelph, University of Ottawa, Brock University, McGill University, Concordia University, and Bishops University; Alberta: University of Calgary; New Brunswick: University of New Brunswick in Saint John; and Nova Scotia: University College of Cape Breton. Students also have the option of pursuing doctoral degrees in education. University of British Columbia, York University, University of Western Ontario, and Concordia University all have programs leading to doctoral degrees. Prior to student teaching, students must take a regimen of courses that pertain to curriculum, teaching, and assessment, as well as developmental and educational psychology. Students who wish to teach at the secondary level must major in their prospective core fields—English or French language, mathematics, history and society (for social studies and civics), or one of the natural sciences.

Informal Education

Informal education in Canada is available to students at the numerous colleges and community colleges throughout the country. One particular program that has been successful in this regard is Adult Basic Education (ABE). The goal of ABE is to provide both credit and noncredit programs and courses to adults who have a variety of reasons for entering or reentering higher education. Many adults wish to increase their level of education or obtain a certificate in a certain field. Others may need courses in order to advance in a particular occupation or place of employment. Another reason for ABE is to provide education for adults who are interested in education throughout the lifespan. ABE also provides adults with skills in specific domains so as to improve chances of employment.

System Economics and Future Prospects

According to the United Nations Development Programme (2010), along with Argentina, Jordan, Ireland, Aruba, Thailand, Syria, and Poland, total public expenditures on education of Canada represented 4.9 percent of the gross domestic product (GDP) in 2007. Given the GDP of Canada at $1.335 trillion, educational expenditure in the country amounts to more than $65.4 billion, or about $13,645 per student (total amount equivalent to US dollars divided by 4,794,000, the approximate number of primary and secondary students in the country). Accordingly, although Canada ranks 75 of 186 countries in terms of percentage of educational expenditure, the country ranks one of the highest in terms of per student educational spending.

Canada is one of the most educationally advanced

Canada Education at a Glance

General Information

Capital	Ottawa
Population	33.3 million
Languages	English, French
Adult literacy rate (ages 15 and over)	99.9%
GDP per capita	US$35,600
People below poverty line	15.9%
Number of phones (landline) per 100 people	54.7
Number of phones (mobile) per 100 people	49.7
Number of Internet users per 100 people	65.6
Life expectancy at birth (years)	80

Formal Educational Information

Enrollment in primary school (ages 6–11)	2.2 million
Enrollment in lower and upper secondary school (ages 12–17)	2.5 million
Number of years of compulsory education	12 (ages 6–17)
Primary school student/teacher ratio	15
Lower and upper secondary school student/teacher ratio	17.7
Primary school gross enrollment ratio (2001)	100%
Secondary school gross enrollment ratio	98%
Tertiary school gross enrollment ratio	58%
Primary school entrants completion rate	100%
Child labor (ages 5–14 years)	no data

Note: Unless otherwise indicated, all data are based on sources from 2011.

countries in the Western world—particularly in primary and secondary education. Although a responsibility of the individual provinces and territories, education has been a key driving force in terms of the country's overall direction on a federal level. Canada was the home of 19 Nobel Laureates, many of whom studied in Canadian universities. In addition, students throughout the world seek college or university education in Canada as well as in the United States.

Daniel Ness and Chia-ling Lin

REFERENCES

Central Intelligence Agency. *The CIA World Factbook*. New York: Skyhorse, 2011. https://www.cia.gov/library/publications/the-world-factbook/index.html.

Nation Master. 2011. www.nationmaster.com.

UNESCO. *Global Education Digest 2012: Comparing Education Statistics Across the World*. Montreal: UNESCO Institute for Statistics, 2012.

———. "Strong Foundations: Early Childhood Care and Education." *Education for All Global Monitoring Report 2007*. Paris: UNESCO, 2006.

UNESCO–IBE. www.ibe.unesco.org/en/worldwide/unesco-regions/europe-and-north-america/canada.html.

United Nations Development Programme. *United Nations Development Report 2010*. New York: Palgrave Macmillan, 2010.

US Department of Labor. *2001 Findings on the Worst Forms of Child Labor*. Washington, DC: Bureau of International Labor Affairs, US Department of Labor, 2002.

World Bank Education Statistics. 2011. www.worldbank.org.

COSTA RICA

Costa Rica is located in the southern part of North America. The official language is Spanish, although English is also spoken. About 94 percent of Costa Ricans are white (including mestizo), 3 percent are black, 1 percent Amerindian, 1 percent Chinese, and 1 percent belong to other racial groups. Nearly three-quarters of the population are Roman Catholic, 14 percent Evangelical, 2 percent Jehovah's Witnesses and other Protestant sects; 5 percent profess other religions, and 4 percent none.

In the sixteenth century, the Spanish conquistadores explored and colonized the region that is now Costa Rica. However, colonization proved unsuccessful because of mosquito-related diseases,

a very warm climate, piracy, and the resistance of native peoples. In 1563 Cartago became the first successful colonial settlement. Its success was due primarily to its cooler, inland location. Costa Rica remained a colony of Spain for more than 250 years. In 1821 the colony joined forces with other nearby colonies in the establishment of the United Provinces of Central America. This confederation fragmented in 1838—less than 20 years later. In the same year, Costa Rica declared its independence from Spain. The Costa Rican economy has a strong tourism industry, technology industry, and agricultural sector as well. The standard of living in Costa Rica is rather high, and land ownership is more prevalent than in other nearby Central American nations.

Educational System

The Costa Rican Ministry of Education controls the educational system in the country. In general, education in Costa Rica consists of public primary and secondary education as well as tertiary education. Although compulsory education in Costa Rica begins at age six, parents have the opportunity to send their children under six years to preprimary school. Compulsory education in Costa Rica spans a period of approximately 11 years, for students between the ages six and 15 years. It is important to note that the Costa Rican constitution (Article 78) states that although this educational period is compulsory, it is not enforced.

Primary School

Although the gross enrollment ratio for primary school is 110 percent, many primary-school-age students do not attend school. This statement is based on the primary net enrollment ratio of 87.5 percent. One reason for the nearly 13 percent rate of children not attending primary school might be that Costa Rica is a largely agrarian society—especially in rural areas of the country. The percentage of Costa Rican students enrolled in secondary school has been much lower. Given that 92 percent of all primary school students generally complete primary school, 39 percent of girls and 37 percent of boys continue in secondary education. Despite these unfavorable numbers, the percentage of students enrolling in secondary school has increased since the 1980s and the student/teacher ratio has fallen from about 30 to 1 in 1980 to about 15 to 1 in both primary and secondary school.

Secondary School

Secondary school in Costa Rica consists of two levels: lower level and upper level. The lower level is a continuation of the primary education curriculum. The upper level prepares college- or university-bound students. Both publicly funded and private educational institutions must adhere to curriculum guidelines set forth by the Ministry of Education. Due to greater financial stability and income, students in Costa Rican private schools often perform at higher levels than do students at public institutions. Private institutions are able to provide additional hours of educational assistance for students that are not available in public institutions. As a result, there is a fairly significant gap in educational equity in terms of socioeconomic class.

Like the educational systems of its neighbors, that of Costa Rica suffers from a relatively high attrition rate, initially at the primary level and most predominantly at the secondary level. Attrition is the result of poor financial resources among families, teenage pregnancy, and disciplinary issues among teenagers. Nevertheless, the earning of a diploma has always been seen as a positive indicator of upward mobility and financial success in Costa Rica.

Costa Rican Special Schools

Costa Rica is one of the few countries in Central America that has developed so-called special schools, which accommodate academically promising students—particularly in mathematics and the sciences. Established by Victor Bujan in 1989, the Colegios Cientificos Costarricenses (Costa Rican Academies of Science) include six schools that are in operation throughout the country. These institutions were modeled after the Texas Academy of Mathematics and Science—a model of a "special school" developed by Julian Stanley. Unlike special schools in Cuba and the United States, Costa Rican special schools are on university campuses and are thus affiliated with Costa Rican universities and technical institutes. Students, then, are instructed by college-level faculty. Moreover, they live in facilities on campus. Students at the Colegios Cientificos receive credit that is transferable

to their undergraduate degree programs. Each student must be under 17 years of age, have a cumulative grade point average above 85 percent, and score at least 150 points (out of 200) on a specialized admissions test. The typical period of schooling is two years, and common courses taken include physics, chemistry, biology, calculus, differential equations, Spanish, history, philosophy, as well as the fine and performing arts. These highly competitive schools graduate about 10 students per year.

Tertiary Education

Higher education in Costa Rica is provided by universities, colleges, and technical and vocational institutions. The country is home to five public universities. Established in 1940, the University of Costa Rica is the oldest university in the country. Located in San Pedro, in the San José province, the university is also the largest, with an annual enrollment of nearly 35,000 students. While public universities are partially subsidized by the Costa Rican government, they have a significant degree of autonomy. To distinguish between public universities, no two institutions can have the same degree program. Private universities, on the other hand, are not obliged to abide by this rule.

Teacher Education

Teacher education programs in Costa Rica are among the most efficient in Central America. In general, Costa Rican primary and secondary school teachers obtain teacher certification through their credential of a baccalaureate from a university as well as several months or years of student teaching. Those seeking secondary credentials must complete a major in a specific field at the university level prior to receiving a baccalaureate degree. Given that teachers in Costa Rica must have teacher certification, the Ministry of Education is responsible for determining qualifications for both curriculum and procedures for becoming a teacher in the country. The Education Ministry is responsible for quality assurance with regard to teacher preparation and professional development during a teacher's candidacy and professional career. The ministry also enforces accountability and encourages improvement in teacher education and preparation. Like educational ministries of neighboring countries, the Ministry of Education in Costa Rica adheres to the commonly held principle that student achievement and success are dependent on so-called high qualified teachers. This notion is a common belief among most government officials who control educational systems throughout the world. Officials generally ignore other factors that influence education: home environment and socioeconomic class are two important factors that are often ignored.

Informal Education

Informal education in Costa Rica is a branch of educational development that is run by the Ministry of Education. Its emphasis is the development and promotion of lifelong learning, as well as general education and holistic learning for all children and adults. Two aims of the informal educational initiative in Costa Rica are to increase enrollment in primary school and prevent attrition in secondary school. Given an 18 percent rate of people living under the poverty line, informal education in the country is also intended to provide comfortable facilities for students whose aim is to improve skills in order to find employment. Like informal education initiatives in neighboring countries, the key objective for informal education in Costa Rica is to prepare all students for opportunities within a global market economy.

System Economics and Future Prospects

According to the United Nations Development Programme (2010), along with Latvia, Estonia, Seychelles, and Mozambique, total public expenditures on education of Costa Rica represented 5 percent of the gross domestic product in 2008 (GDP). Given the GDP of Costa Rica at $51.3 billion, educational expenditure in the country amounts to more than $2.56 billion, about $2,816 per student (total amount equivalent to US dollars divided by 911,000, the approximate number of primary and secondary students in the country). Costa Rica ranks 66 of 186 countries in terms of percentage of educational expenditure.

The literacy rate in Costa Rica has steadily improved from 1992 to the present. According to Central Intelligence Agency *Factbook* (2010) figures, the rate of literacy for individuals over 15 years old in Costa Rica is approximately 95 percent, among the

Costa Rica Education at a Glance

General Information

Capital	San José
Population	4.1 million
Language	Spanish
Adult literacy rate (ages 15 and over)	96%
GDP per capita	US$12,500
People below poverty line (2004)	18%
Number of phones (landline) per 100 people	33.6
Number of phones (mobile) per 100 people	24.2
Number of Internet users per 100 people	24.2
Life expectancy at birth (years)	77

Formal Educational Information

Enrollment in primary school (ages 6–11)	483,000
Enrollment in lower and upper secondary school (ages 12–16)	428,000
Enrollment in tertiary school	1 million
Number of years of compulsory education	11 (ages 6–15)
Primary school student/teacher ratio	24.9
Lower and upper secondary school student/teacher ratio	18.7
Primary school gross enrollment ratio	110%
Secondary school gross enrollment ratio	79%
Tertiary school gross enrollment ratio	25.3%
Primary school entrants completion rate	92%
Child labor (ages 5–14)	5%

Note: Unless otherwise indicated, all data are based on sources from 2011.

highest of the Central American nations. Despite an increase in educational access for Costa Rican children as well as a large increase in the literacy rate, there is much to be done to improve the educational system of Costa Rica. To begin with, the primary school completion rate is at 92 percent; clearly, not all students between six and 15 years old are successful in passing annual examinations at the primary level. In addition, the secondary school gross enrollment rate in Costa Rica is only 79 percent. This indicates that the number of secondary-school-age students actually attending secondary school is even lower. Poor school attendance is also common among rural student populations. Schools that accommodate rural communities often lack adequate facilities and are far from rural populations. Although primary school is free, families, regardless of income, are expected to pay additional fees that are associated with a child's education, such as books and other supplies. Families are also obligated to pay for their children's travel to and from school, a price that many rural families are unable to afford. In the future, one important goal for improving access to education for all Costa

Rican students is to provide information and communications technology (ICT) that will minimize the burdens for rural children and families and will most likely assist in keeping students in school.

Daniel Ness and Chia-ling Lin

REFERENCES

Central Intelligence Agency. *The CIA World Factbook.* New York: Skyhorse, 2011. https.www.cia.gov/library/publications/the-world-factbook/index.html.

Nation Master. 2011. www.nationmaster.com.

UNESCO. *Global Education Digest 2012: Comparing Education Statistics Across the World.* Montreal: UNESCO Institute for Statistics, 2012.

———. "Strong Foundations: Early Childhood Care and Education." *Education for All Global Monitoring Report.* Paris: UNESCO, 2006.

UNESCO–IBE. www.ibe.unesco.org/en/worldwide/unesco-regions/latin-america-and-the-caribbean/costa-rica.html.

United Nations Development Programme. *Human Development Report 2011.* http://hdr.undp.org/en/.

US Department of Labor. 2002. *2001 Findings on the Worst Forms of Child Labor.* Washington, DC: Bureau of International Labor Affairs, US Department of Labor.

World Bank Education Statistics. 2011. www.worldbank.org.

CUBA

Cuba is an island about 90 miles south of Florida (US) in the Caribbean Sea and Atlantic Ocean. The official language is Spanish. More than half of Cubans are mulatto, about 37 percent are white, 11 percent are black, and 1 percent is Chinese. Over 85 percent of the population is Roman Catholic. The remainder of the population comprises those of various Protestant sects, Jehovah's Witnesses, Jews, and followers of Santeria.

After the initial voyages of Columbus in the 1490s, the Amerindian population of Cuba began its steady decline. Cuba was a colony of Spain for nearly four centuries. Havana served as a harbor for ships that brought natural resources from the Americas before they went on their way to Spain. During this time, the island also served as one of a number of receiving outposts of the African slave trade. The slaves who remained on the island worked on the local coffee and sugar plantations. Spanish rule was particularly harsh for the Cuban locals, so much so that independence movements sprang up on many occasions. Hope for independence and success in emancipation from Spain came at the end of the nineteenth century, when the Spanish-American War broke out in 1898. After a three-year period, Cuba finally gained its independence in 1903 after the signing of the Treaty of Paris. Cuba became a communist state in 1959. The United States instituted an embargo on Cuba since 1961, two years after its change in government. To ease economic hardship, the former Soviet Union provided between $4 billion and $6 billion annually to the island nation. Following the breakup of the Soviet Union in the early 1990s, Cuba fell into a recession. Cuba has steadily recovered from its recession since then. The Cuban economy is relatively strong in tourism, sugar, tobacco, construction, nickel, steel, cement, agricultural machinery, and pharmaceuticals. In exchange for petroleum, the Cuban government provides Venezuela with professionals, many of whom are skilled in medicine. This exchange is due in large part to the exceptional system of education in Cuba.

Educational System

Although objective measures do not exist in measuring the preeminence of educational systems in developing countries, it is widespread knowledge that among developing nations, Cuba's educational system is outstanding and is competitive with the educational systems of postindustrial, Organisation for Economic Co-operation and Development (OECD) nations. In many respects, the educational system in Cuba can arguably serve as a blueprint for other educational systems. Cuban education thrives in the areas of science—primarily in chemistry and biology (particularly medicine)—and mathematics. In fact, in a recent study of mathematics achievement in the Caribbean island and Central America region, Cuba ranked first in mathematics and science in each grade level. The study also showed that Cuba ranked first even when considering gender and social class (UNESCO/OREALC 2011). Cuban students also outdo those of other Latin American and Caribbean countries in terms of language skills (see Figure). Moreover, Cuba prides itself on promoting and succeeding in universal teenage and adult literacy, equal academic achievement for males and females

Figure: **Language Achievement Scores (1st Quartile, Median, and 3rd Quartile) Among Third-Grade Students in 11 Latin American and Caribbean Countries**

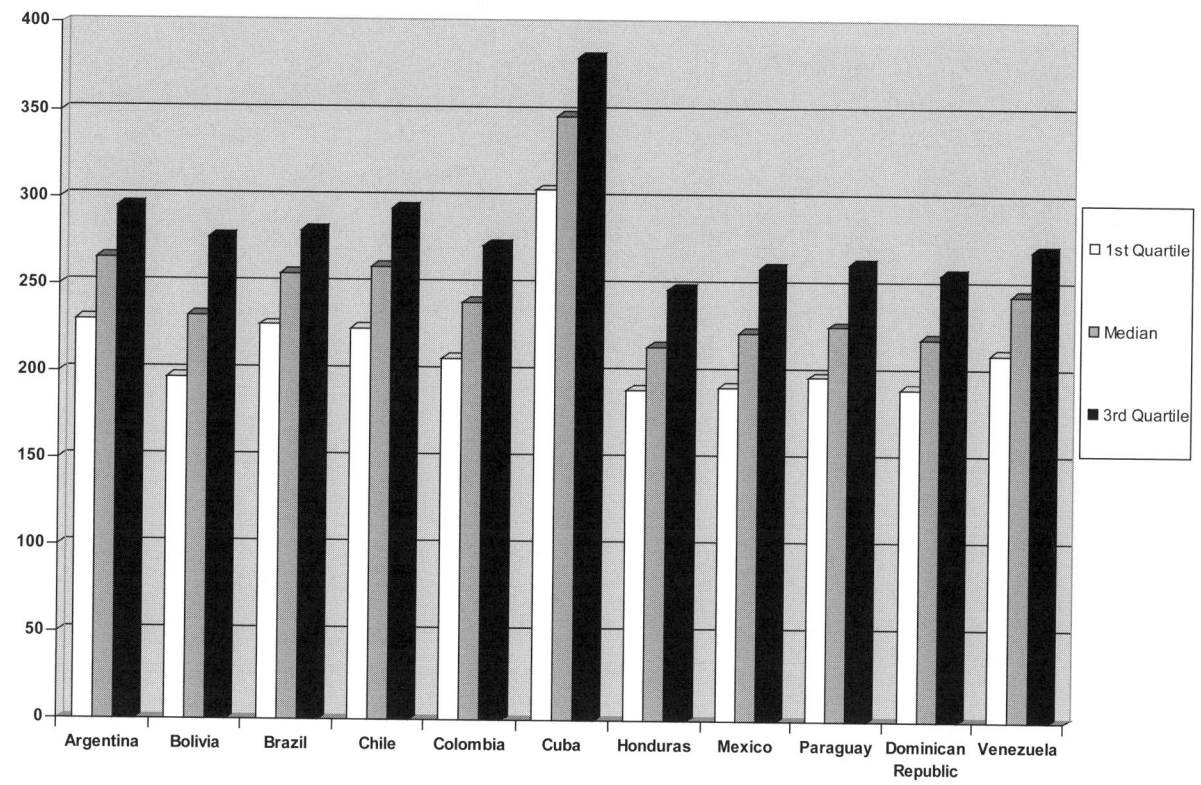

Source: UNESCO/OREALC, 2011.

at all levels of education, outstanding pedagogical knowledge among teachers, and overall excellence in achievement across cultural and economic backgrounds. The following points are important to consider regarding education in contemporary Cuba. First, education is free regardless of social class, which, in and of itself, is relatively negligible given that most citizens are members of the working class. Second, all books, supplies, meals, and transportation to and from school are free. Third, the student-teacher ratio at the primary level is never allowed to be above 25 students per teacher. As of 2015 the government intends to limit the number of secondary school students to 15 per class. Fourth, the average school day in Cuba is 14 hours, thus giving working parents a 12-hour time span that allows them to have day care for their children an hour before and an hour after school. In addition, service is available for parents of children with physical disability whereby teachers go to the homes of students who have limited mobility.

Precompulsory and Compulsory Education

The Cuban educational system pays great attention to education for preschool children. The Cuban government developed a program known as the Children's Circle for children from one to five years old with the intention of fostering the educational and cognitively developmental needs of children below the age of primary education. Unfortunately, lack of economic resources, in part as a result of Cuba's notoriously negative status with other countries throughout the world, has dampened progress in sustaining preschool programs in the country. This resulted in the establishment of a program titled "Educate Your Child," which provides cost-effective preschool preparation for primary education through family-based initiatives. The "Educate Your Child" curriculum includes the development of effective communication skills, the development of early language skills, and a focus on physical development and important habits for both health and cognitive development. This program involves the cooperation of families and their preschoolers in attending classes twice per week during the academic year.

Primary education in Cuba commences at age five and lasts for six years. It is founded upon a Marxist-Leninist model of education that promotes educational inclusion of all members of Cuban society and condemns and disapproves of a capitalist approach to education at all levels. All students, regardless of age and gender, are required to wear school uniforms, which identify grade level based on uniform color. At the age of 11 or 12, primary education students begin their initial three years of secondary education schooling. At the culmination of this initial period, students decide whether to continue with a preuniversity secondary education track or with a vocational-professional secondary education track. In addition to primary- and secondary-level education, there are also more than 430 schools in Cuba that accommodate students with special needs.

Cuban Special Mathematics and Science Secondary Schools

The strong focus on compulsory education in Cuba is the result of it's the country's efforts to promote schools for high-ability students, particularly those in mathematics and science. According to Vogeli (1997), Fidel Castro sponsored an initiative in 1966 whereby the Cuban government authorized the establishment of schools that "[utilize] new methods and [promote] a spirit of investigation" and also serve as "models for the nation's future schools" (p. 71). The first school established for such purposes was the Lenin School, which opened in Havana in 1974. The school enrolls between 2,500 and 3,000 students and employs nearly 50 teachers. It is especially important to note that unlike in high-ability specialized schools in other countries—such as those in the United States, Hungary, Romania, and China—half of the students of the high-ability schools in Cuba are female. Curricula at the Lenin school range from "regular" to "special," and of the very high-ability students, a small proportion of them are prepared for entrance in international mathematics Olympiad competitions. After the success of the Lenin School, 14 other specialized schools for high-ability students were founded—one for each province of the country. One of these schools is the Humboldt Seven School, which is located near Ha-

vana. Compared to the Lenin School, the Humboldt School enrolls one-sixth the number of students, and more than half of the students are female. The Humboldt School, which is a boarding school, is particularly important because its curricula and general format serve as a blueprint for other specialized schools throughout Cuba. For example, the schedule at the Humboldt School, which encourages family involvement, requires students to attend class for 11 days—equivalent to two five-and-a-half-day weeks of school instruction. The students then can return to their homes for a three-day weekend. The Humboldt School is also the first school in Cuba to institute an outreach program, which scouts potentially high-ability and talented students. These students engage in mini-Olympiads for the identification of students who outperform the general student population. All Cuban specialized schools then select some of these high-performing students through the implementation of a two-round examination and possible interview.

Postcompulsory Education

Both primary and secondary education is compulsory in Cuba. Although tertiary education is not compulsory, it is extremely encouraged so that graduates can survive with, at the very least, modest resources and compete as well as possible in the changing global economy. Higher education in Cuba is almost entirely funded by the Cuban government. Higher education is provided by universities, colleges, and institutes offering programs ranging from certificates in learning and achieving proficiency in a trade or vocation to two-year associate degrees, four-year bachelor's degrees, and, after further study of two to four years, master's degrees. Major universities in Cuba include the following institutions: University of Havana (founded in 1728, and one of the oldest institutions of higher learning in the Western Hemisphere); Agricultural University of Havana; University of Camagüey; University of Ciego de Ávila; University of Cienfuegos "Carlos Rafael Rodríguez"; University of Granma; University of Holguín "Oscar Lucero Moya"; University of Matanzas "Camilo Cienfuegos"; University of Pinar del Rio "Hnos Saíz Montes de Oca"; University "Marta Abreu" of Las Villas; University of Santiago de Cuba; Universidad de Ciencias Informaticas; Higher Polytechnic Institute "José Antonio Echevarria"; Instituto Superior Minero Metalúrgico

Dr. Antonio Núñez Jiménez; Universidad Católica de Santo Tomás de Villanueva (established in 1946) repudiated in 1961 by the Cuban government due to the institution's Catholic orientation; Instituto Superior Pedagogico Enrique Jose Varona, La Havana; and La Filial Instituto Superior Pedagogico Enrique Jose Varona, La Isla de la Juventud (Isle of Youth). In 1959 there were only three universities of medicine in Cuba. At present, there are 23.

Curriculum, Assessment, and Instruction

Curriculum in Cuban schools is based on a Marxist-Leninist vision of a purely socialist education—one based on the denouncement of capitalism and the goal of working collectively as a nation to solve societal problems. About 10 percent of time spent in primary education is devoted to "labor education." To this end, students engage in collective gardening in plots that are between 2.5 and 50 acres. Schools that do not have gardens, particularly those that are located in cities, provide opportunities for their students to learn about the growing of food in collective gardens located in the provincial capitals. Both school and government officials emphasize that this education is not production; students learn how to care for gardens for the purpose of gaining knowledge of working collectively, not for the purpose of actually performing labor. Therefore, children are not engaging in child labor. Other forms of labor education in Cuba include woodworking and sewing. Labor education at the secondary level comprises about 5 percent of the student's entire time in school—half that of primary students. In recent years, labor education has been deemphasized due to the perception of other countries that Cuba engages in student exploitation.

Another element of the Cuban education system is the notion of education for values and social cohesion. This part of the curriculum emphasizes what the system perceives as essential in maintaining a socialist form of government and the importance of collectivity in labor and production. Education for values and social cohesion plays a small yet significant part of the curriculum in secondary school.

Other than labor education and education for values and social cohesion, students devote a significant amount of time to the typical academic subjects: mathematics, Spanish, history and civics, the natural sciences, information technologies (that are accessible to students and teachers), health and hygiene, fine arts, and the performing arts. Middle school and high school curricula consist of mathematics, Spanish language and literature, history, geography, foreign language, physics, chemistry, biology, values, the fundamentals of Marxism, computer science and information technologies, physical education, art, and military training. The content of both primary and secondary education is more rigorous than that of other countries. In fact, curriculum methods developed in Cuba are models for curriculum in developing countries around the world.

In addition to the regular primary school curriculum, students at the primary level are expected to learn music and dance, as well as "green" science. This type of science teaches students about environmental issues that affect them daily as well as repercussions of environmental contamination and waste in general. In addition, students are expected to learn about health and proper hygiene. Moreover, since 2010 the Cuban primary curriculum has included Cuban revolutionary history.

Teacher Education

One of the primary reasons for Cuba's success in its educational system has to do with the role of teacher education. Cuba's system of training teachers, like its educational system as a whole, can serve as a blueprint for other nation's systems as well. In stark contrast to other countries, like the United States and Canada, and perhaps many countries of the European Union, the professional status of teachers in Cuba is deemed quite high. In fact, the difference in salary scales between teachers and other professionals in Cuba is insignificant.

Teacher education in Cuba emphasizes basic foundations of knowledge and skills in all subjects, as well as positive values toward education and learning. Preservice and in-service teachers are provided with a balance of content knowledge in the disciplines with pedagogical knowledge. Cuban teacher education also emphasizes a strong link between theory and practice. Both preservice and in-service teachers enroll in programs that are school-based; that is, the primary or secondary school is not disconnected from teacher education study. Rather, it is very much a part of it. Teacher trainers in Cuba seem to be equivalent to college-level professors in the United States. However, unlike in other countries, teacher trainers in Cuba must complete seven years of internship at the grade level for which the candidate intends to train in-service and preservice teachers. Over half of the nearly 150,000 teachers in Cuba have earned master's degrees.

Teachers in Cuba do not think of their profession as second-rate, one with "summers off," frequent vacation periods, or a lack of communication with other teachers and students. In contrast, the teaching profession in Cuba is considered a lifelong endeavor that promotes training and enrichment throughout a teacher's career. In all, there are 15 pedagogical institutes, each of which provides rigorous programs in education for teachers of preschool, primary school, and the intermediate school levels. College-level programs in teacher education are much more rigorous than in the United States, Canada, and many countries in Europe. Cuban teacher education at the preservice level consists of five years of training, a great deal of which emphasizes the liberal arts in addition to pedagogical theory courses. In-service teachers must then spend an additional six years in college. The Cuban program in teacher education is analogous to the medical model in Cuba and in other countries, where premed education lasts for four to five years and is followed by six to seven years of internship and in-field experience.

Despite the variables of home environment, early educational experiences, parent involvement, and the like, the teacher's role in student achievement is nevertheless part of the Cuban education accountability scheme. Teacher evaluation is an ongoing process throughout the country, a process that its administrators use to further teaching progress both in and out of school. The players in the accountability process include the university, members of government, and *colectivos* (teacher work groups). Ongoing teacher assessment is not a local or regional decision—it is nationally mandated. Accountability can range in penalty, depending on the level of student achievement. De Moura (1999) found that teachers whose students perform below the average academic level risk cuts in salary.

Informal Education

Informal education opportunities in Cuba are important for the country's endurance. One of the main

goals of Cuban informal education is to support the developing informal education sector, which includes adults who need additional skills to perform in their occupations. It is also an educational sector devoted to the promotion of critical thinking skills for both young students and adults. Students in these programs are encouraged to engage in independent critical thinking as well as creative projects, particularly those that assist needy individuals. The People in Peril Association (PIPA) is one of the major foundations that has been seminal in the informal education movement in Cuba. Through grants and contributions, PIPA is in the process of searching for innovative curricula that involve new methods of instruction in this particular area. Another mission of informal learning initiatives in Cuba is lifelong learning for both children and adults.

System Economics

Public expenditure on education for Cuba in 2005 was approximately 9.8 percent of the gross domestic product (GDP). Cuba outranks numerous countries in this respect when comparing the country's public expenditure on education with that of the world in the same year (approximately 4.9 percent of GDP), with developing countries (approximately 4.7 percent), and with countries in the Caribbean and Central American region (approximately 5.0 percent). Public expenditure on education in Cuba as a percentage of government expenditure at the end of the 2005 academic year was 16.6 percent. In 2005 the percentage of public expenditure on education was 85.8 percent, over 6 percent lower than the world average and Caribbean average, and nearly 4 percent below the "developing country" average. Spending per student by the end of the 2004 academic year as a percentage of GNP per capita at the primary level was estimated to be nearly 28 percent. Spending as a percentage of GNP per capita at the secondary education level is not known at this time.

Future Prospects

It is important to note that in terms of student success and the ability to find work after school, the system of education in Cuba is one of the most innovative and effective in the world. As noted above, it also serves as a model for numerous countries, both developed and currently developing. The case of education in Cuba can be informative for several reasons. First, education in Cuba has demonstrated that a successful educational system with high-quality teachers does not necessarily need to be based on state or national income or allocation. Instead, it can be grounded on how a modicum of financial resources is coordinated and controlled. In other words, a successful educational system need not be based on high levels of expenditure but on how a limited amount of expenditure is used as a function of that system. The Cuban education system demonstrates how the attention to equity and concern for the social roles of teachers and the children they teach can contribute to educational success. The Cuban education system is also informative in that it shows that effective accountability measures, textbook standards, and teacher training can also be construed as a function of educational success.

No doubt, with the seemingly exponential growth of the Internet and other forms of information and communication technologies, Cuba will be increasingly subject to external influences in the future. Accordingly, it is uncertain at present how the country will be affected in terms of educational investment as a function of economic growth and opportunity. How the educational system of Cuba will compare with those of other countries can only be determined in a matter of time.

Daniel Ness and Chia-ling Lin

REFERENCES

Central Intelligence Agency. *The CIA World Factbook.* New York: Skyhorse, 2011. https://www.cia.gov/library/publications/the-world-factbook/index.html.

"Cuba." In *The Europa World Yearbook*, vol. 1. London: Routledge, 2007.

Cuba Ministry of Education. 2006. "Education Statistics at a Glance." www.moes.gov.bz/.

De Moura, Claudio. *Ugly Schools, Good Schools? Notes from the Education Unit, Sustainable Development Department.* Washington, DC: Inter-American Development Bank, 1999.

Gasperini, Lavinia. *The Cuban Education System: Lessons and Dilemmas.* Country Studies: Education Reform and Management Publication Series 1:5 (2000). ERIC Clearinghouse Document No. 454117.

Human Development Reports. *Commitment to Education: Public Spending.* 2008. http://hdrstats.undp.org/indicators/99.html.

Nation Master. 2011. www.nationmaster.com.

Perusia, Juan Cruz. *Global Education Digest 2007: Cost and Commitments in Educating for All.* Montreal: UNESCO Institute for Statistics, 2007.

UNESCO. *Global Education Digest 2006: Comparing Education Statistics Across the World.* Montreal: UNESCO Institute for Statistics, 2006.

———. "Strong Foundations: Early Childhood Care and Education." *Education for All Global Monitoring Report.* Paris: UNESCO, 2006.

UNESCO–IBE. www.ibe.unesco.org/countries/Cuba.htm.

UNESCO/OREALC. Laboratorio Latinoamericano de evaluación de la Calidad de la Educación, Primer Estudio Internacional Comparativo sobre Lenguaje, Matemática y Factores Associados en Tercero y Cuarto grado. Santiago, Chile: UNESCO, 2011.

UNESCO–UIS. www.uis.unesco.org.

UNICEF. www.unicef.org/infobycountry/cuba.html.

United Nations Development Programme. "Beyond Scarcity: Power, Poverty and the Global Water Crisis." *Human Development Report 2012.* New York: Palgrave Macmillan, 2012.

Vogeli, Bruce R. *Educating the Gifted in Mathematics: An International Panorama.* New York: Trustees of Teachers College, Columbia University, 1997.

World Bank Education Statistics. 2011. www.worldbank.org.

Cuba Education at a Glance

General Information

Capital	Havana
Population	11.3 million
Language	Spanish
Adult literacy rate (ages 15 and over)	99.9%
GDP per capita	US$4,000
People below poverty line	no data
Number of phones (landline) per 100 people	7.5
Number of phones (mobile) per 100 people	1.2
Number of Internet users per 100 people	1.7
Life expectancy at birth (years)	77

Formal Educational Information

Enrollment in primary school (ages 6–11)	826,000
Enrollment in lower and upper secondary school (ages 12–17)	912,000
Tertiary school graduates	7 million
Number of years of compulsory education	12 (ages 6–17)
Primary school student/teacher ratio	10.7
Lower and upper secondary school student/teacher ratio	11
Primary school gross enrollment ratio	102%
Secondary school gross enrollment ratio	94%
Tertiary school gross enrollment ratio	61.5%
Primary school entrants completion rate	94%
Child labor (ages 5–14)	no data

Note: Unless otherwise indicated, all data are based on sources from 2011.

Dominican Republic

The Dominican Republic is one of two nations on the island of Hispaniola. The official language is Spanish. Nearly 75 percent of Dominicans are of mixed ethnicity, roughly 15 percent are white, and 10 percent are black. Almost all of the population belongs to the Roman Catholic Church. Approximately 5 percent of the population are members of other religions or none.

It is commonly believed that early European settlement in the present-day Dominican Republic began with Christopher Columbus's first cross-Atlantic voyage in 1492. The island, named Hispaniola, served as a pivotal location for Spanish ships that were returning from or traveling to the mainland. By 1697 France dominated the western third of the island, which eventually became the Republic of Haiti in 1804. Santo Doming, the eastern two-thirds of the island, sought independence in 1821, but was instead conquered by Haiti for nearly 22 years. The Dominican Republic became an independent nation in 1844, with only a brief period under Spanish rule from 1861 to 1865. The years leading up to World War II proved most unsettling for the country when Rafael Leonidas Trujillo assumed dictatorship of the Dominican Republic in 1930. Trujillo remained dictator until his assassination in 1961. A republican government was then established; however, in the following year the president was deposed in a military coup. Despite regular elections, presidents maintained power for long periods of time—one in particular from 1965 to 1995. The standard of living in the Dominican Republic is relatively low. The adult prevalence rate of HIV/AIDS is approximately 1.7 percent, with about 88,000 Dominicans living with the disease.

Educational System

Preprimary education in the Dominican Republic is not compulsory. All preschools require tuition and fees and are mostly available for parents who can afford them for their children. Compulsory education in the Dominican Republic is a 12-year period for children from six to 17 years old. However, children between the ages of six and 14 years are not required to go to school despite the compulsory education law. About 23 percent of all Dominicans are of primary or secondary school age. Spanish is the most common language of instruction in the country. Given the large school-age population, financial resources are limited in providing the large numbers of students with a high-quality education. As a result, the student/teacher ratios (40.5 to 1 for primary and 30.3 to 1 for secondary) are high compared to the student/teacher ratios of other North American and Latin American countries. Private and parochial schools have attempted to assist public schools as a way to lessen the burdens of large class sizes. Despite these trends, however, the education system in the Dominican Republic ranks higher than those of many of the other Central American countries.

Primary education schools in the Dominican Republic mostly enroll students as young as six and as old as 12 years of age. Primary schools include basic instruction in the Spanish language, mathematics, social studies, and natural sciences. The curriculum also includes sports and physical education, arts and crafts, and music. Secondary schools in the country enroll students as young as 11 or 12 and as old as 17 or possibly 18 years of age. Like high schools in the United States, Dominican secondary education is essentially a continuation of the basic education from primary school; however, subjects become more specified as they do in most secondary schools throughout the world. Although Spanish is the official language used in compulsory education, students living in urban areas are more likely to have opportunities to study foreign languages at both the primary and secondary levels.

Most Dominican students who graduate from secondary schools are eligible to study abroad—particularly in the United States, Canada, or countries in Europe. This is because most schools in the country are accredited by the Dominican Ministry of Education, which has a mutual agreement with the United States Southern Association of Colleges and Schools as well as colleges and universities in Europe that provide the International Baccalaureate. Tertiary study abroad also depends upon socioeconomic class; clearly, most Dominican families are unable to pay tuition for their children, whether in the Dominican Republic or not. Dominican secondary schools provide international college entrance examinations, such as the SAT.

Tertiary education in the Dominican Republic includes both public and private education in universities as well as vocational institutions. To date, there are 34 public and private universities in the country. Although established in 1914, the University of Santo Domingo is the continuation of an older university, the University of Santo Tomás de Aquino (St. Thomas Aquinas University) that was founded in 1538, as a result of an official decree from Pope Paul III to establish the first institution of higher education in the New World. At present, with an enrollment of over 170,000 students in 13 campuses throughout the country, it is the largest tertiary institution in the Dominican Republic. Students who wish to enroll in teacher education programs can do so in schools of teaching and pedagogy, which are generally part of larger universities. Otherwise, the ministry often searches for teachers coming from abroad.

System Economics and Future Prospects

According to the United Nations Development Programme (2010), along with the Solomon Islands and Macau, total public expenditures on education of the Dominican Republic represented 2.2 percent of the gross domestic product in 2007 (GDP). Given the GDP of the Dominican Republic at $84.94 billion, educational expenditure in the country amounts to more than $1.87 billion, about $817 per student (total amount equivalent to US dollars divided by 2,288,000, the approximate number of primary and secondary students in the country). The Dominican Republic ranks 165 of 186 countries in terms of percentage of educational expenditure—one of the lowest in Central America.

The literacy rate in the Dominican Republic has steadily improved from the 1990s to the present. For individuals between the ages of 15 and 24, literacy was at 95 percent in a 2004–2008 study. These data are an indication of a rapidly developing expansion of enrollments at all educational levels in the Dominican Republic. Also, 92 percent of all primary school students are able to complete the primary level. Although showing signs of growth, the Dominican Republic still lags behind other Central American countries in the number of students pursuing tertiary degrees. As in other Central American countries, school attendance is disadvantaged as a result of a lack of adequate

Dominican Republic Education at a Glance	
General Information	
Capital	Santo Domingo
Population	9.8 million
Language	Spanish
Adult literacy rate (ages 15 and over)	87%
GDP per capita	US$8,400
People below poverty line	25%
Number of phones (landline) per 100 people	9.6
Number of phones (mobile) per 100 people	38.7
Number of Internet users per 100 people	10
Life expectancy at birth (years)	73
Formal Educational Information	
Enrollment in primary school (ages 6–11)	1.1 million
Enrollment in lower and upper secondary school (ages 12–17)	1.1 million
Tertiary school graduates	3.1 million
Number of years of compulsory education	12 (ages 6–17)
Primary school student/teacher ratio	40.5
Lower and upper secondary school student/teacher ratio	30.3
Primary school gross enrollment ratio	113%
Secondary school gross enrollment ratio	71%
Tertiary school gross enrollment ratio	32.9%
Primary school entrants completion rate	92%
Child labor (ages 5–14)	10%

Note: Unless otherwise indicated, all data are based on sources from 2011.

facilities at schools and a high student/teacher ratio, particularly in rural parts of the country.

One of the most pressing issues in the Dominican Republic in terms of the country's status as a competitor in the global economy is educational reform. It is clear from the state of the nation's industrial and agricultural economies that changes in education are needed. To be sure, there has been a steady decline in mining, sugarcane production, and tourism. These declines have been particularly evident since the country's entry into the World Trade Organization and the Central American Free Trade Agreement. In grappling with these growing problems, the Ministry of Education in the Dominican Republic has shown signs of progress in virtually all educational sectors within the last 15 years. According to a report issued by the Organization for Economic Co-operation and Development, the Dominican Republic has shown progress, particularly in the areas of educational equity, quality of programs, and the decentralization of fiduciary accountabilities. Nevertheless, serious issues regarding educational access, school overcrowding, a child labor minority, and poverty among one-quarter of the population must be corrected if the country is to be competitive in the global marketplace. One initiative that is helping in this regard is the development of information and communications technology (ICT). This initiative may help the children of rural families stay in school through the secondary level.

Daniel Ness and Chia-ling Lin

REFERENCES

Central Intelligence Agency. *The CIA World Factbook*. New York: Skyhorse, 2011. https.www.cia.gov/library/publications/the-world-factbook/index.html.

Nation Master. 2011. www.nationmaster.com.

UNESCO. *Global Education Digest 2012: Comparing Education Statistics Across the World*. Montreal: UNESCO Institute for Statistics, 2012.

———. "Strong Foundations: Early Childhood Care and Education." *Education for All Global Monitoring Report*. Paris: UNESCO, 2006.

UNESCO–IBE. www.ibe.unesco.org/en/worldwide/unesco-regions/latin-america-and-the-caribbean/dominican-republic.html.

United Nations Development Programme. *United Nations Development Report 2010*. New York: Palgrave Macmillan, 2010.

US Department of Labor. *2001 Findings on the Worst Forms of Child Labor*. Washington, DC: Bureau of International Labor Affairs, US Department of Labor, 2002.

World Bank Education Statistics. 2011. www.worldbank.org.

EL SALVADOR

El Salvador is the smallest country in Central America. The official language is Spanish. Nearly 90 percent of Salvadorans are mestizo, 9 percent white, and 1 percent Amerindian. Approximately 83 percent of the population belongs to the Roman Catholic Church.

El Salvador is a democratic republic. The executive powers reside in a president, who is the chief of state and the head of government. The legislative branch is the unicameral Legislative Assembly. Like nearly all Central American nations, El Salvador was first settled by, and subsequently colonized by, Spain in the sixteenth century. The country's independence from Spain came in 1821. In 1839 El Salvador emancipated from the Central American Federation. The country was in civil war from 1980 to 1992. El Salvador's economy, the third largest in Central America, has been fairly sluggish in recent years. The government has been focusing attention on modifying the country's export markets and encouraging foreign investment. The adult prevalence rate of HIV/AIDS is approximately 0.7 percent, with about 29,000 Salvadorans living with the disease.

Educational System

Preprimary education in El Salvador is not compulsory. With tuition and fees, it is available for parents who can afford it. The preprimary period consists of two to three years of preschool education, the last year of which is equivalent to the Western kindergarten. Compulsory education in El Salvador lasts for nine years. Students enter primary education at age seven and leave at age 15. This nine-year period consists of a basic curriculum devoted to speaking, reading, and writing in Spanish (the official language of the country), basic mathematics, science, history, arts, crafts, and physical education. The primary education period is divided into three sequences: grades 1 through 3, grades 4 through 6, and grades 7 through 9. Grades 1 through 3 introduce children to the basic educational content, such as mastery of the alphabet, early reading ability, and basic arithmetic operations. Unfortunately, the greatest percentage of students repeating grade levels falls into this sequence of grades—particularly in grades 1 and 2. This is problematic for it represents the greatest amount of financial expense and outlay in the Salvadoran education system. This is a major problem, especially in rural communities where agrarian economies are dominant. To illustrate, in 2001, about 14 percent of urban children and 17 percent of rural children repeated the first grade. Although these numbers diminish in subsequent grades, they do remain prevalent; about 3 percent of all students repeat grades from grades 6 to 9.

Grades 4 through 6 represent the second sequence of grades at the primary level. At this point, students hone their skills in language and mathematics, as well as social studies and some science topics. The third and final sequence of primary school, grades 7 through 9, is a period when students begin to determine their progress and future education as evidenced in their academic assessments. Unlike previous grade levels when students are assigned to a single teacher, in grades 7 through 9 students are assigned to different teachers who specialize in particular subjects during the school day (similar to the American junior and senior high school).

Secondary education consists of two tracks. The first track is a two-year period that prepares students for tertiary education. The second track prepares students who are not college or university bound and who wish to hone their skills for a particular vocation. This second track option lasts for three years, the last of which prepares students for a technical degree or basic degree in business.

Tertiary education in El Salvador, a period that lasts for five years, includes both public and private education in universities as well as vocational institutions. Although public higher education is available in El Salvador, it is not entirely free. Accordingly, higher education is not universal, and because it cannot be totally subsidized by the Salvadoran government, educational gaps persist in terms of socioeconomic class and higher education access. The largest and oldest of the public institutions in El Salvador is the University of El Salvador, which was established in 1841 by the then president of El Salvador, Juan Lindo. In addition to helping establish tertiary level institutions, Lindo also spearheaded the development of primary schools in communities with 150 or more inhabitants.

Tertiary education in El Salvador also includes public and private technical and vocational institutes. Teacher training institutes, or normal schools, are located primarily in the country's urban centers. These teacher training schools have an unusual curriculum in that prospective teachers need not take course work in the content areas. Instead, they are expected to focus on pedagogical theories and how these theories reflect educational teaching and instructional methods.

System Economics and Future Prospects

According to the United Nations Development Programme (2010), along with the Bahamas, Slovakia, and Benin, total public expenditures on education of El Salvador represented 3.6 percent of the gross domestic product (GDP) in 2008. Given the GDP of El Salvador at $43.98 billion, educational expenditure in the country amounts to more than $1.58 billion,

about $870 per student (total amount equivalent to US dollars divided by 1,821,000, the approximate number of primary and secondary students in the country). El Salvador ranks 128 of 186 countries in percentage of educational expenditure.

The literacy rate in El Salvador has steadily improved from 1992 to the present. For individuals between the ages of 15 and 21, literacy was at an 87.5 percent rate in 1992, 91 percent rate in 1997, and 94 percent rate in 2000. These promising data are an indication of a rapidly developing expansion of enrollments in all educational levels in the country. Among all Central American nations with the exception of Mexico, El Salvador has had the greatest progress in terms of the number of years of schooling completed among students 15 years old (the last age of primary education) and above. Also, 87 percent of all primary school students are able to complete the primary level. These promising results, however, do not mean that education in El Salvador has been effective in leading to a productive and self-sufficient workforce. For example, other Central American countries, like Costa Rica and Panama, have higher

---

El Salvador Education at a Glance

General Information

Capital	San Salvador
Population	6 million
Language	Spanish
Adult literacy rate (ages 15 and over)	80.2%
People below poverty line (2005)	35.2%
GDP per capita	US$4,900
Number of phones (landline) per 100 people	14
Number of phones (mobile) per 100 people	34.7
Number of Internet users per 100 people	9.2
Life expectancy at birth (years)	72

Formal Educational Information

Enrollment in primary school (ages 7–12)	944,000
Enrollment in lower and upper secondary school (ages 13–18)	877,000
Tertiary school graduates	1.3 million
Number of years of compulsory education	12 (ages 7–18)
Primary school student/teacher ratio	25.6
Lower and upper secondary school student/teacher ratio	no data
Primary school gross enrollment ratio	113%
Secondary school gross enrollment ratio	63%
Tertiary school gross enrollment ratio	19%
Primary school entrants completion rate	87%
Child labor (ages 5–14)	6%

Note: Unless otherwise indicated, all data are based on sources from 2011.

numbers of students pursuing tertiary degrees. As in other Central American countries, school attendance is disadvantaged as a result of an extremely high rate of crime and juvenile delinquency and a lack of adequate facilities at schools, particularly in rural parts of the country. Educational improvement initiatives in El Salvador include the development of information and communications technology that will lessen the burdens for rural children and families and will most likely assist in keeping students in school through the secondary level.

Daniel Ness and Chia-ling Lin

REFERENCES

Central Intelligence Agency. *The CIA World Factbook.* New York. Skyhorse, 2011. https.www.cia.gov/library/publications/the-world-factbook/index.html.

Nation Master. 2011. www.nationmaster.com.

UNESCO. *Global Education Digest 2012: Comparing Education Statistics Across the World.* Montreal: UNESCO Institute for Statistics, 2012.

———. "Strong Foundations: Early Childhood Care and Education." *Education for All Global Monitoring Report.* Paris: UNESCO, 2006.

UNESCO–IBE. www.ibe.unesco.org/en/worldwide/unesco-regions/latin-america-and-the-caribbean/el-salvador.html.

United Nations Development Programme. *United Nations Development Report 2010.* New York: Palgrave Macmillan, 2010.

US Department of Labor. *2001 Findings on the Worst Forms of Child Labor.* Washington, DC: Bureau of International Labor Affairs, US Department of Labor, 2002.

World Bank Education Statistics. 2011. www.worldbank.org.

GUATEMALA

Guatemala is a country located in Central America. The official language is Spanish. However, nearly 40 percent of the population speaks one or more of the 23 officially recognized Amerindian languages. The population of Guatemala in the United Nations 2011 estimate was 13.8 million. Excluding Mexico, Guatemala is the most populous country in Central America. The breakdown in terms of ethnicity is the following: Mestizo and European at 59.4 percent; K'iche at 9.1 percent; Kaqchikel at 8.4 percent; Mam at 7.9 percent; Q'eqchi at 6.3 percent; other Mayan at 8.6 percent; and non-Mayan indigenous at 0.2

percent. Approximately 60 percent of the population belongs to the Roman Catholic Church, 39 percent are members of different Protestant sects, and 1 percent professes indigenous Mayan religions.

For centuries the Mayan civilization flourished in present-day Guatemala. This flourishing came to a close in the sixteenth century, after the arrival of the Spanish conquistadores. For nearly 400 years, from the sixteenth century to the beginning of the nineteenth century, the region was controlled and colonized by the Spanish. The country declared independence, along with some of its neighbors, in 1821. Since then Guatemala has gone through numerous coups and changes of government. The 36-year guerrilla war in the late twentieth century, with more than 100,000 casualties and scores more as refugees, ended in 1996.

Educational System

The educational system in Guatemala is one of the poorest in Central America. Preprimary education in Guatemala is not compulsory. Primary education in Guatemala, on the other hand, is compulsory for a period of six years for students between the ages of seven and 12 years. Since the early 1990s, primary school completion increased dramatically in the country. In 1992 only 39 percent of all Guatemalan children completed primary school. Today, the primary school completion rate is about 74 percent. Unfortunately, however, there is disparity in education access and continuation to the tertiary level when comparing children both in terms of ethnicity and geography. Urban Guatemalan children have much greater educational access than do their rural peers. Moreover, the overwhelming majority of rural children are of Mayan descent; these children do not perform as well as their Ladino peers who live in urban settings. To make matters worse, health and well-being are poor. To illustrate, with 290 deaths per 100,000 live births, the maternal mortality rate in Guatemala is the highest among all the countries in Latin America. According to the Center for Economic and Social Rights, Guatemala has one of the lowest levels of educational spending (2010). Guatemala also has the lowest spending on education and the second-lowest spending on health among all countries in Latin America and the Caribbean.

The educational curriculum in Guatemala demonstrates a gradual inclusion of various subjects in subsequent grade levels. For example, emphasis on mathematics does not begin until third grade. The curriculum includes a focus on the following subjects: reading and writing in first grade; spelling, reading, and writing in the second grade; social studies, natural sciences and technology, and mathematics in the third grade; history and geography in the fourth grade; physical education and art in the fifth grade; and elements of all previously mentioned subjects in the sixth grade. Unfortunately, there is little evidence that teachers or schools are adhering to any performance-based criterion of quality. So, given that there are few, if any, student expectations with regard to ability and performance, it is difficult to identify students' educational growth in Guatemalan schools. In addition, assessment of students' work is based more on student conduct and completion of work than on whether they understand concepts in a specific subject. Schooling is hampered even more in rural areas where school is simply canceled if a teacher is ill for a particular day. Moreover, in the rainy season, schools days are shortened, thus making it all the more difficult to cover school content. Given a high level of agrarian labor in the countryside, school attendance is further hampered by the lack of workers in the fields. UNICEF data suggest that 21 percent of all school-age children are engaged in labor.

Tertiary education in Guatemala is mostly available for a selected number of students, most coming from affluent families. There is one public tertiary institution and 11 private tertiary institutions in Guatemala. The single public tertiary institution is the University of San Carlos of Guatemala, which was established in 1676, making it one of the oldest continuing universities in the Americas. The university began with only five programs, mostly in the areas of law, agriculture and surveying, and theology. At present, the university offers nearly 100 degrees in nearly 50 disciplines and careers. The University of San Carlos of Guatemala is the largest in the country, enrolling more than 146,000 students on 18 campuses throughout Guatemala. The university is also the only public institution in the country that offers degrees in teacher education. Other teacher education programs can be found as separate schools among some of the 11 private universities.

Guatemala Education at a Glance

General Information

Capital	Guatemala City
Population	12.7 million
Languages	Spanish, Amerindian languages (40%)
Adult literacy rate (ages 15 and over)	69.1%
GDP per capita	US$5,000
People below poverty line (2004)	56.2%
Number of phones (landline) per 100 people	8.9
Number of phones (mobile) per 100 people	24.9
Number of Internet users per 100 people	6
Life expectancy at birth (years)	69

Formal Educational Information

Enrollment in primary school (ages 7–12)	2.1 million
Enrollment in lower and upper secondary school (ages 13–17)	1.5 million
Number of years of compulsory education	11 (ages 7–17)
Primary school student/teacher ratio	32.6
Lower and upper secondary school student/teacher ratio	15.4
Primary school gross enrollment ratio	114%
Secondary school gross enrollment ratio	51%
Tertiary school gross enrollment ratio	9.6%
Primary school entrants completion rate	74%
Child labor (ages 5–14)	21%

Note: Unless otherwise indicated, all data are based on sources from 2011.

System Economics and Future Prospects

According to the United Nations Development Programme (2010), along with Andorra, India, Singapore, and the British Virgin Islands, total public expenditure on education of Guatemala represented 3.2 percent of the gross domestic product (GDP) in 2008. Given the GDP of Guatemala at $70.031 billion, educational expenditure in the country amounts to nearly $2.25 billion, about $596 per student (total amount equivalent to US dollars divided by 3,773,000, the approximate number of primary and secondary students in the country). Guatemala ranks 143 of 186 countries in terms of percentage of educational expenditure.

The Educational Ministry of Guatemala is currently seeking to improve education in the country. The ministry's goals are to reach high levels of standards and expectations, find and retain strong leaders, support learning that is student-centered, involve parents and communities in educational initiatives, identify important benchmarks for purposes of assessment and accountability, foster a curriculum that promotes inquiry and challenge, provide professional development for in-service teachers, and maximize the amount of time available for all students to succeed in school. Unfortunately, with lack of financial and material resources and an inadequate mind-set among many Guatemalans about the importance of a strong education, these goals are going to be difficult to reach—especially within a short period of time.

Fortunately, both governmental and nongovernmental organizations have provided support in recent years. The World Bank lent $33 million for educational improvements in order to improve educational access in rural regions of the country. While this infusion of funds helped education access of rural children, the World Bank identified high levels of corruption among contractors and poor levels of educational infrastructure. The ministry needs to invest in technologies that allow children of rural families to benefit from all school subjects. In addition, the country would be wise in establishing law that prevents the labor of children—especially those under 16 years old—who deserve an education that will help them compete in the global economy.

Daniel Ness and Chia-ling Lin

REFERENCES

Center for Economic and Social Rights. *Visualizing Rights: Guatemala, Fact Sheet No. 3*. New York: Center for Economic and Social Rights, 2011.

Central Intelligence Agency. *The CIA World Factbook*. New York: Skyhorse, 2011. https.www.cia.gov/library/publications/the-world-factbook/index.html.

Nation Master. 2011. www.nationmaster.com.

UNESCO. *Global Education Digest 2012: Comparing Education Statistics Across the World*. Montreal: UNESCO Institute for Statistics, 2012.

———. "Strong Foundations: Early Childhood Care and Education." *Education for All Global Monitoring Report*. Paris: UNESCO, 2006.

UNESCO–IBE. www.ibe.unesco.org/en/worldwide/unesco-regions/latin-america-and-the-caribbean/guatemala.html.

United Nations Development Programme. *United Nations Development Report 2010*. New York: Palgrave Macmillan, 2010.

US Department of Labor. *2001 Findings on the Worst Forms of Child Labor*. Washington, DC: Bureau of International Labor Affairs, US Department of Labor, 2002.

World Bank Education Statistics. 2011. www.worldbank.org.

HAITI

Haiti is a Caribbean nation that takes up the western one-third of the island of Hispaniola (the Dominican Republic comprising the eastern two-thirds). The official and most spoken language is French; however, Creole is also a very common language. Based on the 2001 census, about 95 percent of all Haitians are black and 5 percent fall under mulatto or white. About 80 percent of the Haitian population is Roman Catholic, 16 percent fall into one of the Protestant sects, 3 percent under "other," and 1 percent under "none."

Of the countries in the Central American and Caribbean region, Haiti was the first to become an independent republic. However, the country has suffered from numerous calamities and impoverished conditions. The rate of HIV/AIDS among Haitian adults is 5.6 percent (nearly 280,000 cases). Moreover, with a continuously low gross domestic product (GDP), Haiti is the poorest country in North America.

Educational System

According to the Library of Congress's Federal Research Division, Haiti's school-age populations suffer from extremely high levels of illiteracy. On average, the literacy rate of the entire population of Haiti is 53 percent (55 percent for males and approximately 50 percent for females). There are numerous reasons for this low rate. Two reasons are the depressingly high level of poverty of most Haitian citizens and the overwhelmingly agrarian lifestyles. Moreover, 90 percent or more of the primary schools are privately run, usually by religious establishments or organizations with religious affiliations. This indicates that most attendees come from wealthier families.

Precompulsory and Compulsory Education

Accordingly, the notion of compulsory schooling and education is nebulous due to the lack of public educational facilities. The 2010 earthquake in Haiti complicates the role of the educational system even further. This earthquake resulted in an estimated 300,000 casualties, including many deaths, many of whom were children attending school. Moreover, there is a great shortage of educational facilities, school infrastructure (let alone other necessary forms of infrastructure, such as homes for displaced individuals), educational supplies, and teachers.

Preearthquake records indicate approximately 15,200 primary schools in Haiti, again, nearly 90 percent of which are privately run—mostly by international private schools from Canada, the United States, and France, independent church groups, or nongovernmental organizations (NGOs). Most rural children do not attend primary school because their families cannot afford to send them. Instead, they traditionally work in agriculture and livestock. Perhaps more dismal are the enrollment and attrition rates of primary schools. In general, primary schools are nowhere near full capacity; currently, only 67 percent of all primary school age children are enrolled. In 2000 only 64 percent of all children in Haiti were enrolled in primary school. Of these students, less than one-third (30 percent) reach grade 6—the grade level necessary to reach in order to enter secondary school. Of the 30 percent of students who finish primary school, two-thirds (20 percent of the original number of students enrolled in primary school) have the opportunity or the financial means to enter secondary school.

Postcompulsory Education

Despite Haiti's poor educational system and lack of compulsory education for children under the age of 18, the few students who graduate from secondary school may have the opportunity to attend certain forms of higher education, at a college or university or in other public and private institutions. The Haiti Ministry of Education controls the higher education institutions in the country.

There are 23 universities and institutions of higher education in Haiti. Established in 1820, the University of Haiti is the oldest. The earliest schools within the university were the colleges of law and medicine. The remaining universities and institutions were founded after 1960. These include the University of Notre Dame, the University of the Caribbean, and the university affiliated with the Association of Universities of the Francophonie.

Curriculum, Assessment, and Instruction

The primary language of communication in Haiti's schools is French. After 1860, when a concordat with the Vatican was signed, Haitian education was predominantly controlled by the Catholic Church. Despite the emphasis on a Catholic religious education, the model of schooling in the country was predominantly based on the French public school system. As a result, Haitian education adapted the classical European curriculum that included literature, arithmetic, and geometry. These schools increasingly served the more affluent Haitian families, while rural families often did not have access to education. Instead, many children and adolescents in rural parts of Haiti learned basic kills associated with farming and agronomy. This system remained until educational reforms took place in 1978. From that time to the present, the major change in curriculum was the implementation of Haitian Creole as the language of instruction in the first four grades of primary school. The curriculum also grouped children according to academic levels and promoted the learning of concepts rather than strict memorization. Finally, it is important to consider the impact of the 2010 earthquake; the educational system up to that point came to a sudden halt and many lives were lost, both children and adults, as a result of the earthquake. At present, formal education and curriculum implementation are run ad hoc depending on the leadership of each community in the country.

Teacher Education

Due to the chaotic state of the Haitian educational system after the 2010 earthquake, teacher education is not at all a significant concern for most Haitians who are attempting to rebuild their communities and their country. Nevertheless, if the Haitian people are to resurrect what has been devastated in their cities and towns, setting an agenda on improving education in general and identifying qualified teachers in particular will be an essential part of the rebuilding process. It has been suggested that before the earthquake the main cause of poor education in the country was the poor quality of teachers and that a lack of teacher education programs may still be the largest obstacle in improving education in Haiti. Data suggest that nearly 80 percent of Haitian teachers within the last decade had no formal teacher training (see Wolff 2008). And the training that some teachers did have often came from unofficial, nonaccredited private institutions, mostly Christian fundamentalist organizations. Moreover, teachers in Haiti have historically had difficulties in their positions. They receive little, if any, support in terms of content, classroom instruction, student conduct, evaluation of students, and supervision.

Informal Education

Informal education in Haiti is disorganized to a degree, especially after the 2010 earthquake. Most informal education centers are makeshift structures that are used for both informal education and formal education for young students. In terms of informal education, volunteers from other parts of the world, predominantly the United States, are engaged in helping Haitian adults to grapple with daily chores related to health and well-being, not only of themselves, but also of their family and community, as well as to gain knowledge and skills that are needed for everyday livelihood. A tangential objective of informal education at the present time is to prepare all students for opportunities within a global market economy. But this is far from the central purpose of informal education given the country's dire circumstances as a result of extremely poor infrastructure that was devastated after the 2010 earthquake. Prior to the earthquake, the adult (above age 15) literacy rate was 40 to 45 percent of the population. The government attempted to decrease the rate of illiteracy as part of a 200th anniversary initiative commencing in 2004. To an extent, the government was successful: the rate of literacy increased to nearly 53 percent. But it has not improved since. The Peace Corps sent volunteers to Haiti at various times since 1982; however, since 2005, Peace Corps volunteering has been closed. Reopening will depend on the status of the Haitian government.

System Economics

Public expenditure on education for the world in 2005 was approximately 4.9 percent of the gross domestic product, 4.7 percent for developing countries, and 5.0 percent for countries in the Caribbean and Central American region. Public expenditure on education for Haiti is approximately 1.4 percent of its GDP, making Haiti one of the lowest-ranking countries on educational spending on the federal level—177 of 186 countries. Given the GDP of the Haiti at $11.53 billion, educational expenditure in the country amounts to approximately $161.42 million, about $60.30 per student (total amount equivalent to US dollars divided by 2,675,000, the approximate number of primary- and secondary-age students in the country). With a ranking of 177 of 186 countries in percentage of educational expenditure, Haiti has the lowest percentage of GDP allocated for education in the region, the lowest per student educational spending in the region, and the fifth-lowest among countries with populations over 1 million. It is important to note, however, that primary and secondary gross enrollment ratios are 80 percent and 25 percent, respectively. Moreover, the net enrollment ratios are significantly less—the primary net enrollment ratio is only 21.5. This indicates that of the

---

Haiti Education at a Glance

General Information

Capital	Port-au-Prince
Population	9.7 million
Languages	French and Creole
Adult literacy rate (ages 15 and over)	52.9%
GDP per capita (2010)	US$1,200
People below poverty line	80%
Number of phones (landline) per 100 people	1.6
Number of phones (mobile) per 100 people	4.6
Number of Internet users per 100 people	5.7
Life expectancy at birth (years)	62*

Formal Educational Information

Enrollment in primary school (ages 6–11)	1.2 million
Enrollment in lower and upper secondary school (ages 12–18)	1.4 million
Number of years of compulsory education	13 (ages 6–18)
Primary school student/teacher ratio	33.7
Lower and upper secondary school student/teacher ratio	no data
Primary school gross enrollment ratio	80%
Secondary school gross enrollment ratio	25%
Tertiary school gross enrollment ratio	1%
Primary school entrants completion rate	no data
Child labor (ages 5–14 years)	21%

Note: *Postearthquake figures indicate that life expectancy for Haiti was 30 years (see the *CIA World Factbook* 2010). However, prior to 2010, life expectancy was 57. At present, life expectancy is 63 years for females and about 61 years for males.

Unless otherwise indicated, all data are based on sources from 2011.

2.675 million school-age students and 1.389 million primary-school-age students in the country, actual primary school enrollment amounts to slightly less than 300,000 students going to school. The figures for secondary school are expected to be significantly less than the net enrollment figure for primary school, but the exact net enrollment figure for secondary school is unknown at the present time.

Future Prospects

There are numerous problems that Haiti must solve in order to achieve higher rates of literacy as well as human and knowledge capital. One egregious problem is poverty. Haiti is the poorest country in the Western Hemisphere. A second, but no less serious, egregious problem is child slavery. According to the "Free the Slaves" website, parents in rural Haiti who cannot afford to support their children send them to the cities. These children, often referred to as *restavecs* (literally "one who stays with," translated from the French), are engaged in unpaid manual labor. Although parents believe their children will be educated, they seldom are. Also, Haiti has been plagued by hostility and lawlessness. The pandemonium thwarts basic services and prevents humanitarian assistance from reaching the most vulnerable of populations—especially children. Moreover, many schools and health facilities throughout the country have closed because teachers and health-care providers are unable to go to work for fear of violence. Haiti is in dire need of both physical and economic support from more developed nations as a means of not only improving education, but also providing the essential necessities of life for its youth.

The 2010 earthquake has made life in Haiti extremely harrowing and distressing. Although a revamping of the educational system is high on the country's list, there are numerous problems that need development, restructuring, and improvement in Haiti. For example, many people are displaced as a result of the earthquake as well as outright poverty. Nearly one million people need new homes. In addition, the lack of food and clean water is a severe problem that must be resolved in order for children to learn effectively in a classroom environment.

Daniel Ness and Chia-ling Lin

REFERENCES

Central Intelligence Agency. *The CIA World Factbook*. New York: Skyhorse, 2011. https.www.cia.gov/library/publications/the-world-factbook/index.html.

Free the Slaves. *Ending Slavery: The 25 Year Plan*. Washington, DC: Free the Slaves, 2009. www.freetheslaves.net/Page.aspx?pid=183.

"Haiti." In *The Europa World Yearbook*, vol. 1. London: Routledge, 2007.

Nation Master. 2011. www.nationmaster.com.

UNESCO. *Global Education Digest 2012: Comparing Education Statistics Across the World*. Montreal: UNESCO Institute for Statistics, 2012.

———. "Strong Foundations: Early Childhood Care and Education." *Education for All Global Monitoring Report 2007*. Paris: UNESCO, 2007.

UNESCO–IBE. www.ibe.unesco.org/countries/Haiti.htm.

UNESCO–UIS. www.uis.unesco.org.

UNICEF. www.unicef.org/infobycountry/haiti.html.

United Nations Development Programme. "Beyond Scarcity: Power, Poverty and the Global Water Crisis." *Human Development Report 2006*. New York: Palgrave Macmillan, 2006.

Wolff, Laurence. *Education in Haiti: The Way Forward*. Washington, DC: Partnership for Educational Revitalization in the Americas, 2008.

World Bank Education Statistics. 2011. www.worldbank.org.

HONDURAS

Honduras is a country located in Central America. The official language is Spanish, although many Hondurans speak one of the numerous Amerindian dialects. Nearly 90 percent of Hondurans are mestizo (mixed Amerindian and European), 7 percent Amerindian, 2 percent black, and 1 percent white. Almost all of the country's citizens are Roman Catholic, with only 3 percent belonging to one of the Protestant denominations.

Sharing the fate of nearly all of the post-Columbian regions of Central America, Honduras became a part of the Spanish empire in the Americas during the sixteenth century. As a result of waning control of the Spanish during the latter part of the eighteenth century and early nineteenth century, Honduras became one of several countries in the region to assume independence in 1821. As an independent state, the country was an important producer of sugarcane and coffee. However, being prone to both hurricanes and earthquakes, Honduras runs the risk of being vulnerable to poor quality and amounts of its agricultural production. By 1957 Honduras was run almost entirely by military rule and remained a quasi-military dictatorship for nearly 25 years. During the 1980s, the southeastern region of Honduras near the border with Nicaragua became one of the homes of the anti-Sandinista contras who fought along with the El Salvadoran army against Nicaragua's Marxist government. In 1998 Honduras was devastated by Hurricane Mitch, which caused the deaths of over 5,000 people and over $2 billion in damages and economic losses.

After Haiti, Honduras is the second-poorest country in the region. In addition to an unstable economy, there is an unequal distribution of wealth among the people. The unemployment rate is nearly 28 percent—nearly five to six times the unemployment rate of its neighboring countries. Moreover, nearly 53 percent of the population falls below the poverty line.

Educational System

Education in Honduras is compulsory during the primary education period, or for children from seven to 12 years of age. Preprimary education is available mainly in Tegucigalpa, primarily for families that are able to afford it for their children. Unfortunately, Honduran education has had a reputation as one of the bleakest in Central America. Although the primary school gross enrollment ratio is 113 percent, only 79 percent of all primary school children who enroll in primary school complete school. Much of the problem of student attrition has to do with a large agrarian population, particularly in rural communities where sending children to formal schooling hampers a family's ability to maintain crops and livestock, both for subsistence farming and cash crop farming. UNICEF data suggest that 16 percent of all Honduran children are engaged in child labor. Of these children, only 34 percent are able to complete primary school. Given these data, the overwhelming majority of Honduran children who complete primary school live in the cities of Honduras.

Education in Honduras faces similar problems in educational attainment as many sub-Saharan African countries in that although de jure compulsory education lasts for 12 years, de facto compulsory education

is only for six. Moreover, although primary education is free, families are obliged to pay for school supplies, school fees, uniforms, and transportation costs. These factors put rural families at a disadvantage when considering formal education access for their children. Furthermore, the coastal areas of Honduras along the Caribbean Sea, the poorest and most rural part of the country, are susceptible to hurricanes, particularly from July to October. Accordingly, poorly constructed schools are vulnerable to closure and, at times, severe damage as a result of hurricanes.

Honduran secondary education is also rife with obstacles. To begin with, although roughly four out of five Honduran children are able to complete primary school education, about two-thirds of those who do actually enroll in secondary school. Formal secondary school attendance Honduras is mostly a function of both geographical location and socioeconomic class. Poor communities consist of people who generally engage in agricultural labor while those in more affluent communities tend to be more diverse and better educated in terms of their occupations. At present, the principal purpose of attending secondary school is to continue education to the tertiary level.

Tertiary education in Honduras is primarily available for students of affluent families. Both public and private universities in Honduras are almost exclusively in urban areas: Tegucigalpa, La Ceiba, and San Pedro Sula. In total there are 25 public and private universities in the country. The oldest and largest tertiary institution in Honduras is the National Autonomous University of Honduras, which has a matriculated student population of nearly 148,000 students, one of the largest tertiary institutions in Central America. The university was founded in 1847 and, over the course of 165 years, has grown to eight campuses throughout the country.

System Economics and Future Prospects

According to the United Nations Development Programme (2010), along with Egypt, Sierra Leone, Panama, Nepal, Mali, Kuwait, and Gabon, the total public expenditures on education in Honduras represented 3.8 percent of the gross domestic product (GDP) in 1991. Given the GDP of Honduras at $33.77 billion, and assuming that the percentage of educational expenditure has remained the same,

Honduras Education at a Glance

General Information

Capital	Tegucigalpa
Population	7.4 million
Language	Spanish
Adult literacy rate (ages 15 and over)	80%
GDP per capita	US$3,100
People below poverty line (1993)	53%
Number of phones (landline) per 100 people	1.6
Number of phones (mobile) per 100 people	4.6
Number of Internet users per 100 people	5.7
Life expectancy at birth (years)	69

Formal Educational Information

Enrollment in primary school (ages 7–12)	1.1 million
Enrollment in lower and upper secondary school (ages 13–18)	1 million
Number of years of compulsory education	12 (ages 7–18)
Primary school student/teacher ratio	34.1
Lower and upper secondary school student/teacher ratio	33.3
Primary school gross enrollment ratio	113%
Secondary school gross enrollment ratio	66%
Tertiary school gross enrollment ratio	16.4%
Primary school entrants completion rate	79%
Child labor (ages 5–14)	16%

Note: Unless otherwise indicated, all data are based on sources from 2011.

educational expenditure in the country amounts to more than $1.283 billion, about $586 per student (total amount equivalent to US dollars divided by 2,192,000, the approximate number of primary and secondary students in the country). Honduras ranks 119 of 186 countries in terms of percentage of educational expenditure.

Education in Honduras has suffered from several setbacks, including the lack of individual initiative to pursue formal education, particularly among rural families; widespread poverty, with nearly half of the country's population below the international poverty line; and substandard educational infrastructure, particularly in areas outside of Tegucigalpa. Accordingly, the Honduran education system has faced difficulty in keeping children in school at both primary and secondary grade levels. In part, this is a result of an extremely high rate of crime and juvenile delinquency. However, the Honduran Ministry of Education has received grants and other forms of financial support from the United States Agency for International Development (USAID) that enabled the development and growth of the Education for All program (EDUC-

ATODOS). This program has provided children with formal educational opportunities and helped adults finish primary and secondary education programs, especially those who left formal education in order to enter the workforce. In recent years, EDUCATO-DOS has extended the grade levels for people who have dropped out of school in the past. At present, students can return to school to finish secondary level education. Although many of these individuals do not go to college, they now have more skills in various technical vocations that will allow them to diversify their occupational opportunities.

Daniel Ness and Chia-ling Lin

REFERENCES

Central Intelligence Agency. *The CIA World Factbook.* New York: Skyhorse, 2011. https.www.cia.gov/library/publications/the-world-factbook/index.html.

Nation Master. 2011. www.nationmaster.com.

UNESCO. *Global Education Digest 2012: Comparing Education Statistics Across the World.* Montreal: UNESCO Institute for Statistics, 2012.

———. "Strong Foundations: Early Childhood Care and Education." *Education for All Global Monitoring Report.* Paris: UNESCO, 2006.

UNESCO–IBE. www.ibe.unesco.org/en/worldwide/unesco-regions/latin-america-and-the-caribbean/honduras.html.

United Nations Development Programme. *United Nations Development Report 2010.* New York: Palgrave Macmillan, 2010.

US Department of Labor. *2001 Findings on the Worst Forms of Child Labor.* Washington, DC: Bureau of International Labor Affairs, US Department of Labor, 2002.

World Bank Education Statistics. 2011. www.worldbank.org.

JAMAICA

Jamaica is a Caribbean island nation located about 125 miles (200 kilometers) directly south of the eastern part of Cuba and approximately the same distance west of Haiti. The official and most commonly spoken language is English. Based on the 2001 census, about 91 percent of all Jamaicans are black and approximately 9 percent fall under "other" or "unknown." As in some of the other Caribbean island nations, Jamaica's religions are diverse. Over 62 percent of Jamaicans are members of one of the Protestant sects, 2.6 percent are Roman Catholic,

14.2 percent follow other or unspecified religions, and 20.9 profess none.

Jamaica was first inhabited by the Spanish in 1494, when Christopher Columbus made his second voyage to the Americas. The Taino, a native people who inhabited Jamaica for several centuries, were exterminated by the Spanish. The island was used as one of the first key posts in the Western Hemisphere for the Atlantic slave trade. The Spanish controlled Jamaica for well over a century until the English seized the island in 1655 for the purpose of establishing an agrarian economy. The island was then a major colonial base for the production of sugar, cocoa, and coffee. Slavery in Jamaica was abolished in 1834. The nearly quarter of a million former slaves became small-scale farmers. In 1958 Jamaica, along with the other British Caribbean colonies, joined the Federation of the West Indies and gained independence four years later. Economic conditions in Jamaica worsened in the 1970s, contributing to the country's large networks of organized crime. The country's primary concern is its centralized location for illegal drug trafficking and a large number of HIV/AIDS cases. The rate of HIV/AIDS among Jamaican adults is 3 percent (nearly 5,600 cases).

Educational System

According to Nation Master, the duration of compulsory education in Jamaica is only seven years—namely, the primary school period. Families are required to pay school fees for their children. Prior to primary school, parents with enough financial resources have the option to send their young children to preschool. These children are usually between the ages of one and five years. Despite noncompulsory status, preschool attendance in Jamaica is quite high when compared to other countries in Central America and the Caribbean islands. Approximately two-thirds of all parents enroll their children in early childhood programs. They do so for many reasons—the most important of which is lack of supervision when parents are engaged in employment or other forms of labor.

Primary school education in Jamaica is considered compulsory. Students either attend free public schools (which still require parents to pay resources fees) or private preparatory schools if their parents can afford the tuition. Primary school students are usually between the ages of five and 11 years. The key goal of the primary school curriculum in Jamaica is to provide students with a basic understanding of language, mathematical thinking, and social studies. In recent years, there has been more accountability on the part of schools to identify the strengths and weaknesses in students' abilities. To this end, students are assessed at the end of grades 3, 4, and 6 in order to determine levels of achievement and promotion to secondary school levels. At the end of grade 4, for example, students are administered a test in literacy. By the end of grade 6, students are administered a battery of tests that measure their levels of achievement in language, mathematics, and social studies.

Unlike secondary education in the United States and other countries throughout the world, that of Jamaica consists of forms—namely, Forms 1, 2, and 3 for the lower secondary level and Forms 4, 5, and 6 for the upper secondary level. In addition to a continuation of the basic education curriculum from primary school, students at the lower secondary level enroll in courses related to the natural sciences (e.g., earth science, biology, physics) as well as foreign language—particularly French, Spanish, Portuguese, and other languages associated with the region. The first part of upper high school consists of Forms 4 and 5. This is the secondary period when students decide their career selection. Students have latitude in terms of which courses they select. Nevertheless, they must enroll in language and literature and mathematics. Upper-level high schools offer both academic and occupational courses.

Form 6, which consists of a two-year period, is for students who decide to continue to university education. Students who enter Form 6 are highly competitive because the best universities accept students with the highest secondary school average. Students must pass the Caribbean Advanced Proficiency Exam in order to be considered for university acceptance. Unfortunately, students in rural parts of the country have a strong disadvantage for university enrollment because upper-level high schools with Form 6 levels are most common in urban areas. Both primary and secondary schools also include courses on tourism for students who may have a leaning in the direction of hotel management and hospitality studies. The country receives most of its foreign income from the tourism industry.

The primary school gross enrollment ratio in Jamaica stands at 95 percent; however, data indicate that the number of primary school students actually attending preschool is lower. This is evident from the primary-level net enrollment ratio of 90.3 percent. The situation is bleaker in that the percentage (82 percent) of primary students in Jamaica actually completing primary school is even lower. This indicates that even fewer students attend secondary school. Statistics in 2005 indicate that the secondary school gross enrollment rate in Jamaica is 87 percent, but the secondary school net enrollment rate is only 78 percent. Much of the drop in enrollment occurs in rural areas of the country, where agricultural labor is needed the most. Moreover, UNICEF data indicate that child labor between the ages of five and 14 is prevalent in the country at a 6 percent rate. The Jamaican education system also suffers from a rather high student/teacher ratio, about 36 to 1 in primary school. These factors have contributed to the adverse elements of education in Jamaica.

Tertiary education in Jamaica includes universities, liberal arts colleges, professional colleges, technical colleges, teacher training institutes, and human employment and resource training (HEART) centers. Established in 1907, the Northern Caribbean University is the oldest private tertiary institution in Jamaica. The largest university in terms of enrollment is the Mona campus of the University of West Indies. There are eight teacher training colleges in Jamaica. Teachers colleges and educational institutes are separate, autonomous entities and are not affiliated with universities. In addition colleges and universities that offer baccalaureate and graduate degrees, 14 colleges offer degrees that can be completed in less than three or four years. These 14 colleges are analogous to the community college in the United States. They focus on both academic education and technical training. Other tertiary institutions include a college of agriculture and science and a college of sport and physical education. Finally, tertiary programs in Jamaica also include 30 vocational training centers and HEART centers that accommodate adults who may not have upper secondary school diplomas but who wish to learn skills for future employment.

System Economics and Future Prospects

According to the United Nations Development Programme (2010), along with Fiji and New Zealand, total public expenditures on education in Jamaica represented 6.2 percent of the gross domestic product (GDP) in 2008. Given the GDP of Jamaica at $43.98 billion, educational expenditure in the country amounts to more than $23.93 billion, about $2,432 per student (total amount equivalent to US dollars divided by 610,000, the approximate number of primary and secondary students in the country). Jamaica ranks 34 of 186 countries in percentage of educational expenditure.

The literacy rate in Jamaica has steadily improved from 1992 to the present. For individuals between the ages of 15 and 21, the literacy rate is 87.5 percent. Increasing rates in literacy have contributed to the increase in enrollments at all educational levels in the country. These outcomes do not mean that education in Jamaica has been effective in leading to a productive and self-sufficient workforce. To be sure, only 82 percent of all primary school students are able to complete the primary level. As in other Central American countries, school attendance is disadvantaged as a result of a lack of adequate facilities at schools, particularly in rural parts of the country. Moreover, although primary and most of secondary

---

Jamaica Education at a Glance

General Information

Capital	Kingston
Population	2.7 million
Language	English
Adult literacy rate (ages 15 and over)	87.9%
GDP per capita	US$4,900
People below poverty line (2003)	14.8%
Number of phones (landline) per 100 people	12.3
Number of phones (mobile) per 100 people	97.2
Number of Internet users per 100 people	38.4
Life expectancy at birth (years)	73

Formal Educational Information

Enrollment in primary school (ages 6–11)	323,000
Enrollment in lower and upper secondary school (ages 12–16)	287,000
Number of years of primary/secondary education	11 (ages 6–16)
Primary school student/teacher ratio	35.5
Lower and upper secondary school student/teacher ratio	19.3
Primary school gross enrollment ratio	95%
Secondary school gross enrollment ratio	87%
Tertiary school gross enrollment ratio	19%
Primary school entrants completion rate	82%
Child labor (ages 5–14)	6%

Note: Unless otherwise indicated, all data are based on sources from 2011.

education is free, parents are still required to pay fees associated with their children's education. Educational improvement initiatives in Jamaica include the development of information and communications technology that will lessen the burdens for rural children and families and will most likely assist in keeping students in school through the secondary level.

Daniel Ness and Chia-ling Lin

REFERENCES

Central Intelligence Agency. *The CIA World Factbook.* New York: Skyhorse, 2011. https.www.cia.gov/library/publications/the-world-factbook/index.html.

Nation Master. 2011. www.nationmaster.com.

UNESCO. *Global Education Digest 2012: Comparing Education Statistics Across the World.* Montreal: UNESCO Institute for Statistics, 2012.

———. "Strong Foundations: Early Childhood Care and Education." *Education for All Global Monitoring Report.* Paris: UNESCO, 2006.

UNESCO–IBE. www.ibe.unesco.org/en/worldwide/unesco-regions/latin-america-and-the-caribbean/jamaica.html.

United Nations Development Programme. *United Nations Development Report 2010.* New York: Palgrave Macmillan, 2010.

US Department of Labor. *2001 Findings on the Worst Forms of Child Labor.* Washington, DC: Bureau of International Labor Affairs, US Department of Labor, 2002.

World Bank Education Statistics. 2011. www.worldbank.org.

MEXICO

Mexico, formally referred to as the United Mexican States, is a country with a long history of pre-Columbian cultures. Nearly 60 percent of Mexicans are mestizo (mixed Amerindian and European), 30 percent are Amerindian (indigenous Americans), 9 percent are European, and 1 percent is identified as "other." About three-quarters of the country's citizens are members of the Roman Catholic Church, about 6 percent are Protestant, and 17 percent have an unspecified religion or no religion. Over 91 percent of the population 15 years or older is literate. The predominant spoken and written language is Spanish; however, other languages include Mayan, Nahuatl, and related regional dialects.

Mexico was the location of extremely advanced civilizations that reigned for millennia before the Spanish conquest. The Mayan civilization developed techniques in trade and agriculture that many scholars believe to more innovative than those in many Western societies. At one point, presumably in the few centuries prior to Spanish invasion, the population in the region exceeded several million, and transportation facilities, as depicted by historians of the period, were outstanding. Spanish conquistadores and their armies essentially obliterated the Mayan and other Amerindian civilizations in the sixteenth century. Mexico fell under Spanish rule until it gained independence in the early 1800s. A few decades later, in the Mexican-American War, Mexico lost much of what is presently the southwestern portion of the United States, stretching from Texas to northern California. Mexico's economy fell into recession in 1994 when the price of the peso dropped considerably. Current concerns include low wages, unemployment, unequal distribution of income, and lack of advancement for a large portion of the Amerindian population. In 2000 the country regained its two-party system when the Institutional Revolutionary Party was defeated by the newly formed National Action Party.

Mexico's trade has more than tripled since the signing and implementation of the North American Free Trade Agreement (NAFTA) in 1994. Moreover, since that time, the country's industries and seaports were replaced with more modern forms of infrastructure, machinery, and technology. Ninety percent of Mexico's trade is under free trade agreement with over 40 countries, including the Central American nations, the European Union, and Japan.

Educational System

The system of education in Mexico comprises four general levels: preschool (i.e., three years of kindergarten education), compulsory basic education (grades 1 through 9), upper secondary education (grades 10 through 12), and tertiary education. According to Santibañez, Vernez, and Razquin (2004), public schools in Mexico serve 87 percent of all children and adolescents of compulsory school age and upper secondary school age. Unlike decentralized educational systems, such as those in the United States, Australia, or Papua New Guinea, the educational system in Mexico is centralized at the federal level. The Secretaria de Educación is responsible for ratifying the curriculum at each grade level, choosing the textbooks used, hiring school personnel, and determining school staff and faculty salaries. Although each of Mexico's 32 states is formally accountable for its individual education systems on a state level, the country still maintains a centralized education system on a national level.

Without question, education in Mexico within the last 75 years experienced exponential growth—from a one-time fledgling system in the 1930s and 1940s that catered primarily to children of elite families to one that has prepared nearly all of its citizens under 16 years old with the ability to read, write, and calculate. According to Santibañez, Vernez, and Razquin (2004), the number of primary and secondary students in Mexico increased eightfold from the middle of the twentieth century to the present—from about 3.25 million students in 1950 to more than 26 million students today. The country also saw an increase in the number of secondary school students within the last 30 years—from more than 1 million students in 1970 to more than 5 million in 2000. The percentages of students completing ninth grade increased from 10 percent in the middle twentieth century to more than 40 percent of the secondary school population in the 1990s. The Mexican government, therefore, was compelled to grapple with a large growth in students within a 40-year period. The government has attempted to control the educational process through the implementation of standardized exit examinations as well as standardized testing for admission to specified educational institutions. The government has also introduced various teacher evaluation systems for credentialing and certifying productive teachers. The system of education in Mexico is facing the most difficulty in reconciling increased educational opportunities for the mass population, on the one hand, with improving the levels and rigor of education on the other. Another problem that concerns scholars who do research on education is that Mexico lacks a system whereby data regarding student academic performance can be collected. That is, there is no organization in Mexico analogous to the National Center for Education Statistics in the United States, which provides data on student achievement and high-performing schools. As a result, while there is much information on student performance in the Distrito Federál where Mexico City is located, there is little, if any, data on student performance in other states of Mexico.

Preprimary and Compulsory Education

Preprimary education in Mexico is not compulsory. With tuition and fees, it is available for parents who can afford it. The preprimary period in Mexico generally consists of two broad types: nursery school and preschool. Nursery school engages children who are two or three years old in the process of socialization as well as providing day care for working parents. Preschool in Mexico consists of two to three years of education, the last year of which is equivalent to the Western kindergarten. Children are generally between the ages of three and six. Approximately 4 million children are enrolled in preschool in Mexico—about 56 percent of the preschool-age population. The Mexican legislature recently passed a law that will make preschool education compulsory; however, the law is not fully in practice and may take several years to come to fruition.

Compulsory education in Mexico lasts for nine years. Primary education in Mexico is compulsory and free for children and adolescents ages 6 through 15 years. In 1991, after the ratification of the establishment of parochial schooling, the country saw a large increase in the number of parochial schools, particularly in large metropolitan areas. In total, there are about 15 million children enrolled in primary schools. General public primary schools in Mexico enroll about 93 percent of the primary school population. Community and indigenous schools enroll 7 percent of the population. Primary school in Mexico, which includes both primary school and lower secondary school (grades 7 through 9), consists of basic education. The general public primary school curriculum is a uniform national curriculum, and instruction is in Spanish. By contrast, curriculum in indigenous schools is modified in that instruction is given in the local language. These schools are often multigrade schools in which one or two teachers are responsible for teaching all the grade levels. Indigenous schools are most common in the rural regions of Mexico.

It should not be surprising that students in rural regions of Mexico lag behind students in urban areas in reading and mathematics. Approximately 45 percent of urban basic education students achieve reading competency at the sixth grade level but only 15 percent achieve mathematics competency. The percentages are much lower for rural students in both community (multigrade) and indigenous schools. Rural children, on average, have a 29 percent competency level in reading and a 9 percent competency level in mathematics by the sixth grade. Community school children have an 18 percent competency level and 6 percent competency level by the sixth grade for reading and mathematics, respectively. Indigenous school children have a 12 percent competency level and 4 percent competency level by the sixth grade for reading and mathematics, respectively.

Mexican secondary schools focus on academic, vocational, and technical skills. The basic education curriculum found in the primary grades continues into grades 7 through 9, the lower secondary school level. Students who graduate from lower secondary school are not required to continue their education. In fact, only 68 percent of all students complete basic education—the lower secondary school level. Moreover, only 35 percent complete the upper secondary school level (grades 10, 11, and 12). Widespread difficulties have adversely affected coverage of secondary school in rural Mexico—namely, a lack of teachers, a lack of financial and material resources, and poor infrastructure.

One solution that seems to have worked in this regard is distance learning, which seems to have overcome the barriers associated with few educational resources. Distance learning is beginning to operate in rural areas where the construction of secondary schools is too expensive. Although not ideal in educating secondary students, distance learning lectures are delivered to rural communities by satellite television in the form of 15-minute programs. The programs are given in Spanish or translated into the language spoken in the specific region. Distance learning has also alleviated the problem of class size. Rather than a 35 to 1 student/teacher ratio in a typical rural secondary school, class size is reduced to 22 students. Moreover, there is usually one teacher or program facilitator per grade level. In total, approximately 1.2 million students in 16,500 schools are educated through distance learning—20 percent of all students in Mexico. Distance learning enrollments are higher in rural parts of the country—particularly in poor states with high indigenous populations. Since 1995 distance learning education has grown more than 95 percent. It also represents nearly half of all lower secondary school students in the most economically disadvantaged states of Mexico. In contrast, distance education in urban states or more affluent states is used by less than 5 percent of all students.

Within the past few decades, the Mexican government has attempted to address the problem of adult illiteracy. Since the years preceding World War II, the Mexican Educational Ministry has established campaigns to improve the literacy rate of adults. The literacy rate has improved from below 50 percent in the 1940s to more than 91 percent in the 1990s and up to the present time. Initiatives in recent years to eradicate illiteracy in Mexico have been thwarted by recent surges in drug-related violence and growth in juvenile delinquency. Despite efforts to eradicate illiteracy, there are drastic differences in illiteracy rates among the Mexican states. To illustrate, with a 97 percent literacy rate, Distrito Federál (i.e., Mexico City metropolitan area) ranks 1 of 32 in terms of literacy. In contrast, the literacy rate of Chiapas, a state with a large rural population located in southern Mexico, has a literacy rate of 78 percent. To make matters worse, a huge gap exists between males and females, where males have a literacy rate of 83 percent compared to slightly over 70 percent for females—a 13 percent discrepancy. These data are indicative of the rather lackluster schooling for children of rural families compared to children of urban families.

Given levels of literacy and school completion comparisons among states of Mexico, it might be useful to compare states in terms of socioeconomic and demographic indicators. In doing so, it is possible to compare states with regard to percentage of indigenous population, socioeconomic marginality rate, and the human development index. The socioeconomic marginality rate is an index of welfare based on ethnic background. This index has been used primarily in Mexico to determine the existence of positive correlations between indigenous populations and poverty. Results in 2003 indicate that states with the greatest number of indigenous citizens—Chiapas, Oaxaca, Puebla, Guerrero, Hidalgo, Campeche, San Luis Potosí, Veracrúz, and Yucatán—have the highest rates of marginality and some of the lowest rates regarding the human development index. States that have the lowest marginality rates or negative marginality rates—such as Distrito Federál, Colima, Sonora, Quintana Roo, and Baja California—tend to have higher human development indices. It should be clear, then, that positive relationships exist in terms of low graduate rates, illiteracy rates, and poor human development indices, and overall poor quality of education.

Similar to literacy comparisons, the states of Mexico also differ in terms of the percentage of children who complete primary, lower secondary, and upper secondary school. For example, the Distrito Federál, where Mexico City is located, ranks 1 of 32 states in terms of percentage of children finishing primary school, as well as the percentages of adolescents completing both lower secondary school and upper secondary school. The states in Mexico that rank the lowest in numbers of students finishing primary and secondary level education include Chiapas, Guanajuato, Guerrero, Michoacán, Oaxaca, and Zacatecas. These five states graduate the fewest number of upper secondary students and therefore send the fewest number of upper secondary school graduates to college or the university.

Tertiary Education

In contrast to primary and secondary education, tertiary education in Mexico follows the model used in the United States. In general, baccalaureate degrees are usually awarded after four years of study. Master's degrees are generally awarded after two further years, and doctoral degrees are awarded after a minimum of three years beyond the master's degree.

There are at least 130 institutions of higher education in Mexico. Nine are public universities, 32 are national autonomous universities, and 42 are private universities. The two most competitive and largest universities in enrollment are the National Autonomous University of Mexico in Mexico City and the University of Guadalajara. Established in 1551 as the Royal and Pontifical University of Mexico, the National Autonomous University of Mexico (which changed its name in 1920) has the largest enrollment of any tertiary institution in North America with over 300,000 students. With an enrollment of over 200,000 students, the University of Guadalajara was established in 1791, making it the second-oldest university in the country. Although these enrollments are high, collectively, they represent a very small proportion of Mexican students who enter college- or university-level education.

Teacher training institutions are available in Mexico. However, several reports in the last two decades have shown that teacher preparation has been inadequate at both the primary and secondary levels (see Santibañez, Vernez, and Razquin 2004). To begin with, teacher training reforms at the college level were enacted in 1999. However, because secondary education curriculum reforms took place in 1993, there were too few teachers to accommodate the curriculum changes at the secondary level. Thus, there was an intermittent period of six years between the secondary school curriculum reforms and the teacher training reform of 1999. There were few formally trained teachers to accommodate the new secondary curriculum during this time. Second, most preservice secondary education students have only finished a high school degree and therefore do not have adequate content knowledge to teach secondary school students. Third, only 60 percent of all teachers at the primary and secondary levels in Mexico have attended a teacher training institution. Of the 40 percent who did not, most have been awarded a college degree and were hired to fill teaching positions as a result of teacher shortages in various parts of the country. Teacher education at the in-service level has also been seen as unsuccessful because all students, regardless of background or experience, must take the same courses and curriculum.

System Economics and Future Prospects

According to the United Nations Development Programme (2010), along with Dominica, Iran, and Malta, total public expenditures on education in Mexico represented 4.8 percent of the gross domestic product (GDP) in 2007. Given the GDP of Mexico at $1.56 trillion, educational expenditure in the country amounts to more than $74.88 billion, about $2,838 per student (total amount equivalent to US dollars divided by 26,382,000, the approximate number of primary and secondary students in the country). It is important to note, however, that the secondary school gross enrollment rate is 80 percent, indicating that attrition rates are not low in Mexico. Accordingly, per student spending in the country is based on the total number of children and adolescents who are required to enroll in primary and secondary school each school year. Mexico ranks 82 of 186 countries in percentage of educational expenditure.

The literacy rate in Mexico has steadily improved

from the middle twentieth century to the present. For individuals between the ages of 15 and 21, literacy was near 90 percent overall in 1990 and steadily increased to 92 percent today. These data are an indication of a rapidly developing expansion of enrollments at all educational levels in the country. These results, however, do not mean that education in Mexico has been effective in leading to a productive and self-sufficient workforce. Clearly, there are a number of tangentially related problems that have affected poor educational conditions in Mexico—one of them being the recent growth in drug trafficking. It is also evident that the education system in Mexico is far from successful in providing educational access and school-to-work options. This issue is most pressing in rural parts of the country. As indicated above, only 86 percent of all students who begin at the primary level are able to complete the lower secondary school level—that is, the basic curriculum. As in other Central American countries, school attendance is disadvantaged as a result of a lack of adequate facilities at schools, which is, again, most prominent in rural parts of the country. Educational improvement initiatives in Mexico include the development of information and communications technology (ICT) that has reduced the burdens for rural children, adolescents, and their families and will most likely assist in keeping students in school through the secondary level.

It is encouraging that international organizations have maintained a long-standing commitment to foster Mexico's educational progress. Although the improvement of secondary education has been a major factor in the improvement of the country's education system, international organizations, such as the World Bank and the Inter-American Bank, have focused primarily on basic education (grades 1 through 9). These organizations have generated funding for resources as a means of alleviating inequities in educational funding. For the past three decades, both organizations have provided anywhere from $500 million to $1.5 billion in loans and technical assistance to the Mexican government in order to improve education at the basic level. In particular, the World Bank issued $300 million in loans to eradicate illiteracy and to improve educational achievement in the most economically vulnerable parts of the country.

At any rate, the most pressing issues in education in Mexico are connected with education quality and the lack of teachers and resources in certain areas—mainly

---

Mexico Education at a Glance

General Information

Capital	Mexico City
Population	108.7 million
Language	Spanish
Adult literacy rate (ages 15 and over)	91%
GDP per capita	US$10,700
Number of phones (landline) per 100 people	18
Number of phones (mobile) per 100 people	43.7
Number of Internet users per 100 people	17.1
Life expectancy at birth (years)	75

Formal Educational Information

Enrollment in primary school (ages 6–11)	13 million
Enrollment in lower and upper secondary school (ages 12–17)	13.2 million
Number of years of compulsory education	12 (ages 6–17)
Primary school student/teacher ratio	27.3
Lower and upper secondary school student/teacher ratio	17.9
Primary school gross enrollment ratio	109%
Secondary school gross enrollment ratio	80%
Tertiary school gross enrollment ratio	24%
Primary school entrants completion rate	100%

Note: Unless otherwise indicated, all data are based on sources from 2011.

---

rural regions. Poor educational quality is evident from low test scores and generally low achievement in all academic domains throughout the country. As shown above, less than 20 percent of all students achieve satisfactory results in mathematics by sixth grade. Poor quality of education is mostly attributed to poor teacher preparation, a short school day (particularly at the primary level), teacher absenteeism (particularly in rural districts), a lack of transition in the curriculum from primary to secondary school, and a generally poor infrastructure. In addition to educational quality, Mexican education suffers from lack of enrollment, particularly at the lower and upper secondary school levels. According to Santibañez, Vernez, and Razquin (2004), this pressing issue is based on both poor supply (lack of teachers and resources) and demand (lack of educational initiative on the part of students and their families). As such, attrition rates in Mexican lower and upper secondary schools are high. Health and wellbeing is another concern that comprises successful educational outcomes in Mexico. The adult prevalence rate of HIV/AIDS is approximately 0.3 percent, with about 160,000 Mexicans living with the condition.

Daniel Ness and Chia-ling Lin

REFERENCES

Central Intelligence Agency. *The CIA World Factbook*. New York: Skyhorse, 2011. https.www.cia.gov/library/publications/the-world-factbook/index.html.

Nation Master. 2011. www.nationmaster.com.

Santibañez, Lucrecia, Georges Vernez, and Paula Razquin. *Education in Mexico: Challenges and Opportunities*. Los Angeles: RAND Corp., 2004.

UNESCO. *Global Education Digest 2012: Comparing Education Statistics Across the World*. Montreal: UNESCO Institute for Statistics, 2012.

———. "Strong Foundations: Early Childhood Care and Education." *Education for All Global Monitoring Report*. Paris: UNESCO, 2006.

UNESCO–IBE. www.ibe.unesco.org/en/worldwide/unesco-regions/latin-america-and-the-caribbean/mexico.html.

United Nations Development Programme. *United Nations Development Report 2010*. New York: Palgrave Macmillan, 2010.

US Department of Labor. *2001 Findings on the Worst Forms of Child Labor*. Washington, DC: Bureau of International Labor Affairs, US Department of Labor, 2002.

World Bank Education Statistics. 2011. www.worldbank.org.

NICARAGUA

Nicaragua is a country located in Central America. The official language is Spanish. Nearly 69 percent of Nicaraguans are of mixed ethnicity, roughly 17 percent are white, 9 percent are black, and 5 percent Amerindian. Approximately 73 percent of the population belong to the Roman Catholic Church, 15 percent are Evangelical, 1.5 percent Moravian, 0.1 percent Episcopal, 1.9 percent profess other religions, and the remaining 8.5 percent no religion.

In the sixteenth century, the Spanish initially conquered and subsequently colonized the region that is now Nicaragua, specifically along the Pacific coast. In the first half of the nineteenth century, the area was occupied by the British. The region of Nicaragua became independent from Spanish colonization in 1821. Subsequently, the colony joined forces with other nearby colonies in the establishment of the United Provinces of Central America. In 1838 the loosely knit confederation fragmented. In the same year, Nicaragua was declared an independent republic. In the latter half of the nineteenth century, both Spanish and British control of the coasts began to wane. As corruption and bribery seemed to play a

role in the Nicaraguan government during the 1970s, the Marxist Sandinista guerrillas steadily increased in power and eventually assumed leadership in 1979 after a fairly brief civil war. The United States showed its opposition to the Sandinista government in the 1980s by sponsoring so-called contra guerrillas to challenge the Sandinista guerrillas. The country held free elections in 1990, 1996, 2001, and 2006.

Unemployment in Nicaragua, which has the third-lowest per capita income in the Western Hemisphere, is rampant.

Educational System

As directed by the Nicaraguan government, all Nicaraguan children and families have a right to a free and public education. Accordingly, schooling was made compulsory between the ages of seven and 17 years. However, because the country's economy is partially agrarian and mostly industrial, schooling has not been enforced in certain parts of the country. In fact, many children of school age are not attending school. According to UNICEF data, 15 percent of all children (18 percent boys and 11 percent girls) are working, most often in agriculturally related settings. The majority of children who are engaged in labor are rural children who most likely live far from schools. Most rural families live in the eastern part of the country along the Caribbean coast.

Nicaraguan children and adolescents attend school from February to November and have the months of December and January off. The curriculum of the educational system in Nicaragua was greatly influenced by the curriculum of Cuba, which emphasizes the importance of the needs of collective society as opposed to that of the individual or family. Therefore, curriculum focused on medicine, agriculture, and technological innovation. So-called classic curriculum was minimized.

At nearly 38 students per teacher per classroom, the primary school student/teacher ratio in Nicaragua is rather large. The student/teacher ratio for secondary school students is not much lower—about 33 students per teacher per classroom. Educational data from 2005 suggest that the primary school gross enrollment ratio is 112 percent but the primary school net enrollment ratio is only 87 percent. This indicates that there are more school-age students in the country than the schools can enroll; yet only 87 out of 100 children of primary age are actually attending school. Moreover, the survival rate to grade 5, according to 2004 data, is only 53.5 percent. The problem in secondary school is even more acute. While the gross enrollment rate for secondary school students is 66 percent, the net enrollment rate is only 43 percent.

Students are unable to attend institutions of higher education in Nicaragua if they fail the *Bachillerato*, an examination given at the end of secondary school. In certain tertiary institutions, students are expected to take an entrance examination. University education is a period of four or five years of study. However, vocational and technical training usually spans two to three years.

There are eight universities in Nicaragua. The National Autonomous University of Nicaragua is the oldest and largest tertiary institution in the country. There are also a number of private technical and vocational institutes in Nicaragua. Teacher training institutes, or normal schools, are located primarily in urban centers, most notably in Managua. The problem with many teacher training facilities is the lack of infrastructure and resources. In addition, courses emphasize nearly all content at the expense of pedagogical technique. The National Council of Universities is an important branch of the Nicaraguan government because it controls the country's planning and development in addition to tertiary education.

System Economics and Future Prospects

According to the United Nations Development Programme (2010), total public expenditures on education in Nicaragua represented 3.1 percent of the gross domestic product (GDP) in 2003. Given the GDP of Nicaragua at $17.34 billion, educational expenditure in the country amounts to more than $537.5 million, about $350 per student (total amount equivalent to US dollars divided by 1,538,000, the approximate number of primary and secondary students in the country). Nicaragua ranks 146 of 186 countries in percentage of educational expenditure.

Despite socialist elements in the Nicaraguan political system that encouraged a strong educational foundation, education in the country is far from adequate. The country ranks one of the lowest in terms of literacy among all Central American and Caribbean nations. The Sandinistas improved the quality of education since they took power in 1979. They spearheaded efforts to improve primary and secondary education in the 1980s and 1990s: primary, secondary, and even tertiary enrollments increased considerably during these years. In fact, their policies helped increase the gross national product for all education levels from that of years past. It is true that the literacy campaign initiative in 1980 greatly reduced illiteracy in the country. Prior to that year, half of the country could not read or write. By the end of the decade, only 23 percent of the country was illiterate. Nevertheless, more needs to be done in eradicating illiteracy in the country and improving literacy within the educational system.

Within the past several decades, the Nicaraguan system of education has sought to improve education in the country. Its goals have been to reach high levels of literacy and education not solely for students' personal gain but for social and national development. Unfortunately, with lack of financial and material resources, partly due to numerous embargoes relating to the conflict with El Salvadoran rebels in the 1980s, the Nicaraguan education system did not improve as fast as those in other nations did. At present, the country is

Nicaragua Education at a Glance

General Information

Capital	Managua
Population	5.6 million
Language	Spanish
Adult literacy rate (ages 15 and over)	67.5%
GDP per capita	US$3,100
Number of phones (landline) per 100 people	3.9
Number of phones (mobile) per 100 people	19.7
Number of Internet users per 100 people	2.5
Life expectancy at birth (years)	71

Formal Educational Information

Enrollment in primary school (ages 7–12)	856,000
Enrollment in lower and upper secondary school (ages 13–17)	682,000
Number of years of compulsory education	11 (ages 7–17)
Primary school student/teacher ratio	35.7
Lower and upper secondary school student/teacher ratio	32.4
Primary school gross enrollment ratio	112%
Secondary school gross enrollment ratio	64%
Tertiary school gross enrollment ratio	17.9%
Primary school entrants completion rate	72%
Child labor (ages 5–14)	15%

Note: Unless otherwise indicated, all data are based on sources from 2011.

grappling with a rapidly growing school-age population but at the same time is ill-supported in terms of financial resources to provide to public schools. The Nicaraguan government as well as international organizations and nongovernmental organizations need to continue their efforts to improve the educational standing of the country through initiatives that will increase potential for the citizens of the country.

Daniel Ness and Chia-ling Lin

REFERENCES

Central Intelligence Agency. *The CIA World Factbook*. New York: Skyhorse, 2011. https.www.cia.gov/library/publications/the-world-factbook/index.html.

Nation Master. 2011. www.nationmaster.com.

UNESCO. *Global Education Digest 2012: Comparing Education Statistics Across the World*. Montreal: UNESCO Institute for Statistics, 2012.

———. "Strong Foundations: Early Childhood Care and Education." *Education for All Global Monitoring Report*. Paris: UNESCO, 2006.

UNESCO–IBE. www.ibe.unesco.org/en/worldwide/unesco-regions/latin-america-and-the-caribbean/nicaragua.html.

United Nations Development Programme. *United Nations Development Report 2010*. New York: Palgrave Macmillan, 2010.

US Department of Labor. *2001 Findings on the Worst Forms of Child Labor*. Washington, DC: Bureau of International Labor Affairs, US Department of Labor, 2002.

World Bank Education Statistics. 2011. www.worldbank.org.

PANAMA

Panama, located in the southern part of North America, is an isthmus that serves as the link between North America and South America. The official language is Spanish, although English is also spoken, and much of the Panamanian population is bilingual. About 70 percent of Panamanians are mestizo, 14 percent Amerindian and mixed (nonwhite), 10 percent white, and 6 percent Amerindian. Roman Catholics make up nearly 85 percent of the population, followed by Protestants at 15 percent.

The Panamanian isthmus, like other nearby regions, was colonized by the Spanish in the sixteenth century. Spanish colonization was difficult due to malaria and other mosquito-borne diseases, piracy by ships of other European countries, and resistance of native peoples. Panama, like its neighbors, remained a colony of Spain for more than 250 years. In 1821 Panama became part of a federation known as the Republic of Gran Colombia, which included the present-day countries of Colombia, Venezuela, and Ecuador. In 1830, upon the dissolution of Gran Colombia, Panama became part of Colombia. Panama seceded from Colombia in 1903, partially due to US involvement in promoting the construction of a canal, and declared its independence. This independence was under the condition of US sovereignty over the strip of land on both sides of the canal, known as the Panama Canal Zone. Construction on the canal lasted from 1904 to 1914. In 1977 the United States agreed to cede the Panama Canal Zone to Panama by 1999. In 2007 Panama embarked on a plan to widen the canal by nearly twice its original width in order to enable very large ships to traverse the canal. The expected completion of the project will be in 2015. The Panamanian economy has a strong services sector. Services in Panama include tourism, the operation of the Panama Canal, banking, and insurance.

Educational System

Public education in Panama began shortly after the country's independence from Colombia in 1903. The education system in Panama seemed to follow the educational trends of the United Sates. For example, education in the United States during and shortly after World War I followed the progressive education model, whereby students engaged in activities that fostered practical connections with industry and society. Panama followed this model during the 1920s and 1930s.

Preprimary education in Panama is not compulsory. With tuition and fees, it is available for parents who can afford it. The preprimary period consists of two to three years of preschool education, the last year of which is equivalent to the Western kindergarten. Compulsory education in Panama lasts for nine years and consists of six grades of primary school and the first three grades of the secondary period.

Students enter primary education at age six and leave at age 15. This nine-year period consists of a basic curriculum devoted to speaking, reading, and writing in Spanish (the official language of the country), basic mathematics, science, history, arts, crafts, and physical education.

Secondary education consists of two levels: a lower secondary, or middle school level, and an upper secondary level that prepares students for tertiary education. Students must graduate from the lower secondary level in order to enroll into upper secondary level schools. Students who complete the lower secondary level without completing the upper secondary level generally end up practicing a vocation or technical trade. As in primary education, the number of students entering secondary education programs between 1960 and 1985 increased more than fourfold.

Tertiary education in Panama includes both public and private education in universities as well as colleges and vocational institutions. According to the United States Education Department, there are nearly 90 institutions of higher education in Panama. Public higher education is less expensive than private tertiary programs, but it is not entirely free. The largest and oldest of the public institutions in Panama is the University of Panama, which was established in 1935. The University of Panama has an enrollment of nearly 75,000 students and more than 25 schools, including the major liberal arts and sciences, medicine, veterinary medicine, education, architecture, dentistry, and even dolphin training. Tertiary education in Panama also includes public and private technical and vocational institutes. Teacher training institutes, or normal schools, are located primarily in the country's urban centers and as faculties and departments of universities and colleges.

System Economics and Future Prospects

According to the United Nations Development Programme (2010), along with the Bahamas, Slovakia, and Benin, total public expenditures on education in Panama represented 3.8 percent of the gross domestic product (GDP) in 2008. Given the GDP of Panama at $44.82 billion, educational expenditure in the country amounts to more than $1.7 billion, about $2,195 per student (total amount equivalent to US dollars divided by 776,000, the approximate number of primary and secondary students in the country). Panama ranks 115 of 186 countries in percentage of educational expenditure.

Education in Panama made great gains since the country's independence in 1903. By 1930, approximately 25 percent of the country's GDP was

---

Panama Education at a Glance

General Information

Capital	Panama City
Population	3.4 million
Language	Spanish, English (14%)
Adult literacy rate (ages 15 and over)	91.9%
GDP per capita	US$8,200
Number of phones (landline) per 100 people	3.9
Number of phones (mobile) per 100 people	19.7
Number of Internet users per 100 people	2.5
Life expectancy at birth (years)	75

Formal Educational Information

Enrollment in primary school (ages 6–11)	401,000
Enrollment in lower and upper secondary school (ages 12–17)	375,000
Number of years of compulsory education	12 (ages 6–15)
Primary school student/teacher ratio	24.7
Lower and upper secondary school student/teacher ratio	15.8
Primary school gross enrollment ratio	111%
Secondary school gross enrollment ratio	70%
Tertiary school gross enrollment ratio	43.9%
Primary school entrants completion rate	97%
Child labor (ages 5–14)	11%

Note: Unless otherwise indicated, all data are based on sources from 2011.

---

allocated for building an educational infrastructure and improving educational access. Primary education increased exponentially from the 1920s to the 1950s. Adult illiteracy dropped from 75 percent after the end of World War I to 70 percent in the mid-1920s to about 25 percent in the mid-1950s. The illiteracy rate of adults dropped to an all-time low in the 1980s and 1990s with only 5 percent illiteracy in urban areas. Rural areas suffered the most in terms of poor schooling and education. This is so for the very same reasons as in other developing nations; poor school infrastructure in rural areas prevents rural populations, who tend to be hemmed in an agrarian economy, from receiving formal education. In Panama these poor, rural populations tend to be indigenous, Amerindian ethnic minorities. It is also worth noting that most of the ethnic minority population that lives in rural regions of the country has children engaged in mostly agricultural labor. UNICEF data indicate that about 11 percent of the population between the ages of five and 14 are engaged in some form of work. Given the high rate of primary school completion, it would seem that most children engaged in labor also go to school.

At the same time, the successful literacy rates in the country are an indication of a rapidly developing expansion of enrollment at all educational levels in the country. As a developing country, Panama, like Trinidad and Tobago, and possibly Costa Rica, has higher numbers of students pursuing tertiary degrees on average than other Central American and Caribbean countries. Also, 97 percent of all primary school students are able to complete the primary level. Despite problems meeting initiatives regarding access for rural populations, literacy and education access are relatively equal for both genders. In order to reach populations with limited or no educational access, Panamanian leaders will need to establish initiatives that fund the development of information and communications technologies, which, in effect, would tap into rural areas that presently are not benefiting from formal education.

Daniel Ness and Chia-ling Lin

REFERENCES

Central Intelligence Agency. *The CIA World Factbook*. New York: Skyhorse, 2011. https.www.cia.gov/library/publications/the-world-factbook/index.html.

Nation Master. 2011. www.nationmaster.com.

UNESCO. *Global Education Digest 2012: Comparing Education Statistics Across the World*. Montreal: UNESCO Institute for Statistics, 2012.

————. "Strong Foundations: Early Childhood Care and Education." *Education for All Global Monitoring Report*. Paris: UNESCO, 2006.

UNESCO–IBE. www.ibe.unesco.org/en/worldwide/unesco-regions/latin-america-and-the-caribbean/panama.html.

United Nations Development Programme. *United Nations Development Report 2010*. New York: Palgrave Macmillan, 2010.

US Department of Labor. *2001 Findings on the Worst Forms of Child Labor*. Washington, DC: Bureau of International Labor Affairs, US Department of Labor, 2002.

World Bank Education Statistics. 2011. www.worldbank.org.

PUERTO RICO

Puerto Rico is an unincorporated territory of the United States. Languages spoken on the island are predominantly Spanish and English. About 80.5 percent of Puerto Ricans are white, 8 percent are black, 0.4 percent Amerindian, 0.2 percent Asian, and nearly 11 percent of other ethnic backgrounds. Roman Catholics make up nearly 85 percent of the population, followed by Protestants at 15 percent.

The island of Puerto Rico was inhabited by native peoples for centuries prior to European colonization. In 1493, after Columbus's second voyage to America, the island was declared a possession of the Spanish crown. Puerto Rico remained under Spanish control for 400 years until the Spanish-American War, when it was ceded to the United States. In 1917 Puerto Ricans were allowed US citizenship status. In 1967, 1993, and 1998, plebiscites were held in which Puerto Rican voters chose to keep their status as US citizens as opposed to the possibility of becoming a US state or an independent country. Today Puerto Rico is a commonwealth of the United States. The executive powers lie with the president of the United States, who is the chief of state. The head of the island's government is a governor. Puerto Rico has one of the largest industrial sectors of the Caribbean islands. The top industries include tourism, pharmaceuticals, electronics, apparel, and food products.

Educational System

Primary and secondary education in Puerto Rico is run by the government's Department of Education. The system is essentially run as it would be in one of the states of the United States. Compulsory education is also similar—students between the ages of five and 18 are required to attend school. The territory contains about 2,100 primary and secondary schools of which about 1,500 are public and 600 are private (mostly Catholic or parochial). At 94 percent, the literacy rate on the island is perhaps the lowest among the US territories.

At present, there are about 526,000 students on the island, of whom about 372,000 are primary school students and 260,000 are in the age range for secondary school. However, it is estimated that only 154,000 actually attend secondary school. These numbers may indicate that the drop in secondary school students is due to a high attrition rate at secondary grade levels. There are a total of nearly 72,000 school staff members, of whom almost 41,000 are teachers. The rest are support staff and administrators.

Puerto Rico is the only region in the United States in which instruction is given in a language other than English, namely, Spanish. English became the dominant language after the US occupation in 1898. But Spanish reemerged as the dominant language during World War I and has remained the dominant language ever since. Both primary and secondary schools in Puerto Rico are subject to the same federal mandates as the states. For example, in the 1990s, schools in Puerto Rico were expected to participate in Goals 2000 initiatives; in the following decade, in No Child Left Behind regulations; and subsequently, in Race to the Top.

There are approximately 25 institutions of higher education in Puerto Rico. Established in 1903, the largest university is the University of Puerto Rico, with an enrollment of over 60,000 students. It is ranked as one of the best universities in the Caribbean. Teacher training programs are affiliated with certain colleges and universities on the island. In general, as in the 50 states, students in Puerto Rico who want to become teachers must receive a baccalaureate before eligibility for certification.

System Economics and Future Prospects

According to recent figures, the gross domestic product of Puerto Rico amounts to nearly $65 billion. It is estimated that expenditures in education in Puerto Rico during the 2007 academic year amounted to $3.268 billion and that per student spending amounted to about $6,000.

Education in Puerto Rico has faced a number of difficult problems in the past 10 years. To begin with, in 2002, Victor Fajardo, the secretary of the Department of Education of Puerto Rico was involved in a major scandal in which he was convicted of embezzling federal funds allocated for schooling which he used instead to finance political campaigns. These funds were supposed to be used to improve the technological infrastructure of schools on the island and to train teachers in using technology. In addition, this incident may have indirectly contributed, at least in part, to a deficit of three-quarters of a billion dollars in 2005.

Another problem in the territory is attrition. It is estimated that nearly 100,000 secondary school students drop out of school every year. This occurs for a variety of reasons, ranging from the need to earn a living to the belief that schooling is unimportant. Many rural students of Puerto Rico drop out of school so that they can help their families in farm related duties. Indeed, the economic problems after 2007 dampened the educational prospects of many students, given that tertiary education on the island is not free.

Daniel Ness and Chia-ling Lin

Puerto Rico Education at a Glance

General Information

Capital	San Juan
Population	3.9 million
Languages	Spanish, English
Adult literacy rate (ages 15 and over)	94.1%
GDP per capita	US$19,300
Number of phones (landline) per 100 people	28.2
Number of phones (mobile) per 100 people	68
Number of Internet users per 100 people	25.4
Life expectancy at birth (years)	79

Formal Educational Information

Enrollment in primary school (ages 6–11)	372,000
Secondary school age individuals (ages 12–17)	260,000
Number of years of compulsory education	12 (ages 6–17)
Combined primary/secondary school student/teacher ratio	13.8
Primary school gross enrollment ratio (1998)	129%
Secondary school gross enrollment ratio	66%
Tertiary school gross enrollment ratio	41.4%
Primary school entrants completion rate	no data

Note: Unless otherwise indicated, all data are based on sources from 2011.

REFERENCES

Central Intelligence Agency. *The CIA World Factbook.* New York: Skyhorse, 2011. https.www.cia.gov/library/publications/the-world-factbook/index.html.

Nation Master. 2011. www.nationmaster.com.

National Center for Education Statistics. *The Digest of Education Statistics.* Washington, DC: US Department of Education, 2011.

UNESCO. *Global Education Digest 2012: Comparing Education Statistics Across the World.* Montreal: UNESCO Institute for Statistics, 2012.

———. "Strong Foundations: Early Childhood Care and Education." *Education for All Global Monitoring Report.* Paris: UNESCO, 2006.

UNESCO–IBE. www.ibe.unesco.org/en/worldwide/unesco-regions/europe-and-north-america/united-states.html.

United Nations Development Programme. *United Nations Development Report 2010.* New York: Palgrave Macmillan, 2010.

US Department of Labor. *2001 Findings on the Worst Forms of Child Labor.* Washington, DC: Bureau of International Labor Affairs, US Department of Labor, 2002.

World Bank Education Statistics. 2011. www.worldbank.org.

TRINIDAD AND TOBAGO

Trinidad and Tobago constitute a Caribbean island nation located about 12.5 miles (20 kilometers) off the coast of Venezuela. The official language is English, but Caribbean Hindustani, French, Spanish, and Chinese are also common. The population estimate for 2011 was 1.2 million. Based on the 2000 census, about 40 percent of all Trinidadians and Tobagonians are Indian (from South Asia), 37.5 percent are African, 20.5 percent are of mixed ancestry, and 2 percent are unspecified. As in other Caribbean island nations, Trinidad and Tobago's religions are diverse. Approximately 26 percent of the residents are Roman Catholic, 22.5 percent Hindu, nearly 8 percent Anglican, 7 percent Baptist, 7 percent Pentecostal, 5.8 percent Muslim, 4 percent Seventh Day Adventist, almost 6 percent from another Protestant Christian sect, and 14 percent categorized as other, unspecified, or none.

Trinidad and Tobago was first colonized by the Spanish in the sixteenth century. For the next several centuries, the islands became increasingly profitable as a strong sugar-producing colony. By the early 1800s, the islands were controlled by Great Britain. Sugar production waned after 1834, when slavery was banned. To increase sugar production, Great Britain shipped laborers from India to the islands. This move subsequently helped not only sugar production but the cocoa industry as well. Oil was discovered in Trinidad (as well as nearby Venezuela) in 1910 and further increased the colony's natural wealth. Trinidad and Tobago was declared independent in 1962 and remains one of the Caribbean's most economically flourishing countries, due to its rich petroleum production. Tourism also has become a major industry in the country, particularly on the island of Tobago.

Educational System

The Trinidad and Tobago public educational system has been modeled on the educational system of the United Kingdom. Private and parochial schools are available, however, for a fee. Compulsory education in Trinidad and Tobago, consisting of both primary and lower secondary school, lasts for 11 years and serves children between the ages of five and 16 years.

The country's literacy rate of nearly 99 percent represents one of the highest in the region, which includes the Caribbean, Central America, and northern South America.

Although children begin primary schooling at five years of age, Trinidadian and Tobagonian children in preschool have a greater level of content instruction than do preschoolers in other regions of the world. They learn to read and write at much earlier ages than their North, Central, and South American counterparts.

At five years old, students begin formal primary school and remain in this period of schooling for seven years. Unlike most educational systems in the world, Trinidad and Tobago sanctions exit examinations for the primary school level. As discussed below, exit examination practice plays a major part of the Trinidad and Tobagonian educational system. In fact, the Caribbean Examinations Council, a special government organization, controls the testing and assessment of students in the country. This examination, the Secondary Entrance Examination, determines which secondary school Trinidadian and Tobagonian children will attend.

Secondary school in Trinidad and Tobago is a schooling period that lasts for at least five years. At the end of the secondary school period, students must register to take the Caribbean Secondary Education Certificate (CSEC) examinations or the General Certificate of Education "O" ("ordinary") level, which is still administered in other British Commonwealth countries and was the equivalent examination taken in the United Kingdom prior to 1988. Students with high scores on the CSEC examination may opt to remain in secondary school and enter the upper secondary school level for two years. At the end of this two-year period, students are eligible to take the Caribbean Advanced Proficiency Examination (CAPE) or the United Kingdom equivalent—the General Certificate of Education "A" ("advanced") level.

Tertiary education in Trinidad and Tobago is free to all students to the baccalaureate level who successfully pass the CAPE or the British equivalent examination. Some postgraduate degrees are free, depending on the area that the federal government is subsidizing at a particular time. The universities in the country include the University of the West Indies (with a campus in the town of St. Augustine), the University of the Southern Caribbean in Port of Spain, and the

University of Trinidad and Tobago in Wallerfield. Students who exit lower secondary school have the option of attending other educational institutions that emphasize vocational and technical training as well as professional studies. These institutions include the College of Science, Technology and Applied Arts of Trinidad and Tobago (the polytechnic institute of the country), the School of Business and Computer Science, the School of Accounting and Management, BorderCom International, Roytec, and the Trinidad and Tobago Hospitality and Tourism Institute. The government of Trinidad and Tobago also subsidizes students from less affluent families who have high academic potential.

Teacher training is available at the university level. All teachers must have a qualification from an accredited university or related institution of higher education in order to be eligible to teach in the country. There are different gradations of teachers in Trinidad and Tobago. In other words, teachers begin with the title of "assistant teacher" and eventually become "teacher" when they have more experience. Assistant Teacher II teachers need a minimum of five levels of mathematics, English, and science at the "Ordinary" level in order to be eligible for certification. At the next level, Assistant Teacher III, teachers need a minimum of five levels at the "Ordinary" level in English and mathematics. They must also successfully pass the Caribbean Examination Council's examinations that will make them eligible for "Advanced" levels. These teachers must also specialize in a field of interest.

System Economics and Future Prospects

According to the United Nations Development Programme (2010), along with South Korea and Malawi, total public expenditures on education in Trinidad and Tobago represented 4.2 percent of the gross domestic product (GDP) in 2002. Given the GDP of Trinidad and Tobago at $27.1 billion, educational expenditure in the country amounts to more than $1.138 billion, about $5,197 per student (total amount equivalent to US dollars divided by 219,000, the approximate number of primary and secondary students in the country). Trinidad and Tobago ranks 102 of 186 countries in percentage of educational expenditure.

Trinidad and Tobago Education at a Glance

General Information

Capital	Port of Spain
Population	1.2 million
Languages	English, Caribbean Hindustani, French, Spanish, Chinese
Adult literacy rate (ages 15 and over)	98.6%
GDP per capita	US$19,800
Number of phones (landline) per 100 people	30.6
Number of phones (mobile) per 100 people	75.7
Number of Internet users per 100 people	15.1
Life expectancy at birth (years)	67

Formal Educational Information

Enrollment in primary school (ages 5–11)	121,000
Enrollment in lower and upper secondary school (ages 12–16)	98,000
Number of years of compulsory education	11 (ages 5–16)
Primary school student/teacher ratio	17.5
Lower and upper secondary school student/teacher ratio	19.4
Primary school gross enrollment ratio	100%
Secondary school gross enrollment ratio	81%
Tertiary school gross enrollment ratio	12.1%
Primary school entrants completion rate	91%
Child labor (ages 5–14)	1%

Note: Unless otherwise indicated, all data are based on sources from 2011.

Trinidad and Tobago is by far the leading country in the Caribbean and Central American region in terms of educational productivity, literacy, numeracy, and overall school-to-work success. The Trinidad and Tobago government's promotion and advocacy of education for its youth have contributed to the country's overall economic success in the region. Education is free for all children and adolescents between the ages of three and 21, or when a student completes a baccalaureate. Given the country's relatively small area, most Trinidadians and Tobagonians, whether urban or rural, have adequate access to send their children to school. Rather than the government using information and communication technologies for the purpose of reaching distant populations of students (as in other countries in the region), students engage in these technologies as an academic endeavor or as a means of becoming adept in their use and applications as well as in their engineering and construction.

Daniel Ness and Chia-ling Lin

REFERENCES

Central Intelligence Agency. *The CIA World Factbook*. New York: Skyhorse, 2011. https.www.cia.gov/library/publications/the-world-factbook/index.html.

Nation Master. 2011. www.nationmaster.com.

UNESCO. *Global Education Digest 2012: Comparing Education Statistics Across the World*. Montreal: UNESCO Institute for Statistics, 2012.

———. "Strong Foundations: Early Childhood Care and Education." *Education for All Global Monitoring Report*. Paris: UNESCO, 2006.

UNESCO–IBE. www.ibe.unesco.org/en/worldwide/unesco-regions/latin-america-and-the-caribbean/trinidad-and-tobago.html.

United Nations Development Programme. *United Nations Development Report 2010*. New York: Palgrave Macmillan, 2010.

US Department of Labor. *2001 Findings on the Worst Forms of Child Labor*. Washington, DC: Bureau of International Labor Affairs, US Department of Labor, 2002.

World Bank Education Statistics. 2011. www.worldbank.org.

UNITED STATES OF AMERICA

The United States, a constitutionally based federal republic, has one of the largest educational systems in the world. The most frequently spoken language is English (82.1 percent), followed by Spanish (10.7 percent), other Indo-European dialects (3.8 percent), and languages from East Asia (2.7 percent). The ethnicity is 81.7 percent white, 12.9 percent black, 4.2 percent Asian, and 1 percent Amerindian and Alaska native. The census of the United States must take into account populations having more than one ethnic background in future estimates. More than half of the population are members of one of the Protestant sects, 24 percent are Roman Catholic, 2 percent Mormon, 1 percent Jewish, 1 percent Muslim, 10 percent follow other religions, and 10 percent none. There are nearly 1 million Americans living with HIV/AIDS (0.6 percent among American adults). Although the number of cases gradually decreased since 2000, the trend seems to be changing, with an ever-increasing number of new cases since 2007.

History of Education in the United States

The history of education in the United States can generally be divided into three periods: (1) from the colonial era to the 1830s; (2) from the commencement of public education in the 1830s, propelled by the educational reformer Horace Mann, to World War II; and (3) since World War II, a period highlighted by the GI Bill of Rights in 1944 and the Supreme Court's *Brown v. Board of Education* decision in 1954, both landmark events that contributed greatly to an increase in the number of people entering both K–12 education and higher education institutions.

Early American Education (1607–1835)

Education was a staple in American life since the early colonial period. With the exclusion of Spanish colonization of the Americas, early colonial America was populated mainly by English, Dutch, French, and Swedish settlers—with the overwhelming majority from England. English settlers were diverse in terms of religious belief as well as the purpose for leaving the mother country. The early colonists who were members of the Virginia company left England in an effort to increase wealth, while the early colonists of New England left the mother country as a result of religious conflict and persecution of the Puritans—a radical Calvinist sect—by the Anglican Church. Regardless, however, of the purpose of exodus, American colonists established institutions of education shortly after their arrival and creation of settlements in the colonies.

It should be noted that the schools of the fledgling American republic were founded and patronized by the political and social elite. Schools were seen as both free and public, but not in the way that twenty-first-century Americans construe the terms. The terms "free" and "public" did not mean free for all people in the United States. Schooling was not free for slaves or children of people who could not afford it. "Free" meant that school was open to all, that is, the "public," who could afford an education. In fact, a number of politicians and thinkers of the early republic believed that receiving an education was for the most part determined by the will of the head of the household to send children (mostly sons) to school. Thomas Jefferson, for example, a leading proponent of education, argued that a society that compels school for all children against the will of the parents would be worse than parents who refuse to send their children to school. In sum, the meaning of free and public schooling in the early years of the United States had an entirely different meaning than it does today.

It should also be noted that schooling that was "free" and "public" in the eighteenth- and early nineteenth-century meanings of the terms was by no means secular. In fact, the notion of schooling and education at that time meant not simply becoming a literate individual but also a religious and moral one as well. In fact, members of the Continental Congress of 1785 argued that religion and morality, in addition to knowledge, were fundamental to a strong central government and a growing and developing society.

The Need for an Educational System

From the founding of the fledgling government in the early 1780s to the first years of the Jackson presidency in the late 1820s, moderate to severe economic recessions occurred every two to five years. The United States suffered a severe economic panic in 1825 as stocks crashed due to unsound American land investments in Latin America. Another panic occurred toward the end of the 1820s as a result of the English Crown's decision to forbid American trade with British colonies. Poor economic conditions, compounded by a dramatic increase in European immigrants, particularly from Germany and Ireland, hastened the commonly accepted need for a literate and well-informed citizenry. One major goal of the creators of the US Constitution was to equip the country's citizens with knowledge for both obtaining a vocation and promoting self-government. However, it took nearly 40 years for interest in public education to become a central issue. Demand for public schooling crested in the 1830s—the height of the Jacksonian presidency. Working parents insisted on the establishment of free schools so that their children would have the same opportunities to succeed in society as the children of wealthy families. The Workingmen's Party of Philadelphia made education a key issue in 1830 by insisting that public schooling would increase access to economic opportunity and, at the same time, reduce crime and possibly eliminate poverty.

The Early Nineteenth-Century American School Context

Prior to the onset of compulsory education in America, schools were erratic and unpredictable places depending on the context and setting. One fact that is surprising today, but at the same time self-evident is that schooling, especially in northern states where temperatures fell below freezing during the winter, often lasted for just three to four months out of the year. Rarely would the school year begin before April and end after October—quite the contrary to the academic school year today. In places like northern New York or western Massachusetts, the school year would perhaps begin in June and end in September. During that period, it was normal for a teacher to board with the family of each of the children of the school, perhaps a week at a time per family. Teachers were poorly paid, almost as low as unskilled manual laborers. Female teachers were paid less than male teachers. Corporal punishment in the form of flogging was the norm, so much so that in numerous instances when flogging was extensive, rebellions would often break out between parents and teachers. Education laws were lax, and almost no regulations associated with schooling were followed. Although education was for affluent individuals in the North, schools in the South were even more elitist than in the North; schooling was only for children of individuals who could afford it and who wanted it.

American Education from 1835 to World War II

Schooling in the eighteenth century and the first two decades of the nineteenth century accommodated, for the most part, students whose families could afford it. Education was primarily a means to prepare clergy, lawyers, and political leaders. The notion of schooling as a means for growing an economy and for competing in a so-called global marketplace was not remotely an issue at the time for most Americans.

Horace Mann and Compulsory Education

The leaders of Massachusetts had required towns to maintain schools since the 1630s—the early years of the Massachusetts colony. The first indications of a statewide school system in the United States occurred in the 1830s with a movement for public education led by Horace Mann, a Massachusetts attorney. Mann, an abolitionist, changed the conception of "free" and "public" when it came to education. Albeit not exactly the same in meaning as we think today, the notion of free and public education for Mann meant the improvement of society through a strong national economy and industrial base. To achieve this goal, Mann believed, required a more open education that required more children to enroll in schools. Initially, Mann sponsored the establishment of a Massachusetts state board of education and subsequently served as its secretary. Not only did he spearhead the notion of free education for the masses, but he also led the creation of the first state-run normal school for the training of teachers in Lexington, Massachusetts. He also established a Massachusetts state association for teachers and a minimum school year of six months for the children and adolescents of the Commonwealth of Massachusetts. Mann's primary impetus for urging the creation and promotion of a public school system was his premise that schooling for all children would lead to social stability and economic opportunities.

Based on his 12 reports to the Massachusetts state government, Mann proposed his philosophy of education and what he regarded as most important in terms of what students should learn—the curriculum—and how they should learn it. As seen clearly in these reports, Mann was a progenitor of the pragmatist approach to education. He strongly believed in the necessity of a curriculum that corresponded to the students' lives as adults and their rights and responsibilities as informed citizens. For example, rather than progressing from arithmetic to algebra, Mann believed that after learning arithmetic, students should apply these skills toward a specific occupation, such as bookkeeping, surveying, or engineering. He also disparaged recitation and other forms of rote learning, specifically as it is associated with the learning of language. Curiously, although there was a clear separation of church and state as identified in the Constitution, Mann argued for Christian religious instruction, but using a nondenominational approach. In his seventh report, Mann urged that the United States adopt the Prussian method of instruction, particularly the approach that Mann himself observed when he visited Prussia. This method involved the training of teachers, the

requirement for all students to attend kindergarten, student testing and assessment, and a set curriculum for each grade level. Mann faced constant criticism and opposition from a number of groups. Boston schoolteachers, for example, argued that he was out of touch with the everyday happenings of the classroom. Although the country was moving into a preindustrial economy, particularly in the North, much of the region remained agrarian. Farmers were reluctant to lose their children's labor to an extended school calendar. Taxpayers did not want to pay for better school buildings, teachers, books, and the normal schools. In addition, given many Americans' negative attitudes toward Europe, any comparison of European models as exceeding the levels of American methods, regardless of subject, was viewed as offensive by a number of his opponents. Also, members of various Christian denominations objected to the generalized Christianity he had proposed.

Despite several years of criticism, other states and other governments consulted Mann about establishing public educational systems. Education leaders from Great Britain, for example, admired his approach to universal compulsory education. His legacy is clearly evident not only in the United States but around the world. Although there has always been an American suspicion of state-funded welfare programs, Mann's promulgation of universal compulsory education proved to be one such program that Americans in general have agreed to live with.

Although slow to respond to Mann's initiative in the North (clearly in response to sectional disputes prior to and during the American Civil War), North Carolina was the key state in the South to lead efforts in the movement toward state-supported education. By the 1860s, nearly two-thirds of the state's white school-age population attended school, on average, for four months out of the year, much less time than in Massachusetts during the same period. This was due to the fact that North Carolina's economy relied heavily on children's assistance in agriculture and farming. Unlike the northern states in antebellum America, there was a general sentiment in favor of an aristocratic class. Although the South had a higher number of college graduates than any other region of the country, it produced far fewer public school students. Moreover, the number of illiterate white students in the South exceeded half a million, far greater than those in the North.

It is important to note that Mann's educational initiative was also in response to the mass migration of people from Europe, predominantly Ireland and Germany, who fled their mother countries due to famine and poor economic conditions. Schooling, thought Mann and other political leaders in the North, would provide a sense of Americanization for newly arriving immigrants; it would help the economy by providing both a moral and intellectual program for creating an effective American workforce. To accommodate the largest immigration of Catholics in United States history, both public and Catholic parochial schools opened in nearly all urban centers and townships throughout the North. As a result of autonomy given to school leaders, many of whom were recent immigrants, schooling ruled by the elite was soon modified so that more control was given to the general citizenry.

Education in the United States During the Late Nineteenth Century

Although American public education in its inception was led by individuals with highly optimistic views of education for the masses, it was far from ideal. The spread of public education from the years immediately following the American Civil War to the period after World War I was primarily due to an effort to "Americanize" children of immigrants. As a result of more citizen control of schools and education in general, by the late nineteenth century local school boards, not politicians or elites, governed schools. During this time, schools were dependent on city councils for financial stability. School districts were generally small, but by 1890 there were over 120,000 of them. Immigrants saw schooling as a means for upward economic mobility. As a result, first- and second-generation immigrants attempted to take control of most urban school boards. Irish immigrants were the most dominant group. Most Irish immigrants' first language was English, so they had an advantage in this regard over other groups. They were often the leaders of school boards in Boston, Chicago, and San Francisco. Jewish leaders held sway in the education system in New York City.

By the 1890s, nearly all Americans finished elementary school. By the first two decades of the twentieth century, the number of students graduating from secondary school was growing at a rapid rate. More-

over, there was a great deal of competition among new high schools that were cropping up in towns throughout the country. In general, this competition, along with a decentralized and overall democratic system, dramatically improved the American educational system and made it one of the most successful systems in the world. Nevertheless, by the end of the nineteenth century, language and mathematics curricula consisted primarily of rote memorization and sentence diagramming. Students had little exposure to concepts and inquiry. This was to change with the progressive education movement.

The Early Twentieth Century and Progressivism in Education

The work of John Dewey had a profound effect on schooling in turn-of-the-century America. For one thing, Dewey and other so-called progressive educators claimed that learning by recitation or rote memorization was the wrong way to gain knowledge. Instead, in addition to reading, students must engage in the act of learning for its own sake. In other words, phonics was replaced by whole-word recognition (a debate that has continued to the present), and mathematics learning went from memorization of times tables to more hands-on and visual practice that fostered concepts. Progressive educators were also interested in increasing student preparation for the workforce. Girls were trained in home economics, such as sewing and cooking, while boys were engaged in mechanical training, metal- and woodworking (called "industrial arts" in the late twentieth century), and agricultural studies.

In a way, the situation in the United States paralleled efforts in France to prepare children of rural French, mostly agrarian, families for life and work in Paris. Intentions for the development of the first intelligence test are a case in point. Alfred Binet (1857–1911), the inventor of the well-known intelligence quotient (IQ), devised the first intelligence test with the goal of identifying the intellectual strengths and weaknesses of young French children whose families migrated to the cities in order to find employment in industry and commerce. Based on the individual test results, a child would be placed in the appropriate educational school and environment for future preparation.

Some, but not all, progressive educators of the

early twentieth century espoused the notion of individual differences in learning, arguing that some students were born with more aptitude than others. Unfortunately, the American situation diverged from the French case; Binet and his colleagues and political supporters were not concerned with IQ in terms of hereditary disposition while the American educators were. A number of Americans, on the other hand, believed that children were born with different IQs and therefore needed to be educated differently. This belief among American educators, political leaders, and some psychologists led to some of the gloomiest periods in American history. Racism became rampant. African American and immigrant men, mostly those from southern and eastern Europe, were sent to the front lines during World War I because they generally performed more poorly than did those from northern European countries on IQ tests, which was almost entirely an indication of cultural differentiation and not intellectual ability.

American Education Since World War II

As a result of a number of educational initiatives after World War II, American education, many education scholars would argue, became the leading international education system. One of these initiatives was the GI Bill of 1944. This bill allowed veterans returning from World War II the opportunity to receive higher education and enabled those without a secondary education to graduate from high school with the newly created General Education Development (GED) degree. This federally subsidized education helped veterans compete in a growing workforce that essentially demanded new skills for each subsequent decade. This period also saw tremendous growth in infrastructure. Never before in United States history was there so much primary and secondary school construction throughout the country. In addition, more and more people settled in areas of the country that were at one time considered desolate regions but are currently booming and growing rapidly in terms of population (e.g., Clark County, Nevada and Maricopa County, Arizona). According to the National Center for Education Statistics (2011), the total number of elementary and secondary schools in the United States reached 93,295.

In addition to these initiatives, the Supreme Court case of *Brown v. Board of Education* in 1954 changed the course of American education in terms of race and civil rights. It can be argued that this case had a major impact on the civil rights movement in the years that followed. The court declared that the separation of schools based on race—in other words, separate schools for black and white children—was unconstitutional. This decision dramatically changed the direction of education in years to come. There was one major problem, however: although de jure segregation on the basis of race was struck down, de facto segregation continued. The ensuing civil rights movement helped strike down de facto segregation; nevertheless, it still exists to a lesser degree in certain regions of the country.

It appears that another major education shift is anticipated—especially given economic downturns during the latter part of the first decade of this century. At present, education leaders and politicians are grappling with controversial issues that will affect American youth and the education system in some way. These individuals are presently debating the role of various educational constituents and whether they foster or thwart educational progress. The following questions are currently being debated in the United States. What role will education and teacher unions (and unions in general) play in years to come? If education unions are vulnerable to collapse, what will be the direction of American education? Will schools become for-profit institutions? What changes will occur in how teachers are trained? What is the future of public education as we know it? Will any other model of schooling take its place? And if so, what will it be, and will it be more beneficial than the status quo?

The answers to these questions are unclear. What is known, however, is that the systems of government in the United States have mechanisms that attempt to delay any immediate change that may occur, and if immediate change does occur, people have the right to vote against it.

Educational System

With a population that surpassed the 300 million mark in 2006, the United States of America is one of the world leaders in educational infrastructure, technology, curriculum, and policy. There are over 120,000 kindergarten through grade 12 (henceforth,

K–12) schools in the United States, and approximately 100,000 of them are public institutions. With nearly 3,500 colleges and universities, the United States has the largest system of higher and adult education in the world. Public K–12 institutions in the United States are largely funded by local and state governments that obtain the overwhelming majority of public education funds through residential property taxes. Since the late 1970s, federal budgets have steadily increased funding that has been earmarked for education. Although school districts and communities generally welcome federal funding, they resist federal control of public schools and are strongly in favor of local control.

Precompulsory and Compulsory Education

Compulsory schooling throughout the United States commences with kindergarten, for children approximately five years of age. School attendance prior to the kindergarten level—such as nursery school or preschool—is not compulsory. Nevertheless, 64 percent (nearly two-thirds) of all American children attend preschool prior to kindergarten. The 12 grades of compulsory education are divided into various configurations depending on the state, county, school district, or smaller administrative unit. In some districts and administrative units, primary school consists of grade 1 through 8, followed by high school, which consists of grades 9 through 12. In others, grades 1 through 4 is primary school, 5 through 8 is middle school, and 9 through 12 comprises high school. In yet another configuration, grades 1 through 6 is primary school, 7 through 8 or 7 through 9 is junior high school, and 9 through 12 or 10 through 12 (depending on whether junior high school is two or three years in duration) is high school.

Postcompulsory Education

Postcompulsory education in the United States is tertiary education, mostly in the form of colleges and universities. Colleges and universities may be public or private as well as nonprofit or for-profit institutions.

The two-year community college is an American invention that was conceived in the late nineteenth century and came to fruition in 1901 with the opening of Joliet Junior College in Joliet, Illinois. The American community college has historically been an economic boon for the United States because it has served as the educational backbone of the nation's industrial and professional workforce. There are more community colleges in the United States than in any other country. After World War II, with the passing of the GI Bill, community colleges were teeming with students, many of whom were former military personnel. In addition, the Higher Education Act of 1965 made higher education much more accessible. Accordingly, there was dramatic growth in the number of community colleges built in the United States from the 1950s through the 1970s. Traditionally, the purpose of the American community college was twofold: to prepare academically inclined students for transfer to four-year colleges or universities or to prepare students for technical and vocational training and subsequent entry into the workforce. Within the last two decades, a new purpose emerged: to prepare students for lifelong learning and continuing education.

The United States has also been a world leader in its universities. The Quacquarelli Symonds (QS) World University Rankings in 2010 show that 106 of the leading 600 world universities are in the United States—more than one-sixth of the world's leading universities. The QS World University top 20 ranking includes 13 universities in the United States: Harvard University, Yale University, Massachusetts Institute of Technology, University of Chicago, California Institute of Technology, Princeton University, Columbia University, University of Pennsylvania, Stanford University, Duke University, University of Michigan, Cornell University, and Johns Hopkins University.

In addition to the community college, the comprehensive university was in many respects an American invention. Comprehensive universities were an outgrowth of land-grant universities that were labeled as such because they were given federal funds to promote programs outside the realm of a classical education—the dominant curriculum of colleges and universities before 1850—but not necessarily excluding it. Due to changes in social class, a growing economy, and a burgeoning industrial base, the Morrill Land-Grant Acts of 1862 and 1890 allowed for the infusion of finances to a select number of eastern universities to promote agricultural science, engineering, and professional studies that require advanced scientific methods. Shortly thereafter, a number of land-grant universities were founded in the Midwest and Far West. The first land-grant university was Michigan State University, followed by Pennsylvania State University in 1855. The oldest land-grant university is Rutgers University in New Brunswick, New Jersey. Established in 1766, Rutgers University became a land-grant institution in 1864. Cornell University was established as a land-grant university when it was founded in 1865, serving as the only land-grant institution in New York. The entire University of California system is based on the land-grant model.

Curriculum, Assessment, and Instruction

American curriculum, assessment, and instruction are constructs that are difficult to generalize because they are so diverse and depend on the school setting and mission of the educational institution. For example, the curriculum practices of most American public schools differ from those of parochial schools precisely because their missions are different; parochial schools are not public and therefore do not receive local, state, or federal funds. They are almost entirely dependent on their communities, small to large tuitions, and more or less centralized organizations (e.g., Catholic dioceses, National Council of Churches for Protestant schools, or Hillel for Jewish schools) that may offer financial support.

American curriculum and instructional practices also differ based on geographic location. Some states require all or most of the students in the state to use the same textbooks, chosen in part thanks to the capitalist enterprise of textbook publishers who exhibit their publications to the state education departments for their approval. These states, mostly in the South and West, include Alabama, Arkansas, California, Florida, Georgia, Idaho, Indiana, Kentucky, Louisiana, Mississippi, Nevada, New Mexico, North Carolina, Oklahoma, Oregon, South Carolina, Tennessee, Texas, Utah, Virginia, and West Virginia. States that do not have textbook adoption policies grant local districts the autonomy to select textbooks.

American curriculum within the last several decades also reflects changes related to the influx of immigrants of different religious backgrounds, changes in law, changes related to technology and the Internet,

and changes of emphasis based on educational significance. Civics, which was at one time considered an essential subject, has been modified and diversified; the subject presently consists of separate secondary school courses in government, history, and geography. The mathematics curriculum traditionally emphasized calculus as the capstone mathematics course in the last year of high school and as the gateway subject for college-level credit. Other mathematical subjects, such as statistics and computer mathematics, have recently taken the place of calculus or at least have served as a substitute. Theoretical physics, which was at one time the capstone natural science course, lessened in significance. Integrated science subjects, such as organic chemistry and earth and marine or environmental science, have served as substitutes.

Methods of instruction in the United States have varied greatly in the last few decades. From the early days of compulsory education to the 1970s, classrooms were mostly teacher-centered. In other words, the process of teaching and learning centered on the teacher, who had sole authority in presenting content to students. By the 1970s, with a growing interest in how the mind and brain acquire knowledge and how people learn in general, classrooms had become more student-centered and knowledge-centered. This form of instruction was greatly influenced by the theories of Jean Piaget. A decade later, research centered on social psychological theories (predominantly those of Lev Vygotsky) showed that student learning was most productive when teachers provide assistance rather than bestowing information; in other words, best practice suggests that teachers present a topic and then support and encourage students to engage in inquiry. Modes of instruction have changed as well. Information and communication technologies have transformed the ways in which students learn, and they are being modified as time progresses.

Each state has its own set of forms of assessment for students. Most states have a set of examinations in at least three subjects—usually English, mathematics, and natural science—from grade 3 to grade 6, the last three or four years of elementary school. These states also mandate end-of-year examinations in most subjects in middle school and high school. It is important to note that local and state tests often fail to demonstrate student academic potential. Assessments are made easier because school district leaders do not want to show poor quality in student performance. As a result, student test scores have increased dramatically. This inappropriate conduct on the part of school principals, district superintendents, and other educational authorities reached its peak under the Bush administration's No Child Left Behind law, when districts would be denied funding and forced to close schools for alleged poor performance. Evidence of increased test scores can be demonstrated by comparing student test scores from the National Assessment of Educational Progress (NAEP), a national test in English, mathematics, and science, with the same students' scores on state examinations. Results indicate a large gap between state and national assessments: scores on the NAEP examination are much lower than those on individual state examinations.

Teacher Education

All states require that teachers receive a minimum of an undergraduate education and earn a baccalaureate prior to full-time teaching. Moreover, each state in the Union has its own requirements regarding specific emphases, depending on the grade level or subject of interest. Nearly all state education departments emphasize teacher training credentialing and accreditation as part of their reform efforts to improve teacher quality. This reform effort, however, is paradoxical in that college and university education schools and departments are rushing to become accredited with their state education departments through national accreditation agencies, predominantly the National Council for the Accreditation of Teacher Education (NCATE), yet, at the same time, recent federal and state initiatives have downplayed the role of teacher education institutions at the tertiary level. Some education scholars have even predicted that with the exception of perhaps the 10 or 11 preeminent colleges of education, schools of education at the tertiary level will be on the wane.

Informal Education

There are numerous forms of informal education programs in the United States. Given the large growth in the number of citizens of Latino and Chicano background, numerous programs, specifically in large cities, attempt to eliminate gaps in education due to language. Accordingly, English as a Second Language

(ESL) programs and Teaching English to Speakers of Other Language (TESOL) programs are quite common. These programs are often housed in primary or secondary schools—nearly always after school hours. They are also available at the community college or college level, mostly in the form of continuing education. Besides learning the most commonly spoken language of the United States, learning English allows recent immigrants from all over the world to communicate with employers and other hiring personnel in order to get a new job.

Also, informal education provides adults in particular with skills that they might need to increase their potential in the jobs they already have. There are numerous examples of this interest in informal education. Many employers send employees to educational sites in order to prepare them for skills that they will need to utilize on the job, from operating motorized equipment to learning a new computer program. In other instances, numerous informal educational institutions offer certificates upon program completion, which is oftentimes the equivalent of a college degree. For example, pre-service and in-service teachers are now able to receive certification in nontraditional higher education settings, such as museums and nonprofit foundations. Some workplaces encourage informal education in the form of arts, crafts, music, or even yoga, depending on the place of work.

In addition to helping with employment possibilities, informal education in the United States also provides lifelong learning.

System Economics

According to the United Nations Development Programme (2010), along with Ethiopia and the Netherlands, total public expenditures on education in the United States represented 5.5 percent of the gross domestic product (GDP) in 2007. Given the GDP of the United States at $14.72 trillion, educational expenditure in the country amounts to more than $736 billion, about $14,556 per student (total amount equivalent to US dollars divided by 50,564,000, the approximate number of primary and secondary students in the country).

It should also be noted that a large amount of revenue for education on a local, district, and regional level is generated from property taxes in a particular

Figure: **Federal, State, and, Local Government Spending per Student, 2010**

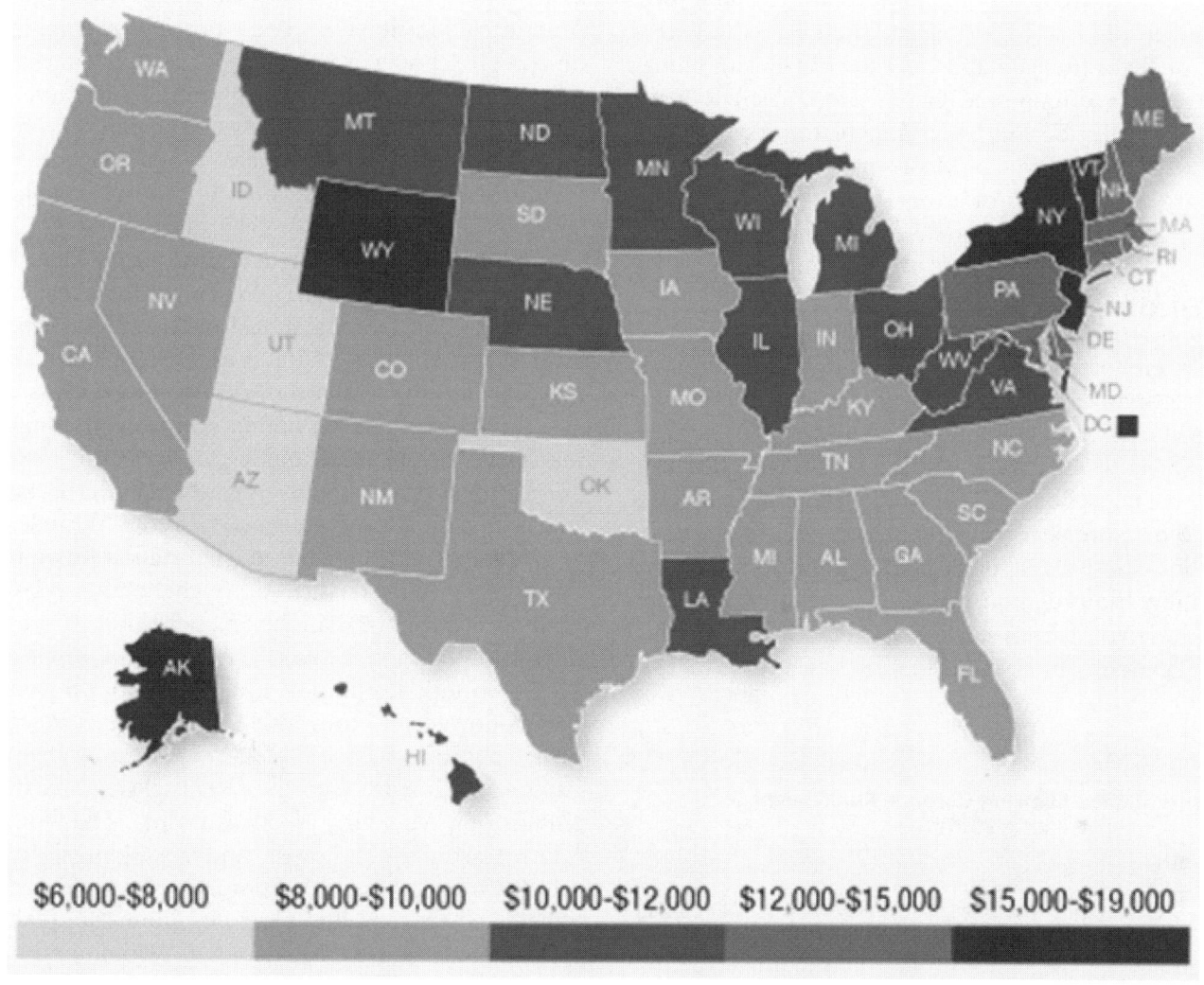

$6,000-$8,000 $8,000-$10,000 $10,000-$12,000 $12,000-$15,000 $15,000-$19,000

Sources: US Census Bureau. Vo, Lam Thuy. "How Much Does The Government Spend To Send A Kid To Public School?" *Planet Money.* 2012. www.npr.org/blogs/money/2012/06/21/155515613/how-much-does-the-government-spend-to-send-a-kid-to-school.

town or community. Since education laws are primarily the responsibility of each state, most per student spending is generated locally and not nationally. When considering federal, state, and local government spending combined (in other words, not solely federal spending as indicated above), the average spending per child amounts to $10,615. The map in the Figure shows spending per student (2010) in each of the 50 states when considering federal, state, and local authority monies. Some states, such as Alaska, New York, New Jersey, Vermont, and Wyoming, per student spending amounts to $15,000 to $19,000 annually, while per student spending in Arizona,

Idaho, Oklahoma, and Utah falls between $6,000 and $8,000 annually (a difference of $7,000).

Secretaries of Education

The United States of America is the first country to assign a federal cabinet member whose charge is to direct the educational system. The initial stimulus to form such a position began in the Carter administration, when President Jimmy Carter appointed Shirley Mount Hufstedler as the first secretary of education. In chronological order, the secretaries of education and the presidents they served under are as follows:

Shirley Mount Hufstedler of Colorado (Carter), Terrel Howard Bell of Idaho (Reagan), William John Bennett of New York (Reagan), Lauro Fred Cavazos Jr. of Texas (Reagan and George H.W. Bush), Lamar Alexander of Tennessee (George H.W. Bush), Richard Wilson Riley of South Carolina (Clinton), Roderick Raynor "Rod" Paige of Mississippi (George W. Bush), Margaret Spellings of Texas (George W. Bush), and Arne Duncan of Illinois (Obama).

Future Prospects

Contemporary trends in American education show little, if any, indication of what the future holds for American schoolchildren and adolescents. We can see, however, an overarching trajectory of what education for the masses has meant to its constituents for the last 200 or more years of its existence. The single-room schoolhouse was at one time an innovation. But mass immigrations demonstrated that change was needed in how youth were to be educated. Within the last half century, American education has become mecha-

nistic and highly bureaucratized, so much so that many critics believe that another dramatic change in American education is needed—possibly an emphasis on charter schools or more school choice. Time will tell whether the charter school model will serve as the premier model or whether the notion of public school education will still take the lead. At present, it is unclear as to whether charter schools have had any impact on educational progress.

It has also been indicated in this chapter that despite numerous advances and contributions of the American educational system to the world at large, schooling in the United States also has its shortcomings. Unlike nearly all countries of Europe (France and the Czech Republic are exceptions), the United States falls behind most postindustrial nations in its position on corporal punishment. Given that education is state run and not fully centralized by the federal government, each state has its own legislation on the corporal punishment issue. Although the State of New Jersey was the first to ban the practice in 1867, it took over 100 years for the next state—Massachusetts in 1971—to take the initiative. Since 1971, 29 states have followed suit. Currently, 20 states sanction corporate punishment (see Table). In 13 states (Alabama, Arkansas, Florida, Georgia, Kentucky, Louisiana, Mississippi, Missouri, North Carolina, Oklahoma, South Carolina, Tennessee, and Texas) more than 1,000 students receive corporal punishment annually while in seven states (Arizona, Colorado, Idaho, Indiana, Kansas, New Mexico, and Wyoming) fewer than 1,000 students do.

In addition, some education researchers and political leaders criticize the role of school and teacher unions, arguing that unions thwart the educational process by preventing the firing of poor teachers. It is important, however, to reach a middle ground with regard to this issue. It is likely that few people wish to see US schools serving only elite groups or to return to a time when only wealthy families could afford an education and female teachers were grossly underpaid. Unions have demonstrated the ability and commitment to prevent these situations from happening. At the same time, it is important that union leaders reach compromise with political and educational leaders so that the education system remains a driving force for the American economy.

Daniel Ness and Chia-ling Lin

Table: **States Allowing Corporal Punishment**
(period ending 2011)

State	Number of students hit annually	Percentage of students	Ranking by percentage[1]
Alabama	33,716	4.5	3
Arizona	16	negligible	19
Arkansas	22,314	4.7	2
Colorado	8	negligible	18
Florida	7,185	0.3	12
Georgia	18,249	1.1	7
Idaho	111	0.4	11
Indiana	577	0.5	10
Kansas	50	0.01	17
Kentucky	2,209	0.3	12
Louisiana	11,080	1.7	5
Mississippi	38,131	7.5	1
Missouri	5,159	0.6	9
New Mexico	705	0.2	14
North Carolina	2,705	0.2	14
Oklahoma	14,828	2.3	4
South Carolina	1,409	0.2	14
Tennessee	14,868	1.5	6
Texas	49,197	1.1	7
Wyoming	0	0	20
US total	223,190	0.46	

[1] Given that some states in the list have the same percentage of students receiving corporal punishment, the ranking by percentage of these states will have the same ranking (i.e., states ranked 7th and 14th).

United States of America Education at a Glance

General Information

Capital	Washington, DC
Population	301.1 million
Languages	English, Spanish;
	Indo-European languages;
	Asian and Pacific island languages
Adult literacy rate	
(ages 15 and over)	99%
GDP per capita	US$44,400
People under poverty line	12%
Number of phones (landline) per 100 people	89
Number of phones (mobile) per 100 people	72.9
Number of Internet users per 100 people	68.2
Life expectancy at birth (years)	78

Formal Educational Information

Enrollment in primary school (ages 6–11)	24.5 million
Enrollment in lower and upper secondary school (ages 12–17)	25.9 million
Number of years of compulsory education	12 (ages 6–17)
Primary school student/teacher ratio	15.4
Lower and upper secondary school student/teacher ratio	15
Primary school gross enrollment ratio	99%
Secondary school gross enrollment ratio	94.7%
Tertiary school gross enrollment ratio	82.7%
Primary school entrants completion rate	99%
Child labor (ages 5–14)	no data

Note: Unless otherwise indicated, all data are based on sources from 2011.

REFERENCES

Center for Effective Discipline. "States Allowing Corporal Punishment." Corporal Punishment in Schools by State. 2008. www.stophitting.com.

Central Intelligence Agency. *The CIA World Factbook.* New York: Skyhorse, 2011. https.www.cia.gov/library/publications/the-world-factbook/index.html.

Certification Map. "Where Do You Want to Teach?" Certification Map: Teacher Certification Made Simple. www.certification-map.com.

Johnson, Dale, Bonnie Johnson, Stephen J. Farenga, and Dan Ness. *Stop High-Stakes Testing: An Appeal to America's Conscience.* Lanham, MD: Rowman & Littlefield, 2008.

National Center for Education Statistics. *Overview of Public Elementary and Secondary Students, Staff, Schools, School Districts, Revenues, and Expenditures: School Year 2004–05 and Fiscal Year 2004.* Washington, DC: US Department of Education, 2011.

Nation Master. 2011. www.nationmaster.com.

Peterson, Paul E. "Education." In *Understanding America: The Anatomy of an Exceptional Nation,* ed. Peter H. Schuck and James Q. Wilson, 411–447. New York: Current Affairs, 2006.

UNESCO. *Global Education Digest 2012: Comparing Education Statistics Across the World.* Montreal: UNESCO Institute for Statistics, 2012.

———. "Strong Foundations: Early Childhood Care and Education." *Education for All Global Monitoring Report 2007.* Paris: UNESCO, 2007.

UNESCO–IBE. www.ibe.unesco.org/en/worldwide/unesco-regions/europe-and-north-america/united-states.html.

UNESCO–UIS. www.uis.unesco.org.

US Census Bureau. http://2010.census.gov/2010census/.

Vo, Lam Thuy. "How Much Does the Government Spend to Send a Kid to Public School?" Planet Money. 2012. www.npr.org/blogs/money/2012/06/21/155515613/how-much-does-the-government-spend-to-send-a-kid-to-school.

World Bank Education Statistics. 2011. www.worldbank.org.

SOUTH AMERICA

INTRODUCTION

The present section discusses the educational systems of 12 countries and one region in South America. The educational systems of South American countries seem to show the least number of disparities of any region in the world. As a whole, South America is a continent that is neither the world's most destitute nor the world's most affluent. The mean per capita income ranges from about the equivalent of $10,000 to $16,000 per household. The continent's overall rate of natural population increase is slightly less than 1 percent, clearly not as high as countries of central Africa that have an average rate of increase at 2.3 percent or as low as most developed nations that have an average increase of about 0.35 percent. Car ownership is one of the single most important predictors of economic growth and income status. The rate of car ownership in South America is approximately 104 cars per 1,000 people. This predicts the overall wealth of South America to be within the second seventh of the world's population. Rates of personal computer ownership and Internet usage are not only indicators of income status but also access to education. This is due to a positive correlation between Internet usage and schooling. The number of personal computers in South America equals approximately 10 units per 100 people, and the number of Internet users on the continent number approximately 30.5 Internet users per 1,000 people—again falling within the range of the second seventh of the world's population.

More related to educational access is the rate of literacy. The literacy rate of countries of South America is approximately 93 percent of the population. Finally, the number of years of education is clearly an indication of the educational access and economic health of a nation. In addition, it affects the population in that the more education a woman attains, the less likely she is to bear children. The average number of years of education in South America is 14 years. These 14 years comprise between 8 and 13 years of compulsory education as well as preschool, the upper secondary noncompulsory level, and tertiary education. Again, the population of South America falls within the second seventh of the world's population in terms of literacy and educational access.

It is important to emphasize, however, that a large number of alienated groups desire educational access and the ability to read and write, but instead have been subjugated to particular lifestyles that do not allow for upward economic mobility. This situation has been perpetuated in part by sporadic military juntas and strongmen who have usurped control of various governments in South America within the last 150 years. Amerindian populations that have been historically alienated in their own countries have little alternative; most live in agrarian regions where a child's labor is an essential part of a family's livelihood. As a result, schooling is more of a burden for these families than a benefit.

Despite their overall mediocre standing in terms of educational access, some of the countries of South America have extremely poor and in some cases abhorrent social policies. For example, Peru's constitution sanctions child labor and compulsory education simultaneously. It should be evident that this policy greatly diminishes the quality of education for students who are obligated to work and attend school at the same time. Although child labor is generally low in South America, it is nevertheless prevalent in all countries of the continent. As expected, countries with high rates of poverty have high rates of child labor. So one will find higher rates of child labor in Peru, Ecuador, and Bolivia, and lower rates in Chile, Argentina, and Uruguay. The poorer countries also have regions with rather large rural populations, particularly Amerindian groups. These areas are known to have few resources and no running water or power sources in some cases. Amerindian children often do not complete their primary school education because they are required to travel long distances in order to attend school. In many instances, families must pay travel expenses—fees that make the cost of living prohibitively expensive.

Daniel Ness and Chia-ling Lin

ARGENTINA

Argentina is a country located in the southern part of South America. The official language is Spanish, although many residents speak English, French, Italian, and German. Approximately 97 percent of Argentinians are white (most of whom are Spanish or Italian). The remaining 3 percent are mestizo with mixed white and Amerindian ancestry or non-white. Although 92 percent of all Argentinians are Roman Catholic, only about 20 percent practice the religion. Approximately 2 percent of the population are members of one of the Protestant sects, 2 percent are Jewish, and the remaining 4 percent profess no religion.

The earliest signs of human inhabitance in the region of Argentina were approximately 13,000 years ago (about 11,000 BCE) in the area that is now called Patagonia. Native civilizations in the region had flourished for at least 12,000 years. By 1480 much of the northwestern part of Argentina was conquered by the Incan Empire, remaining in its possession until the 1530s. The first conquistadores from Spain arrived in Argentina through the Rio de la Plata and set up a post in present-day Buenos Aires. Shortly after the arrival of European settlers, much of the population of the native civilization was exterminated as a result of both Spanish colonization and disease. By 1816 the region known as the United Provinces of the Rio Plata declared independence from Spanish rule. Several years later, three provinces—Bolivia, Paraguay, and Uruguay—splintered into independent nations, and the region

remaining was Argentina. This event spawned heavy immigration to Argentina from Europe in ensuing decades, particularly between 1860 and 1930. Most of the European immigrants came from Spain and Italy. Most of Argentina's troubles came from internal conflicts between civilians and the military. The country also had political difficulties between those who embraced a federalist position and those who embraced a unitarian position. After World War II, Argentina's ruler, Juan Perón, led his government through authoritarian rule. After Perón and a number of unsuccessful governments, a military junta took command of Argentina in 1976. After the Falkland Islands crisis with the United Kingdom, Argentina was once again under democratic rule, and with the exception of the economic crisis from 2001 to 2002, the country has remained politically and economically successful for over 30 years.

Educational System

Along with the systems of Chile, Uruguay, and to some extent Brazil, the educational system in Argentina is one of the most successful in South America. Historically, many countries' educational systems were spearheaded by progressive individuals who attempted to ensure that the economic status of their respective countries was on par with those of other developing or developed nations. Clearly, Horace Mann was an early sponsor of compulsory education in the United States, and José Pedro Varela was a seminal educational figure in the early years of the Republic of Uruguay. In the same light, Domingo Faustino Sarmiento established the importance of education institutions in Argentina. As president of the country from 1868 to 1874, Sarmiento was concerned that Argentina was falling behind other developed nations, particularly certain European nations, in the education of its citizens. Accordingly, Sarmiento initiated communication with European schoolmasters to send their most highly qualified students to establish schools and libraries in Argentina. By 1884 Argentina had become one of the first countries in South America to establish a free, mostly secular, compulsory system of education. The separation of religion from schools and other educational establishments created a rift between the Argentine government and the Catholic Church. Secularism in Argentina did not begin with the establishment of compulsory schooling. It had begun nearly 75 years earlier with the May 1810 revolution that declared the country independent. Part of the rift between church and state was a result of the efforts of early Argentinians to separate themselves politically and in other ways from Spanish imperialist powers. Moreover, the country's revised constitution of 1853 contained an amendment that allowed for the freedom of Catholic and other religious worship within the borders of a secular state. Argentina, then, represents one of the first examples of separation of church and state with respect to Catholic (although not Protestant) doctrine. However, after 1947, the merging of church and state had taken place under the presidency of Juan Perón and even at a greater level under the military junta leader Pedro Aramburu, one of Perón's successors. As a result, federal funding of educational institutions was partially allocated to parochial schools throughout the country—particularly Catholic institutions. Due to economic downturns in the 1980s, the Argentine government issued a law that decentralized secondary school education. Since 1992 the administration of secondary schools in Argentina was primarily the responsibility of each of the 23 provinces. Despite these decentralization efforts, spending in education increased steadily since the 1990s.

Preprimary and Compulsory Education

Prior to 2006 education was compulsory in Argentina for children between the ages of six and 14 years. However, under a new education statute that was passed in 2006 by the Chamber of Deputies in the bicameral Congress of Argentina, students are required to attend school for a total of 13 years. The last year of preprimary education—often kindergarten—is the first compulsory year of education.

Data from the Argentine Ministry of Education website suggests that the number of children attending preprimary schools exceeds an enrollment of 1.3 million students. This accounts for approximately 60 percent of the population of children between the ages of three and five. The last year of preprimary education in the country is compulsory and serves all children prior to grade 1 who are six years of age. In addition, the government's "Early Years" National Infant Development Programme is aimed at support-

ing families in the raising of children from ages one to four, emphasizing social, emotional, and cognitive development.

Basic education comprises two three-year terms of primary school (grades 1 through 6) and the first three-year term of secondary school (grades 7 through 9); however, many primary schools are arranged under an older system that includes grade 7. The last three years of secondary school (grades 10 through 12) are also compulsory; students cannot apply to tertiary institutions if they do not graduate from secondary school. At present, there are over 4.1 million children of primary school age in the country. The student/teacher ratio at this level is 22 students per teacher, and the primary school enrollment ratio is 113 percent. According to UNESCO, the overwhelming majority of children eligible to attend primary school are actually enrolled. This conclusion supports the country's primary net enrollment ratio of 98.6 percent. Moreover, the primary school entrants' completion rate is 99 percent, further supporting this conclusion. Curriculum at this level includes the reading and writing of Spanish, mathematics, basic natural science, social studies, physical education, art, and music.

Secondary school includes both lower and upper cycles, the first of which is a three-year period and the second a three- or four-year period. The estimated number of children and adolescents of secondary school age in Argentina is approximately 4.1 million individuals. The student/teacher ratio at the secondary school level is approximately 17 students per teacher. The secondary school gross enrollment rate and net enrollment rate are 86 percent and 80 percent, respectively. Although generally lower than those of other developed nations, these rates are the highest among Latin American nations. The curriculum at the secondary level includes natural science specialization courses (i.e., biology, chemistry, physics), secondary mathematics courses (algebra, geometry, and precalculus), and a greater emphasis on Spanish literature, the mastery of a foreign language in certain instances, and more courses in the areas of government and history. In order to be eligible for university acceptance, students must attend secondary school for a period of five years or more and successfully pass the baccalaureate examination at the end of the secondary level.

Tertiary Education

Argentina prides itself not only on its overall success in the preprimary, primary, and secondary education system; the country also has a number of internationally renowned institutions of higher education. There are at least 97 universities in the country—45 public and 52 private institutions. The National Technological University is a leading polytechnic institute that enrolls some 75,000 students every year. It is the most competitive polytechnic university in Argentina and perhaps the most competitive in South America. The university offers the most diverse programs in engineering of any polytechnic university in the region. Moreover, with its 30 campuses, the university serves Argentine students throughout the country. The Buenos Aires campus is the central facility of the university. The largest university in the country, however, is the University of Buenos Aires. Founded in 1821, the university enrolls 308,594 students annually, thus making it the second-largest university in Latin America (the National Autonomous University of Mexico ranks the first in Latin America). The university graduated four Nobel laureates—more than any other university in the Spanish-speaking world. The university houses 13 schools that include the following disciplines: agronomy; architecture, design, and urban planning; engineering; dentistry; medicine; law; economics; veterinary medicine; pharmacy and biochemistry; philosophy and literature; social sciences; psychology; and natural science.

It is important to note that public universities in Argentina are subsidized by the government and free for all who are accepted and who complete secondary education requirements. One of the main dilemmas concerning Argentine students at public universities is that many of them must seek employment upon graduating from secondary school. Therefore, these individuals lead busy lives by working full-time and going to the university seeking tertiary diplomas or certificates. On the one hand, successful students in this situation are desirable candidates in that at the end of their program, they will have both experience and a degree in their field. However, many students who pursue this route end up dropping out of the university because full-time employment and study often adversely affects student output. Students who seek graduate level study may do so in research-based academic fields as well as medicine and engineering.

Doctorates include doctor of philosophy, doctor of medicine, and doctor of law degrees. Most postgraduates, however, pursue master's degrees.

Teacher Education

Teacher training programs in Argentina are housed at many of the public and private universities as well as teacher training institutes and normal schools. From 1871 to 1921, teacher education took place primarily at the Sarmiento Teachers' College, which was perhaps one of the first teacher education institutions in the Western Hemisphere. After it had closed in 1921, programs took place in normal secondary schools. After the 1970s, however, preservice teachers were trained in tertiary-level institutes and particularly in university-level programs. At present, preprimary, primary, and lower secondary school preservice teachers who will be expected to teach the basic education curriculum are trained in higher teacher training institutes for a period of two and a half years. In addition, a half-year student teaching experience must follow course work. Preservice teachers for secondary school must enroll in a university program and specialize in an area of expertise. Although the country's education system ranks higher than those of other Latin American nations, a large segment of the teacher population earns at or below the poverty line. At the same time, government and organizational initiatives have helped raise teacher standards and reputations. One of the more recent innovations in teacher training in the country concerns of "Online Teacher Training" and "Shortening Distances," two initiatives sponsored by the Instituto Nacional de Formación Docente de Argentina (National Teacher Training Institute of Argentina) and UNESCO Montevideo.

System Economics and Future Prospects

According to the United Nations Development Programme (2010), along with Aruba, Canada, Ireland, Poland, Syria, and Thailand, total public expenditure on education in Argentina represented 4.9 percent of the gross domestic product (GDP) in 2007. Given the GDP of Argentina at $609 billion, educational expenditure in the country amounts to nearly $30 billion, about $3,628 per student (total amount

---

Argentina Education at a Glance

General Information

Capital	Buenos Aires
Population	41.7 million
Languages	Spanish, English, Italian, German, French
Adult literacy rate (ages 15 and over)	97.2%
GDP per capita	US$15,200
Number of phones (landline) per 100 people	21.8
Number of phones (mobile) per 100 people	54.8
Number of Internet users per 100 people	24.8
Life expectancy at birth (years)	76

Formal Educational Information

Enrollment in primary school (ages 6–11)	4.1 million
Enrollment in lower and upper secondary school (ages 12–17)	4.1 million
Number of years of compulsory education	13 (ages 5–17)
Primary school student/teacher ratio	21.8
Lower and upper secondary school student/teacher ratio	17.3
Primary school gross enrollment ratio	113%
Secondary school gross enrollment ratio	86%
Tertiary school gross enrollment ratio	65%
Primary school entrants completion rate	99%
Child labor (ages 5–14)	7%*

Note: *Refers to part of the country.
Unless otherwise indicated, all data are based on sources from 2011.

---

equivalent to US dollars divided by 8,226,000, the approximate number of primary and secondary students in the country). Argentina ranks 69 of 186 countries in percentage of educational expenditure. Recent UNESCO figures, however, indicate that Argentina's Education Financing Act No. 26075 of 2010 has raised educational expenditures to 6 percent of the country's GDP.

The educational system in Argentina has historically been one of the most successful in Latin America. Despite an annual per capita gross income of slightly over $14,700, Argentines have been able to maintain a progressive education system that enables nearly all citizens a right to go to school. However, there have been some problems with educational access. The most egregious issue is the problem of child labor in the western part of the country. Most of these children between the ages of five and 14 years are members of Amerindian groups that have historically been alienated by the majority. As a result, these children are expected to meet the same requirements as their peers who are not obligated to work for a living

or help out with family subsistence. Many of these children often do not remain in school past grade 5, while others have difficulty in managing to complete their secondary education.

Through information and communication technologies as well as other modes of discourse, the country has been increasingly successful in reaching its rural populations—particularly those in the rural regions near the Andes highlands and Patagonia.

Daniel Ness and Chia-ling Lin

REFERENCES

Center for Economic and Social Rights. *Visualizing Rights: Argentina, Fact Sheet No. 3*. New York: Center for Economic and Social Rights, 2010.

Central Intelligence Agency. *The CIA World Factbook*. New York: Skyhorse, 2011. https.www.cia.gov/library/publications/the-world-factbook/index.html.

Nation Master. 2011. www.nationmaster.com.

UNESCO. *Argentina: Early Childhood Care and Education (ECCE) Programs*. Geneva: UNESCO, 2006.

———. *Global Education Digest 2012: Comparing Education Statistics Across the World*. Montreal: UNESCO Institute for Statistics, 2012.

———. "Strong Foundations: Early Childhood Care and Education." *Education for All Global Monitoring Report*. Paris: UNESCO, 2006.

UNESCO–IBE. www.ibe.unesco.org/en/worldwide/unesco-regions/latin-america-and-the-caribbean/argentina.html.

United Nations Development Programme. *United Nations Development Report 2010*. New York: Palgrave Macmillan, 2010.

US Department of Labor. *2001 Findings on the Worst Forms of Child Labor*. Washington, DC: Bureau of International Labor Affairs, US Department of Labor, 2002.

World Bank Education Statistics. 2011. www.worldbank.org.

BOLIVIA

Bolivia is a country located in south-central South America. The country has three official languages: Spanish, Quechua, and Aymara. Approximately 30 percent of Bolivians are Quechuan, 30 percent are mestizo (mixed white and Amerindian), 25 percent are Aymara, and 15 percent are white. Roman Catholicism is the religion of 95 percent of the population. The remaining 5 percent of the population belong to Protestant Christian sects.

Civilizations inhabited the region of Bolivia for more than 13,000 years. Indigenous populations lived in both the Andean highlands and the eastern lowlands for at least 10,000 years. By the year 1000 a large part of the area comprising Bolivia had become part of the Incan Empire, and it remained so until the 1530s. The first conquistadores from Spain arrived in the Andean highlands by the mid-sixteenth century. A large part of the native indigenous population was exterminated as a result of both Spanish colonization and disease. With the help of Simon Bolívar, the famous independence fighter (Bolivia is named in his honor), Bolivia was emancipated from Spanish rule in 1825. Unfortunately, the Bolivian government suffered more than 200 coups between independence and the late twentieth century. In 1982 Bolivia established democratic civilian rule. However, problems related to poverty, social and political turmoil, and the production of illegal drugs have caused a great deal of tension in the political process. Bolivians elected Evo Morales, a member of the Movement Toward Socialism party, in December 2005 with the hope of solving much of the country's difficulties associated with poverty, poor education, and social inequities.

Educational System

Although the Bolivian government allocates a fairly significant percentage of its gross domestic product (GDP) to education, schooling in the country is in need of improvement. As in some of its neighbors, a number of factors may account for the need of improving the educational system. First, UNESCO data indicate that child labor in the country has reached 22 percent. It should be evident that countries that have such a large percentage of their citizens between five and 14 years engaged in labor more than likely have poor school enrollments. Second, there is a rather large rift between educational access of urban children and rural children. Students in Bolivia's urban centers tend to have greater access to better schools and schools in general. As a result, student enrollment in the two environments differs as well; students in rural communities average about four years of schooling while those in urban areas attend school for at least 10 years.

Preprimary education in Bolivia is not compulsory. Primary education in Bolivia is compulsory for a

period of seven years for students between the ages of seven and 14 years. Secondary school continues for an additional four years. Since the early 1990s, primary school completion increased dramatically in the country. The primary school student/teacher ratio is roughly 24 students per teacher. The primary school gross enrollment ratio is 113 percent. Yet the primary school net enrollment ratio is 95 percent—thus indicating that there is a student population that is not attending school and is not completing grade 6, the last year of primary school. The student/teacher ratio for secondary school is also about 24 students to one teacher. The lower and upper secondary school gross enrollment ratio is about 89 percent. But the net enrollment ratio for this group is 72 percent, indicating that nearly 30 percent of all students within this age group are either not finishing secondary school or not enrolling in it altogether.

The basic education curriculum in Bolivia includes a focus on the following subjects: reading and writing, science, mathematics, Bolivian history and geography, physical education, and art. Unfortunately, there is little evidence that teachers or schools are adhering to any performance-based criterion of quality. In rural areas, school is simply canceled if a teacher is ill for a particular day or if there are shortages of personnel. Given a high level of agrarian labor in the countryside, school attendance is hampered by the lack of workers on the fields. UNICEF data suggest that 22 percent of all school-age children are engaged in labor.

Tertiary education in Bolivia is mostly available for a selected number of students, most coming from affluent families. There are 10 public universities and 23 private universities in Bolivia. The University of San Francisco Xavier in Sucre was established in 1624, making it one of the oldest continuing universities in the Americas. The university was initially intended to educate young men of the aristocracy of South America in the areas of law and theology. In the nineteenth century, the University of San Francisco Xavier became an educational center for intellectuals who advocated independence of all Spanish colonies. As a result, the university is symbolically known as the location that instigated the Bolivian War of Independence, which led to the independence of several countries on the continent. At present, the university offers courses in several disciplines in the arts, sciences, humanities, medicine, and law. The university with the largest enrollment is the University of San Andrés in La Paz, founded in 1830. It has an enrollment of over 37,000 students.

Initially, teacher training in Bolivia took place in makeshift normal schools in La Paz and in rural areas. At present, many universities are taking the initiative to create programs and departments of education. One of the most successful cases is the teacher training program at Nur University in Santa Cruz. The primary goal is to provide teachers with a strong foundation in teaching reading and writing. It is believed that many students leave primary school as a result of a poor language curriculum, and if students learn to read and write successfully, they will be more inclined to continue their schooling.

System Economics and Future Prospects

According to the United Nations Development Programme (2010), along with Saint Lucia, total public expenditure on education of Bolivia represented 6.3 percent of the GDP in 2006. Given the GDP of Bolivia at $19.18 billion, educational expenditure in the country amounts to more than $1.2 billion, about $446 per student (total amount equivalent to US dollars divided by 2,711,000, the approximate number of primary and secondary students in the country). Bolivia ranks 31 of 186 countries in percentage of educational expenditure—the highest rank of any country in South America.

The educational situation of Bolivia demonstrates that the infusion of financial resources or allocation of funds for education does not necessarily translate into a better education system. It is also important to note that although the country allocates a large part of its revenue for education, its gross national product is lower than that of most countries in South America. Some observers have criticized Bolivian teacher unions for initiating teacher strikes, thereby shortening the number of school days for students (Contreras and Talavera 2003). However, this observation can be seen as superficial when considering the poor wages of teachers and lack of veneration of the teaching profession in the country.

The Educational Ministry of Bolivia is currently seeking to improve education in the country. The ministry's goals are to reach high levels of standards and expectations, find and retain strong leaders,

---

Bolivia Education at a Glance

General Information

Capitals	Sucre (constitutional capital)
	La Paz (government seat)
Population	10.1 million
Languages	Spanish, Quechua, Aymara
Adult literacy rate (ages 15 and over)	86.7%
GDP per capita	US$3,100
Number of phones (landline) per 100 people	7.1
Number of phones (mobile) per 100 people	26.6
Number of Internet users per 100 people	5.3
Life expectancy at birth (years)	66

Formal Educational Information

Enrollment in primary school (ages 6–11)	1.4 million
Enrollment in lower and upper secondary school (ages 12–17)	1.3 million
Number of years of compulsory education	8 (ages 7–14)
Primary school student/teacher ratio	24.2
Lower and upper secondary school student/teacher ratio	23.6
Primary school gross enrollment ratio	113%
Secondary school gross enrollment ratio	89%
Tertiary school gross enrollment ratio	no data
Primary school entrants completion rate	98%
Child labor (ages 5–14)	22%

Note: Unless otherwise indicated, all data are based on sources from 2011.

---

support learning that is student-centered, involve parents and communities in educational initiatives, identify important benchmarks for purposes of assessment and accountability, foster a curriculum that promotes inquiry and challenge, provide professional development for in-service teachers, and maximize the amount of time available for all students to succeed in school. Unfortunately, with lack of financial and material resources and an inadequate mind-set among many Bolivians about the importance of a strong education, these goals are going to be difficult to reach—especially within a short period of time.

Fortunately, both governmental and nongovernmental organizations (NGOs) have provided support in recent years. For example, the NGO Enda Tiers Monde has provided funding for the education of street children in Enda, an urban area near La Paz. Enda Tiers initially provides a curriculum of art, physical education, and manual skills, giving students the opportunity to gain experience in various vocations. Other NGOs that have contributed to the education system in Bolivia are the World Bank,

USAID, and UNICEF. In addition to these programs, the government has promoted an educational reform that involves the decentralization of power, thus providing more autonomy in rural regions of the country. This decentralization has also led to improvements in teacher training and the provision of instruction in local languages. The ministry needs to invest in technologies that allow children of rural families to benefit from all school subjects. In addition, the country would be wise to establish law that prevents the labor of children—especially those under 16 years—who deserve an education that will help them compete in the global economy.

Daniel Ness and Chia-ling Lin

REFERENCES

Central Intelligence Agency. *The CIA World Factbook*. New York: Skyhorse, 2011. https.www.cia.gov/library/publications/the-world-factbook/index.html.

Contreras, Manuel E., and Maria Luisa Talavera. "The Bolivian Education Reform 1992–2002: Case Studies in Large-Scale Education Reform." In *Country Studies: Education Reform and Management Publication Series* 2:2. Washington, DC: World Bank, 2003.

Nation Master. 2011. www.nationmaster.com.

UNESCO. *Global Education Digest 2012: Comparing Education Statistics Across the World*. Montreal: UNESCO Institute for Statistics, 2012.

———. "Strong Foundations: Early Childhood Care and Education." *Education for All Global Monitoring Report*. Paris: UNESCO, 2006.

UNESCO–IBE. www.ibe.unesco.org/en/worldwide/unesco-regions/latin-america-and-the-caribbean/bolivia.html.

United Nations Development Programme. *United Nations Development Report 2010*. New York: Palgrave Macmillan, 2010.

US Department of Labor. *2001 Findings on the Worst Forms of Child Labor*. Washington, DC: Bureau of International Labor Affairs, US Department of Labor, 2002.

World Bank Education Statistics. 2011. www.worldbank.org.

BRAZIL

Brazil is the largest country in South America in both area and population. The official language is Portuguese; however, some Brazilians also speak Spanish, English, French, and Italian. The region of Brazil was controlled by Portuguese conquerors and explorers at the beginning of the sixteenth century. Although claimed by Portugal in 1500, the first settlement in what is now Brazil was in 1532. In 1534 a series of conflicts took place that eventually led to the displacement and extermination of many native tribes. Given the suitable environment for sugarcane production, the Portuguese used the vast lands for producing sugar and exporting the commodity throughout the world. Sugar was a major boon for the Portuguese government. As a result, Portuguese authorities sanctioned the importation of people from West Africa to engage in slave labor. For the next century or more, Portuguese Brazil imported more slaves from Africa than any other country in the Western Hemisphere. The vast territory of Brazil eventually became independent from its mother country in 1822 and became a republic in 1889. For nearly 50 years, commencing in the 1930s, the country was ruled and governed by a military junta. By 1985 civilian rule was once again restored. As a result, the country has seen economic growth and strengthened its service, industry, and agriculture sectors. Brazil is the economic superpower of South America. The country possesses a great deal of natural resources to supply its large number of diversified industries and agricultural base. The country has a relatively high rate of literacy, about 89 percent. However, more than 10 percent of Brazilians ages 15 and older are unable to read or write.

Educational System

The earliest evidence of formal education in the Portuguese territory of Brazil was the teaching of reading and writing that was promoted by the Jesuit order. The Jesuits, in fact, had a stranglehold on education throughout the sixteenth century, not only in South America, but in East Asia and Africa as well. Many Brazilian males who learned how to read and write under Jesuit guidance were sent to Portugal to study at the University of Coimbra, one of the oldest universities in Europe. By the eighteenth century, the Jesuit missionary assignment placed a great deal of its emphasis on converting people in South America to Catholicism, mostly in Brazil. To be sure, education and the promotion of literacy were the modus operandi in religious conversion to Roman Catholicism. Nevertheless, the more than three-century period between the beginning of Portuguese colonization of Brazil in the early sixteenth century and the late nineteenth century came to be one of the gloomiest periods in Brazilian history. Slavery was rampant as Portuguese landowners used slaves from Africa largely for sugarcane production and mining. Unlike their Portuguese counterparts, no slaves were formally educated. After the Marquis of Pombal expelled most of the Jesuits from the colony, a number of institutions were founded that specialized in particular academic and scientific domains. For example, the Sociedade Cientifica (Scientific Society) was established in Rio de Janeiro in 1772. Roughly 30 years later, a school for botany opened its doors in Salvador, Bahia. In 1800 the Aula Prática de Desenho e Figura (Classroom Practice and Figure Drawing Institute) opened its doors in Rio de Janeiro, serving as the first school of fine arts in the region.

Modern educational influences in Brazil have emanated from early twentieth-century developments in socialist, anticolonialist philosophies. Perhaps the most important Brazilian educator and educational theorist was Paulo Freire. Born in Recife in 1921, Freire developed the notion of critical pedagogy, a term that refers to the analytical review of the typical curriculum and pedagogical practices that have served to alienate the overwhelming number of oppressed people in Brazil. Strongly influenced by the philosophies of Jean-Paul Sartre, Karl Marx, Louis Althusser, Ivan Illich, and Antonio Gramsci, Freire combined his studies of philosophy, particularly the subfield of phenomenology, with law, his primary major at the University of Recife. This combination of interests served as the bedrock of his conviction of praxis in education. Praxis in education concerns the importance of the interrelationship between education for research and knowledge with education in practice, that is, as a dialogic, two-way communicative experience between teacher and student. After being imprisoned for more than two months for what Brazilian authorities called "subversive" ideas in his teachings, Freire was exiled from Brazil in 1964 and did not return to his homeland until 1979. One of his most influential publications is *Pedagogy of the Oppressed*, which he wrote in 1968. This book examines the duality of the oppressor and the oppressed. He maintains that oppressed groups are wholly schooled in systems that promote and foster a so-called banking model of education, whereby students are seen in terms of empty vessels that can be simply told what to learn based on what the state wants them to learn. Freire's contributions to Brazilian education

included methods of bringing disadvantaged social and ethnic groups in the country out of poverty through progressive education techniques—practices that are encouraged even today by numerous landless peoples throughout the country.

Preprimary, Primary, and Secondary Education

There are roughly 10.8 million children of preschool age in Brazil and approximately 37.4 million children and adolescents of primary and secondary age (nearly one-quarter of the population of the entire country)—thus making Brazil the most populous country in South America in terms of people between the ages of about four and 17 years. Preprimary schools in Brazil are not compulsory. However, a large sector of the preschool-age population attends preschools. Parents can begin sending their children to preprimary institutions at two years of age. However, the majority of children attending preprimary institutions are between three and five years of age. Publicly funded preschools are predominantly available in large urban areas. In fact, families in the northern and western parts of the country, particularly in the Amazonian highlands, find preschools few and far between, some even more than 185 miles (300 kilometers) away, and thus cannot afford to send their children to preschool or a related preprimary institution. Like other preprimary institutions throughout the world, preschool curricula in Brazil emphasize the integration of social, emotional, psychomotor, and intellectual development in young children as a preparation for primary school.

Schooling in Brazil is compulsory for all children between seven and 14 years of age—eight to nine years in total. This comprises the full primary school period as well as a so-called lower secondary period of two to three years. The primary school student/teacher ratio in Brazil is about 26 children for every teacher. Due to the infusion of resources in the Brazilian education sector, there seems to be an indication of a shift in what will be defined as compulsory in the future (i.e., whether compulsory education will be extended). The basic curriculum at the primary level consists of arithmetic, basic science, Portuguese, social studies and community, music, art, and physical education.

The gross enrollment rate for primary school children in Brazil is 140 percent. Yet only 95 percent of all children are actually attending school, as indicated by the country's net enrollment ratio for primary school attendance. The secondary school student/teacher ratio is about 17 students for every teacher. While the gross enrollment ratio for secondary students in Brazil is 106 percent, the net enrollment ratio for this age group is only 78 percent, indicating that more than 20 percent of all students of secondary school age are not attending school. Secondary education is divided into two parts: middle education and secondary (high school) education. Middle education, which is essentially a continuation of the basic education in primary school, lasts for three years. The end of middle school serves as the end of compulsory education. The last three years of secondary education (the so-called upper secondary period) consists of more specified courses (e.g., mathematics, physics, biology, chemistry, philosophy, social science, Portuguese language and literature, a foreign language, geography, and history).

Tertiary Education

Although tertiary education in Brazil has traditionally been available mostly for a selected number of students, most coming from affluent families, more and more students from lower- and middle-class backgrounds are attending universities thanks to the country's commitment to increase the educational standing of its citizens. There are believed to be a total of 171 public and private universities in Brazil. About two-thirds of these universities are located in the southeastern part of the country, the majority in the states of São Paulo, Rio de Janeiro, Paraná, Rio Grande do Sul, Mato Grosso do Sul, and Espírito Santo. Perhaps the most competitive university in Brazil is the University of São Paulo. Founded in 1934, it enrolls approximately 88,000 students per year. Although the main campus is in São Paulo, the university serves students at 10 additional campuses. The University of São Paulo has the largest number of programs in the country. In total the university has more than 40 schools and institutes that specialize in specific academic and professional domains. A second highly competitive university in Brazil is the University of Campinas, which is also located in the state of São Paulo. The University of Campinas, which was founded in 1966, enrolls about 32,000

students per year and has 23 colleges and schools. Tertiary students attending certain universities may be eligible to enter master's programs and doctoral programs. Baccalaureates in Brazil usually take one or two years more than in most European colleges and universities.

Students in secondary school must pass a qualifying examination known as the *Vestibular*, which is a high-stakes test that determines one's entrance into undergraduate education in a university. Undergraduate education usually takes between four and six years to complete. In addition to colleges and universities, the country has competitive polytechnic universities and institutes. These schools include Instituto Tecnológico de Aeronáutica (Aeronautics Institute of Technology) in São José dos Campos and the Instituto Militar de Engenharia (Military Institute of Engineering) in Rio de Janeiro. Established in 1792, the Instituto Militar de Engenharia is the third oldest polytechnic institution in the world, and the oldest in the Western Hemisphere.

Teacher Education

Nearly all publicly funded and some privately funded universities in Brazil have teacher education and training programs. As in similar programs in the United States, students must attend a university- or college-level program in order to become a teacher at the primary or secondary school level. Teacher training in Brazil suffers from the lack of content knowledge of a large proportion of schoolteachers throughout the country. Current initiatives thus focus on the improvement of teacher education. In general, preservice and in-service teachers have scored low on examinations that measure ability in mathematics and Portuguese. In addition, prospective teachers have been shown to score poorly in these subjects during primary school and secondary school study. According to the report of the International Commission of Education for the Twenty-First Century titled *Education: The Treasure Within*, published by UNESCO, one of the primary ways of improving teacher education in Brazil and in other countries with similar poor outcomes is to ensure the improvement of recruiting teachers, course content in the main subject areas (i.e., mathematics, language, basic science, and history), and teachers' working conditions. Moreover, it will be necessary to improve the reputation of teachers and their social status in Brazilian society in order for education for all to be successful.

Informal Education

There are essentially two models of informal education in Brazil. One model is based on programs that typically provide opportunities for adult laborers who decide to return to school to gain new skills in order to work in higher-paying occupations. A large proportion of this adult population consists of individuals over the age of 15 who are unable to read or write. Current UNESCO data suggest that between 16 million and 17 million Brazilian adults are illiterate. To be sure, about 25 percent of the population in the northern two-thirds of the country is illiterate—more than three times the rate in southern Brazil. Moreover, about 14 million Brazilian adults have received no schooling or at most one year of schooling. Based on these statistics, the Brazilian Ministry of Education has collaborated with nongovernmental agencies to initiate funding in the development of primary and vocational education programs for adults over 15 years of age who have had very little, if any, education. Accordingly, the federal government has allocated funding to each of the 26 states based on the number of people who are estimated to be illiterate or lacking primary education or vocational skills—particularly to those states whose Human Development Index is less than 0.500. In essence, the northern part of Brazil receives most of the funding and resources for adult informal education programs.

A second model of informal education entails the schooling of landless peasants who have traditionally been economically disadvantaged. On April 17, 1996, during a demonstration in the state of Pará, federal police opened fire and killed 22 peaceful marchers. In one respect, this sad event was a result of informal education practice. In another, it was a major influence on a growing movement to educate people of all landless communities in terms of their rights, general knowledge in mathematics and literacy, and praxis—the integration of research with practice. Education is an important goal for encamped (i.e., lacking permanent residences), landless peasants; it is essential for these families to be educated so that they can improve their economic conditions by understanding how Brazilian law and government practice affect their current standing and livelihood.

Informal education for landless workers may help them find access to land for subsistence. Informal education of this sort is usually held at regional schools throughout the country. In addition, the Florestan Fernandes National School in Guararema, near São Paulo, was built specifically for educating and training economically disadvantaged populations. The school trains students in agronomy for subsistence and seeks to inspire students and help them find their occupational niche as a means of gaining a more dignified livelihood.

System Economics and Future Prospects

According to the United Nations Development Programme (2010), along with Yemen, Slovenia, Belarus, and Grenada, total public expenditure on education in Brazil represented 5.2 percent of the gross domestic product (GDP) in 2007. Given the GDP of Brazil at $2.194 trillion, educational expenditure in the country amounts to nearly $114 billion, about $3,050 per student (total amount equivalent to US dollars

---

Brazil Education at a Glance

General Information

Capital	Brasilia
Population	203.4 million
Languages	Portuguese, Spanish, English, French
Adult literacy rate (ages 15 and over)	88.6%
GDP per capita	US$8,800
Number of phones (landline) per 100 people	22.3
Number of phones (mobile) per 100 people	45.4
Number of Internet users per 100 people	13.6
Life expectancy at birth (years)	72

Formal Educational Information

Enrollment in primary school (ages 7–10)	14 million
Enrollment in lower and upper secondary school (ages 11–17)	23.4 million
Number of years of compulsory education	11 (ages 7–17)
Primary school student/teacher ratio	26
Lower and upper secondary school student/teacher ratio	16.7
Primary school gross enrollment ratio	140%
Secondary school gross enrollment ratio	106%
Tertiary school gross enrollment ratio	23.8%
Primary school entrants completion rate	111%
Child labor (ages 5–14)	6%

Note: Unless otherwise indicated, all data are based on sources from 2011.

divided by 37,406,000, the approximate number of primary and secondary students in the country). Brazil ranks 57 of 186 countries in percentage of educational expenditure.

The Brazilian Ministry of Education's objectives in the long run are to help students reach high levels of standards and expectations, find and retain effective teachers, support learning that is student-centered, involve parents and communities in educational initiatives, identify important benchmarks for purposes of assessment and accountability, foster a curriculum that promotes inquiry and challenge, provide professional development for in-service teachers, and maximize the amount of time available for all students to succeed in school. The ministry needs to invest in technologies that allow children of rural families, particularly in the northern two-thirds of the country, to benefit from all school subjects. In addition, the country will need to eliminate the labor of children—especially those under 16 years—who deserve an education that will help them compete in the global economy.

It is important to note that forms of slavery still exist today in Brazil. There are an estimated 50,000 slave laborers working on sugarcane plantations throughout the country, despite the fact that slavery was declared illegal in 1888. This abominable statistic demonstrates the need for harsh sanctions against those who continue to perpetuate the dastardly practice of slavery. Fortunately, in recent years, the Brazilian government has warranted and successfully issued a number of raids on farms that practice slavery. Accordingly, the Brazilian government and Ministry of Education will need to provide formal emancipatory education for former slaves for their own economic success and as a means of eradicating the practice of slavery so that the country can be seen on the world stage as a respectable nation.

Brazil has come a long way in terms of its standing in educational access and progress. The Organisation for Economic Co-operation and Development (OECD) presented education data that indicate dramatic increases in ability in mathematics, reading, and science knowledge from 2000 to 2010. Although Chile and Argentina outperform all countries in South America in assessment, Brazil shows the greatest gains in students' increased ability in these content areas. These increases in international test scores, however, should not be taken as a sign that all is well in educa-

tion in Brazil. At present, two-thirds of all students 15 years of age or older are able to work with basic arithmetic at most. OECD data also emphasize that more needs to be done to improve Brazilian students' abilities in analytical reasoning; only 1 of every 100 students is considered a "high-performing" student. Clearly, more needs to be done to eliminate poverty and illegal labor practices in the country. Only then will it be possible to see strong gains and high achievement among the country's student population and in the education system as a whole—on par with the systems of other developed countries in the world.

Daniel Ness and Chia-ling Lin

REFERENCES

Central Intelligence Agency. *The CIA World Factbook*. New York: Skyhorse, 2011. https.www.cia.gov/library/publications/the-world-factbook/index.html.

EFA. "Strong Foundations: Early Childhood Care and Education." *Education for All Global Monitoring Report*. Paris: UNESCO, 2006.

Freire, Paulo. *Pedagogy of the Oppressed*. New York: Herder and Herder, 1970.

Movimento Dos Trabalhadores Rurais Sem Terra. *Education and Political Training Sector*. Chicago: Friends of the MST, 2011.

Nation Master. 2011. www.nationmaster.com.

Phillips, Tom. "Brazilian Taskforce Frees More Than 4,500 Slaves after Record Number of Raids on Remote Farms." *Guardian*, January 3, 2009.

UNESCO. *Global Education Digest 2006: Comparing Education Statistics Across the World*. Montreal: UNESCO Institute for Statistics, 2006.

UNESCO–IBE. www.ibe.unesco.org/en/worldwide/unesco-regions/latin-america-and-the-caribbean/brazil.html.

United Nations Development Programme. *United Nations Development Report 2010*. New York: Palgrave Macmillan, 2010.

US Department of Labor. *2001 Findings on the Worst Forms of Child Labor*. Washington, DC: Bureau of International Labor Affairs, US Department of Labor, 2002.

World Bank Education Statistics. 2011. www.worldbank.org.

CHILE

Chile is a country located in the southern part of South America. The official language is Spanish, although there are many residents who speak Italian and German. Approximately 95 percent of Chileans are white and white-Amerindian. The remaining 3 percent are Amerindian or from another ethnic group. Approximately 70 percent of all Chileans are Roman Catholic, about 15 percent are Evangelical, and 1 percent is Jehovah's Witnesses. About 6 percent are non-Christians, and roughly 8 percent are nonbelievers.

Chile became an independent nation in 1810; however, it was not until 1818 that Chilean militia overpowered Spanish forces. The present-day northern administrative divisions were annexed by Chile during the War of the Pacific that involved Peru and Bolivia. Thus, in 1883, the Chilean government acquired the province of Antofagasta from Bolivia and the provinces of Tarapacá, Tacna, and Arica from Peru. In 1891 Chile went through civil war when rebel forces backed by the Roman Catholic Church attempted to overthrow the leadership of José Manuel Balmaceda, a member of the Liberal Party.

Salvador Allende, a Marxist-Leninist, was elected president in the 1970s and instituted most of his initiatives early on in his presidency. On September 11, 1973, military forces led by General Augusto Pinochet seized power from the Allende government. Pinochet banned all political parties and suspended the Chilean constitution. As a result of Pinochet's coup d'état, thousands of Allende supporters were arrested and many of these individuals were executed or exiled. Some were even tortured by a number of his secret police. Pinochet installed himself as president even though his policies were comparable to a dictatorship.

Civilian rule was restored in 1989, when Patricio Aylwin was elected president after the first election in 16 years of totalitarianism under August Pinochet. Under Aylwin's leadership, the previous Pinochet regime was charged with numerous human rights violations. Since 1990 the country's economy has steadily grown, and levels of poverty have dropped considerably. At present, Chile, along with Argentina, has transitioned into a strong economic power in South America.

Educational System

Preprimary education in Chile is not compulsory. Nevertheless, it has played a role in the Chilean education system for more than a century. With the encouragement of German educationists, preschool education became one component of the Chilean system of education in the early twentieth century. Enrollment in preschool was slow for several decades. Only in 1960 did preschool enrollment grow to significant levels. By 2000 the number of parents enrolling their children in preschool surpassed the 250,000 mark. The majority of these children attends kindergarten—usually considered the final year of the preprimary years.

Compulsory Education

Compulsory education in Chile includes primary and secondary education for students between the ages of six and 17. The duration of compulsory education in the country is 12 years. The primary and secondary school student/teacher ratio is about 25 students for every teacher. Virtually all students at the level of grade 8 complete their primary education. The primary school entrants' completion rate percentage of 123 percent accounts for older students who return to school to complete their basic curriculum requirements. This rate will eventually level off in the future. The secondary school gross enrollment rate is at 91 percent because secondary school was made compulsory in 2003 and not all students who fall within the appropriate secondary level age have completed secondary school, mostly students in poor, rural communities.

Primary Education

Primary education in Chile is compulsory for a period of eight years—eight grade levels—for students between the ages of six and 13 years. Chilean primary education is considered a basic curriculum that covers the Spanish language, mathematics, basic natural science in some schools, and social studies. The intentions of the early leaders of the republic were progressive in education; they wanted to institute schooling as early as 1812. However, as a result of limited resources, civil war, and occasional conflict with neighboring countries, this goal was unable to be realized for nearly a century. From 1920 to about 1930, basic education study was mandatory for a four-year period, between the ages of six and 10 years. From 1930 to 1965, primary education was compulsory for a period of six years—for students ages six to about age 11. In 1965 the Ministry of

Education in Chile established an education reform that mandated an eight-year period of education for all children ages six to 13 years.

Secondary Education

Prior to 2003, secondary education was not mandatory in Chile. The Pinochet government and Chilean military rule in general had been quite antagonistic toward a governmental, centralized system of support for secondary education and higher education. This position was the result of higher education's overall influence on socialist politics and an effort on the part of military leaders and right-wing politicians to limit educational access, especially to poor and working populations, as much as possible. Under the presidency of Ricardo Lagos, who survived the Pinochet regime, secondary education became a compulsory part of education in Chile and an important part of the country's education system. The law was added to the Chilean constitution in 2003.

Secondary education in Chile is generally divided into two modules. The first module is an academic track that emphasizes the natural sciences and humanities. By grade 11, students who excel academically have the option of focusing on one or two subjects related to mathematics, the natural sciences, humanities, and social sciences. These students are more often university-bound than are other students. The second module is a technical and vocational track that prepares students with skills that will make them competitive for entering the Chilean workforce. Public schools generally emphasize the technical and vocational module. Unfortunately, preference for the first module that emphasizes the arts and sciences is usually given to secondary school students of private schools. Students whose family incomes are low will more than likely attend public schools.

Tertiary Education

Tertiary education in Chile consists of both public and private institutions of education. There are currently 75 universities in Chile. The governments under Eduardo Frei and Salvador Allende in the 1960s and early 1970s provided greater educational access to universities. There are eight so-called traditional universities: the University of Chile (established in 1842), University of Santiago (established in 1849

as the School of Arts and Crafts and later as the Technical University of the State), Pontifical Catholic University of Chile (established in 1888), University of Concepción (established in 1919), Pontifical Catholic University of Valparaíso (established in 1928), Federico Santa María Technical University (established in 1929 in Valparaíso), Southern University of Chile (established in 1954 in Valdivia), and Catholic University of the North (established in 1956 in Antofagasta). The University of Chile in Santiago is the oldest and largest institution of its kind in the country, with a total enrollment of nearly 28,000 students. The University of Santiago is the premier polytechnic institution in the country.

Teacher Education

University departments and programs in education are the primary settings for teacher training in Chile. This training lasts between four and five years. Preservice teachers are prepared in different ways, depending on the level (preprimary, primary, or secondary levels). Each university has its own university entrance examination that all education applicants must pass in order to continue in teacher training. The country itself does not have official certification procedures for new teachers. Universities handle both the education and the certification process. Accordingly, there is no form of monitoring the quality and effectiveness of newly graduated teachers. In recent years, there has been an initiative to deemphasize behaviorist methodologies in teaching and instruction, and, instead, greater emphasis on a cognitive approach to learning.

Informal Education

Recent census figures indicate that more than 4.5 million Chilean citizens 15 years or older have fewer than eight years of schooling. This statistic greatly diminishes their potential in the economic market. Despite the fact that the Chilean government allocated significant funding to education after 1990, many adult workers in Chile need to retool themselves to gain new skills, especially adults who were unable to attend school during the military regime between 1973 and 1989. The most adversely affected populations in this regard are the indigenous populations in Chile, particularly those in the highly concentrated

Chile Education at a Glance

General Information

Capital	Santiago
Population	16.8 million
Languages	Spanish, Italian, German, English
Adult literacy rate (ages 15 and over)	95.7%
GDP per capita	US$12,700
Number of phones (landline) per 100 people	21.1
Number of phones (mobile) per 100 people	64.9
Number of Internet users per 100 people	41.1
Life expectancy at birth (years)	77

Formal Educational Information

Enrollment in primary school (ages 6–11)	1.5 million
Enrollment in lower and upper secondary school (ages 12–17)	1.7 million
Number of years of compulsory education	12 (ages 6–17)
Primary school student/teacher ratio	25.2
Lower and upper secondary school student/teacher ratio	25.2
Primary school gross enrollment ratio	104%
Secondary school gross enrollment ratio	91%
Tertiary school gross enrollment ratio	47.8%
Primary school entrants completion rate	123%
Child labor (ages 5–14)	3%

Note: Unless otherwise indicated, all data are based on sources from 2011.

region of La Araucanía in central Chile. This region also has the highest percentage of families and individuals living in poverty. Recent developments in Chile include the promulgation of informal or nonformal schooling, particularly for indigenous populations. Most of the country's poor are employed in small and medium-sized companies that hire fewer than five employees. Accordingly, these individuals have the greatest need to improve their skills if the company should become insolvent.

System Economics

According to the United Nations Development Programme (2010), along with Mauritius, total public expenditure on education of Chile represented 3.4 percent of the gross domestic product (GDP) in 2007. Given the GDP of Chile at $260 billion, educational expenditure in the country amounts to nearly $9 billion, about $2,667 per student (total amount equivalent to US dollars divided by 3,315,000, the approximate number of primary and secondary students in the country). Chile ranks 129 of 186 countries in percentage of educational expenditure.

Future Prospects

Since the early 1990s, the educational system in Chile has become one of the most successful in South America. Despite an annual per capita gross national product of slightly over $15,000, Chile has managed to maintain a streamlined education that gives nearly all its citizens a right to go to school. Through information and communication technologies as well as other modes of discourse, the country has been successful in reaching its rural populations as well. The F-50 Villa Las Estrellas School on the Antarctic continent is one successful example of rural education in a remote region under Chilean jurisdiction. The school is run by two teachers for approximately 15 students between grades 1 and 8. The community also has access to library facilities. In addition, there is also a kindergarten on the premises that is headed by one teacher and attended by about five students.

Daniel Ness and Chia-ling Lin

REFERENCES

Central Intelligence Agency. *The CIA World Factbook*. New York: Skyhorse, 2011. https.www.cia.gov/library/publications/the-world-factbook/index.html.

Nation Master. 2011. www.nationmaster.com.

UNESCO. *Global Education Digest 2012: Comparing Education Statistics Across the World*. Montreal: UNESCO Institute for Statistics, 2012.

———. "Strong Foundations: Early Childhood Care and Education." *Education for All Global Monitoring Report*. Paris: UNESCO, 2006.

UNESCO–IBE. www.ibe.unesco.org/en/worldwide/unesco-regions/latin-america-and-the-caribbean/chile.html.

United Nations Development Programme. *United Nations Development Report 2010*. New York: Palgrave Macmillan, 2010.

World Bank Education Statistics. 2011. www.worldbank.org.

COLOMBIA

The Republic of Colombia has a population of over 45 million and is the third-largest Spanish-speaking nation in the world after Mexico and Spain.

Approximately 58 percent of Colombians are of mixed Spanish and native Indian descent (mestizo); 20 percent are white; 18 percent are Afro-Colombian (black and mulatto); 3 percent mixed black and Native American; and 1 percent Native American. Although the majority of the population is Spanish-speaking, there are over 60 aboriginal languages throughout Colombia. With respect to religion, approximately 90 percent of Colombians are Roman Catholic.

Educational System

Since the 1960s, the Revolutionary Armed Forces of Colombia (*Fuerzas Armadas Revolucionarias de Colombia*), commonly known by the acronym FARC, has had a great impact in society and education. FARC was established as a Marxist-Leninist revolutionary guerrilla organization with the goal of seizing power and control in Colombia through an armed revolution. FARC funds itself primarily through extortion, kidnapping, and participation in the illegal drug trade. In reaction to FARC and civil unrest, Colombia adopted goals for education that include respect for human rights, peace, and democracy. Cultural, scientific, technological advancement and environmental protection are also high priorities in Colombia's education system. Currently, Colombia's education system comprises approximately 9 million students, with 60,000 schools and 400,000 teachers employed in primary and secondary education.

Preschool

Preschool is a component of the formal basic education system in Colombia. Roughly 80 percent of preschools are public, providing education for children three to five years of age. In 2008, 48 percent of children under six years of age were enrolled in preschool. The first two levels of preschool, *prejardín* and *jardín*, offered to children three and four years old, are not compulsory, whereas *Transición* is the only compulsory level in preschool. *Transición* is tuition-free and attended by children five years of age.

Primary Education

Primary education is a part of the formal compulsory education system. In 2008 the net enrollment rate at the primary level was 90 percent. Primary education consists of five elementary grades (students six to 10 years of age) and four secondary grades (students

11 to 14 years of age). In 2007 and previous years, Colombia spent the largest portion of its allocation of public spending on primary education. Funds distributed to primary education amounted to 41 percent of the total 12.6 percent designated for use in all levels of education (i.e., preprimary, primary, secondary, and tertiary) (UNESCO 2007). In the same year, the completion rate in primary education was 107 percent and the primary to secondary transition rate was 99 percent.

Secondary Education

Secondary education is also part of the compulsory education system. This level consists of both an academic track and a technical track for students between the ages of 14 and 17. The academic track enhances student learning in the fields of science, arts, and humanities. The technical track prepares students for employment in social services or industrial occupations. In 2008 the net enrollment rate for secondary school was 71 percent, an increase of 14 percent from 2005.

Postsecondary Education

Higher education is led by the Colombian government through the country's Institute for the Promotion of Higher Education (Instituto Colombiano de Estudios Fiscales [ICEF]). ICEF monitors the quality of tertiary schools throughout Colombia. A report by UNESCO indicated that in 2008, 35 percent of the total population of tertiary age were attending tertiary education institutions. Higher education in Colombia is available to students who have completed secondary education and have passed a highly competitive exam required for admission to any public postsecondary institution. Such institutions offer a variety of degrees in areas of science, technology, and humanities through undergraduate, graduate, and postdoctorate programs. In the capital city of Bogotá, there are over 100 higher education technology institutes and universities. Throughout Colombia, there are seven public national universities and 24 departmental (regional) universities.

The National University of Colombia is the largest higher education institution, with over 43,000 students. In 2009 the National University launched a campaign to promote science and technology in education. The Colombian government also endeavors to find solutions that widen availability of higher education through virtual education by investing in technological advancements. The University City of Valle paves the way for such ventures; the school has eight satellite campuses in other Colombian cities.

Private Education

Colombia's private education comprises 14 Catholic universities and 25 nonsectarian universities. Approximately 20 percent of students in primary school and 35 percent of students in secondary school will attend a private institution, while 65 percent of students in higher education already attend private school. One significant contributor to the private-public partnership is the Coffee Growers of Colombia—one of the world's largest nongovernmental associations (NGA) in the coffee community. The goal of the NGA is to support the state and provide aid, such as educational materials and teacher training, to remedy deficiencies and weaknesses throughout the educational system. Another goal is to extend rural education up to grade 11. Other educational contributions include building, equipping, and improving the quality of rural education and health centers.

Curriculum, Instruction, and Assessment

The government of Colombia requires that the national curriculum include math, environmental science, social sciences, art, humanities, physical education, technology, and ethics and human values. However, school curricula are based primarily on the decisions of school administrators and usually reflect individual school characteristics. Further, Colombian schools are encouraged to include content pertaining to regional traditions.

Education in Colombia consists of levels, cycles, and grades. A level is defined as the stages of education (preschool, elementary school, secondary school, high school, and university), cycles are the combination of phases within each level, and grades are composed of organized and implemented plans of study per academic study year. The annual academic calendar consists of 40 hours per week with a required 20-week semester and an hourly

requirement of pedagogical content. Preschools have a 25-hour-per-week requirement to teach children reading skills, and elementary and secondary education has a requirement of an additional five hours. The annual total number of hours allowed for pedagogical activities (instruction hours) is a minimum of 1,000 hours for preschool and 1,200 for elementary and secondary education. In addition, a 10-hour weekly instruction in cultural, sports, and social activities is provided based on the interest of students. Furthermore, bilingual education was made compulsory in many non-Spanish-speaking areas given that Colombia's constitution recognizes many non-Spanish languages as official languages.

In 1976 coffee companies established and funded the *Escuela Nueva* (EN) or New School model in rural areas of Colombia to address educational inequalities in primary education. The mission of the EN is to integrate school life and community, develop students' self-esteem, and encourage student activism in democratic school decision making (Mora 2005). The EN employs a multigrade teaching method whereby one or two teachers instruct children of different grades in one classroom; allows students to advance at their individual pace; promotes group work, peer instruction, and mentorship; and encourages students to actively take part in their own learning as opposed to rote learning. Currently more than 30,000 rural schools use the EN model in Colombia. Studies have shown that the EN has improved educational achievement, reduced student dropout, and successfully increased community participation in educational advancement. In addition to Colombia, millions of students worldwide benefit from Escuela Nueva Foundations.

In 1991 the Ministry of National Education and ICEF created an evaluation exam of basic education known as the "Knowledge" test. This test was given to students in grades 5 to 9 to assess their academic performance in language, mathematics, natural science, social science, and social duties. Before acceptance into college, students in the eleventh grade must take a standardized test similar to the American Scholastic Aptitude Test (SAT). In addition to national standardized tests, academic promotion is often contingent on students' competency in homework assignments, projects, class participation, and general exams. However, children schooled under the EN model have much more flexibility in grade level advancement.

Teacher Education

In 1997 the Ministry of National Education included an additional level of postsecondary schooling known as the *Normales*. The *Normales* are two-year institutions dedicated to teacher training for preschool and elementary school levels. There were 138 institutions accredited in 2001 to assist in increasing the quality of teaching in Colombia. Teacher education in Colombia consists of two phases depending on the level of teaching interest. Phase I requires training in two-year institutions known as *Las Escuelas Normales Superiores*, which are accredited by the Ministry of National Education to train teachers for preschool and primary school levels. Phase II is for those interested in teaching at higher levels of education or who desire a degree in education. Phase II requires either a high school degree or completion of Phase I, and also a passing score on a national exam (developed and published by ICEF), before allowing advancement to a four-year undergraduate education program at a university. Education students attending *Normales Superiores* are required to take 12 hours per week of intense courses (in all basic subjects including pedagogy, epistemology, humanities, sociocultural concepts, and practical training) for two years. In order to teach grade levels beyond primary school, student teachers must select a program with a particular plan of study directed toward their teaching interest in various subjects (e.g., math or science).

The Colombian Ministry of National Education does not require teacher certification upon employment; rather students' grade level denotes their pay scales, as delineated in the National Teachers Scale (*Escalafón Nacional Docente*). There are 14 grade levels in the National Teachers Scale and an increase in salary comes with each progressing level. Salary increases are also dependent on teaching experience and teacher training courses taken.

For students interested in continual teacher training, the *Sistema Nacional de Capacitación Docent*, a national system of teacher training that is a component of the Ministry of National Education, guarantees educators constant training and opportunities for increase in pay scales. ICEF collaborates with the ministry and Colombian universities for the promotion and continuance of teacher training programs.

Nonformal Education

Nonformal education provides skills to improve the quality of life for Colombians. Due to high competitiveness in admission and often lack of accessibility to higher education, nonformal education is an alternative to tertiary education. Colombia's National Services of Learning (*El Servicio Nacional de Aprendizaje*), more commonly known as SENA, was established in 1957. SENA, comprising more than 200,000 programs and 21,000 instructors, offers the labor force free educational programs in technical fields in order to improve occupational skills. SENA is also involved in virtual education. By the end of 2007, it was estimated that 1.2 million Colombians were benefiting from virtual programs.

System Economics

Studies have shown that income disparity in Colombia is significant. In 2008 the Gini Coefficient, which measures inequality of income distribution, was high at .058. However, educational spending totaled 12.6 percent of the total Colombian governmental expenditure in 2007, or 4.9 percent of the national gross domestic product of US$401.1 billion. Forty-one percent of the total national expenditure on education in 2007 was allocated to primary education, while 29 percent was given to secondary education, 26 percent to tertiary education, and 4 percent distributed to unnamed educational sources.

Gender and Education

Colombia's pattern of armed conflict has given the country the second-highest number of internally displaced refugees in the world. In the capital city of Bogotá, up to 77 percent of displaced children are out of school; according to Connolly, Hayden, and Levin (2007), many of these children are in their formative years. Displaced children often end up as child soldiers and, in some cases, in domestic and sexual slavery.

Despite civil unrest, 2006 UNESCO statistics reveal that Colombia is one of 19 out of 25 Latin American and Caribbean nations to have achieved gender parity in primary school with a gender parity index (GPI) of 0.98. In the same year, secondary schools achieved a GPI of 1.11, and tertiary schools, 1.09; however, Colombia has yet to reach the Millennium Development Goal of universal primary education (UPE), as only 88 percent of all children are enrolled in primary school, 65 percent in secondary school, and 31 percent in higher education. UPE is reached when the net enrollment rate reaches 95 percent. Gender parity is achieved when the GPI of the gross enrollment ratio is between 0.97 and 1.03.

Studies conducted by UNESCO in 2006 show that male and female school enrollment rates were comparable. For instance, 65 percent of both males and females were enrolled in preprimary school (preschool levels of *pre-jardín*, *jardín*, and *transición*). Primary school enrollment numbers were also similar between the two genders as 88 percent of girls were enrolled in primary school, compared to 89 percent of boys. In secondary school enrollment, girls gained a slight increase in enrollment with 68 percent versus 61 percent for boys. Female enrollment continued to stay ahead of male enrollment as 32 percent of females were reported to have attended higher education compared to 30 percent of males. Furthermore, the region of Latin America and the Caribbean shows only 3 percent of all children not in compulsory school in comparison to other regions of the world, including South and West Asia (with 24 percent) and sub-Saharan Africa (with 47 percent). Of the 3 percent of children not enrolled in compulsory school in the Latin America and Caribbean region, 47 percent are females.

Due to civil strife, violent outbreaks, and a desire to improve human rights and encourage economic growth, the Colombian government instigated seven social development strategies in 1994, one of them especially targeted to women. The Policy for Equity and Women's Participation was specially implemented to meet the needs of women though improvements in educational acquisition, health care, employment, human rights and justice, and rural development. Each of these sectors seeks to eliminate impediments to equality, encourage and improve political participation, support women's human rights, and eliminate violence against women. The National Department for Women's Equality (NDWE), implemented in 1996, promotes awareness, provides technical assis-

tance, and enhances cooperation at national, regional, and local levels.

Technology and Education

In 2006 Colombia developed its Ten-Year Education Plan (*El Plan Decenal de Educación*) with the goal to create a strong foundation in science, technology, and innovation. In order to improve the quality and access of education in Colombia, companies such as Didáctica and universities have worked on developing virtual information classrooms (*aulas informáticas virtuales*).

Over the years, a number of Colombian programs have been developed to enhance computer literacy and access. For instance, Microsoft's Learning Initiative, part of the Computers for Education program, comprises two subprograms: (1) Fresh Start for Donated Computers, and (2) Integrating ICT Skills into Teaching and Learning. These subprograms have provided computer training for teachers and distributed more than 71,000 refurbished computers to over 7,000 schools. Additionally, the program has provided free upgrades on selected Microsoft Windows products and significantly reduced pricing on Microsoft Office. The Colombian Education Ministry and Ecopetrol have also collaborated to increase computer access throughout the country. Together, they signed an alliance to provide 490 personal computers, Internet access to 35 schools, and computer training for 175 teachers.

Dilemmas and Challenges: Future Prospects

Colombia has a long and complex history of armed conflict with FARC. Human Rights Watch (2005) estimated that 20 to 30 percent of the guerrillas in FARC are children less than 18 years of age. According to the Humanitarian Action Report (2007), between 5,000 and 6,000 children in Colombia are enrolled in nonstate armed entities. Children who try to escape or leave FARC are known to suffer frightening consequences such as torture or death by a firing squad. Poverty is another problem in Colombia. The country's unequal income distribution has produced high levels of poverty. The United Nations *Human Development Report* (2008) indicates that 14 percent of Colombians have an income of less than

$1 per day and 27 percent earn less than $2 per day. Nevertheless, the nationwide poverty rate dropped from 56 percent in 2002 to 45 percent in 2006. Additionally, the extreme poverty rate decreased from 22 percent in 2002 to 12 percent in 2006. Studies in 2008 showed that a factor contributing to Colombia's poverty was its high unemployment rate of 11.8 percent. Educational and vocational opportunities for the rural population are much more limited compared to those offered in large cities. Nearly 38 percent of Colombian teachers are not qualified to teach and thus often work in rural areas. Consequentially, many of the poorest and most isolated regions trail far behind the more developed in rates of educational access.

One future initiative of the Colombian government is the improvement of health care, environmental sustainability, and unemployment as the country endeavors to meet Millennium Development goals by 2015. Colombia also has goals to increase education coverage, provide equity and accountability, and to ensure that funding is properly distributed. Other goals include universal primary schooling, promotion of gender equity, and empowerment of women. Another initiative concerns Colombia's role in improving the quality of education with the Ten-Year Plan. Beginning in 2006, the Ten-Year Plan, with a deadline in 2016, aims to address challenges in education such as pedagogical renewal and the integration of science and math into classrooms.

Alma S. Boutin-Martinez, Rose Wong, and Mavel Moreno

REFERENCES

Central Intelligence Agency. *The CIA World Factbook.* New York: Skyhorse, 2011. https.www.cia.gov/library/publications/the-world-factbook/index.html.

Connolly, Paul, Jacqueline Hayden, and Diane Levin. *From Conflict to Peace Building: The Power of Early Childhood Initiative—Lessons from Around the World.* Washington, DC: National Association for the Education of Young Children, 2007.

Ecopetrol. *Ecopetrol Supports Colombia's Education.* 2007. www.ecopetrol.com.co/english/contenido.aspx?catID=313&conID=39293.

Georgetown University. Political Database for the Americas (*Base de Datos Politicos de las Ameritas*). 2011. http://pdba.georgetown.edu.

Human Rights Watch. *U.N. Security Council to Discuss Colombia's Child Soldiers.* 2005. www.hrw.org/news/2005/02/21/colombia-armed-groups-send-children-war.

Ministry of Education. *Pruebas Saber.* 2012. http://menweb.mineducacion.gov.co/saber/.

Mora, José G. Public-Private Partnerships in Latin America: A Review Based on Four Case Studies. Conference Proceedings. *Mobilizing the Private Sector of Public Education.* Kennedy School of Government, Harvard University, October 5–6, 2005.

Nation Master. 2011. www.nationmaster.com.

Servico Nacional de Aprendizaje (SENA). 2009.

UNESCO–IBE. "Colombia." In *World Data on Education: A Guide to the Structure of National Education Systems,* 6th ed. 2007. www.ibe.unesco.org/en/services/resources-studies/world-data-on-education.html.

UNESCO Ministerio de Educación. *El Desarrollo de la Educación: Informe nacional de Colombia.* 2008. www.ibe.unesco.org/National_Reports/ICE_2008/colombia_NR08_sp.pdf.

United Nations Development Programme. *Human Development Report: Colombia.* 2008. http://hdr.undp.org/en/.

US Department of State. *Colombia.* 2009. www.state.gov.

World Bank Education Statistics. 2011. www.worldbank.org.

Colombia Education at a Glance

General Information

Capital	Bogotá
Population	44.3 million
Languages	Spanish, Queschua, and 80 indigenous languages currently used
Adult literacy rate (ages 15 and over)	92.8%
GDP per capita	US$8,600
People below poverty line	49.2%
Number of phones (landline) per 100 people	17.3
Number of phones (mobile) per 100 people	49.2
Number of Internet users per 100 people	10.7
Life expectancy at birth (years)	72

Formal Educational Information

Enrollment in primary school (ages 6–10)	4.7 million
Enrollment in lower and upper secondary school (ages 11–16)	5.6 million
Number of years of compulsory education	11 (ages 6–16)
Primary school student/teacher ratio	26.5
Secondary school student/teacher ratio	24.6
Lower and upper secondary school student/teacher ratio	24.6
Primary school gross enrollment ratio	112%
Secondary school gross enrollment ratio	78%
Tertiary school gross enrollment ratio	29.3%
Primary school entrants completion rate	97%

Note: Unless otherwise indicated, all data are based on sources from 2011.

ECUADOR

Ecuador is a country located in South America. The official language is Spanish. However, a large part of the Ecuadorian population speaks Quechua or one of the many other Amerindian languages. The breakdown in terms of ethnicity is the following: mestizo and European at 65 percent; Quechua at 25 percent; Spanish at 7 percent; and black at 3 percent. Approximately 95 percent of the population belongs to the Roman Catholic Church. Only 5 percent of the population consists of members of other religions.

For centuries, the Incan civilization flourished in present-day Ecuador. The Inca domination ended in 1533 when Spanish conquistadores took over the region. The region of present-day Ecuador was called the territory of Quito (which is presently the capital city of the country) and was under Spanish rule for more than 150 years. In 1717 Quito became a territorial acquisition of New Granada (present-day Colombia) under New Granada's viceroyalty. Between 1819 and 1822, Quito, New Granada, and Venezuela established Gran Colombia, a federation that became independent from Spain. The country's present name was changed in 1830, when this region of Gran Colombia withdrew and became an independent nation. Shortly after this point, Charles Darwin visited the Galapagos Archipelago, a stretch of islands off the coast of Ecuador and under the country's jurisdiction, where he found additional support for the theory of evolution. Ecuador lost territory in a number of skirmishes and wars with its neighbors in the early twentieth century. Within the past several decades, officials have been elected to office, but not without dispute. To this day, Ecuador ranks as one of the least politically stable countries in South America. Civilian protests have recently contributed to recalls of the country's presidents.

Educational System

The educational system in Ecuador is one of the poorest in South America, both in terms of financial and physical resources. The system has the most difficulty in reaching rural areas of the country. In the last several decades of the twentieth century, government spending on education was steadily increasing, and there was some hope that this infusion of funds would translate to a more efficient system. However, this did not happen, and after 2000, there was a steady decline of government funding for education and schooling. At 1 percent of the government's total gross domestic product (GDP), educational expenditure in Ecuador is one of the lowest in the world.

Similar to the educational systems of most developing countries in parts of South America, Central America, Africa, and parts of Asia, the system in Ecuador is able to fund only the minimal schooling costs for each student. Families are required to pay for additional fees and transportation costs to and from school. This expense puts a tremendous burden on rural families because they tend to be poorer than urban families, and since they live farther from school buildings than urban dwellers for the most part, they must bear the brunt of paying more fees for their children's school transportation.

Nevertheless, all children must attend school for their basic education requirements, which, according to the constitution of Ecuador, is a period of nine years. Preprimary education in Ecuador is not compulsory. Primary education in the country, on the other hand, is compulsory for a period of six years from grades 1 through 6, for students between the ages of six and 11. The primary school student/teacher ratio is about 23 students for every teacher. The gross enrollment ratio for primary school is 117 percent. This percentage is rather high because a number of students older than those attending grade 6 are eligible to attend primary school. The secondary school student/teacher ratio is about 13 students for every teacher. This ratio seems low because the number of students continuing beyond the nine-year compulsory period is quite low. Moreover, many students, especially children and adolescents in rural parts of the country, do not attend school because their life circumstances are difficult; many families are struggling financially, and agricultural laborers, including children, are greatly needed. UNICEF data show that child labor might be at the 8 percent mark. These data corroborate the low secondary school enrollment ratio of 61 percent. Children who finish the basic education requirement at the primary level are required to continue their schooling in the lower secondary school, which enrolls students in grades 6 through 8—students from 12 to about 15 years old.

Tertiary education in Ecuador is mostly available for a selected number of students, most coming from affluent families. There are approximately 20 universities in Ecuador. The Central University of Ecuador is the largest university in the country and one of the oldest in South America. Established in 1826, the university was the result of the merging of the University of Quito (established in 1622 after the formation of the Quito Territory) and the University of Saint Thomas Aquinas (established in 1688). It is important to note that this unification of the two older universities occurred shortly before the country's change of name from Quito to Ecuador in 1830. The Central University of Ecuador also has the most offerings of any university in the country. In addition to a school of arts and sciences, the university also offers programs in architecture, business administration, economics, agriculture, medicine and related disciplines (such as dentistry, veterinary medicine, and pharmacology), the social sciences, engineering and mining, and law. Other large universities include the National Polytechnic School (established in 1869), Universidad Católica de Santiago de Guayaquil (established in 1962), the University of the Pacific (established in 1997), and the Technical University of Quevedo (established in 1984).

Teacher education in Ecuador is somewhat haphazard and is not based on any consistent curriculum for training teachers. In sum, Ecuadorian teacher education has undergone similar difficulties as teacher education systems of other developing countries—namely, although teacher education programs are housed in the universities, there is little, if any, articulation between university teacher education programs and established education policy or procedure with regard to certification or credentialing. Historically, there has been a significant gap between how teachers were prepared in their programs and their actual practice in schools. These problems are consistent with Ecuadorian teacher preparation today. The problem with most teacher education programs is not one of teacher education curriculum per se, but one of content. Teachers are simply not prepared to teach the content that their students are expected to learn in order to be promoted to subsequent grade levels.

System Economics and Future Prospects

According to the United Nations Development Programme (2010), total public expenditure on education

Ecuador Education at a Glance

General Information

Capital	Quito
Population	13.7 million
Languages	Spanish, Quechua
Adult literacy rate (ages 15 and over)	91%
GDP per capita	US$4,500
People below poverty line	38.5
Number of phones (landline) per 100 people	12.4
Number of phones (mobile) per 100 people	45.4
Number of Internet users per 100 people	4.5
Life expectancy at birth (years)	77

Formal Educational Information

Enrollment in primary school (ages 6–11)	1.7 million
Enrollment in lower and upper secondary school (ages 12–17)	1.6 million
Number of years of compulsory education	9 (ages 6–15)
Primary school student/teacher ratio	23.1
Lower and upper secondary school student/teacher ratio	13.3
Primary school gross enrollment ratio	117%
Secondary school gross enrollment ratio	61%
Tertiary school gross enrollment ratio	20%
Primary school entrants completion rate	101%
Child labor (ages 5–14 years)	8%

Note: Unless otherwise indicated, all data are based on sources from 2011.

in Ecuador represented 1 percent of the GDP in 2001. Given the GDP of Ecuador at $155.3 billion, educational expenditure in the country amounts to nearly $2.25 billion, about $457 per student (total amount equivalent to US dollars divided by 3,402,000, the approximate number of primary and secondary students in the country). Ecuador ranks 172 of 186 countries in percentage of educational expenditure.

The Educational Ministry of Ecuador is currently seeking to improve education in the country. The ministry's goals are to reach high levels of standards and expectations, find and retain strong leaders, support learning that is student-centered, involve parents and communities in educational initiatives, identify important benchmarks for purposes of assessment and accountability, foster a curriculum that promotes inquiry and challenge, provide professional development for in-service teachers, and maximize the amount of time available for all students to succeed in school. Unfortunately, given the lack of financial and material resources and an inadequate mind-set among many Ecuadorians about the importance of a strong education, these goals are going to be difficult to reach—especially within a short period of time.

Fortunately, both governmental and nongovernmental organizations have lent support in recent years. While this infusion of funds helped rural children gain access to education, there remain high levels of corruption among contractors and poor levels of educational infrastructure, especially in the Andes region and northwestern section of the Amazonian basin in the eastern part of the country. The ministry needs to invest in technologies that allow children of rural families to benefit from all school subjects. In addition, the country would be wise in establishing law that prevents the labor of children—especially those under 16 years—who deserve an education that will help them compete in the global economy.

Daniel Ness and Chia-ling Lin

REFERENCES

Boulianne, Real, and Cynthia Weston. "Discrepancy between Preparation and Practice in Teacher Education: An Ecuadorian Study." *Teaching and Teacher Education* 3:2 (1987): 99–107.

Central Intelligence Agency. *The CIA World Factbook*. New York: Skyhorse, 2011. https.www.cia.gov/library/publications/the-world-factbook/index.html.

Nation Master. 2011. www.nationmaster.com.

UNESCO. *Global Education Digest 2012: Comparing Education Statistics Across the World*. Montreal: UNESCO Institute for Statistics, 2012.

———. "Strong Foundations: Early Childhood Care and Education." *Education for All Global Monitoring Report*. Paris: UNESCO, 2006.

UNESCO–IBE. www.ibe.unesco.org/en/worldwide/unesco-regions/latin-america-and-the-caribbean/ecuador.html.

United Nations Development Programme. *United Nations Development Report 2010*. New York: Palgrave Macmillan, 2010.

US Department of Labor. *2001 Findings on the Worst Forms of Child Labor*. Washington, DC: Bureau of International Labor Affairs, US Department of Labor, 2002.

World Bank Education Statistics. 2011. www.worldbank.org.

GUYANA

Guyana is a South American nation. The country was a colony of the Netherlands from the seventeenth century to the early nineteenth century, at which time it became a colony of the United Kingdom. As a result of the end of black slavery in the 1820s, the British sent indentured servants from India and others from the East Indies to work on the colony's abundant sugar plantations. Guyana became independent from Great Britain in 1966 and was controlled by a number of socialist leaders. Since the 1990s, the country has been generally politically stable, and free and fair elections have prevailed for the most part. About 50 percent of all Guyanese are Christian. About 35 percent are Hindu—the largest percentage of Hindu population on the continent. About 10 percent of the population is Muslim, and 5 percent are members of other religions.

Educational System

Education in Guyana is compulsory for a period of nine years. This period consists of six years of primary education and the first three years of a seven-year secondary school period. Preprimary education in the country is usually a two-year period for children between the ages of three and six years. Although not compulsory, most parents send their children to the prekindergarten (ages four and five) or kindergarten levels (ages five and six). In the 1970s and 1980s, Guyana was grappling with improving early childhood education; teachers were not trained adequately, both in terms of content and child development. In recent years, UNICEF and other nongovernmental organizations have provided assistance in improving preprimary education in the country.

Primary education begins at the first-grade level (ages six or seven) and continues to the sixth grade. Primary schools in Guyana can be found in three settings: elementary schools (grades 1 through 6); primary/secondary schools (grades 1 through 9—the last three grades are the first three grades of secondary education); and extended schools (preprimary grades through grade 9). The curriculum in Guyanese schools is similar to that in American schools in that the four common subjects of language arts, social studies, mathematics, and natural science are taught. The student/teacher ratio at the primary school level is about 26 students for every teacher. The primary school gross enrollment ratio is 132 percent, indicating that the number of students of all ages enrolled in primary school is greater than the actual number of students who are typically within the age range of six to 11 years. It is not surprising, then, that 126 percent of all primary school entrants complete primary school. However, this does not mean that all students of primary grade levels are enrolled in primary school; the net enrollment ratio amounts to only 89 percent. The secondary school student/teacher ratio in Guyana is 16 to 17 students for every teacher. The secondary gross enrollment ratio is 102 percent. However, the net enrollment ratio is only 67 percent, indicating that far fewer students of the age group are actually enrolled.

Most students who successfully complete their secondary education programs have the option of attending, if accepted, the University of Guyana or any of the several specialized colleges in the country. Otherwise, students must apply to colleges or universities abroad. Established in 1963, the University of Guyana in Georgetown is the preeminent university in the country. Operating on two campuses, the university is divided into eight schools: arts, natural sciences, social sciences, education and humanities, health sciences, technology, agriculture and forestry, and continuing education.

In Guyana there are also several colleges that specialize in various fields. The Critchlow Labour College is an important institution that serves as both a formal educational institution and a center for training adults in new skills for different professions. It was established in 1967 as part of the Guyanese labor movement, which has historically attempted to serve the working populations of postcolonial Guyana. The country is also home to the Cyril Potter College of Education, which was founded as the Teachers' Training Centre in 1928. The college is the primary institution that trains teachers throughout the country. Teachers who graduate from Cyril Potter College are usually automatically approved for certification and qualification to teach in Guyanese schools. Nevertheless, students who graduate from other programs are considered for educational positions. In addition to the University of Guyana and these colleges, there are numerous state and private institutions in the areas of business and management, nursing, and technical vocations.

System Economics and Future Prospects

According to the United Nations Development Programme (2010), along with Belgium, total public expenditures on education in Guyana represented 6.1 percent of the gross domestic product (GDP) in 2007. Given the GDP of Guyana at $5.069 billion,

educational expenditure in the country amounts to more than $309 million, or $1,995 per student (total amount equivalent to US dollars divided by 155,000, the approximate number of primary and secondary students in the country). Guyana ranks 35 of 186 countries in percentage of educational expenditure, the second-highest educational expenditure in South America (Bolivia ranks higher).

Education is compulsory at the primary and the first of two secondary school levels in Guyana. But a large percentage of students do not complete school beyond the fifth-grade level, and even fewer continue to secondary school. As in neighboring countries, school attendance is hampered as a result of poor education for teachers, a lack of adequate facilities at schools, and difficulty in reaching large rural populations. Also, many families are unable to afford the fees that are associated with a child's education. Although public education in Guyana is free, families often are required to pay for books and supplies as well as travel to and from school—especially in rural districts. Rural families find it extremely difficult to

---

Guyana Education at a Glance

General Information

Capital	Georgetown
Population	744,768
Languages	English, Amerindian dialects, Creole, Caribbean Hindustani, Urdu
Adult literacy rate (ages 15 and over)	98.8%
GDP per capita	US$4,800
People below poverty line	no data
Number of phones (landline) per 100 people	12.4
Number of phones (mobile) per 100 people	45.4
Number of Internet users per 100 people	4.5
Life expectancy at birth (years)	66

Formal Educational Information

Enrollment in primary school (ages 6–11)	87,000
Enrollment in lower and upper secondary school (ages 12–16)	68,000
Number of years of compulsory education	9 (ages 6–15)
Primary school student/teacher ratio	26.2
Lower and upper secondary school student/teacher ratio	16.5
Primary school gross enrollment ratio	132%
Secondary school gross enrollment ratio	102%
Tertiary school gross enrollment ratio	9.9%
Primary school entrants completion rate	126%
Child labor (ages 5–14)	16%

Note: Unless otherwise indicated, all data are based on sources from 2011.

send their children to schools mainly because fees are expensive and children are needed by their families for agricultural labor, particularly in the rural north and east. To make matters worse, UNICEF data show that about 16 percent of Guyanese children between five and 14 years engage in labor. This factor strains educational access especially for economically disadvantaged populations. In addition, families find educational alternatives; given the diversity of religious faiths in the country, many families send their children to schools run by particular religious denominations rather than public schools. Therefore, an important goal for the Guyanese government is to invest in services that will make it affordable and motivating for families to send their children to public schools. One way to do this is to develop and foster information and communications technology (ICT) that will lessen the burdens for children and families and will most likely keep students in school through the secondary level.

Daniel Ness and Chia-ling Lin

REFERENCES

Central Intelligence Agency. *The CIA World Factbook*. New York: Skyhorse, 2011. https.www.cia.gov/library/publications/the-world-factbook/index.html.

Nation Master. 2011. www.nationmaster.com.

UNESCO. *Global Education Digest 2012: Comparing Education Statistics Across the World*. Montreal: UNESCO Institute for Statistics, 2012.

———. "Strong Foundations: Early Childhood Care and Education." *Education for All Global Monitoring Report*. Paris: UNESCO, 2006.

UNESCO–IBE. www.ibe.unesco.org/en/worldwide/unesco-regions/latin-america-and-the-caribbean/guyana.html.

United Nations Development Programme. *United Nations Development Report 2010*. New York: Palgrave Macmillan, 2010.

US Department of Labor. *2001 Findings on the Worst Forms of Child Labor*. Washington, DC: Bureau of International Labor Affairs, US Department of Labor, 2002.

World Bank Education Statistics. 2011. www.worldbank.org.

PARAGUAY

Paraguay is a landlocked country located in South America. The official languages are Spanish and Guarani. In terms of ethnicity, mestizos (Spanish or other European and Amerindian) constitute 95 percent of the population. Approximately 90 percent of the population belongs to the Roman Catholic Church. About 6 percent of the population are members of Protestant groups and about 3 percent are members of another form of Christianity, members of other religions, or have no religion.

Paraguayan independence from Spain occurred in 1811, but the country's declaration of independence from Argentina, its neighbor, did not occur until 1842. Paraguay underwent years of war with Brazil, Bolivia, and Argentina, its three neighbors. The country was defeated by Brazil, Argentina, and Uruguay in the War of the Triple Alliance (1854–1870), one of the bloodiest wars to take place in South America. More than half of the country's inhabitants perished. The overwhelming number of those who survived were women and children; only 28,000 of approximately 150,000 adult males managed to survive the war. As a result of the war, Paraguay was forced to cede territory to Argentina and Brazil. Another devastating war was the Chaco War, which the Paraguayans fought with Bolivia in the 1930s. Although Paraguay lost much of its army, it gained territory from Bolivia. After 35 years of military dictatorship under Alfredo Stroessner, regular and free elections were resumed in the country in 1989.

Educational System

The educational system in Paraguay is unique compared to those of other South American countries. Given its relatively poor standing from a historical perspective, illiteracy in the country has remained rather low in comparison to that of some of its neighbors. The military dictatorship from 1954 to 1989 under Alfredo Stroessner's presidency did not help the country's educational standing by any means. Like Augusto Pinochet and other military despots during his time, Stroessner downplayed the role of education in the fear that strong educational systems would be a threat to his control. Given relative stability in the country's democratic process in recent years, Paraguay's educational system has steadily been improving.

Preprimary, Compulsory, and Secondary Education

The general sequence of schooling and educational levels in Paraguay starts with preprimary, noncompulsory education, which begins when children are three years of age. This is followed by prekindergarten and kindergarten, for children from three to five years, followed by preschool for children ages five and six. Compulsory education in Paraguay is a period of nine years, from grade 1 (ages six or seven years) to grade 9 (ages 14 or 15 years). At present, there are about 937,000 primary school students attending school in Paraguay. Students are presented with a basic curriculum providing foundational skills in language, reading, writing, and mathematics, as well as physical education and art. The primary school student/teacher ratio is about 20 students per teacher. The primary school gross enrollment ratio is 104 percent. However, about 89 percent of all students entering first grade are able to complete primary school.

Grades 7 through 9 at the compulsory stage, regardless of school type, are usually considered the lower secondary education level. At present about 869,000 students are enrolled in the lower secondary grade levels or the upper secondary grade levels combined. Secondary education—namely, high school—is a noncompulsory period for students with strong academic abilities. These students must complete three years of course work before they graduate and apply to the university level. Less affluent children and adolescents from urban and rural environments are at a disadvantage because they have traditionally had limited resources, and subsistence farming has compelled them to stay home and work in the fields rather than go to school. It should be noted that 15 percent of all children between the ages five and 14 are engaged in child labor, and the overwhelming majority of them are rural indigenous children and young adolescents. The lower and upper secondary school student, teacher ratio is roughly 12 students per teacher. Unfortunately, the secondary school enrollment ratio in Paraguay is 64 percent, one of the lowest in South America.

Tertiary Education

Tertiary education in Paraguay is available for a selected number of students, most coming from affluent families. This is not surprising given that roughly 25 percent of all postsecondary-age students enroll in one of the country's universities or related tertiary institutions. There are approximately 32 universities in Paraguay, of which 8 are public and 24 are private. Established in 1889, the Universidad Nacional de Asunción (National University of Asunción) is the oldest university in Paraguay. In fact, more than a century had passed when, in 1993, the next university—Universidad Nacional de Concepción—was established. The fact that no institution was established in the intervening years is plausible: The country endured a succession of several wars from the late nineteenth century to the middle of the twentieth century; and Stroessner's dictatorship frustrated any possibility of the establishment of a university. The National University of Asunción is also the largest university in the country, with an enrollment of more than 36,000 students. The university has 12 schools and 14 regional campuses. In addition, the National University of Asunción is the primary university with a traditional arts and sciences curriculum. The National University of Itapua is another well-known public university in Paraguay. Assuming they have the correct credentials, students with interests in engineering, medicine, and other polytechnic disciplines apply to the National University of Itapua.

Teacher education in Paraguay takes place within the university or in separate teacher training institutes—formerly called normal schools when they initially appeared in 1896. Paraguayan teacher education has undergone similar difficulties as teacher education systems of other developing countries. There is little, if any, articulation between university teacher education programs and established education policy or procedure with regard to certification or credentialing. Historically, there has been a significant gap between how teachers were prepared in their programs and their actual practice in schools. These problems are consistent with Paraguayan teacher preparation today. Teacher education programs emphasize instructional techniques at the expense of content matter. As a result, students are not receiving the content they need to succeed and advance to subsequent educational levels. Teachers are simply not prepared to teach the content that their students are expected to learn in order to be promoted to subsequent grade levels. There are some programs, however, that are attempting to ameliorate the problem of school attrition in indigenous rural communities.

Paraguay Education at a Glance

General Information

Capital	Asunción
Population	6.4 million
Languages	Spanish, Guarani
Adult literacy rate (ages 15 and over)	94%
GDP per capita	US$4,800
People below poverty line	32%
Number of phones (landline) per 100 people	4.8
Number of phones (mobile) per 100 people	28.3
Number of Internet users per 100 people	3
Life expectancy at birth (years)	75

Formal Educational Information

Enrollment in primary school (ages 6–11)	937,000
Enrollment in lower/upper secondary school (ages 12–17)	869,000
Number of years of compulsory education	12 (ages 6–17)
Primary school student/teacher ratio	19.6
Lower/upper secondary school student/teacher ratio (2003)	11.8
Primary school gross enrollment ratio	104%
Secondary school gross enrollment ratio	64%
Tertiary school gross enrollment ratio	24.5%
Primary school entrants completion rate	89%
Child labor (ages 5–14)	15%

Note: Unless otherwise indicated, all data are based on sources from 2011.

System Economics and Future Prospects

According to the United Nations Development Programme (2010), along with Oman and Greece, total public expenditure on education of Paraguay represented 4 percent of the gross domestic product (GDP) in 2008. Given the GDP of Paraguay at $33.27 billion, educational expenditure in the country amounts to over $1.33 billion, about $737 per student (total amount equivalent to US dollars divided by 1,806,000, the approximate number of primary and secondary students in the country). Paraguay ranks 103 of 186 countries in percentage of educational expenditure.

The Educational Ministry of Paraguay is currently seeking to improve education in the country. The ministry's goals are to reach high levels of standards and expectations, find and retain strong leaders, support learning that is student-centered, involve parents and communities in educational initiatives, identify important benchmarks for purposes of assessment and accountability, foster a curriculum that promotes inquiry and challenge, provide professional development for in-service teachers, and maximize the amount of time available for all students to succeed in school. Unfortunately, given a lack of financial and material resources and an inadequate mind-set among many Paraguayans about the importance of a strong education, particularly those who must work in order to survive, these goals are going to be difficult to reach—especially within a short period of time.

Fortunately, both governmental and nongovernmental organizations have been supportive in recent years. The ministry needs to invest in technologies that allow children of rural families to benefit from all school subjects. In addition, the country would be wise to establish law that prevents the labor of children—especially those under 16 years—who deserve an education that will help them compete in the global economy.

Daniel Ness and Chia-ling Lin

REFERENCES

Central Intelligence Agency. *The CIA World Factbook.* New York: Skyhorse, 2011. https.www.cia.gov/library/publications/the-world-factbook/index.html.

Nation Master. 2011. www.nationmaster.com.

UNESCO. *Global Education Digest 2012: Comparing Education Statistics Across the World.* Montreal: UNESCO Institute for Statistics, 2012.

———. "Strong Foundations: Early Childhood Care and Education." *Education for All Global Monitoring Report.* Paris: UNESCO, 2006.

UNESCO–IBE. www.ibe.unesco.org/en/worldwide/unesco-regions/latin-america-and-the-caribbean/paraguay.html.

United Nations Development Programme. *United Nations Development Report 2010.* New York: Palgrave Macmillan, 2010.

US Department of Labor. *2001 Findings on the Worst Forms of Child Labor.* Washington, DC: Bureau of International Labor Affairs, US Department of Labor, 2002.

World Bank Education Statistics. 2011. www.worldbank.org.

PERU

Peru is a country located on the Pacific coast of South America. The official languages are Spanish and Quechua. In addition, there are numerous speakers of Aymara and other languages native to the Amazonian basin in the northeastern part of the country. In terms of ethnicity, Amerindians make up 45 percent of the population and mestizos (Spanish or other European and Amerindian) represent 37 percent of the population. Europeans make up 15 percent, and blacks, Japanese, and Chinese another 3 percent of the population. Approximately 81 percent of the population belongs to the Roman Catholic Church. Most of the remaining population are not members of any religion or are members of unspecified religions. A very small minority of the population are non-Catholic Christians.

Peru was the home of numerous civilizations prior to Spanish colonization in the early sixteenth century. The most prominent civilization was the Inca Empire, which flourished for centuries in the region that is now Peru. Incan rule ended in 1533 when Spanish conquistadores took over the region that includes present-day Peru, Bolivia, Ecuador, southern Colombia, and a small section of northwestern Brazil. Spain controlled the region for almost three centuries. In 1821 Peru declared its independence. The Spanish military was finally defeated in 1824. One of the outcomes of the War of the Pacific in 1883 was that Peru (along with Bolivia) was forced to cede large amounts of its southern territory to Chile. During the 1980s, the country witnessed a great deal of political instability with the possibility of violent uprisings and coups. The election of Alberto Fujimori in 1990 eased tensions in this regard. However, Peru witnessed an economic downturn in the late 1990s. The economy has remained stagnant and has not shown signs of improvement ever since.

Educational System

Peru has the second-longest compulsory education period in South America (Argentina has the longest). At the same time, the Peruvian educational system is rather unexceptional when compared to those of other South American countries. Despite a rather large schooling infrastructure and a plethora of teachers and teacher candidates, many do not have the required content skills to teach, as evidenced by the Ministry of Education's national examination for teachers. The system has the greatest difficulty in reaching rural areas of the country, which tend to be inhabited by the nation's poorest populations. Although government spending on education has been increasing slowly, education funding has not shown

signs of efficiency in the system. To make matters worse, Peruvians are allowed to begin entering the labor force at age 12, although they are required to attend school to the age of 16. This inconsistency puts poor children who must engage in labor at a great educational disadvantage when compared to their slightly more affluent peers who do not need to contribute to the family income and instead are able to focus on their school studies. In addition, these students are at a disadvantage in terms of where they are expected to attend school; in general, school infrastructure in rural Peru is substandard and lacks basic necessities. Indeed, these students are unable to compete with more affluent students who live primarily in urban areas.

Preprimary and Compulsory Education

Half of all Peruvian children from three to five years old are enrolled in one of several forms of preschool, making the country a leading proponent of education during early childhood. This period provides an academic, physical, and emotional basis for children's education at the primary and secondary levels. Unfortunately, most of the children who do not enter preschool are poor rural children whose families rely on family labor and subsistence farming.

Regardless of setting, all children are required to attend primary and secondary school from grades 1 through 11, or ages six through 16. The last year of the preprimary education period is compulsory in Peru. Students attend primary school between the ages of six and 11 years. The primary school student/teacher ratio is about 25 students for every teacher. The gross enrollment ratio for primary school is 112 percent. This percentage is rather high because a number of students older than those attending grade 6 are eligible to attend primary school. The secondary school student/teacher ratio is about 17 students for every teacher. This ratio is not high because the rate of students continuing beyond sixth grade (age 11) is strongly correlated to the number of children who by age 12 decide to enter the workforce—i.e., those engaged in child labor. Children and adolescents in rural parts of the country either do not attend school or find school somewhat of a burden because their life circumstances are often difficult; families struggle to earn income, and both textile and agricultural sectors are greatly in need of low-skilled children to run machines and perform other types of manual labor. According to data provided by UNICEF, child labor in Peru is approximately 34 percent. It is important to note that females outnumber males in terms of child labor. As a result, there is great disparity not only in socioeconomic class, but also in ethnicity and gender with regard to child labor. Despite these adverse circumstances, the Ministry of Education in Peru has initiated programs that allow working children to complete their 11 years of compulsory schooling. Although the secondary school gross enrollment ratio is 92 percent, the actual percentage of adolescents who are attending secondary school is low; the secondary school net enrollment ratio shows that only 70 percent of all eligible individuals are actually enrolled in school. These data corroborate the UNICEF data on child labor in Peru.

Children who finish the basic education requirement at the primary level are required to continue their schooling at the secondary school level, which enrolls students in grades 7 through 11—students from ages 12 to about 16 years. Peruvian secondary schools are divided into two phases—an initial two-year phase that continues the basic education of the primary school years and a second three-year phase that is supposedly equipped to prepare students for a university or technical education. The second phase is divided into two separate systems: one for continuing secondary school students and another for adults who did not complete their secondary studies and are returning to gain new skills.

Tertiary Education

Tertiary education in Peru consists of the university and technical college. Established in 1551, the National University of San Marcos is a public university in Lima and one of the oldest universities in the Americas. Its enrollment, both undergraduate and graduate, is approximately 33,000 students, the most of any state-run higher education institution. The National University of San Marcos has colleges of health sciences, humanities, social sciences, natural sciences, engineering, and business sciences. The largest private university is the University of San Martin of Porres, which enrolls about 32,000 students annually. With about 50 professional studies, the Universidad Nacional Federico Villareal has

the highest number of programs. The most common courses of study in universities throughout Peru are accounting and business management. All told, there are 78 universities, of which 33 are state and 45 are private. Although 3 million students graduate from secondary school in Peru every year, only one-sixth of this population (about 500,000) actually attend higher education institutions. Indigenous Peruvians are at an educational disadvantage in terms of the number of students who attend and graduate from the university level.

Teacher education is available as one of several programs in most Peruvian universities. However, pedagogical courses are greatly emphasized at the expense of content knowledge. As a result, children in Peruvian schools perform quite poorly, even with respect to peers in neighboring countries. Approximately 200,000 of the country's 250,000 teachers who were administered a content specialty examination by the Education Ministry of Peru were able to solve elementary problems in mathematics, and about one-third failed a reading comprehension examination.

Peru Education at a Glance

General Information

Capital	Lima
Population	28.6 million
Languages	Spanish, Quechua
Adult literacy rate (ages 15 and over)	87.7%
GDP per capita	US$6,600
People below poverty line	54%
Number of phones (landline) per 100 people	7.8
Number of phones (mobile) per 100 people	19.5
Number of Internet users per 100 people	16
Life expectancy at birth (years)	70

Formal Educational Information

Enrollment in primary school (ages 6–11)	3.5 million
Enrollment in lower/upper secondary school (ages 12–16)	2.9 million
Number of years of compulsory education	11 (ages 6–16)
Primary school student/teacher ratio	25.3
Lower/upper secondary school student/teacher ratio (2003)	16.6
Primary school gross enrollment ratio	112%
Secondary school gross enrollment ratio	92%
Tertiary school gross enrollment ratio	33.5%
Primary school entrants completion rate	99%
Child labor (ages 5–14)	34%

Note: Unless otherwise indicated, all data are based on sources from 2011.

System Economics

According to the United Nations Development Programme (2010), along with Liberia, total public expenditure on education in Peru represented 2.7 percent of the gross domestic product (GDP) in 2008. Given the GDP of Peru at $276.9 billion, educational expenditure in the country amounts to nearly $7.5 billion, about $1,138 per student (total amount equivalent to US dollars divided by 6,572,000, the approximate number of primary and secondary students in the country). Peru ranks 151 of 186 countries in percentage of educational expenditure.

Future Prospects

Despite encouraging data supporting a fairly strong educational system, there is a starkly unequal balance favoring affluent Peruvian families in terms of educational access. One primary factor that contributes to unequal educational access is the overwhelming number of school-age children who are engaged in labor, most evident among children in rural families. As a consequence, nearly 200,000 children drop out of school, particularly after they complete their primary education, every year and join the workforce.

In addition to the problem of unequal access, school infrastructures differ in terms of schools for more affluent children in comparison to those whose family incomes are low or below the poverty line. The Peruvian Education Ministry instituted some initiatives to rectify some of the problems in the country's education system. To "accommodate" working children, the government instituted a so-called shift initiative that allows working children to attend school at different times of the day. The Peruvian Ministry of Education has issued a mandate that encourages teachers to provide more time for working children whose grades fall below their peers'. This is not necessarily an advantage because it places undue strain on teachers as well as working students.

Daniel Ness and Chia-ling Lin

References

Central Intelligence Agency. *The CIA World Factbook*. New York: Skyhorse, 2011. https.www.cia.gov/library/publications/the-world-factbook/index.html.

D'Andrea, Marisol. *Peru: Inequality of Education for Indigenous Groups, the Neglected Class*. Toronto: Ontario Institute for Studies in Education, 2007.

Nation Master. 2011. www.nationmaster.com.

UNESCO. *Global Education Digest 2012: Comparing Education Statistics Across the World*. Montreal: UNESCO Institute for Statistics, 2012.

UNESCO–IBE. www.ibe.unesco.org/en/worldwide/unesco-regions/latin-america-and-the-caribbean/peru.html.

UNICEF. www.unicef.org/infobycountry/peru.html.

United Nations Development Programme. *United Nations Development Report 2010*. New York: Palgrave Macmillan, 2010.

World Bank Education Statistics. 2011. www.worldbank.org.

SURINAME

Suriname is a country in the northern part of South America. Originally, the Spanish occupied the region in the sixteenth century, and it was occupied by the British in the following century. It changed hands presumably because the region was not as beneficial as other areas in terms of agricultural production. The Netherlands occupied and colonized the region in 1667 and held on to it until the country's independence in 1975. The history of Suriname in the nineteenth century follows that of Guyana at about the same time; after the abolition of slavery in 1863, the Dutch brought indentured laborers from Java in the East Indies and from India to work the fields. After independence in 1975, the country was ruled by a socialist government ruling under martial law. Democratic civilian elections were held in 1991 and continue to the present. Despite the country's rather small population, religion is quite diverse. Approximately 27 percent of the population are Hindu, 25 percent Protestant, 23 percent Catholic, 20 percent Muslim, and 5 percent follow local indigenous religions. Languages are diverse too. Dutch is the official language but most people communicate in English as well. Other common languages include Sranang Tongo, Caribbean Hindustani, and Javanese.

Educational System

Education in Suriname is free and compulsory for a seven-year period—between the ages of six and 17 years. Education in the country has been supported by efforts from the government as well as religious groups—particularly the Roman Catholic and Moravian Churches. Classroom instruction is conducted in Dutch; however, instruction in a number of religious affiliated schools is conducted in other languages. The primary and secondary school student/teacher ratios are 17 to 1 and 15 to 1, respectively. The primary school gross enrollment ratio is 120 percent, but the net enrollment ratio is much lower—94 percent. Even fewer students enroll into or graduate from secondary school. The secondary gross enrollment rate is approximately 87 percent, yet the net ratio is only about 74 percent. The literacy rate of Surinamese citizens over 15 years of age is nearly 90 percent. Much of the illiterate population lives in rural areas in the southern parts of the country.

Most Surinamese students eligible for university education travel abroad in order to complete their higher education studies. Those who remain in Suriname have only one option—Anton de Kom University. Founded in 1882 in Paramaribo, Anton de Kom University began as the Geneeskundige School, which translates as "Medical School." Accordingly, the School of Medicine is not only the first specialization of Anton de Kom University, but also one of the university's main functions. The university has developed departments and programs in a variety of fields that include law, business and administration, engineering, architecture, information technologies, agricultural science, environmental sciences, education, and the humanities.

System Economics and Future Prospects

According to the United Nations Development Programme (2010), there are no data on current levels of education expenditure as a percentage of gross domestic product (GDP) in Suriname. The most recent data (2008) show approximately 3.5 percent of the country's GDP allocated for educational purposes. Assuming this percentage to be the same today, and given the GDP of Suriname at $4.794 billion, educational expenditure in the country would amount to nearly $168 million, or $1,598 per student (total amount equivalent to US dollars divided by 105,000, the approximate number of primary and secondary students in the country).

The system of education in Suriname has been somewhat successful in elevating the economic sta-

Suriname Education at a Glance	
General Information	
Capital	Paramaribo
Population	470,784
Languages	Dutch, English, Sranang Tongo, Caribbean Hindustani
Adult literacy rate (ages 15 and over)	89.6%
GDP per capita	US$7,100
People below poverty line	70%
Number of phones (landline) per 100 people	17.2
Number of phones (mobile) per 100 people	49.5
Number of Internet users per 100 people	6.4
Life expectancy at birth (years)	73
Formal Educational Information	
Enrollment in primary school (ages 6–11)	55,000
Enrollment in lower/upper secondary school (ages 12–17)	50,000
Number of years of compulsory education	12 (ages 6–17)
Primary school student/teacher ratio	17.1
Lower/upper secondary school student/teacher ratio (2003)	15.1
Primary school gross enrollment ratio	120%
Secondary school gross enrollment ratio	87%
Tertiary school gross enrollment ratio	12.4%
Primary school entrants completion rate	87%
Child labor (ages 5–14)	6%

Note: Unless otherwise indicated, all data are based on sources from 2011.

tus of the country. However, it is in great need of improvement. A significant percentage of students do not finish primary school—given the precipitous drop in enrollment from primary school to secondary school. School attendance suffers from a lack of adequate facilities at schools and difficulty in reaching large rural populations. Rural families are often unable to afford fees associated with a child's education, such as the cost of books and supplies. The Surinamese government and education leaders must find alternative ways to alleviate problems related to poverty so that children in poor families will be able to gain an education.

Daniel Ness and Chia-ling Lin

REFERENCES

Central Intelligence Agency. *The CIA World Factbook*. New York: Skyhorse, 2011. https.www.cia.gov/library/publications/the-world-factbook/index.html.

Nation Master. 2011. www.nationmaster.com.

UNESCO. *Global Education Digest 2012: Comparing Education Statistics Across the World.* Montreal: UNESCO Institute for Statistics, 2012.

———. "Strong Foundations: Early Childhood Care and Education." *Education for All Global Monitoring Report.* Paris: UNESCO, 2006.

UNESCO–IBE. www.ibe.unesco.org/en/worldwide/unesco-regions/latin-america-and-the-caribbean/suriname.html.

United Nations Development Programme. *United Nations Development Report 2010.* New York: Palgrave Macmillan, 2010.

US Department of Labor. *2001 Findings on the Worst Forms of Child Labor.* Washington, DC: Bureau of International Labor Affairs, US Department of Labor, 2002.

World Bank Education Statistics. 2011. www.worldbank.org.

URUGUAY

Uruguay is a country located in the southern part of South America. The official language is Spanish. Other languages include Portunol and Brazilero—a mix between Portuguese and Spanish that is spoken near the border of Brazil. Approximately 88 percent of Uruguayans are white, 8 percent are mestizo, and 4 percent are black. About 66 percent of all Uruguayans are Roman Catholic. About 2 percent of the population is Protestant and 1 percent is Jewish. The remaining population is either non-Christian or follows no religion.

Educational System

Public education in Uruguay is centralized and administered through national cabinets, such as the Ministry of Education. The National Board of Education, via the Central Directive Council, is responsible for preschool, elementary school, middle school (lower secondary school), high school, and technical school administration and curriculum. The Ministry of Education and Culture supervises the country's day-care system and its private universities to ensure that degrees are consistent with international weighting systems. Uruguay is a country that advocates universal education for all children. As one of the few welfare states on the continent, Uruguay was known since the late nineteenth and early twentieth century as a leader in education as a means of economic success and citizenship. The country's education system underwent a major reform in the late 1990s that has challenged the traditional format of educational systems in the world.

Compulsory Education

Education in Uruguay is compulsory for a period of at least 11 years, including two years of preprimary education (preschool for ages for and five), primary school, and the first three years of secondary school. Primary education consists of a period of six grade levels, for students between the ages of six and 11 years. Education is free in all public institutions up to the tertiary (university) level and is secular. Initial education—preschool education and primary school education (grades 1 through 6)—is part of the educational reform movement that began in 1995 as part of extended compulsory education. Uruguayan primary education is considered a basic curriculum that covers the Spanish language, mathematics, basic natural science in some schools, and history and culture of the region. About 337,000 students in Uruguay are enrolled in grades 1 through 6. The primary school student/teacher ratio is about 21 students per teacher and has remained at this number for the last two decades. The primary school gross enrollment ratio in Uruguay is 109 percent and the primary net enrollment ratio is 100 percent.

Secondary education in Uruguay is generally divided into lower secondary and upper secondary levels, both lasting for three years. Students enter lower secondary school at age 12 and enter upper secondary school at age 15. The lower secondary level emphasizes the common comprehensive education that follows primary school. By grade 10, students focus on specific areas of interest. Upper secondary education is free but not compulsory. Therefore, most Uruguayan students enroll in the upper secondary school because it is essential for university acceptance. Students who enter the lower secondary junior high school can attend either public or private high schools. Students can also enroll in the University of the Republic of Uruguay (Universidad del Trabajo del Uruguay [UTU]), which offers a three-year junior high school education. Senior high school is available at both public and private schools. Students who are under 15 years of age but have completed the junior high school three-year cycle are eligible to enter the UTU to enter a so-called technical education cycle. Nevertheless, students with both basic and technical knowledge can enter the UTU as university students. Senior high school is divided into a humanities component, scientific/biological component, and artistic component. There are also senior high schools in the country that emphasize vocational training. Completion of senior high school is necessary in order to be accepted to any of the country's universities.

Tertiary Education

Students who enter one of the country's universities must have earned a *bachillerato*. Students are to attend the university for at least four years in order to be eligible to graduate. Public or state-run universities and other forms of tertiary education are under the auspices of the National Board of Education. The country is home to one public university, namely, the University of the Republic. Founded in 1849, the University of the Republic is the oldest and by far the largest higher education institution in the country, enrolling more than 80,000 students every year. The university is home to 15 colleges as well as seven separate schools, which offer a vast array of programs in academic and technical disciplines. The University of the Republic has annexed several locations in urban areas throughout the country as a means of increasing tertiary education access. There are also four private universities in Uruguay: the Catholic University of Uruguay, the University ORT of Uruguay, University of Enterprise (Universidad de la Empresa), and the University of Montevideo. Established in 1942 by Russian Jewish émigrés but open to all, the University ORT of Uruguay is the largest private university in the country, enrolling about 8,000 students annually. "ORT" is the abbreviation of a Russian term that translates roughly to "polytechnic institution."

Teacher Education

Teacher education programs in Montevideo and throughout Uruguay have been some of the most successful in South America. In general, teacher education programs are provided by teacher training colleges, whose curricula emphasize both content and pedagogy. Students who wish to become teacher candidates and obtain a degree at the university must complete all of their compulsory education require-

ments as well as the three-year senior high school cycle. The National Board of Education in Uruguay controls the certification of teachers as well as the certification of technical professionals in the country. Students wishing to pursue teacher or professor degrees in Uruguay must enroll in the Normal School (*Institutos Normales*, also known as *Magisterio*) in Montevideo, the Normal Experimental School de la Costa, or in one of 21 teacher training institutes in the country. Instruction at technical colleges requires that students obtain a degree at the Normal Institute of Technical Education. Candidates for professor of secondary education positions must obtain their degrees at the Artigas Teacher Training Institute in Montevideo or at teacher training institutes and regional centers located throughout the country.

Informal Education

Recent figures indicate that citizens of Uruguay earn tertiary degrees at far higher rates than citizens of other countries of South and Central America. In addition, the literacy rate for people 15 years or older accounts for more than 98 percent of the

Uruguay Education at a Glance	
General Information	
Capital	Montevideo
Population	3.3 million
Language	Spanish
Adult literacy rate (ages 15 and over)	98.5%
GDP per capita	US$14,300
People below poverty line	27.4%
Number of phones (landline) per 100 people	28.9
Number of phones (mobile) per 100 people	17.3
Number of Internet users per 100 people	19
Life expectancy at birth (years)	76
Formal Educational Information	
Enrollment in primary school (ages 6–11)	337,000
Enrollment in lower/upper secondary school (ages 12–17)	332,000
Number of years of compulsory education	11 (ages 5–15)
Primary school student/teacher ratio	20.8
Lower/upper secondary school student/teacher ratio (2003)	14.7
Primary school gross enrollment ratio	109%
Secondary school gross enrollment ratio	105%
Tertiary school gross enrollment ratio	40.5%
Primary school entrants completion rate	91%
Child labor (ages 5–14)	8%

Note: Unless otherwise indicated, all data are based on sources from 2011.

population. One of the main purposes of informal education practice in Uruguay is to educate adults who are pursuing changing careers or possibly gaining higher-level skills for possible increased economic mobility. As stated above, older individuals are able to attend one of the UTU sites as a means of earning degrees, most often either a lower secondary or upper secondary degree in one of the technological or vocational disciplines, that may not have been possible for these individuals at an earlier time.

System Economics

According to the United Nations Development Programme (2010), along with Pakistan, Madagascar, Georgia, Cameroon, Bahrain, Albania, and Turkey, total public expenditure on education in Uruguay represented 2.9 percent of the gross domestic product (GDP) in 2007. Given the GDP of Uruguay at $48.43 billion, educational expenditure in the country amounts to nearly $1.405 billion, about $2,100 per student (total amount equivalent to US dollars divided by 669,000, the approximate number of primary and secondary students in the country). Uruguay ranks 148 of 186 countries in percentage of educational expenditure.

Future Prospects

In the past few decades, the educational system in Uruguay has become one of the most successful in South America. Despite an annual per capita gross national product of slightly over $14,300, Uruguay has been able to maintain a progressive education system that enables nearly all its citizens to go to school. As a technologically advanced nation in South America, Uruguay is a participant in the One Laptop per Child Initiative, which, in part, provides laptop computers to ministries of education throughout the world which then distribute one laptop for each child. There have been drawbacks, however. Most significant is that the survival rate to grade 5 is 91 percent, and the rate of completing the last primary school grade is slightly below 90 percent. Albeit not low, these rates are by no means encouraging.

Daniel Ness and Chia-ling Lin

REFERENCES

Central Intelligence Agency. *The CIA World Factbook*. New York: Skyhorse, 2011. https.www.cia.gov/library/publications/the-world-factbook/index.html.

Nation Master. 2011. www.nationmaster.com.

UNESCO. *Global Education Digest 2012: Comparing Education Statistics Across the World*. Montreal: UNESCO Institute for Statistics, 2012.

———. "Strong Foundations: Early Childhood Care and Education." *Education for All Global Monitoring Report*. Paris: UNESCO, 2006.

UNESCO–IBE. www.ibe.unesco.org/en/worldwide/unesco-regions/latin-america-and-the-caribbean/uruguay.html.

United Nations Development Programme. *United Nations Development Report 2010*. New York: Palgrave Macmillan, 2010.

US Department of Labor. *2001 Findings on the Worst Forms of Child Labor*. Washington, DC: Bureau of International Labor Affairs, US Department of Labor, 2002.

World Bank Education Statistics. 2011. www.worldbank.org.

VENEZUELA

Venezuela is a country located on the Caribbean coast of South America. The official language is Spanish; however, numerous indigenous dialects are also spoken throughout the country. The country is home to Spanish, Italian, Portuguese, Middle Eastern, German, African, and indigenous populations. Approximately 96 percent of the population belongs to the Roman Catholic Church. Most of the remaining population consists of people who are members of no religion or are members of Protestant Christian sects or unspecified religions.

Venezuela was the home of several civilizations prior to Spanish colonization in the early sixteenth century. The Spanish had ruled the region for nearly 300 years when, in 1830, the three countries of Gran Colombia—Venezuela, Colombia, and Ecuador—became independent states. Venezuela has been more or less stable since that time. Within recent years, the country has undergone political changes that have been an attempt to help underrepresented populations achieve better living conditions.

Educational System

According to the UNESCO *Education for All Global Monitoring Report* (2010), Venezuela's Education Index increased by more than 5 percent between 1999 and 2007. This index measures educational progress in terms of access, equality, and quality of instruction. These data are based on results from universal primary education, increased rates of adult literacy, decrease in the gender gap, and retention of students in school beyond grade 5. Venezuela currently ranks 59 out of 128 countries that have an Education Index. The country ranked 64 of 128 in 2007. Within the last three decades, the literacy rate in Venezuela increased dramatically. At present the literacy rate is 93 percent, one of the highest in South America. As of 1999 the Venezuelan government added to its constitution a mandate that calls for at least nine years of compulsory education. The general structure of educational levels that apply to other countries in the region also apply with Venezuela, of course with some exceptions. In general, compulsory education begins with six years of primary school, for children six to 11 years old, followed by three years of lower secondary school, for children 12 to 14 or 15 years old.

Preprimary and Compulsory Education

Although preprimary education is not compulsory, most Venezuelan children from the age of three to five are enrolled in one of several forms of preschool, making the country a leading proponent of education during early childhood. This period provides an academic, physical, and emotional basis for children's education at the primary and secondary levels. Unlike in neighboring countries, the Venezuelan Ministry of Education and the government in general have attempted to ameliorate the problems associated with the preschool education of poor rural children, whose families rely on family labor and subsistence farming.

Regardless of setting, all children must attend school for their basic education requirements for a period of nine years. All six years of primary education in the country are compulsory. The primary school student/teacher ratio is about 21 students for every teacher. The gross enrollment ratio for primary school is 105 percent. This percentage is rather high because a number of students older than those attending grade 6 are eligible to attend primary school. Although Venezuela does not condone

child labor, engaging children in the workforce can contribute to a lower primary net enrollment ratio. The primary completion rate for primary entrants is at 92 percent. The secondary school student/teacher ratio is about 11 students for every teacher. Again, child labor may play a role in this low student/teacher ratio. The secondary school gross enrollment ratio is 75 percent. The secondary school net enrollment ratio is 63 percent, indicating that many adolescents and young adults are still not completing school and thus lack middle- to high-level skills and abilities for upward mobility.

Venezuelan children and adolescents in rural parts of the country tend to have greater difficulty in attending school than their urban counterparts. They either do not attend school after a few years of primary education or they find attending school a burden because their life circumstances are often difficult; families struggle to earn income, and various fields of labor are greatly in need of low-skilled children and adolescents to run machines and perform other forms of manual labor. According to data provided by UNICEF, child labor in Venezuela is approximately 8 percent. Although this percentage seems low by South American standards, it is significant in that it affects rural populations at a much greater rate than it does urban populations. Despite these adverse circumstances, the Ministry of Education in Venezuela, most significantly under President Hugo Chavez, has initiated programs that allow all Venezuelans, regardless of socioeconomic class, to complete school.

Children who finish the basic education requirement at the primary level are required to continue their schooling at the lower secondary school level, which enrolls students in grades 7 through 9—students from ages 12 to about 14 or 15 years. Venezuelan secondary schools are divided into two phases—an initial three-year phase that continues the basic education of the primary school years and a second two-year phase, known as "diversified education," when students identify what they would like to study at the tertiary education level. Upon completion of "diversified education" in grades 10 and 11, students have the title of Bachelor of Science, bachelor of humanities, or technician of the sciences. Students with these titles are able to apply to one of the nearly 100 tertiary education institutions in the country.

Tertiary Education

Prior to the Venezuelan constitution of 1999, different types of tertiary-level institutions were labeled as public and private entities. For example, prior to a recent surge in the number of free higher education institutions, there were 17 public universities and 18 private universities. Technical schools were also labeled in this manner. In order to address the inequities of educational access between poor and more affluent Venezuelans, higher education was declared free in the constitution of 1999. It accounts for 35 percent of the total education budget. Tertiary education in Venezuela consists of the university and technical college. Established in 1721, the Central University of Venezuela in Caracas is the largest higher education institution in the country and one of the oldest universities in South America. Its enrollment, both undergraduate and graduate, is roughly 58,000 students. The Central University of Venezuela has 11 schools that consist of 40 departments. Departments are determined by discipline or area of study.

At present, only a small percentage of Venezuelans attend higher education institutions. Recent figures indicate that tertiary-level students account for only 11 percent of all students in the country. Moreover, students from the top 20 percent of all Venezuelan families in terms of socioeconomic status make up approximately 70 percent of the country's university enrollments.

To help rectify this situation, the Bolivarian University of Venezuela was established in 2003 under the initiation of President Hugo Chavez. The impetus for its creation was the government's Mission Sucre—a scholarship program whose aim is to improve the well-being and economic advancement of poor and rural Venezuelans or those who were traditionally excluded from obtaining secondary or higher education credentials. The student enrollment of Bolivarian University of Venezuela is approximately 200,000, but due to new enrollments following the development of new branches of the university, this figure is only an estimate. The university offers programs in the following areas: agroecology, architecture, social communication, education, animation, environmental management, social management and urban planning, public health management, medicine, law, and political sciences. The university has branches in at least nine locations throughout the country. The Bolivarian University accepts all students who have completed one of the secondary degrees (described above). However, if students do not possess these credentials, they are accepted on the basis of completing them.

Teacher education in Venezuela is obtainable through its universities. The present goal of the Ministry of Education is to promote a centralized curriculum that emphasizes socialist values. Student teachers, then, have a diverse curriculum that includes expertise in content as well as teaching methods. Given the wide array of educational levels and the current objective to universalize education, teacher education in the country has become an important area of study at the university level.

System Economics and Future Prospects

According to the United Nations Development Programme (2010), along with Niger, Japan, Luxembourg, Brunei, and Togo, total public expenditure on education in Venezuela represented 3.7 percent of the gross domestic product (GDP) in 2007. Given the GDP of Venezuela at $344.1 billion, educational expenditure in the country amounts to nearly $12.732 billion, about $2,098 per student (total amount equivalent to US dollars divided by 6,070,000, the approximate number of primary and secondary students in the country). Venezuela ranks 117 of 186 countries in percentage of educational expenditure.

Since 2000 Venezuela has made significant headway in its focus on education. Some of the objectives that the Ministry of Education set out to accomplish have been infant and early childhood education, control of the gender gap (so that both boys and girls are given an equal educational footing), the universalization of primary school teaching and learning, literacy promotion among children and adults, and the improvement of skill sets for adults.

Despite recent efforts to make education free to all Venezuelans, regardless of socioeconomic class, education access remains a major issue that Venezuela must confront in order to maintain steady economic growth. Only 11 percent of the college- and university-age population actually attends an institution of higher education. The remaining 89 percent of the population either graduate from one

```
┌─────────────────────────────────────────────────────────┐
│              Venezuela Education at a Glance              │
│                                                           │
│  General Information                                      │
│  Capital                                          Caracas │
│  Population                                  27.6 million │
│  Language                                         Spanish │
│  Adult literacy rate (ages 15 and over)               93% │
│  GDP per capita                                 US$7,200  │
│  People below poverty line                          37.9% │
│  Number of phones (landline) per 100 people          13.9 │
│  Number of phones (mobile) per 100 people              48 │
│  Number of Internet users per 100 people             11.7 │
│  Life expectancy at birth (years)                      73 │
│                                                           │
│  Formal Educational Information                           │
│  Enrollment in primary school (ages 6–11)    3.3 million  │
│  Enrollment in lower/upper secondary                      │
│     school (ages 12–16)                      2.7 million  │
│  Number of years of compulsory                            │
│     education                               9 (ages 6–15) │
│  Primary school student/teacher ratio                  17 │
│  Lower/upper secondary school                             │
│     student/teacher ratio                              11 │
│  Primary school gross enrollment ratio               105% │
│  Secondary school gross enrollment ratio              75% │
│  Tertiary school gross enrollment ratio             39.3% │
│  Primary school entrants completion rate              92% │
│  Child labor (ages 5–14)                               8% │
│                                                           │
│     Note: Unless otherwise indicated, all data are based  │
│  on sources from 2011.                                    │
└─────────────────────────────────────────────────────────┘
```

of the secondary education levels—with or without a terminal degree—or leave school shortly before or at the end of grade 6.

Although recent government-sponsored educational objectives have gained significant amount of traction in recent years, the lack of resources for these children is still a problem. The ministry needs to make the improvement of the well-being of all children its priority by closing the gap that prevents working children from attaining equal education access. In addition, the country's leaders will need to invest in technologies that allow children and adults of rural families to benefit from school.

Daniel Ness and Chia-ling Lin

REFERENCES

Central Intelligence Agency. *The CIA World Factbook.* New York: Skyhorse, 2011. https.www.cia.gov/library/publications/the-world-factbook/index.html.

Nation Master. 2011. www.nationmaster.com.

UNESCO. *EFA Global Monitoring Report.* Washington, DC: UNESCO, 2010. www.unesco.org/new/en/education/themes/leading-the-international-agenda/efareport/.

———. *Global Education Digest 2012: Comparing Education Statistics Across the World.* Montreal: UNESCO Institute for Statistics, 2012.

———. "Strong Foundations: Early Childhood Care and Education." *Education for All Global Monitoring Report.* Paris: UNESCO, 2006.

UNESCO–IBE. www.ibe.unesco.org/en/worldwide/unesco-regions/latin-america-and-the-caribbean/venezuela.html.

United Nations Development Programme. *United Nations Development Report 2010.* New York: Palgrave Macmillan, 2010.

US Department of Labor. *2001 Findings on the Worst Forms of Child Labor.* Washington, DC: Bureau of International Labor Affairs, US Department of Labor, 2002.

World Bank Education Statistics. 2011. www.worldbank.org.

Post-Soviet Nations

Introduction

The present section discusses the educational systems of 15 countries that, prior to 1991, made up the Union of Soviet Socialist Republics (the Soviet Union). These countries are grouped together for a number of reasons. First, due to their inclusion as part of the former Soviet Union, the formal education systems of these countries, with a few exceptions (Russia and some of the European former Soviet republics) more or less originated and developed at the same time. So similarities between several countries in this section will be evident to the reader. Second, given the nature of these fledgling education systems, most have kept similar curricula for primary and secondary students. Consequently, much of the Soviet-era curriculum has remained fairly constant. An exception to the rather consistent curriculum is the nationalistic tendency of many of these countries to change the language of instruction from Russian to the second official language of the country (e.g., Uzbek in place of Russian). Third, the formal education systems in this group of countries, again with some exceptions (most notably, Estonia, Latvia, and Lithuania, which are members of NATO and the European Union), have witnessed decline. This decline makes this group of nations an anomaly in terms of the trend in formal education infrastructure throughout the world; in fact, most countries of the world have seen some sort of growth and development, whether small or prodigious, within the last two to five decades.

One major reason for this phenomenon of decline was the formation of fledgling governments, particularly those in central and southwestern Asia, that were obligated to meet the needs of their citizens without the aid of Moscow, which they had enjoyed during the Soviet years. Accordingly, the education systems of these new nations became subordinate to other pressing issues, such as providing enough food, attempting to eliminate government corruption by newly elected or appointed leaders, reducing unemployment and poverty, and improving health care.

Another reason that may have contributed to the decline of these post-Soviet new education systems is a commonly held belief that education attainment is a privilege and not a right. This conception, even by some holding political office, has contributed to greater infusion of funding to higher education than to preprimary, primary, and secondary education. This is clearly evident when examining the number of universities and other tertiary-level institutions that were founded and built in most of the 15 countries after 1991, that is, after the dissolution of the Soviet Union. The construction of hundreds of new higher education institutions during the post-Soviet era explains in part why primary and secondary education is at a disadvantage in these countries.

A third reason may have to do with institutionalized or illegal social policies that are often tacitly condoned by governments—the most egregious being the practice of child labor. UNICEF data show that nine of the 15 countries—Armenia, Azerbaijan, Georgia, Belarus, Kazakhstan, Kyrgyzstan, Moldova, Ukraine, and Tajikistan—engage children between the age of seven and 14 years in various sorts of labor. In fact, data on child labor in Moldova, an eastern European country, show that 32 percent of the population in this age group is working; in Georgia, 18 percent of the children between 7 and 14 years are engaged in labor, and in Tajikistan, roughly 10 percent. It should be evident that child labor practices would contribute to the decline of a country's system of education as a result of low enrollment; to be sure, governments and education ministries tend to hold or divert funding to other areas than schooling and education if children are not showing up in class. Another egregious problem concerns poor populations. Children of poor urban or rural families are strongly disadvantaged in their educational attainment in this region of the world. Rural households are particularly disadvantaged by the need to pay for transportation between school and home. These families are often burdened to pay additional fees for their children's education.

A fourth and related reason for the decline in primary and secondary education is chronic racism. In eastern European post-Soviet nations, this problem is most notable against minority populations, particularly the Roma. Antiziganism, racism directed at Roma children and adults, exists not only within the community but within political leadership as well. Education access is an example of implicit racism in that Roma children are often funneled into schools that have poor curriculum and infrastructure. As a result, Roman and other poor and minority populations are unable to experience the same positive opportunities as their more fortunate peers.

Despite many setbacks and the gradual decline of many education systems in the region after 1991, education in the region has the potential to experience growth in coming decades. This is because the region as a whole has access to important natural resources that, if developed and cultivated properly, can lead to positive economic advancement. Fighting government and private corruption, ending child labor, and instituting a plan that will provide equity and opportunities for all people will be initial steps in reversing the declining educational trend in the region.

Daniel Ness and Chia-ling Lin

Armenia

Armenia is a landlocked country in west-central Asia. Armenia was controlled by the Roman Empire in the first few centuries of the Common Era. During the early Middle Ages, the area was initially controlled by the Byzantine Empire and subsequently by Arabs

and Persians. In 1828 the Ottoman Empire relinquished the eastern region of Armenia to the Russian Empire. The western region of Armenia remained with the Ottomans for nearly a century. By World War I, the Ottoman Turks had displaced millions of Armenians from their homes and communities. The Turks engaged in genocide of a large segment of the Armenian population. By 1917 it is estimated that nearly 1 million Armenians had perished. The eastern region declared independence in 1918 only to be taken over by the Soviet Union in 1920. As a result, the Armenian population region of Nagorno-Karabakh fell under control of the Azerbaijani part of the Soviet Union and has not been turned over to Armenia to the present day. Armenia became independent from the Soviet Union in 1991. Since that time, Armenia and Azerbaijan, a predominantly Muslim country, have been in conflict. This conflict has resulted in Turkey's boycott of Armenian imports and exports. Nearly all Armenians are Christian. The overwhelming majority are members of the Eastern Orthodox Church.

Educational System

Like other post-Soviet republics, Armenia benefited greatly during the Soviet era in terms of educational access for all children and adolescents. Fortunately, much of the centralized curriculum that Armenian children were offered under Soviet control has been emulated by the current Ministry of Education in Armenia. One important outcome in Armenia's case is the country's current literacy rate of 100 percent of the population aged 15 and older, which is perhaps due to the strict, centralized system of education and the level of importance that Armenia devotes to education in improving its market economy. Nevertheless, it is important to consider that the rate of student attrition in the country is rising. As a result, the Armenian educational system has declined significantly since the country's independence. This unfortunate statistic is making it difficult for the Armenian government to keep its commitment of providing a successful education for all Armenian children. Since 1994 there has been some intervention by nongovernmental organizations to improve the education system so that Armenian students can gain competitiveness. One of the more recent nongovernmental initiatives in Armenian education is the Transparent Education in Armenia Project, whose goal is to provide a more active education for Armenian youth. This project attempts, in part, to provide a curriculum that fosters awareness of civic behavior, such as corrupt practices in government and politics, as well as empowerment in school progress. The United States Agency for International Development (USAID) and the Education Development Center have been pivotal organizations in this initiative.

Preprimary education in Armenia emphasizes children's physical, social, and moral development, as well as skills in communication. In general, preschool is available for children between the ages of three and six years. At present, there are about 700 preschools accommodating nearly 45,000 children. However, there were more preschools in Armenia during the Soviet era. Funding by the state for preschool has gradually fallen since 1991. As a result, preschool attendance dropped precipitously, from nearly 50 percent enrollment in 1987 to slightly over 20 percent enrollment in 2006. As a result, most Armenian children enter compulsory education with little or no background in subject knowledge.

Education in Armenia is compulsory for nine years—grades 1 to 9, or ages seven through 15 years. Students attend primary education for a rather short period of three years and continue at the lower secondary level for six years. At present, there are nearly 125,000 primary-school-age children and nearly 400,000 secondary-school-age children and adolescents in Armenia. The student/teacher ratio at the primary school level is about 21 students per teacher. Given this rate, there are between 5,000 and 6,000 primary school teachers in Armenia. The primary school gross enrollment ratio is 94 percent. The net enrollment ratio for primary school in the country is 79 percent, indicating that over 20 percent of the primary school population is not in attendance. Unfortunately, only 87 percent of all primary school entrants finish primary school. The secondary school student/teacher ratio is about 10 students for every teacher. At this rate, there are anywhere from 39,000 to 40,000 secondary school teachers. While the secondary gross enrollment ratio in the country is 88 percent, the net ratio is 85 percent, indicating that 15 percent of the secondary-school-age population is dropping out of school.

Most students who successfully complete their secondary education programs are strongly encour-

aged to attend one of the country's universities or technical colleges. There are at least 14 universities and approximately 90 technical colleges in Armenia. The oldest and largest institution in the country is Yerevan State University, in the country's capital. Founded in 1919, Yerevan State University enrolls about 10,000 undergraduate and graduate students each academic year. The programs in mathematics and natural sciences are what make Yerevan State University competitive in the region. There are nine faculties in the School of Exact Sciences and 10 faculties in the School of Humanitarian Sciences. In addition to comprehensive universities, other universities in Armenia include the American University of Armenia, Russian-Armenian State University, Armenian State Institute of Physical Culture, Eurasia International University, Yerevan State Medical University, Yerevan State Linguistic University, Yerevan State Institute of Economy, the Yerevan State University of Architecture and Construction, and Armenian State Pedagogical University (ASPU). ASPU was founded in 1922 and has prepared Armenian teachers in over 20 fields in education for more than 90 years.

Armenia Education at a Glance

General Information

Capital	Yerevan
Population	2.9 million
Language	Armenian
Literacy rate	99%
GDP per capita	US$5,700
People below poverty line (2004)	35%
Number of phones per 100 people	20
Number of Internet users per 100 people	5
Number of Internet hosts	8,163
Life expectancy at birth (years)	72

Formal Educational Information

Primary school age population	124,000
Secondary school age population	398,000
Primary school age population	4%
Number of years of primary education	3 (ages 7–9)
Student/teacher ratio (primary)	21
Student/teacher ratio (secondary)	10
Primary school gross enrollment ratio	94%
Primary school entrants completing primary school	87%
Secondary school gross enrollment ratio	88%
Child labor (ages 5–14)	4%

Note: Unless otherwise indicated, all data are based on sources from 2011.

System Economics and Future Prospects

According to the United Nations Development Programme (2010), along with Singapore and Madagascar, total public expenditures on education in Armenia represented 3 percent of the gross domestic product (GDP) in 2007. Given the GDP of Armenia at $17.27 billion, educational expenditure in the country amounts to more than $518 million, or $993 per student (total amount equivalent to US dollars divided by 522,000, the approximate number of primary and secondary students in the country). Per student spending was greater during the Soviet era. Armenia ranks 134 of 186 countries in percentage of educational expenditure.

According to UNICEF, about 4 percent of all Armenian children between 5 and 14 years of age are engaged in labor. As a result, the government and the Ministry of Education must grapple with high rates of attrition of students, particularly those in secondary schools. The dropping preschool enrollment has only exacerbated the school dropout problem, since students are increasingly failing to understand the importance of education as it contributes to society. Due to an education system that is losing its ability to maintain school attendance along with a rigorous curriculum, Armenia has been the recipient of funding from nongovernmental agencies. More time is needed to determine the effects of recent educational initiatives by nongovernmental agencies before it is possible to assess improvement.

Daniel Ness and Chia-ling Lin

REFERENCES

Central Intelligence Agency. *The CIA World Factbook.* New York: Skyhorse, 2011. https.www.cia.gov/library/publications/the-world-factbook/index.html.

Nation Master. 2011. www.nationmaster.com.

UNESCO. *Global Education Digest 2012: Comparing Education Statistics Across the World.* Montreal: UNESCO Institute for Statistics, 2012.

———. "Strong Foundations: Early Childhood Care and Education." *Education for All Global Monitoring Report.* Paris: UNESCO, 2006.

UNESCO–IBE. www.ibe.unesco.org/en/worldwide/unesco-regions/europe-and-north-america/armenia.html.

United Nations Development Programme. *Human Development Report 2011.* http://hdr.undp.org/en/.

US Department of Labor. *2001 Findings on the Worst Forms of Child Labor.* Washington, DC: Bureau of International Labor Affairs, US Department of Labor, 2002.

World Bank Education Statistics. 2011. www.worldbank.org.

AZERBAIJAN

Azerbaijan is a central Asian country that was part of the former Soviet Union. In ancient times and through the Middle Ages, the region of Azerbaijan was inhabited by Turkic peoples. It was controlled by numerous empires since ancient times, namely, the Persian Empire, Greek rule under Alexander, Roman rule, and later Muslim groups, particularly Arabian rule. The country fell under Russian control in the middle of the nineteenth century. After the Bolshevik Revolution, Azerbaijan was an independent nation for about three years, but in 1920 it ceded control to the Soviets. It became independent a second time in 1991 after the fall of the Soviet Union. Since that time, Azerbaijan has been in conflict with Armenia, which controls a stretch of territory that divides the larger part of the country from a smaller part that is landlocked between Armenia and Iran. Nagorno-Karabakh, a region of Azerbaijan that is entirely within the country's boundaries, presents another dispute between the two nations because this area is inhabited by a large Armenian population. After Soviet occupation, the country lost between 15 and 20 percent of its territory as a result of these disputes and must support more than half a million of its citizens that have been displaced. The country has potential, however, to achieve an economic windfall if it taps recently found sources of petroleum.

The overwhelming majority of Azerbaijani are Azeri. Other groups include Russians, Dagestani, and Armenians.

Educational System

Like the preprimary systems of other post-Soviet countries, that of Azerbaijan during the Soviet era was highly successful in preparing young children for formal education at the primary level. Despite the seemingly positive aspects of independence, preprimary attendance in Azerbaijan declined shortly after Soviet rule, primarily as a result of poor funding and poor teacher education and qualification procedures. At present, there are approximately 340,000 children of preschool age, but only about 108,000 (less than 32 percent) attend day-care facilities or preschools. As a result of a reduction in state funding, preschool education is a financial burden for many families. Like other post-Soviet nations, Azerbaijan has seen a rise in home-based preschool, which tends to soften much of the financial burden for families.

Education in Azerbaijan is compulsory for a period of 11 years for children between the ages of six and 16 years. This compulsory period consists of four years of primary education, five years of lower secondary school, and two years of upper secondary school. The compulsory education years comprise a basic curriculum that considers essential subjects—Azerbaijani, Russian, mathematics, basic natural science, physical education, art, and music. Azerbaijani students must attend the two-year upper secondary level in order to be eligible for university enrollment.

The student/teacher ratio at the primary school level is 12 to 13 students for every teacher. The primary school gross enrollment ratio is 96 percent. However, the net enrollment rate for primary school is approximately 12 percent percentage points lower (84 percent), indicating that about 16 percent of all children at the primary level are not attending school. The secondary school student/teacher ratio in Azerbaijan is about eight students for every teacher. The secondary gross enrollment ratio in the country is 83 percent. However, the net enrollment rate is much lower—approximately 78 percent, thus indicating that roughly 22 percent of Azerbaijani adolescents do not attend school, a complete turn of events from school attendance prior to 1991, when school attendance was strictly enforced. About 97 percent of all students reach the last year of primary school (about nine years of age). However, only 92 percent of all primary-school-age students actually complete primary school. Ironically, although schooling in Azerbaijan is compulsory for an 11-year period, the average number of years that Azerbaijani students attend school is 9.6 years. One major question, then, would be how compulsory education is enforced in the country.

Azerbaijani students who successfully complete their secondary education programs are generally encouraged to pursue a degree at one of the universities in the country. There are 24 public and private universities in Azerbaijan. Established in 1919, Baku State University is the country's oldest institution; it is estimated that the university enrolls over 20,000 students annually. Baku State University has 16 departmental faculties and two research institutes that are devoted to applied mathematics and theoretical physics. With an enrollment of about 17,000, the Azerbaijan State Economic University, founded in 1930, is a large institute of economics in the region. Established in 1920, the Azerbaijan State Oil Academy is a leading, highly specialized mining and engineering institution in the region. Other high-ranking institutions in the country include the Azerbaijan Medical University, Azerbaijan University of Languages, Baku Academy of Music, Azerbaijan State University of Culture and Arts, and Baku Slavic University. Founded in 1991, Khazar University in Baku was one of the first institutions in the former Soviet Union to introduce a westernized system of higher education—one emphasizing law, engineering and applied science, business and management, medicine, and education. The School of Education at Khazar University maintains programs in elementary education, mathematics and computer sciences, chemistry and biology, history and geography, Azerbaijani language and literature, education administration, and history and philosophies of education. Students need to acquire a baccalaureate to be eligible to teach in state compulsory education schools. Students also have the opportunity to continue for doctorates in educational fields.

System Economics and Future Prospects

According to the United Nations Development Programme (2010), along with Kazakhstan, the Philippines, and Indonesia, total public expenditures on education in Azerbaijan represented 2.8 percent of the gross domestic product (GDP) in 2009. Given the GDP of Azerbaijan at $90.15 billion, educational expenditure in the country amounts to more than $2.5 billion, or $1,382 per student (total amount equivalent to US dollars divided by 1,826,000, the approximate number of primary and secondary students in the country). Per student spending was greater during the Soviet era. Azerbaijan ranks 141 of 186 countries in percentage of educational expenditure.

Azerbaijan Education at a Glance

General Information

Capital	Baku
Population	8.1 million
Language	Azerbaijani
Literacy rate	99%
GDP per capita	US$7,500
People below poverty line (2004)	49%
Number of phones per 100 people	14
Number of Internet users per 100 people	8
Number of Internet hosts	880
Life expectancy at birth (years)	66

Formal Educational Information

Primary school age population	559,000
Secondary school age population	1.2 million
Primary school age population	7%
Number of years of primary education	4 (ages 6–9)
Student/teacher ratio (primary)	13
Student/teacher ratio (secondary)	8
Primary school gross enrollment ratio	96
Primary school entrants completing primary school	97%
Secondary school gross enrollment ratio	83%
Child labor (ages 5–14)	7%*

Note: *Refers to part of the country.
Unless otherwise indicated, all data are based on sources from 2011.

With a near 100 percent literacy rate, Azerbaijan, along with the other countries of the Caucasus region, has the highest rate of literacy among the nations in western Asia and even eastern Europe. Despite the high literacy in the country, the formal educational system in Azerbaijan has declined since independence. With the end of the Soviet period, there was a steady decrease in organization in the administrative and academic levels of the country's Ministry of Education, and there was a steady drop in school enrollment at nearly all education levels. The present goal of the Azerbaijani Ministry of Education is to rebuild the educational infrastructure in the country to preindependence levels. A number of nongovernmental organizations have helped to assuage the burden of family fiduciary responsibility with regard to education within the last decade, mostly in the form of funding for students of poor families, the purchase of educational resources, and travel between home and school. These organizations have also been instrumental in recent years with regard to improvements in teacher education in the country.

Daniel Ness and Chia-ling Lin

REFERENCES

Central Intelligence Agency. *The CIA World Factbook*. New York: Skyhorse, 2011. https.www.cia.gov/library/publications/the-world-factbook/index.html.

Nation Master. 2011. www.nationmaster.com.

UNESCO. *Global Education Digest 2012: Comparing Education Statistics Across the World*. Montreal: UNESCO Institute for Statistics, 2012.

———. "Strong Foundations: Early Childhood Care and Education." *Education for All Global Monitoring Report*. Paris: UNESCO, 2006.

UNESCO–IBE. www.ibe.unesco.org/en/worldwide/unesco-regions/europe-and-north-america/azerbaijan.html.

United Nations Development Programme. *Human Development Report 2011*. http://hdr.undp.org/en/.

US Department of Labor. *2001 Findings on the Worst Forms of Child Labor*. Washington, DC: Bureau of International Labor Affairs, US Department of Labor, 2002.

World Bank Education Statistics. 2011. www.worldbank.org.

BELARUS

The Republic of Belarus is a landlocked country in eastern Europe. The region of Belarus has always been associated with Russia both politically and economically, perhaps more than any of the other former Soviet republics. Unlike many of the other republics of the Soviet Union, Belarus was not an independent nation prior to 1991. Even after its formal separation from Russia, it still has kept close ties with Russia, even to the present day. In 1999 leaders of both Belarus and Russia signed a treaty that has attempted to bring the two countries closer together economically. The goals of the treaty, however, have yet to be achieved. Moreover, there has been political strife in recent years because the country's administration has censored the press and forbidden a democratic form of government.

About 80 percent of all Belarusians are members of the Eastern Orthodox Church. The remaining 20 percent of the population belong to the Roman Catholic, Protestant, Jewish, and Muslim faiths.

Educational Systems

Formal education in Belarus is run by the country's Ministry of Education. Under a decree established in 1994, education in the country became decentralized.

Accordingly, each province of the country oversees its schools at the primary and secondary levels. Education levels in Belarus consist of preprimary, primary, lower and upper secondary, and higher education. Education is compulsory during the primary and lower secondary levels, when students are taught a so-called basic curriculum.

Preprimary education in the former Soviet Union had become successful in preparing young children for formal education at the primary level. As a result, Belarusian children showed evidence of strong academic achievement in primary and secondary school. However, since independence, Belarusian's preprimary attendance has declined, primarily as a result of a lack of funding in this educational sector. Between 1992 and 1997, the number of preschool institutions declined from nearly 5,000 schools to 4,500 schools—a drop of nearly 50,000 children. Nevertheless, some families send their children to nursery schools that accommodate children from six months to three years of age. Kindergartens are available for children between the ages of three and six years.

Education in Belarus is compulsory for a period of nine years for children between the ages of six and 14 years. This period consists of four years of primary education and five years of lower secondary school. In addition to this compulsory period, most students who graduate from lower secondary school continue for an additional three years of upper secondary school. Compulsory education years comprise a basic curriculum that considers essential subjects—Russian, Belarusian, mathematics, basic natural science, physical education, art, and music. Belarusian students must attend the upper secondary level in order to be eligible for university enrollment.

The student/teacher ratio at the Belarusian primary school level is about 16 students for every teacher. The primary school gross enrollment ratio is 95 percent. However, the net enrollment rate for primary school is approximately 89.5 percent, indicating that 10 to 11 percent of all children at the primary level are not attending school. The secondary school student/teacher ratio in Belarus is 9 to 10 students for every teacher. The secondary gross enrollment ratio in the country is 96 percent. Data show, however, that 10 to 11 percent of all secondary-school-age adolescents are not attending school. This statistic is based on a secondary school net enrollment ratio

of 89.2 percent. Outcomes regarding completion of primary school in the country are more promising; nearly all students reach the last grade in primary school and about 95 percent of all students at the primary level complete primary school.

Belarusian students who successfully complete their secondary education programs are generally encouraged to pursue a degree at one of the universities or vocational institutions in the country. There are approximately 56 higher education institutions in Belarus. Two are comprehensive universities, eight are so-called classical universities, two are professional agricultural universities, two are professional universities of economics, four are professional universities of medicine, two are professional pedagogical universities specializing in teacher training, six are professional technological universities, seven are professional universities in various fields (i.e., sports, culture and arts, environmental studies, food-related studies, and linguistics), two are professional academies associated with the armed forces, two are professional arts academies, two are professional academies that specialize in agriculture and veterinary medicine, six are economics institutes, two are emergency control institutes, five are institutes for social sciences, three are higher colleges, and one is a university in exile (i.e., European Humanities University, which is a Belarusian university located in Lithuania). The largest and one of the most competitive research universities in the country is the Belarusian State University, located in Minsk. Founded in 1921, the university enrolls about 31,000 students annually. About 2,000 of these students are from other countries. The university has 16 faculties and four educational institutes. Teacher education is available in the pedagogical institutes or at universities that have pedagogical faculty.

System Economics and Future Prospects

According to the United Nations Development Programme (2010), along with Hong Kong, Australia, Germany, Niger, and Saint Lucia, total public expenditures on education in Belarus represented 4.5 percent of the gross domestic product (GDP) in 2009. Given the GDP of Belarus at $128.4 billion, educational expenditure in the country amounts to more than $5.778 billion, or $4,455 per student (total amount equivalent to US dollars divided by 1,297,000, the approximate number of primary and secondary students in the country). Per student spending was greater during the Soviet era. Belarus ranks 83 of 186 countries in percentage of educational expenditure.

With a near 100 percent literacy rate, Belarus has one of the highest rates of literacy among the nations in the former Soviet bloc of eastern Europe. Despite this advantage, the country's formal system of education has been in steady decline since independence. With the end of the Soviet period, the Education Ministry in the republic was forced to regroup its mission and vision for educating Belarusian youth. As a result, there was considerable lack of organization from the start, which thus contributed to a drop in school enrollment throughout the fledgling nation. The present goal of the Belarusian Ministry of Education is to rebuild the educational infrastructure and finance each sector of the education system in an egalitarian manner. Various nongovernmental organizations have helped in this regard within the last decade, mostly in the form of funding for students of former peasant families, travel between home and school, and teacher education improvements.

According to UNICEF, approximately 5 percent of all children in Belarus between five and 14 years of age are engaged in labor. As a result, the government and the Belarusian Ministry of Education must grapple with high rates of attrition of students, particularly those in secondary schools. The problem of attrition is compounded by a dropping preschool enrollment. The social ills of child labor and a dwindling preschool enrollment have possibly led to students' misconceptions about the importance of education as it contributes to society. Due to an education system that is losing its ability to maintain school attendance along with a rigorous curriculum, Belarus has been the recipient of funding sources from nongovernmental agencies. More time is needed to assess improvement in the Belarusian educational system as a result of recent NGO initiatives.

Daniel Ness and Chia-ling Lin

REFERENCES

Central Intelligence Agency. *The CIA World Factbook.* New York: Skyhorse, 2011. https.www.cia.gov/library/publications/the-world-factbook/index.html.

Nation Master. 2011. www.nationmaster.com.

UNESCO. *Global Education Digest 2012: Comparing Education Statistics Across the World.* Montreal: UNESCO Institute for Statistics, 2012.

————. "Strong Foundations: Early Childhood Care and Education." *Education for All Global Monitoring Report.* Paris: UNESCO, 2006.

UNESCO–IBE. www.ibe.unesco.org/en/worldwide/unesco-regions/europe-and-north-america/belarus.html.

United Nations Development Programme. *United Nations Development Report 2010.* New York: Palgrave Macmillan, 2010.

US Department of Labor. *2001 Findings on the Worst Forms of Child Labor.* Washington, DC: Bureau of International Labor Affairs, US Department of Labor, 2002.

World Bank Education Statistics. 2011. www.worldbank.org.

Belarus Education at a Glance

General Information

Capital	Minsk
Population	9.7 million
Languages	Belarusian, Russian
Literacy rate	99%
GDP per capita	US$8,100
People below poverty line (2004)	27%
Number of phones per 100 people	34
Number of Internet users per 100 people	35
Number of Internet hosts	33,641
Life expectancy at birth (years)	70

Formal Educational Information

Primary school age population	383,000
Primary school age population	4%
Number of years of primary education	4 (ages 6–9)
Student/teacher ratio (primary)	16
Student/teacher ratio (secondary)	9
Primary school gross enrollment ratio	95%
Primary school entrants completing primary school	99%
Secondary school gross enrollment ratio	96%
Child labor (ages 5–14)	5%

Note: Unless otherwise indicated, all data are based on sources from 2011.

ESTONIA

The Republic of Estonia is located in northeastern Europe on the Gulf of Finland to the north and the Baltic Sea and the Gulf of Riga to the west. Since medieval times, Estonia has been under Swedish, Danish, German, and Russian control. The country became independent for the first time in 1918. However, 22 years later, the country became a republic of the former Soviet Union. Estonia became independent again in 1991 after the end of Soviet power. In 2004 the country became a member of NATO and the European Union.

There is great religious diversity in Estonia. Approximately 33 percent of the population is Christian. Most of these individuals are Lutheran. The remaining Christian population is Orthodox or Roman Catholic. The religion of about 32 percent of the population is unspecified, and about 34 percent of the population has no religious affiliation.

Educational System

Preprimary education in Estonia is one of the few preprimary systems that has been successful both during and after the Soviet era in preparing young children for formal education at the primary level. Although preschool education is not compulsory, most children are sent to preprimary institutions. Of the nearly 50,000 preschool-age children in the country, nearly 47,000—about 93.6 percent—attend preschool or kindergarten. Funding for preprimary education in Estonia is based on local and municipal budgeting along with nominal fees that parents must pay in order for their children to attend preschool.

Education in Estonia is compulsory for a period of nine years for children between the ages of seven and 15 years. This period consists of six years of primary school and three years of lower secondary school. Although the last three years of secondary school (for students ages 16 to 18) are not compulsory, the overwhelming majority of this age group does attend. The compulsory education years comprise a basic curriculum that considers essential subjects—Estonian, Russian, mathematics, basic natural science, physical education, art, and music.

The student/teacher ratio in Estonian primary schools is approximately 14 students for every teacher. The primary school gross enrollment ratio is nearly 100 percent. The net enrollment rate for primary school is about 95 percent. The secondary school student/teacher ratio in Estonia is about 10 students for every teacher. The secondary gross enrollment ratio in the country is nearly 100 percent. The net enrollment ratio for secondary school is close to 90 percent, indicating that most students complete their secondary education; a small minority attempt to enter the workforce either after graduation from

lower secondary school or while attending upper secondary school.

Estonian students who successfully complete their upper secondary education programs are generally encouraged to pursue a degree at the university level. There are about 22 higher education institutions in Estonia. Two are public, comprehensive, doctoral-granting universities, 10 are public professional universities or academies, and 10 are private universities. Established in 1632, the University of Tartu is the oldest university in the country. The annual enrollment of the University of Tartu is about 17,000 students. The university is renowned for its research in the fields of molecular and cell biology in particular and the natural sciences in general. Other important areas of study at the University of Tartu include linguistics, semiotics, and cognitive psychology. Tallinn University, the second comprehensive institution, is a rather new university that was established as a result of the merger between the Tallinn Pedagogical University and the Estonian Academic Library with former institutes of technology, humanities, and social sciences. Tallinn University serves roughly 10,000 students annually. The Tallinn University of Technology is the only polytechnic institution in the country. The Estonian Academy of Music and Theater is the preeminent institution of the performing arts in the region. Teacher training for both the primary and secondary school levels takes place at several universities in the country. For example, Tallinn University has a Department of Education Studies, which prepares primary and secondary school teachers as well as curriculum specialists. Instruction at the tertiary level requires that teachers or professors obtain degrees at the university level in a specific area of study.

System Economics and Future Prospects

According to the United Nations Development Programme (2010), along with Syria, Argentina, Poland, Grenada, Ireland, and Canada, total public expenditures on education in Estonia represented 4.9 percent of the gross domestic product (GDP) in 2007. Given the GDP of Estonia at $24.65 billion, educational expenditure in the country amounts to more than $1.2 billion, or $6,039 per student (total amount equivalent to US dollars divided by 200,000, the approximate number of primary and secondary

Estonia Education at a Glance

General Information

Capital	Tallinn
Population	1.3 million
Languages	Estonian (67%), Russian (30%)
Literacy rate	96%
GDP per capita	US$20,300
People below poverty line (2004)	5%
Number of phones per 100 people	34
Number of Internet users per 100 people	67
Number of Internet hosts	729,534
Life expectancy at birth (years)	72

Formal Educational Information

Primary school age population	80,000
Secondary school age population	120,000
Primary school age population	6%
Number of years of primary education	6
Student/teacher ratio (primary)	14
Student/teacher ratio (secondary)	10
Primary school gross enrollment ratio	100%
Primary school entrants reaching grade 5	99%
Secondary school gross enrollment ratio	100%
Child labor (ages 5–14)	no data

Note: Unless otherwise indicated, all data are based on sources from 2011.

students in the country). Per student spending was greater during the Soviet era. Estonia ranks 64 of 186 countries in percentage of educational expenditure.

Estonia has a 100 percent literacy rate. At present, along with the educational systems of Latvia and Lithuania, Estonia's education system ranks as one of the most successful of the post-Soviet systems. Estonia is one of the leading centers of telecommunication and technology in the region. Despite these positive trends in education, it is important to note Estonia's rising unemployment rate. At present, the unemployment rate is 10.2 percent, and the increase in unemployment between 2007 and 2009 was 9.3 percent, the second-highest increase in the world. Only Spain's was higher.

Daniel Ness and Chia-ling Lin

REFERENCES

Central Intelligence Agency. *The CIA World Factbook*. New York: Skyhorse, 2011. https.www.cia.gov/library/publications/the-world-factbook/index.html.

Nation Master. 2011. www.nationmaster.com.

UNESCO. *Global Education Digest 2012: Comparing Education Statistics Across the World*. Montreal: UNESCO Institute for Statistics, 2012.

———. "Strong Foundations: Early Childhood Care and Education." *Education for All Global Monitoring Report*. Paris: UNESCO, 2006.

UNESCO–IBE. www.ibe.unesco.org/en/worldwide/unesco-regions/europe-and-north-america/estonia.html.

United Nations Development Programme. *United Nations Development Report 2010*. New York: Palgrave Macmillan, 2010.

US Department of Labor. *2001 Findings on the Worst Forms of Child Labor*. Washington, DC: Bureau of International Labor Affairs, US Department of Labor, 2002.

World Bank Education Statistics. 2011. www.worldbank.org.

GEORGIA

Georgia is a west Asian country that was part of the former Soviet Union. In the middle of the nineteenth century, Georgia came under Russian rule, and after a three-year period of independence (1918–1921), Georgia was taken over by the Soviet Union. Independence was achieved again in 1991 after the breakup of the Soviet Union. Since that time, there have been numerous conflicts regarding the regions of Abkhazia and South Ossetia, both of which are within the boundaries of Georgia but are outside the jurisdiction of the Georgian government. Nevertheless, democratization has been gradually occurring in the country since 2000.

About 83 percent of all Georgians are Russian Orthodox Christian. About 10 percent of the population are Muslim, 4 percent belong to the Armenian-Gregorian branch of the Greek Orthodox Church, 1 percent are Roman Catholic, and the remaining have no religious affiliation.

Educational System

Education in Georgia is supervised by the Ministry of Education and Science. The primary languages of instruction are Georgian and Russian. Schooling in the country consists of preprimary education, basic education at the primary and lower secondary levels, upper secondary education, and higher education.

Preprimary education in Georgia during the Soviet era was highly successful in preparing young children for formal education at the primary level. However, indicators seem to suggest that preschool and kindergarten enrollment in the country had dropped in the fledgling years of the republic shortly after independence. Nevertheless, enrollment in early childhood education has grown since 1999, when the preschool enrollment figure was 35 percent of the population of children between three and six years. By 2002, 43 percent of the preschool-age population in Georgia was enrolled. Seven years later, 63 percent of the population of this age group was enrolled.

Education in Georgia is compulsory for a period of nine years for children between the ages of six and 14 years. This period is fairly consistent with those of neighboring nations, which expect students to attend school for a period between 9 and 11 years. In Georgia duration of primary school is a period of six years. The duration of lower secondary school is a period of three years—from ages 12 to 14 years. The system encourages students to attend the last two years of secondary school in order to be eligible for university or trade school enrollment. The compulsory education years comprise a basic curriculum that considers essential subjects—Georgian, Russian, mathematics, basic natural science, physical education, art, and music.

The student/teacher ratio at the primary school level in Georgian schools is 14 to 15 students for every teacher. The primary school gross enrollment ratio is 94 percent. However, the net enrollment rate for primary school is approximately 87 percent, indicating that about 13 percent of all children at the primary level are not attending school. Data and statistics regarding Georgia's primary education completion rate have been erratic within the last two decades. Primary school completion showed promising outcomes between 1999 and 2001. However, the percentage of students completing primary school fell from 100 percent in 2001 to 84 percent in 2006. The secondary school student/teacher ratio in Georgia is 9 to 10 students for every teacher. The secondary gross enrollment ratio in the country is 83 percent. However, net enrollment ratio data for secondary school indicate that 13 percent of the population between the ages of 12 and 18 are not attending school.

Georgian students who successfully complete their secondary education programs are generally encouraged to pursue a degree at one of the universities in the country. There are 41 universities in the country—18 public universities and 23 private universities. In addition, the country is home to 58 private, nonuniversity institutions of higher education. Established in 1918, Tbilisi State University, in

the country's capital, is Georgia's oldest and largest institution. It is also the oldest higher education institution in the Caucasus region. Tbilisi State University enrolls about 35,000 students annually. The university maintains six schools: the Faculty of Exact and Natural Sciences, Faculty of Humanities, Faculty of Social and Political Sciences, Faculty of Economics and Business, Faculty of Law, and Faculty of Medicine. The recently established International School of Economics is a highly selective, autonomous college of Tbilisi State University that emulates the curricula of New Economic School of Moscow. Other high-ranking institutions in the country include Ilia State University, Batumi Shota Rustaveli State University, Akaki Tsereteli State University, Telavi Iakob Gogebashvili State University, the Georgian Technical University, Gori University, Batumi International University, the Tbilisi State Medical University, the Tbilisi Vano Sarajishvili State Conservatory, and the Tbilisi State Academy of the Arts. Primary education teachers attend specialized teacher training institutions where they receive a *Datskebiti Skolis Mastsavlebeli*—a certificate for teaching in primary school. Secondary school teachers are trained at either the same teacher training institutes or at one of the country's

---

Georgia Education at a Glance

General Information

Capital	Tbilisi
Population	4.6 million
Languages	Georgian (71%), Russian (9%), Armenian (7%), Azeri (6%), other (7%)
Literacy rate	100%
GDP per capita	US$3,800
People below poverty line (2004)	54%
Number of phones per 100 people	14
Number of Internet users per 100 people	22
Number of Internet hosts	110,680
Life expectancy at birth (years)	76

Formal Educational Information

Primary school age population	341,000
Secondary school age population	370,000
Primary school age population	7%
Number of years of education (primary/secondary)	6/5
Student/teacher ratio (primary)	14
Student/teacher ratio (secondary)	9
Primary school gross enrollment ratio	94%
Primary school entrants reaching grade 5	79%
Secondary school gross enrollment ratio	83%
Child labor (ages 5–14)	18%

Note: Unless otherwise indicated, all data are based on sources from 2011.

comprehensive universities. Students attend one of these institutions for a period of five years, at the end of which time they receive the *Sashualo Skolis Mastsavlebeli*, which is the certificate for teaching at the secondary school level.

System Economics and Future Prospects

According to the United Nations Development Programme (2010), along with Andorra, Uganda, Chad, Guatemala, the British Virgin Islands, and Mauritius, total public expenditures on education in Georgia represented 3.2 percent of the gross domestic product (GDP) in 2009. Given the GDP of Georgia at $22.32 billion, educational expenditure in the country amounts to more than $714 million, or $1,005 per student (total amount equivalent to US dollars divided by 711,000, the approximate number of primary and secondary students in the country). Per student spending was greater during the Soviet era. Georgia ranks 31 of 186 countries in percentage of educational expenditure.

Like that of its neighbors, Georgia's literacy rate is 100 percent; the country ranks, along with Azerbaijan, Russia, and Armenia, as having the highest rate of literacy in the region. Despite this success, Georgia's formal system of education has suffered from decline since independence. With the end of the Soviet period, the Education Ministry in the republic lacked organization, and there was a drop in school enrollment throughout the nation. According to UNICEF, 18 percent of all children between five and 14 years of age are engaged in labor. As a result of the abhorrent conditions of putting children to work—let alone the overwhelmingly high percentage of children engaged in labor—the government and the Ministry of Education must grapple with high rates of attrition of students, particularly those in secondary schools. The present goal of the Georgian Ministry of Education is to rebuild the educational infrastructure in the country. Due to relatively recent independence, Georgia has been the recipient of numerous funding sources, primarily from nongovernmental organizations, which have assisted in ameliorating the hardships of families with regard to fiduciary responsibilities in sending children to school.

Daniel Ness and Chia-ling Lin

REFERENCES

Central Intelligence Agency. *The CIA World Factbook*. New York: Skyhorse, 2011. https.www.cia.gov/library/publications/the-world-factbook/index.html.

Nation Master. 2011. www.nationmaster.com.

UNESCO. *Global Education Digest 2012: Comparing Education Statistics Across the World*. Montreal: UNESCO Institute for Statistics, 2012.

———. "Strong Foundations: Early Childhood Care and Education." *Education for All Global Monitoring Report*. Paris: UNESCO, 2006.

UNESCO–IBE. www.ibe.unesco.org/en/worldwide/unesco-regions/europe-and-north-america/georgia.html.

United Nations Development Programme. *United Nations Development Report 2010*. New York: Palgrave Macmillan, 2010.

US Department of Labor. *2001 Findings on the Worst Forms of Child Labor*. Washington, DC: Bureau of International Labor Affairs, US Department of Labor, 2002.

World Bank Education Statistics. 2011. www.worldbank.org.

KAZAKHSTAN

The Republic of Kazakhstan became independent from Russia in 1991. Many European Russians migrated to Kazakhstan in order to expand the region's agricultural production. As a result, native Kazakhs were close to being outnumbered by European Russians. The rate of unemployment (7 percent) and poverty (17 percent) in Kazakhstan is much lower than in neighboring Central Asian nations. This is mainly a result of the country's large supply of natural resources. Kazakhstan's government has been relatively stable since 1991 and, accordingly, has focused on improving the level of petroleum production and the mining of both precious metals and standard metals and minerals for industrial use and for export.

About 47 percent of all Kazakhstani are Muslim, and 44 percent are members of the Russian Orthodox Church. The remaining 9 percent of the population have no religious affiliation.

Educational System

The national body responsible for education in Kazakhstan is the Ministry of Education and Science. The aim of the ministry is to appropriate state funds for the purpose of educating Kazakh youth, adolescents, and young adults. The ministry also attempts to provide guidance for all educational and scientific institutions in the country.

Preprimary education in Kazakhstan during the Soviet era was highly successful in preparing young children for formal education at the primary level. Despite setbacks in the Kazakh preschool and kindergarten program within the past two decades, the government is making an effort to ensure that all families have a right to send their children between the ages of four and five years to preschool and kindergarten. At present, there are a total of 848,000 preschool-age children in Kazakhstan. Approximately 136,000, or 16 percent, of them are enrolled in a preschool or kindergarten. Kindergartens in Kazakhstan differ from those of other post-Soviet systems in that Kazakh kindergartens emphasize cognitive development and language. Since 1991, preschool and kindergarten infrastructure in the country has been in decline. Recent initiatives through the help of nongovernmental organizations (NGOs) have helped to deal with the problems of poorly built schools as well as the lack of resources for students.

Education in Kazakhstan is compulsory for a period of 10 years for children between the ages of six and 15 years. The compulsory education period comprises a basic curriculum introduced in the five years of primary school and continued for the five years of the so-called general secondary level (for children 10 to 15 years old). The curriculum emphasizes essential subjects—Kazakh, Russian, mathematics, basic natural science, physical education, art, and music. Kazakh students who are 16 and 17 years old must attend the upper two-year secondary level (Gymnasium) in order to be eligible for university enrollment.

The student/teacher ratio at the primary school level is 16 to 17 students for every teacher. The primary school gross enrollment ratio is 105 percent. However, the net enrollment rate for primary school is approximately 91 percent, indicating that about 9 percent of all children at the primary level are not attending school. It is encouraging to note that the survival rate to the last primary grade in Kazakhstan is nearly 100 percent. The primary school completion rate in is 107 percent because a percentage of the population older than 11 years of age has graduated from the primary school level. The secondary school student/teacher ratio in Kazakhstan is about 11 students for every teacher. The secondary gross enrollment ratio in the country is 95 percent. The secondary net enrollment ratio is approximately 89 percent, indicating that 11 percent of the secondary-school-age population is not attending secondary school.

Kazakh students who successfully complete their secondary education programs are generally encouraged to pursue a degree at one of the universities in the country. In Kazakhstan, there are three general levels of university education. The first level is called basic higher education, which leads students toward the baccalaureate. A second level is scientific-pedagogical higher education, which provides education for students pursuing the master's degree and doctorate. A third level is called specialized higher education, which is provided for students who wish to obtain a degree in a vocational or trade profession. Given Kazakhstan's location and history, languages of instruction in Kazakh universities include primarily Kazakh and Russian. However, English, German, French, Chinese, and Arabic are also used for instruction.

There are an estimated 75 higher education institutions in Kazakhstan. Most of the universities are state-run and subsidized by the government. The major strength of Kazakh universities is that they emphasize applied approaches to both arts and the natural and social sciences. This was essentially the mission of these institutions, especially during Soviet rule, given that theoretical-based and research-based education was primarily the function of Russian universities. Established in 1934, the Al-Farabi Kazakh National University in Almaty is the country's oldest and largest institution. With an enrollment of about 20,000, the Kazakh National University is divided into 13 schools: Faculties of Mechanics and Mathematics, Physics, Biology, Chemistry, Geography, History, Philology and Language, Journalism, International Relations, Eastern Studies, Political Science and Philosophy, Economics and Business, and Law. A second leading university in Kazakhstan is the L.N. Gumilev Eurasian National University in Astana, the country's capital. The university is known primarily for its emphasis in applied arts and sciences as well as education, engineering, information technology, and applied physics and technical sciences. In addition to certain comprehensive universities, such as the Eurasian National University, primary education teachers attend specialized pedagogical institutes where they receive a certificate for teaching in primary school. Secondary school teachers are trained at one of the country's comprehensive universities. Students attend one of these institutions for a period of five years, at the end of which time they receive the Specialist's Diploma for teaching at the secondary school level. Six of the 14 provinces and three cities have pedagogical universities: Kazakh National Pedagogical University in Almaty, the Aktobe State Pedagogical Institute, the Kostanay State Pedagogical Institute, the Pavlodar State Pedagogical Institute, the Semey State Pedagogical Institute, and the Taraz State Pedagogical Institute.

In 2000 the Ministry of Education of Kazakhstan collaborated with the ministries and governments of Kyrgyzstan and Tajikistan in chartering the first international university of the world—namely, the University of Central Asia. Currently under construction, the university will have three campuses—one in each of the three nations. At present, however, research and education activities are conducted in office space in the capital cities of the three countries. The campus in Kazakhstan will be located in Tekeli, a small city near Almaty, the country's largest city.

System Economics and Future Prospects

Due to limited data, it is difficult to know the total public expenditures on education in Kazakhstan. However, 1991 data show that the country's expenditures represented 9.4 percent of its gross domestic product (GDP). Assuming that this percentage is the same today, and given the GDP of Kazakhstan at $37.72 billion, educational expenditure in the country would amount to close to $3.5 billion, or $518 per student (total amount equivalent to US dollars divided by 6,841,000, the approximate number of primary and secondary students in the country). Nevertheless, given the spending on education in neighboring countries, it is surmised that per student spending was greater during the Soviet era and that some decline in education expenditure has occurred since then.

With a near 100 percent literacy rate, Kazakhstan, along with Uzbekistan, has the highest rate of literacy among the nations in Central Asia. Despite this success, Kazakhstan has been in steady decline with regard to its education system since independence.

Kazakhstan Education at a Glance	
General Information	
Capital	Astana
Population	15.4 million
Language(s)	Kazakh, Russian
Literacy rate	99%
GDP per capita	US$9,400
People below poverty line	19%
Number of phones per 100 people	22
Number of Internet users per 100 people	15
Number of Internet hosts	53,984
Life expectancy at birth (years)	67
Formal Educational Information	
Primary school age population	932,000
Secondary school age population	2 million
Primary school age population	6%
Secondary school age population	13%
Number of years of education (primary/secondary)	4/7
Student/teacher ratio (primary)	17
Student/teacher ratio (secondary)	11
Primary school gross enrollment ratio	105%
Primary school entrants completing primary school	99%
Secondary school gross enrollment ratio	95%
Child labor (ages 5–14)	2%

Note: Unless otherwise indicated, all data are based on sources from 2011.

With the end of the Soviet period, the Education Ministry in the republic lacked organization, and there was a drop in school enrollment throughout the nation. The present goal of the Ministry of Education of Kazakhstan is to rebuild the educational infrastructure in the country. This initiative began in 2003 with the infusion of $600,000 from the Asian Development Bank. Moreover, the United States Agency for International Development, the World Bank, and other nongovernmental organizations in collaboration with the Peace Corps have attempted to help by ameliorating the burdens of poor families grappling to pay for their children's educational fees, particularly those associated with travel between home and school, books and related supplies, and teacher education improvements.

Daniel Ness and Chia-ling Lin

References

Central Intelligence Agency. *The CIA World Factbook*. New York: Skyhorse, 2011. https.www.cia.gov/library/publications/the-world-factbook/index.html.

Nation Master. 2011. www.nationmaster.com.

UNESCO. *Global Education Digest 2012: Comparing Education Statistics Across the World*. Montreal: UNESCO Institute for Statistics, 2012.

————. "Strong Foundations: Early Childhood Care and Education." *Education for All Global Monitoring Report*. Paris: UNESCO, 2006.

UNESCO–IBE. www.ibe.unesco.org/en/worldwide/unesco-regions/asia-and-the-pacific/kazakhstan.html.

United Nations Development Programme. *United Nations Development Report 2010*. New York: Palgrave Macmillan, 2010.

US Department of Labor. *2001 Findings on the Worst Forms of Child Labor*. Washington, DC: Bureau of International Labor Affairs, US Department of Labor, 2002.

World Bank Education Statistics. 2011. www.worldbank.org.

KYRGYZSTAN

Kyrgyzstan is a landlocked central Asian country that used to be part of the former Soviet Union. The Kyrgyz Republic became independent from Russia in 1991. Initially, the president maintained overwhelming power over the country. Demonstrations in Bishkek in 2005 and 2006, however, led to a reformulation of the country's constitution, which eventually included a passage that balanced the power between the president and the legislature. Current social and political concerns include reducing the number of corrupt politicians in government positions, expanding democratization, and improving relations between different ethnic groups.

The country's population was 5.5 million in the 2011 estimate. About 75 percent of all Kyrgyzstani are Muslim. The remaining population is Russian Orthodox or has no religion. Kyrgyzstan comprises an area of 76,641 square miles (198,500 square kilometers)—slightly smaller than the state of South Dakota. With an unemployment rate of about 18 percent and a poverty rate of more than 40 percent, Kyrgyzstan is rated the second-poorest country in Central Asia.

Educational System

In Kyrgyzstan it is desirable to be associated with schools and education. There is a very high premium put on receiving an education, which is considered a status symbol for many Kyrgyz families. Even at a time that the country's economy is vulnerable, Kyrgyz parents believe that the opportunity to provide education for children is essential. Since the country's independence in 1991, the numbers of universities and tertiary-level students have quadrupled in Kyrgyzstan. On the face of it, the increase in universities and university enrollment seems quite promising. However, the Kyrgyzstan government is implementing reforms in higher education at the expense of draining funds from secondary education. As a result, Kyrgyz secondary students, and primary students to a degree, have been sidelined as university officials maintain prematurely that economic outcomes as a result of university growth have been successful. Accordingly, the educational system in Kyrgyzstan is seemingly contradictory in that higher education appeals to parents, while, at the same time, students are being shortchanged in their secondary education. Moreover, there seems to be an inherent level of corruption in that private universities are allowed to award state diplomas.

Preprimary education in Kyrgyzstan has only recently been considered as a major influence on primary and secondary education. Laws are currently being considered that would make preprimary education mandatory in the country. At present, 11 percent of the country's children under age six attend kindergarten—the year before the primary education levels.

Education in Kyrgyzstan is compulsory for a period of nine years for children between the ages of six and 14. This period consists of four years of primary education and five years of secondary school. These compulsory education years comprise a basic curriculum that considers essential subjects—Russian, Kyrgyz, mathematics, basic natural science, physical education, art, and music. An upper secondary school period of three years is not compulsory, but most families strive to send their children to the upper secondary level for the purpose of eligibility for university enrollment. Most state-funded schools were built during the Soviet era and were based on the philosophical foundations of the former Soviet Union. In addition to state-run institutions, children and adolescents have the opportunity to attend religious schools—primarily Muslim—which were banned prior to 1991.

The student/teacher ratio at the primary school level is about 24 students for every teacher. The primary school gross enrollment ratio is 97 percent. However, the net enrollment rate for primary school is about 86 percent, indicating that not all children at the primary level are attending school. The secondary school student/teacher ratio in Kyrgyzstan is about 14 students for every teacher. The secondary gross enrollment ratio in the country is 86 percent. However, the net enrollment ratio is only 81 percent, again indicating that much smaller numbers of students of the age group are actually enrolled.

Most students who successfully complete their secondary education programs are strongly encouraged to attend one of the many Kyrgyz universities. There are at least 54 higher education institutions in the country. Although comprehensive universities exist, Kyrgyzstan is known primarily for its specialized professional universities, particularly those in medicine and in engineering and technology. The institutions with the largest enrollments include Kyrgyz State University, the oldest university in the country; Kyrgyz Technical University; Kyrgyz Medical Institute; Osh State University; Kyrgyz-Russian

Slavonic University; and the Asian Medical Institute. Osh State University has an enrollment of some 27,000 students. It was originally founded as the Osh Pedagogical Institute, a teacher training college, and was reorganized in 1992 to include more diverse disciplines. The Kyrgyz Technical University was established in 1954 during the Soviet period and served as one of the largest polytechnic universities in central Asia.

System Economics and Future Prospects

According to the United Nations Development Programme (2010), along with Israel, Cape Verde, and Finland, total public expenditures on education in Kyrgyzstan represented 5.9 percent of the gross domestic product (GDP) in 2008. Given the GDP of Kyrgyzstan at $11.85 billion, educational expenditure in the country amounts to more than $700 million, or $551 per student (total amount equivalent to US dollars divided by 1,270,000, the approximate number of primary and secondary students in the country). Per student spending was greater during the Soviet era. Kyrgyzstan ranks 31 of 186 countries in percentage of educational expenditure.

In recent years, Kyrgyzstan has been the recipient of numerous initiatives and funding through government subsidies and programs funded by nongovernmental agencies. Despite recent initiatives in improving the country's education system, Kyrgyzstan's educational system is rife with problems ranging from political corruption to ethnic tension and high rates of poverty. Proper organizational arrangements of processes and administration of the educational system as well as the proper allocation of funding could rectify some of these problems.

Daniel Ness and Chia-ling Lin

REFERENCES

Central Intelligence Agency. *The CIA World Factbook*. New York: Skyhorse, 2011. https.www.cia.gov/library/publications/the-world-factbook/index.html.

DeYoung, Alan J. *Lost in Transition: Redefining Students and Universities in the Kyrgyz Republic*. Charlotte, NC: Information Age, 2011.

Nation Master. 2011. www.nationmaster.com.

Kyrgyzstan Education at a Glance	
General Information	
Capital	Bishkek
Population	5.2 million
Languages	Kyrgyz (64%), Uzbek (14%), Russian (13%), Dungan, Ukrainian, Uygur
Literacy rate	99%
GDP per capita	US$2,100
People below poverty line	40%
Number of phones per 100 people	10
Number of Internet users per 100 people	16
Number of Internet hosts	97,976
Life expectancy at birth (years)	69
Formal Educational Information	
Primary school age population	438,000
Secondary school age population	832,000
Primary school age population	8%
Secondary school age population	16%
Number of years of education (primary/secondary)	4/7
Student/teacher ratio (primary)	24
Student/teacher ratio (secondary)	14
Primary school gross enrollment ratio	97%
Primary school entrants completing primary school	99%
Secondary school gross enrollment ratio	86%
Child labor (ages 5–14)	4%

Note: Unless otherwise indicated, all data are based on sources from 2011.

UNESCO. *Global Education Digest 2012: Comparing Education Statistics Across the World.* Montreal: UNESCO Institute for Statistics, 2012.

———. "Strong Foundations: Early Childhood Care and Education." *Education for All Global Monitoring Report.* Paris: UNESCO, 2006.

UNESCO–IBE. www.ibe.unesco.org/en/worldwide/unesco-regions/asia-and-the-pacific/kyrgyzstan.html.

United Nations Development Programme. *United Nations Development Report 2010.* New York: Palgrave Macmillan, 2010.

US Department of Labor. *2001 Findings on the Worst Forms of Child Labor.* Washington, DC: Bureau of International Labor Affairs, US Department of Labor, 2002.

World Bank Education Statistics. 2011. www.worldbank.org.

LATVIA

The Republic of Latvia is located in northeastern Europe on the Gulf of Riga to the west. In medieval times, Latvia was controlled by Germanic armies that eventually converted pagan groups in the region to Christianity. Latvia was controlled by both Polish and Lithuanian forces in the sixteenth century. The country became independent for the first time in 1918. However, the country eventually became one of the republics of the Soviet Union in 1940. Latvia once again became independent in 1991 after the end of Soviet rule. In 2004 the country became a member of NATO and the European Union. Religions in the country include members of the Lutheran Church, Roman Catholic Church, and Russian Orthodox Church.

Educational System

Education in Latvia is has been strongly influenced by German education. Germanic Christian missionaries established schools as part of monasteries in Latvia as early as the thirteenth century. German, then, was the principal language of instruction for at least three centuries. During the seventeenth, eighteenth, and nineteenth centuries, Latvian began to be used more frequently, not only in general discourse but in the teaching of language and school instruction. Part of the reason for including Latvian during instruction was to promote literacy through the recitation and reading of religious writings. Education for the masses emerged during the second half of the nineteenth century.

Preprimary education in Latvia is similar to that of Estonia and Lithuania. In general, preschools in the country have been fairly successful both during and after the Soviet era in preparing young children for formal education at the primary level. Preschool education in Latvia is not compulsory; however, the majority of children are sent to preprimary institutions. Of the nearly 74,000 preschool-age children in the country, nearly 63,000—about 85 percent—attend preschool or kindergarten. Funding for preprimary education in Latvia is based on local government budgets. Parents must also contribute to their children's preschool education and care.

Education in Latvia is compulsory for a period of nine years for children between the ages of seven and 15 years. As in Estonia, compulsory education in Latvia consists of six years of primary school and three years of lower secondary school. The last three years of secondary school (for students ages 16 to 18) are not compulsory, although more than 90 percent of the population of this age group do attend. The compulsory education years comprise a basic curriculum that considers essential subjects—Latvian, Russian, mathematics, basic natural science, physical education, art, and music.

The student/teacher ratio in Latvian primary schools is approximately 12 students for every teacher. The primary school gross enrollment ratio is nearly 95 percent. The net enrollment rate for primary school is about 90 percent, indicating that a minority of primary-school-age students are either not promoted to subsequent grade levels or are taken out of school for some reason. The survival rate to the last primary school grade is nearly 100 percent, and the rate of primary school completion is about 92 percent of the population for that level. The secondary school student/teacher ratio in Latvia is about 11 students for every teacher. The secondary gross enrollment ratio in the country is nearly 100 percent. Data regarding net enrollment ratio for secondary school in Latvia are currently unavailable, but are believed to be encouraging in terms of the number of Latvian secondary students continuing to the tertiary level. Parents whose children drop out of the basic education curriculum have the option of sending their children to basic vocational programs. Upper secondary-school-age adolescents have three options: general secondary education schools, which are attended by most students at this level for a period of three years; secondary vocational schools, which are attended by students who opt out of university-bound schools for a period of four years; and vocational program schools, which are attended by lower secondary school students who transition to upper-level vocational programs for a period of two to three years.

There are four options for tertiary education in Latvia: university baccalaureate programs, which are intended to prepare students who wish to continue for postgraduate education; university-level professional programs; applied professional programs; and college preparation programs geared for adults who are either returning to school or for adolescents who left school and wish to return. Latvian students who successfully complete their upper secondary education programs are generally encouraged to pursue a degree at the university level. There are at least 25 university- or academy-level education institutions in Latvia. Six of these institutions are comprehensive universities and 19 are professional universities or academies with distinct specializations. The University of Latvia is the largest university in the country, having an annual enrollment of about 22,000 students. The university consists of 13 faculties, including specializations in natural sciences, social sciences, humanities, theology, education, law, and medicine. The Riga Technical University is one of the oldest technical universities in the region. Established in 1862, the purpose of the Riga Technical University was to prepare students in a number of engineering and architectural fields in order to maintain industrial competitiveness with countries of western Europe. The institution enrolls approximately 16,000 students annually. In addition to these higher education institutions, there are a number of specialized academies that aim to promote excellence in the areas of economics, music, law, fine arts, business and industry, travel and telecommunication, and military studies. Teacher preparation in Latvia is offered at the university level where preservice teachers enroll in teacher training and pedagogical courses while pursuing a specified content area of study.

System Economics and Future Prospects

According to the United Nations Development Programme (2010), along with Seychelles, Aruba, and

Latvia Education at a Glance	
General Information	
Capital	Riga
Population	2.2 million
Languages	Latvian (58%), Russian (58%), Lithuanian
Literacy rate	100%
GDP per capita	US$16,000
People below poverty line	no data
Number of phones per 100 people	29
Number of Internet users per 100 people	56
Number of Internet hosts	289,478
Life expectancy at birth (years)	72
Formal Educational Information	
Primary school age population	83,000
Secondary school age population	262,000
Primary school age population	3.5%
Secondary school age population	11.5%
Number of years of education (primary/secondary)	4/8
Student/teacher ratio (primary)	12
Student/teacher ratio (secondary)	11
Primary school gross enrollment ratio	95%
Primary school entrants completing primary school	98%
Secondary school gross enrollment ratio	99%
Child labor (ages 5–14)	no data

Note: Unless otherwise indicated, all data are based on sources from 2011.

Mozambique, total public expenditures on education of Latvia represented 5 percent of the gross domestic product (GDP) in 2007. Given the GDP of Latvia at $32.2 billion, educational expenditure in the country amounts to more than $1.6 billion, or $4,667 per student (total amount equivalent to US dollars divided by 345,000, the approximate number of primary and secondary students in the country). Per student spending was greater during the Soviet era. Latvia ranks 57 of 186 countries in percentage of educational expenditure.

Latvia has a 100 percent literacy rate. At present, along with the educational systems of Lithuania and Estonia, Latvia's education system ranks as one of the most successful of the post-Soviet systems. Latvia is one of the leading countries in the post-Soviet region in the area of information and communication technologies. Given the country's limited natural resources, Latvia's focus on building its education system is perhaps its greatest asset for the future.

Daniel Ness and Chia-ling Lin

REFERENCES

Central Intelligence Agency. *The CIA World Factbook*. New York: Skyhorse, 2011. https.www.cia.gov/library/publications/the-world-factbook/index.html.

Nation Master. 2011. www.nationmaster.com.

UNESCO. *Global Education Digest 2012: Comparing Education Statistics Across the World*. Montreal: UNESCO Institute for Statistics, 2012.

———. "Strong Foundations: Early Childhood Care and Education." *Education for All Global Monitoring Report*. Paris: UNESCO, 2006.

UNESCO–IBE. www.ibe.unesco.org/en/worldwide/unesco-regions/europe-and-north-america/latvia.html.

United Nations Development Programme. *United Nations Development Report 2010*. New York: Palgrave Macmillan, 2010.

US Department of Labor. *2001 Findings on the Worst Forms of Child Labor*. Washington, DC: Bureau of International Labor Affairs, US Department of Labor, 2002.

World Bank Education Statistics. 2011. www.worldbank.org.

LITHUANIA

The Republic of Lithuania is located in northeastern Europe on the Gulf of Riga to the west. In medieval times, Lithuania was controlled by Germanic armies that eventually converted pagan groups in the region to Christianity. By the sixteenth century, the present-day region of Lithuania became part of a two-state union, commonly known as the Polish-Lithuanian commonwealth—a monarchy that also included Polish forces. The country became independent for the first time in 1918. However, it eventually became one of the republics of the Soviet Union in 1940. From 1940 to 1944, however, the country was occupied by Nazi Germany. Lithuania once again became independent in 1991 after the end of Soviet rule. Religions in the country include members of the Roman Catholic Church (approximately 80 percent of the population), the Russian Orthodox Church (about 4 percent), and the Lutheran Church (about 2 percent). About 5.5 percent of the population does not specify a religion, and 10.5 percent of the population has no religious affiliation.

Educational System

Although preprimary education in Lithuania has been fairly successful both during and after the Soviet era in preparing young children for formal education at the primary level, it falls behind the preprimary systems of Latvia and Estonia in terms of percentage of children attending preschool. Although preschool education is not compulsory, slightly over half of children are sent to preprimary schools. Of the nearly 129,000 preschool-age children in the country, nearly 81,500—about 63.2 percent—attend preschool or kindergarten. The curriculum and teaching practices in early childhood education in Lithuania are run by the Ministry of Education and Research.

Education in Lithuania is compulsory for a period of nine years for children between the ages of seven and 15 years. This period consists of six years of primary school and three years of lower secondary school. Although the last three years of secondary school (for students ages 16 to 18) are not compulsory, the overwhelming majority of this age group does attend. The compulsory education years comprise a basic curriculum that considers essential subjects—Lithuanian, Russian, mathematics, basic natural science, physical education, art, and music.

The student/teacher ratio in Lithuanian primary schools is approximately 14 students for every teacher. The primary school gross enrollment ratio is 94 percent. The net enrollment rate in 2005 for primary school was about 88 percent, which demonstrates that primary school enrollment in Lithuania is lower than primary school enrollments in neighboring countries. The secondary school student/teacher ratio in Lithuania is about 10 students for every teacher. The secondary gross enrollment ratio in the country is nearly 100 percent. The net enrollment ratio for secondary school is close to 94 percent, indicating that most students complete their secondary education while a small percentage attempt to enter the workforce either after graduation from lower secondary school or while attending upper secondary school.

The two basic types of higher education institutions in Lithuania are universities (or academies) and colleges. There are both public and private universities and colleges in the country. Lithuanian students who successfully complete their upper secondary education programs most often pursue a degree at the university level. There are over 20 universities and professional academies in Lithuania. The oldest and largest university in the country is Vilnius University, which enrolls about 22,000 students per year. Established in 1579, Vilnius University is the oldest university in the Baltic States. Although Vilnius University was founded by Jesuit priests, it was influenced greatly during the following century by important leaders and theologians who were Jewish or Protestant. Vilnius University is divided into 14 faculties, five institutes, three research centers, and six research, recreation, and support divisions. Other competitive higher education institutions in Lithuania include Kaunas University of Technology, Mykolas Romeris University, the Lithuanian Academy of Music and Theater, the Vilnius Gediminas Technical University, and the Vilnius Pedagogical University.

Teacher training for both the primary and secondary school levels and for educational research takes place at either departments or programs at several universities or at pedagogical universities that specialize in the training of teachers. For the most part, teachers who plan to teach at the preprimary or primary level must receive a baccalaureate from a university. Preservice secondary school teachers receive preparation at Vilnius University, Vilnius Pedagogical University, Šiauliai Pedagogical University, Vytautas Magnus University, or Klaipėda University. Students can also seek enrollment in four-year programs at private universities or colleges in the country. Higher education institution instructors must seek the doctorate in order to teach at the university or college level.

System Economics and Future Prospects

According to the United Nations Development Programme (2010), along with Dominica, Iran, and Serbia, total public expenditures on education in Lithuania represented 4.7 percent of the gross domestic product (GDP) in 2007. Given the GDP of Lithuania at $56.22 billion, educational expenditure in the country amounts to more than $2.642 billion, or $4,603 per student (total amount equivalent to US dollars divided by 574,000, the approximate number of primary and secondary students in the country). Per student spending was greater during the Soviet era. Lithuania ranks 74 of 186 countries in percentage of educational expenditure.

Lithuania has a 100 percent literacy rate. The country's education system is one of the most successful of the post-Soviet systems. Along with its northern neighbors, Lithuania is one of the leading countries in the post-Soviet region in the area of information and communication technologies. However, the country's educational system faces difficulty in competing with its western European neighbors in the global market. This is evident when comparing Lithuania's per capita GDP with those of its northern and western neighbors.

Daniel Ness and Chia-ling Lin

REFERENCES

Central Intelligence Agency. *The CIA World Factbook*. New York: Skyhorse, 2011. https.www.cia.gov/library/publications/the-world-factbook/index.html.

Nation Master. 2011. www.nationmaster.com.

UNESCO. *Global Education Digest 2012: Comparing Education Statistics Across the World*. Montreal: UNESCO Institute for Statistics, 2012.

———. "Strong Foundations: Early Childhood Care and Education." *Education for All Global Monitoring Report*. Paris: UNESCO, 2006.

UNESCO–IBE. www.ibe.unesco.org/en/worldwide/unesco-regions/europe-and-north-america/lithuania.html.

Lithuania Education at a Glance

General Information

Capital	Vilnius
Population	3.5 million
Languages	Lithuanian (82%), Russian (8%), Polish (6%)
Literacy rate	100%
GDP per capita	US$15,300
People below poverty line	4%
Number of phones per 100 people	22
Number of Internet users per 100 people	50
Number of Internet hosts	1.1 million
Life expectancy at birth (years)	75

Formal Educational Information

Primary school age population	159,000
Secondary school age population	415,000
Primary school age population	4.5%
Secondary school age population	11.5%
Number of years of education (primary/secondary)	4/8
Student/teacher ratio (primary)	14
Student/teacher ratio (secondary)	10
Primary school gross enrollment ratio	94%
Primary school entrants completing primary school	98%
Secondary school gross enrollment ratio	100%
Child labor (ages 5–14)	no data

Note: Unless otherwise indicated, all data are based on sources from 2011.

United Nations Development Programme. *United Nations Development Report 2010.* New York: Palgrave Macmillan, 2010.

US Department of Labor. *2001 Findings on the Worst Forms of Child Labor.* Washington, DC: Bureau of International Labor Affairs, US Department of Labor, 2002.

World Bank Education Statistics. 2011. www.worldbank.org.

MOLDOVA

The Republic of Moldova is a landlocked country in southeastern Europe. Moldova was inhabited by several tribes since ancient times. The region was the location of numerous invasions by various groups from both European and Asian lands. The region became the Principality of Moldavia in 1359 and eventually became the eight eastern counties of present-day Romania. Moldova was incorporated into the Soviet Union after World War II. The country became independent in 1991. In 2001 Moldova was the only post-Soviet republic where the Communist Party won an election.

Approximately 98 percent of all Moldovans are members of the Eastern Orthodox Christian faith. The remaining 2 percent of the population consists of members of Protestant sects and Judaism. Moldova's gross domestic product (GDP) for 2010 amounted to $11.01 billion. Moldova is the poorest nation in Europe. More than 11 percent of Moldovans live on less than $2 per day.

Educational System

There are five types of primary schools in Moldova: primary schools, gymnasia, lyceums, general schools, and special schools. Primary schools cater to students in grades 1 through 4. These schools provide students with a basic curriculum that includes Russian and Romanian. Mathematics and the natural sciences are also emphasized early on in Moldovan children's schooling. Of the roughly 188,000 primary-level students in Moldova, only 12,000 attend the four-year primary school. Most children at this level attend the gymnasia, lyceums, or general schools. Gymnasia enroll students from grades 1 through 9, thereby including a primary level component. Similarly, Lyceums are schools that enroll students from grades 1 through 12. Students who enter lyceums must pass the Baccalaureate examination. General schools also enroll students from grades 1 through 12; however, general school students are unable to continue their studies in academic disciplines traditionally provided in higher education institutions. Special schools accommodate students, grades 1 through 11, who have physical or psychological conditions that impede learning ability.

Secondary schools in Moldova include the following nine types: gymnasia (from grade 5 to grade 9), lyceums (grade 5 to grade 12), general schools (grade 5 to grade 11), evening schools (grade 5 to grade 12), trade schools (grade 12), vocational schools (grade 10 to grade 12), vocational lyceums (grade 10 to grade 12), *colegii* (grade 10 or 11 to grade 12), and special schools (grade 5 to grade 11). Curriculum in both the gymnasia and lyceums continues and emphasizes the basic education curriculum of primary education. Gymnasia graduates decide whether to attend vocational schools or continue to the *colegii*, which prepare students for university education. Students in general schools or evening schools are not allowed to attend the university. Twelfth-grade students enrolled in the lyceums and vocational lyceums are the only secondary-level students permitted to take the baccalaureate examination, which determines the eligibility of university-bound students. Successful lyceum students attend universities while successful vocational lyceum students usually attend polytechnic universities. Due to the strong emphasis on tracking, access to secondary schools that prepare tertiary-bound students is usually based on socioeconomic class—students from affluent families gain access and students from less affluent families do not. Accordingly, the secondary school gross enrollment rate is 82 percent.

In total, there are 30 higher education institutions in Moldova, 16 public and 14 private. These institutions include universities, polytechnic universities, colleges, normal schools, and agricultural institutions. Less than half of all university-level faculty hold doctorates. This can be contrasted with a more than 90 percent rate of doctorates among faculty in the United States, Canada, most countries in Europe, Australia, and New Zealand. The two largest public universities in Moldova are the State University of Moldova in Chişinău and Alecu Russo State University of Bălţi. Both universities were established shortly after the end of World War II with the aim of developing postwar educational infrastructure in the Soviet Union.

Moldova Education at a Glance

General Information

Capital	Chişinău
Population	4.3 million
Languages	Moldovan (sub-dialect of Romanian), Russian, Gagauz
Literacy rate	99%
GDP per capita	US$2,000
People below poverty line (2004)	30%
Number of phones per 100 people	26
Number of Internet users per 100 people	20
Number of Internet hosts	482,181
Life expectancy at birth (years)	70

Formal Educational Information

Primary school age population	188,000
Secondary school age population	448,000
Primary school age population	4.5%
Secondary school age population	10.5%
Number of years of primary education	4/7
Student/teacher ratio (primary)	17
Student/teacher ratio (secondary)	12
Primary school gross enrollment ratio	91%
Primary school entrants completing primary school	97%
Secondary school gross enrollment ratio	82%
Child labor (ages 5–14)	32%

Note: Unless otherwise indicated, all data are based on sources from 2011.

System Economics and Future Prospects

According to the United Nations Development Programme (2010), along with Saint Kitts and Nevis, total public expenditures on education in Moldova represented 9.6 percent of the gross domestic product in 2009, thus making Moldova the country with the highest education expenditure as a percentage of GDP in Europe. Given the GDP of Moldova at $11.01 billion, educational expenditure in the country amounts to more than $1 billion, or $1,662 per student (total amount equivalent to US dollars divided by 636,000, the approximate number of primary and secondary students in the country). Despite its large percentage of education expenditure, per student spending is one of the lowest in Europe. Moldova ranks 7 of 186 countries in percentage of educational expenditure.

Despite a 99 percent literacy rate, Moldova's socioeconomic and educational infrastructure has suffered from decline since the country's independence in 1991. The Education Ministry lacks resources for its schools, thereby contributing to a drop in school enrollment. Another reason for a steady drop in enrollment is child labor. According to UNICEF, 32 percent of all children between five and 14 years of age are engaged in labor. This is one of the highest rates of child labor in the region. This factor most likely accounts for the high rate of attrition of students, particularly those in secondary schools.

Due to the poor economic circumstances of Moldova, there are close to 1,800 nongovernmental agencies working with the Moldovan government to improve the adverse conditions in the country, ranging from the poor economy to problems in health care and education. Nongovernmental organizations helping the nation in the sphere of education have supported initiatives to supply funding that will alleviate travel burdens for schoolchildren as well as funding allocated for educational supplies and materials.

Daniel Ness and Chia-ling Lin

REFERENCES

Center for Economic and Social Rights. *Visualizing Rights: Moldova, Fact Sheet No. 3.* New York: Center for Economic and Social Rights, 2011.

Central Intelligence Agency. *The CIA World Factbook.* New York: Skyhorse, 2011. https.www.cia.gov/library/publications/the-world-factbook/index.html.

Nation Master. 2011. www.nationmaster.com.

UNESCO. *Global Education Digest 2012: Comparing Education Statistics Across the World.* Montreal: UNESCO Institute for Statistics, 2012.

———. "Strong Foundations: Early Childhood Care and Education." *Education for All Global Monitoring Report.* Paris: UNESCO, 2006.

UNESCO–IBE. www.ibe.unesco.org/en/worldwide/unesco-regions/europe-and-north-america/republic-of-moldova.html.

United Nations Development Programme. *United Nations Development Report 2010.* New York: Palgrave Macmillan, 2010.

US Department of Labor. *2001 Findings on the Worst Forms of Child Labor.* Washington, DC: Bureau of International Labor Affairs, US Department of Labor, 2002.

World Bank Education Statistics. 2011. www.worldbank.org.

RUSSIAN FEDERATION

Russia is the largest country in the world in terms of area. The official language is Russian, although numerous languages of border countries as well as minority languages are also spoken. It is the eighth-largest country in the world in terms of population, which is mainly Russian (80 percent). Other groups include Tatar (4 percent), Ukrainian (2 percent), Bashkir (1 percent), Chuvash (1 percent), and other or unspecified populations (12 percent). At present, religion in Russia is sanctioned; however, it had been forbidden for more than seven decades under the Soviet system from 1917 to 1991. Accordingly, about 70 percent of the residents are either nonbelievers or nonpracticing believers. Russian Orthodox Christianity is the religion of about 15 percent of the population, Islam about 10 percent, and other types of Christianity about 2 to 5 percent of the population.

The official name of the country is the Russian Federation. The former Soviet system after World War II had become a generally strong and vibrant economic and military superpower. However, as a result of growing technological advances, it was difficult for the Soviet government to remain a semiclosed system, operating in isolation from Western economies. Consequently, in the 1980s Mikhail Gorbachev, the last Soviet general secretary, adopted glasnost (openness) and perestroika (restructuring) as a means of modernizing Soviet society. In 1991 ethnic tension—along with years of economic deprivation for many Soviet citizens—led to the splintering of the Soviet Union into 15 independent nations, the Russian Federation being one of them. The Russian Federation under Vladimir Putin severely handicapped Chechen rebels, who invaded areas surrounding Chechnya, a predominantly Muslim republic of the Russian Federation. Nevertheless, there are still periods of sporadic violence in the Caucasus region of Russia.

The country is grappling with widespread corruption, as well as an infrastructure that needs overhauling and refurbishing. Russia's economic status has improved over the last decade as a result of oil exports. Nevertheless, about 13 percent of the population lives below the international poverty line and approximately 8 percent of the population is out of work.

Educational System

The present-day Russian education system is best seen through the reforms and transitions that occurred before, during, and after the fragmentation of the Soviet Union in 1991. Since the 1917 Revolution, the state put a very high premium on education and a highly skilled society. The literacy rate is nearly 100 percent—essentially on par with the United States, Western Europe, and other developed countries. This section discusses the Russian education system in terms of its administration, educational levels, and general consistencies that are apparent in preprimary schools, compulsory schools, and institutions of higher education.

Administration

The constitution of the Russian Federation guarantees the right to a formal education for all Russian citizens. Education in the Russian Federation is generally administered at the federal level, although processes of decentralization are currently under way. More specifically, education is under the auspices of the Ministry of Education and Science in Russia, which oversees all primary schools, secondary schools, and postsecondary institutions, universities, and institutions of science. The ministry is also responsible for assessment, school accreditation, and curriculum. The Ministry of Education and Science in the Russian Federation is a relatively new entity. Established in 2004 under the Decree of the President of the Russian Federation No. 314, it took over the responsibilities of the functions under the Ministry of Education in the Russian Federation—the ruling body of education prior to 2004. As for education, the ministry is accountable for activities related to scientific innovation, technological improvements, basic and general education curriculum, and science towns—cities and towns in the Russian Federation that are specifically developed in order to contribute scientific advances. The ministry is also responsible for intellectual property, trademarks, and patents.

Education Levels

The education system in Russia comprises three general levels: preprimary, primary, and secondary education. Primary school and the first part of secondary school are compulsory. The last two years of secondary school (i.e., high school) and higher education institutions are not compulsory. Compulsory education is free in the Russian Federation.

Precompulsory and Compulsory Education

As indicated above, preprimary education in Russia is not compulsory. Nevertheless, nearly 60 percent of all Russian children between five and six years of age are enrolled in kindergarten. Of this population, 67 percent of all preschool aged children whose families live in urban areas attend kindergarten while only 43 percent of those whose families live in rural regions attend kindergarten. The first school experience is preprimary school, which is diverse in terms of type. Some preprimary institutions in Russia emphasize introduction to early content while others place more focus on socialization. A third, more common type of preprimary school is analogous to day care, which provides elements of socialization and serves as a location where children can be looked after while parents are working. The fourth and most prevalent preprimary level is kindergarten—a level that is considered a preparatory year for entrance into first grade. Preprimary education, intended for children entering at age three and exiting at age five, usually lasts for three years; however, some preprimary institutions enroll children younger than three years.

Compulsory education lasts for 9 or 10 years—namely for children from six to 15 years old—and covers what is referred to as basic general education. The type of school that provides the first half of this basic education is the primary general school, which lasts for four years and provides a so-called basic education curriculum for students between the ages of six and nine years. At present, there are approximately 4 million primary-school-age children in Russia. The primary gross enrollment rate is 129 percent, and approximately 94 percent of all children complete primary school. Children who do not complete primary school are most likely learning disabled or physically disabled.

Compulsory education continues with the first five years of secondary education. The first and longer part of secondary schooling lasts from about age 10 to age 15. The school that provides the first five years of secondary education in Russia is called the basic general secondary school. The last two to three years of secondary education, for students from 15 through 17 years old, are not compulsory. Students in secondary school at these grade levels attend advanced secondary (senior) school. At age 15,

students who do not pursue an academic track generally enter the professional or vocational training system—known as the *Professional'no-tekhnicheskoe uchilishche*. These schools are somewhat analogous to two-year junior colleges, but differ in that they accommodate students who have finished basic education requirements and seek professional education. After a one-and-a-half to two-year period, students can continue for their professional license for an additional two to three years. These students often enroll in the non-university-level higher education institution known as the technical college. Students in these institutions are between the ages of 15 and 19 years. The duration of compulsory basic secondary school is six years and that of senior secondary school is two additional years. The estimated total number of secondary school students is 12.7 million, which amounts to roughly 9 percent of the general population of the country.

Postcompulsory Education

Russia ranks high in the number of people who have been awarded tertiary education degrees. More than half of all Russians have tertiary degrees from higher education institutions throughout the country. In general, there are eight types of higher education institutions in Russia: the university; technical university; university-level academy; university-level institute; conservatory; college (non-university-level higher education institution); technical school (non-university-level higher education institution); and technical institution for vocational studies. In addition, there are seven types of credentials at the higher education level: certificate of secondary (complete) general education (for students who completed secondary school); diploma of secondary vocational education; diploma of incomplete higher education; baccalaureate degree; specialist diploma; master's degree; and doctor of philosophy degree. Most universities in Russia are quite competitive and require students to pass entry examinations. College and university students, especially those enrolled in Asian Russian institutions, have the opportunity to enroll in distance education courses; however, this depends on the infrastructure of the university and whether the institution maintains the capacity to offer courses to students in both urban areas and remote regions.

Figure: **Russian Education System Scheme of Education Levels**

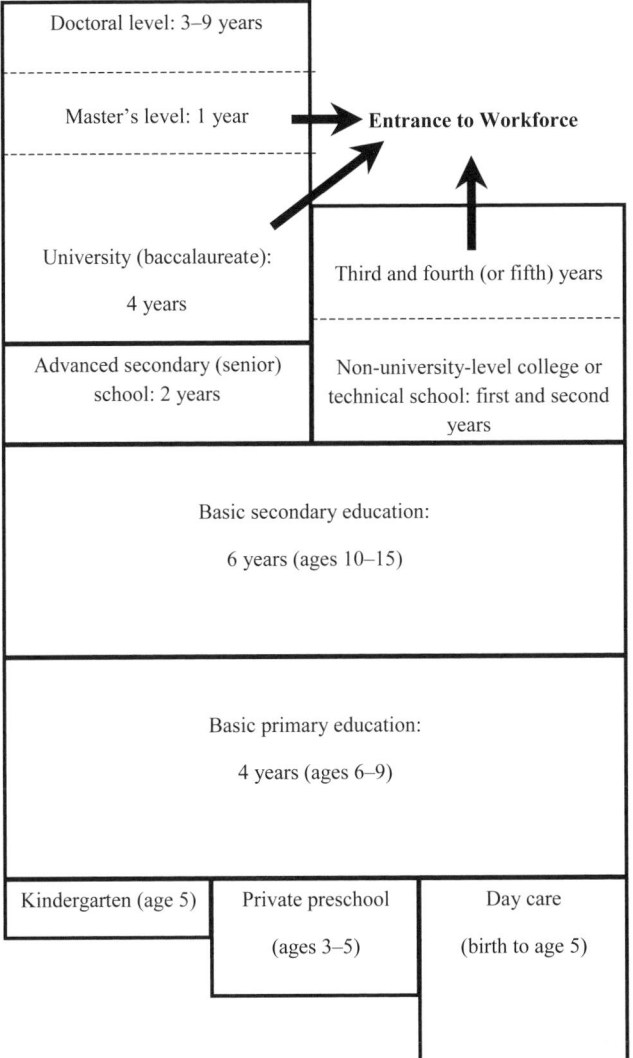

Entrance to Workforce

| Doctoral level: 3–9 years |
| Master's level: 1 year |
| University (baccalaureate): 4 years |
| Third and fourth (or fifth) years |
| Advanced secondary (senior) school: 2 years |
| Non-university-level college or technical school: first and second years |
| Basic secondary education: 6 years (ages 10–15) |
| Basic primary education: 4 years (ages 6–9) |
| Kindergarten (age 5) | Private preschool (ages 3–5) | Day care (birth to age 5) |

Entrance to Workforce

In terms of the structure of the higher education system in Russia, funding is provided both by state institutions and nonstate higher education institutions. Approximately half of all students in state institutions pay for their tuition. All students in nonstate institutions must pay for their tuition and related fees. Based on the types of higher education indicated above, there are three general levels: incomplete higher education (about two years); baccalaureate (*bakalavr* degree) programs that last at least four years; and postgraduate programs (similar to those in the United States and other developed nations) that range from master's programs for about two years to doctoral programs that can require from five to 15 additional years after university entrance.

In the non-university-level first stage, students can obtain a "diploma of incomplete higher education" (*diplom o nepolnom vysshem obrazovanii*), a dysphemism for "associate degree" in US community colleges. Students who earn these initial diplomas are eligible for mid-level skilled entrance occupations and professions that do not require the baccalaureate. At the university-level second stage, students may be eligible to earn the baccalaureate after at least four years of study. In state-run institutions, the national government controls half of all programs and the university regulates the other half of the curriculum. Courses of study include those in the natural sciences, humanities, social sciences, and professional studies. Students must defend a diploma project in order to be awarded a degree. The university-level third stage is for students who hold a baccalaureate and plan to study for a specialist diploma or master's degree. These students must complete all courses and defend a thesis before sitting for final examinations. Students can earn the master's degree by completing at least one year of course work beyond the baccalaureate or entering a program for five or six years that awards postgraduate degrees. The specialist diploma allows students to continue for a doctorate or enter a profession upon graduation. The university-level fourth stage, known as *Kandidat Nauk* (en route PhD) is for students who wish to pursue doctorates. These programs are extremely competitive, and course work lasts for at least three years. Upon completion of course work, students must complete qualifying examinations in the specialized program of study. Afterward, students at this level must conduct independent research and defend a dissertation. Upon successful completion, students are awarded the *Doctor Nauk* (PhD) degree.

There are a total of 447 universities in Russia. These universities do not include postsecondary technical and vocational institutions, nor do they include nonuniversity colleges, some of which are teacher training institutes for preservice primary school teachers (see below). Of the total number of universities, 381 are in European Russia and the remaining 66 institutions are in Siberia. The curricular foci of these universities range from arts and science universities to polytechnic universities, agricultural institutions, medical schools, law schools, and institutions of various professional disciplines. Established in 1755, the Lomonosov Moscow State University is the oldest and largest university in Russia. According to the Quacquarelli Symonds (QS) World University Rankings in 2010, Moscow State University ranks as one of the top 100 universities in the world. Other high-ranking universities in Russia include Saint Petersburg State University, Novosibirsk State University (Siberia), Tomsk State University (the oldest university in Siberia, established in 1887), and the State University Higher School of Economics.

Curriculum, Assessment, and Instruction

Discussion of curriculum, assessment, and instruction in Russia focuses on the content, delivery of content, and testing of content in two environments: general schooling and gifted (i.e., high ability) schools. It is important to note, however, that students of all intellectual levels in Russia attend typical primary and secondary schools and often do not enter specific schools based on academic ability.

General Schooling

Schooling for all grade levels begins in September and ends in May. End-of-grade examinations occur in June. The academic year is divided into four parts with one week of break in November, two weeks of break in January, and one additional week of break in March. Individual subject periods range from 40 minutes to 45 minutes (similar to those in the United States) with anywhere from five-minute to 25-minute intervals between periods. Curriculum in the Russian primary school consists of several subjects. Children must study the Russian language unless the students' native language is not Russian. In this case, students must study their native language along with learning Russian as a second language. Other subjects include reading, mathematics, basic topics in natural science, physical education, art, and music. In general, the curriculum is mandated by the central government. However, teachers and school administrators have been given slightly more autonomy in recent years with regard to what they teach, but mostly to how they teach the content.

The curriculum in the typical Russian secondary school comprises the following subject matter: Russian language and literature, Russian history, one or more foreign languages, mathematics, biology, chemistry, physics, geography, world history, physical education, industrial (manual) labor courses (mostly for males), cooking and crafts (mostly for females), art, music, and astronomy. At the senior high school, noncompulsory level, students may also enroll in advanced algebra and geometry classes as well as calculus and advanced levels of foreign language. Students attend school from 8:00 AM to 1:00 PM or 2:00 PM for five and sometimes six days (including Saturdays) per week.

Assessment at the secondary school level is based on a rubric system of grades identified as 2 (the lowest grade) through 5 (the highest grade). The rubric system generally adheres to the following outline: 2—below satisfactory; 3—satisfactory; 4—good; and 5—excellent. The pass/fail cutoff is between 2 and 3: thus 2 is failing and 3 is passing. Higher education institutions use rubric systems as well: unsatisfactory, pass, satisfactory, good, and excellent. The only grade of failing at the university level is "unsatisfactory."

Gifted and Talented Curriculum

Gifted education in the Russian Federation is now a growing movement and part of the curriculum. From the turn of the century to the years preceding World War II, gifted education was intensively examined by researchers. However, by 1936, the Soviet government forbade research in gifted education because it was thought to be associated with capitalism and elitist philosophies. This was especially the case in its association with intelligence (IQ) testing. However, although the Soviet government significantly downplayed the role of gifted education, it nevertheless remained a major component in the Soviet education system. In particular, the Soviet Union sponsored extracurricular programs that were geared to students who greatly excelled in the areas of science, mathematics, the arts, music, and sports. The key component of gifted education in the Soviet Union and in present-day Russia has been interdisciplinary learning that was spearheaded by a number of Russian psychologists and educators at the beginning of the twentieth century—most notably Pavel Petrovich Blonsky, who focused on psychological testing for innate abilities. Despite harsh critique on the part of the Soviet government, Blonsky's work and that of his contemporaries served as the blueprint for future endeavors in the promotion of gifted education in Russia. The fragmentation of the Soviet Union in the first few years of the 1990s led to the collapse of the funding for these so-called extracurricular programs for high-ability students.

The integrated gifted education curriculum in Russia emphasizes three main mechanisms: (1) the course of study in gifted education must be thematic and interdisciplinary; (2) gifted education must adhere to basic subject courses that are mandatory for all schools—namely, Russian language and literature, mathematics, natural sciences, computer science, history, sports, arts, and music; and (3) gifted curriculum must include advanced courses in English and German. Thematic content depends on the age level of the students in a gifted program. For example, young children will often learn subjects based on the thematic unit of origin—in other words, where things come from. Content for older students might be centered on a thematic unit of invention or interrelation so that they can find their own solutions to solve world problems. Students are enrolled into gifted programs based on the results of a short cognitive abilities test, a play lesson—which allows the administrator (i.e., teacher or psychologist) to analyze five or six children at a time in a period of constructive play, and an individual interview. Identification of high-ability students in Russian schools involves intellectual abilities that exceed others within the particular age group; creativity and novelty when engaged in certain situations; and traits of curiosity, persistence or commitment to particular tasks, and a penchant for engaging in complex situations.

Teacher Education

Teacher training in Russia has historically been one of the most rigorous of all teacher education environments. Preservice teachers can apply for one of three different levels: basic primary, basic secondary, and high school or postcompulsory level. Teacher training of preprimary and basic primary (i.e., elementary) schoolteachers occurs in the non–university-level educational institutions. These institutions are colleges (also known as *tekhnikums*) that offer courses of study that last two years to nearly five years. The first two years consist of course work followed by two

to three years of teacher training within the school setting. Some universities also have teacher training programs that last for a full five-year period. Both options provide teachers with credentials to teach at the preprimary and primary levels.

Preservice secondary school teachers must pursue coursework at the university level. Students must attend a secondary-level university program for at least five years. This course of study includes both pedagogical content knowledge as well as content in a specific discipline (e.g., mathematics, one of the natural sciences, Russian, foreign language). Most, but not all, universities in Russia have programs or faculties of secondary education teacher training.

Preservice training of teachers for high school and other forms of higher education must enroll in a university program and must have postgraduate credentials. Teachers at the college (i.e., nonuniversity) or university level must enroll in programs that offer a doctorate, most often the PhD degree. Graduates generally begin as lecturers and are appointed on a year-to-year basis. Tenure is granted by the universities to professors who are promoted from the "lecturer" level to "professor" level.

Informal Education

The notion of adult or informal education has played a significant role in terms of lifelong learning in European education as well as national curricula in non-European countries throughout the world. However, only recently has informal and adult education in Russia been considered an important part of the country's education system. As a result, informal education in Russia lags behind programs in other countries—both in developing and postindustrial societies. Meschtyb (2000) has argued that adult education for both indigenous and nonindigenous Russians has been severely lacking. Accordingly, adult or informal education can serve many purposes. First, it can support intercultural tolerance. Second, it has the potential of providing skills to adults who can potentially work in occupations that require different qualifications. Third, it has the potential of both familiarizing adults and others with information and communication technologies as well as reaching remote regions where education access may be inadequate or lacking in resources. Within the last decade, there have been a number of successful initiatives in various districts of Russia. The European Association for the Education of Adults (2011) has demonstrated that successful adult education programs place great emphasis on intercultural tolerance, citizenship education, and programs for disadvantaged populations—including women, people of varying socioeconomic status and ethnicity, and older populations.

At present, nongovernmental organizations have been instrumental in promoting informal education in Russia and in other countries throughout the world. In Russia, organizations that have led the mission of informal education for young people and adults include the Znanie Society, the Siberian Adult Education Association, the Pskov Adult Education Association, and several regional public organizations. The so-called All-Russia Znanie Society was established during the Soviet era by eminent scientists as a means of disseminating scientific knowledge to students and adults throughout the vast country. Given the country's transition in the 1980s and 1990s, the Znanie Society has modified its mission to a degree in order to include a wider array of purposes, including spreading scientific knowledge, discussing philosophical and ethical issues involving intercultural relationships, and fostering skill improvement for the purpose of upward economic mobility. Courses and seminars provided by the Znanie Society are designed to encourage professional development and provide new skills and abilities. Moreover, in recent years, there has been a trend toward the study of management, marketing, finance, paralegal studies, and other courses of study that were at one time considered forbidden.

System Economics

According to the United Nations Development Programme (2010), along with Colombia, Antigua and Barbuda, and Croatia, total public expenditures on education in Russia represented 3.9 percent of the gross domestic product (GDP) in 2006. Given the GDP of Russia at $2.229 trillion, educational expenditure in the country amounts to more than $87 billion, about $5,226 per student (total amount equivalent to US dollars divided by 16,634,000, the approximate number of primary and secondary students in the country). Accordingly, although Russia ranks 104 of 186 countries in percentage of educational expenditure, the country ranks one of the highest in terms of per stduent educational spending.

Future Prospects

The system of education in Russia is in transition from an entirely state-governed, centralized system in the Soviet era of the twentieth century to one based on market economy and quasi-privatized organization in the twenty-first century. Although not decentralized, the educational system seems to be moving in the direction of decentralization of schools.

Despite a strong educational system, the Russian government is in the position of identifying ways in which the focus of education can be either redirected or modified in order to address urgent problems in the country. To begin with, the curriculum in Russia does not seem to address the issues of poverty, particularly in the country's ethnic republics; child mortality; lack of financial resources for subsidizing health care; tobacco and drug addiction; HIV/AIDS and other infectious diseases; and the promotion of equality among historically alienated groups—particularly women and ethnic minorities. UNESCO's *National Human Development Report: Millennium Development Goals in Russia: Looking into the Future* (2010) addresses one of the key issues facing education in Russia today: although the system of education provides access to formal education, it still lags behind other nations in reducing social inequities in terms of distribution of wealth and resources. The UNESCO report states clearly that less emphasis should be placed on indicators that demonstrate across-the-board access and more emphasis on indicators that demonstrate high educational quality for social and ethnic groups. In sum, from an analytical perspective, formal education in Russia demonstrates high levels of performance when compared with other countries. It is second only to Canada in the number of individuals who have completed tertiary degrees. In addition, Russia has a surplus of highly skilled people who graduated from demanding technical institutions. At the same time, the country is grappling with the fact that the high level of education in Russia is not addressing the social inequalities and standard of living of its citizens. In other words, high levels of education do not translate to a high standard of living. The UNESCO report addresses the need for the Russian government to engage in several endeavors. First, the country will need to articulate strategies that make vocational institutions and universities more efficient so that graduates can compete in the changing labor market. Second, vulnerable populations—such as physically and learning disabled individuals and children in remote rural areas—need access to education. Third, research has demonstrated that preschool education is directly correlated with success in the workforce. Accordingly, the central government will need to accommodate preschool-age children who live in rural parts of the country and those from low-income households. Fourth, there is great disparity in financial and physical resources among the various subregions (oblasts, okrugs, and state republics) of the country. These disparities must be eradicated so that students of one region can gain the same high-quality access as students of another region. Finally, the curriculum, particularly at the secondary school level, must address practical high-level skills so that competition would be possible. The Programme for International Student Assessment (PISA) is one particular indicator that addresses this problem. PISA results indicate that, despite the high levels of formal education, 15-year-old students in Russia score an average of 60 points below students of other countries that participate in the Organisation for Economic Cooperation and Development (OECD).

Although not an overwhelmingly pressing issue, school violence has been problematic in Russia, especially after the collapse of the Soviet Union. Russian authorities are particularly wary of school violence, especially after the Beslan school massacre involving Chechen Muslim extremist terrorists in North Ossetia in September 2004.

It is also worthy of note that secondary education and higher education in Russia are in a state of transition. One of the major transitional reforms is the process of decentralizing these systems of education from the centralized system that was prized by the Soviet government. A second major reform concerns the development of a new financial apparatus for fostering the transition from secondary school to the university. In past decades, secondary and higher education was funded by the state. At present, there are greater numbers of private organizations that are funding secondary education and universities throughout the country. In addition, the new system in Russia is attempting to provide greater academic freedom for university faculty and their students.

Daniel Ness and Chia-ling Lin

REFERENCES

Central Intelligence Agency. *The CIA World Factbook*. New York: Skyhorse, 2011. https.www.cia.gov/library/publications/the-world-factbook/index.html.

European Association for the Education of Adults. *Adult Education for New Russia*. 2011. www.eaea.org/index.php?k=11988.

GED. *Global Education Digest 2012: Comparing Education Statistics Across the World*. Montreal: UNESCO Institute for Statistics, 2012.

International Association of Universities, World Higher Education Data Base. *Russia: Structure of Educational System*. Paris: UNESCO National Information Centre on Academic Recognition and Mobility, Ministry of Education and Science of the Russian Federation, 2006.

Meschtyb, Nina. *Adult Education and Indigenous Peoples in Russia*. Hamburg, Germany: UNESCO Institute for Education, 2000.

Nation Master. 2011. www.nationmaster.com.

Russian Federation Education at a Glance

General Information

Capital	Moscow
Population	138.7 million
Languages	Russian, other languages (depending on region)
Literacy rate	99%
GDP per capita	US$12,200
People below poverty line	18%
Number of phones per 100 people	31.5
Number of Internet users per 100 people	32.5
Number of Internet hosts	10.3 million
Life expectancy at birth (years)	66

Formal Educational Information

Primary school age population	3.9 million
Secondary school age population	12.6 million
Primary school age population	3%
Secondary school age population	9%
Number of years of education (primary/secondary)	4/6
Student/teacher ratio (primary)	16.5
Student/teacher ratio (secondary)	9.5
Primary school gross enrollment ratio	129%
Primary school entrants completing primary school	94%
Secondary school gross enrolment ratio	91%
Child labor (ages 5–14)	no data

Note: Unless otherwise indicated, all data are based on sources from 2011.

Nikolaev, Denis, and Dmitry Chugunov. *The Education System in the Russian Federation: Education Brief 2012.* Washington, DC: World Bank, 2012.

Shcheblanova, Elena, and Natalia Shumakova. "Gifted Education in Russia: A Special Programme at a Moscow School." *European Council for High Ability News* 21:1 (2007): 1, 3.

UNESCO. *National Human Development Report in the Russian Federation: Millennium Development Goals in Russia: Looking into the Future.* Moscow: UNESCO, 2010.

UNESCO–IBE. www.ibe.unesco.org/countries/russia.htm.

UNESCO–UIS. www.uis.unesco.org.

UNICEF. www.unicef.org/infobycountry.

World Bank Education Statistics. 2011. www.worldbank.org.

TAJIKISTAN

Tajikistan is a landlocked central Asian country that was part of the former Soviet Union. The Republic of Tajikistan became independent from Russia in 1991. The country went through five years of civil war between 1992 and 1997. Since then, there have been no major instances of war. After years of Soviet rule, the people of Tajikistan have attempted to adapt to the new economic market. At present, however, Tajikistan ranks as the poorest country of the former Soviet Union. The unemployment rate in Tajikistan is 12 percent. Although that is not the highest unemployment rate in the region, the Tajik people live in dire poverty. Current data show a poverty rate of 64 percent. Current social and political concerns include reducing government corruption, improving relations between different ethnic groups, and increasing economic standing. The country has also played a role in combating global terrorism.

About 85 percent of all Tajikistani are Sunni Muslim and 5 percent are Shiite Muslim. About 10 percent of the population are either Russian Orthodox Christian or have no religious affiliation.

Educational System

Although not exemplary, preprimary education in Tajikistan during the Soviet era was somewhat successful in providing primary school preparation. Unfortunately, since independence, the country's preprimary attendance has declined. At present, between 7 and 10 percent of the country's children under age six attend preschool or kindergarten. For many families, public preschool education is a financial burden because costs to run these institutions have increased.

Education in Tajikistan is compulsory for a period of 11 years for children between the ages of six and 16 or 17 years. This period consists of four years of primary education, five years of lower secondary school, and two years of upper secondary school. The compulsory education years comprise a basic curriculum that considers essential subjects—Russian, Tajik, mathematics, basic natural science, physical education, art, and music. Students must attend upper secondary level in order to be eligible for university enrollment.

The student/teacher ratio at the primary school level is about 22 students for every teacher. The primary school gross enrollment ratio is 100 percent. However, the net enrollment rate for primary school is about 97 percent, indicating that about 3 percent of all children at the primary level are not attending school. The secondary school student/teacher ratio in Tajikistan is about 16 students for every teacher. The secondary gross enrollment ratio in the country is 83 percent. However, the net enrollment ratio is only 80 percent, again indicating that much smaller numbers of children in that age group are actually enrolled. In light of these data, about 25 percent of all children and adolescents eventually drop out of school.

Similar to families in neighboring countries to the north, particularly former Soviet republics, most Tajik families encourage students who successfully complete their secondary education programs to pursue a degree at one of the Tajik universities. There are about 35 universities in the country. Like most of the universities in Kyrgyzstan to the north, those of Tajikistan are known primarily for professional study, particularly in the areas of medicine, engineering, and technology. The institutions with the largest enrollments include Khujand State University, one of the oldest universities in the country; Tajik State National University; Tajik State Pedagogical University; Tajikistan University of Technology; Tajikistan State University of Law, Business, and Politics; Tajikistan Humanitarian International University; Khorugh State University; and the University of Central Asia in Khorog.

System Economics and Future Prospects

According to the United Nations Development Programme (2010), along with Benin, Japan, and Anguilla, total public expenditures on education in Tajikistan represented 3.5 percent of the gross domestic product (GDP) in 2008. Given the GDP of Tajikistan at $14.61 billion, educational expenditure in the country amounts to more than $511 million, or $269 per student (total amount equivalent to US dollars divided by 1,905,000, the approximate number of primary and secondary students in the country). Per student spending was greater during the Soviet era. Tajikistan ranks 119 of 186 countries in percentage of educational expenditure.

In recent years, Tajikistan has been the recipient of financial support, primarily from government subsidies and programs funded by nongovernmental agencies. For example, CARE, a major humanitarian organization, has assisted in school attendance through programs that enable children in primary school to benefit from schooling. Part of this assistance is in the form of school meals as well as increases in teacher salaries. In attempting to improve economic conditions, the government is in the process of becoming a member of the World Trade Organization. Nevertheless, Tajikistan's educational system is in dire need of improvement. Political corruption and high rates of poverty are two aspects of education that must be rectified. In addition, the government of Tajikistan also must grapple with illegal child labor practices. At present, UNESCO data suggest that 10 percent of all Tajikistani children between five and 14 years are engaged in labor.

Daniel Ness and Chia-ling Lin

REFERENCES

Central Intelligence Agency. *The CIA World Factbook.* New York: Skyhorse, 2011. https.www.cia.gov/library/publications/the-world-factbook/index.html.

DeYoung, Alan J. *Lost in Transition: Redefining Students and Universities in the Kyrgyz Republic.* Charlotte, NC: Information Age, 2011.

Nation Master. 2011. www.nationmaster.com.

UNESCO. *Global Education Digest 2012: Comparing Education Statistics Across the World.* Montreal: UNESCO Institute for Statistics, 2012.

Tajikistan Education at a Glance	
General Information	
Capital	Dushanbe
Population	7.4 million
Languages	Tajik, Russian
Literacy rate	100%
GDP per capita	US$1,300
People below poverty line	64%
Number of phones per 100 people	5
Number of Internet users per 100 people	8
Number of Internet hosts	1,504
Life expectancy at birth (years)	65
Formal Educational Information	
Primary school age population	696,000
Secondary school age population	1.2 million
Primary school age population	9%
Number of years of education (primary/secondary)	4/7
Student/teacher ratio (primary)	22
Student/teacher ratio (secondary)	16
Primary school gross enrollment ratio	100%
Primary school entrants completing primary school	100%
Secondary school gross enrollment ratio	83%
Child labor (ages 5–14)	10%

Note: Unless otherwise indicated, all data are based on sources from 2011.

———. "Strong Foundations: Early Childhood Care and Education." *Education for All Global Monitoring Report.* Paris: UNESCO, 2006.

UNESCO-IBE. www.ibe.unesco.org/en/worldwide/unesco-regions/asia-and-the-pacific/tajikistan.html.

United Nations Development Programme. *United Nations Development Report 2010.* New York: Palgrave Macmillan, 2010.

US Department of Labor. *2001 Findings on the Worst Forms of Child Labor.* Washington, DC: Bureau of International Labor Affairs, US Department of Labor, 2002.

World Bank Education Statistics. 2011. www.worldbank.org.

TURKMENISTAN

Turkmenistan is a country in central Asia. Russia took control over the region of Turkmenistan in 1865 and again in 1885. The region became a republic of the Soviet Union in 1924 and maintained the Soviet school infrastructure for the next 70 to 80 years. The Republic of Turkmenistan became independent from Russia in 1991. The Turkmenistani government's recent identification of large petroleum and natural gas reserves has been seen as a windfall for the country's economy.

About 90 percent of all Turkmenistani are Muslim. The remaining population is mostly Eastern Orthodox. Turkmenistan's gross domestic product (GDP) for 2010 amounted to $36.64 billion. With an unemployment rate of approximately 60 percent and a poverty rate of more than 30 percent, Turkmenistan is considered one of the most destitute countries in Central Asia.

Educational System

Given Turkmenistan's relatively small population in a rather large area, the Soviets provided strong educational foundations in the region. The system seemed to have contributed to a current literacy rate of about 99 percent of the population aged 15 and older. Unfortunately, the Turkmen educational system has declined significantly for at least a decade since the country's independence. Since 2005 there has been some intervention by nongovernmental organizations to improve the curriculum so that Turkmen students can gain competitiveness on the world stage. The country is currently in the process of redefining its curriculum to fit the needs of its citizens.

Preprimary education in Turkmenistan has only recently been considered influential on subsequent schooling. The Early Childhood Development Project in the country has teamed up with the Ministry of Health and the Ministry of Education to develop a national framework for the schooling of children in preprimary education. Training materials developed by the Early Childhood Development Project help teachers at this level promote child motor and intellectual development in the early years. Currently, there are typically four years of preschool, for children ages 3 through 6, but most children are not enrolled for this entire period. However, due to limited data, the percentage of families that enroll their children in preschool is somewhat unclear.

Education in Turkmenistan is compulsory for a period of 10 years for children between the ages of seven and 17. This period consists of three years of primary education and six to seven years of secondary school. The compulsory education years comprise a basic curriculum that considers essential subjects— Turkmen, Russian, mathematics, basic natural science, physical education, art, and music. In 364 of the reported 1,764 schools in the country, curriculum is taught in Uzbek, Kazak, or Karakalpak—depending on the region of the country that the school is located. There is a five-year lower secondary level that is essentially a continuation of the basic curriculum. Before graduation, students are tested to determine which upper secondary school they will attend. One type of upper secondary school is a continuation of study that prepares students for university education. A second type prepares students for a technical or vocational education. The remaining students do not continue their education. Most state-funded schools were built during the Soviet era and were based on the Soviet political model. Since the independence of Turkmenistan, children and adolescents have had the opportunity to attend religious schools. However, these schools do not provide the rigor that the state run schools do.

No data exist regarding the student/teacher ratio at the primary school or secondary school levels; however, given the student population at approximately 1 million students and a reported 1,764 schools in the country, a somewhat rough estimate of students per school would number more than 600 children and adolescents. The primary school gross enrollment ratio is 97 percent. The secondary gross enrollment ratio is 90 percent. One encouraging statistic is that 100 percent of all primary school entrants reach grade 5.

Most students who successfully complete their secondary education programs are strongly encouraged to attend one of the country's universities or technical colleges. There are at least 14 universities and approximately 90 technical colleges in Turkmenistan. The oldest and largest institution in the country is the Turkmen State University in Ashgabat, the country's capital. Founded in 1950, Turkmen State University enrolls about 11,000 students each academic year. In addition to comprehensive universities, other universities in Turkmenistan include the State Academy of the Arts, the Turkmen State Pedagogical Institute, the Turkmen National Institute of World Languages, the Turkmen State Medical Institute, a police academy, a music conservatory, and a number of polytechnic institutes.

System Economics and Future Prospects

Recent data on total public expenditures on education of Turkmenistan do not exist. However, 1995 data show that the country's expenditures represented 4.3 percent of its gross domestic product. Due to gradual deterioration of the education system for at least a decade after the country's independence, it is difficult to have confidence that the rate is the same today. However, assuming that this percentage is the same, and given the GDP of Turkmenistan at $36.64 billion, educational expenditure in the country would amount to close to $1.6 billion, or $1,434 per student (total amount equivalent to US dollars divided by 1,099,000, the approximate number of primary and secondary students in the country). Per student spending was greater during the Soviet era.

Turkmenistan has been the recipient of funding sources from nongovernmental agencies, particularly UNICEF. This is a result of the country's rather high rate of unemployment and poverty since emancipation in 1991. Since 2005, however, the educational system and the Ministry of Education have undergone organizational reform through the assistance of nongovernmental organizations and the government to a lesser extent. This reorganization has been somewhat successful in recent years.

Daniel Ness and Chia-ling Lin

Turkmenistan Education at a Glance

General Information

Capital	Ashgabat
Population	4.9 million
Languages	Turkmen (72%), Russian (12%), Uzbek (9%), other (7%)
Literacy rate	99%
GDP per capita	US$8,500
People below poverty line	58%
Number of phones per 100 people	10
Number of Internet users per 100 people	1.5
Number of Internet hosts	794
Life expectancy at birth (years)	68

Formal Educational Information

Primary school age population	295,000
Secondary school age population	804,000
Primary/secondary school age population	22%
Number of years of education (primary/secondary)	3/7
Student/teacher ratio (primary/secondary)	no data
Primary school gross attendance ratio	97%
Primary school entrants reaching grade 5	100%
Secondary school gross enrollment ratio	90%
Child labor (ages 5–14)	no data

Note: Unless otherwise indicated, all data are based on sources from 2011.

REFERENCES

Central Intelligence Agency. *The CIA World Factbook.* New York: Skyhorse, 2011. https.www.cia.gov/library/publications/the-world-factbook/index.html.

Nation Master. 2011. www.nationmaster.com.

UNESCO. *Global Education Digest 2012: Comparing Education Statistics Across the World.* Montreal: UNESCO Institute for Statistics, 2012.

———. "Strong Foundations: Early Childhood Care and Education." *Education for All Global Monitoring Report.* Paris: UNESCO, 2006.

UNESCO-IBE. www.ibe.unesco.org/en/worldwide/unesco-regions/asia-and-the-pacific/turmenistan.html.

United Nations Development Programme. *United Nations Development Report 2010.* New York: Palgrave Macmillan, 2010.

US Department of Labor. *2001 Findings on the Worst Forms of Child Labor.* Washington, DC: Bureau of International Labor Affairs, US Department of Labor, 2002.

World Bank Education Statistics. 2011. www.worldbank.org.

UKRAINE

The Republic of Ukraine is located in southeastern Europe. By the eighteenth century, Ukraine had come under Russian rule. Ukraine became independent after the Bolshevik Revolution of 1917, but its independence was short-lived. In 1920 Ukraine fell under Soviet rule. Between the World Wars, the region suffered famines, most notably the famine of 1932 to 1933. It is hard to determine the death toll of famine during this time because various scholarly sources give different estimates. It is possible, though, that the number of deaths resulting from famine exceeded 4 million. As a result of the end of the Soviet period, Ukraine became independent again in 1991. Despite independence, corrupt Ukrainian leadership stalled efforts to move the country forward both educationally and economically. A series of peaceful protests and civil resistance during the latter part of 2004, known as the Orange Revolution, helped to impede government corruption and rigged elections.

Approximately 62 percent of all Ukrainians are Orthodox Christian. This population includes members of the Ukrainian Orthodox Church of Kiev, Ukrainian Orthodox Church of Moscow, Orthodox Christians with no jurisdiction, and Greek Catholics. The remaining 38 percent of the population consist of Protestants, Jews, and those who have no religious affiliation.

Educational System

Like preschoolers in other former Soviet republics, those of Ukraine were well prepared at the preprimary level for entrance into primary school. However, shortly after independence, Ukrainian preprimary attendance declined due to inadequate funding for educational resources at early childhood levels. At present, there are over 1.145 million preschool-age children in Ukraine. Yet only 56 percent of these children (641,760 children) have been sent to preschools and kindergartens.

Until 2001 education in Ukraine was compulsory for a period of nine years for children between the ages of seven and 15 years. Students were also encouraged to continue in school for another two years of secondary education (ages 16 and 17 years) so they could prepare themselves for entering a higher education institution. This period is consistent with those of neighboring nations: four years of primary education, five years of lower secondary school, and two years of upper secondary school. Recent education reforms, however, have led the Ukrainian government to increase the duration of compulsory education from nine years to 12 years as a means of encouraging Ukrainian youth to pursue tertiary education. The compulsory education years comprise a basic curriculum that considers essential subjects—Russian, Ukrainian, mathematics, basic natural science, physical education, art, and music. The student/teacher ratio at the primary school level is about 17 students for every teacher. The primary school gross enrollment ratio is 102 percent. However, the net enrollment rate for primary school is about 90 percent, indicating that about 10 percent of all children at the primary level are not attending school. The secondary school student/teacher ratio in Ukraine is about 11 students for every teacher. The secondary gross enrollment ratio is 93.5 percent. However, only 84 percent of all Ukrainian children and adolescents are attending secondary school. This indicates that roughly 16 percent of the student-age population at the secondary level is not attending school. Fortunately, the primary school completion rate is nearly 105 percent; this means that many older students in Ukraine are completing their primary school educa-

tion. Moreover, about 98 percent of all Ukrainian children enter the last year of the primary grade. One of the main reasons why students drop out of school early is that they do not see the relevance of schooling and education to the context of the outside world and the everyday working environment.

Higher education in Ukraine consists of four types: vocational schools; colleges and related institutions that offer baccalaureate degrees; universities, conservatories, and academies that provide both undergraduate and professional education; and universities that provide postgraduate courses in addition to undergraduate education. Ukrainian students who successfully complete their secondary education programs are generally encouraged to pursue a degree at one of the universities in the country. There are approximately 150 universities, academies, and conservatories throughout the 24 oblasts and several municipalities of Ukraine. Established in 1661, Lviv University is the country's oldest institution. Founded in the Jesuit tradition by the Polish king John II Casimir, Lviv University has had a turbulent history. Initially, it was granted the ability to issue diplomas in the areas of theology and law. By 1772 the university was under the auspices of Austria. Lviv University was closed by Austrian authorities between 1805 and 1817 as a result of the Napoleonic Wars. By the 1870s, the university was considered to be the leading Polish-language university in the world. The Nazis closed the university during part of World War II. However, in 1944, the university was taken over by the Red Army, and, since then, it has been under Ukrainian authority. Lviv University has 18 faculties as well as 13 research divisions and enrolls about 11,500 students annually.

The second oldest institution in the country (founded in 1804), the University of Kharkiv, enrolls approximately 15,000 students per year. The University Ranking by Academic Performance has ranked the university as the most competitive in the country. The third oldest university in Ukraine is Taras Shevchenko National University of Kiev, founded in 1834. The university enrolls roughly 20,000 students annually and continues to rank high among Ukrainian universities as one of the most competitive in the region. In addition to university education, the Ukrainian Ministry has promoted so-called nontraditional studies for adults who return to school. To this end, the ministry developed distance learning programs for working adults who wish to broaden their skill base. In addition, certain institutions of higher education have programs that are based on lifelong learning for adults who return to school to obtain a degree that they may have been unable to earn in the past.

There are three types of teacher education institutions in Ukraine: institutions that train teachers at the preprimary and primary levels; those that train prospective teachers at the secondary levels; and those that train teachers at the nonuniversity tertiary levels. The four main universities of pedagogy are the National Dragomanov Pedagogical University in Kiev, the Nizhyn Pedagogical University, the South Ukrainian State Pedagogical University in Odessa, and the Ternopil National Pedagogical University. Numerous other universities that do not specialize in teacher education per se have individual departments or schools of education that prepare teachers.

System Economics and Future Prospects

According to the United Nations Development Programme (2010), along with Vietnam and the Netherlands, total public expenditures on education in Ukraine represented 5.3 percent of the gross domestic product (GDP) in 2007. Given the GDP of Ukraine at $136.6 billion, educational expenditure in the country amounts to more than $7.24 billion, or $1,230 per student (total amount equivalent to US dollars divided by 5,888,000, the approximate number of primary and secondary students in the country). Per student spending was greater during the Soviet era. Ukraine ranks 48 of 186 countries in percentage of educational expenditure. Half of all funding for all levels between preprimary education and secondary education is supplied by local governments, while the other half is supplied by the Ukrainian government.

With a near 100 percent literacy rate, Ukraine has one of the highest rates of literacy in the region. Despite this success, however, Ukraine has suffered from decline in its formal system of education since independence. With the end of the Soviet period, the Education Ministry in the republic was provided limited resources for its schools, and there was a drop in school enrollment throughout the nation. Another reason for a steady drop in enrollment is child labor. According to UNICEF, 7 percent of all

Ukraine Education at a Glance	
General Information	
Capital	Kiev
Population	45.4 million
Languages	Ukrainian (67%), Russian (24%), other languages (7%)
Literacy rate	99%
GDP per capita	US$7,800
People below poverty line	29%
Number of phones per 100 people	29
Number of Internet users per 100 people	23
Number of Internet hosts	1 million
Life expectancy at birth (years)	68
Formal Educational Information	
Primary school age population	1.7 million
Secondary school age population	4.1 million
Primary/secondary school age population	13%
Number of years of education (primary/secondary)	4/7
Student/teacher ratio (primary)	17
Student/teacher ratio (secondary)	11
Primary school gross enrollment ratio	102%
Primary school entrants reaching grade 5	98%
Secondary school gross enrollment ratio	93%
Child labor (ages 5–14)	7%

Note: Unless otherwise indicated, all data are based on sources from 2011.

children between five and 14 years of age are engaged in labor. As a result of the abhorrent practice of putting children to work—let alone the high percentage of children engaged in labor—the government and the Ministry of Education must grapple with high rates of attrition of students, particularly those in secondary schools.

The Ukrainian Ministry of Education is said to be in the process of rebuilding the educational infrastructure in the country. Various nongovernmental organizations have attempted to ameliorate the problems that have been thrust upon the Ukrainian education system within the last decade, such as the lack of funding for students of poor families and rural dwellers, the burden of family fees associated with supplies and travel between home and school, and poor teacher quality.

Daniel Ness and Chia-ling Lin

REFERENCES

Center for Economic and Social Rights. *Visualizing Rights: Ukraine, Fact Sheet No. 3.* New York: Center for Economic and Social Rights, 2010.

Central Intelligence Agency. *The CIA World Factbook.* New York: Skyhorse, 2011. https.www.cia.gov/library/publications/the-world-factbook/index.html.

Nation Master. 2011. www.nationmaster.com.

UNESCO. *Global Education Digest 2012: Comparing Education Statistics Across the World.* Montreal: UNESCO Institute for Statistics, 2012.

————. "Strong Foundations: Early Childhood Care and Education." *Education for All Global Monitoring Report.* Paris: UNESCO, 2006.

UNESCO–IBE. www.ibe.unesco.org/en/worldwide/unesco-regions/europe-and-north-america/ukraine.html.

United Nations Development Programme. *United Nations Development Report 2010.* New York: Palgrave Macmillan, 2010.

US Department of Labor. *2001 Findings on the Worst Forms of Child Labor.* Washington, DC: Bureau of International Labor Affairs, US Department of Labor, 2002.

World Bank Education Statistics. 2011. www.worldbank.org.

UZBEKISTAN

Uzbekistan is a landlocked central Asian country that was part of the former Soviet Union. The region of Uzbekistan was under Russian control in 1864 and eventually became part of the Soviet Union in 1924 after some resistance by Uzbek forces. The Republic of Uzbekistan became independent from Russia in 1991. Since then, the country has focused its attention on petroleum reserves and mining in order to increase its economic status. Although it has a low unemployment rate of 3 percent, Uzbekistan has a poverty rate of about 33 percent. Current social and political concerns include reducing government corruption, cooperation among different ethnic groups, and combating terrorism. Tashkent, the fourth-largest city during the Soviet era, has recently become a major terrorist target, due to the Uzbek government's cooperation with international military and secret service agencies.

About 88 percent of all Uzbekistani are Muslim. About 12 percent of the population are either Russian Orthodox Christian or have no religious affiliation.

Educational System

Preprimary education in Uzbekistan during the Soviet era was highly successful in preparing young children for formal education at the primary level. Unfortunately, since independence, preprimary attendance of Uzbekistan has declined, primarily as a result of poor funding and poorly trained teachers. UNICEF data show that preschool attendance dropped from 35 percent during the Soviet period to less than 20 percent after 1998. For many families, preschool education is a financial burden because costs to run these institutions have increased since state funding has been reduced. Moreover, parents do not want to send their children to state-run preschools that are overenrolled. In recent years, however, home-based preschool has been on the increase in Uzbekistan; it eliminates much of the financial burden for families and at the same time uses standards-based early childhood curriculum that prepares children for primary school.

Education in Uzbekistan is compulsory for a period of 11 years for children between the ages of seven and 17 years. This period is consistent with those of neighboring nations: four years of primary education, five years of lower secondary school, and two years of upper secondary school. The compulsory education years comprise a basic curriculum that considers essential subjects—Russian, Uzbek, mathematics, basic natural science, physical education, art, and music. Uzbek students must attend the upper two-year secondary level in order to be eligible for university enrollment.

The student/teacher ratio at the primary school level is roughly 24 students for every teacher. The primary school gross enrollment ratio is 100 percent. However, the net enrollment rate for primary school is about 78 percent, indicating that about 22 percent of all children at the primary level are not attending school. The secondary school student/teacher ratio in Uzbekistan is about 11 students for every teacher. The secondary gross enrollment ratio in the country is 95 percent. No data are available for the country's net enrollment ratio for secondary education. However, in light of the gross and net enrollment data for primary school that show lack of school attendance, it would be safe to suggest that secondary enrollment is significantly less than 95 percent.

Uzbek students who successfully complete their secondary education programs are generally encouraged to pursue a degree at one of the universities in Uzbekistan. It is important to note, however,

Uzbekistan Education at a Glance

General Information

Capital	Tashkent
Population	28.1 million
Languages	Uzbek (74%), Russian (14%),
	Tajik (4.5), other languages (7.5)
Literacy rate	99%
GDP per capita	US$2,000
People below poverty line	33%
Number of phones per 100 people	6.5
Number of Internet users per 100 people	9.0
Number of Internet hosts	47,718
Life expectancy at birth (years)	65

Formal Educational Information

Primary school age population	2.3 million
Secondary school age population	4.5 million
Primary school age population	8%
Number of years of education (primary/secondary)	4/7
Student/teacher ratio (primary)	24
Student/teacher ratio (secondary)	11
Primary school gross enrollment ratio	100%
Primary school entrants completing primary school	96%
Secondary school gross enrollment ratio	95%
Child labor (ages 5–14)	no data

Note: Unless otherwise indicated, all data are based on sources from 2011.

that higher education enrollment dropped nearly 13 percentage points from 1991, the year of the country's independence, to 2001. There are approximately 65 higher education institutions in the country. Of these institutions, 14 universities and 20 polytechnic institutes are accountable to the Ministry of Higher and Secondary Specialized Education of Uzbekistan. Established in 1918, the National University of Uzbekistan in Tashkent is the country's oldest institution and enrolls approximately 10,000 students annually. With an enrollment of about 10,000, the Tashkent State University of Economics is the largest university emphasizing economics in Central Asia. The university maintains the largest university library in the region. Like the educational ministries in Kyrgyzstan, the Ministry of Education and Higher and Secondary Specialized Education in Uzbekistan has allocated a large percentage of its education spending to higher education since 1991. The Westminster International University in Tashkent is a relatively new institution (founded in 2002) that has been successful in attracting students with high academic credentials. Other high-ranking institutions in the country include the Moscow National University in Tashkent, Namangan State University, Tashkent University of Information Technologies, the University of World Economy and Diplomacy, and the Management Development Institute of Singapore.

System Economics and Future Prospects

Due to limited data, it is difficult to know the total public expenditures on education in Uzbekistan. However, 1991 data show that the country's expenditures represented 9.4 percent of its gross domestic product (GDP). Assuming that this percentage is the same today, and given the GDP of Uzbekistan at $37.72 billion, educational expenditure in the country would amount to close to $3.5 billion, or $518 per student (total amount equivalent to US dollars divided by 6,841,000, the approximate number of primary and secondary students in the country). Nevertheless, given the spending on education of neighboring countries, it is surmised that per student spending was greater during the Soviet era and that education expenditure has declined since then.

With a near 100 percent literacy rate, Uzbekistan, along with Kazakhstan, has the highest rate of literacy among the nations in central Asia. Despite this success, however, Uzbekistan has suffered from decline in its formal system of education since independence. With the end of the Soviet period, the Education Ministry in the republic lacked organization, and there was a drop in school enrollment throughout the nation. The present goal of the Ministry of Education of Uzbekistan is to rebuild the educational infrastructure in the country. Various nongovernmental organizations have helped in this regard within the last decade, mostly in the form of funding for students of poor families, travel between home and school, and teacher education improvements.

Daniel Ness and Chia-ling Lin

REFERENCES

Central Intelligence Agency. *The CIA World Factbook*. New York: Skyhorse, 2011. https.www.cia.gov/library/publications/the-world-factbook/index.html.

Nation Master. 2011. www.nationmaster.com.

UNESCO. *Global Education Digest 2012: Comparing Education Statistics Across the World.* Montreal: UNESCO Institute for Statistics, 2012.

———. "Strong Foundations: Early Childhood Care and Education." *Education for All Global Monitoring Report.* Paris: UNESCO, 2006.

UNESCO–IBE. www.ibe.unesco.org/en/worldwide/unesco-regions/asia-and-the-pacific/uzbekistan.html.

United Nations Development Programme. *United Nations Development Report 2010.* New York: Palgrave Macmillan, 2010.

US Department of Labor. *2001 Findings on the Worst Forms of Child Labor.* Washington, DC: Bureau of International Labor Affairs, US Department of Labor, 2002.

World Bank Education Statistics. 2011. www.worldbank.org.

GLOSSARY

.ac.. Part of a uniform resource locator (URL) that stands for "academic institution," most often higher education institutions throughout the world but not in the United States (e.g., www.ox.ac.uk, which is the URL for the University of Oxford).

***.edu.** Internet domain extension that directs individuals to educational websites, particularly those of American colleges, universities, community colleges, and other education-based institutions.

accreditation (educational). The process or status of approval of an institution that engages in compulsory schooling or certifies teachers for the education profession.

actual age. The age of a child or adult (used in comparison to *mental age*).

adult education. The teaching and instruction of adults or individuals who have completed compulsory education. Adult education is most often associated with workplace education, continuing education programs in colleges and universities, or educational extension programs at secondary schools and institutions of higher education.

agricultural education. Education involving the growing of crops and raising of livestock for maximizing production. Agricultural education also involves soil management, water conservation, fertilizer use, and food and nutritional education.

aim. The purpose of an educational unit or course of study.

algorithm. A psychological or written device that, when used correctly, has 100 percent accuracy when solving a problem. *Compare* heuristic.

alternative education. Education that involves nonformal or informal education practices for individuals of all ages and for all educational reasons.

American Federation of Teachers. An international union for teachers based in the United States.

ancient universities (also called medieval universities). The oldest institutions of higher education in Europe. Institutions founded primarily in Italy, England, France, Spain, Scotland, and Germany from the eleventh to fourteenth centuries. The primary purpose was to educate elite young men in the trivium and quadrivium, as well as religion and law. Ancient universities existed in Asia, particularly in India and China; however, these institutions did not offer degrees.

andragogy. A theory that emphasizes the equal importance of adult education with education of children (pedagogy).

anti-bias curriculum. A plan and organization of content and subject matter that aim to address problems associated with racism, sexism, and all forms of oppression that were traditionally ignored in school teaching and learning.

applied academics. A course of study that involves learning transfer—the ability to use formal academic subjects in the workplace or in practice.

apprenticeship. A form of education that involves the preparation of skilled practitioners within a certain applied or professional domain. Apprentices (or novices) are often involved in vicarious learning or hands-on learning with an expert.

assessment. *See* authentic assessment, formative assessment, summative assessment.

authentic assessment. A method of testing or measuring the ability of students using everyday or real-life activities without the use of standardized tests.

autodidact. Self-taught individual (also known as automath).

behaviorism. A theoretical position emanating from the empiricist tradition of John Locke that emphasizes the importance of stimuli and responses as well as positive and negative reinforcements in controlling what is learned.

benchmark. A threshold of knowledge that a student must possess in order to meet a particular educational standard.

bilingual education. The teaching and learning of content in two or more languages. It can also refer to the teaching and learning of two or more languages.

boarding school. A school that houses and educates students. Dormitories and food facilities are available in or near the school. Although they originated in the United Kingdom, boarding schools are prevalent in countries throughout the world.

Bologna Process. An international initiative whose mission is to standardize higher education acceptance procedures and graduation requirements throughout Europe and parts of Asia.

Brown v. Board of Education of Topeka, Kansas. A 1954 landmark US Supreme Court decision that ended racial segregation in public schools and cleared the way for future civil rights legislation.

Catholic school. A type of parochial school funded by the Catholic Church, often emphasizing conservative values. In some instances, these values are not aligned with the beliefs of certain groups or people whose principles are not endorsed by the church.

certification. A designation that indicates the achievement of earning the qualification of performing a particular job. Certification is often associated with the qualification for becoming a teacher. However, in a larger educational context, certification can also refer to the qualification that enables one to engage in any specified vocation or profession. The intention of certification is that the candidate has reached a knowledge level of appropriate skill sets and dispositions that will entitle that individual to apply for employment in the specified area of expertise. Professional certification refers to state or nationally approved qualification of a given profession. Licensure is a type of certification that is required by law or federal mandate.

charter school. An educational institution, invented in the United States, which is funded by federal, state, and local government taxes, but, unlike the public school, it is not subject to regulations and accountability procedures. This is because families can select the charter school of their choice but cannot select the public school, which is based on district statutes that enforce student attendance based on community or region of residence.

child labor. A form of either sanctioned or forced labor of children in their formative years, usually between and including the ages of five to 14.

classical education. The education that was dominant during Greek and Roman antiquity or formal education in medieval times. Classical education can also refer to Confucian or Taoist traditions in China.

classroom management. The ability of teachers to control student behavior in class so that instruction can take place with little interruption.

coeducation. Often referred to as "coed," a form of education that became widespread in the 1960s, particularly in colleges and universities, involving the integration of males and females in the same formal school environment.

cognitive development. A theoretical position emanating from the rationalist philosophies of Jean-Jacques Rousseau and Immanuel Kant that emphasizes the importance of the mind in gaining knowledge (unlike behaviorism, which emphasizes stimulus and response).

cognitive map. A psychological representation that involves coding, storage, recall, and decoding of information for the purpose of identifying a specific location or spatial representation of a given entity or group of entities.

collaborative learning. A type of education that involves shared and common effort on the part of students and their peers and teachers.

college. Generic term that refers to an institution of higher education where individuals seek baccalaureate degrees and sometimes master's degrees. Older definitions often include elite preparatory upper secondary schools as colleges.

community college. A concept and institution that began in the United States in 1901 and is the most attended type of institution in the country today, although these schools also exist in other countries. Community colleges generally have two missions: to provide secondary school graduates with the academic prerequisites for transfer to a four-year college or university, and to provide students with middle- to high-level skills in order to enter the workforce. Students who complete the community college program can earn an associate's degree. Although community colleges are often considered a "two-year college," most students do not complete their degrees within that time period.

comparative education. The study of systems and institutions of learning of one country or culture in relation to another.

compulsory education. Mandatory education according to a country's federal law or statute. Compulsory education is not necessarily public education or free.

computer-based earning. The process of acquiring new knowledge through the use of computers and other electronic forms of technology.

concept. A mental construct that is associated with groupings of facts as a means of problem solving, not the process of solving problems. *Compare* procedure.

concept map. A system of arranging content visually for the purpose of knowledge acquisition.

constructivism. A contemporary psycho-educational philosophy that stems from the research of Jean Piaget in describing how knowledge develops.

content. A characteristic of a curriculum having to do with the study of a distinct academic field.

cooperating teacher. A full-time teacher who works with a teacher candidate (i.e., student teacher) and allows the candidate to perform teaching duties in the classroom for the purpose of gaining teaching experience.

cooperative education. A form of education that involves the integration of academic training with practical work experience—the two usually fluctuating from one semester to the next.

cooperative learning. Learning that takes place, usually in groups, whereby students engage in discourse with their peers for mutual learning experience.

corporal punishment. A form of retribution by which certain state or national laws permit schools or school districts to use physical force on students who allegedly exhibit what is deemed poor behavior by school staff or administrators. Countries that allow corporal punishment include many in the Middle East, Central Asia, East Asia, Africa, and most in North and South America. Twenty states in the United States maintain corporal punishment procedures on the books.

course. A unit of study, usually in a single academic or vocational area that usually lasts from one week to four months.

creativity. A human ability that enables one to summon and utilize cognitive structures—memory, problem solving, and the like—for the purpose of synthesizing plans, new concepts and constructs, or methods through the processes of insight and innovation.

criterion-reference tests. Assessments that measure a student's knowledge in terms of what is expected knowledge for a given age.

critical pedagogy. Nonoppressive teaching and learning whereby teachers engage students in questioning and challenging dominant cultural constructs.

critical thinking. A way of approaching education and learning through the process of dialogue by questioning commonly held assumptions.

cultural learning. The manners and customs by which a cultural group passes information and content from one generation to the next.

curriculum. The body of knowledge that a person or state deems important for another person or group of people to learn, usually for the purpose of improving society. Curriculum is often considered the program of study in which content is defined, arranged, and emphasized.

degree. A level of achievement in an educational institution that indicates the completion of a period of education and is formalized through the awarding of a diploma.

distance education. A process of teaching and learning via computer technology that can reach long distances and that involves the dissemination of knowledge through the Internet.

diversity. A contemporary catchphrase that most often refers to different ethnicities. The term is more effective when referring to differences concerning multiple variables (e.g., ethnicity, geography, economic variation).

dyscalculia. The inability to perform arithmetic operations or solve mathematical problems.

dyslexia. A neurological disorder that is marked by physical impairment in the areas of reading and writing. Dyslexia is not correlated with intelligence.

education reform. A program of systemic district, regional, or national change in educational practice (i.e., teaching and learning) and administration. Also referred to as *educational reform.*

educational evaluation. Assessment or appraisal of an educational body or curriculum for the purpose of school improvement and educational progress as a whole.

educational leadership. The process of administration of a district's, state's, or country's system of education.

educational policy. Rules and regulations that pertain to the administration of education in a particular district, region, or country.

educational psychology. The study of human learning in both nonformal and formal educational settings. This area of inquiry includes cognitive psychology, social psychology, school psychology, physical development, and social and emotional development.

educational research. Study or investigation involving the ways in which students and teachers interact in the formal and informal environments of teaching and learning. Educational research is generally categorized as a field of social science. It implements elements of psychology and sociology.

educational software. Software that is intended to be used with computer hardware or a similar electronic device for the purpose of self-directed learning of a given subject.

educational technology. The implementation and use of technological tools for the purpose of teaching and learning. Such technology includes computer hardware and software, calculators, hands-on or visual manipulatives, whiteboards, video home system (VHS) or digital video discs (DVDs), and the like, as well as nonelectronic technology.

e-learning. A process of learning through the use of computer technology, such as e-mail, the Internet, computer graphics, and the like, that can be used as a method of instruction in the classroom or as a form of distance education.

elementary school. A generic title for a type of school with a basic curriculum for students in the first five or six grade levels. The more universal term is "primary education." See *Primary Education.*

empirical knowledge. The acquisition of facts and concepts that is based on information from the senses, particularly observable information. Empirical knowledge differs from other forms of knowledge in that it is based on experience, not on intuition, reason, or innate concepts or abilities.

epistemology. A branch of philosophical inquiry that investigates the origin and study of knowledge. The term stems from Greek (*episteme*, knowledge, and *–ology*, study of).

e-portfolio. Also called an electronic portfolio: an organized collection of media-related records that are intended to demonstrate one's ability in a particular field.

equity in education. The principle that all students, regardless of race, ethnicity, religion, gender, age, geographical location, socioeconomic class, or sexual orientation, are entitled to a satisfactory education.

exchange student. A secondary- or tertiary-level student who studies in another country and lives with a host family, which, in turn, sends a relative, often a son or daughter, to the country of the hosted student. Exchange programs are common within the context of foreign language and speech acquisition.

experiential education. A method of discourse and education that involves learning by doing, or engaging students in active participation in a particular area of inquiry.

extracurricular activities. Activities occurring before or after school and sometimes during school that typically require voluntary participation on the part of the student. These activities include sports, academically related clubs, and theater, music, and artistic programs.

forbidden knowledge. Ideas and concepts that are traditionally banned in a particular region or country, most often for political or religious reasons.

formal knowledge. The knowledge acquired as a result of using concepts, universal symbols, and procedures learned in a school or similar setting.

formative assessment. A method of measuring students' abilities through question-and-answer or observation formats and without the use of standardized tests.

functional illiteracy. The inability to read and write as a means of functioning in everyday society. It is important to note, however, that someone who is functionally illiterate may still be able to read and write in an academic or nonfunctional setting.

Future Problem-Solving Program. An international competition involving nearly 250,000 students from North America, parts of Europe, East Asia, Australia, and New Zealand. The purpose of the program is to compete in various levels of problem-solving activities. Results of the competition are often compared as part of an international ranking.

gifted education. Also called education for high-ability students: a form of education tailored for students who excel in most educational subjects, particularly language, mathematics, and the natural sciences.

global education. The idea that the dissemination of knowledge should have at least three goals: to improve the socioeconomic status of all people, to prepare students for new forms of employment in the twenty-first century, and to solve problems associated with global warming and the preservation of the earth's resources.

grammar school. Generic term that most often is synonymous with "elementary school," but can also be more comprehensive and include many or all levels of elite education, particularly in countries that were formerly colonized by European countries.

gross enrollment ratio (GER). The total number of children of all ages divided by the total number of children in the official school age group.

gymnasium. An upper secondary school (analogous to the senior high school level) most common in Western European countries, particularly German-speaking countries, that is usually noted for its academic rigor. In some countries, however, the gymnasium refers to the lower secondary school while the lyceum is the upper secondary school.

habituation. A psychological process that involves nonassociative learning and the diminution of reaction to a given stimulus over time.

heuristic. A psychological or written device that has less than 100 percent accuracy when attempting to solve a problem. *Compare* algorithm.

hidden curriculum. Content knowledge that is usually presented in a nonformal manner—that is, not within the classroom or school context. Examples of hidden curriculum include experiential learning among peers outside of the classroom and informal

discussions on the Internet, in virtual chat rooms, or in venues on or off campus, such as an auditorium, where students and faculty gather.

high school. Generic term that refers to a secondary education institution.

high-stakes testing. An often discriminatory form of assessment, which includes standardized testing, that is mostly used to determine a student's promotion to the next grade.

higher education. Generally defined as "tertiary education" (*see* tertiary education), but more specifically defined as academic college or university education.

homeschooling. A form of compulsory education in which the student is permitted to be formally instructed at home. Curriculum benchmarks that are enforced in public and private schools must be met in the homeschooling context as well.

illiteracy. The inability to read and write in one's native language and, therefore, in any language.

inclusion. A method of schooling that combines all students in one class regardless of their cognitive abilities.

informal education. A form of learning that usually does not result in the earning of a degree and that can involve students of all ages for the purpose of learning for its own sake or to gain a skill.

informal knowledge. The knowledge acquired through everyday or spontaneous activities.

inquiry. A student-centered form of learning that promotes study through scientific investigation, hypothesizing, or questioning.

instruction. The way or means by which content or the curriculum in general is disseminated.

instructional technology. A type of instruction that involves the use of various forms of technology for the purpose of increasing the skill levels of workers and making them more desirable in multiple businesses and industries within the workforce.

instructional theory. An approach to education that investigates the best or most desirable means of promoting and fostering student learning, mostly through educational objectives in taxonomic form.

intelligence. A term referring to one's knowledge at any given time, not one's aptitude based on heredity, the latter being the most frequent use of the term.

intelligence quotient. A controversial numerical value that is determined by multiplying a person's *mental age* by 100, then dividing the product by the person's *actual age*.

international education. Informal and formal engagement in practices that involve teaching and learning in all cultural or national contexts.

international poverty line. The monetary threshold at which one earns an adequate standard of living in a particular country. It is generally a crude predictor of a country's quality of education.

intrinsic motivation. Interest and engagement in a particular activity for its own sake and without external incentive.

junior high school. The level of education after primary school and before senior high school. It is usually the first or lower secondary education period.

kindergarten. A generic term that has different meanings depending on the country where it is used, but mainly suggests the first year of schooling before formal instruction commences in the first grade.

kinesthetic learning. A form of educational practice whereby students actively engage in the learning process through physical activity and not merely by watching or listening.

knowledge transfer. A concept that refers to one's ability to employ academic expertise for practical uses or necessities—for example, an engineer's knowledge of integration in calculus as a means of determining the appropriate gauge for constructing railroad track.

learning. The process of acquiring knowledge, procedures, and concepts for the purpose of educational advancement or the improvement of skill sets for employment.

learning by teaching. The process of allowing students to engage in the teaching process as they gain knowledge and practice in a certain academic or practical skill or ability.

learning disability. An overused term to describe someone who is unable or has difficulty to engage in acquiring knowledge. Unless related to organic or physiological constraints (such as neurological dysfunction, blindness, deafness), learning disabilities are often used as social constructs that sometimes impede progress in the classroom. Administrative bodies often ignore this finding.

lesson planning. The activity of creating and developing a procedure that a teacher can follow in order to provide academic instruction for students.

lesson study. A research-based procedure whereby teachers who are engaged in professional development examine lessons in order to maximize effectiveness. These lessons are presented are presented to students, and subsequently examined a second or third time for additional feedback on the efficacy and usefulness of content.

liberal arts. A program of study that involves academic disciplines in the humanities and the sciences and, at the same time, excludes subjects pertaining to specific vocations and professions.

licensure. *See* certification.

lifelong learning. A philosophy of education that embraces learning, training, and inquiry throughout the life span for the purposes of personal edification, the enhancement of career goals, the acquisition of skills for market desirability, and continuous and purposeful discourse that emphasizes learning for the sake of learning.

literacy. The ability to read and write in one's native language.

literacy rate. The percentage of a total population who can read and write in the official, native, or common language of a particular country. It mostly refers to individuals older than primary school students (usually 15 or older) who can read and write.

manipulative. A physical device that is used for the purpose of making connections between students' everyday, concrete (informal) knowledge with conventionally systematic, and often abstract and scientifically based, concepts(formal knowledge).

master of European business (MEB). A degree from European universities and some Asian universities that identifies individuals with skills in the fields of global economics and business.

mastery learning. An educational method emphasizing that all children can learn content if given the appropriate conditions and environment in which to study.

mental age. The age at which an individual is performing intellectually or cognitively. See *Actual Age.*

metacognition. A process that involves one's own ability to regulate the acquisition of knowledge.

middle school. Generic term that is often synonymous with "junior high school," but can also refer to an institution that includes the last one or two grades of primary education and the first one or two grades of secondary education.

motivation. The force or incentive that gives an individual intention and purpose for engaging in a particular activity.

multiculturalism. A philosophical view connected with educational practice that emphasizes tolerance of all ethnic groups.

multiple intelligences. A theory of human intelligence proposed by Howard Gardner that espouses forms of intellect or aptitude other than the language, numerical, and visual-spatial domains.

National Assessment of Educational Progress (NAEP). A national assessment in the United States that measures American students' verbal and quantitative abilities.

National Council for the Accreditation of Teacher Education (NCATE). An organization that accredits teacher education schools and colleges in the United States and in other countries throughout the world, but, to date, does not have valid or reliable methods of determining so-called successful teacher training institutions.

National Labor Relations Board v. Yeshiva University. A case in 1980 involving the signing of a petition of the Yeshiva University Faculty Association with the National Labor Relations Board affirming that the association represented a bargaining agent for the faculty of Yeshiva University. The US Supreme Court concluded that all Yeshiva University faculty members were managerial or supervisory personnel and were not employees within the context of the National Labor Relations Act. This case served as a precedent for numerous institutions of higher education in both the United States and abroad (under different legislation).

National Postgraduate Representative Body. A society of scholars, primarily in European countries, that represents students enrolled in doctoral and master's programs. The society consists of numerous organizations that represent graduate students in various countries.

net enrollment rate (NER). The total number of children enrolled in school and in the official school age group divided by the total number of children in the official school age group.

NGO. Abbreviation for "nongovernment organization." NGOs can be both national and international organizations.

nontraditional education. *See* alternative education.

normal school. An institution that prepares students who wish to become teachers. Normal schools originated in the United States but are now most common in Asia, Australia and New Zealand, and parts of Europe.

norm-referenced tests. Assessments that measure a student's knowledge in comparison to that of other students.

note taking. The ability to write information that is provided in classroom lectures or related learning environments for the purpose of retrieving and reviewing material at a later time or date.

numeracy. A portmanteau of the words "numerical literacy," which refers to an individual's level of mathematical knowledge, particularly in basic knowledge of numbers and operations of numbers.

objective. A statement of a goal that students must follow in order to succeed in a particular course of study.

obscurantism. The inculcation of dogmas, often in religious contexts, for indoctrination purposes that impedes free thinking and reason.

observational learning. The process of gaining knowledge and skills by observing, imitating, or replicating the behavior of an expert. One major aspect of observational learning is vicarious reinforcement, whereby the learner performs a task soon after observation.

Office of Educational Research and Improvement (OERI). An offshoot of the US Department of Education that investigates research and best practices in education.

open-ended instruction. A method of teaching that involves a student's problem-solving ability as a means of finding a solution or answer.

outdoor education. Learning that takes place outside of the formal school context, particularly in the outside environment. Outdoor education is often analogous to environmental education, involving field trips or excursions to state or national parks, wildlife sanctuaries, and the like.

parochial school. An educational institution funded by a religious denomination that often discriminates on the basis of religion, sexual orientation, or personal values.

peace education. Education involving the teaching and learning of compassion for others, conflict resolution, and ways of contributing to a cleaner, more peaceful, nonviolent planet.

pedagogy. The study of teaching and methods of instruction.

phonics. A method of learning how to read by decoding words according to sounds, such as phonemes. *Compare* whole language.

portfolio. A collection of a student's work that shows progress over time.

postsecondary education. *See* tertiary education.

predictive power. An indication of the strength of a statistical tool that is used for testing a dependent variable in a scientific investigation. The stronger the predictive power, the better the researcher will be able to determine the viability of a theory or hypothesis that is intended to support a particular study. Predictive power also enables the scientific researcher to support the use of specific numbers of participants or data in an experiment.

preprimary education. An umbrella term that refers to all forms of education prior to a compulsory educational period, usually catering to children less than six years of age.

preschool. Generic term for a type of preprimary schooling that usually provides some academic instruction but focuses mostly on social interaction and play.

primary education. Period of schooling for children between the ages of five and 13 years. Primary school is the first compulsory educational period.

primary school. *See* primary education.

private school. An institution of learning that is funded by tuition, private organizations, corporations, or individual sponsors and not by government or taxpayers' money.

problem-based learning (PBL). A method of learning that involves the fostering and development of students' cognitive abilities as a means of acquiring knowledge. This type of learning often involves open-ended situations necessitating collaborative efforts by a group of students.

problem finding. One's intentional search for or discovery of situations (i.e., problems) that require resolution, not for the sake of finding problems, but to determine possible glitches that can arise when accomplishing a particular task or project. Creativity and intuition are important in the process of problem finding.

problem solving. A method or process of answering a question that involves an individual's prior knowledge in a particular academic domain. It often but not always is placed in the context of extended questions within the domains of mathematical or scientific thinking that requires resolution. The individual or system of artificial intelligence must employ methods of accessing previously learned knowledge and apply that knowledge to the situation at hand.

procedural knowledge. *See* procedure.

procedure. A mental construct that refers to the process by which one solves specified tasks or problems; it does not refer to the concepts associated with those problems. Procedural knowledge is needed in order to enable one to develop skills to solve problems involving procedures or algorithms.

professional certification. *See* certification.

professional development school (PDS). An educational institution that usually partners with a teacher training college or center for the purpose of providing student teaching preparation for preservice teachers.

Program for International Student Assessment (PISA). A unique international assessment that aims to consider differences in socioeconomic class and academic ability.

public school. An institution of learning that is funded by the state or federal government of a given nation. Some public institutions are funded in part by tuition and subsidized by taxes.

pupil/teacher ratio. *See* student/teacher ratio.

quadrivium. Four of the seven disciplines—arithmetic, geometry, music, and astronomy—that were taught in ancient universities.

recitation. The repetition of words, phrases, or sentences for the intended purpose of memorizing information. Recitation is often imposed by the teacher.

reliability. A score indicating that a test is consistent in how it demonstrates an individual's abilities or knowledge in a particular domain.

rote learning. The process of acquiring knowledge through memorizing information. Rote learning is antithetical to critical thinking, complex or advanced problem solving, and so-called deep understanding.

rubric. An assessment system whereby students or candidates are graded based on learning objectives that are connected with regional or national standards.

scaffolding. A term emanating from the theories of Lev Vygotsky and coined by psychologist Jerome Bruner: a method by which an adult or peer provides prompts or assistance to another individual who is seeking to learn or answer a question.

school discipline. A concept that refers to a code of conduct that students must adhere to; poor behavior results in some form of punishment. *See* corporal punishment.

secondary education. Period of schooling after primary school. Secondary school may be compulsory depending on the country and may be divided into lower and upper levels.

secondary school. *See* secondary education.

Secretary's Commission on Achieving Necessary Skills (SCANS). A committee under the jurisdiction of the US Department of Labor that investigates the most efficient ways to educate students with the skills necessary for the twenty-first century labor market and workforce.

self-efficacy. The level at which people perceive or recognize their general capability in a given task.

self-esteem. The level of self-worth of an individual. Identifying oneself as "poor" in mathematics may contribute to lower self-esteem; however, one's self-perception as a "poor" carpenter or automobile mechanic may contribute to lower self-efficacy.

senior high school. A term most often synonymous with the comprehensive upper level secondary school.

service learning. An approach to education that enables students to learn academic subjects as a means of better serving their communities and improving the well-being of society in general.

situated cognition. Knowledge that is acquired as a result of working or learning within a given context, particularly where the knowledge can be applied, and not in a school setting.

skill. A learned ability that enables an individual to perform specified actions.

social learning. *See* observational learning.

Socratic method. A method of teaching that involves asking students questions and challenging student answers that are in the form of assumptions. The Socratic method is outlined in the Dialogues of Plato that were written in the fourth century BCE.

special education. The education of students who are lacking in some aspect of their social, academic, or physical development. This form of education is tailored for students whose needs cannot be met by traditional educational and schooling practices.

standardized testing. A form of high-stakes assessment that involves a student's ability to answer a question based on a particular criterion or benchmark (usually multiple-choice, essay, or short-answer formats).

standards. Term used to denote locally, regionally, nationally, or internationally agreed-upon or "universal" thresholds of academic ability in school subjects.

STEM. An acronym for "science, technology, engineering, and mathematics" that refers to programs in various countries throughout the world, the success of which is often seen as an indicator of a country's economic success and ability to compete in the global marketplace.

student activism. Student-inspired movements that are organized for the purpose of changing elements within a system of education.

student-centered learning. A form of teaching and learning that emphasizes students' ways of knowing. This form of learning avoids traditionally teacher-centered lecture and recitation formats and instead employs methods of instruction that engage student interaction in the learning process.

student teacher. A student in a school of education or normal school who is placed in a school with a cooperating full-time, experienced teacher for the purpose of gaining real-time teaching experience.

student/teacher ratio. The number of students taught by a teacher, usually in a single classroom.

summative assessment. A method of measuring students' abilities through the use of standardized testing procedures.

tabula rasa. Latin for "blank slate," the term used by the seventeenth-century English philosopher John Locke to describe the nature of knowledge in early childhood.

taxonomy in education. A classification system that divides the purpose of formal learning into various categories. Benjamin Bloom's taxonomy is by far the most common.

teaching. The act of providing instruction for others, usually students, for the purpose of educating and providing knowledge.

technology education. The teaching and learning of the ability to develop and use tools in shaping the natural environment for particular purposes or goals.

tertiary education. A period of schooling after secondary school. Tertiary education is not compulsory.

Training. The acquisition of knowledge that is based on content in vocational and technical areas.

Trends in International Mathematics and Science Study (TIMSS). Formerly the Third International Mathematics and Science Study, TIMSS is an international assessment that takes place every four to six years.

trivium. Three of the seven ancient disciplines—grammar, logic, and rhetoric—that were taught in ancient universities.

two-year college. *See* community college.

UNESCO. United Nations Educational, Scientific and Cultural Organization: an international organization with the mission of eradicating poverty through education, intercultural dialogue, and human rights legislation.

UNICEF. United Nations International Children's Fund is an international organization created by the United Nations General Assembly in 1946 with the aim of helping children who live in adverse situations and conditions throughout the world.

United Nations Children's Fund. *See* UNICEF.

United Nations Educational, Scientific, and Cultural Organization. *See* UNESCO.

university. An institution of higher education that is devoted to both research and the development of future experts and leaders within individualized academic fields. Degrees offered at the university level include baccalaureates, master's degrees, and doctorates.

validity. The score indicating that a testing instrument measures exactly what it was originally designed to measure.

vicarious reinforcement. The ability to obtain a skill merely by watching and observing an expert in the field.

virtual learning. A method of education that involves the use of computer or Internet technology.

virtual learning environment. A learning situation involving the use of software systems that enable students' acquisition of knowledge and the teacher's ability to administer and manage content.

visual learning. A teaching method that promotes the use of graphic organizers for concept development. Graphic organizers include concept maps, concept webs, and slides.

vocational education. A type of learning that can be either formal or informal and that prepares students in traditionally nonacademic subjects—particularly those that provide skills needed to enter the workforce.

voucher. A controversial certificate that enables parents to send their children to nonpublic schools, such as charter schools that are funded by local, state, or federal tax revenue or parochial schools which are private.

West Virginia State Board of Education v. Barnette. A 1942 court decision stating that students cannot be forced to salute the flag.

Westside Community Board of Education v. Mergens. A 1990 court case that allowed a student in a public school in Omaha, Nebraska, to establish an extracurricular Bible club on school premises.

whole language. A method of learning how to read that emphasizes context at the expense of learning phonemes as a means of reading comprehension. *Compare* phonics.

World Bank. An international organization whose primary purpose is to provide international loans and, at times, donations to countries in need of physical infrastructure, most particularly for the building of education facilities. The World Bank database is a frequently cited source for international education.

Yeshiva Law. *See National Labor Relations Board v. Yeshiva University.*

zone of proximal development. Term associated with the work of Lev Vygotsky that is defined as the difference between a student's actual knowledge (in the present) and potential knowledge (in the future), that is, increased cognitive abilities that are mediated by adult or peer intervention.

INDEX

Notes: Numbers in bold designate volume. Page numbers followed by *t* indicate tables; *f* indicate figures.

REFERENCE